From Masters of Slaves to Lords of Lands

Today we think of land as the paradigmatic example of property, while in the past, the paradigmatic example was often a slave. In this seminal work, James Q. Whitman asserts that there is no natural form of ownership. Whitman dives deep into the long Western history of this transformation in the legal imagination – the transformation from the ownership of humans and other living creatures to the ownership of land. This change extended over many centuries, coming to fruition only on the threshold of the modern era. It brought with it profound changes, not only in the way we understand ownership but also in the way we understand the state. Its most dramatic consequence arrived in the nineteenth century, with the final disappearance of the lawful private ownership of humans, which had been taken for granted for thousands of years.

James Q. Whitman is a professor at Yale Law School. He is the author of numerous books and articles, including *Hitler's American Model*, *The Verdict of Battle*, *The Origins of Reasonable Doubt*, and *Harsh Justice*, and the recipient of many awards.

See the Studies in Legal History series website at
http://studiesinlegalhistory.org/

Studies in Legal History

EDITORS

Lisa Ford, *University of New South Wales*
Thomas McSweeney, *William & Mary Law School*
Reuel Schiller, *University of California College of the Law, San Francisco*
Taisu Zhang, *Yale Law School*

Other books in the series:

Marie-Amélie George, *Family Matters: Queer Households and the Half-Century Struggle for Legal Recognition*
Simon Devereaux, *Execution, State and Society in England, 1660–1900*
Giuliana Perrone, *Nothing More than Freedom: The Failure of Abolition in American Law*
Christian G. Fritz, *Monitoring American Federalism: The History of State Legislative Resistance*
Ada Maria Kuskowski, *Vernacular Law: Writing and the Reinvention of Customary Law in Medieval France*
E. Claire Cage, *The Science of Proof: Forensic Medicine in Modern France*
Kristin A. Olbertson, *The Dreadful Word: Speech Crime and Polite Gentlemen in Massachusetts, 1690–1776*

(Continued after the Index)

From Masters of Slaves to Lords of Lands

The Transformation of Ownership in the Western World

JAMES Q. WHITMAN
Yale University

Shaftesbury Road, Cambridge CB2 8EA, United Kingdom

One Liberty Plaza, 20th Floor, New York, NY 10006, USA

477 Williamstown Road, Port Melbourne, VIC 3207, Australia

314–321, 3rd Floor, Plot 3, Splendor Forum, Jasola District Centre, New Delhi – 110025, India

103 Penang Road, #05–06/07, Visioncrest Commercial, Singapore 238467

Cambridge University Press is part of Cambridge University Press & Assessment, a department of the University of Cambridge.

We share the University's mission to contribute to society through the pursuit of education, learning and research at the highest international levels of excellence.

www.cambridge.org
Information on this title: www.cambridge.org/9781009497534

DOI: 10.1017/9781009497541

© James Q. Whitman 2025

This publication is in copyright. Subject to statutory exception and to the provisions of relevant collective licensing agreements, no reproduction of any part may take place without the written permission of Cambridge University Press & Assessment.

When citing this work, please include a reference to the DOI 10.1017/9781009497541

First published 2025

A catalogue record for this publication is available from the British Library

A Cataloging-in-Publication data record for this book is available from the Library of Congress

ISBN 978-1-009-49753-4 Hardback

Cambridge University Press & Assessment has no responsibility for the persistence or accuracy of URLs for external or third-party internet websites referred to in this publication and does not guarantee that any content on such websites is, or will remain, accurate or appropriate.

For Bill Ewald

Contents

Acknowledgments *page* viii

Introduction: Owning Humans, Owning Land – Two
Primitive Modes of the Property Imagination 1

PART I MASTERS OF MEN AND BEASTS

1 Hierarchy and the Hunt for Prey: Early Human Ownership 37
2 Masters of Men and Beasts: The Early Roman *Fantasia* of Ownership 75
3 The *Dominus* Enters the Law 125
4 Classical Roman Slave Law: The Just Hunt for Human Prey 160
5 An Empire of the Chieftainship over People 208

PART II FROM MASTERS TO LORDS

6 Introduction to Part II: From *Pierson* v. *Post* to *Johnson* v. *M'Intosh* 231
7 From Slavery to Feudalism: The Great Hypothesis 236
8 From Masters to Lords in Late Antiquity 291
9 From the Law of Owning Humans to the Law of Owning Land: The Early Modern Culmination 333
Conclusion: From Man the Killer to Man the Tiller 385

Bibliography 395
Index 435

Acknowledgments

This book has been a long time in the writing, and I have accumulated debts to many readers, some of whom I fear that I may have forgotten. I ask them to forgive me.

The project began as a lecture at the Clough Center of Boston College Law School, before a lively and thoughtful audience. I have presented subsequent versions in various fora, including the University of Michigan Law School, the University of Pennsylvania Law School, Stanford Law School, Yale Law School, William and Mary Law School, the American Society for Legal History, the Oxford Centre for Socio-Legal Studies, and the Works-in-Progress Workshop of the American Society for Comparative Law. I benefited especially from the opportunity to present the project in its late stages at the Collège de France, on the invitation of Dario Mantovani. I am grateful to the participants in all of these venues for their responses and suggestions.

I have been blessed by the generosity of many readers who took the time to read portions, or even the entirety, of earlier drafts. My warmest thanks to Ari Bryen, Clifford Ando, Zachary Hertz, John Hudson, Dario Mantovani, Lauren Benton, Richard Ross, Nathaniel Hay, Charles Donahue, R. H. Helmholz, Joseph Manning, Anthony Kronman, David Grewal, Kaius Tuori, Tom McSweeney, Tamar Herzog, Stuart Banner, Taisu Zhang, Emanuele Conte, William Ewald, Carol Rose, Robert Ellickson, and Henry Smith. E. A. R. Brown was not only generous with her thoughts; she provided me with notes of her own research. The book was meat for innumerable conversations with my wife Sara McDougall, to whom I owe an enormous intellectual debt in this as in all things. I have dedicated it to Bill Ewald, who has been my treasured intellectual companion from the first moment of the conception of the project. I am proud to see this book appear in the distinguished series of the American Society for Legal History, which has been my scholarly home, and the home of so many others, for decades.

Introduction: Owning Humans, Owning Land – Two Primitive Modes of the Property Imagination

"There is nothing which so generally strikes the imagination, and engages the affections of mankind," wrote William Blackstone, eminent author of the *Commentaries on the Laws of England*, in 1766, "as the right of property."[1] This line, one of the most quoted in the literature of the law, states a familiar truth about human psychology: The thought of property kindles desire; we like to imagine ourselves as owners. But what sorts of objects "engage our affections"? When property "strikes our imagination," what is it that we imagine?

For Blackstone himself, there was one answer first and foremost: *land*. He famously celebrated the right of property as "that sole and despotic dominion over the external things of the world, in total exclusion of the right of any other individual in the universe" – and then went on to explain that by "the external things of world" he had in mind in particular "the dominion of land," of "a determinate spot of ground" or "a particular field." Only as a sort of afterthought did he add "or … a jewel."[2] When the right of property struck the imagination of William

---

[1] William Blackstone, *Commentaries on the Laws of England, Book II: Of the Rights of Things*, ed. Simon Stern (Oxford, 2016), 1.

[2] The jewel example was conventional in the Roman legal tradition, from which Blackstone presumably took it: *D.* 1.8.3. Florus 6 *inst.*: *Item lapilli, gemmae ceteraque, quae in litore invenimus, iure naturali nostra statim fiunt.* "The external things of the world" was also a conventional phrase, notably in the Thomist tradition. See Thomas Aquinas, *Summa theologiae* I-II q. 69, a. 3, obj. 5: "*affluentia exteriorum bonorum.*" Available at www.corpusthomisticum.org/sth2055.html; Domingo de Soto, Relectio de Dominio, §19, in Domingo de Soto, *Relecciones y opusculos*, ed. Jaime Brufau Prats

Blackstone, what sprang to his mind first was the thought of an eighteenth-century Englishman as "sole and despotic" proprietor of real estate. In this, he was a typical representative of the common law tradition, a legacy of a centuries-old feudal order in which there was no condition more socially desirable than being the lord of lands.[3]

Two and half centuries later, land still reigns at the center of the property law imagination in common-law America. The word "property," as the Merriam-Webster dictionary reports, signifies "something owned or possessed: *specifically*: a piece of real estate."[4] When speakers of American English describe themselves as owning "property," what they mean is that they own land. There is something paradoxical about this, since land is by no means as economically or socially important in modern America as it was in the England of Blackstone.[5] Today, people's fortunes depend at least as much on their pension funds as on their real estate, and American social status no longer derives from being baronial lord of a manor. Nevertheless, when Americans hear the word "property," what springs to their minds first is still what sprang to the mind of Blackstone: the image of acreage. As Carol Rose, the most insightful of property scholars, suggests, when we think about property, we begin by "picturing" it;[6] and in America what we picture first is land.

Nor is it just a matter of how Americans form their mental pictures. It is also a matter of how they define their rights. Being a real estate holder carries considerable legal benefits in the United States.[7] One example is

---

(Salamanca, 1995), 136: "Appropriatio bonorum exteriorum." For the use of "external goods" in Ockham and the Franciscan tradition, Annabel Brett, *Liberty, Right and Nature* (Cambridge, 1997), 58–59.

[3] For the focus on land, see Simon Stern, "Editor's Introduction to Book II," in Blackstone, *Commentaries on the Laws of England: Book II*, vii–ix. I will discuss scholarly reservations about the "feudal" character of medieval law in Chapter 7.

[4] Available at www.merriam-webster.com/dictionary/property.

[5] An observation made by Bernard Rudden, "Things as Things and Things as Wealth," *Oxford Journal of Legal Studies* 14 (1994): 82–83 [81–97], and elaborated powerfully by Katharina Pistor, *The Code of Capital* (Princeton, 2019), 5–6 and *passim*.

[6] Carol Rose, *Property and Persuasion: Essays on the History, Theory and Rhetoric of Ownership* (New York, 1994), 1.

[7] Catalogued by commentators such as Benjamin Barros, "Home as a Legal Concept," *Santa Clara Law Review* 46 (2006): 255–306; Stephanie Stern, "Residential Protectionism and the Legal Mythology of Home," *Michigan Law Review* 107 (2009): 1093–1144; and classically Margaret Jane Radin, "Property and Personhood," *Stanford Law Review* 34 (1982): 957–1015.

the home mortgage interest deduction, a massive public subsidy for private ownership, unmatched in other countries. Another is the American conception of the right of privacy, strongly defined as privacy within the walls of the home.[8] Then there is the homestead exemption in the law of bankruptcy, the rule that allows insolvent Americans, unlike defaulting debtors elsewhere, to keep their homes out of the clutches of their creditors.[9] But the most dramatic example is the "castle doctrine" in criminal law: This is the rule that gives Americans the quasi-feudal, if not despotic, privilege of using deadly force when they believe they have been attacked within their own domains.[10] "[T]he use [of] arms in defense of hearth and home," the Supreme Court has declared, is sanctified by the Constitution itself.[11] In America, the state's monopoly of violence terminates at the homeowner's doorstep.

This more or less taken-for-granted assumption that property involves, in the first instance, the ownership of real estate, and maybe even the right to kill anyone who intrudes on it, comes so naturally to contemporary Americans that they may be surprised to learn that it is

---

[8] I explore this in James Q. Whitman, *The Two Western Cultures of Privacy: Dignity versus Liberty*, Yale Law Journal 113 (2004): 1151–1221.

[9] E.g., Barros, "Home," 284–285.

[10] To put it technically, the rule absolves them of the duty to retreat, though the belief in question must in principle be reasonable. In practice, and in cultural understanding, the castle doctrine extends much further. It would be out of place to discuss all the complexities and variations of the doctrine in this book. Cases of Americans making legally dubious use of the privilege are legion, and often both tragic and shocking. See, e.g., Jack Healy, Glenn Thrush, Eliza Fawcett, and Susan C. Beachy, "In a Nation Armed to the Teeth, These Tiny Missteps Led to Tragedy," *New York Times*, April 20, 2023, available at www.nytimes.com/2023/04/20/us/wrong-house-shootings-guns.html, which includes the heart-rending statement of the mother of one victim: "I know people have the right to protect their dwellings." T. Markus Funk argues that American self-defense law is not distinctively permissive. See Funk, "Busting the Durable Myth That U.S. Self-Defense Law Uniquely Fails to Protect Human Life," *Oxford University Comparative Law Forum* 2 (2023), available at https://ouclf.law.ox.ac.uk/busting-the-durable-myth-that-u-s-self-defense-law-uniquely-fails-to-protect-human-life/#post-1490; Funk and Eugene Volokh, "U.S. Self-Defense Law – 'Harsh' by International Standards?" *Bloomberg Law Insights* (10 March 2022), available at https://news.bloomberglaw.com/us-law-week/u-s-self-defense-law-harsh-by-international-standards. This is not the place to conduct a debate on that topic, but I note that Funk's account of German law relies on pre-1945 law, and that his argument draws on law-on-the-books rather than law-in-action. In any case, my observations here turn on the cultural significance of the home, and not on the broader questions of self-defense law that are his subject.

[11] *District of Columbia v. Heller*, 554 U.S. 570, 633 (2008). This is not of course about the castle doctrine, but it can be taken as an expression of the same cultural values.

not universal. Isn't land the first image that springs to mind everywhere when people hear the word "property"? Doesn't the law everywhere respect the owner's right to "despotic dominion" within "hearth and home"? And indeed, it is the case that in most parts of the "modern West," as three Oxford legal historians tell us, "we tend to assume that land is the archetypal form of property."[12] But land is not the only "archetypal form" to be found in human societies. The right of property has "struck the imagination and engaged the affections" differently in other legal cultures, both in the present and in the past.

Present-day Europe offers some examples. In Germany, for one, the dictionary definition of property dismisses the idea of property as "land" as "antiquated."[13] There, as elsewhere in Continental Europe, it goes without saying that what Blackstone called the "Gothic castle" of feudal law has been demolished:[14] German property law is post-feudal, and so real estate plays a significantly lesser role in German thinking and teaching, while the German rate of homeownership is notoriously low.[15]

Germans may have another reason for rejecting the idealization of land as well: They live in a country where the ideology of "Blut und Boden," "blood and soil," once put the link between Germans and their land at the center of Nazi politics.[16] As one Nazi lawyer gushed in 1933, the year Hitler took power, "the ground and soil of Germany must be the very foundation of our state and our life, our homeland, the basis of the psychological conditions for the existence of our *Volk*, our best and most beautiful possession, indeed sacred!"[17] Hitler's

---

[12] Georgy Kantor, Tom Lambert, and Hannah Skoda, "Introduction," in Kantor, Lambert, and Skoda, eds., *Legalism: Property and Ownership* (Oxford, 2017), 10 [1–27].

[13] Available at www.duden.de/rechtschreibung/Eigentum. Some of the same "post-feudal" attitude is also present in French real property law, which is marked by its systematic distrust of landlords.

[14] See Bridget Marshall, "Romanticism, Gothic and the Law," in Kieran Dolin, ed., *Law and Literature* (Cambridge, 2018), 143 [142–156].

[15] See, e.g., Leo Kaas, Georgi Kocharkov, Edgar Preugschat, and Nawid Siassi, "Reasons for the Low Homeownership Rate in Germany," available at www.bundesbank.de/en/publications/research/research-brief/2020-30-homeownership-822176#:~:text=Germany%20has%20high%20transfer%20taxes,potentially%20tilt%20incentives%20towards%20renting.

[16] See the documents collected in Gustavo Corni and Horst Gies, eds., *Blut und Boden: Rassenideologie und Agrarpolitik im Staat Hitlers* (Idstein, 1994).

[17] Hans Dölle, "Das bürgerliche Recht im nationalsozialistischen Staat," *Schmollers Jahrbuch für Gesetzgebung* 57 (1933), 669. Quoted in Justus Wilhelm Hedemann, *Die Fortschritte des Zivilrechts im XIX. Jahrhundert* (Berlin, 1935), 2.2:348.

Introduction 5

foreign policy too turned on the acquisition of *Lebensraum*, of new lands for racial Germans as the Nazis defined them. In Germany, it may be easier to see how the "affection" for land can degenerate into something frightening and dangerous than it is in America.[18]

But the most provocative examples of how the property imagination can vary come from the societies of the past. For in past times and places, the paradigmatic example of property was frequently not land, but a human being.

Ancient Roman law is a prime example. The Romans certainly owned land, which was no less financially desirable in their agrarian society than it was in Blackstone's England.[19] But the economic importance of land did not dictate the language of the law: When we open an introductory text composed for ancient Roman law students, we discover that the basic formula for claiming ownership was not "I declare that this land is mine," but "I declare that this *man* is mine."[20] "This man" regularly served as the standard example of property in Roman law, appearing over and over again in the formulaic language of the law.[21] The imagery of the ownership of humans cropped up throughout Roman legal terminology and symbolism. To take an example familiar to historians of slavery, the standard Roman term for "owner," *dominus*, had the core meaning of "slavemaster";[22] that fact led Orlando Patterson to conclude, in his classic study *Slavery and Social Death*, that the "idiom of power" in ancient Roman property law was the idiom of the master/slave relationship.[23] Much more can be said as well. As we shall see in the pages of this book, for example, the Romans treated the capture and enslavement of enemies in war as a paradigm justification for property rights.[24]

All this hints at a deep-seated contrast between the ancients and the moderns: Where "despotic dominion" over a piece of land was what first struck the property imagination of William Blackstone in 1766, what first struck the property imagination in Rome, two millennia

---

[18] This is not much present in the mind of Germans today, as far as I know, but it was in the 1950s. See the discussion of the "Odium" associated with the National Socialist "Mythos" after 1945 in Heinz Haushofer, *Ideengeschichte der Agrarwirtschaft und Agrarpolitik* (Munich, Bonn, and Vienna, 1958), 399.
[19] For the comparison, Keith Hopkins, *Conquerors and Slaves* (Cambridge, 1978), 52.
[20] Gai. *Inst.* 4.16.   [21] Below, Chapter 2.   [22] Below, Chapter 2.
[23] Orlando Patterson, *Slavery and Social Death* (Cambridge, MA, 1982), 32.
[24] Below, Chapter 3.

earlier, often seems to have been "despotic dominion" over a man. If there had been a Roman Merriam-Webster, it is tempting to speculate that one of its entries might have read, "*Property*. Something owned or possessed: *specifically*: a human being."[25]

Nor is Rome the only example of a legal culture whose property law has revolved in some way around "despotic dominion" over humans, rather than "despotic dominion" over land. The law of precolonial West and South Africa is another case, and a particularly intensively studied one.[26] Here is how historian John Thornton describes the law of precolonial Africa: "Slaves were the only form of private, revenue-producing property recognized in African law. By contrast, in European legal systems, land was the primary form of private, revenue-producing property."[27] "Across precolonial West Africa," as another scholar writes, "wealth, power, and prestige were measured primarily in people, not in land."[28] The anthropologist Jack Goody formulates it this way: Where feudal Europe had "the chieftainship over land," precolonial Africa had "the chieftainship over people."[29] Scholars struggle mightily over the interpretation of this African law of "the chieftainship over people," so different from European law, and on its face so disturbing. Africanists make a point of noting that it resembled the law of ancient Rome.[30]

And Rome and precolonial Africa are not alone. "The higher value given to control over people rather than ownership of land was not

---

[25] This would be the case if the term defined were *mancipium*. See below, Chapter 2.
[26] E.g., Seymour Drescher, *Abolition: A History of Slavery and Anti-Slavery* (Cambridge, 2009), 18.
[27] John Thornton, *Africa and Africans in the Making of the Atlantic World, 1400–1680* (Cambridge, 1992), 74. Lauren Benton argues that Thornton exaggerates the differences between Europe, notably Spain, and Africa. Benton, *Law in Colonial Cultures: Legal Regimes in World History, 1400–1900* (Cambridge, 2002), 50–51. This is not a debate into which I will enter, but the burden of my argument is that the contrast is best understood as one in the conceptual world of the law, not in the realities on the ground. That contrast, as we shall see, does not by any means imply that the European regimes I study were in fact based exclusively on landownership.
[28] James H. Sweet, "Defying Social Death: The Multiple Configurations of African Slave Family in the Atlantic World," *William and Mary Quarterly* 70 (April 2013): 255 [251–272].
[29] Jack Goody, *Technology, Tradition and the State in Africa* (Oxford, 1971), 30.
[30] Suzanne Miers and Igor Kopytoff, *Slavery in Africa: Historical and Anthropological Perspectives* (Madison, WI, 1977), 7. Further discussion below, Chapters 1 and 2.

a peculiarity of Africa," remarks the world historian Jürgen Osterhammel:

> [T]he status of Russian magnates before the emancipation of the peasantry in 1861 was measured more by their serfs or "souls" than by the size of their estate, and around the same time in Brazil the importance of a landowner depended on the number of his slaves. In early nineteenth-century Batavia, no European who wanted to count as somebody could afford to arouse the suspicion that he was skimping on the number of his black slaves.[31]

"The idea of land as form of private, revenue-producing property," we can read of another example, "was absent in Comanche culture, and livestock and slaves in a sense took the place of landed private property."[32] The anthropologist Marshall Sahlins makes similar observations in his *Stone Age Economics*: In the "primitive structure of production," Sahlins notes, rights to productive resources grow not out of the ownership of "farmlands, pastures, hunting or fishing territories," but out of "the hold on persons."[33] Economists, for their part, build models designed to explain why, in some societies of the past, the sources of wealth lay "in the ownership of peasants and not of land."[34]

These examples, drawn from widely different continents, centuries, and social science disciplines, are by no means all identical, but they do suggest a common pattern; and taken together they present the mystery that is my point of departure in this book. As we survey human legal cultures, past and present, we encounter two contrasting ways in which the right of property has "struck the imagination and engaged the affections of mankind": Some cultures have put "higher value on control over people"; some have put higher value on "ownership of land." In some the right of property has been paradigmatically claimed by the declaration *this land is mine*, in some by *this man is mine*. In some owners have been, if you will, house-proud, in some slave-proud.

---

[31] Jürgen Osterhammel, *Transformation of the World*, trans. P. Camiller (Princeton, 2014), 223.
[32] Pekka Hämäläinen, *The Comanche Empire* (New Haven, 2009), 5.
[33] Sahlins, *Stone Age Economics*, new ed. (New York, 2017), 84–85; below, Chapter 1.
[34] Evsey Domar, "The Causes of Slavery or Serfdom: A Hypothesis," *Journal of Economic History* 30 (1970): 19 [18–32].

This contrast in human cultures of ownership, documented in the work of so many historians and social scientists, is powerful evidence of a basic truth about property, which was forcefully stated by David Hume: There is, Hume insisted, no "natural" form of property. Ownership is a complex human institution, paralleled among other animals only in its barest essentials;[35] and like all human institutions, it is shaped by cultural differences. "A man's property," as Hume put it in his *Treatise of Human Nature*, "is some object related to him. This relation is not natural, but moral, and founded on justice";[36] and "justice," in Hume's account, is the product of the conventions of human society. The evidence of these various societies makes it clear enough that those conventions can take divergent forms.

Two divergent forms in particular: owning humans and owning land. I am going to call these the two primitive modes of the property imagination. They can be called "primitive" in two senses of the word. On the one hand, they are "primitive" in the sense that they seem to constitute root conceptions of ownership, "archetypal forms" that have played a peculiarly prominent role in human thinking about what counts as property. As Blackstone writes, we *imagine* property; as Rose writes, we *picture* it; we start from a paradigmatic image of some thing or some creature that we might desire to own. Cognitive psychologists tell us that the human mind depends on "prototypes" or "exemplars" in order to make sense of the world, core instances by which it can categorize and evaluate what it perceives.[37] Owning humans and owning land seem, in these sundry cultures, to constitute the prototypes or exemplars – the images of property that have sprung first to the mind, the first entries in the dictionary. They are also, and as I shall argue in this book not coincidentally, the objects of ownership that have laid the foundations of "wealth, power, and prestige," the

---

[35] See below, Chapter 1.
[36] Hume, *A Treatise of Human Nature*, David Fate Norton and Mary J. Norton, eds. (Oxford, 2000), 315. There are of course two senses in which we may speak of the non-"natural" character of property: first, that there is no natural right of property, second that there is no natural form. My concern in this book is with the second.
[37] For discussion of a vast literature, Emmanuel Pothos, Andy J. Wills, John Paul Minda, and J. David Smith, "Prototype Models of Categorization: Basic Formulation, Predictions, and Limitations," in Pothos and Wills, *Formal Approaches in Categorization* (Cambridge, 2011), 40–64.

claims of right that justified the control of productive resources, defined high social status, and licensed violence.

Owning humans and owning land can be called "primitive" in a second sense as well: These are both conceptions of ownership that stand in some tension with what we should not be embarrassed to call civilization. The urge to own human beings is an impulse whose dangers we can all appreciate; in modern eyes, slavery has come to count as the definitional violation of human rights. A culture in which humans are perceived as objects of ownership, we all recognize, is a culture of evil. But as phenomena like the ideology of *Blut und Boden* and the American "castle doctrine" signal, the urge to own land carries dangers as well. Ethologists identify two basic drives in animal behavior, social dominance – the exercise of power by high-ranking animals over other, submissive, members of the species – and territoriality.[38] Ever since Robert Ardrey's 1966 bestseller *The Territorial Imperative*, it has been a commonplace that the second of these, territoriality, lies at the root of "the animal origins of property and nations," driving wars and other efforts, private and public, to claim *Lebensraum*.[39] Yet the study of these various legal cultures suggests that territoriality is not the only "animal origin" of human property law; dominance plays a part too; and both dominance and territoriality are worrisome. Both draw on disturbing wellsprings in human psychology. Both reflect the fact that human animals, in the dark words of Adam Smith, "love to domineer."[40]

* * *

This book is a study of these two patterns by which property "strikes the imagination, and engages the affections." As I aim to show, the contrast takes us deep into the mysteries of the human institution of ownership. I also have a historical thesis: Western property law bears the marks of a transformation, from an ancient world in which the property imagination centered heavily on the mastership over humans

---

[38] See below, Chapter 1.
[39] Ardrey, *The Territorial Imperative: A Personal Enquiry into the Animal Origins of Property and Nations* (New York, 1966).
[40] Smith, *An Inquiry into the Nature and Causes of the Wealth of Nations*, ed. Edwin Cannan (New York, 1994), 418. Smith had slavery in mind. As I shall try to show, the same urges are found in the ownership of land.

and other living creatures, to a modern world, in which the property imagination came to center on lordship over land.

That transformation has left many traces. Some of our most important property law doctrines originated in an ancient Roman legal culture whose property concepts regularly turned on the paradigm of the capture and subjugation of both human beings and animals. Over many centuries, however, those same doctrines came to turn on the paradigm of the settlement and cultivation of the soil. The long history of this transformation reached its culmination in the late eighteenth and nineteenth centuries, which saw the final disappearance of slavery from Western law. Indeed, as I will argue in the closing chapter, we cannot fully answer the great question of why the ownership of human beings lost its legitimacy in Western law unless we come to terms with the many centuries of silent transformation in the property imagination that preceded its disappearance.

Such is the history that this book sets out to retrace. Before diving in, it is essential to state one point as emphatically as possible: This is a book about the legal imagination, not about the realities of what people have in fact owned. To put it differently, this is not a history of property law in the narrow sense. The history of property law in the narrow sense is, quite properly, largely history of the mechanics of market and labor relations and of wealth distribution. By contrast, this book is a study of mentalities and ideologies – of how the law has imagined and justified ownership, and of how owners have imagined and justified themselves. In Patterson's elegant words, it is a study in the history of "idioms of power."

Those idioms of power have never been dictated in any simple or straightforward way by economic interests. Patterson was speaking of ancient Rome when he used the phrase "idiom of power," and the Roman example serves well to make the point. It is not the case that the ancient Romans only owned slaves and did not own real property. Far from it. Economic historians have thoroughly demonstrated the importance of landownership in the agrarian civilization of Rome. In particular, they have thoroughly discredited the old belief, held once upon a time by figures like Karl Marx and Max Weber, that the ancient Greco-Roman world had "slave economies."[41] But economic history

---

[41] See below, Chapter 7.

can never give an adequate account of the institution of ownership. Regardless of where their economic interests may have lain, when the Romans reached for paradigm examples of property rights, they displayed a striking habit of grasping at the capture and enslavement of an imaginary man, much as people in precolonial Africa and elsewhere did. This Roman idiom of power certainly bore *some* relationship to the Roman economics of slavery – but only some.[42] In any case, as thoughtful historians emphasize, no study of the economic interests of slaveholders can do full justice to the significance of slavery in Roman society. The master/slave idiom of power shaped Roman understandings of status and authority in realms well outside the limits of the master/slave relationship itself.[43]

Comparable observations can be made about the Britain of Blackstone. It is not the case that slavery had no place in the British economy of 1766, even if Blackstone tried to deny that it had any place in the common law.[44] Quite the contrary: As economic historians now vigorously maintain, a heavy proportion of British wealth grew out of the barbarities of the Atlantic slave trade.[45] But the sources of eighteenth-century wealth did not determine the shape of the eighteenth-century property imagination; the language of the law did not simply translate into black letter the language of economic interest. When Blackstone celebrated "despotic dominion," what he celebrated

---

[42] See the sage assessment of Aldo Schiavone, *The Invention of Law in the West*, trans. Jeremy Carden and Antony Shugaar (Cambridge, MA, 2012), 362–365.

[43] Bodel, "Slave Labour and Roman Society," in Bodel and Paul Cartledge, eds., *The Cambridge World History of Slavery, Vol. 1: The Ancient Mediterranean World* (Cambridge, 2011), 314 [311–336]: "we must approach the question as primarily a cultural rather than an economic issue"; sim. Keith Bradley, "Slavery in the Roman Republic," ibid., 245 [241–264]: "the proportion of slaves in the overall Roman population during the conquest remains indeterminate. What continue to be important therefore are institutional indicators of the predominance of slavery in Roman culture."

[44] Blackstone, *Commentaries on the Laws of England, Book I: Of the Rights of Persons*, ed. David Lemmings (Oxford, 2016), 272–273.

[45] E.g., Padraic X. Scanlan, *Slave Empire: How Slavery Built Modern Britain* (London, 2020). Nor is that the only way in which Blackstone's vision of the law departed from the realities: "Sole and despotic dominion" was not in fact a correct description of English property law. David Schorr, "How Blackstone Became a Blackstonian," *Theoretical Inquiries in Law* 10 (2009): 103–126; Carol Rose, "Canons of Property Talk, or Blackstone's Anxiety," *Yale Law Journal* 108 (1998): 601–632. As we shall see in Chapter 9, Blackstone was in this respect typical of early modern treatise writers.

was despotic dominion over land. The same can be said of other Britons as well – for example, of Jane Austen, a woman, as scholars argue, who idealized landholdings even as her family accumulated wealth from the slave trade, which meets with "dead silence" in her novels.[46] The point is, once again, not one about how British fortunes were amassed, but one about how, in Blackstone's own beautiful phrase, property "struck the [British] imagination and engaged [British] affections."

By the same token, and not least, the fact that contemporary Americans think first of a plot of land when they hear someone utter the word "property," and brandish their right "to use arms in defense of hearth and home," does not by any means imply that real estate is the most important factor in the contemporary American economy. What it tells us instead is something about the American culture of ownership, and something troubling at that.

Economic analysis is incapable of making sense of all this. Most especially, it is incapable of making sense of a critical feature of ownership upon which I will lay much emphasis in the chapters that follow: The claim of ownership commonly lays the legal foundation for some sort of claim to the right to use violence. The "castle doctrine" in American law is an obvious example;[47] on the larger international stage the same is true of territorial disputes in war. As both suggest, assertions of the right to lands often imply assertions of the right to resort to force, and at the limit to kill, whether in the course of defending those rights or in the course of acquiring them. *I am the homeowner*, says the American, ***ergo*** *I can take the life of this intruder, and it will be no murder*. Claims to the ownership of humans obviously license violence as well. *I am the slaveowner*, says the Roman whose behavior is deplored by Seneca, ***ergo*** *I can order this slave flogged for any reason I like*.[48] The same is true of the violence visited by husbands on the wives

---

[46] Edward Said, *Culture and Imperialism* (New York, 1993), 96 and generally 80–97. See the thoughtful and measured discussion of Devoney Looser, "Breaking the Silence: Exploring the Austen Family's Complex Entanglements with Slavery," *Times Literary Supplement*, May 21, 2021, available at www.the-tls.co.uk/articles/jane-austen-family-slavery-essay-devoney-looser/.

[47] Daniel Sharfstein, "Atrocity, Entitlement and Personhood in Property," *Virginia Law Review* 98 (2012): 635–690.

[48] Sen. *Ira* 3.35.2, in Robert Kaster and Martha C. Nussbaum, trans., *Seneca: Anger, Mercy, Revenge* (Chicago, 2010), 90.

they are understood to "own," by fathers on the children they "own," by the "owners" of animals, and more. "Ownership" does not just ground rights to buy and sell. It grounds rights to command, coerce, beat, and at times kill. No purely economistic theory of property that fails to reckon with this centrally important fact about the human institution of ownership can possibly count as complete.

The fact that ownership grounds rights to command, coerce, beat, and at times kill is especially important because it helps us to understand a fact about human societies upon which I will lay much emphasis in this book: The "idioms of power" of ownership are commonly akin to the "idioms of power" of rulership; the models used to conceive and justify the private exercise of "despotic dominion" are also the models used to conceive and justify the state exercise of "despotic dominion." In some legal cultures, rulers are understood to exercise power over peoples; in others they are understood to exercise power over territories. "Rulership," as Hugo Grotius wrote in 1625, "can take two possible subject matters. The primary type is rulership over persons ... as for example over a horde of men, women and children seeking a new place to settle. The secondary type is rulership over a place, which is called 'territory.'"[49] Cultures with Grotius' "primary" type, rulership over persons, tend also to be cultures with ownership of humans, as we shall see; cultures with territorial rulership, the type that Grotius deemed "secondary," tend also to be cultures with territorial ownership. "Sovereignty and property," in the words of the marvelously learned historian of international law Martti Koskenniemi, "are the yin and yang of power," and each must generally be seen in light of the other.[50] Goody's phraseology handsomely captures this consonance between yin and yang, rulership and ownership: In some cultures, the law generally presupposes the "chieftainship over land," both when it comes to owners and when it comes to rulers; in others, it generally presupposes the "chieftainship over people."

* * *

---

[49] Grotius, *De jure belli ac pacis*, ed. Jean Barbeyrac (Utrecht, 1773), 1:233–234 (2.3.4.1): *Imperium duas solet habere materias sibi subjacentes, primariam personas, quae materia sola interdum sufficit, ut in exercitu virorum, mulierum, puerorum quaerente novas sedes; et secundariam locum, qui dicitur territorium.* For further discussion of the phrase "interdum sufficit" see below, Chapter 8.

[50] Koskenniemi, *To the Uttermost Parts of the Earth: Legal Imagination and International Power, 1300–1870* (Cambridge, 2021), 959.

The chapters that follow make use of many examples from anthropology and comparative history. But their core focus is on the long history of the Roman legal tradition, which established the basic terms for Western property thinking in both the civil law and the common law worlds, and many of the basic terms for the Western understanding of rulership as well. The "West," as I will speak of it in this book, is the West of the Roman legal tradition.

At its ancient origins, the book argues, Roman law bore an unmistakable kinship with the law of societies like those of precolonial Africa, the Southwest of the Comanches, and many others worldwide that put "higher value on the control over people." This was not, be it said one last time, a matter of the Roman economic realities of any period. The Romans certainly always owned land. But as we shall see, the ancient Roman understanding of the nature of land tenure was often different from the modern understanding, while the Roman idiom of power – its legal terminology, symbolism, and normative tropes – was rich in the language of the capture and ownership of humans, alongside something closely related: the capture and ownership of beasts.

The association between slaves and beasts was close indeed, as is often the case in slave societies; and the law presupposed that both were acquired in much the same way. Slaves were paradigmatically captured in war, while beasts were paradigmatically captured in the hunt; and warmaking and hunting were linked in Antiquity: War was a form of hunting, only with human instead of animal prey, one of its principal aims being to enslave one's opponents. "There is a hunting of man," as Plato put it; "the whole art of war is hunting."[51] Aristotle spoke in the same terms,[52] and so, centuries later, did Max Weber: "In Antiquity, war is always also a hunt for slaves."[53] Roman property law imagery drew on both kinds of hunt, and its property law teachings and terminology often pictured the owner as a man of arms, who seized and subjugated both wild beasts and free men. Ancient Roman law,

---

[51] Plat. *Soph.* 222c, in Harold North Fowler, trans., *Plato: Theaetetus, Sophist*, Loeb Classical Library 123 (Cambridge, MA, 1921), 284–285. This passage is concerned with more than just war; I will have more to say about it in Chapter 3.
[52] Arist. *Pol.* 1256b, in H. Rackham, trans., *Aristotle: Politics*, Loeb Classical Library 264 (Cambridge, MA, 1932), 36–37.
[53] Weber, "Die sozialen Gründe des Untergangs der antike Kultur," in Weber, *Gesammelte Aufsätze zur Sozial- und Wirtschaftsgeschichte* (Tübingen, 1924), 293 [289–311].

like ancient vases, ancient poems, and ancient mosaics, was festooned with figures of hunters and warriors, often shown bearing down on their victims, spear or sword in hand. In this, I will argue, the law bore a kinship with classical Greco-Roman religion, in which, as the historian of religion Mircea Eliade writes, "warriors, conquerors, and military aristocracies carr[ied] on the symbolism and ideology of the paradigmatic hunter."[54]

The Roman legal sources that feature this "symbolism and ideology of the paradigmatic hunter" can strike the modern reader as savage. They are studded with ugly slave-society formulae such as "I declare that this man is mine"; their doctrines on the acquisition of property casually lump together animal and human prey; their basic terminology makes use of words meaning "master of slaves and beasts"; and they ascribe the chilling power of life and death to a *paterfamilias* who ruled as a kind of absolute chieftain over a Roman household that commingled his descendants, his slaves, and his animals.[55] The law takes it for granted that the enslavement of enemies in war is inherently legitimate; indeed, as we shall see in Chapter 4, the jurists understood it to be a matter of basic justice that enemies should be treated as potential human prey to be hunted down. Roman ideology of imperial rule spoke in the same tones of insouciant brutality: The Romans, as Myles Lavan writes, often declared that the peoples of the world had been made "slaves to Rome."[56] At their most disturbing moments, the ancient Roman texts even call to mind Friedrich Nietzsche's notorious account of the "blond beast" of Antiquity – the dominant male who behaved as a "magnificent animal of prey, roving in search of booty and victory";[57] for "booty and victory" were indeed much the stuff of ancient Roman property symbolism and ideology.

But we must not allow ourselves to be fooled by the savage imagery in the sources. The law, as the great ancient historian M. I. Finley warns, "often give[s] a false picture of what [was] actually being done

---

[54] Eliade, *A History of Religious Ideas*, trans. Willard Trask (Chicago, 1978), 1:35.
[55] Below, Chapter 2.
[56] Lavan, *Slaves to Rome: Paradigms of Empire in Roman Culture* (Cambridge, 2013).
[57] Nietzsche, *Zur Genealogie der Moral*, Bk I, §11: "Auf dem Grunde aller dieser vornehmen Rassen ist das Raubthier, die prachtvolle nach Beute und Sieg lüstern schweifende *blonde* Bestie nicht zu verkennen," in Giorgio Colli and Mazzino Montanari, eds., *Nietzsches Werke: historisch-kritische Ausgabe* (Charlottesville, 1995), 6.2:289.

in society."⁵⁸ Contemporary classicists have put great energy into showing that the Roman socio-economic realities give the lie to the legal texts. The Roman *paterfamilias* did not really enjoy the power of life and death that the law ascribed to him; that is a "myth."⁵⁹ Roman slaves were not really enemies who had been captured on the field of battle; that is a "myth" too.⁶⁰ The peoples of the Empire were not really the slaves of Roman masters, any more than the Roman economy really depended on the slave mode of production. Most broadly, the Romans, though they engaged in forms of casual violence that shock us today, were not really Nietzschean "blond beasts" (although, as Chapter 2 will recount, Nazi ideologues believed they were, holding that archaic Rome was the home of a race of conquering Aryan warriors).

The reality, contemporary Roman law scholars insist, is that the ancients were market actors like us, who responded to the same economic incentives that we respond to, trading, lending, and borrowing; among other things, they were "feverishly engaged" in real estate deals.⁶¹ It would be no more correct to conclude from the prevalence of master/slave language in the Roman legal sources that ancient Rome had a slave economy (the conclusion once drawn by not only by Marx and Weber, but by many other scholars as well) than it would be to conclude from the reading of an American casebook that the most important economic factor in the contemporary United States is land, or to conclude from a reading of Blackstone that slavery had no place in the eighteenth-century British economy. An "élite mentality" pervades the sources, as Finley insisted; but that mentality, as Walter Scheidel and Sitta von Reden write, had doubtful "real-life impact."⁶² The ancient terminology and symbolism are not blueprints of the workings of ancient economies. They are articulations of an ancient legal imagination. They are expressions of the ways in which the

---

⁵⁸ Finley, *Ancient Slavery and Modern Ideology*, expanded ed., ed. Brent Shaw (New York, 1998), 193.
⁵⁹ Brent Shaw, "Raising and Killing Children: Two Roman Myths," *Mnemosyne* Ser. 4, 54 (2001): 31–77.
⁶⁰ Harper, *Slavery in the Late Roman World*, AD 275–425 (Cambridge, 2011), 34.
⁶¹ Elizabeth Rawson, "The Ciceronian Aristocracy and Its Properties," in M. I. Finley, ed., *Studies in Roman Property* (Cambridge, 1976), 86 [85–102].
⁶² Scheidel and von Reden, "Introduction," in M. I. Finley, *The Ancient Economy*, Scheidel and von Reden, eds. (New York, 2002), 3 [1–10].

Romans, in the words of Kyle Harper, "conceived of and justified" ownership.[63]

But it is the premise of this book that ways of conceiving and justifying matter. The legal imagination, as Koskenniemi writes, is a motive force in human societies; our modes of picturing and justifying supply us with "both an interpretation of the world and a recipe for dealing with its problems."[64] Rome may not have had a slave economy; but that is not the end of the matter. When the law calls a man a master, it invites him to behave like a master. The haunting reflections of Thomas Jefferson, master of hundreds of slaves, cry out to be quoted: "The whole commerce between master and slave is a perpetual exercise of the most boisterous passions, the most unremitting despotism on the one part, and degrading submissions on the other. Our children see this, and learn to imitate it; for man is an imitative animal."[65] Jefferson was echoing Hume, who described the behavior of American slaveholders, and their resemblance to ancient Romans, with characteristically disabused eloquence:

> The little humanity, commonly observed in persons, accustomed, from their infancy, to exercise so great authority over their fellow-creatures, and to trample upon human nature, were sufficient alone to disgust us with that unbounded dominion. Nor can a more probable reason be assigned for the severe, I might say, barbarous manners of ancient times, than the practice of domestic slavery; by which every man of rank was rendered a petty tyrant, and educated amidst the flattery, submission, and low debasement of his slaves.[66]

Law does not just grease the gears of the economy. It teaches "manners," and sometimes "barbarous" ones. The human being, Jefferson's "imitative animal," takes cues from other human beings, and it takes cues from the conceptualizations of the law as well.

And the law is always in the business of giving cues. It has to be, for the simple Humean reason that there is no "natural" form of property. The law imposes a conceptual order on the world – what the philosopher and jurist William Ewald calls a "framework of

---

[63] Harper, *Slavery in the Late Roman World*, 34.
[64] Koskenniemi, *Uttermost Parts*, 952.
[65] Jefferson, *Notes on the State of Virginia* (Baltimore, 1800), 163 (= Query 18).
[66] Hume, "Of the Populousness of Ancient Nations," in Hume, *Political Discourses*, 2nd ed. (Edinburgh, 1752), 161–162 [155–262].

cognition";[67] and that conceptual order counts as "law" because it both guides and justifies the conduct of those it classifies as owners. As the Marxist tradition puts the point, the exercise of property rights is always bound up with some sort of justificatory ideology.

The ingenious definition of "ideology" of the Marxist philosopher Louis Althusser lends itself particularly aptly to the long history of Western ownership that I will recount in this book: Ideology, Althusser wrote, is "the imaginary relationship of individuals to their real conditions of existence."[68] It is a familiar Marxist charge that "the imaginary relationship" of modern Western owners "to their real conditions of existence" takes a form drawn from the labor theory of John Locke: We conceive of and justify ownership as the supposed reward for productive effort. "'Property created by the owner's labor' in civilized society," Friedrich Engels sneered, "is an ideal fiction of the jurists and economists, the last lying legal pretense by which modern capitalist property still props itself up."[69] Or as Patterson more gracefully phrases it, the fiction that ownership is always the reward for labor is our way of "cloth[ing] the beastliness" of the property order.[70] The ancient Roman sources strike us as savage, the first Part of this book argues, because the Romans had an alien vocabulary of lying pretense. Instead of justifying ownership as the reward for productive labor, they tended to justify it as the reward for success in the manly pursuits of war and the hunt, letting their beastliness go, to the modern eye, unclothed.

* * *

The argument of this book, then, is that Western law bears the marks of a long-term transformation – but not a transformation from the economics of slavery to the economics of landownership. It bears the marks of a transformation in the "idioms of power" of the law. The history of Western property law is, in some very considerable measure, a history of how the law of an ancient

---

[67] Ewald, "Comparative Jurisprudence (I): What Was It Like to Try a Rat?" *University of Pennsylvania Law Review* 143 (1995): 1940 [1889–2149].

[68] Althusser, "Idéologie et appareils idéologiques d'État," available at http://classiques.uqac.ca/contemporains/althusser_louis/ideologie_et_AIE/ideologie_et_AIE.pdf.

[69] Engels, *Der Ursprung der Familie, des Privateigenthums, und des Staats* (Hottingen-Zürich, 1884), 155. I have taken the English translation from the text available at www.marxists.org/archive/marx/works/1884/origin-family/ch09.htm.

[70] Patterson, *Slavery and Social Death*, 18.

culture whose understanding of "despotic dominion" centered on the subjugation of human and animal prey, and the rule over peoples, was transformed into a law of modern cultures whose understanding of "despotic dominion" came to center on the settlement and cultivation of land, and the rule over territories.

The transformation can be traced in the history of some of the most important doctrines that the West has inherited from ancient Rome. One especially significant example is the history of the Roman law of *occupatio*, the law of how to acquire things that have never been owned before. There are few property law doctrines that have attracted more intense interest among contemporary historians than *occupatio*. European conquests from the sixteenth century onward often turned on the *occupatio* of land, justified as the taking of *res nullius*, a thing belonging to no one, or later as the taking of *terra nullius*, land belonging to no one; for that reason, historians of European colonialism and imperialism have devoted reams of writing to it.[71] To early modern and modern Westerners it seemed obvious that land was the paradigmatic form of property to be acquired through "occupation." Kant, for instance, declared that the only possible subject of such appropriation was "the soil";[72] in this he was echoing Locke, Rousseau, and many other early modern authors, and anticipating later theorists of the soil such as Carl Schmitt, all of whom took it for granted that land was necessarily the primary object of acquisition.

Yet as we shall see, the ancient Roman doctrine of *occupatio* on which this was based had virtually nothing to do with land. Ancient Roman *occupatio* was a doctrine about hunting down wild animals and enslaving enemies in war. *Occupatio* began, as A.-J. Arnaud writes, as law of the hunt for living creatures and mobile spoils – it was law of "the mastery of hunters over their game, the mastery of fishers over their catch ... war captives ... and booty";[73] and as a matter of imperial rule, too, the classical Romans "conquered

---

[71] See the discussion in Lauren Benton and Benjamin Straumann, "Acquiring Empire by Law: From Roman Doctrine to Early Modern European Practice," *Law and History Review* 28 (2010): 1–36.

[72] Kant, *Philosophy of Law*, trans. W. Hastie (Edinburgh, 1887), 87.

[73] Arnaud, "Reflexions sur l'occupation du droit romain," *Revue historique du droit* 46 (1968), 186; cf. 188 [183–210]. Further discussion below, Chapter 4.

peoples, not land."⁷⁴ Only centuries later was *occupatio* transformed into law for the "occupiers" of the soil, in Europe and in the wider conquered world, undergoing what Arnaud calls a "radical transformation" that "operated on the foundation and form of our conception of the law of property."⁷⁵ The law of first acquisition was born as law of tracking and capturing living prey, not what it became for Western colonizers and John Locke, a law of "discovering," settling, and cultivating land.

Signs of the same "radical transformation ... that operated on the foundation and form of our conception of the law of property" can be detected throughout Western law, both in the forms of ownership and in the forms of rulership. A second important example involves the semantic history of the Roman terminology highlighted by Patterson in his account of the Roman idiom of power: *dominus*, and its derivative form *dominium*. *Dominus* and *dominium* are the principal terms for "owner" and "property" in the Western tradition. *Dominium* is the term that appears, for example, in Blackstone's familiar formula "despotic dominion." The power exercised by the *dominus* over his *dominium* lies at the foundation of the distinctive Western way of understanding property. According to this Western way of owning, the rights of the owner are "absolute": The owner, the *dominus*, is deemed to have the unshackled power to use, abuse, and destroy his possessions without regard to the interests of any other person.

At its origins, as Patterson observes, this "absolute" conception was the product of an ancient Roman slave society: *Dominus* meant "master," and its core meaning referred to the ownership of slaves.⁷⁶ The law extended this slave-word to all objects of ownership: Owners, in the jargon of the law, were called "masters" of everything they possessed, animate and inanimate alike. Nevertheless, in everyday ancient Latin usage, *dominus* never ceased to mean "master," and Patterson is by no means the only observer to argue that these terms

---

[74] Benjamin Isaac, *Limits of Empire: The Roman Army in the East*, rev. ed. (Oxford, 2000), 395.
[75] Arnaud, "Reflexions sur l'occupation," 199.
[76] The term *erus* was also used, possibly in particular by slaves in addressing their masters. For discussion of the two terms, see Luigi Capogrossi Colognesi, *Proprietà e signoria in Roma antica*, 2nd ed. (Rome, 1994), 257–287. See further the discussion below, Chapters 2 and 3.

never lost their conceptual roots in the ancient master/slave relationship. The formidable Roman law scholar Max Kaser, for example, described the Romans of the Imperial period as men who liked to call themselves "masters" not only when they spoke of their slaves or beasts, but also of their inanimate possessions.[77] We shall see more about the Roman liking for calling themselves "masters" in Chapter 3. In Chapter 5, we shall see that they often used the same symbolism and ideology to describe their rule over their Empire: There too, they described themselves as *domini*, masters; the idiom of power in Roman rulership was much the same as the idiom of power in Roman ownership; sovereignty and property, Koskenniemi's yin and yang, both sounded in the chieftainship over people.[78]

In subsequent centuries, however, *dominus* and *dominium*, this ancient language of the master and his slave-holdings, literal and metaphorical, underwent a series of striking semantic transformations, which have been chronicled by scholars such as Paolo Grossi and Alain Guerreau. In the parlance of the Middle Ages, *dominium* came to signify primarily the ownership of land; but it also signified the right to rule over the dependents on that land, "covering simultaneously power over land and men."[79] As Grossi, the master Italian historian of property law, formulates it, the "juridical experience" of Western ownership changed: Where in Antiquity it revolved around the paradigmatic figure of the household master, whose "absolute" rule over humans and other living creatures was conceptually extended to his rule over things, in the Middle Ages, it came to revolve around the paradigmatic figure of the feudal noble, maintaining a manorial court and enjoying a variety of privileges.[80] Medieval *dominium* thus stood somewhere midway between ancient slavery and modern landownership, encompassing

---

[77] Max Kaser, *Eigentum und Besitz im älteren römischen Recht* (Weimar, 1943), 308.
[78] Kaser, *Eigentum un Besitz*, 302–306.
[79] Guerreau, *Le féodalisme: un horizon théorique* (Paris, 1980), 181. Of course the term had an immense variety of meanings, beginning with the *dominium* exercised by God. For the fuller range of meanings, see http://ducange.enc.sorbonne.fr/dominus. In quoting Guerreau, I do not mean to suggest that the meaning of *dominium*, a subject of voluminous discussion among medievalists and historians of political theory, ends there. My purpose is only his: To contrast its usage in describing owners with that of classical Roman law. Much more treatment of the term will be found in the chapters that follow.
[80] Grossi, *Le situazioni reali nell'esperienza giuridica medievale* (Padua, 1968), discussed below, Chapter 8.

both control of land and control of human beings; it intermingled Goody's chieftainship over land with his chieftainship over people. But beginning especially in the second half of the eighteenth century, the semantics of the terms shifted further: *Dominium* took on a more restricted sense, as purely the ownership of "the external things of the world," without any accompanying right to rule over persons, a development that can be traced in the thought of Enlightenment figures such as Hume, Smith, Blackstone, and Kant. Most of these Enlightenment authors were consciously anti-feudal; but none of them ceased to think of property in the first instance as property in land.[81]

Many comparable instances of the same "radical transformation" can be given as well; and it is important to recognize that they extend beyond the law of property. They also include a "radical transformation" in conceptions of rule, and of the very nature of law itself. Kingship is a key example. In the early Middle Ages, there was a King of the Franks, the chief of what medievalists call a "state as a collectivity of persons"; from the later Middle Ages onward, there came to be a King of France, the chief over a "land-surface state."[82] The transformation in the conceptualization of ownership was thus paralleled by a transformation in the conceptualization of rulership, from Grotius' primary form, "rulership over people," to his secondary form, "rulership over a place, which is called 'territory.'"

In tandem with this transformation from rulership over people to rulership over land came a changing conception of what counted as a realm. Premodern states did not ordinarily have sharp boundary lines; their edges were marches and fluid frontier zones.[83] As the anthropologist Alain Testart writes, they lacked a "territorial base," exercising instead "primarily power over humans and not over things."[84] Only in the later Middle Ages, and especially from the sixteenth century onward, did Europeans come to think of the world as sharply divided by borders of the familiar modern kind, just as the properties of landowners were

---

[81] Another closely related term underwent a similar transformation: *servus*, which meant "slave" in Antiquity, came in time to mean "serf." See below, Chapter 7.
[82] With many complications discussed below in Chapters 5 and 8.
[83] Below, Chapter 5.
[84] Testart, *Éléments de classification des sociétés* (Paris, 2005), 82.

divided by sharply drawn boundaries.[85] Only in the late eighteenth and nineteenth centuries, as historians of state power such as Lauren Benton and Charles Maier have demonstrated, do we find a clearly established commitment to the proposition that European states, like the private owners of land, should occupy contiguous and clearly demarcated territories, rather than existing as scattered domains whose populations were subject to the personal rule of the same monarch.[86] Only at that very late date do both a concept of property founded in the ownership of land, and the territorial state, congeal into their modern forms.

It was in the midst of the same late medieval and early modern transition to a law centered on landownership and territorial rule that the concept of the *ius soli*, of citizenship by virtue of birth on the soil of a particular territory, came fully to the fore. More generally, the later Middle Ages and early modern period witnessed a slow movement from personal law to territorial law: In Antiquity Romans lived, at least in principle, by the law of the Romans, Jews lived by the law of the Jews, and so on.[87] By the sixteenth, seventeenth, and eighteenth centuries, monarchs demanded increasingly that all live by the uniform law of the land.

* * *

Not least, it was during the same transformative centuries, from the late medieval period into the nineteenth century, that landownership came gradually to displace slaveownership in Western law. Just as where once there had been a King of the Franks there came to be a King of France, where once there had been owners of human beings, there came to be owners of land.

This great shift had many manifestations, among them a development much discussed among historians of slavery: Beginning in the later Middle Ages, "free-soil" doctrines emerged in northwestern Europe. It came to be the rule that, while humans might lawfully be acquired and owned anywhere else, most particularly in Africa and the New World,

---

[85] Below, Chapter 5 and Friedrich Kratochwil, "Of Systems, Boundaries, and Territoriality: An Inquiry into the Formation of the State System," *World Politics* 39 (1986): 27–52.

[86] Benton, *A Search for Sovereignty: Law and Geography in European Empires, 1400–1900* (Cambridge, 2010); Maier, *Once within Borders: Territories of Power, Wealth and Belonging since 1500* (Cambridge, MA, 2016).

[87] But with many complications discussed in Chapter 5.

there were no slaves on the territory of France or the Netherlands or England.[88] Free-soil doctrines probably first began to appear in thirteenth-century cities including Toulouse and Bologna.[89] They became important throughout northwestern Europe from the latter part of the sixteenth century onward, especially in France.[90] In England, where such free-soil doctrines had already been vaguely enunciated in the sixteenth century,[91] they reappeared in Lord Mansfield's epoch-making 1772 decision in Somerset's Case, the great decision that opened the way for British anti-slavery campaigns.[92]

These free-soil doctrines, be it emphasized, were not an expression of an abolitionist commitment to universal human rights. It is hardly the case that late sixteenth-century French law, for example, showed a dedication to the dignity and equality of all persons. None of these teachings held that slavery itself was universally impermissible, only that it was repugnant to the law of the territory in which the court in question sat. This was law that freed lands, not humans. The long history of free soil reached its climax in the nineteenth-century United States, where free-soil doctrines were incorporated into the Northwest Ordinance and the Missouri Compromise, serving as the basis of the Antebellum condominium between North and South. But over time, as all Americans know, a growing crisis in the idea of free soil, which culminated in its rejection by the Supreme Court in *Dred Scott v. Sandford*, played a crucial role in triggering the American Civil War.[93] The Civil War, seen in the large historical perspective of legal history, was thus the closing chapter in a centuries-long reorientation

---

[88] Sue Peabody and Keila Grinberg, eds., *Free Soil in the Atlantic World* (New York, 2015).

[89] Below, Chapter 9.

[90] Drescher, *Abolition*; Sue Peabody, *There Are No Slaves in France: The Political Culture of Race and Slavery in the Ancien Régime* (Oxford, 1996).

[91] Hulsebosch, "Somerset's Case at the Bar: Securing the 'Pure Air' of English Jurisdiction within the British Empire," *Texas Wesleyan Law Review* 13 (2006/7): 699 [699–710].

[92] *Somerset v. Stewart*, 98 ER 499 (1772).

[93] *Dred Scott v. Sandford*, 60 U.S. (19 How.) 393 (1857). The reasoning of the opinion turned, most familiarly, on whether Black people could be citizens. But the facts of the case involved the classic free-soil claim that Dred Scott had become free upon setting foot on the soil of Illinois and Wisconsin Territory, and much of the decision is devoted to that doctrine. I will not enter here into the debate over how much Dred Scott mattered for the outbreak of the Civil War, beyond observing its importance within the long free-soil tradition.

away from the ownership of humans and toward the ownership of land, whose beginnings must be traced back more than a half millennium before Appomattox.

And by the latter half of the nineteenth century, this transformation was sufficiently advanced that the law throughout the West would recognize only owners of land, not owners of humans. As I will argue in the final chapter, this implies an account of the final disappearance of lawful slavery that is in tension with those that mostly prevail in the current literature.

The nineteenth-century disappearance of lawful slavery (or, as I will be careful to insist, the disappearance of lawful *private* enslavement[94]) is the threshold event in the rise of the modern culture of human rights, and there are correspondingly intense debates over its causes. Scholars defend two conflicting principal views. One school, whose thought dates back to Adam Smith, holds that slavery proved to be economically unsustainable. As industrial capitalism developed, according to the classic version of this interpretation, slavery was outcompeted by wage labor. That explanation was once taken for granted by most historians,[95] but it has little support today. In its place, a second school now dominates. Far from being economically unsustainable, this second school now maintains, slavery was flourishing in the late eighteenth and early nineteenth centuries, and indeed grew more profitable with the rise of transborder capitalism. It was only through the actions of leaders driven by the urge for moral reform, notably ones motivated by Christian convictions, that this highly lucrative institution was finally stamped out.

There is much power in this literature, which includes the work of great scholars from Adam Smith to David Brion Davis. Yet the long history of the law of ownership recounted in this book points toward a far older, far deeper, and considerably more mysterious process of change. The disappearance of slavery from Western property law

---

[94] As I will emphasize below, Chapter 9, enslavement to the state, rather than declining in the nineteenth century, was on the upswing.

[95] This owes much to the seminal work of Eric Williams, who compelled historians to give closer attention to the place of slavery within the capitalist economy; Williams, *Capitalism and Slavery* (Chapel Hill, 1944). For discussion and extensive citation from current literature, see Holly Brewer, "Slavery, Sovereignty, and 'Inheritable Blood': Reconsidering John Locke and the Origins of American Slavery," *American Historical Review* 122 (2017): 1041 and 1041 n. 7 [1038–1078].

cannot be understood if we focus only on the events and ideas of the eighteenth and nineteenth centuries, and it cannot be understood if we consider only economic forces or abolitionist beliefs. Indeed, it cannot be understood if we focus only on the history of slavery and not on the larger history of the property imagination. The end of slavery was only one aspect of a "radical transformation" that did indeed "operate on the foundation and form of the law of property," and the foundation and form of our conception of rulership as well. The "control over people" had been gradually giving way to the control over land long before the rise of either industrial capitalism or abolitionism. Observed through the long lens of general legal history, the disappearance of lawful slavery looks like the product of an immensely slow process of transformation in the imaginative relationship between humans and "the external things of the world," a "deep history," in the phrase of historian Daniel Lord Smail, that unfolded over at least a millennium and a half.[96]

Understanding that deep history is indispensable for our understanding of the causes of the end of lawful slavery. It is also indispensable for reckoning with the consequences. We speak as though the historic alternative to slavery has been freedom, but that is not quite right. The truth is that the alternative has typically been a different form of subjection, founded in the ownership of land. The history of the decline of slavery is not the history of the triumph of liberty in some simple way. Instead, it has regularly been the history of what the Marxist tradition has always called the passage "from slavery to serfdom."[97] Marx and his followers dated that transition from one form of oppression to another to the decline and fall of the Western Roman Empire. But the fact is that it is a transition that has taken place many times, under many names, in the Western world. It has been identified in various episodes dating to Late Antiquity and the Middle Ages; but transitions "from slavery to serfdom" also occurred repeatedly in the early modern and modern centuries. This includes the treatment of indigenous populations by the Spanish colonizers, and the fate of former slaves in early nineteenth-century Haiti: In both

[96] Smail, *On Deep History and the Brain* (Berkeley, 2008); Andrew Shryock and Daniel Lord Smail, *Deep History: The Architecture of Past and Present* (Berkeley, 2011).
[97] Below, Chapter 7.

cases, the miseries of slavery were succeeded by the miseries of a form of serfdom. Not least, it includes the history of the United States: The Civil War abolished slavery, but it did not abolish domination based on the ownership of land. The result was that many oppressed early nineteenth-century slaves became oppressed late nineteenth- and early twentieth-century sharecroppers and other laborers effectively tied to the soil. The slaves once again became serfs of a kind; the masters once again became lords.

These dismal *sequelae* belong to the history of abolition too; and we are all too likely to miss them if we root our conception of human rights too exclusively in the abolitionist campaign against the immorality of "property in man."[98] What Smith called the "love [of] domineer[ing]" and St. Augustine called the *libido dominandi*, the "lust for domination," does not make itself felt in the institution of the ownership of human beings alone.[99] It makes itself felt in the institution of ownership *tout court*. Truncated histories of slavery and its abolition – histories that omit the *longue durée* of the history of the Western property imagination – will never suffice for a reckoning with all the dimensions of the human exercise of power.

The Plan of This Book

This book takes the form of an extended essay on the history of the transformation in the legal imagination sketched in this Introduction, focusing on key doctrines in the Roman legal tradition, such as *occupatio* and the conception of *dominium*, alongside changes in the conceptualization of rulership, and the causes of the disappearance of lawful slavery. I make no claim to offer a history of the economics of Western property relations. Nor do I provide an exhaustive account of Roman property law. My aim is narrower: It is to track the history of crucial teachings whose conceptual coloration has changed over the long centuries of the Western legal tradition. I ask specialists in the field to understand the ambitions of this book: I do not pretend to say everything

---

[98] The slogan quite familiar in the Revolutionary Era, as Sean Wilentz emphasizes. Wilentz, *No Property in Man: Slavery and Anti-slavery at the Nation's Founding* (Cambridge, MA, 2018).

[99] Augustine, *De civitate Dei, Libri I–X*, Corpus Christianorum, series Latina 47 (Turnhout, 1955), 1.

that can be said. *Of course* there is more to Roman property law than what I investigate here.

Part I is dedicated to explicating the mystery of the imaginative orientation of the ancient sources. As it sets out to show, Roman property law can only be understood against the background of comparative anthropology and ethology, and of comparative religion as well.

Chapter 1 sets the stage with the anthropology and ethology of ownership. There is a lively literature on the very early history of human property. Social scientists compare human territoriality and dominance to territoriality and dominance among other animals, such as birds, lions, and house cats, examine claims to the ownership of prey in hunter-gatherer societies, and dissect the forms of nonmodern, non-Western land tenure. The chapter reviews this literature, and sketches a contrast between two patterns in ownership culture, one more strongly oriented toward Goody's "chieftainship over people" and toward hunting norms, the other more strongly oriented toward the "chieftainship over land." Rights in land exist in both types of culture. But in the chieftainship over people, widespread throughout the non-Western, nonmodern world, rights in land take the form of what anthropologists call "use rights," granted out by chiefs in accordance with "the status or position in society" of the rights-holders. Rights in land, in such a use-rights system, can be described, in ethological terms, as a function of the social dominance order: They are distributed by a chief, the human cousin of the alpha male of other primates, and they presuppose "control over people rather than ownership of land."

The chapter also emphasizes a second topic, of particular importance for understanding the anthropological background to ancient Roman law: Studies of early human property focus in particular on the ownership of prey in the hunt. The chapter places this research in the context of the anthropology of hunting, as well as the accounts of the origins of classical religion found in the work of two great historians of religion, Walter Burkert and Mircea Eliade, both of whom argued that the structures of classical Greco-Roman sacrificial religion could be traced back thousands of years to the hunting practices of the Paleolithic.

Chapters 2, 3, and 4 turn to the Roman property law teachings that have been foundational in the formation of the Western legal tradition – teachings on the nature of ownership and the law of enslavement. Chapter 2 begins with archaic Roman property law, a body of mysterious sources whose symbolism and terminology show a striking orientation toward the ownership of living creatures, human and animal. That symbolism and terminology was seized upon by many of the leading scholars and thinkers of the past, who believed it offered clues to the origins of human society, supposedly based exclusively on the ownership of slaves and beasts and lacking the ownership of land. Those interpretations have been rightly dismissed today. Modern scholarship has been heavily dedicated to reconstructing the socio-economic realities; scholars often deploy their learning to dispel the "myths" in the sources. Yet, as the chapter argues, the myths matter; "idioms of power" cannot simply be written off; we must take the imagery and symbolism of the archaic sources seriously. The chapter brings the anthropology of property law to bear on the interpretation of these mysterious sources, and describes the long intellectual and political history of their interpretation and ideological use.

Chapter 3 turns to the formation of high classical Roman property law, with its terminology of the *dominus*, the "master," and its "absolute" conception of ownership. This classical master/slave language once played a fundamental role in Western intellectual and political history: The rise of the *dominus*, with his 'absolute' power, was the topic of extensive analysis and controversy, and it figured prominently in the ideologies of Communism and Fascism, both of which blamed classical Roman property law for the evils of capitalism. Those ideologically charged arguments have been essentially forgotten by contemporary scholars. The chapter sets out to revive this forgotten debate. Drawing on Roman social history, the chapter argues that the appearance of the new terminology of the *dominus* in classical law can be linked to important social changes in the nature of Roman elite power: the *dominus* became a newly dominant figure throughout Roman culture. The chapter closes by arguing that Roman property law bore a kinship to classical Greco-Roman religion. Eliade and Burkert both believed that the ideology of classical religion rested on orientations that can be tracked back to the hunters of Paleolithic. Ancient Roman property law can be seen in the same light: It too carried on the "symbolism and ideology of the paradigmatic hunter."

Chapter 4 turns to the classical Roman law of slavery. The classical jurists, the chapter argues, had no doubts about the legitimacy of the hunt for human prey in war. Quite the contrary: they thought of the capture and enslavement of enemies as a paradigm of just acquisition – though they insisted, importantly, that enslavement had to take place through war, and not through mere brigandage. In order to enter into their cultural world, with its serene acceptance of the hunt for human prey through war, we must overcome two widespread misconceptions. The first is that the ancient understanding of slavery was dominated by the Aristotelean doctrine of the natural slave, which defined a class of inferior persons born to serve. The second is that the ancient Roman jurists, even though they lived in a slave society, were motivated by humane sentiments, and were even "pioneers of human rights." The chapter argues that both these familiar interpretations of the ancient sources are serious misreadings, which obscure the assumptions of the ancient jurists and distort the place of Roman slave law in Western history. It is essential that we come to terms with the ancient belief system: We will not understand the long historical arc of the Western law of slavery if we do not recognize that the classical jurists did not see any need for justification for slavery beyond the fact of victory in battle or in the sack of cities; only in the early modern period did two new justifications appear in the law, the theory of natural slavery and the theory of the consent of the victim. The chapter closes by discussing how the jurists used the model of the hunt for human and animal prey as the basis for analogical reasoning. The key test of the normative centrality of a property doctrine, the chapter argues, is whether that doctrine is used in the making of such analogies: The classical Roman practice of building analyses on the model of the hunt for prey, both human and animal, is telling, in the same way that the modern American practice of looking to the analogy of land is telling.

Chapter 5 addresses the nature of Roman imperial rule. Roman ownership and Roman rulership, the chapter suggests, both sounded in the "chieftainship over people." Roman historians have often argued that rulership in the Roman Empire was modeled on the household powers of the Roman *paterfamilias*. In particular, as Lavan and other recent scholars have suggested, Roman rule made heavy use of the ideology of the master/slave relationship; the idiom of power of Roman rulership, on this account, turned on the rhetoric of

Introduction

enslaving the peoples of the world. The chapter surveys these interpretations, with the purpose of highlighting the conceptual connections between Roman ownership and Roman rulership, Koskenniemi's yin and yang. Just as the modern territorial state is conceptualized in ways that are in close harmony with the modern private ownership of land, the classical Roman understanding of rule was in harmony with the Roman understanding of household domination.

Part II of the book shifts gears, turning to the question of how the classical Roman orientation declined, and eventually gave way to the strong orientation toward land and its cultivation characteristic of modern Western property law and most closely associated with the philosophy of John Locke. As the chapters in this Part argue, the transformation was a matter of the legal historical *longue durée* – a centuries-long process of cultural change, whose beginnings can be traced to Late Antiquity, but whose consummation cannot be dated before the late eighteenth and nineteenth centuries.

Chapter 7 begins with the most famous explanation for the transformation of Western law. This is the socio-economic explanation embraced by Marx, Weber, and many other scholars, including the great medievalist Marc Bloch. These classic thinkers all subscribed to the same great hypothesis: that Western social evolution had been determined by a passage "from slavery to feudalism," from the ownership of humans in the slave economies of Antiquity to the ownership of land in the feudal economies of the Middle Ages; and though they differed sharply over the causes and the chronology of the change, they all thought that socio-economic factors of some kind were at work. Their various theories have been generally abandoned today, primarily because they rested on claims about economic history that have been proven dubious. But it is the contention of this book that economic history never suffices for a full understanding of the human institution of ownership. What Marx and Weber thought of as socio-economic history must be reinterpreted as history of the legal imagination. The chapter investigates the origins of the classic theories, and makes the case that the classic thinkers erred by mistaking the imaginative orientations in the legal sources for the economic realities. The theories of Marx, Weber, and their many followers have been rightly rejected by social and economic historians; but their works testify to a profound change in the law, which has indeed undergone a sort of transition "from slavery to feudalism."

Chapters 8 and 9 set out to shift the focus from economic history to the history of cultural change in the law, in order to trace the immensely long history of the (imaginative) passage from slavery to feudalism in the law of the West. Chapter 8 begins in Late Antiquity. Marx and Weber both regarded Late Antiquity as the period of pivotal change, when an ancient slave economy collapsed. Their interpretations have been almost universally abandoned, but many scholars have argued that Late Antiquity witnessed the rise of a new legal orientation that was more "land-based." This literature has pointed to two explanatory factors in particular: the decline of classical *polis* culture amidst the deurbanization of Late Antiquity, and the rise of Christianity. The chapter draws together the threads of this literature, in order to develop an account of late antique cultural change. Classical Roman property law, it argues, had its context in classical cities. The relative decay of urban dominance and the rise of Christianity tended to undermine the classical foundations of the law of both ownership and rulership. The Roman Empire was reconceived in more territorial terms, while, as Chris Wickham has powerfully argued, the relative deurbanization of the Empire led members of the elite to relocate their bases of power to the countryside. The consequent shifts in elite culture certainly did not result in any decisive and thoroughgoing transformation of the understanding of ownership and rulership, but they can be linked with other developments that tended to displace the center of gravity of ancient culture from the cities and into the countryside. The shifts can also be linked with religious change: The triumph of Christianity did not result in the end of slavery; but it did bring with it the destruction of religious practices that had been infused with "the symbolism and ideology of the paradigmatic hunter."

Chapter 9 lays out the case that the culmination of the transformation of Western ownership culture must be dated to the late eighteenth and nineteenth centuries. The great scholars who addressed the classic problem of the passage from slavery to feudalism, from Marx to Weber to Bloch, dated the change to Late Antiquity, or, more commonly, the post-Carolingian period. The chapter sums up the evidence for the proposition that Arnaud's "radical transformation that operated on the foundation and form of our conception of property law" should properly be understood as the product of a far slower process of change, which only came to fruition in the age of Blackstone and after, and which witnessed the triumph of renewed "absolute" conception of property, now firmly centered on land, the related triumph of the territorial conception of the state, and the abolition of the private ownership of human beings. The chapter traces the rise of an early modern conception of property, which held that acquisition was primarily acquisition of land, that the ownership of land was necessarily exclusive, and that it was established through cultivation rather than mere occupation. It shows how the venerable law of use rights found a home under a new doctrinal rubric, eminent domain, and discusses the transformation of the ancient law of enslavement through war. As early modern lawyers and philosophers wrestled the ancient sources on slavery, they undertook a task that the Roman jurists had never undertaken: to find justifications for slavery beyond the mere fact of victory. Paradoxically, the early modern decline of the inherited conception of slavery began in these efforts to justify the institution, either through norms of consent or through the Aristotelean theory of natural slavery. The chapter further draws on the work of historians of the state such as Benton, Maier, and Annabel Brett, all of whom date the rise of a territorial understanding of sovereignty to the later eighteenth century, the age of the triumph of the absolute ownership of land.

The Conclusion sums up and reflects.

PART I

MASTERS OF MEN AND BEASTS

1

Hierarchy and the Hunt for Prey: Early Human Ownership

In the "modern West," observe Georgy Kantor, Tom Lambert, and Hannah Skoda, "we tend to assume that land is the archetypal form of property."[1] So we do; it is easy to multiply examples, not only from the literature of the law, but also from philosophy, economics, and *belles lettres*. The most florid statement of this commonplace modern Western belief came from Carl Schmitt, the matchlessly clever legal philosopher who put his pen in the service of Hitler in the 1930s. Myth, Schmitt declared in his 1950 *Nomos of the Earth*, revealed the primordial centrality of land:

> In mythical language, the earth became known as the mother of law. This signifies a threefold root of law and justice. First, the fertile earth contains within herself, within the womb of her fecundity, an inner measure, because human toil and trouble, human planting and cultivation of the fruitful earth is rewarded justly by her with growth and harvest ... Second, soil that is cleared and worked by human hands manifests firm lines, whereby definite divisions become apparent ... Third and last, the solid ground of the earth is delineated by fences, enclosures, boundaries, walls, houses, and other constructs. Then, the orders and orientations of human social life become apparent ... Law is bound to the earth and related to the earth. This is what the poet means when he speaks of the infinitely just earth: justissima tellus.[2]

---

[1] Georgy Kantor, Tom Lambert, and Hannah Skoda, "Introduction," in Kantor, Lambert, and Skoda, eds., *Legalism: Property and Ownership* (Oxford, 2017), 10 [1–27].
[2] Schmitt, *The Nomos of the Earth in the International Law of the Jus Publicum Europaeum*, trans. G. L. Ulmen (Candor, N.Y., 2003), 42.

"[T]he great primeval acts of the law," Schmitt continued, staked out claims on the earth, "appropriating land, founding cities, and establishing colonies."[3] The very Greek word for law, *nomos*, was proof of the foundational importance of these "primeval acts." For *nomos*, Schmitt asserted, a word derived from the Greek root *nem-*, "to distribute," originally meant nothing other than "the distribution of land."[4] The division of the earth by *nomos* thus gave birth to law itself. It established the basis for the international order as well. Without the division of the globe into territories, there could be no states; and without states there could be no international law. The whole planet, like the private holdings on it, must of necessity be divided by "enclosures, boundaries [and] walls," delineating the independent zones of territorial domination of its sovereign entities.

Schmitt's account of the *nomos* of the Earth, the original act of carving the surface of the planet up into the holdings of private owners and eventually territorial states, marked the mystic climax of a Western legal tradition that had been gathering strength since the early sixteenth century. Over the course of the early modern period, it gradually became a European commonplace that the planet should be mapped and divided. "The whole world," it was widely believed by the late eighteenth century, "is best managed when divided among private owners."[5] During the same centuries, it became something of a commonplace that the "primeval acts of the law" involved staking out claims on land; Locke and Rousseau are only the most familiar examples. It also became conventional to think of states as resembling private landowners: By the end of the eighteenth century, the integrity of European states was coming to depend on their capacity to erect well-demarcated and well-policed borders around contiguous territories.[6] It further became conventional to think of law as intimately bound up with the state's monopoly of violence within those borders: European law came to be territorial law, law that applied to all persons once they crossed a fixed boundary and set foot

---

[3] Ibid., 44. [4] Ibid., 67–69.
[5] Carol Rose, "The Comedy of the Commons: Custom, Commerce, and Inherently Public Property," *University of Chicago Law Review* 53 (1986): 712 [711–781].
[6] Charles Maier, *Once Within Borders: Territories of Power, Wealth and Belonging since 1500* (Cambridge, MA, 2016).

in the domain of a sovereign.[7] Europeans had been exporting these ideas of the territorial division of the planet to the rest of the humanity during more than four centuries of "appropriating land [and] establishing colonies," in a process that culminated in the scramble for Africa in the final decades of the nineteenth century, which largely completed the division of the earth among sovereigns with a territorial base.[8] Two generations later, the same ideas drove the *Blut und Boden* ideology of the Nazi movement in which Schmitt participated.

But over recent decades, social scientists and historians have systematically punctured Schmitt's myth. It is not the case that the division of "the solid earth" by "fences, enclosures [and] boundaries" can be traced back to the "primeval legal acts" of human history. The early human relationship to land almost certainly looked quite different. Rights in many or most societies of the past have been primarily rights in the *resources* on the land, not in the land as such; and those rights have been governed by the hierarchical structure of the community, taking the form of "use rights" granted out by chiefs or other social superiors. As for Schmitt's account of the history of *nomos*: It is dubious at best. Scholars now believe that the original usage of *nomos* involved the distribution, not of land, but of meat and drink, and that its earliest history should be traced back to hunter-gatherer rituals for sharing out meat after the kill. (We shall see more about such meat and drink sharing practices as this chapter goes along.) The application of the term to the distribution of land was a very late development.[9]

Nor is it the case that states have always and everywhere been defined by their capacity to erect and police well-defined borders around contiguous territories. Most states in most past times and

---

[7] Maier, *Once Within Borders*; and e.g., Dieter Grimm, *Types of Constitutions*, text at n. 27, available at www.oxfordhandbooks.com/view/10.1093/oxfordhb/9780199578610.001.0001/oxfordhb-9780199578610-e-6.

[8] Benton, *A Search for Sovereignty: Law and Geography in European Empires, 1400–1900* (Cambridge, 2010). Schmitt's own view was different. Schmitt, *Nomos of the Earth*, 217–223.

[9] See now the discussion of a philosopher, Thanos Zartaloudis, *The Birth of Nomos* (Edinburgh, 2019), 22–30. For a forceful earlier focus on the distribution of meat, with the distribution of land appearing only late, see Gerhard J. Baudy, "Hierarchie, oder: die Verteilung des Fleisches," in Burkhard Gladigow and Hans J. Kippenberg, eds., *Neue Ansätze in der Religionswissenschaft* (Munich, 1983), 164 [131–174]. See further Richard Seaford, *Money and the Early Greek Mind* (Cambridge, 2004), 39–47. Further discussion below, this chapter.

places had, not fixed delineated boundaries, but fluid frontier zones; and in past centuries, rulership was conceived primarily as rulership over a people, not rulership over a territory. It is not even the case that law has always been bound up with the territorial monopoly of violence. The law of Antiquity and the Middle Ages was largely personal, not territorial: Individuals were often thought of as subject to the law of the community to which they belonged, not the law of the place in which they happened to find themselves.[10]

If we are to make sense of the long history of Western property law, we cannot begin with Schmitt's supposed "primeval acts" of the division of the earth. Instead, we must understand how and why the modern Western way of thinking arose, and what alternatives it displaced.

* * *

If the "infinitely just earth" was not primevally divided up into private plots of land, with "fences, enclosures [and] boundaries," as Schmitt insisted, what *did* early human property look like? Schmitt's fable has been discarded today, but social scientists have not given up on the effort to reconstruct the primeval forms of human ownership. Quite the contrary: The problem of early human forms of property is the subject of a vibrant literature, especially among anthropologists. That literature wanders down some strange pathways, for example comparing humans to birds and spiders. Nevertheless, it makes for essential background reading to the history of Western property law that begins in ancient Rome.

Current research suggests several conclusions about the very early history of human property. Humans, like other animals, have probably always made some sort of territorial claims. Those claims, however, have by no means always taken the form of landownership familiar in the modern Western world.[11] To be the modern Western "owner" of land is, at its notional core, to be something like its territorial ruler, with the power, in principle, to bar entry by others and enjoy sole access to its fruits. Such exclusive ownership probably did exist early

---

[10] With many complications to be discussed in Chapter 5.
[11] E.g., James M. Acheson and Roy J. Gardner, "Strategies, Conflict, and the Emergence of Territoriality: The Case of the Maine Lobster Industry," *American Anthropologist* 106 (2004): 297 [296–307].

on in human societies to a limited extent, in the form of control over circumscribed areas such as garden plots.

But with regard to the larger territorial ranges of communities, rights in land looked different, typically taking the form of what anthropologists call "use rights." A system of use rights does not accord exclusive quasi-sovereign rights in particular tracts. Instead, as the phrase suggests, it allots rights to the use of resources on the tract. Those rights to resources are generally granted out by chiefs or other figures in authority, in line with the social hierarchical order of the community. "Land tenure systems," as one anthropologist describes this widespread pattern, "are characterized by a coexistence of multiple rights that are often held by different persons as a function of their status or position in society."[12] The distinction between such a "status or position"-oriented system and the modern practice of landownership must be stated carefully. The distinction is *not* that there are no rights in land in the former. It is that rights in land, in societies more oriented toward use rights, must always be viewed against the background of the hierarchical structure of society: Rights in land exist; but they can only be understood in light of the rights-holder's place in the communal rank order. But land, importantly, is not the only object of rights that is of interest for the study of early human property. Anthropological studies focus on something else as well: the ownership, or quasi-ownership, of animal prey.

Most of the work of anthropologists has developed in response to an age-old question, first posed in Antiquity: whether there was ever "primitive communism," a primordial phase in the history of human societies when there was no ownership at all, and in particular no ownership of land – an age, in the words of Jean-Jacques Rousseau, when "the earth belonged to no one."[13] Belief that in the beginning "the earth belonged to no one" was widespread among the ancients. Virgil, for example, sang of a happy era at the dawn of history when

---

[12] Christian Lund, *Local Politics and the Dynamics of Property in Africa* (Cambridge, 2008), 16. Cf. Maurice Godelier, "Territory and Property in Primitive Society," in M. von Cranach, K. Foppa, W. Lepenies, and D. Ploog, eds., *Human Ethology: Claims and Limits of a New Discipline* (Cambridge, 1979), 141 [133–155].

[13] Jean-Jacques Rousseau, *Discourse of the Origin of Inequality*, trans. Donald Cress (Indianapolis, 1992), 44.

"no tillers subjugated the land: even to mark possession of the plain or apportion it by boundaries was sacrilege ..."[14] A particularly influential statement came from Cicero, who declared that land was "by nature common property," and only artificially appropriated and distributed. Like David Hume, centuries later, Cicero was at pains to deny that ownership was a "natural" institution:

There is ... no such thing as private ownership established by nature; instead property becomes private either through appropriation by those who found it lying empty sometime in the past, or through conquest in war, or by decree of law, or by private bargain, or contractual stipulation, or distribution by lot ...[15]

The same view established itself in the Latin Christian tradition, whose leading figures regularly denounced private property as a product of the sin of avarice, which had simply not existed before the Fall.[16] The Christian tradition made its way into the writings of St. Thomas More, from More to other utopian authors such as Tommaso Campanella, and finally into Rousseau's great lament in the *Discourse of the Origin of Inequality*:

The first person who, having enclosed a plot of land, took it into his head to say this is mine and found people simple enough to believe him was the true founder of civil society. What crimes, wars, murders, what miseries and horrors would the human race have been spared, had someone pulled up the stakes or filled in the ditch and cried out to his fellow men: "Do not listen to this impostor. You are lost if you forget that the fruits of the earth belong to all and the earth to no one!"[17]

---

[14] Verg. G. 1.121–129, in H.Rushton Fairclough, trans., *Virgil: Eclogues; Georgics; Aeneid: Books 1–6*, rev. by G. P. Goold, Loeb Classical Library 63 (Cambridge, MA, 1916), 106–107; cf. Sen. *Oct.* 398–406, in John G. Fitch, ed. and trans., *Seneca: Tragedies, Vol. II: Oedipus; Agamemnon; Thyestes; Hercules on Oeta; Octavia*, Loeb Classical Library 78 (Cambridge, MA, 2004), 548–551; Tib. 1.3.43–44, in F. W. Cornish, J. P. Postgate, J. W. Mackail, trans., *Catullus; Tibullus; Pervigilium Veneris*, rev. G. P. Goold, Loeb Classical Library 6 (Cambridge, MA, 1913), 206–207. For a deathless general survey of ancient authors, see John Selden, *Mare Clausum, seu de Dominio Maris* (Leiden, 1636), 9–12 (Lib. I, ch. 4).

[15] Cic. *Off.* 1.21, in Walter Miller, trans., *Cicero: On Duties*, Loeb Classical Library 30 (Cambridge, MA, 1913), 22–23.

[16] Peter Garnsey, *Thinking about Property: From Antiquity to the Age of Revolution* (Cambridge, 2007), 59–83; Arthur Lovejoy, "The Communism of St. Ambrose," *Journal of the History of Ideas* 3 (1942): 458–468.

[17] Rousseau, *Discourse of the Origin of Inequality*, trans. Cress, 44.

This venerable belief, that in the infancy of humanity the earth was "the common possession of all men," was very slow to die. Nineteenth-century historians, anthropologists, and early sociologists uniformly predicated a primitive human stage of communal ownership. As Henry Maine asserted in his 1861 *Ancient Law*, "joint-ownership, and not separate ownership, is the really archaic institution." Lewis Henry Morgan produced a particularly important account in his 1877 *Ancient Society, or Researches in the Lines of Human Progress from Savagery, through Barbarism to Civilization*, drawn from his long experience living among the Iroquois:

> [T]he property of savages was inconsiderable ... Rude weapons, fabrics, utensils, apparel, implements of flint, stone and bone, and personal ornaments represent the chief items of property in savage life ... Lands, as yet hardly a subject of property, were owned by the tribes in common, while tenement houses were owned jointly by their occupants ...[18]

Morgan's description of "the property of savages" shaped much of late nineteenth-century thought, notably that of Karl Marx and Friedrich Engels;[19] and primitive communism remained a basic tenet of the Marxist tradition deep into the twentieth century. No less an authority than Stalin laid down the Marxist line in 1938: Human history, Stalin decreed from Moscow, began in primitive communism. Only later in the course of social evolution was it succeeded by the stages of slavery, feudalism, and capitalism.[20]

But like most ideas promoted by Stalin, this one is in bad odor today. Anthropologists and historians alike reject the hypothesis of primitive communism, on the basis of a wide range of evidence, from archeology to animal ethology to the ethnography of hunter-gatherers. Thus ancient economic historians now confidently conclude that "private property existed before states or formal legal

---

[18] Morgan, *Ancient Society, or Researches in the Lines of Human Progress from Savagery, through Barbarism to Civilization* (New York, 1877), 527–528.

[19] Marx, *The Ethnological Notebooks of Karl Marx (Studies of Morgan, Phear, Maine, Lubbock)*, transcribed and ed. with an introduction by Lawrence Krader (Assen, 1974); Engels, *Der Ursprung der Familie, des Privateigentums, und des Staats, im Anschuß an Lewis H. Morgans Forschungen* (Hottingen-Zürich, 1884).

[20] Joseph Stalin, "The Five Main Types of Relations of Production," in *History of the Communist Party of the Soviet Union (Bolsheviks)*, now in David Brandenberger and Mikhail Zelenov, eds., *Stalin's Master Narrative* (New Haven, 2019), 266–267.

institutions."[21] And indeed, the archeological and literary evidence for some form of early property in land is bountiful. Some of the most striking evidence takes the form of boundary stones, often elaborately carved, which survive from all over the ancient world. "You must not move your neighbor's boundary marker," admonishes Deuteronomy in a typical statement.[22] We find law of boundary stones far and wide, for example in the ancient Near East,[23] among the Aztecs,[24] or in ancient Arabia.[25] The Romans even worshiped their boundary stones and brought them offerings.[26] We shall see much more about boundary-stone cults in the chapters that follow.

To be sure, archeology and written evidence can only take us just so far back in human history. But anthropologists believe that they can push back much further, through studies of animal ethology, human ethnography, and the reconstruction of the early evolution of the genus *Homo*. Some of the most stimulating work is drawn from ethological studies of nonhuman animals. Patterns of behavior that ethologists call "territorial" are found throughout the animal world. Ethologists do not entirely agree on how to define territoriality, and as recent work emphasizes, it is far from clear that animal behavior should be interpreted in terms drawn from human experience.[27] Nevertheless, it has often been said that the near ubiquity of animal territoriality

---

[21] Joseph Manning, "Property," forthcoming in *Cambridge Comparative History of Ancient Law*.

[22] Deut. 19:14, NRSV. For a treatment discussing this admonition alongside the Roman *terminus* and other aspects of Roman and other ancient traditions, see Karl-Heinz Ziegler, "Grenze," in *Reallexikon für Antike und Christentum* (Stuttgart, 1950–2022), 12: cols. 1095–1107. The meaning of the Hebrew term is not entirely clear. The term is גְּבוּל (*gebul*), usually translated as "boundary" or "territory." The term here is interpreted as boundary marker in almost all standard translations. For a valuable general survey of ancient boundary stones on the basis of the scholarship available at the time, including the Hebrew tradition, see Giulia Piccaluga, *Terminus: i segni di confine nella religione romana* (Rome, 1974), 27–93.

[23] Ursula Seidl, *Die babylonischen Kudurru-Reliefs: Symbole mesopotamischer Gottheiten* (Göttingen, 1989).

[24] Frances Berdan, *The Aztecs of Central Mexico: An Imperial Society* (New York, 1982), 98.

[25] D. 47.11.9. Ulpianus 9 *de off. procons.*, discussed in Ari Bryen, *Law as Books*, forthcoming.

[26] Below, Chapter 2.

[27] Ambika Kamath and Ashton Wesner, "Animal Territoriality, Property and Access: A Collaborative Exchange between Animal Behaviour and the Social Sciences," *Animal Behaviour* 164 (2020): 233–239. For problems in definition, also Wayne

proves that human animals too must always have claimed some sort of rights in land. The economist Herbert Gintis has made a particularly energetic effort to exploit this research, arguing that studies of animal territoriality decisively disprove the classic claims of Rousseau and other believers in primitive communism. An immense variety of nonhuman creatures, writes Gintis in an article on "the evolution of property," "own" territory. That fact suffices to prove that the idea of primitive communism is nonsense:

> The dominant view in Western thought, from Hobbes, Locke, Rousseau, and Marx to the present, is that private property is a human social construction that emerged with the rise of modern civilization ... However, evidence from studies of animal behavior, gathered mostly in the past quarter century, has shown this view to be incorrect. Various territorial claims are recognized in non-human species, including butterflies ... spiders ... wild horses ... finches ... wasps ... non-human primates ... lizards ... and many others ... In non-human species, that an animal owns a territory is generally established by the fact that the animal has occupied and altered the territory (e.g., by constructing a nest, burrow, hive, dam, or web, or by marking its limits with urine or feces). In humans there are other criteria of ownership, but physical possession and first to occupy remain of great importance.[28]

Human ownership, on this account, is in essence no different from the territorial claims of, for example, house cats, whose behavior has been studied by animal ethologists such as Paul Leyhausen.[29]

But how exactly does human territoriality function? Precisely what sorts of claims on land can we guess our early ancestors would have made? Just how much are we like our pet cats? Attempts to answer these questions have been guided by ethological studies of one kind of animal in particular: Early human behavior is thought to have resembled the behavior of birds. Here, the leading theory was proposed by the evolutionary biologist Jerram Brown, who argued in

---

L. Linklater, "Territorial Tuatara? – A Hypothesis Still to Be Tested," *New Zealand Journal of Ecology*, 35 (2011): 308–311.

[28] Gintis, "The Evolution of Private Property," *Journal of Economic Behavior and Organization* 64 (2006): 1–16.

[29] See Leyhausen, "Dominance and Territoriality as Complemented in Mammalian Social Structure," in A. H. Esser, ed., *Behavior and Environment: The Use of Space by Animals and Men* (New York, 1971), 22–33, for an extremely stimulating discussion on the relationship between rank and space.

1964 that bird territoriality is driven by a kind of cost/benefit analysis. The key factor for birds is the "defendability" of resources:

[W]hen a food supply cannot be feasibly defended, because of its mobility or transient nature, generally no territorial system is evolved to defend it; and the territory, if present, may be restricted only to the nest and the area reachable by the parents on the nest.[30]

Brown offers the illustration of "a simple form of territoriality" in the Brandt's cormorant (*Phalacrocorax penicillatus*), a handsome seabird found on the Pacific coast of North America. The territorial claims of the Brandt's cormorant are circumscribed to an area in which it can fight off competitors:

The territory consists of the nest and a barren area extending a few feet or more around it. It is used in the attraction of a mate, for copulation, and defense of the family. All food is obtained from the sea under conditions which make the defense of a feeding area completely impractical if not impossible. Consequently, no matter how intense competition for food might be, the evolution of a territory used for feeding would be blocked through lack of defendability. On the other hand, the small area used for mating and family defense is feasibly defendable, and competition for the often limited optimal nesting space probably intensifies the necessity of defense of the nesting territory in this species.[31]

The bird's "ownership," to the extent that it is appropriate to use such a human term, is limited to its nesting area.

Taking their cue from the work of Brown and other evolutionary biologists, economic anthropologists argue that human animals are like the Brandt's cormorant:[32] From the earliest history of the species, they have probably claimed relatively exclusive control over some, but only some, territories – namely those that are worth the cost of defending against competition from other humans. Rada Dyson-Hudson and Eric Alden Smith, the authors of the leading statement,

---

[30] Jerram Brown, "The Evolution of Diversity in Avian Territorial Systems," *Wilson Bulletin* 76, no. 2 (1964): 160 [160–169].

[31] Ibid., 162–163.

[32] One of the most influential economic anthropologists, James Acheson, goes so far as to argue that the defendability hypothesis explains the full spectrum of human property claims on the planet even in complex human societies down to the present. Acheson, "Private Land and Common Oceans: Analysis of the Development of Property Regimes," *Current Anthropology* 56 (2015): 28 [28–55].

formulate the general principle: "territoriality is expected to occur when critical resources are sufficiently abundant and predictable in space and time, so that costs of exclusive use and defense of an area are outweighed by the benefits gained from resource control."[33] Alden Smith and Benjamin Chabot-Hanowell identify garden plots and, curiously, livestock as leading examples of such "defensible" objects of property:

[I]f resource X is dense and predictable enough to be economically defensible, but resource Y is not, the simplest expectation is territorial defense of X but not Y. An example is the pattern of land use and property rights found among many East African cattle herders, where garden plots and livestock are claimed as property by individuals or households, but grazing land is communally owned by the "tribe" (ethnic group).[34]

There is obviously something odd in speaking of livestock as a kind of "territory"; I will return to the question of the ownership of beasts (and the related ownership of slaves) later. For the moment, let me just note, lest all this ethological argument seem too wildly remote from the subject of this book, that garden plots and livestock also seem to have been privileged objects of ownership in early Roman law.[35] Let me further note, on the topic of "defendability," that the Roman literature derived the very word "territory" from the verb *terreo*, "to scare off."[36]

These ethological analyses of human territoriality certainly do not leave much room for the hypothesis of primitive communism; Gintis is surely right about that. At the same time, it is essential to emphasize what this anthropological work does not purport to show: Contrary to what Gintis argues, it does not purport to explain the ownership of land

---

[33] Dyson-Hudson and Alden Smith, "Human Territoriality: An Ecological Reassessment," *American Anthropologist* 80 (1978): 21 [21–41]. For a useful summary of the literature, with roots in the work on birds by Brown, see Benjamin Chabot-Hanowell and Eric Alden Smith, "Territorial and Non-territorial Routes to Power: Reconciling Evolutionary Ecological, Social Agency, and Historicist Approaches," in James Osborne and N. Parker Van Valkenburgh, eds., *Territoriality in Archaeology* (Washington, D.C., 2015): 75 [72–86].
[34] Chabot-Hanowell and Smith, "Territorial and Non-territorial Routes to Power," 77.
[35] Below, Chapter 2.
[36] Julius Frontinus, *De controversiis* 1.1.8, in Carolus Thulin, ed., *Corpus agrimensorum Romanorum*, Teubner (Leipzig, 1913): *territorium est quidquid hostis terrendi causa constitutum est*. This etymology took on quite a life in medieval law. See Dante Fedele, *The Medieval Foundations of International Law: Baldus de Ubaldis (1327–1400)* (Leiden, 2021), 204–205.

as we know it today. Modern Western landownership has two critical features: It is individual; and it is exclusionary: The law ordinarily presupposes a sole "owner," and further generally guarantees that owner the right against "physical invasion" by others.[37] This is the "sole and despotic dominion ... in total exclusion of the right any other individual in the universe" of Blackstone, and it is commonly called "Blackstonian" ownership.

Anthropologists are careful to emphasize that the human territoriality they describe does not involve ownership in the full Blackstonian sense. This is partly because claims to territory are not necessarily wholly exclusionary.[38] Territoriality, as anthropologist Elizabeth Cashdan carefully defines it, consists in "the maintenance of an area 'within which the resident controls or restricts use of one or more environmental resources.'"[39] This "control or restriction of one or more resources" does not necessarily rule out entry into the territory by others – the claim is a claim on the resources, not on the land as such – and ethnographic studies suggest that the boundaries of such territories are often more porous than is the case in modern Western landownership. The "territories" in question are something like the "territories" of street-level drug dealers or traveling sales representatives: They are territorial rights of exploitation; and as such they do not require the prevention of entry by outsiders who do not challenge those rights. In this respect, as anthropologist Tim Ingold observes, human territoriality resembles the territoriality of other animals such as lions.[40] We shall see that the same is true of the territoriality of most premodern states. The modern conception of territory that must be fenced off, and of rights that are necessarily disturbed by the presence of an intruder, is quite distinctive, and it constitutes a comparatively recent development in the history of human societies, in many respects dating only to the latter part of the eighteenth century, as we shall see in Chapter 9.

---

[37] E.g., Henry Smith, "Exclusion and Property Rules in the Law of Nuisance," *Virginia Law Review* 90 (2004): 965–1049.
[38] E.g., Elizabeth Cashdan, "Territoriality," in David Levinson and Melvin Ember, eds., *Encyclopedia of Cultural Anthropology* (1996) 4:1301–1305.
[39] Cashdan, "Territoriality among Human Foragers: Ecological Models and an Application to Four Bushman Groups," *Current Anthropology* 24 (1983): 47 [47–66].
[40] Ingold, *The Appropriation of Nature: Essays on Human Ecology and Social Relations* (Iowa City, 1987), 133–134.

Moreover, the territoriality that economic anthropologists study is by no means typically individual. "[T]raditional systems of land tenure among nonindustrial peoples," Cashdan explains,

> exist everywhere, even though they do not fit easily into Western ideas of land ownership. Rights to land are typically obtained through kinship, either from one's parents (as among the !Kung Bushmen) or from one's lineage (as among most pastoralists and subsistence horticulturalists). Land rights can be manipulated to the extent that kinship and fictive kinship ties can be manipulated, but access is not usually such without such ties. Because land cannot be sold in [traditional] systems, nor can individual users dispose of land as they wish Western concepts of land ownership can be misleading...[41]

"Traditional systems of land tenure" are a function of real and fictive kin relations; they involve not the ownership of land, but what is better called the allotment of the use of land in line with the interpersonal organization of the society in question. Contrary to the thesis of Gintis, the economic anthropology of territoriality thus gets us, at best, only part of the way to settling the question of how Blackstonian exclusive landownership emerged.

* * *

The study of territoriality does not exhaust the literature of anthropology on early human ownership, however. Anthropologists also think that they can identify another important form of ownership, or quasi-ownership, that does not involve land. This has to do with the claims that attach to the capture of animal prey among hunter-gatherers.

The study of hunter-gatherers has long been regarded as particularly valuable for understanding human evolution. As Richard B. Lee and Irven DeVore write in a seminal 1968 study, "[c]ultural man has been on earth for some 2,000,000 years; for over 99 percent of this time he has lived as a hunter-gatherer."[42] That fact that the human species formed almost entirely in hunter-gatherer conditions suggests that

---

[41] Cashdan, "Territoriality" (1996), 1302–1303.
[42] Lee and DeVore, "Problems in the Study of Hunters and Gatherers," in Lee and DeVore, eds., *Man the Hunter* (Chicago, 1968), 3 [3–12]. Current literature emphasizes that hunter-gatherers have also frequently engaged in agriculture. See for the earliest history, e.g., Ian Hodder, "The Lady and the Seed," in Mehmet Özdogan, Harald Hauptmann, and Nezih Basgelen, eds., *From Village to Cities* (Istanbul, 2003), 132 [129–137].

even modern behavioral patterns, the products of 2 million years of evolution, can be supposed to reflect the "lifestyle of Upper Paleolithic hunter-gatherers," in the words of Christopher Boehm.[43] "Our intellect, interests, emotions and basic social life," down into the present, according to this anthropological view, "all are evolutionary products of the hunting adaptation."[44] This hunting adaptation, dating far back in hominin history, brought with it the use of lethal weapons; and as evolutionary anthropologists emphasize, those weapons could be turned on fellow humans just as they could be turned on animal prey: Humans became far more efficient killers of their conspecifics than other primates had ever been. Much follows, anthropologists believe, from this fact: the fact that early humans, armed with spears, became what the great historian of Greek religion Walter Burkert calls *Homo necans*, the spear-wielder, "man the killer."[45] We shall see in the next chapter that the spear continued to feature prominently as a symbol of ownership in Roman law.

The norms of the hunt have figured in studies of early property concepts in particular, a topic on which anthropologists have produced a rich and stimulating literature. That literature turns on the problem of the individual ownership of prey. Hunters hunt in bands. If several hunters are pursuing the same animal, which one of them can be said to "own" the game when it is finally taken? Different societies give different answers, which have been much studied by ethnographers since the late nineteenth century. Some of those answers are summarized by J. H. Dowling:

There are a number of alternative ways of ascribing to a single person ownership of collaboratively acquired animals. Among the Central Eskimo the person who first sees a young seal or polar bear owns that animal regardless of who actually kills it ... Among the Copper Eskimo it is the first person who inflicts a wound on the animal who owns it, even though the wound is a minor one and the animal would escape if another hunter did not assist in its killing ... The Andamanese assign the ownership of the slain pig or dugong to the man who inflicts the first serious wound; minor wounds give the inflictor

---

[43] Boehm, *Hierarchy in the Forest* (Cambridge, MA, 1999), 3.
[44] Sherwood Washburn and Chet Lancaster, "The Evolution of Hunting," in Lee and Devore, eds., *Man the Hunter*, 293 [293–303].
[45] Burkert, *Homo necans: Interpretationen altgriechischer Opferriten und Mythen*, 2nd ed. (Berlin, 1997), at e.g., 25.

no rights in the animal ... Among the White Knife Shoshoni, the man who kills an animal owns it ... As a final alternative, the Bushmen of the South African Kalahari desert ascribe ownership to the person who owns the arrow or spear that kills the animal, even though the missile is shot or thrown by another ...[46]

In the next two chapters we shall see that the same problem also appeared in the Roman law of *occupatio*, which offered its own solution to the question of which hunter owns a given piece of prey.

When it comes to animal prey, at least, some form of individual ownership arguably existed very early on in human history. Yet here again, we must be careful not to suppose that we are in the presence of modern Western concepts. Dowling and other anthropologists are careful to note that the form of "ownership" that accrues to individual hunters under these various rules differs from "ownership" of the modern Western kind. This is because the "owner" does not enjoy exclusive rights over the meat of the killed animal. Meat is always shared among members of the community, as has probably been the case since very early on in hominin evolution.[47] In consequence, the "ownership" of the killed prey consists, not in Blackstonian "sole and despotic dominion," but in the right to *distribute* meat, which carries great prestige. It is the prospect of such prestige that gives individuals the incentive to hunt, as anthropologist Nicolas Peterson explains:

Without such a mechanism for identifying the successful hunter, it would be difficult to motivate people to hunt in the presence of an ethic of sharing, since

---

[46] Dowling, "Individual Ownership and the Sharing of Game in Hunting Societies," *American Anthropologist* 70 (1968): 504 [502–507] (citations omitted). For another example, Robert Bailey, "The Behavioral Ecology of Efe Pygmy Men in the Ituri Forest, Zaire," *Anthropological Papers, Museum of Anthropology, University of Michigan* 86 (Minneapolis, 1991) 33. Useful analysis of literature and discussion of sharing practices in Nobuhiro Kishigami, "A New Typology of Food-Sharing Practices among Hunter-Gatherers, with a Special Focus on Inuit Examples," *Journal of Anthropological Research* 60 (2004): 341–358.

[47] For a detailed examination of the evidence, see Brian M. Wood and Ian C. Gilby, "From *Pan* to Man the Hunter: Hunting and Meat Sharing by Chimpanzees, Humans, and Our Common Ancestor," in Martin Muller, Richard Wrangham, and David Pilbeam, eds., *Chimpanzees and Human Evolution* (Cambridge, MA, 2017), 339–382; Carel P. van Shaik and Judith Burkart, "Mind the Gap: Cooperative Breeding and the Evolution of Our Unique Features," in Peter M. Kappeler and Joan B. Silk, eds., *Mind the Gap: Tracing the Origins of Human Universals* (Berlin, 2009), 477–496.

everybody would sit around waiting for others to hunt, knowing they would automatically receive a portion. By identifying a hunter with the right to distribute, hunters are motivated to hunt because they receive substantial prestige by being so identified.[48]

The hunt is followed by collective feasting on the prey, over which the successful hunter presides. In this connection, it is worth repeating that the Greek term for law highlighted by Schmitt, *nomos*, is derived from the root *nem-*, "to distribute"; and that the primary early instances of the use of the verb *nemein*, attested in Homer, involve the distribution, not of land, but of meat and drink; in particular, as Sitta von Reden writes, they involve "food distribution . . . by a leading warrior."[49] It is also worth emphasizing that the value in the right to distribute meat lies in the fact that it carries "substantial prestige." What we see here is a culture of "ownership" in which what individuals set out to maximize is, not their wealth, but their status. We shall see more examples shortly of individuals who seek to maximize their status through the distribution of goods to others rather than maximizing their wealth in the familiar modern Western fashion.

It is important to stress a last point as well: Such ceremonies, which I will call "rites of distribution," continued to feature in legal and religious history for millennia. In Chapter 3, we will see that comparable ceremonies governed the distribution of booty among victorious warriors from Antiquity down into the nineteenth century. Just as the hunt for animal prey ended with the festive sharing of meat, the hunt for booty in war ended as the chief distributed shares of the take. Another such rite of distribution will feature especially prominently in the chapters that follow: As Burkert and many other students of ancient religion emphasize, the killing of animals and the

---

[48] Peterson, "Demand Sharing: Reciprocity and the Pressure for Generosity among Foragers," *American Anthropologist* 95 (1993): 866 [860–874]. For more discussion, see Morton Fried, *Evolution of Political Society: An Essay in Political Anthropology* (New York, 1967), 34, 65–67; Ingold, *Appropriation of Nature*, 223–229; Alain Testart, "Game Sharing Systems and Kinship Systems among Hunter-Gatherers," *Man* (N.S.) 22 (1987): 287–304.

[49] Von Reden, *Money in Classical Antiquity* (Cambridge, 2010), 158, contrasting "food distribution among a group of equals (*daiesthai*) [with] the sharing out of pieces by a leading warrior (*nemein*)"; and the discussion of Seaford, *Money and the Early Greek Mind*, 49.

distribution of their meat, this hominin practice with an immensely deep evolutionary history, is also found in the animal sacrifices of classical Greco-Roman Antiquity, in which the killing of the victim was followed by a communal feast.

This close association between hunting practices, feasting, and animal sacrifice is frequently noted by anthropologists. "[T]he principles of sacrifice," writes Ingold, "are prefigured in the hunt."[50] It is precisely this resemblance between early human hunting and classical sacrificial ritual that led Burkert to analyze classical religion as religion of *Homo necans*, "man the killer," displaying "tracks of biology" that reach back into the earliest phases of the evolution of human societies[51]; and that led Mircea Eliade to analyze classical religion as the religion of "warriors, conquerors, and military aristocracies [who] carr[ied] on the symbolism and ideology of the paradigmatic hunter."[52] As I will argue in the next three chapters, the same "symbolism and ideology" can be detected in ancient Roman property law.

* * *

The work of economic anthropologists thus suggests that human animals have always made some strong territorial claims, though probably only to limited "defensible" zones such as garden plots, comparable to the nesting areas of birds. It also suggests that there are intimations of a kind of "ownership" of prey among hunter-gatherers, conferring the right to distribute meat, and ownership of livestock as well. Studies further indicate that hunter-gatherer societies, in their more complex variants, have incorporated slavery within their systems of social stratification.[53] But there is nothing in

---

[50] Ingold, "From the Master's Point of View: Hunting Is Sacrifice," *Journal of the Royal Anthropological Institute* 21 (2015): 24–27. See further Jonathan Z. Smith, "The Bare Facts of Ritual," *History of Religions* 20 (1980): 112–127; Ingold, "Hunting, Sacrifice and the Domestication of Animals," in *The Appropriation of Nature*, 243–276; Valerio Valeri, "Wild Victims: Hunting as Sacrifice and Sacrifice as Hunting in Huaulu," *History of Religions* 34 (1994): 101–131; classically Karl Meuli, "Griechische Opferbräuche," in *Gesammelte Schriften*, ed. Thomas Gelzer (Basel, 1975), 2:948–1021 [907–1021].

[51] Burkert, *The Creation of the Sacred: Tracks of Biology in Early Religions* (Cambridge, MA, 1988).

[52] Eliade, *A History of Religious Ideas*, trans. Willard Trask (Chicago, 1978), 1:35.

[53] E.g., Jeanne E. Arnold, "The Archaeology of Complex Hunter-Gatherers," *Journal of Archaeological Method and Theory* 3 (1996): 77–126; Alain Testart, "The Significance

this literature that points to anything quite like the modern Western Blackstonian conception of ownership. The same can be said of studies on the mechanics of "traditional systems of land tenure" in communally controlled zones, which characteristically involve what anthropologists call "use rights," rights in resources assigned in accordance with the social hierarchical structure of the community.

In their explanations of how "traditional systems of land tenure" function, anthropologists draw on a conceptualization of property that dates back to the early twentieth-century work of Bronisław Malinowski and E. Adamson Hoebel, as well as the work of the philosophers of legal realism. Malinowski, Hoebel, and many subsequent anthropologists argue that the modern Western conception of ownership is out of place in the interpretation of property in many non-Western societies. This is because the modern Western conception imagines property as an unmediated relationship between persons and things. Modern Western ownership is an *in rem* right, a right "in a thing": In the modern Western world, we believe that we can offer a complete account of the right of a person to "own" a thing without any consideration of that person's relationship to other persons.

Not so in many non-Western cultures, in which it is commonly the case that property is understood, not as a direct *in rem* relationship between a person and a thing, but instead as a function of relationships within an assemblage of persons. Malinowski made the point in an influential 1926 account of rights in canoes among Trobriand islanders: Examining an intricate complex of shared canoe-rights, he concluded that "[o]wnership can be defined neither by such words as 'communism' nor 'individualism.'"[54] Canoe-rights, rather than being the subject of either individual or joint ownership, were functions of a shifting web of "duties, privileges and mutualities,"[55] as different parties took control over a given canoe at different moments, on the basis of complex interpersonal relationships.

Canoe-rights, like rights to prey in hunter-gatherer societies, are thus lodged in a system of social relations; they are rights to the use

---

of Food Storage among Hunter-Gatherers: Residence Patterns, Population Densities, and Social Inequalities," *Current Anthropology* 23 (1982): 528, 530 [523–537].

[54] Malinowski, *Crime and Custom in Savage Society* (London, 1926), 20–21.

[55] Ibid. Cf. E. Adamson Hoebel, "Fundamental Legal Concepts as Applied in the Study of Primitive Law," *Yale Law Journal* 51 (1942): 951–966.

of the canoe, not rights of ownership; and the same is true of "use rights" in land, which, as their name suggests, are rights, not in the land as such, but in the resources of the land. Marshall Sahlins explains the workings of use rights in his classic *Stone Age Economics*, here describing what he calls the "primitive mode of production":

> The household in the tribal societies is usually *not* the exclusive owner of its resources: farmlands, pastures, hunting or fishing territories ... Where these resources are undivided, the domestic group has unimpeded access; where the land is allotted, it has claim to an appropriate share. The family enjoys the *usufruct*, it is said, the use-right ...[56]

Use rights thus involve what the property theorist Henry Smith calls a "governance strategy" rather than an "exclusion strategy":[57] They confer rights to exploit the resources of land, without conferring the right to fence the land off "in total exclusion of the right of any other individual in the universe." Such use rights, Sahlins tells us, are not "owned" but "allotted." But how does the process of this allotment work? What sort of "governance" determines rights? The answer lies in what Sahlins calls "political control." Even the simplest societies have a hierarchical authority structure, in the form of a chieftainship or of the internal hierarchy of the family; and it is that structure that determines who is assigned which privileged claims.

Sahlins illustrates the pattern of political control over the allotment of resources using the example of an ideal-typical tribal chieftainship, operating on principles of gift exchange. Gift-exchange principles, which have been much studied by anthropologists since the early twentieth century, are easily misunderstood. Gift exchange is not a form of selfless giving. It is best understood as a form of self-interested exchange. But it is a form of self-interested exchange that rests on principles different from those of market orders, and in which actors are engaged in a different kind of utility maximization. In the ideal-typical market order, self-interested individuals aim to maximize their wealth. In an ideal-typical gift-exchange order, by contrast, actors often aim to maximize, not their wealth, but their social status; and

---

[56] Sahlins, *Stone Age Economics*, new ed. (Abingdon and New York, 2017), 84–85, and 97 for "primitive structure of production."

[57] Smith, "Exclusion versus Governance: Two Strategies for Delineating Property Rights," *Journal of Legal Studies* 31 (2002): S453–S487.

higher-ranking individuals frequently achieve that end, not by accumulating resources in their own hands, but by distributing resources to others. The classic example of such a gift-exchange order is a "Big Man" society of the kind that Malinowski described in Melanesia. In Malinowski's famous example, the Big Man oversees the distribution of yams to the community, without himself claiming any greater share of yams than anyone else. Indeed, as the work of anthropologists has repeatedly shown, high-status individuals in a gift-exchange order, far from acting acquisitively, may even impoverish themselves in order to magnify their social standing through largesse.[58] Like the "owners" of the prey killed among hunters and gathers, or the Homeric "leading warriors" who assert their primacy through the distribution of meat and drink, they aim to maximize their prestige through exercising the authority to distribute, rather than by laying claim to a larger share.

Land tenure in Sahlins' "primitive mode of production" can helpfully be thought of as fitting within the classic gift-exchange logic:[59] The chief asserts and maintains his rank, not by accumulating lands in his own hands, but by distributing use rights in land to less high-ranking members of the community. "Chiefdoms," in the definition of the anthropologist Elman Service, "are redistributional societies with a permanent central agency of coordination."[60] From season to season, the chief determines which households will exercise rights in those tracts that are not held as a commons. This is the "political control" of which Sahlins speaks. It is a system of communal ownership in the bare sense that it assumes a certain territory claimed by a certain community. But it is not a system of the communism of coequal rights in land. Far from assuming equality, it assumes, and reinforces, the superior status of the chief. The group is collectively territorial, but within the group the

---

[58] For the current state of play on the most famous example, see M. E. Harkin, "Potlatch in Anthropology," in James D. Wright, ed., *International Encyclopedia of the Social and Behavioral Sciences* (Amsterdam, 2015), available at www.sciencedirect-com.yale.idm.oclc.org/referencework/9780080970875/international-encyclopedia-of-the-social-and-behavioral-sciences.

[59] Although Sahlins himself does not make the connection.

[60] Service, *Primitive Social Organization: An Evolutionary Perspective*, 2nd ed. (New York, 1971), 134.

distribution of rights in land is determined by a distinctively human form of dominance ordering.

Such "political control" over the distribution of use rights in land has been identified by anthropologists and historians in societies all over the world, not only in the tribal chieftainships that Sahlins took as his ideal type, but in much more complex societies as well. Many of the most revealing cases have been studied by historians of the Western encounter with non-Western societies from the sixteenth century onward. The typical consequence of that encounter was not the displacement of some supposed primitive communism. Instead, the arrival of Western traders and conquerors commonly (though not invariably[61]) brought a confrontation between a Western attachment to landownership[62] and a widespread non-Western pattern of use rights in resources allotted, in line with the widespread human norm, through political control.

William Cronon, the historian of the clash between Western settlers and indigenous chieftainships in colonial Southern New England, gives a frequently quoted account of that encounter in his *Changes in the Land*: "What the Indians owned – or, more precisely, what their villages gave them claim to – was not the land but the things that were on the land during the various seasons of the year. It was a conception of property shared by many of the hunter-gatherer and agricultural peoples of the world, but radically different from that of the invading Europeans."[63] Cronon's much-cited description, it should be said, is a shade misleading. He speaks of "villages" giving claims, which might all too easily be taken to imply egalitarian sharing, or some version of primitive communism. That is not right, and Stuart Banner chooses more precise, and more hard-edged, language in his own account of the same encounter, *How the Indians Lost Their Land*. Banner emphasizes that it was "village *chiefs*" who accorded rights:[64] What the English colonists encountered were not communistic

---

[61] See, e.g., from a classic author, Leopold Pospisil, *Anthropology of Law: A Comparative Theory* (New York, 1971), 274.
[62] See below, Chapter 9, for a more thorough discussion.
[63] Cronon, *Changes in the Land: Indians, Colonists and the Ecology of New England* (New York, 1983), 60, 62, 65.
[64] Banner, *How the Indians Lost Their Land: Law and Power on the Frontier* (Cambridge, MA, 2009), 20, emphasis added.

villagers, but communities whose common territories were exploited and cultivated by families subject to the political control exercised by sachems. Other New World societies too, though they differed immensely, as Allan Greer shows, had real property regimes that functioned against the background of some form of hierarchical control.[65]

Parallel observations have been made about an immense variety of societies, from Hawaii[66] to New Zealand[67] to Africa,[68] to the pre-Columbian Inca,[69] to Ancient India,[70] many of them with much more highly articulated social hierarchies than the tribal bands of colonial Southern New England. Precolonial Africa has been the subject of especially probing work. Antony Hopkins, for example, in a study of the mid nineteenth-century British annexation of Lagos, has shown how Western conceptions of private landownership clashed with use rights in a highly developed agrarian order. Lagos was not a world of tribal bands, but it *was* one in which chiefs distributed land rights as a means of asserting and cementing their authority: "Allocation of use rights was important as a means of settling followers and of building up a power base of dependents, some free men but most of slave status, by attaching them to the entourage of the chief concerned."[71] The intrusion of the British shattered this system of land allotment as an instrument of entourage-building, replacing it with the Western style of private landownership; what the arrival of Western power brought was, neither the destruction of primitive communism, nor the theft of land

---

[65] Greer, *Property and Dispossession: Natives, Empires and Land in Early Modern North America* (Cambridge, 2018), at e.g., 30–31 (reading Nahua real property against background of hierarchical social ordering), 40–41 (sachems in Atlantic coastal societies), 50 (on "power" and "control" among the Innu). Greer rightly emphasizes the variety among these societies, but I allow myself to hope that he would agree that they seem to have shared an orientation toward dominance relations of some kind in the understanding of rights in land.

[66] E.g., Jocelyn Linnekin, "The Hui Lands of Keanae: Hawaiian Land Tenure and the Great Mahele," *Journal of the Polynesian Society* 92 (1983): 172 [169–188].

[67] Stuart Banner, "Two Properties, One Land: Law and Space in Nineteenth-Century New Zealand," *Law and Social Inquiry* 24 (1999): 807–852.

[68] Martin Chanock, *Law, Custom and Social Order: The Colonial Experience in Malawi and Zambia* (Portsmouth, N.H., 1998), 231.

[69] Godelier, "Territory and Property," 136–137.

[70] Romila Thapar, *From Lineage to State* (Oxford, 1984), 104.

[71] Hopkins, "Property Rights and Empire Building: Britain's Annexation of Lagos, 1861," *Journal of Economic History* 40 (1980): 784 [777–798].

previously owned in fee simple by the local population, but the erosion of the local authority structure. Martin Chanock, surveying a range of African studies, gives a similar account: In precolonial society, "people were linked to land through their membership of groups. It was their group standing which gave them access to land and consequently their concern was with maintaining their position linked to other persons rather than with rights in land."[72] This is the state of affairs that Goody tries to capture through his phrase "chieftainship over people."[73]

Discussion of precolonial African societies has centered on one particular aspect of this chieftainship over people: the master/slave relationship. Slavery was "an integral feature of almost every ancient society of Europe, Africa and Asia."[74] There is thus nothing particularly surprising or shocking about its presence in precolonial Africa. Nevertheless, African slavery has inevitably seemed disturbing to modern Western observers, accustomed, since the late eighteenth century, to thinking of "property in man" as the foulest violation of human rights and sharply conscious of the horrific history of the Atlantic slave trade. This is, as one specialist puts it, an "explosively sensitive" topic,[75] and it is not easy to find comfortable ways of talking about it.

Anthropologists have proposed a variety of ways of defusing it. Goody suggests an economic approach: Precolonial Africa, he argues, was oriented toward the chieftainship over people rather than the chieftainship over land because in Africa, by contrast with Europe, people were scarce whereas land was plentiful. It is not that the Africans were somehow more vicious exploiters of their fellow human beings than the Europeans; it is rather that it is always the relatively scarce factor of production that comes to be defined as "property" in every society.[76] I will return to this economic argument at the end of this chapter.

---

[72] Chanock, Law, *Custom and Social Order*, 281.
[73] Jack Goody, *Technology, Tradition and the State in Africa* (Oxford, 1971), 30.
[74] Jeffrey Fynn-Paul, "Empire, Monotheism and Slavery in the Greater Mediterranean Region from Antiquity to the Early Modern Era," *Past & Present* 205 (2009): 7 [3–40].
[75] Joseph C. Miller, "Breaking the Historiographical Chains: Martin Klein and Slavery," *Canadian Journal of African Studies/Revue canadienne des études africaines* 34 (2000): 513 [512–531]; Sean Wilentz, *No Property in Man: Slavery and Anti-slavery at the Nation's Founding* (Cambridge, MA, 2018).
[76] Goody, *Technology, Tradition and the State*, 25. In this, Goody was echoing but not citing the work of a year earlier (presumably unknown to him) by the economist Evsey Domar. See below.

Another influential approach to the problem was suggested by the anthropologist James L. Watson, in an essay contrasting African slavery with the more noxious form found in such settings as antebellum America. Antebellum slavery conformed to what Watson calls a "closed model": Enslaved persons, deemed racially inferior, were permanently excluded from membership in the dominant society. African slavery, by contrast, operated on an "open model," of a kind found in many parts of the world: Slaves were not regarded as inherently inferior, and they could eventually be freed and integrated into full membership in the dominant order. Indeed, enslavement was used as means of recruiting new members. In that sense, African slavery was categorically different from the slavery into which African captives were thrown in the New World. (Roman slave law, as we shall see, assumed an open model as well.[77])

But the most widely cited effort to cope with the explosive challenge of African slavery comes from historian Suzanne Miers and anthropologist Igor Kopytoff. Miers and Kopytoff insist that we must not surrender to our instinctive shock when we hear the word "slavery," for the word can mean quite different things in different contexts. The "slaves" of precolonial Africa were simply one group in a larger socio-economic order organized around what Miers and Kopytoff call "rights-in-persons." Free persons were also subject to claims of right; slaves simply sat on the lowest rung of a social order in which most individuals were in some sense the property of a small stratum of masters. The domination over *all* persons was conceptualized through the language of ownership; the very fabric of society was woven out of the ownership of some humans by others. Younger members of lineages, for example, were understood to be property just as slaves were; the reality is that most persons in these societies were located on a "slavery to kinship continuum."[78]

And in this orientation toward rights-in-persons, Miers and Kopytoff argue, African societies were not utterly different from

---

[77] James L. Watson, "Slavery as an Institution, Open and Closed Systems," in Watson, ed., *Asian and African Systems of Slavery* (Berkeley, 1980), 1–15. For the application to Rome, Peter Temin, "The Labor Market of the Early Roman Empire," *Journal of Interdisciplinary History* 34 (2004): 513–538.

[78] Miers and Kopytoff, *Slavery in Africa: Historical and Anthropological Perspectives* (Madison, WI, 1977), 23–24.

Hierarchy and the Hunt for Prey 61

European ones, which after all also recognized such relations. They cite in particular a famous example from Roman law, to which we will return:

> Rights-in-persons exist in almost all social relationships. Thus, children have the right to support and protection from their parents, who have the right to demand obedience from them; a husband in many Western societies could until recently expect domestic services from his wife in return for material support from him, and they had exclusive rights to each other's sexual activity, adultery on either side being grounds for divorce ... Such rights-in-persons may cover not just a person's services but his entire person – thus, the father in ancient Rome could kill or sell his children ... the position of the so-called "slave" can only be understood in the general cultural context of these rights.[79]

What differentiated Africa from Europe was not that the latter was a realm of perfect freedom, whereas the former was a realm of servitude. Both worlds were ones in which some persons dominated others; a Roman father (so Miers and Kopytoff believe[80]) could even "kill or sell his children." What distinguished the two was rather that domination rested more on rights-in-things in Europe. In the European world, it was regularly the case that the rich ruled by virtue of being rich; in Africa, it was always the case that the status superiors ruled by virtue of being status superiors. These were simply two different styles of inequality. Sahlins gives a sharp formulation to the contrast: "[T]he two systems of property work differently," he explains, "the one (chieftainship) a right to things realized through a hold on persons, the other (bourgeois) a hold on persons realized through a right to things."[81] The contrast is not one between slavery and freedom, but one between exploitation by masters (ruling persons) and exploitation by lords (ruling lands).

* * *

The various societies described by these anthropologists and historians are not all simple tribal chieftainships of the kind analyzed by Sahlins. But they *are* all societies whose social orders diverge sharply from what Schmitt imagined in *The Nomos of the Earth*. Schmitt declared that it was the division of the earth that gave rise to "the orders and

---

[79] Miers and Kopytoff, *Slavery in Africa*, 7.
[80] We shall see in the next chapter that it is not so simple.
[81] Sahlins, *Stone Age Economics*, 93.

orientations of human social life." In these societies, the reverse holds, in one fashion or another: It is "the [political and hierarchical] orders and orientations of human social life" that govern the forms of land tenure. These are all societies in which the distribution of rights in land is obedient, in one way or another, to the dictates of human hierarchy.

The contrast can be pictured as a contrast in the way the law draws its map of the real property order. In the eyes of Schmitt and modern Westerners, the map of property in land is a plat, parceling out "the solid earth" into plots held by owners in fee simple. This plat identifies rights-holders who are relatively immune to "political control" within their own domains; and it is taken for granted that "[t]he whole world ... [is] divided among private owners."[82] In these numerous non-Western and nonmodern societies, by contrast, the working map of rights in land is not a plat, but a chart of the social hierarchy, tracing the threads of political control in the web of the "hold on persons." The ultimate governing principle is not who owns which acreage, but who ranks where on the social scale of inferiors and superiors. To put it (cautiously) in the language of ethology, the ultimate governing principle has to do, not with individual territoriality, but with another pattern studied by ethologists: social dominance.[83]

The ethological concept of dominance certainly must be used cautiously. Human rank-ordering looks different from the rank-ordering found among other animals. The evolutionary anthropologist Bernard Chapais states the contrast this way: Dominance among other primates flows from physical intimidation. Among chimpanzees and others of our cousins, alpha males achieve their dominance, in the words of Richard Wrangham, through "physical and often bloody fights."[84] By contrast, Chapais argues, human rank is a matter of

---

[82] Rose, "Comedy of the Commons," 712.
[83] The distinction between dominance and territoriality poses some inevitable definitional challenges. For discussion, see Christine R. Maher and Dale F. Lott, "Definitions of Territoriality Used in the Study of Variation in Vertebrate Spacing Systems," *Animal Behaviour* 6 (1995): 1581–1597; John H. Kaufmann, "On the Definitions and Functions of Dominance and Territoriality," *Biological Review* 58 (1983): 1–20.
[84] Richard Wrangham, *The Goodness Paradox: The Strange Relationship between Virtue and Violence in Human Evolution* (New York, 2019), 159–160. Cf. Wrangham, "Evolution of Coalitionary Killing," *American Journal of Physical Anthropology* 110 (1999): 1–30.

Hierarchy and the Hunt for Prey 63

"prestige," acquired through "competence" in activities "from hunting to shamanism."[85] The "dominant" human is not necessarily the most physically powerful one, but the most skilled.

Now, the generalizability of Chapais' analysis must not be overstated. This is partly because some ethologists deny that rank-ordering among other primates in fact involves pure physical intimidation. There are studies arguing that other dominant primates "generously" distribute food to subordinates just as human Big Men do.[86] But more importantly, for my purposes, it is because physical intimidation is so often clearly present in human societies. Chapais, like other evolutionary anthropologists, is concerned with the transition to hunter-gatherer societies, which are famously egalitarian.[87] More complex human societies look different, however, with patterns of dominance that unquestionably involve violent coercion, as the anthropologists Kent Flannery and Joyce Marcus emphasize.[88] The institution of slavery certainly rests on physical intimidation, and so do many other relationships in complex human societies that take of the form of what German law traditionally calls by the chilling phrase *besondere Gewaltverhältnisse*, substate "special relationships licensing violence." Historical examples of such "special relationships licensing violence" are multitudinous. They can include, for instance, those between husbands and wives, parents and children, creditors and debtors, teachers and pupils. Indeed, the claim of ownership, as I suggested in the Introduction, frequently implies some sort of claim to the right to do violence. It is in the essential nature of ownership that it often grounds a *besonderes Gewaltverhältnis*.

Nevertheless, it is true, and important, that the rank-ordering of most of the cultures surveyed in this chapter is remote from a rank-ordering based purely on physical intimidation. Whether the issue is

---

[85] Chapais, "Competence and the Evolutionary Origins of Status and Power," *Human Nature* 26 (2015): 162 [161–183].
[86] E.g., Jörg Massen, Lisette van den Berg, Berry Spruit, and Elizabeth Sterk, "Generous Leaders and Selfish Underdogs: Prosociality in Despotic Macaques," *PLos One* 5 (2010): e9734.
[87] Though even that egalitarianism, as Christopher Boehm famously argues, operates against the background of a threat of violence against upstarts. See Boehm, *Hierarchy in the Forest*.
[88] Flannery and Marcus, *The Creation of Inequality: How Our Prehistoric Ancestors Set the Stage for Monarchy, Slavery and Empire* (Cambridge, MA, 2012).

the distribution of meat in the hunt or the distribution of use rights in land, these are cultures of the maximization of status, and this maximization of status is indeed arguably distinct from dominance among other animals. Ethologists disagree over the proper definition of dominance, but the definitions ordinarily involve "priority of access to resources."[89] The dominant individual, among other animals, is not only the most physically intimidating one, but the one that gets more. The human pattern on display in these various cultures is distinctive, if not unparalleled, for the simple reason that it is not necessarily the case that the dominant individual gets more.

Nevertheless, if human dominance hierarchy is not synonymous with dominance hierarchy in other animals, I believe it is right to insist that these nonmodern, non-Western patterns of property relations are shaped not just by territoriality, but by human forms of dominance as well. The societies described by these anthropologists and historians are not ruled by the happy egalitarian harmony of primitive communism. They are societies that revolve around "group *standing*," in Chanock's words, and the "concern" of individuals with "maintaining their position." They are societies in which, in the classic language of legal realism, there is no "ownership" understood as a direct and unmediated relationship between persons and things. Instead, as anthropologists since Malinowski and Hoebel have emphasized, rights in things are a function of the relationships among persons.[90] But it must be underlined that there is nothing inherently egalitarian about the relationships among the persons in question. There is no justification for romanticizing some supposed non-Western pattern of communal sharing, or imagining that defining ownership as a relationship between persons is a formula for establishing unmarred human harmony. Property relations are inextricably tied up with patterns of human power. Human societies may well sometimes count as egalitarian in some ways;[91] but *property*

---

[89] E.g., Carlos Drews, "The Concept and Definition of Dominance in Animal Behaviour," *Behaviour* 125 (1993): 288 [283–313].

[90] Arthur L. Corbin, "Legal Analysis and Terminology," *Yale Law Journal* 29 (1919): 165 [163–173]; and the discussion in E. Adamson Hoebel, *The Law of Primitive Man: A Study in Comparative Legal Dynamics* (Cambridge, MA, 1967) (orig. 1954), 47; cf. Pospisil, *Anthropology of Law*, 296: "As has been pointed out so often in anthropological literature, the term ownership in itself is unsatisfactory and misleading."

[91] For an immensely subtle and stimulating discussion, Boehm, *Hierarchy in the Forest*.

is an inherently inegalitarian institution. Conceptions of property differ, and differ starkly, as this book aims to show; but there is no conception of property that does not result in placing some humans higher on the scale of rank or wealth than others.

*　*　*

In the remaining pages of this book, I will try to show that the work of the anthropologists and ethologists is of indispensable value for understanding the ancient Roman property law that lies at the headwaters of the Western tradition, and the later history of Western property law as well. Before passing to that larger history, though, I would like to stress one last point: The contrast between the two patterns of ownership culture that are my subject in this chapter are not well explained through conventional economic analysis.

There are two bodies of economic literature that purport to explain these divergent patterns of social organization. One line of argument sets out to explain why the law protects private property in land, and more broadly in "farmlands, pastures, hunting or fishing territories." The second sets out to explain why the law, in some societies, protects private property in humans. Neither provides an explanation that is fully adequate.

Let me begin with the work of economists who set out to explain why the law protects private property in land and other forms of territory. On that question there is a familiar, and immense, literature, which begins with two seminal articles of the 1960s, Harold Demsetz's "Toward a Theory of Property Rights," and Garrett Hardin's "Tragedy of the Commons."[92]

Like many others writing in later decades of the Cold War, the makers of this "tragedy of the commons" literature were concerned with explaining the ineluctability of the failure of communism; and to that end, they focused on resource management. As a theoretical matter, Demsetz and Hardin argued, communal ownership could never result in the sustainable exploitation of territorial resources, once those resources reached a certain threshold value. This is because individual exploiters would have incentives to overexploit.

---

[92] Demsetz, "Toward a Theory of Property Rights," *American Economic Review* 57 (1967): 347–359; Hardin, "The Tragedy of the Commons," *Science* (N.S.) 162 (1968): 1243–1248.

Only private property holders would properly internalize the externalities of resource exploitation, and accordingly only a system founded in exclusive private property rights could succeed in sustaining a pool of valuable resources. Demsetz illustrated this theory with an example taken from the anthropologist Eleanor Leacock's study of the fur trade in early eighteenth-century Canada. As beaver pelts became more valuable with the appearance of French traders, a system emerged among the indigenous Montagnais of the Labrador Peninsula, under which families were allotted rights in particular hunting territories.[93] It was only the establishment of such rights, Demsetz argued, that permitted owners to manage the population of beavers, avoiding overhunting. Private property, he concluded, evolved in response to the challenges of sustainable resource management.

The subsequent theoretical literature has developed more complex accounts of the sustainable management of communal resources, but without departing from the basic premises of Demsetz. The Nobel-Prize-winning economist Elinor Ostrom blazed the trail in 1990: Through close studies of what she called "common-pool resources" in various parts of the world, Ostrom showed that while unregulated forms of collective ownership might be doomed to fail, under the right conditions certain kinds of commons could survive indefinitely. The success stories, which included mountain communities in Switzerland and Japan, displayed "the side-by-side existence of private property and communal property in settings in which the individuals involved have exercised considerable control over institutional arrangements and property rights."[94] Numerous studies since have followed Ostrom's lead, dissecting the rules of the internal governance that permit, or even require, some degree of the collective ownership or management of common pools.

This "tragedy of the commons" problem, which plays a starring role in contemporary scholarship on property law, is often said to demonstrate the necessity of Blackstonian private property rights: Only exclusive ownership, law students are taught, can succeed in

---

[93] Leacock, "The Montagnais 'Hunting Territory' and the Fur Trade," *American Anthropologist* 56, no. 5, pt. 2, memoir no. 78 (October 1954).

[94] Ostrom, *Governing the Commons: The Evolution of Institutions for Collective Action* (Cambridge, 1990), 61.

Hierarchy and the Hunt for Prey 67

maintaining sustainable resource exploitation. Without it, society would perish.

Yet the anthropology surveyed in this chapter suggests otherwise. Private property in the Blackstonian sense is not in fact the only possible solution to the tragedy of the commons. The problem can be solved just as well by a system of use rights. Use rights are rights in resources, not rights in land as such; and as long as the social hierarchy that exercises "political control" is in good order, a system of use rights in resources fully suffices to avoid the dangers of the tragedy of the commons. The innumerable use-rights systems described by anthropologists and historians are, indeed, nothing other than well-ordered systems of rights in resources without exclusive Blackstonian ownership.

Such is the lesson, indeed, of the very study on which Demsetz built his original case for the tragedy of the commons hypothesis, Leacock's work on Montagnais hunting rights in the early eighteenth century. Leacock's argument had, in fact, nothing to do with Blackstonian ownership. She wrote about the "seasonal allotment" of rights in the resources of beaver furs, which gradually became "relatively stabilized."[95] Indeed, she made a point of noting that "land [in the Montagnais system] has no value as 'real estate' apart from its products. What is involved is more properly a form of usufruct than 'true' ownership."[96] The rights in question, she moreover emphasized, were rights only to the *furs* of beavers; the animals themselves remained available to be eaten by others in case of need. Her rights in resources were thus very limited indeed.[97] This bears no resemblance to a system of Blackstonian exclusive rights in an "owned" territory from which intruders are barred. What Leacock's work suggests instead is exactly what the work of other anthropologists suggests. Nothing in the tragedy of the commons dynamic can explain why Blackstonian ownership should ever arise. If the issue is sustainable resource management, "political control" can comfortably do the job.[98]

Scholars who work in the tragedy of the commons vein do know about use rights. Property theory is conducted by legal and economic

---

[95] Leacock, "Montagnais 'Hunting Territory,'" 15.
[96] Ibid., 1–2 and generally on these opening pages.   [97] Ibid., 2, 15.
[98] I am grateful to Charlie Donahue for emphasizing this point to me.

scholars who are often admirably well read, and property theorists are well aware that property rights in territories, in early stages of development, commonly take that form. "[I]ndividual tenure," as Smith, the theorist of "governance strategies," observes, "probably started out as a system of usufruct."[99] Robert Ellickson, in his influential article "Property in Land," gives particular attention to the dynamics of a primitive order in which "pre-literate groups" manage land through the assignment of usufructs. A system of usufruct, he argues, arises naturally in the course of the evolution of cooperation:

Imagine that several dozen unallied family units live in a fertile valley... [T]he valley residents discern that it is mutually advantageous for all of them to honor a primary norm that entitles each family to keep the crops it has grown, and also a secondary norm that obligates all valley families to punish internal deviants and external marauders who fail to respect private property in crops. Out of this primordial soup emerges the private usufruct on intensively used land.[100]

But why usufruct rather than Blackstonian exclusive ownership? Ellickson invests considerable ingenuity into explaining the prevalence of usufruct in preliterate societies, despite what he presumes to be its relative inadequacy as an institution for the management of resources. His explanation puts the accent on technology. Preliterate societies, Ellickson argues, lack both the technological capacity to engage in permanent improvement of land and the technological capacity to record title. Moreover, land in places such as his "fertile valley" are likely to be so plentiful that permanent improvements are not imperative for efficient management of land resources. But those are conditions that pertain only in preliterate societies. As practices of land improvement and recording techniques develop, usufruct inevitably gives way to ownership of the familiar modern Blackstonian kind.[101]

Yet there is nothing in the logic of resource management that requires us to suppose that Blackstonian ownership would inevitably arise out of the "primordial soup" of social evolution. Why would property theorists think otherwise? The answer is that they have not

---
[99] Smith, "Exclusion versus Governance," 458–459.
[100] Ellickson, "Property in Land," *Yale Law Journal* 102 (1993): 1366 [1315–1400].
[101] Ibid., 1367.

Hierarchy and the Hunt for Prey 69

recognized the extent to which a system of use rights can be managed through norms of social hierarchy, providing the foundation for a fully functional "governance strategy." The makers of this literature have familiarized themselves with anthropology – up to a point. But only up to a point. They find nothing to say about the operation of rank-ordering that features so prominently in the literature of so much of social science, and that has been my theme throughout this chapter.[102] The "political control" whose presence has been detected in so much of the human world by anthropologists and historians simply does not figure in their work. When these property theorists imagine the evolution of property rights, they speak in terms of coequal actors (or, as the case may be, coequal households) engaging in bargaining, or evolving unconscious patterns of mutual accommodation.

Yet it is the logic of social dominance that structures a system of use rights.

This lack of interest in, if not blindness to, the prevalence of hierarchical ordering in human societies follows from two methodological prejudices in the tragedy of the commons literature, both of which must be studiously laid aside if we are to understand the long-term development of the Western property tradition. The first is a prejudice in favor of methodological individualism, which can make it difficult to reckon with the operation of hierarchical authority in human societies.[103] The attachment to methodological individualism runs deep in the literature, which has framed its analyses for decades around the problems of "individuals [who] have a common or collective interest"[104] – the problems, in the words of Ostrom, of how "individuals … have exercised … control over institutional arrangements and property rights."[105] Property theorists of course

---

[102] While Ellickson does acknowledge the contrast between "hierarchy and democracy," ibid. 1348–1349, he does not explore the social scientific literature on the social foundations of hierarchy.

[103] Even in Ellickson's case, methodological householdism, which, it seems fair to say, is the same thing writ slightly larger. Of course, a careful use of the methodological individualism of the kind advocated by Max Weber is fully able to account for the sort of hierarchical ordering that this chapter investigates. What I question is an approach that abstracts entirely from the social position of individuals and so carries the dangers found in this literature.

[104] Mancur Olson, *The Logic of Collective Action* (Cambridge, MA, 1965), 7.

[105] Ostrom, *Governing the Commons*, 61.

understand that their subject is ultimately the functioning of groups: Rights in a commons must be the products of a process of "group consensus,"[106] or decisions by the "group ... acting as a corporate body."[107] Nevertheless, their understanding of how groups operate assumes a process of coequal bargaining, or at least a process of autonomous individual responses to pressures leading to "the evolution of cooperation."

But to suppose that the internal workings of "the group" are the product of bargaining among socially undifferentiated actors is to engage in heroic understatement of the element of human domination at work in so many of the orders that anthropologists and historians study. To say that is not to say that societies are all governed by dominance relations of the kind described by Sahlins and so many other scholars. Ostrom may well have succeeded in identifying examples of relatively egalitarian orders in regions like the Swiss Alpine highlands. But if we imagine that *all* property orders are the products of egalitarian bargaining or accommodation, we blind ourselves to vast stretches of the human experience, and to key evidence for the nature of human property psychology and ownership culture.

As for the second methodological prejudice: This is the assumption that property rights evolve purely as a response to the demands of sustainable resource management. This core methodological assumption lies at the foundation of Demsetz's seminal article on the evolution of property rights. The subsequent literature has advanced greatly in subtlety; but Demsetz's basic assumption has never been abandoned.

And of course it is true that rules of property must conduce to the sustainable management of resources. If they did not, human society would indeed not survive. Nevertheless, the work of anthropologists and historians suggests powerfully that there is much more to cultures of ownership than that. The human world is not composed of small, coequal groups, discovering ways to coexist without exhausting their shared resources. It is made up of human animals who are attached to the maximization of rank and power; and the dynamics of property

---

[106] Thomas Merrill, "The Property Strategy," *University of Pennsylvania Law Review* 160 (2012): 2061 [2061–2095].

[107] Ellickson, "Property in Land," 1368.

law inescapably reflect that fact. This is as true of the ideal-typical "bourgeois" order described by Sahlins as it is of his ideal-typical tribal chieftainship. Property rules do not just secure the efficient management of resources. They secure the accumulation of "wealth, power and prestige" as well; and the "tragedy of the commons" line of analysis leaves us far too few ways of talking about that.

* * *

The Demsetz/Hardin line of literature is by far the best-known body of work on the economics of the evolution of property law. But there is another economic line of argument that deserves attention as well. This is a literature that sets out to explain why some societies display the ownership of humans.

That effort was made, in particular, by the economist Evsey Domar, who asked in 1970 why some societies depend on "the ownership of peasants and not of land."[108] The answer, Domar concluded, lies in whether land or labor is the scarcer factor of production. Where land is abundant but people are few it is the ownership of humans that can "yield an income."[109] The same economic analysis was proposed a year later, independently, by Goody, as we have seen: Africa differed from Europe, Goody argued, because in Africa "the population is small [but] land is plentiful."[110] On this account, the explanation for the contrast between the ownership of people and the ownership of land lies in the most familiar and basic of market forces: It is always the scarcer resources that are the most highly valued, and that are therefore protected by the law as "property." Where land is inexhaustibly abundant, it will no more be the subject of ownership than air.

There is some real power in this argument. It is true enough that if productive land were in infinite supply, and there were no transaction costs to taking possession of it, there would be no economic pressure to make it the object of property rights. But here again, economic analysis

---

[108] Domar, "The Causes of Slavery or Serfdom: A Hypothesis," *Journal of Economic History* 30 (1970): 19 [18–32]. For a recent elaboration, see Nils-Petter Lagerlöf, "Slavery and Other Property Rights," *Review of Economic Studies* 76 (2009): 319–342.

[109] Domar, "Causes of Slavery or Serfdom," 19.

[110] Goody, *Technology, Tradition and the State*, 25. For a reserved but respectful treatment, see Watson, "Slavery as an Institution," 11–13.

cannot yield a fully satisfactory answer to the question of why some cultures are oriented toward "the control over people" where others are oriented toward "the ownership of land." This is partly because many historical cases are not well explained by the Domar/Goody hypothesis. We shall see, for instance, that the use of slave labor expanded dramatically in Republican Rome. Though Domar and Goody may have some insight to offer on the Roman case, it would be strained to argue that large-scale slavery took hold in Roman Italy because "the population [grew] small but the land [grew] plentiful."

But the deeper reason for doubt lies elsewhere. The chieftainship over people is a principle of social organization that includes many features that have little to do with wealth maximization. As critics of Domar point out, slaves have often been kept, not because they "yield an income," but as luxury goods that "consumed more than they produced"[111] – as a means of displaying rank, not a means of procuring wealth.[112] Slaves, as Orlando Patterson writes, are "likely to be nonproductive, and are held ... mainly for prestige or political purposes."[113] The same observation was made by the economic historian Karl Bücher, a man upon whose work I will draw quite a bit in the chapters that follow. Bücher emphasized, at the turn of the last century, how much the Romans invested, not just in return on their slave capital, but in the expensive prestige display of slaveownership:

> When the master shows himself in public, a great crowd of slaves walks in front of him (*anteambulones*), another follows him (*pedisequi*); the *nomenclator* gives him the names of those he encounters who wish to be greeted; his *distributores* and *tesserarii* hand out bribes to the populace and give them his electioneering slogans.[114]

Max Weber, on whom the influence of Bücher ran deep, portrayed the society of Rome in much the same way: "The posh high-class houses of the Roman aristocracy [*die vornehmen Häuser des Römeradels*]

---

[111] Watson, "Slavery as an Institution," 14.
[112] Cf. Keith Hopkins, *Sociological Studies in Roman History*, ed. Christopher Kelly (Cambridge, 2018), 347: "Slavery ceased to be a major method of procuring wealth, while it long survived as a method of displaying it."
[113] Patterson, *Slavery and Social Death*, 24.
[114] Bücher, *Die Entstehung der Volkswirtschaft* (Tübingen, 1893), 27.

consumed slaves in massive quantities."[115] Neville Morley, in a similar vein, writes vividly of "the ingenuity displayed by the Roman elite in the use of slaves to impress visitors and enhance their own public presence, such as Livia's 'pet child' (delicium) and the dwarfs and other curiosities that ... fascinated Romans in the slavemarket."[116] Slaves were indeed often objects of display – of "conspicuous consumption," in the famous phrase of Thorstein Veblen[117] – and nothing in the Domar/Goody hypothesis can make sense of that.[118]

It is critical to underline a further point as well: The ownership of humans involves more than just slavery. Many classes of persons have been deemed property in various societies. Women are frequently regarded as "owned" by their menfolk; and as Miers and Kopytoff point out, younger members of lineages in the precolonial African societies that interested Goody were understood to be "owned" just as slaves were. The same is true of the law of ancient Rome, which, like precolonial Africa, assumed a "slavery to kinship continuum." The "ownership" of humans in such settings is not just a mode of economic exploitation. It is mode of expression in a system of social hierarchy in which the language of ownership is a language of rank.

Not least, the contrast between control over people and control over land is not restricted to the internal organization of households. It also makes itself felt in the forms of the state. The anthropologist Alain Testart makes the point that is made by many other social scientists as well: Premodern states, he observes, typically lacked a clearly defined "territorial base." They were organized instead as rulerships over peoples; their political power was "primarily power over humans and not over things."[119] Economics alone cannot explain why we see

---

[115] Weber, *Wirtschaft und Gesellschaft*, ed. Johannes Winckelmann, 5th ed. (Tübingen, 1985), 798.
[116] Morley, "Slavery under the Principate," in John Bodel and Paul Cartledge, eds., *The Cambridge World History of Slavery, Vol. 1: The Ancient Mediterranean World* (Cambridge, 2011), 278 [265–286]. Joachim Marquardt huffily wrote that such displays cast "[a]n unpleasant light on the perversity of these times." Marquardt, Privatleben der Römer (Leipzig, 1879), 1:149.
[117] Veblen, *The Theory of the Leisure Class: An Economic Study of Institutions* (New York, 1902), 68–101.
[118] For discussion and further literature, see also Stanley Engerman, "Some Considerations Relating to Property Rights in Man," *Journal of Economic History* 33 (1973): 46 [43–65].
[119] Testart, *Éléments de Classification des Sociétés* (Paris, 2005), 82.

this structural consonance between state and society, between rulership and ownership, yin and yang. There may be some measure of truth in the Domar/Goody hypothesis; but in the end it explains much too little.

Certainly, it leaves us too few ways of understanding the ancient Roman foundations of Western property law, to which I now turn.

2

Masters of Men and Beasts: The Early Roman *Fantasia* of Ownership

"The father in ancient Rome," write Suzanne Miers and Igor Kopytoff, in their effort to explain the culture of the ownership of humans in precolonial Africa to modern Western readers, "could kill or sell his children."[1] Their purpose, in invoking this notorious rule of ancient Roman law, on its face so ghoulish, is to show that Africa was not categorically different from the rest of the world. Precolonial African societies made use of slavery, in ways that seem shocking to us today; but it is misleading to focus too much on the plight of the African slave, since younger members of lineage groups, though juridically free, were also deemed to be owned. African societies were organized along a "slavery to kinship continuum," in which being human property was a pervasive condition; and something similar was true of ancient Rome, where the property rights of the *paterfamilias* even extended to the *vitae necisque potestas*, the "power of life and death."

The Roman comparison certainly sounds compelling. But is it correct? Classicists will rush to protest that Miers and Kopytoff are confused about the actual workings of Roman law. A host of careful studies has shown that the Roman realities were not in fact as ghoulish as the letter of the law implies. The ancient sources do speak of the father's "power of life and death"; and it may be possible that in some archaic period, now lost in the mists of Roman prehistory, the heads of

---

[1] Suzanne Miers and Igor Kopytoff, *Slavery in Africa: Historical and Anthropological Perspectives* (Madison, WI, 1977), 7.

clans enjoyed such an unbridled authority. But in the periods for which we have historical documentation, the powers of the father were in practice "hedged round with social restrictions."[2] While Roman literature includes some dramatic tales of fathers putting their sons to death, those tales are few in number, and they reveal more about the "myths" of the law than they do about the realities of Roman society.[3] The truth is that the father's power of life and death was "not a quotidian reality, but a pure concept."[4] Miers and Kopytoff are dealing in legends, not facts.

Yet for all that, the use that they make of Roman law is not wholly unjustified. The proposition that Roman fathers could kill their children may be a myth, a ghoulish expression of the Roman legal imagination, not a sober description of the Roman realities; but the myths of the law are part of its workings. The law is not simply in the business of providing a workaday description of the world. It is in the business of measuring and judging the world against some ideal model; and in property law the business of measuring and judging requires some imaginative account of why owners are entitled to own, and what powers they ought to enjoy. Property law, as Carol Rose writes, depends on "stories, allegories and metaphors" that can serve to explain the foundations of ownership.[5] Giambattista Vico, the extraordinary genius of the early Enlightenment, put the point in his own enchanting terms: The law, Vico wrote, requires a "poetic logic," a non-Cartesian mode of thinking that makes sense of the workings of the world through *fantasia*, imagination.[6] And while classicists have amply demonstrated that the "quotidian reality" of Rome was not as savage as the Roman sources imply, we must not ignore the fact that

---

[2] Bruce Frier and Thomas McGinn, *A Casebook on Roman Family Law* (Oxford, 2004), 191.
[3] Brent Shaw, "Raising and Killing Children: Two Roman Myths," *Mnemosyne* Ser. 4, 54 (2001): 31–77.
[4] Thomas, "Vitae necisque potestas," in Thomas, ed., *Du châtiment dans la cité: supplices corporels et peine de mort* (Rome, 1984), 512 [499–548].
[5] Rose, *Property and Persuasion: Essays on the History, Theory and Rhetoric of Ownership* (New York, 1994), 5–6.
[6] Vico, *La scienza nuova*, ed. Paolo Rossi (Milan, 1958), 27–28 and often. For Vico's theory of "imaginative universals," I have benefited from Donald Phillip Verene, *Vico's Science of Imagination* (Ithaca, N.Y., 1981), 65–94.

the *fantasia* in those sources spoke of the ownership of human beings totally subject to the power of their masters.

Whatever the prosaic realities, the law of ancient Rome did indeed imagine a property order in which the paradigmatic owner was an all-powerful ruler, the chieftain over an extended household that commingled slaves and kin. The descendants of this figure were indeed his lawful possessions just as much as his slaves and his inanimate objects were, and his authority over the persons and things that he owned was indeed unbounded: He held the absolute power to use and destroy his things at will; and in a parallel way, he held the power of life and death. As the great Roman law scholar Max Kaser described the logic of this "absolute" ownership in the ancient sources, the Roman father was permitted to kill his children for the same reason that he was permitted to smash his crockery or slaughter his sheep.[7] They were all *his* – or so the legal theory held.[8]

And the legal theory of this fearsome figure does not only matter for understanding the culture of ancient Roman law. The ancient Roman myth of the unbounded powers of the master/owner lived on in later centuries: It is the source of the "absolute" conception of ownership that we still make use of in the modern market-oriented West. This is indeed one of the most remarkable facts of Western legal history: The modern market conception of ownership, so basic to the way that we think about law, is a conception that originally formed in an ancient slave society. Orlando Patterson puts the point succinctly. Rome produced "a startlingly new legal concept: the idea of the absolute ownership of things," and that idea "became pivotal in [the] private law" of the Western world.[9]

This chapter and the next trek back to the ancient origins of this "startling legal concept," "absolute" ownership, which was born in the myth of the utter power of the Roman household master and lives on as the basis for the conceptualization of property rights in modern

---

[7] Kaser, "Der Inhalt der Patria Potestas," *Zeitschrift der Savigny-Stiftung für Rechtsgeschichte (Romanistische Abteilung)* 53 (1938): 62 [62–87].
[8] The legal theory, it is important to emphasize, did not describe the reality with regard to any form of property, animate or inanimate. See, e.g., Éva Jakab, "Property Rights in Ancient Rome," in Paul Erdkamp, Koenraad Verboven, and Arjan Zuiderhoek, eds., *Ownership and Exploitation of Land and Natural Resources in the Roman World* (Oxford, 2015), 107–131.
[9] Patterson, *Slavery and Social Death* (Cambridge, MA, 1982), 28–29.

market societies. In the previous chapter, we saw how the characteristic modern Western conceptualization of property contrasts with what is found in many other human societies. Property in most nonmodern, non-Western cultures has been understood as a function of relationships among persons. Rights in property, on this conception, rather than conferring absolute power on any individual, are lodged in a web of interpersonal "duties, privileges and mutualities," which necessarily exclude the possibility that any single person could claim exclusive control.[10] A property law of this kind can never be understood outside the context of a larger social order of duties and responsibilities.

Modern Western ownership looks very different: It is conceived, in the canonical definition of William Blackstone, as "sole and despotic dominion ... in total exclusion of the right of any other individual in the universe."[11] The vivid bombast of Samuel Pufendorf's eighteenth-century English translator gives perfect expression to this conception of "sole and despotic dominion": "the Property I claim over a Thing, implies a Right of using, spoiling, and consuming it, to procure my Advantage, or to satisfy my Pleasure; so that what way soever I dispose of it, to say it was my own, shall be a sufficient Excuse."[12]

To say it is my own, shall be a sufficient Excuse. This is the absolute conception of ownership characteristic of modern Western market orders. Like so much of Western law, it is a conception that we have inherited from ancient Rome. But the original version of this conception had a very different coloration from ours. The right to "us[e], spoil[] and consum[e]" things was, as Kaser tells us, conceptually linked to the notional authority of the *paterfamilias* to exercise the power of life and death over persons. The paradigmatic Roman formula for claiming ownership was *I declare that this man is mine*. *Dominus*, the classical word for "owner," meant "master"; the "idiom of power" of ancient Roman property law, as Patterson writes, sounded in the master/slave (and, as I shall emphasize, master/beast) relationship. The word *paterfamilias* has its source in slavery too: As

---

[10] Bronisław Malinowski, *Crime and Custom in Savage Society* (London, 1926), 20–21.
[11] Blackstone, *Commentaries on the Laws of England, Book II: Of the Rights of Things*, ed. Simon Stern (Oxford, 2016), 1.
[12] Pufendorf, *Of the Law of Nature and Nations*, trans. anon. (Oxford, 1703), Bk. 6, ch. 3, paragraph 7, p. 125.

we shall see in this chapter, it is derived from *famulus*, "slave." In Kaser's evocative description, the Romans had a liking for calling themselves "masters" not just when they spoke of their slaves or their beasts, but with regard to all of their possessions, animate and inanimate alike.[13]

Roman owners were imagined as all-powerful masters, free to dispose of the people under their control just as they were free to dispose of their goods and their beasts. Miers and Kopytoff are not wrong to see a family resemblance between this law and the law of precolonial Africa, or of the many other non-Western, nonmodern legal cultures that gave "higher value to control over people," studied by anthropologists and surveyed in the previous chapter. Indeed, I will insist in this chapter that this Roman law can only be understood in light of comparative anthropology.

But as we contemplate this law, we must bear in mind the truth that classicists so often hammer home: The study of Roman legal teachings is not the study of Roman socio-economic realities. We must always be wary of the fallacy to which Miers and Kopytoff succumb, and to which so many have succumbed before and after them; we must remember that the Roman legal sources often give, as M. I. Finley writes, "a false picture of what [was] actually being done in society."[14] Much of the time, indeed, ancient Roman property law teachings should not be thought of as "law" in the sense that we ordinarily use the term today. They were not simply a body of technical solutions to live legal problems. They must be read, as Sinclair Bell and Paul du Plessis write, alongside "other written expressions of the Roman mind, such as poetry and prose";[15] they must be interpreted alongside other examples of what Clifford Ando calls "Roman social imaginaries."[16] They constituted a corpus of inherited beliefs and doctrines that did indeed serve as something like

---

[13] Max Kaser, *Eigentum und Besitz im älteren römischen Recht* (Weimar, 1943), 308, and the further discussion below, Chapter 3.

[14] Finley, *Ancient Slavery and Modern Ideology*, expanded ed., ed. Brent Shaw (New York, 1998), 193.

[15] Bell and du Plessis, "Introduction: The Dawn of Roman Law," in Bell and du Plessis, eds., *Roman Law before the Twelve Tables: An Interdisciplinary Approach* (Edinburgh, 2020), 5 [1–5].

[16] Ando, *Roman Social Imaginaries: Language and Thought in the Context of Empire* (Toronto, 2015).

scripture, revered, but embodying norms that often squared poorly with the day-to-day workings of Roman life.

But to say that Roman law served as something like scripture is, of course, not to say that it did not matter, either in its own time or in later centuries.

This chapter and the next trace the development of the Roman law of absolute ownership, with its slave-society coloration. This chapter begins with archaic Roman property law, a body of mysterious sources whose terminology and symbolism display a striking orientation toward the ownership of living creatures, human and animal. Its purpose is to interpret these early Roman sources in light of the anthropology presented in Chapter 1. As we saw, nonmodern, non-Western societies have generally been characterized by "the chieftainship over people": Rights in land, in such an order, are "use rights," granted out through the "political control" exercised by chiefs, in a property order rooted in the primacy of the hierarchical structure of the society in question. We further saw that anthropologists focus on property rights in prey among hunter-gatherers. The chapter brings this anthropological work to bear on the concepts and symbolism of early Roman property law. The figure of the *paterfamilias* belonged to a larger imaginative universe of the "chieftainship over people"; early Roman rights in land followed the pattern of use rights found throughout most of the human world; and the early Roman property concepts presupposed the hunt for prey that anthropologists have identified as the home of much early understanding of the property. The chapter closes with the ancient doctrine of greatest interest for modern historians: *occupatio*, the law of first acquisition understood as law of "the mastery of hunters over their game, the mastery of fishers over their catch ... war captives ... and booty."[17]

The next chapter turns to an epoch-making development in the era of the fall of the Roman Republic: the entry of the classical figure of the *dominus*, the "master," into the law, and the rise of the classical doctrine of absolute ownership.

* * *

---

[17] A.-J. Arnaud, "Reflexions sur l'occupation du droit romain," *Revue historique du droit* 46 (1968): 186, 188 [183–210]. Further discussion below, Chapter 4.

Masters of Men and Beasts

It is important to set the stage with a rapid review of general Roman history, and the place of Roman law within it. At some point in the late Bronze or early Iron Age, from roughly 1200 to 900 BCE, Indo-European peoples, among them the ancestors of the Latins, descended into the Italian peninsula. The founding of the city of Rome itself was traditionally dated to the early Iron Age, in the mid eighth century BCE. Roman tradition held that early Rome, at first little more than a collection of villages, was ruled by kings, who were expelled in a republican uprising in 509 BCE. That probably approximates something like the truth. There was likely some transition from a monarchical to an oligarchical republican form of government around the end of the sixth century. The republican oligarchy survived thereafter for a half millennium, enduring through an extraordinary process of Roman expansion that began in earnest in the early fourth century BCE, and continued through the conquest of most of the world known to the Romans by the middle of the first century.

From the late second century into the late first century BCE, however, the conquering Republic came under fierce, and ultimately fatal, internal political pressure, which ended with the consolidation of power by Octavian after the Battle of Actium in 31 BCE. Under Octavian, who took the regnal name Augustus, Rome entered the first age of the Roman Empire, the age of the so-called "Principate," during which the legal forms of the Republic were technically preserved while Rome was in reality subject to the rule of a monarch. The Principate survived until the crisis years of the mid third century CE, an age of near disintegration in some parts of the Empire.[18] Toward the end of the third century, under Diocletian and his successors, a new form of the imperial government emerged, usually called the "Dominate" (so named because the Emperor came routinely to be addressed as *dominus*, "master"). During the Dominate, fidelity to the trappings of the Roman Republic diminished, while the Empire was subjected to new forms of territorial rule. Meanwhile, in the early

---

[18] See the account in Olivier Hekster, *Rome and Its Empire, AD 193–284* (Edinburgh, 2015), which is careful to avoid excess in describing the crisis. The end of the Principate could reasonably be dated to the Severans. From the point of view of the legal historian, however, the continuity of the tradition into the Severan period is manifest. For simplicity of exposition I have left that question aside.

fourth century, Constantine, the first Christian emperor, transferred the seat of power from Rome to Constantinople, inaugurating a long line of eastern emperors, of whom the most famous, Justinian, reigned in the middle decades of the sixth century.

The history of ancient Roman law is written against the broad background of this millennium and a half of general Roman history. It can be broken up into five rough principal periods. The first is the archaic period, stretching from the Bronze Age down to the early fourth century BCE. This period is full of mystery. Our knowledge of archaic Roman law rests on scanty later sources, generally preserved only in the accounts of historians, antiquarians and jurists writing about legendary events and traditions dating centuries before their own time. Those sources include most prominently the fragments of the Twelve Tables, traditionally dated to 451–450 BCE, but surviving only in quotations from later authors. The fragments of the Tables are full of fascination, and they have been seized upon by many authors, among them figures such as Vico, Henry Maine, and Friedrich Nietzsche, as evidence somehow unveiling the mysteries of the primeval stages of human history. But the reality is that they are highly problematic sources, and relatively late ones; and it is difficult to find ways of supplementing or elucidating them.[19] Despite those difficulties, the study of ancient Roman property law must begin in the archaic period, since archaic concepts of property never disappeared from ancient Roman doctrine. As we shall see in more detail shortly, those archaic concepts revolved around the capture and ownership of living creatures, human and animal.

The second period is the age of the Middle Republic, a period of extraordinary Roman conquests, first of Italy and then of the larger Mediterranean basin. During this era, sometimes called the period of "preclassical" Roman law, the evidentiary record grows. A body of legislation altered the law, while new procedures and new legal magistracies emerged. As for the sensational conquests of the period, they resulted in a development of particular importance for the history of property law: The expanding Republic acquired a vast *ager publicus*, "public land" in Italy, of immense value in an agrarian

---

[19] Though archeologists and philologists can claim scattered successes. See now the contributions in Bell and du Plessis, eds., *Roman Law before the Twelve Tables*.

society. The legal and political history of the Republic was marked by conflict over which Romans would enjoy rights in the rich resources of this conquered land, and what forms those rights would take.

The third period is the age of the Late Republic, the era of the crisis and collapse of republican government. During the Late Republic, scholars detect the influence of Greek philosophy on Roman law; like the rest of Roman culture, the law grew in sophistication as it digested Greek teachings. In the same period, a class of professional jurists began to emerge. Meanwhile, the Late Republic witnessed a crucial development: the triumph of a form of private ownership in Rome's conquered "public land." This involved in particular the consolidation of *latifundia*, large-scale plantations[20] exploited through mass slave labor and owned by Romans of enormous wealth. During this period of growing juristic sophistication, the privatization of formerly public land, and the appearance of great slave plantations, a new property terminology took hold: *Dominus*, "master," became the key term for "owner," along with a derivative term for property, *dominium*, "that which belongs to a master." It was in this period that the classical conception of absolute ownership began to assume its mature shape.

The fourth, high classical period belongs primarily to the Principate. It was the classical jurists, most of whom served in high imperial office, whose elegant debates over the law established the basic principles and approaches of the Western legal tradition. In particular, classical property law developed a subtle body of doctrine about the rights of the *dominus* over his *dominium*. The classical period came to an end along with the Principate, in the middle decades of the troubled third century CE. With very few exceptions, we possess no original sources for the work of the classical jurists. Our main source is the *Digest* of Justinian, compiled in the early sixth century CE, during the last of our periods, Late Antiquity. The texts preserved in the *Digest* were edited at the time of their compilation, hundreds of years after their authors lived; and they may already have been edited in earlier periods.[21] That

---

[20] I am aware that the use of the term "plantation" carries risks, since it implies a misleading comparison with the American antebellum South. Nevertheless, it is difficult to find a useful English-language alternative.

[21] Aldo Schiavone, *The Invention of Law in the West*, trans. Jeremy Carden and Antony Shugaar (Cambridge, MA, 2012), 28–29; and now the doubts expressed by

means that classical Roman law, like the Roman law of earlier periods, can only be reconstructed with a dose of speculation.

* * *

The law that took shape over these many centuries is often described as Rome's single most important contribution to the sum of human knowledge, the only product of Roman civilization that equaled Greek philosophy, art, and literature in power and originality. Hans Julius Wolff, an eminent German-Jewish legal historian who fled the Nazis and eventually found a home at the University of Oklahoma, sounded a typical paean for his Stetson-wearing American audience in 1951:

> Roman law is not only the best-known, the most highly developed, and the most influential of all the legal systems of the past; apart from English law, it is the only one whose entire and unbroken history can be traced from early and primitive beginnings to a stage of elaborate perfection in the hands of skilled specialists.[22]

Quite so. But how should we understand the "early and primitive beginnings"?

That question has been the arena of stark conflict between two competing schools of interpretation – on the one hand, an older school that I will call, borrowing the language of economic history, the "primitivists"; on the other, a newer school, the "modernists." The primitivist school built its interpretations on the language and symbolism of the early sources, which display a conspicuous orientation toward the ownership of humans and beasts. Primitivists took that language more or less at face value, treating it as evidence for the socio-economic realities of archaic Rome. Early Roman society, according to various primitivist interpretations, was dominated by warriors, hunters and slaveholders. The patterns of behavior of these early Romans were very different from those of modern market actors. Ruled by the values of war and the hunt, archaic Rome was unacquainted with property in land, recognizing only the ownership of living creatures. Indeed, it was a society so different from ours that it

---

Detlef Liebs, "Wenn Fachliteratur Gesetz wird," *Zeitschrift der Savigny-Stiftung für Rechtsgeschichte (Romanistische Abteilung)* 135 (2018): 395–473.
[22] Wolff, *Roman Law: An Historical Introduction* (Norman, OH, 1951), 5.

was unacquainted with the very concept of "property" itself. Only very late in Roman history, with the fall of the Republic and the appearance of the new terminology of *dominus* and *dominium*, in the view of primitivists, did Roman property law begin to assume a doctrinal shape recognizable to the modern eye; only then did it come to boast a general theory founded in an abstract concept of "property."

Such primitivist interpretations were prevalent in studies of Roman law throughout the nineteenth and early twentieth centuries, and not just among scholars: They exercised a profound influence on the development of both Western social thought and Western political ideologies. Leading Western thinkers from Vico to Max Weber built their accounts of early human development on the archaic Roman sources, believing that early Roman law offered key evidence for the course of human social evolution. Communists and Fascists too constructed their ideologies in part on primitivist interpretations of the same archaic texts, as we shall see.

But primitivist interpretations no longer feature much in the modernist contemporary literature. Skeptical of the old reconstructions of archaic Roman society, eager to dispel the "myths" in the Roman legal texts, and intent on consigning communist and fascist interpretations to the past, most contemporary specialists live by the motto that the legal sources "give[] a false picture of what [was] actually being done." The archaic world, they contend, was not in fact all that different from ours. Human actors have always been the same human actors. Despite their weird terminology, the archaic Romans must have been more or less market-oriented just as we are, exchanging things in pretty much the same way that we do today, and owning land just as we do. Such modernist interpretations have largely swept the field over the last fifty years or so, and they have succeeded in demolishing many fallacies. Just as we now understand that the *paterfamilias* did not really wield the power of life and death, we now understand much more broadly that archaic law is no good guide to archaic socio-economic realities.

But this modernist triumph has come at a cost; for it has distracted us from the authentic strangeness of the sources. Primitivist scholars misinterpreted those sources when they treated them as unproblematic evidence for Roman socio-economic realities; the Roman sources should often be treated more as kind of sacred text than as "law" in the sense that we use the term; they are indeed populated by myths. But sacred texts matter, and they must be interpreted on their own terms.

* * *

The quarrel between primitivists and modernists begins with a great question that we already encountered in the previous chapter: whether or not early Romans owned land. As we saw, there is a venerable tradition, extending back to the poets and philosophers of Antiquity, which holds that human history began in the primitive communism – a time, in the words of Rousseau, when "the earth belonged to no one."[23] As Virgil put it, in the beginning "no tillers subjugated the land: even to mark possession of the plain or apportion it by boundaries was sacrilege..."[24] That belief remained strong down into the early twentieth century, embraced in one form or another by almost all leading European social thinkers. As Friedrich Engels explained in his *Origins of the Family, Private Property and the State*, the history of Roman law began in the "common ownership of land," which had existed since what Engels called "the *Urzeit*," the primeval beginnings of human society.[25] The archaic Roman sources, for Engels as for many others, thus opened a window into the earliest history of humanity itself.

But as we also saw, the hypothesis of primitive communism is universally rejected by social scientists today. Early human societies unquestionably featured the ownership of land, though that ownership was probably limited to defensible zones such as garden plots. Ownership of those plots was typically complemented by rights in larger communally controlled areas, which were commonly governed through a system of "use rights," in which chieftains, exercising what Marshall Sahlins calls "political control," granted access to the resources of tracts on a seasonal or other provisional basis.

The same venerable debate over primitive communism has played itself out in the conflict between primitivists and modernists. Engels

---

[23] Jean-Jacques Rousseau, *Discourse of the Origin of Inequality*, trans. Donald Cress (Indianapolis, 1992), 44.
[24] Verg. G. 1.121–129, in H. Rushton Fairclough, trans., *Virgil: Eclogues; Georgics; Aeneid: Books 1–6*, rev. by G. P. Goold, Loeb Classical Library 63 (Cambridge, MA, 1916), 106–107.
[25] Engels, *Der Ursprung der Familie, des Privateigentums, und des Staats, im Anschuß an Lewis H. Morgans Forschungen* (Hottingen-Zürich, 1884), 118. Engels' account, it should be emphasized, was quite subtle and well informed.

was typical of primitivist interpreters, who often held that there was no ownership of land in archaic Rome. Modernist scholars, by contrast, have devoted much of their firepower to proving the contrary.[26] Luigi Capogrossi Colognesi, the preeminent figure in the field, makes the case, largely on the basis of the fragments of the Twelve Tables:

> From the XII Tables on, legal instruments were honed or even created from scratch to extend the protection of private property. Rules of this period suggest a relatively compact world made up of small-scale owners, whose utmost autonomy was stressed, while also being required to cooperate in matters of intersubjective interest. Plots of land were regulated by very visible boundaries, which were protected also by religious sanctions. They appear to have been linked within a network of agricultural pathways, which were often shared between various owners. In addition, the conduct of individual owners was regulated in order to prevent their causing harm to their neighbours.[27]

There is also a Roman tradition according to which Romulus, the legendary founder of the city, allotted two *iugera* of land, a plot of about an acre and quarter, to each Roman as a *heredium*, a holding to be passed on from generation to generation. The tale of the Romulan *heredia* is obviously tinged with myth, but scholars believe that it contains a kernel of truth.[28]

On the basis of such evidence, modernist scholars insist that the Romans did indeed own land, and they are unquestionably right. The myth of primitive communism has been smashed when it to comes to early Roman law, just as it has been smashed more generally. But it is essential that we not stop there. Though the early Romans certainly owned plots of land, it is a mistake to ignore the differences between the archaic Roman world and ours; and the differences are critical to our understanding of the long history of Western property law.

This is partly because, although they owned land, they almost certainly did not own large stretches of it. Scholars agree that early

---

[26] For literature supporting this conclusion, see Saskia Roselaar, *Public Land in the Roman Republic: A Social and Economic History of ager publicus in Italy, 396–89 B.C.* (Oxford, 2010), 22, and 22 nn. 22–23.

[27] Capogrossi Colognesi, "Ownership and Power in Roman Law," trans. Thomas Roberts, in Paul J. DuPlessis, Clifford Ando, and Kaius Tuori, eds., *Oxford Handbook of Roman Law and Society* (Oxford, 2016), 525–526 [524–536].

[28] Discussion and references in Roselaar, *Public Land*, 20 and 20 n. 9.

Roman landholdings were "limited in scope."[29] Two *iugera* of land, the traditional measure of a *heredium*, is enough for a garden plot, but not more – not enough to sustain a family.[30] Specialists accordingly conclude that Romans of the archaic period must also have made use of considerable stretches of land held in common.[31] As the classicist Christopher Smith observes, early Rome must have had some version of what Elinor Ostrom calls "the side-by-side existence of private property and communal property."[32]

That communal property presumably lay in the *ager publicus*,[33] the "public land" of Rome, in which, as scholars reconstruct it, tracts were granted out "in revocable possession," probably by the chiefs of clans or tribes whose precise structure remains mysterious, but whose heads clearly exercised some form of what legal historians have called "political" power.[34] The nature of this "revocable possession" in early Rome's "public land," allotted by Iron Age chieftains of some uncertain sort exercising some uncertain sort of "political power," has long been one of the most fiercely debated topics in Roman history. Ancient historians have expended great energy in the effort, as yet inconclusive, to solve the mystery of who these chiefs were, and how exactly revocable possession in archaic "public land" of Rome worked.[35] But scholars have not been the only ones concerned with the topic. The history of early Roman land tenure also stirred

---

[29] Richard E. Mitchell, "*Ager publicus*: Public Property and Private Wealth during the Roman Republic," in Michael Hudson and Baruch Levine, eds., *Privatization in the Ancient Near East and Classical World* (Cambridge, MA, 1996), 253 [253–291].

[30] E.g., Roselaar, *Public Land*, 25: "If private holdings were as small as two iugera, as is suggested by the sources, then ager publicus must have been very important, because such a small amount was not sufficient to support a family."

[31] Ostrom, *Governing the Commons: The Evolution of Institutions for Collective Action* (Cambridge, 1990), 61.

[32] Smith, "Becoming Political: Middle Republican Quandaries," in Seth Bernard, Lisa Maria Mignone, and Dan-el Padilla Peralta, *Making the Middle Republic: New Approaches to Rome and Italy, c. 400–200 BCE* (Cambridge, 2023), 260 [253–269].

[33] Though see D. W. Rathbone, "The Control and Exploitation of *ager publicus* in Italy under the Roman Republic," in J.-J. Aubert, ed., *Tâches publiques et entreprises privées dans le monde romain* (Neuchâtel, 2003), 140 [135–178]. It is not clear to me what justifies the assumption that it was conquered land even in the earliest periods. See the discussion and literature in Roselaar, *Public Land*, 89 n. 9.

[34] For this interpretation since Pietro Bonfante, see Luigi Capogrossi Colognesi, *Proprietà e signoria in Roma antica* (Rome, 1980), 191–194.

[35] See now the comprehensive treatment of Roselaar, *Public Land*. "Revocable possession": Max Kaser, *Das römische Privatrecht* (Munich, 1954–1959), 1:122.

considerable intellectual excitement among Western political thinkers and leaders from the early modern period into the nineteenth century. Ancient Roman practices always seemed to provide a model for the later West, and the fact that early Roman land rights were somehow limited seemed a matter of momentous political significance: It seemed, figures from Machiavelli onward concluded, to offer a Roman precedent for restrictions on private property.[36]

So how exactly did revocable possession in Rome's early "public land," this supposed warrant for limits on private property, work? The classicists who continue to wrestle with the problem do not, to my knowledge, exploit the literature of anthropology. Yet its relevance is patent, and patently significant.[37] As we saw in the previous chapter, the pattern of "the side-by-side existence of private property and communal property" is widespread. In particular, anthropologists point to private ownership in garden plots; archaic Rome is not exceptional in this respect.[38]

Nor is archaic Rome exceptional in the allotment of rights in communal territory through "political control." Quite the contrary: It seems right, and indeed essential, to recognize that revocable possession in the archaic *ager publicus*, granted out by tribal or clan chiefs, represented a Roman variant on the system of use rights that anthropologists identify throughout the nonmodern, non-Western world. Archaic land tenure in the communally held land of Rome evidently (and unsurprisingly) bore a kinship to the kinds of land tenure familiar from studies of the indigenous peoples of colonial Southern New England, of early nineteenth-century Hawaii, of precolonial Africa, of Maori New Zealand, of the Aztecs, of the

---

[36] Alfred Heuss, *Barthold Georg Niebuhrs wissenschaftliche Anfänge* (Göttingen, 1981); Arnaldo Momigliano, "New Paths of Classicism in the Nineteenth Century," in Momigliano, *Studies on Modern Scholarship*, eds. G. W. Bowersock and T. J. Cornell (Berkeley, 1994), 223–285.

[37] Though it certainly cannot solve all our interpretive problems. In particular, we remain in the dark about the exact structures of hierarchical dominance that would have determined the allotment of rights. For a general survey of the literature, see Ella Hermon, "Approches historiographiques," in Hermon, ed., *La question agraire à Rome: droit romain et société* (Como, 1979), 22–24 [19–29]; Attilio Mastrocinque, "Propriété foncière archaïque et modèles d'interprétation modernes," ibid., 101–102 [101–109]; Luigi Capogrossi Colognesi, "Alcuni problem di storia romana arcaica: *ager publicus, gentes* e *clienti*," *Bolletino dell'Istituto di Diritto Romano* 12 (1980): 29–65.

[38] Discussion above, Chapter 1.

Gangetic Plain in the first millennium BCE, and of innumerable other societies investigated by social scientists and surveyed in Chapter 1.[39] In all of these societies, as we saw, the organizing principle was hierarchical: The map of rights in land was not a plat, delineating the sovereign domains of autonomous Blackstonian owners, but a chart of the social hierarchy, tracing the threads of political control in the web of Marshall Sahlins' "hold on persons," in which rights in land were use rights, granted out by chiefs. Such was the state of affairs in most of the human world of the past, and such seems to have been the state of affairs in early Rome.

* * *

"Limited in scope," private ownership of land in early Rome was thus not identical with private ownership today; we must not allow ourselves to overstate the significance of the modernist demonstration that there was no primitive communism. There is another important sense, too, in which early Roman owners were not like us. Rights in land in early Rome (and later centuries as well) rested on cultural presuppositions that were deeply alien to our own.

This begins with the "religious sanctions" mentioned by Capogrossi Colognesi.[40] These involved consecrated boundary stones. We saw in the last chapter that many ancient societies marked off plots with sacred boundary stones. The Greeks, to take one familiar example among many, set up herms bearing phalluses, a form perhaps also found among the Babylonians.[41] As Walter Burkert remarks, the threatening display of the erect penis is found in other primates as well.[42] Comparably strange cultic practices existed in Rome: The

---

[39] See the fuller discussion above, Chapter 1.

[40] For a discussion laying emphasis on the religious background, see Okko Behrends, "Bodenhoheit und privates Bodeneigentum im Grenzwesen Roms," in Behrends and Capogrossi Colognesi, eds., *Die römische Feldmesserkunst* (Göttingen, 1992), 194–201 [192–284].

[41] Walter Burkert, *Homo necans: Interpretationen altgriechischer Opferriten und Mythen*, 2nd ed. (Berlin, 1997), 70, citing Franz X. Steinmetzer, *Die babylonischen Kudurru als Urkundenform* (Paderborn, 1922), 114–115. Steinmetzer, however, notes that the phallic character is "*not always* evident to the naked eye." Ursula Seidl, expressing some skepticism, observes that the phallic form of Babylonian Kudurrus is attributed to them by Steinmetzer, not expressly by the Babylonians themselves. Seidl, *Die babylonischen Kudurru-Reliefs: Symbole mesopotamischer Gottheiten* (Göttingen, 1989), 68.

[42] Burkert, *Homo necans*, 70.

Romans, the sources tell us, "sacrificed to [their boundary stones] yearly."[43] We cannot know the details of the archaic Roman cult, but the documentation for later periods brings home how exotic ancient landownership is when viewed from the modern standpoint. In the ceremonies in which Roman boundary stones were first erected, they were anointed with unguent, dressed in veils, and crowned; an animal sacrifice was immolated and offered, torches were lit, and blood was poured into the ditch in which they were set.[44] They were further celebrated in an annual religious festival, the Terminalia, on the day of which neighboring owners crowned the boundary stone that separated their holdings with a garland, offered it grain, honeycombs and wine, and ritually sacrificed a lamb or a suckling pig, upon which they then feasted together.[45] The land holdings of these human owners, moreover, sat alongside numerous sacred parcels owned by the gods themselves, marked by their own divine stone monuments.[46] We must not close our eyes to the strangeness of the past. The Roman experience of land was not synonymous with that of the modern suburban homeowner.

In other respects too, it is essential for our grasp of the history of property law to recognize that the modern understanding of private landownership never fully took hold in Antiquity, even long after the archaic period. The modern conception of private landownership is essentially an idea of rights established by sweat of the brow and market forces; our watchwords are still ordinarily the ones given by

---

[43] See Giulia Piccaluga, *Terminus: i segni di confine nella religione romana* (Rome, 1974), 17–19, 293–325. As Piccaluga explains, there is some conflict in the ancient sources. I follow her reading.

[44] This is the account of Siculus Flaccus, *De condicionibus agrorum* 1.1, in Carolus Thulin, ed., *Corpus agrimensorum Romanorum*, Teubner (Leipzig, 1913), 105; also in M. Clavel-Lévêque, D. Conso, F. Faory, J.-Y. Guillamin, and P. Robin, eds., *Siculus Flaccus: Les conditions des terres* (Naples, 1993), 24–27. There is some uncertainty on this topic, since Dionysius of Halicarnassus, echoed by Plutarch, tells us that blood sacrifices were not offered to *termini*. In her careful study, making use of comparative as well as Roman material, Piccaluga credits the account of Siculus Flaccus against these Greek-language authors. Piccaluga, *Terminus*, 17–19, 293–325.

[45] Ov. *Fast.* 2.655–656, in James G. Frazer, trans., *Ovid: Fasti*, rev. G. P. Goold, Loeb Classical Library 253 (Cambridge, MA, 1931), 104–105. The link between the Terminalia and Roman property division was highlighted by the great Italian legal historian Pietro Bonfante, *Corso di diritto romano* (Rome, 1926), 211.

[46] For a survey, see John Scheid, *An Introduction to Roman Religion*, trans. Janet Lloyd (Edinburgh, 2003), ch. 5.

Locke: "As *much Land* as a Man Tills, Plants, Improves, Cultivates, so much is his *Property*."[47] Such ideas are not completely absent from ancient literature; but they can be strikingly hard to find. Ancient authors assumed that land would generally be acquired, not through the Lockean investment of productive labor, but as war booty, or through allotment by authoritative decree. The law of war booty was especially prominent: Conventional ancient language referred to land as "spear-won";[48] the symbolism of property law, as Okko Behrends remarks, had its specific source in the law of war.[49] Cicero comes somewhat closer to the modern understanding. He has even been described as a theorist of property whose ideas were little different from modern ones.[50] But we must read our Cicero closely: Even he presupposed that rights in property should be largely acquired through conquest or allotted "by decree of law ... or distribution by lot." His famous passage deserves to be quoted again:

[P]roperty becomes private either through appropriation by those who found it lying vacant sometime in the past, or through conquest in war, or by decree of law, or by private bargain, or contractual stipulation, or distribution by lot ...[51]

This is remote indeed from Locke. The idea that land should ordinarily be allotted by dominant authorities, or seized by force of arms, did not disappear among the Romans: Roman authors continued to explain that land rights arose through conquest and subsequent distribution as booty,[52] and they continued to recognize

---

[47] Locke, *Two Treatises of Government*, ed. Peter Laslett (Cambridge, 1988), 290 (Treatise 2, §32).
[48] For "spear-won" property, see Walter Schmitthenner, "Über eine Formveränderung der Monarchie seit Alex. d. Gr.," *Saeculum* 19 (1968): 32–46.
[49] Behrends, "Bodenhoheit und privates Bodeneigentum," 271, and generally 271–274.
[50] See the appropriately skeptical discussion of Christopher Pierson, *Just Property: A History in the Latin West* (Oxford, 2013), 45–52.
[51] Cic. *Off.* 1.21, in Walter Miller, trans., *Cicero: On Duties*, Loeb Classical Library 30 (Cambridge, MA, 1913), 22–23.
[52] Siculus Flaccus, *De condicionibus agrorum* 1.1, in Thulin, ed., *Corpus agrimensorum Romanorum*, 102: *Occupatorii autem dicuntur agri quos quidam arcifinales vocant ... quibus agris victor populus occupando nomen dedit. Bellis enim gestis victores populi terras omnes ex quibus victos eiecerunt publicaverunt atque universaliter territorium dixerunt, intra quos fines iuris dicendi ius esset.* Also in Clavel-Lévêque et al., *Siculus Flaccus*, 14–15.

the authority of Roman rulers to confiscate landholdings.⁵³ Roman property law never disengaged itself from the presumption, so widespread in human societies, that rights in land depended in some way on the dictates of the sociopolitical hierarchy.

* * *

The quarrel between primitivists and modernists does not end with the question of primitive communism in land. The early Roman terminology and symbolism of ownership, with their orientation toward the domination over humans and beasts, has divided scholars, social thinkers, and ideologues as well.

Here the debate begins with a striking, and for most modern readers baffling, primitivist claim: Archaic Roman society was so profoundly different from modern society that it did not even possess a general concept of "property." To understand what that claim could possibly mean, it is necessary to start with some basic property law theory.

To the modern mind, it seems obvious that there must be a general concept of "property." To quote Blackstone once more, we take it for granted that it is a part of the human condition that "the external things of the world" "engage the affections of mankind." Modern property theorists, eager to illustrate the supposed naturalness of the abstract concept of property, often point to child psychology: The basic ideas of *meum* and *tuum*, "mine" and "thine," they observe, take hold early on in the psychological development of children. By the age of two or so, we all understand what property is, just as we understand the rudiments of trade. We become market actors as soon as we develop a sense of self.⁵⁴

Modern accounts of the psychology of this purportedly universal and inborn institution of *meum* and *tuum* are pitched at the highest level of abstraction: They divide the world up under two maximally general headings, "things" and "persons." "Things" is a capacious and undifferentiated modern category, lumping together virtually the entirety of the nonhuman world: Essentially all objects, entities and claims can count equally as legal "things," and therefore as potential

---

⁵³ E.g., *SC de Pisone Patre*, ll. 90–100, and the commentary in Werner Eck, Antonio Cabbalos, and Fernando Fernández, *Das senatus consultum de Cn. Pisone patre* (Munich, 1996), 211–215. My thanks to Ari Bryen for suggesting this point.

⁵⁴ Michael Heller and James Salzman, *Mine! How the Hidden Rules of Ownership Control Our Lives* (New York, 2021), 1, start from this familiar claim, while arguing the adult rules develop great complexities.

"property," available to be bought and sold. The only entities that indisputably can*not* count as legal "things" are human beings. "Persons" is a similarly undifferentiated category: It assumes the formal equality of all individuals, ascribing no relevance to differences in their social standing or social roles. For purposes of property law, they are all simply potential owners.

All of that may seem to belong self-evidently to the nature of property, and indeed of human existence. Yet as anthropologists and historians have shown, this mode of understanding the relationship between humans and the world is by no means universal. It may be true that toddlers everywhere think in terms of *meum* and *tuum*, and perceive their world as full of undifferentiated "things"; but adult societies have generally displayed more complex and nuanced understandings, dividing "the external things of the world" up into distinct and incommensurable categories, often subject to transfer through disparate rituals. I cannot resist quoting the most famous literary evocation of a world divided into incommensurable categories, Jorge Luis Borges' invention of a Chinese classification of animals into:

1. those that belong to the Emperor,
2. embalmed ones,
3. those that are trained,
4. suckling pigs,
5. mermaids,
6. fabulous ones,
7. stray dogs,
8. those included in the present classification,
9. those that tremble as if they were mad,
10. innumerable ones,
11. those drawn with a very fine camelhair brush,
12. others,
13. those that have just broken a flower vase,
14. those that from a long way off look like flies.[55]

Borges' list is delicious fiction; but it is in fact the case that such practices of organizing the things of the world into incommensurable

---

[55] Borges, "The Analytic Language of John Wilkins," in Borges, *Other Inquisitions, 1937–1952*, trans. Ruth L. C. Simmons (New York, 1968), 103 [101–105].

categories is found throughout human history. Moreover, property procedures in many societies, rather than establishing absolute property rights, good against all the world, establish relative property rights, good in particular ways against particular persons playing particular social roles.[56]

The archaic Roman sources present a variant on this widespread human pattern of sorting "the external things of the world" into different and incommensurable categories. In fact, it has been argued that archaic Latin, while it included the possessives *meum* and *tuum*, did not even have any general word for "thing." (The word *res*, it is argued, did not mean "thing" but "legal dispute."[57]) Instead, four different property terms appear in the early sources, none of which is easy to decipher. First comes a pair of terms that appear in the surviving fragments of the Twelve Tables, sometimes coupled together, sometimes used separately:[58] *familia*, a term derived from *famulus*, "slave," and *pecunia*, a word derived from *pecus*, "domesticated animal." Alongside these two slave- and beast-words comes a second mysterious pair, not found in the fragments of the Tables but clearly dating to the archaic period: *res mancipi*, "things subject to the hand-gripping power," and *res nec mancipi*, "things not subject to the hand-gripping power." None of these four archaic terms can be translated by the modern word "property," because none of them served as a general umbrella term for all possible objects of ownership. Instead, each archaic term was used for a particular class of things, creatures, or persons that might be owned, subject to peculiar claims of right and sometimes peculiar rituals of transfer. At the same time, a case can be made that early Roman procedures protected only relative, and not absolute rights; we shall see more about that in a moment.

---

[56] E.g., Sharon Hutchinson, "The Cattle of Money and the Cattle of Girls among the Nuer, 1930–83," *American Ethnologist* 19 (1992): 294–316.

[57] See Yan Thomas, "*Res*, chose et patrimoine (note sur le rapport sujet–objet en droit romain)," *Archives de philosophie du droit* 25 (1980): 413–426. For a similar claim, Gennaro Franciosi, *Studi sulle servitù prediali* (Naples, 1967), 18–19.

[58] For doubts about the place of *pecunia*, see Mario Bretone, "Sesto Elio et le Dodici Tavole," *Labeo* 41 (1995): 66–82; and M. Crawford, "'*Pecunia*' in the Twelve Tables," in Martin Price, Andrew Burnett, and Roger Bland, eds., *Essays in Honour of Robert Carson and Kenneth Jenkins* (London, 1993), 137 [135–138]: "One cannot in the end prove that *familia pecuniaque* stood ... anywhere in the Tables. But the contrary arguments are weak and arbitrary."

* * *

This early classification of "the external things of the world" into four distinct categories fueled centuries of primitivist speculation about the origins of Roman law, and beyond that about the origins of human society itself.

I begin with *familia*, derived from "slave," and *pecunia*, derived from "domesticated animal." Efforts to plumb the mysteries of these two archaic slave- and beast-words have taken various tacks over the centuries. Their presence in the Twelve Tables played, to begin with, a leading role in the development of the classic hypothesis of primitive communism in land. After all, these seem to be the most ancient denominators of property; yet the ownership of land is conspicuously absent from the etymologies of both. Doesn't that imply that in the earliest phases of the development of Roman society, and more broadly human society – during Friedrich Engels' *Urzeit* – there was only ownership of humans and beasts, not of land? So primitivist readers of the archaic sources often concluded.[59]

But the etymologies of *familia* and *pecunia* were not only invoked by believers in primitive communism in land. Many thinkers and scholars built their theories on the basis of the derivation of *familia* from *famulus*. Here it is important to emphasize that the modern word "family" is a false friend. The modern "family" denotes a restricted group linked by ties of blood (real or fictive), and ties of affection (also real or fictive). The ancient *familia*, by contrast, included slaves alongside descendants, as well as animals, inanimate objects, and the household religious cult.[60] And within this assemblage of slaves, kin, things, beasts, and idols, it was the slaves that had conceptual pride of place: The word *familia*, derived from *famulus*, meant literally something like "slave-gang," "slave-holdings," or "slave-stuff," all subject to the power of the *paterfamilias*, the "father of the *familia*."[61]

---

[59] On these interpretations, see Pietro Bonfante, Storia del diritto romano (Milan, 1958) 1:192; Gennaro Franciosi, "Gentiles familiam habento," in Franciosi, ed., *Ricerche sulla organizzazione gentilizia romana* (Naples, 1995), 44 [5–49]; Roselaar, *Public Land*, 21.

[60] On the sense of *familia*, Thomas, "Res, chose et patrimoine"; for the household cult, Scheid, *Introduction to Roman Religion*, 165.

[61] Heinrich Honsell, Theo Mayer-Maly, and Walter Selb, *Römisches Recht*, 4th ed. (Berlin, 1987), 62.

The etymological slave-basis of the terms *familia* and *paterfamilias*, striking as it is, played a crucial part in the formation of primitivist interpretations of archaic Roman society, and (once again) much more broadly in the formation of Western thought.[62] The association of *familia* with slavery informed, for example, Vico's seminal *New Science* (first edition 1725), the book sometimes described as the pioneer work of Western social science.[63] Drawing on the archaic law of the *paterfamilias* and its connection to *famulus*, Vico argued that Roman Republican history was a history of a kind of proto-class conflict between dominant patricians, imagined as slavemasters and living by the values of a heroic age, and subordinate plebeians.[64] Henry Maine, author of the seminal modern work on legal history *Ancient Law* (1861), produced his own theory on the basis of the same etymology, which seemed to him to support his interpretation of legal history as a tale of the evolution "from status to contract": In the beginning, everything turned on the status relationship between master and slave, and more broadly between the master of the extended household and his many dependents.[65] Both Vico and Maine influenced Marx, as we know from his ethnological notebooks.[66] Engels, in his own seminal *Origins of the Family*, asserted that the etymological link between *familia* and *famulus* proved that slavery, alongside the subjection of women within the *familia*, played the dominant socio-economic role in early legal evolution, and later Marxist authors followed him.[67]

The Marxist interpretation of early Roman law remains by far the best known of these older theories of the *familia*. But the study of this slave-word also played a formative role in other, less well-remembered, schools of social and political thought as well. Particularly prominent

[62] E.g., Jean Bodin, *Les six livres de la République* (Paris, 1986), 1:85 [= Bk. 1, ch. 5].
[63] With later editions, and continuing to inspire one of the finest of social scientists. Marshall Sahlins, *The New Science of the Enchanted Universe* (Princeton, 2023).
[64] See the useful discussion in Donald Phillip Verene, *Vico's New Science: A Philosophical Commentary* (Ithaca, N.Y., 2016): 257.
[65] Maine, *Ancient Law: Its Connection with the Early History of Society and Its Relation to Modern Ideas*, 10th ed. (London, 1908), 184.
[66] Marx, *The Ethnological Notebooks of Karl Marx (Studies of Morgan, Phear, Maine, Lubbock)*, transcribed and ed. with an introduction by Lawrence Krader (Assen, 1974).
[67] Engels, *Der Ursprung der Familie, des Privateigentums, und des Staats, im Anschuß an Lewis H. Morgans Forschungen* (Hottingen-Zürich, 1884), 61.

among these was the main nineteenth-century rival to Marxist economics – the so-called "primitivist" school of economic history, whose influence was especially strongly felt by the most profound of social thinkers, Max Weber. The core claim of economic primitivists was that ancient economies were not market economies of the modern kind, populated by modern market actors. Instead, they were organized around the semi-self-sufficient extended household, ruled by a household chieftain, for which primitivists used the Greek term *oikos*.

The claim that Antiquity had *oikos* economies, rather than market economies, was first mounted by one of the most inventive social theorists of the nineteenth century, and a man who deserves to be rescued from near-oblivion: Johann Karl Rodbertus (1805–1875), a figure of such prominence is his day that Engels felt obliged to deny that Marx had plagiarized his ideas.[68] Rodbertus was the holder of an expansive Pomeranian estate called Jagetzow, a lord of lands, but one who promoted socialism, and a scholar who advocated an economics sensitive to historical difference.[69] Drawing on the writings of Aristotle and Xenophon and the texts of Roman law, this country magnate proposed that the ancient economy was dominated by the semi-autarkic *oikos*, which was ruled by the "*oikos*-lord," who exercised the absolute power of a Roman *paterfamilias*, which made him "in the undivided fullness of power the owner of workers, land and capital in one person."[70]

Rodbertus' successors followed his lead in juxtaposing ancient *oikos* economies against modern market economies, and in exploiting both Aristotle and archaic Roman property law. *Familia* and *pecunia*, primitivist economic historians held, reflected the internal structure of the autarkic *oikos* household. "Roman property was divided," as one author explained, "*in actual reality as in its conceptual language*, into two main categories, *familia* and *pecunia*. The first describes property in humans, the second describes property in things."[71] The classic

---

[68] Engels, "Vorwort," in Karl Marx, *Das Kapital, Band II: das Circulationsprocess des Kapitals* (Hamburg, 1885), viii [iii–xxiii].
[69] As Udo Engbring-Romang nicely writes, Rodbertus is "a well-known figure who remains unknown." Engbring-Romang, *Karl Rodbertus (1805–1875)* (Pfaffenweiller, 1990), 1.
[70] Rodbertus, "Zur Geschichte der römischen Tributsteuern," *Jahrbücher für Nationalökonomie und Statistik* 4 (1865): 344, and *passim* [341–427].
[71] H. von Scheel, "Die wirtschaftlichen Grundbegriffe im Corpus Iuris Civilis," *Jahrbücher für Nationalökonomie und Statistik* 6 (1866): 336 [325–344]. Emphasis added.

statement of how "actual reality" was reflected in Roman "conceptual language" came from Karl Bücher (1847–1930), an imposingly cultivated figure who counts as the most important of the primitivist economists. The Roman *familia*, Bücher argued, echoing Rodbertus, was the equivalent of the Greek *oikos*, ruled by the "master's right of the slaveholder"; and the prominence of slave language in its terminology showed that the Roman *oikos* economy was associated with an ancient social order that rested on slaves and slave labor.[72] Weber offered similar, though subtler, interpretations, as we shall see in later chapters.

Alongside Marxists and economic primitivists, there was another twentieth-century group as well, to whose work I will be giving a fair bit of attention in this chapter and the next: the legal historians of Nazi Germany. It may seem strange to discuss Nazi-era scholarship in any way seriously, rather than letting it drop in horror. Yet the Nazi period cannot be read out of our legal history (or indeed our history more broadly). This is partly because the Nazi movement was deeply bound up with, and even inspired by, ideas developed by legal historians. Indeed, there has probably never been a political ideology that drew so heavily on "stories, allegories and metaphors" from the history of the law, or that commanded the allegiance, and often the enthusiasm, of so many leading legal historians.[73] If the profession of economics reached the zenith of its political influence in the United States after 1980 or so, the profession of legal history, sad to say, reached its own zenith of political influence in the Germany of the 1930s and 1940s.

But it is not just that legal history influenced Nazism. It is also that the experience of Nazism informed the theories of some of the most brilliant legal historians of the twentieth century. Much of the important work on Roman law of the 1930s and 1940s was done by those who fled.[74] But much of it was done by those who stayed,

---

[72] Bücher, *Die Entstehung der Volkswirtschaft* (Tübingen, 1893), 23, 27–28.
[73] Joachim Rückert, Michael Stolleis, and Dieter Simon, eds., *Rechtsgeschichte im Nationalsozialismus. Beiträge zur Geschichte einer Disziplin* (Tübingen, 1989); Franz-Stefan Meissel, "Deutsche Rechtsgeschichte im nationalsozialistischen Staat," in Ulrike Davy, Helmut Fuchs, Herbert Hofmeister, Judith Marte, and Ilse Reiter, eds., *Nationalsozialismus und Recht* (Vienna, 1990), 412–426.
[74] See now Kaius Tuori, *Empire of Law: Nazi Germany, Exile Scholars and the Battle for the Future of Europe* (Cambridge, 2020).

working inevitably, and sometimes eagerly, under the aegis of the Nazi movement. Our understanding of the Roman culture of masters owes something to the insights of scholars who were themselves working in a German culture of a self-proclaimed master race; we shall see more about them in the next chapter.

Roman property law was a particular focus in Nazi-era writings. Indeed, it was a topic of intense, and even obsessive, National Socialist interest. From its inception, the Party proclaimed itself the enemy of "the materialistic world order," and dedicated itself to overthrowing the "bourgeois-individualistic system."[75] And that system, the Nazi Party Program of 1920 declared, was rooted in classical Roman property law. The classical Roman absolute conception of ownership, the law of the *dominus* and his *dominium*, the Party preached, was a vector of societal corruption: Cosmopolitan in spirit, it left no room for an understanding of property as a social institution, embedded in the communal needs of the *Volk*.

But Nazi beliefs about Roman property law did not end there. According to Nazi teachings, Roman law had not been corrupt from its archaic inception. Nazi histories were always histories of racial degeneration, and that was true of their account of ancient Rome as well. It was a basic tenet of Nazi historiography that Rome had originally been founded by Nordic warriors, the blond and blue-eyed kin of the master race of Germany, who had subjugated the inferior races of Italy in a campaign of Bronze Age conquest.[76] Only in later centuries did this great "Nordic foundation" in the hills of Latium undergo a process of degeneration, as the Romans foolishly allowed themselves to be welcoming of inferior races. Eventually, the law of Roman imperial society, hopelessly polluted by race mixing, had succumbed to the influence of Semites; and by the classical period it had become the embodiment of the degenerate cosmopolitan

---

[75] NSDAP, Parteiprogramm, 24 February 1920, Point 19: "Wir fordern Ersatz für das der materialistischen Weltordnung dienende römische Recht durch ein deutsches Gemein-Recht," available at www.documentarchiv.de/wr/1920/nsdap-programm.html.

[76] See Johann Chapoutot, "The Denaturalization of Nordic Law: Germanic Law and the Reception of Roman Law," in Kaius Tuori and Heta Björklund, eds., *Roman Law and the Idea of Europe* (London, 2019), 113–26.

materialism the Nazis believed it to be in the twentieth century, the "jew-ified" law of an Empire that was a "cesspool of peoples."[77]

Before this later history of degeneration, though, archaic Rome, according to Nazi ideology, had been the realm of a pure Aryan master race, and for that reason archaic Roman property law demanded respectful attention. High school students were taught that the archaic Roman *paterfamilias* was a prototypical Aryan master, charged with guaranteeing the racial purity of the *familia* that he ruled.[78] As for *familia* and *pecunia*: Their terminology revealed the contours of Aryan masterhood. "It is clear," wrote a Roman law scholar of the period, "that in the archaic period he [the master] had the right of rule over persons free and unfree and large animals."[79] We shall see more in Chapter 3 about the Nazi belief that Aryan warrior-values infused the archaic Roman society made up of masters over humans and beasts.

* * *

None of these primitivist efforts at uncovering the "actual reality" beneath the "conceptual language" of *familia* and *pecunia*, from Maine to Marx to Bücher to Weber to the Nazis, whether mounted by Roman law specialists or social theorists, commands much support, if any, among the modernist scholars who generally rule the scene today. The hypothesis of primitive communism in land, as we have seen, has been roundly rejected. The fact that the basic terms for archaic property in the Twelve Tables have etymologies that omit it proves nothing about the socio-economic realities. Even if they did not have an abstract word for "thing," there is no contest today about the common-sense proposition that the early Romans grasped the difference between *meum* and *tuum*. As for the notion that archaic Roman law was the law of a conquering Aryan master race: It would be hard indeed to find anybody who would defend that.

---

[77] Albert Halbe, *Eigentum als Verdienst: eine Kampfschrift gegen und für Alle* (Breslau, 1931), 45–46.
[78] Walther Gehl, *Geschichte: 6. Klasse. Oberschulen/Gymnasien und Oberschulen in Aufbauform* (Breslau, 1940), 74.
[79] Karl Friedrich Thormann, *Der doppelte Ursprung der mancipatio: ein Beitrag zur Erforschung des frühromischen Rechtes unter Mitberücksichtigung des nexum* (Munich, 1943), 64–65. Thormann was himself Swiss, and it is not my intention to call his book a Nazi work. I cite it for purposes of capturing the scholarly mentality of the period.

In the wake of the long chronicle of failed attempts at excavating the socio-economic realities underlying *familia* and *pecunia*, the study of the archaic property terminology of the Twelve Tables has more or less ground to a halt. Most of the contemporary literature finds little of interest to say about the two terms, whatever their vivid etymologies; the reflex among specialists is to declare that they can never be successfully interpreted, or that they were simply interchangeable words for "property," from which no useful conclusions can be drawn.[80] This reluctance to engage with the strangeness of the sources is understandable, after so many failed, and sometimes repellant, efforts at interpretation. It is particularly understandable that specialists in Roman law should want to put Nazi-era interpretations behind them.

Nevertheless, we must not give up too quickly. Primitivist scholars were indeed wrong to suppose that archaic terminology provides the key to understanding the social structure of Rome "in actual reality as in its conceptual language." There is no hope of reconstructing archaic realities on the basis of archaic terminology. "[A]ny illusion of catching Roman private property *in statu nascendi*," as the great ancient historian Arnaldo Momigliano wrote, "must be abandoned."[81] But there is more to understanding property law than reconstructing the realities. The presence of slave- and beast-words for property in the Twelve Tables is not evidence for the socio-economic workings of early Rome, least of all that it was the home of an Aryan master race. But it *is* evidence for archaic ways of imagining ownership, and that is not a matter of no significance. We must not simply brush off the fact that the archaic Roman conceptual vocabulary turned on what we might call, altering the language of Africanists, the "beast–slave–kin continuum."

There is especially wise reflection on this point is to be had from Kaser (1906–1997), the most sensitive historian of early Roman property law, and a man to whose work I will return repeatedly in this chapter and the next. Kaser was a scholar who straddled the

---

[80] On the difficulties, see generally Claire Feuvrier-Prévotat, "Le concept de la *familia pecuniaque* dans la loi des XII Tables," in Hermon, ed., *Question agraire à Rome*, 59–79. See also György Diósdi, "Familia pecuniaque," *Acta antiqua Academiae scientarum hungaricae* 12 (1964): 99, dating the shift by the time of the Twelve Tables [87–105].

[81] Arnaldo Momigliano, "The Origins of Rome," in A. E. Astin, F. W. Walbank, M. W. Frederiksen, and R. M. Ogilvie (eds.), *Cambridge Ancient History* 7.2 (Cambridge, 1989), 99 [52–112].

Masters of Men and Beasts

primitivist/modernist divide. On the one hand, he brought a healthy skepticism to the most aggressive primitivist efforts to reconstruct the exact economic circumstances of archaic Roman society. At the same time, though, he was unwilling to dismiss the differences between early Roman and modern property law that cry out in the sources; and this was true of his treatment of *familia* and *pecunia*. If those terms did not permit a reliable reconstruction of Roman social realities, he held, they nonetheless reflected a truth: the truth that archaic Roman "concept formation" was different from ours. In describing the pattern of this archaic concept formation, Kaser used a stock German phrase, found notably in the Luther Bible.[82] The early Roman conceptualization of property, he wrote, whatever the elusive realities, turned on the ownership of "Gesinde und Vieh," "slaves (and other household subjects and dependents) and animals."[83]

Gesinde und Vieh is a pair of terms Luther used to describe the wealth of the Old Testament patriarchs,[84] and the scriptural comparison is apt and helpful. Like Abraham or Isaac, the Roman *paterfamilias* was imagined by the law as owning "many slaves and servants and flocks" (Gen. 26:14). This is scriptural language that must be interpreted with every bit as much caution as the Roman texts must. When the Old Testament spoke of the patriarchs in this way, it did not imply that they owned no land. Land played every bit as significant a role in the Old Testament texts as it did in early Rome, whether the land in question was the holy promised land of Canaan or the tomb of patriarchs in the Cave of Machpelah at Hebron or the individual holdings of the Hebrews, marked off by sacred boundary stones.

Nevertheless, crucial scriptural passages, especially in Genesis and Psalms, omitted land from the things of the world subject to human dominion, just as archaic Roman terminology did. This begins, indeed, with the first chapter of Genesis: "God said, 'Let us make mankind in

---

[82] Tob. 11:3, in the 1912 version: "wenn dirs gefiel, so wolten wir vorhin ziehen und dein weib so gemach lassen hernach ziehen mit dem gesinde und vieh."

[83] Kaser, *Das römische Privatrecht* (Munich, 1954–1959), 1:45 ("unentwickelte Begriffsbildung"), and 45 n. 13 for further literature.

[84] E.g., Gen. 26:12–14, in the wonderful sixteenth-century language: "Und Isaak seete in dem Lande | und krieg desselben jars hundertfeltig | denn der HERR segnete ihn. Und er ward ein grosser Mann | gieng und nam zu | bis er fast gros ward | daß er viel guts hatte an kleinem und großem vieh | und ein gros Gesinde. Biblia das ist: die gantze heilige Schrifft: Deudstch" (n.p.: 1545).

our image, in our likeness, so that they may rule over the fish in the sea and the birds in the sky, over the livestock and all the wild animals, and over all the creatures that move along the ground'" (Gen. 1:26; cf. Gen. 9:2); the grant of God was a grant of the rulership over living creatures, with no mention of land; and many subsequent passages characterized wealth in what was evidently its paradigmatic form in the texts of Genesis as they have come down to us: "sheep and cattle ... and slaves male and female" (Gen. 12:16).[85] "You have given them dominion over the works of your hands," says Psalm 8:

> you have put all things under their feet:
> [7] all sheep and oxen,
>   and also the beasts of the field,
> [8] the birds of the air and the fish of the sea,
>   whatever passes along the paths of the seas.

These are scriptural passages that demand to be read alongside the Roman texts, which also spoke of creatures that swim, crawl, and fly; indeed, as we shall see in Part II of this book, the Roman and scriptural sources were intricately interwoven in the formation of early modern property thought after 1492.

Whether found in scripture or in the archaic Roman sources, these are texts that look passing strange in our eyes. Why, when we know perfectly well that there was ownership of land in both cases, did these texts speak only of the ownership of living creatures? As we struggle with these ancient expressions of what Kaser called "undeveloped" concept formation,[86] I think it may help to reflect on the cognitive challenge that the conceptualization of ownership presents. "Ownership" is not easy for the mind to picture. The "relation" between owner and object, as David Hume said, is not "natural."[87] It bears no resemblance to forces such as gravity or magnetism. The link between owner and object must always be imagined; and as humans imagine it, they may find it cognitively easiest to start from the model of the ownership of living creatures. The relationship between myself and my dog, myself and my horse, or myself and

---

[85] In the Luther Bible version, "Schafe, Rinder, Esel, Knechte und Mägde."
[86] Kaser, *Das römische Privatrecht*, 1:45.
[87] Hume, *A Treatise of Human Nature*, ed. David Fate Norton and Mary J. Norton (Oxford, 2000), 315.

Masters of Men and Beasts

slave, is easily grasped. It is a relationship between two creatures that can look each other in the eye; it can be comprehended through the familiar experience of command and obedience, what Peter Birks calls "superiority and control":

> The possessive "my" either does or does not connote superiority and control ... "My wife," nowadays, implies neither superiority nor control. In Roman society, "my wife," "my son" and "my child" did imply superiority and were not at first clearly differentiated from "my slave," "my house" and "my horse."[88]

Such relations of "superiority and control" are easy to understand. The relation between a person and an inanimate object is not. What can it mean to say that I have a "relation" with a chair, or a rock, or a plot of land? For that reason, perhaps, it is not wholly surprising that we discover in these ancient texts a formation of concepts that begins with the domination of humans and beasts.

In any case, the domination of humans and beasts is what we find, just as much present in the scriptural texts as in the Roman legal ones; what is true of the Psalm is true of Roman *familia* and *pecunia*. We cannot treat those terms as direct evidence of the archaic social structure of Rome. Primitivists were wrong to suppose otherwise. But, as Kaser suggests, the sources do cast a shaft of light, if only a faint one given the immense historical distances involved, on the taken-for-granted normative orientation of an archaic Roman world that imagined property, in the first instance, as a catalogue of "sheep and cattle ... and slaves male and female." Nor did this cease to be the case after the archaic period: It is worth noting that legal language of the Middle Republic continued to speak of property in the same way, as consisting in "men ... pack mules and horses and mares,"[89] or "slaves male and female and four-footed and domestic animals."[90]

---

[88] Birks, "The Roman Law Concept of Dominium and the Idea of Absolute Ownership," *Acta juridica* (1985): 25 [1–37].

[89] These are the terms of the law of *postliminium*, on which see further Chapter 4 and generally Maria Floriana Cursi, *La struttura del "postliminium" nelle Repubblica e nel Principato* (Naples, 1996), 251–252.

[90] Lex Aquilia: *Ut qui servum servamve alienum alienamve quadrupedem vel pecudem iniuria occiderit, quanti id in eo anno plurimi fuit, tantum aes dare domino damnas esto.* D. 9.2.2.pr. Gaius 7 *ad ed. provinc.*

It would be a mistake to conclude from any of these catalogues that the Romans of the archaic period, or the Middle Republic, did not own land, a least to the extent of garden plots, just as it would be a mistake to think that archaic Roman property law substantiates the claims of Communists or Nazis. But it would be equally mistaken to pass over in silence the Roman habit of enumerating the possessable things of their world as a catalogue of *Gesinde und Vieh*, humans and beasts.

* * *

The other two early Roman terms for property, the mysterious paired opposition *res mancipi/res nec mancipi*, "things subject to the hand-gripping power" and "things not subject to the hand-gripping power," lend themselves to the same interpretation. To see why, we must begin by digging into some difficult problems surrounding the "power" of the archaic *paterfamilias* and the nature of early Roman procedures.

The law of the *paterfamilias* turned on his *potestas*, his "power." But what was "power"? The classical jurists, working centuries after the archaic period, distinguished among three kinds of "power": *manus, mancipium*, and *potestas*. *Manus*, meaning "hand," was a term used in the classical period for the power over women, and *potestas*, usually translated as "control or command," was a term used for the power over slaves, male descendants, and inanimate things. *Mancipium*, "the hand-gripping power," was used for a mysterious category of things called *res mancipi*, to which we will return. *Mancipium* was also used for children. The classical jurists were careful in distinguishing among these different types of "power," but early Roman law did not have any such sophistication, and scholars believe that it made no such fine distinctions.[91] Instead, most scholars surmise, in the earliest phases basic procedures and concepts centered on only one concept: *Manus*, "hand," was used for every form of power. Archaic power was the power of the master's gripping "hand."[92]

The most striking evidence for this lies in the extensive use of hand symbolism: Women and men, beasts and things, were all claimed through a ritual seizure by the metaphorical, and sometimes literal,

---

[91] E.g., Filippo Gallo, "Osservazioni sulla signoria del 'paterfamilias,'" in *Studi in onore di Pietro de Francisci* (Milan, 1956), 2:200–206 [195–236].
[92] See generally Kaser, *Das römische Privatrecht*, 1:50–51.

hand of the powerful master. Primitive legal systems often operate through such symbolic acts. As Jakob Grimm, collector of German fairy tales and pioneering legal historian, wrote in a famous essay on "Poetry in Law," the earliest forms of law operate through "exceedingly simple" symbols, presented through vivid verbal and visual ritual; it is the enactment of the symbolic ritual that impresses the spectator with the binding character of the legal obligation.[93] Hands often feature in such symbolic ritual enactments: The hand, observes André Leroi-Gourhan, the great interpreter of Stone Age cave painting, has played a central role in human ritual as far back as our evidence extends.[94] The power of "exceedingly simple" hand symbolism can still be felt in modern folklaw practices, such as shaking hands to seal a contract, or placing a wedding ring on the finger of a spouse. These are gestures that have no juridical significance in themselves. Nevertheless, they seem to trigger some intuitive lay sense that a legal relationship has been created; hand symbolism has the power to bring home to us that there *is* a contract, that there *is* a marriage. The ritual early Roman seizure by the hand of a "powerful" owner is a leading example of such hand symbolism, close in spirit to magic, though not itself a magical act.[95]

The symbolic seizure by the hand, vivid ritual that it is, is omnipresent in early Roman law. The hand-based ritual that has perhaps attracted the most attention in the Western tradition is the archaic means of claiming contested property. The Twelve Tables declared that claims on property were to be made by "the right of both laying the hand on it," using a term associated with hand-to-hand combat.[96] We cannot be absolutely certain what practice is meant by this evocative language, but it probably describes an archaic procedure

---

[93] Grimm, *Von der Poesie im Recht* (Darmstadt, 1957), 48.
[94] Leroi-Gourhan, *Le geste et la parole: technique et langage* (Paris, 1964), 262.
[95] See the discussion of Gerhard Dulckeit, "Zur Lehre vom Rechtsgeschäft im klassischen Römischen Recht," in *Festschrift Fritz Schulz* (Weimar, 1951), 1:162–163 [148–190].
[96] Gell. 20.10: *ex iure manum consertum*. As Dario Mantovani observes, the ancients themselves were not sure how to interpret this archaic terminology. Mantovani, *Les juristes écrivains de la Rome antique: les œuvres des juristes comme littérature* (Paris, 2018), 71 n. 136, and the discussion in Joseph Howley, "Why Read the Jurists? Aulus Gellius on Reading across Disciplines," in Paul J. Du Plessis, ed., *New Frontiers: Law and Society in the Roman World* (Edinburgh, 2013), 28 [9–30].

called the *legis actio sacramento in rem*, "claiming a thing by means of a sacred wager," which took the form of a fictive contest between warriors, involving both the ritual grasping by hand and the use of what may have been a symbolic warrior's spear, all staged as a conflict over an imaginary slave.

Our best information about this archaic property procedure comes from the jurist Gaius, probably a native of the provinces who moved to the city of Rome in the mid second century CE. This was the Age of the Antonines, often described as the high era of the Empire – "the period in the history of the world," as Edward Gibbon famously declared at the opening of his *Decline and Fall of the Roman Empire*, "during which the condition of the human race was most happy and prosperous."[97] Working in this noontide of the classical Empire, Gaius gave himself over to the study of early Rome. One of the great figures in the creation of the Western legal tradition,[98] he has been described as a man with an immigrant's fervor for Roman history, a "juristic conservative" who "ran a real risk of appearing to be entrapped in the morass of an apparently irrelevant obsession with distant antiquity."[99] Precisely because he was so devoted to the study of archaic law, his writings are sometimes uncertain evidence for the state of Roman law in his own day; but they are our most important source for early Roman legal history.

As Gaius recounted the archaic procedure of "claiming a thing by means of a sacred wager," the two disputants appeared before a Roman magistrate. Both claimed rights as *quirites*, their rights under the ancient system of personal law, as members of the community of Romans. The fictive combat ensued. Trial by combat, in primitive legal systems, is typically understood as kind of wager between the two contestants over who will prevail.[100] That seems to be

---

[97] Gibbon, *History of the Decline and Fall of the Roman Empire* (New York, 1893), 1:316.
[98] E.g., Donald R. Kelley, "Gaius Noster: Substructures of Western Social Thought," *American Historical Review* 84 (1979): 619–648.
[99] Jill Harries, "Lawyers and Citizens from Republic to Empire: Gaius on the Twelve Tables and Antonine Rome," in Claudia Rapp and H. A. Drake, eds., *The City in the Classical and Post-Classical World: Changing Contexts of Power and Identity* (Cambridge, 2014), 64, 74 [62–80].
[100] Discussion with citation to further literature in James Q. Whitman, *The Verdict of Battle: The Law of Victory and the Making of Modern War* (Cambridge, MA, 2012), 80–83.

Masters of Men and Beasts 109

the case with this early property procedure, which required the two claimants to make a ritual wager. In describing the contestation that followed, Gaius quoted standard Roman formulaic language – language in which the example of property was the ownership of a human being. The passages in capitals are his quotations from the relevant legal formulas, which laid down the ritual words to be spoken by the disputants:

> The claimant, holding a rod, and then laying hold of the actual thing in dispute, such as a man [*uelut hominem*], said: "I DECLARE THAT THIS MAN IS MINE [*meum esse*] BY THE RIGHT OF THE QUIRITES. SEE! IN ACCORDANCE WITH WHAT I HAVE STATED, I HAVE PLACED MY STAFF UPON HIM"; and, at the same time, he laid the rod upon the man. His opponent then said and did the same thing. When both of them had asserted their claims, the Praetor said: "BOTH OF YOU RELEASE YOUR HOLD UPON THE MAN"; and they did so. The one who first asserted his claim, then put the following question to the other: "I ASK WHETHER YOU WILL STATE ON WHAT GROUND YOU MAKE THIS CLAIM?" and he replied, "I ASSERTED MY RIGHT TO HIM BY PLACING MY STAFF UPON HIM."[101]

Gaius, and the Roman formula he quotes, thus ask us to picture a slave cowering between two men, both claiming the rights of a master.

It deserves every emphasis that the example of the property provided in this vivid procedural tableau was "this man"; the *legis actio sacramento in rem* is unmistakably a procedural expression of an "idiom of power" founded in the capture and ownership of human beings. To be sure, "this man" was merely the paradigm example. Humans were not the only form of property that could be claimed through this form of fictive combat. Gaius, who was committed to developing a general abstract concept of "things," was quick to observe that the same procedure could easily be used for any mobile goods. Even land was claimed through a staged contest over a clump of earth.[102] There is obviously something a bit comical in this use of the ritual for land,[103] and primitivist scholars

---

[101] Gai. *Inst.* 4.16. I have adapted and altered the translation in Francis de Zulueta, ed. and trans., *The Institutes of Gaius* (Oxford, 1946), 237, in consultation with other available translations.
[102] Gai. *Inst.* 4.17.
[103] As the ancients observed: Cic. *Mur.* 12.26, in C. Macdonald, trans., *Cicero: In Catilinam 1–4; Pro Murena; Pro Sulla; Pro Flacco*, Loeb Classical Library 324 (Cambridge, MA, 1976), 216–217.

sometimes maintained that the sheer clumsiness of staging a ritual battle over a clod of dirt was, once again, proof of primitive communism in land. It is clear, they argue, that land had become a subject of ownership only late in the development of Roman law; in the earliest phases, it was not yet the object of property litigation.[104] That sort of interpretation is (here as elsewhere) not persuasive as an account of the Roman socio-economic realities. The early Romans unquestionably owned land, and the fact that their terminology and procedural imagery spoke first of owning humans is not evidence to the contrary.

At the same time, their terminology and procedural imagery *did* speak first of the ownership of human beings. The definitional example that Gaius gave was "this man"; and the same was true of Roman law more broadly.[105] Contemporary scholars can be much too quick to pass over this brute fact about the sources. Many of them obscure the prominence of "this man" as the exemplary Roman form of property in this and other texts, reformulating and retranslating the operative phrase as "I declare that this *thing* belongs to me."[106] Even one of the most insightful commentators deals with the difficulty by substituting "cow" for "man."[107] Yet these are modern rewritings of the ancient sources, introduced by scholars who are too reluctant to conjure seriously with the symbolism of ancient Roman law. Rewriting the sources is not permitted. When the Romans recited the most basic formulae of their property law, they did not say "this thing" or "this cow." They said "this man," and they said it over and over again. There is no warrant for refusing to give that fact its full weight, and no excuse for failing to ask why they took a human being as their exemplar of property.

---

[104] Still, with regard to mancipatio, in W. W. Buckland and Arnold D. McNair, *Roman Law and Common Law* (Cambridge, 2008), 61. For a thoughtful statement, see Paul Frédéric Girard, *Manuel élémentaire du droit romain*, 3rd ed. (Paris, 1901), 255–277.

[105] As did Gaius elsewhere: Gai. *Inst.* 2.13; 4.93–94; 4.36.

[106] E.g., Alan Watson, *Rome of the XII Tables: Persons and Property* (Princeton, 1975); Birks, "Roman Law Concept," 5, translating formula as "the thing which is the subject of this action"; Barry Nicholas, *An Introduction to Roman Law*, rev. and ed. Ernest Metzger (Oxford, 2008), 117.

[107] Birks, "Roman Law Concept," 3: "for the Roman jurists it is not quite enough to put down the absence of learning about the concept of ownership solely to their natural bias against abstract questions. There is more to it. Their habit of mind was to attend to the thing owned, whether corporeal (a cow) or incorporeal (a right)."

In any case, the procedure is full of puzzles. What does the rod, which would remain associated with the symbolism of ownership in later Roman law,[108] symbolize? Gaius himself offered what seems the most natural interpretation: The use of the rod was a symbolic expression of the primacy of booty-taking in war as a mode of the acquisition of property: "The rod was employed instead of a spear, as an emblem of lawful ownership, for whatever was taken from an enemy a man considered to be absolutely his own."[109] Gaius wrote many centuries after the time of the Twelve Tables, and we cannot assume that his understanding of the procedure was the same as that of the archaic period; nor can we exclude other possible interpretations of the mysterious rod. Nevertheless, the proposition that archaic procedure served as a symbolic enactment of war fits comfortably with the imagery of hand-to-hand combat in the language of the Twelve Tables. It fits with the writings of other classical authors who understood property to be the fruit of war. It fits within the larger conceptual universe oriented toward the enslavement of enemies through war and the taking of other kinds of booty, of which we shall encounter many more examples, both in this chapter and especially in Chapter 4.

So alongside early Roman terminology that speaks of property as consisting in "slaves male and female and four-footed and domestic animals," we have an early Roman procedure that seems to depict symbolically a contest between warriors over the ownership of a man, presumably imagined as taken captive in combat. How should we interpret this? As in the case of *familia* and *pecunia*, this is a question that gripped many later Western minds. There is a long primitivist history, down (once again) into the Nazi period, of arguments that it reveals the truth about the structure of archaic Roman society, and therefore of the beginnings of human history: Rome began in fact as a community of warriors, and private property began in fact as war booty, and especially human war booty, claimed by the spear.

---

[108] For a sketch of the development, Honsell, Mayer-Maly, and Selb, *Römisches Recht*, 515–523. The term *festuca* ordinarily means stalk. The significance of the association with the vegetable stalk, if there was one, is difficult to parse out.

[109] Gai. *Inst.* 4.16: *festuca autem utebantur quasi hastae loco, signo quodam iusti dominii, quod maxime sua esse credebant quae ex hostibus cepissent.*

The font of this warrior interpretation of archaic Roman society is found in the writings of the incomparably brilliant historian and philosopher of law Rudolf von Jhering (1818–1892). Jhering is little remembered today outside the precincts of legal history; but he was one of the major revolutionary thinkers of the nineteenth century, as important in his field as Darwin and Marx in theirs, and his arguments had a powerful impact not only on the law, but also on the thought of figures like Max Weber. Much of his work turned on the disturbing claim that law had to be understood against the background of the realities of force and power, and he was always eager to uncover the truth of violence beneath the surface of legal doctrine.

His interpretation of archaic Roman law was the original source of his philosophical views. The earliest Roman terms for property, Jhering observed, in pages that have lost none of their power, were all etymologically variations on "to seize by force"; and they reflected the truth that the early Romans regarded the "paradigm case" (*Hauptfall*) of acquisition to be the taking of booty in war.[110] It was for this reason that the spear was the symbol of ownership.[111] The fictive combat seen in the *legis actio sacramento in rem*, with its tableau of combat, belonged to an archaic warrior culture, and its conception of property rights, like those of the rest of the law, reflected the nearness of archaic law to violence. This had an implication of considerable significance: It was in the nature of the warrior orientation that the procedure gave rise to relative, not absolute rights: It determined only which of the two warrior disputants was entitled to the slave claimed by both, without purporting to exclude the rights of any other potential claimant.[112] This was not yet a procedure that assumed the absolute conception of ownership of the classical law; it did not establish a right of ownership in Blackstonian "total exclusion of the right of any other individual in the universe." It could not. In a world accustomed to the legitimacy of private violence, and the use of the spear to claim ownership, there could be no such thing as absolute property rights, good against all persons and protected by law.

Jhering's interpretation of archaic procedure as the product of a warrior society, cognizant of the truth of violence, close to the war

---

[110] Rudolf von Jhering, *Der Geist des römischen Rechts auf den verschiedenen Stufen seiner Entwicklung*, 5th ed. (Leipzig, 1891), 1:110–111.
[111] Ibid., 113.   [112] Jhering, *Geist des römischen Rechts*, 2.2:636–37.

Masters of Men and Beasts

of all against all, and incapable of (indeed uninterested in) guaranteeing absolute property rights, had an enormous subsequent influence.[113] Among his readers was Weber, whose understanding of law as "the monopoly of violence" was deeply indebted to Jhering. (It was Jhering who coined the original version of that famous phrase.)[114] Jhering's theories also had, unsurprisingly and depressingly, an influence on Nazi thought. The Nazi-era literature held that the archaic procedure of the *legis actio sacramento in rem* was nothing less than the original Aryan form of claiming property, used by a warrior race dedicated to the capture of slaves and beasts "with the gripping hand." The inferior races that the Romans had conquered had a different, and feebler, conception of ownership, while the very name for the community of conquering Romans, *quirites*, meant nothing other than "spear-men."[115]

It is especially important for the history of Roman law scholarship that Jhering's ideas were adopted by one of the most brilliant authors to emerge during the Nazi period, Kaser, the eminent authority on Roman property law upon whom I have so often relied in this chapter. Kaser was not a Nazi believer; but he accepted the thesis that early Roman procedure started from the idea of combat as a way of laying claims,[116] and gave rise only to relative rights.[117] His endorsement of the relative rights hypothesis, which he developed with unparalleled sophistication, was his most important contribution to the primitivist

---

[113] Cf. also Ludwig Mitteis, *Römisches Privatrecht bis auf die Zeit Diokletians* (Leipzig, 1908), 87–88.

[114] James Q. Whitman, "Aux origines du 'monopole de la violence,'" in C. Colliot-Thélène and J.-F. Kervégan, eds., *De la société à la sociologie* (Lyons, 2002), 71–91.

[115] Thormann, *Der doppelte Ursprung*, 64–65, 94. For *quirites* as "Speermänner," ibid., 83–89 and often. This was one of the etymologies offered by ancient authors, though it is by no means agreed upon today. See Michiel de Vaan, *Etymological Dictionary of Latin and Other Italic Languages* (Leiden, 2008), s.v. "quiris" [509–510]. Again, I cite Thormann as an important author of the period, not as a Nazi ideologue.

[116] Kaser, "Über 'relatives Eigentum' im altrömischen Recht,"*Zeitschrift der Savigny Stiftung für Rechtsgeschichte (Romanistische Abteilung)* 102 (1985): 6 [1–39]: "Kampfsituation," but substituting *ius* for *vis*.

[117] He continued to defend his position, with modifications. See Kaser, "Über relatives Eigentum," and the discussion of his arguments and its critics in Francesco Giglio, "The Concept of Ownership in Roman Law," *Zeitschrift der Savigny Stiftung für Rechtsgeschichte (Romanistische Abteilung)* 135 (2018): 76–107, here esp. 83–84.

tradition, and it became one of the most vigorously contested claims in studies of Roman property law.

So were Jhering and Kaser right? Is it true that archaic Roman property law was warrior law, a law of "spear-men," giving rise only to relative rights, in a society only a step removed from the war of all against all? Is it true, as Nazis might naturally suppose, that law is never more than a thin veil laid over the face of violence? It goes without saying that any interpretation that attracted the support of the Nazis is one we ought to think twice about, and these interpretations have been among the principal targets of modernist critique. Not without reason: They are no more persuasive than the cognate interpretations that take *familia* and *pecunia* as proof that early Rome was really a society familiar only with the ownership of slaves and beasts. It defies common sense to suppose that all property originated in war booty.[118] It is self-evident, as contemporary scholars insist, that people in early Rome, like people everywhere, acquired and distributed property in a wide variety of ways.

Nor, as Kaser's many critics have argued, does it make good sense to suppose that the archaic procedure in practice resolved only relative rights as between the two parties to the action. This dramatic fictive trial by combat was enacted in the public forum, where it could be witnessed by the entire community. As a matter of the social reality, it must have resulted in some sort of definitive disposition of the claim.[119] In any case, as the litigants laid their rod upon the slave at issue, they pronounced the ritual phrase *meum esse*, "he's mine." It is hard to believe that they were not claiming absolute rights, and there is plenty of room to interpret the mysterious details of the Roman procedure in ways that suggest that that is what they were claiming.[120] Kaser's belief that Roman property law began with relative rights is routinely dismissed today, a leading casualty of the rejection of primitivist interpretations.[121]

But here again we must not go overboard with our modernist critiques. The symbolism of archaic Roman procedure does not prove

---

[118] See the critique of Fernand de Visscher, "Mancipium et res mancipi," *Studia et documenta historiae et iuris* 2 (1936): 276 [263–324]: "un squelette sur lequel l'imagination ne trouve que trop beau jeu à s'exercer" ("a skeleton which the imagination takes all too much pleasure in fleshing out").

[119] Luigi Capogrossi Colognesi, *La struttura della proprietà e la formazione dei "iura praediorum" nell'età repubblicana* (Milan, 1969–1976), 1:123.

[120] Alan Watson, *Rome of the XII Tables*, 126; Birks, "Roman Law Concept," 28.

[121] Though see now the effort in Giglio, "Concept of Ownership in Roman Law," 81–82.

the supposed precarious nature of archaic Roman property, in a society plunged into a near-war-of-all-against-all, but it does not tell us nothing. Gaius struck the right note, and it repays the effort to turn back to his text. He did not say that Roman law was *really* law for warriors, or that booty was the only form of property. What he said was that capture was regarded as the most perfect form of the acquisition of property, and therefore the form used ritually to signify ownership. "The rod was employed instead of a spear, as an emblem of lawful ownership, for whatever was taken from an enemy a man considered to be absolutely his own." This does indeed assume what we know to be true about early Roman society, namely that there was a great deal of war-making and seizure of booty, human, animal, and inanimate. What it does not assume is that archaic Roman property consisted only, or even primarily, in booty. What Gaius said is that the law of property generalizes from a normative principal case – in Jhering's term, a *Hauptfall* – and that the normative principal case, in archaic Roman property law as he understood it in the mid second century CE, was the seizure of booty, and in particular of human booty, in war.

It is also surely true, as so many scholars have observed, that early procedures cannot in fact have established only relative rights.[122] But here again, we must not minimize the significance of its symbolism. Yes, the procedure played out in the public forum, and so it must *de facto* have established some sort of generally recognized rights. The fiction of combat between warriors was in the fullest sense a fiction. Yet it was a fiction that purported to speak to the accepted understanding of how property rights justly arose. In Chapter 4, I will have more to say about the idea that the seizure of human prey in war was the paradigm of just acquisition, and more about how classical jurists based their analogical reasoning on the paradigmatic case, the *Hauptfall*, of the capture and enslavement of the enemy.

* * *

Gaius used the same paradigmatic example of the ownership of humans in describing other early procedures as well, all involving the

---

[122] Kaser eventually conceded as much to his critics, recognizing that early Roman property law created relative rights merely as a matter of procedural protections, not as a matter of the substantive content of the rights in question. Kaser, "Über 'relatives Eigentum,'" 3.

same symbolic seizure by hand; and these others are crucial for his explanation of the archaic distinction between *res mancipi* and *res nec mancipi*, "things subject to the hand-gripping power" and "things not subject to the hand-gripping power."

The most important of these hand-symbol procedures is *mancipatio*, a form of ritualized fictive sale. *Mancipatio* did not involve the symbolic courtroom battle, but the term itself literally means "grasping by hand," being derived from *manus*, "hand," and the Latin root *cap-*, meaning "to seize or grasp." Gaius describes the ceremony as follows:

Mancipatio is ... a sort of imaginary sale. It is performed as follows. After no fewer than five witnesses (who must be Roman citizens above the age of puberty) have been called together, as well as another person of the same condition who holds a bronze balance in his hand and is called the "balance holder," the so-called purchaser, holding a piece of bronze in his hands, says: "I DECLARE THAT THIS MAN BELONGS TO ME BY THE RIGHT OF THE QUIRITES, AND BE HE PURCHASED BY ME WITH THIS PIECE OF BRONZE, AND BRONZE BALANCE." Then he strikes the scales with the piece of bronze, and gives it to the so-called vendor as purchase money.[123]

The fictive sale through *mancipatio*, which placed persons, animals, and things in the "power" of their purchaser, was complemented by a reverse ritual. Human beings – not only slaves, but also sons – could be freed through "e-mancipation" or "manu-mission," both terms meaning the release from the hand of their master.[124]

Alongside *mancipatio* comes another very old procedure, *in iure cessio*, "ceding property before the law." This was a simpler means of transferring property, presumably used as a device for avoiding the burdensome ritual required by *mancipatio*. *In iure cessio* permitted a transfer through a collusive action in which the defendant simply declined to contest the claim of the plaintiff.[125] According to Gaius, it is the use of the transfer rituals *mancipatio* and *in iure cessio* that lies in the background of the archaic distinction between *res mancipi* and *res nec mancipi*. The first of these is the class of things that must be

---

[123] Gai. *Inst.* 1.119. Again, I have altered the translation in Zulueta, ed., *Institutes of Gaius*, 39.
[124] See Honsell, Mayer-Maly, and Selb, *Römisches Recht*, 70–71 on *manumissio vindicta*.
[125] Gai. *Inst.* 2.24.

transferred by *mancipatio* or *in iure cessio*. *Res nec mancipi* included everything else.

There are reasons to suspect that Gaius misunderstood the origins of the two categories;[126] but there is no doubt that the distinction existed, and that it must be explained. Which were the *res mancipi*, the "hand-gripped things," only to be transferred through special rituals? The list that has come down to us begins with "italic soil" (i.e. land in Italy or land elsewhere treated as though it were in Italy), as well as servitudes on land. It continues with slaves – indeed, the association with the ownership of humans was so close that the word *mancipium*, "hand-gripped thing," was a synonym for "slave" in ancient Latin.[127] The list then concludes with "animals that are tamed by the back and the neck, such as oxen, mules, horses, and asses," i.e. animals that had to be saddled or yoked. Land, slaves, and "animals tamed by the back and the neck": What shall we make of this?

Contemporary specialists almost uniformly repeat an answer that was first given by the great Roman historian Barthold Georg Niebuhr (1776–1831), a pioneer of the savvy use of the ancient Roman sources to reconstruct ancient Roman realities. Land, slaves, and animals, Niebuhr argued, had an obvious common context: They were the objects of ownership especially important for agriculture, and the special status given to *res mancipi* is evidence that early Roman law was a law of farmers.[128] Niebuhr's interpretation has never lost its grip: It remains more or less orthodoxy today that the *res mancipi* were the specially prized possessions of farmers. *Res mancipi* is thus the last remaining topic on which scholars still believe that they can use archaic terminology to reconstruct archaic realities.

---

[126] Strictly speaking, the term should mean "thing of *mancipium*," not of "thing of *mancipatio*." On the difficulties of interpreting the term *res*, see above, n. 57.

[127] Visscher, "Mancipium et res mancipi," 310–313, finds this mysterious, and seeks a complex explication in the supposed Etruscan origins of slavery.

[128] E.g., Watson, *Rome of the XII Tables*, 137; D. H. van Zyl, *History and Principles of Roman Private Law* (Durban, 1983), 130; more cautiously "the household in early Roman society": Paul du Plessis and Andrew Borkowski, *Borkowski's Textbook on Roman Law*, 5th ed. (Oxford, 2015), 159. For Niebuhr: *Römische Geschichte, neue Ausgabe* (Berlin, 1873), 1:373. The earlier failure to come up with a satisfying account of what made these what Cornelis van Bynkershoek analyzes as the "most precious" things for the Romans is described in Bynkershoek, "Opusculum de rebus mancipi et nec mancipi," in Bynkershoek, *Opuscula* (Leiden, 1752), 109–110 [101–135].

But are they right? As the occasional critic observes, it is not clear that this standard view of the *res mancipi* can be squared with the lists that have come down to us, or with early Roman history as historians now understand it. Archaic Rome was not a simple farming community – among other things, it was engaged in warfare – and the Twelve Tables are not a law directed simply to managing agricultural relations. Nor is it clear that the things included under the heading *res mancipi* are the things that would have mattered most for the practice of farming.[129] Slaves were certainly in use on farms, though there were probably not very many of them in early Rome.[130] It is certainly the case that there were horses and oxen, though they were more difficult to use in Antiquity than in later periods, since the collar harness and frontal yoke that make it fully efficient to put them to work them as draft animals had not yet been invented.[131] But "animals tamed by the back and neck" excludes the most economically important of animal possessions for ancient farmers: pigs, goats, and sheep.[132] Even the inclusion of land is a bit puzzling: Why "Italic" land, a category clearly dating to the age of Roman imperialistic expansion, long after the archaic period?[133]

Summing much of this up in a superb 1936 article, the Belgian legal historian Fernand de Visscher vigorously contested the claim that the archaic *res mancipi* constituted the prized possessions of farmers. The category of *res mancipi* was not about the economics of farming at all, but about the archaic conception of the nature of ownership: The *res mancipi* were the things that emblematized the hand-gripping power of

---

[129] Visscher, "Mancipium et res mancipi," 264–275.
[130] Keith Bradley, "Slavery in the Roman Republic," in John Bodel and Paul Cartledge, eds., *The Cambridge World History of Slavery, Vol. 1: The Ancient Mediterranean World* (Cambridge, 2011), 244 [241–264].
[131] See Pierre Bonnassie, "Survie et extinction du régime esclavagiste dans l'Occident du haut moyen âge (IVe–XIe s.)," *Cahiers de civilisation médiévale* 28 (1985): 331 [307–343].
[132] Niebuhr, aware of the difficulty posed by the absence of small animals, tried to deal with it by conjecturing that the complex rituals of transfer were "not worth the effort" when it came to goats. *Römische Geschichte*, 1:373.
[133] As Thomas H. Watkins pointedly observes, "Italia as a legal entity is a prerequisite of *ius italicum*." Watkins, "Coloniae and *ius italicum* in the Early Empire," *Classical Journal* 78 (1983): 320 [319–326]. Cf. Watkins, "Roman Citizen Colonies and Italic Right," in C. Deroux, ed., *Studies in Latin Literature and Roman History, I* (Brussels, 1979): 70–72 [59–99].

the master, the class of "what could be seized by hand and subjected to the will" of the *paterfamilias*. That is why they included beasts that had to be saddled and tamed, but not pigs, goats, and sheep: The *res mancipi*, the things "subject to the hand-gripping power," were the forms of property that rested on the idea of *taming*, of "the power to give commands, the domestic *imperium*."[134] Even the mention of land had to be seen in the same light: For what mattered about land, Visscher argued, was that it represented the territory over which the domestic master exercised his rule, since every master requires a domain.[135]

Visscher's interpretation, like the interpretations of Kaser, has been the target of energetic modernist critique. Capogrossi Colognesi, in particular, declares that Visscher was a victim of the "irrationalism" of the interwar years, which led him to underappreciate the ancient socio-economic realities.[136] Yet there is nothing "irrationalist" about the effort to make sense of the conceptual universe of an alien legal system, much though the conceptions in question may seem weird to us; and we abandon much deep wisdom when we spurn the scholarship of the interwar years. Visscher, in my opinion, had it right, or at least mostly right.[137] The list of *res mancipi* is not evidence for how the archaic economy worked, any more than any of the other early sources are. It is

---

[134] Visscher, "Mancipium et res mancipi," 294.   [135] Ibid., 295–300.
[136] Capogrossi Colognesi, *Struttura della proprietà*, 1:109, and generally 16–17, 105–120, 203–275, and esp. 352–353. For his views more generally, focusing on the third century BCE and after, see Capogrossi Colognesi, *Struttura della proprietà*, 1:408–462; Capogrossi Colognesi, "Le regime de la terre à l'époque républicaine," in *Terre et paysans dépendants dans les sociétés antiques* (Paris, 1979), 323–325 [313–388]. For critiques more broadly, Honsell, Mayer-Maly, and Selb, *Römisches Recht*, 145–146.
[137] The doubts have to do with his treatment of land. Raymond Monier, "Du *mancipium* au *dominium*, essai sur l'apparition et le développement de la notion de propriété en droit romain," in Monier, "Cours de droit" (unpublished manuscript, 1947), 14–15, argues that Visscher was wrong in imagining that land was an object of archaic ownership at all. I see no way of determining whether this is so. The formula as we have it manifestly long postdates the archaic period – *solum italicum* is clearly not an archaic term. It is impossible to say what the ur-concept of *res mancipi* may have been, but we should certainly hesitate as we interpret a formula so obviously introduced late in the development of the tradition. Nevertheless, it may indeed be the case that land entered the archaic catalogues comparatively late. For the late introduction of land into the law of *postliminium*, see below, Chapter 4, and for the *legis actio sacramento in rem*, above. It seems perfectly possible that the development of the *res mancipi* followed the same course.

evidence of the character of Roman concept formation; and in that respect the special status of the *res mancipi*, as Visscher argued, shares the orientation toward the *potestas* of the master traced throughout this chapter. It is revealing that the classical jurists, when they discussed *res mancipi*, had nothing to say about farming. They devoted themselves to something else entirely: the question of what counted as taming. This was a problem that divided the rival schools of the classical jurists, as Gaius recounts:

Res mancipi are lands and houses on Italic soil, likewise slaves, and animals that are tamed by the back and neck, such as oxen, mules, horses, asses [as well as servitudes in the countryside] ... These animals our authorities [i.e. those of Gaius' own school of interpretation, the Sabinians] hold to be *res mancipi* as soon as they are born: but Nerva and Proculus and other authors of the opposite [Proculian] school hold that they become *res mancipi* only when they have been broken in, or, if they cannot be broken in owing to their extreme wildness, that they become *res mancipi* when they reach the usual age for breaking in. Further, wild beasts such as bears and lions are *res nec mancipi*, as are animals such as elephants and camels; it does not matter that such animals [elephants and camels] are commonly tamed by the back and neck.[138]

It is entertaining to discover the interest of the classical jurists in the decidedly post-archaic problem of the classification of elephants and camels. (This Mediterranean preoccupation with exotic animals was one the Roman jurists shared with the Jewish translators of the Septuagint, the Greek version of the Hebrew Bible, who worried in the third century BCE about whether giraffe meat was kosher.)[139] But why did such questions matter at all, if the concern of the law was with the needs of farmers? Why vest so much legal significance in the question of exactly when and how beasts can be deemed broken in by their masters?

* * *

The distinction between wild and tamed beasts was not confined to the law of *res mancipi*. We have already seen that *pecunia* comes from *pecus*, meaning specifically domesticated animal. Other examples can

---

[138] Gai. *Inst.* 2.14a–17, again altering the translation in Zulueta, *Institutes of Gaius*, 69–71. Cf. Bruce Frier, "Bees and Lawyers," *Classical Journal* 78 (1982–1983): 105–106 [105–114], on the difficulties posed by wild animals.
[139] See, with references to further literature, Maja Miziur-Moździoch, "How a Sheep Turned into a Giraffe: The Case of Deuteronomy 14:5," *Vetus Testamentum* 70 (2020): 753–758.

be given too: Ancient Roman law often worked with a basic distinction between two classes of beasts, the wild and the domesticated. This was a distinction, as we shall see, that paralleled the equally basic distinction between the two classes of humans, the free and slave. Chapter 4 will go more deeply into the parallel between wild animals that have not yet been tamed and free humans who have not yet been enslaved.

It is particularly important that the capture and taming of wild beasts played a central role in another topic touching on hand symbolism, and one, as we have seen, of the greatest importance for the history of later Western property law and Western imperial expansion: the doctrine of *occupatio*; and it is with *occupatio* that I close this chapter.

Ancient *occupatio* was the first of the examples of acquisition given in the Roman texts, and thus the core model of how ownership should be conceptualized.[140] *Occupatio* is of course the source of the modern word "occupation," and to modern Western ears it will naturally suggest the occupation of land. Any other use of the term will seem to us odd; we would not speak of "occupying" a wild animal or "occupying" an enemy defeated in war. Correspondingly, the modern Western understanding of *occupatio* centers, in a characteristically modern Western way, on land. It follows that the doctrine of acquisition through *occupatio* in modern law is the doctrine of *terra nullius*,[141] of the right to claim ownership of land that belongs to no one.

But in Antiquity *occupatio* had a different sense. *Occupatio*, like *mancipatio* and *mancipium*, is a derivative from the root *cap-*, "to seize by hand"; and while the term could be used for land (Cicero in particular used it that way[142]), the doctrine as we find it in the classical legal sources barely touches on land at all. Instead, it is

---

[140] What came to be called, in the early modern period, the "original mode" of acquisition. Grotius, *De jure belli ac pacis*, ed. Jean Barbeyrac (Utrecht, 1773), 1:233 (2.3.4.1). Cf., e.g., on Gershom Carmichael, Andrew Fitzmaurice, *Sovereignty, Property and Empire* (Cambridge, 2014), 133.

[141] A phrase only in use since the nineteenth century. Fitzmaurice, *Sovereignty, Property*, 31.

[142] Lauren Benton and Benjamin Straumann, "Acquiring Empire by Law: From Roman Doctrine to Early Modern European Practice," *Law and History Review* 28 (2010): 14 [1–36]. The later *agrimensores* also spoke of *ager occupatorius*, but that terminology postdates the material in this discussion. See Paula Botteri, "La définition de l'*ager occupatorius*," *Cahiers du Centre Gustave Glotz* 3 (1992): 45–55.

a doctrine of the *occupatio*, the seizure, of wild animals and defeated enemies in war. As A.-J. Arnaud, the historian of the transformation of ancient Roman law in the modern world, writes, the ancient doctrine of *occupatio* was about "the mastery of hunters over their game, the mastery of fishers over their catch ... war captives ... and booty."[143] The account preserved in the *Digest* of Justinian gives the flavor of the doctrine in its ancient form. It begins, like the first chapter of Genesis, with "the fish in the sea and the birds in the sky, ... the livestock and all the wild animals, ... all the creatures that move along the ground," and then extends the model of capture to other topics by analogy:

[D. 41.1.1pr. 2] Gaius, *Common Matters or Golden Things*, Book 2 ... (1) [A]ll animals which are captured on land, on sea, or in the air, that is to say, wild beasts and birds, as well as fish, become the property of those who take them ... (3) For what does not belong to anyone by natural law becomes the property of the person who first acquires it.

[D. 41.1.5.7] Those things that we seize from the enemy automatically become ours ...

[D. 41.1.7pr.] To such an extent is this true that even men who are free become the slaves of the enemy; but, still, if they escape from the power of the enemy they will recover their pristine liberty.[144]

We shall see in Chapter 4 that the jurists extended the basic analogy of the capture of living creatures through *occupatio* to a wide range of other topics.

The ancient hunting orientation of *occupatio* is, if it needs to be said again, no guide to the ancient socio-economic realities. The fact that the ancient doctrine of *occupatio* did not turn, in the modern Lockean way, on the settlement and cultivation of land does not for a moment signify that the Romans did not care about land, did not conquer it, or did not "occupy" it in the modern sense of the term. Far from it. There was perhaps no form of property more important for the development of Roman property law, and Roman Republican politics, than the conquered land of the *ager publicus*; we shall see more about that in the next chapter. What the doctrine of *occupatio* tells is only something about Roman imaginative reflexes in conceptualizing and justifying ownership.

---

[143] A.-J. Arnaud, "Reflexions sur l'occupation du droit romain," *Revue historique du droit* 46 (1968), 186; cf. 188 [183–210]. Further discussion below, Chapter 4.

[144] For the placement of these passages, see Otto Lenel, *Palingenesia iuris civilis* (repr. Frankfurt a.M., 2004), 1: col. 253.

And those reflexes, here as so often, centered on the *Hauptfall*, the paradigmatic case, of the "seizure" of wild beasts and defeated enemies.[145]

There is no mistaking the culture that lies in the background of all this law: As Arnaud and Yan Thomas emphasize, this is law of a culture oriented toward hunting and war, the two activities that Weber deemed to be characteristic of the all-male bands of traditional societies.[146] The texts on *occupatio*, like the other property doctrines this chapter has investigated, must be interpreted as part of that culture, as cantos in what Vico called the "serious poem" of Roman law.[147] These are sources that cry out to be read alongside Genesis, and alongside the innumerable ancient Mediterranean celebrations, verbal and visual, in poems, plays, vases, and frescoes, of hunters and warriors as well. A snatch of ancient verse can serve as one from an inexhaustible list of examples. Here is the "Song of Hybrias the Cretan," recorded by the Greek rhetorician Athenaeus around the turn of the third century CE:

> I have great wealth – a spear and a sword
> and the good shield of animal hide, skin's protector;
> for with this I plough, with this I reap,
> with this I tread the sweet wine from the grape-vine,
> with this I am named master of vassals.
>
> Those who dare not wield a spear and a sword
> and the good shield of animal hide, skin's protector:
> all these men, falling around my knee,
> worship me, calling me
> master and great king.[148]

The Roman legal sources are a good bit less exuberant, but the idea that wealth is acquired by the spear and the sword, and consists in a fondness for being called master of men, perhaps ideally ones "falling

---

[145] For the association of the *libertas naturalis* of humans with that of wild animals: Mario Talamanca, "L'antichità e i 'diritti dell'uomo,'" *Atti dei Convegni Lincei* 174 (2001): 73–75 [41–91]. In Aristotle's scheme, domestic animals ranked just below humans, with slaves and barbarians a step up from them. Peter Garnsey, *Ideas of Slavery from Aristotle to Augustine* (Cambridge, 1996), 110–114.

[146] Weber, *Wirtschaft und Gesellschaft*, ed. Johannes Winckelmann, 5th. ed. (Tübingen, 1985), 154.

[147] Vico, *Scienza nuova*, 507: "il diritto romano fu un serioso poema ... e l'antica giurisprudenza fu una severa poesia."

[148] Ath. 15.50.24, in C. D. Yonge, trans., *The Deipnosophists; or, Banquet of the Learned, of Athenaeus* (London, 1853–1854), 1112.

around my knee," resounds through them, as does more broadly the idea of property as "spear-won."

The Roman legal texts cry out, too, to be read alongside the work of the anthropologists. We saw in the last chapter that the literature of anthropology has long pointed to property in prey as the prime example of quasi-ownership among the hunter-gatherers they study, with a history that probably extends back to the Upper Paleolithic. I quote once again a few of the rules catalogued by ethnographers:

> Among the Central Eskimo the person who first sees a young seal or polar bear owns that animal regardless of who actually kills it ... Among the Copper Eskimo it is the first person who inflicts a wound on the animal who owns it, even though the wound is a minor one and the animal would escape if another hunter did not assist in its killing ... The Andamanese assign the ownership of the slain pig or dugong to the man who inflicts the first serious wound; minor wounds give the inflictor no rights in the animal ...[149]

The classical Roman law of *occupatio* offers its own solution to the same problem, so well known to anthropologists; and the jurists juggled other solutions, such as wounding, as well.[150] That does not mean that Roman law did not give distinctive answers, or that doctrine of the classical period, to which I now turn, was not marked by uncommon sophistication. But the problem itself is extraordinarily old.

---

[149] J. H. Dowling, "Individual Ownership and the Sharing of Game in Hunting Societies," *American Anthropologist* 70 (1968): 504 [502–507].

[150] Cf. D. 41.1.5.1. Gaius 2 *rer. cott.*: *Illud quaesitum est, an fera bestia, quae ita vulnerata sit, ut capi possit, statim nostra esse intellegatur.*

3

The *Dominus* Enters the Law

In the era of the fall of the Republic and the transition to monarchy – "a century of anarchy, culminating in civil war and military tyranny," as Ronald Syme described it in his *Roman Revolution* of 1939[1] – Roman property law underwent an epochal transformation. The archaic concepts of property described in the previous chapter did not simply vanish. *Familia* and *pecunia*, the slave- and beast-words of the Early and Middle Republic, survived in the law, as did *res mancipi* and *res nec mancipi*, the language of the master's gripping hand. The archaic procedures were not formally abolished for centuries.

Nevertheless, beginning perhaps at the end of the second century BCE, a new language took hold: the language of the *dominus*, the "master," and its derivative form *dominium*.[2] The transformation extended, moreover, well beyond the introduction of a novel terminology. Legal reasoning entered new realms of abstraction as well. Archaic law, as we saw in the last chapter, had no abstract term for "property." Classical law, by contrast, growing steadily in sophistication, turned increasingly to problems in the general nature of property as such, now treated under the heading *dominium*, for which the jurists developed a large body of subtle doctrine. "The very end of the Republic and the rise of the Empire," as an influential account explained in 1948,

---

[1] Syme, *The Roman Revolution* (Oxford, 1939), 2.
[2] And later on, *proprietas*, "that which is one's own."

were marked by profound transformations, not only in Roman political institutions, but also in certain conceptions of private law. This is the epoch when the notion of *dominium* progressively substitutes itself for *mancipium*; it is also the epoch when the distinction between *res corporales* and *res incorporales* [corporeal and incorporeal things], passing from philosophy into law, assumes its place alongside the division into *res mancipi* and *res nec mancipi*.[3]

It was from this period on that absolute ownership, the "startlingly new legal concept," in the words of Orlando Patterson, that "became pivotal in [the] private law" of the Western world, began to assume its mature shape.[4]

What can explain this new birth of the law, contemporaneous with the death of the Roman Republic? That question once loomed large, not only in the work of scholars, but also in Western ideological battles. Roman law was not a subject of interest only to specialists in pre-1945 Europe. Ideologues on both the Left and the Right took an interest – indeed at times an obsessive interest – in it as well. Both extremes of the political spectrum shared a hatred for classical Roman property law, which they blamed for the evils of capitalism;[5] and on both the Left and the Right the origins of the Roman conception of absolute ownership, the property law doctrine that supposedly lay at the foundation of those evils, were traced to the social and political upheavals of the fall of the Roman Republic.

For Karl Marx and his followers, the triumph of classical absolute ownership was linked to the emergence of new patterns of class

---

[3] Raymond Monier, "La date d'apparition du 'dominium,'" in *Studi in onore di Siro Solazzi* (Naples, 1948), 357 [357–374]. Classically Monier, "Du *mancipium* au *dominium*, essai sur l'apparition et le développement de la notion de propriété en droit romain," in Monier, "Cours de droit" (unpublished manuscript, 1947), and e.g., among many Luigi Capogrossi Colognesi, *Proprietà e signoria in Roma antica*, 2nd ed. (Rome, 1994), 184–186. There is no shortage of debate about the significance of this moment. This is particularly true to the extent the claim is that there was no concept of property earlier on. For arguments dating the transaction to more abstract thought earlier see Yan Thomas, "*Res*, chose et patrimoine (note sur le rapport sujet–objet en droit romain)," *Archives de philosophie du droit* 25 (1980): 425 [413–426]. See also Michèle Ducos, "Les juristes romains et le domaine agraire," in E. Hermon, ed., *La question agraire à Rome: droit romain et société* (Como, 1999), 121–122 [121–129]; cf. Rodolfo Ambrosino, "Le applicazioni innovative della 'mancipatio,'" in *Studi in memoria di Emilio Albertario* (Milan, 1953), 2:583 n. 23 [2:575–617].
[4] Patterson, *Slavery and Social Death* (Cambridge, MA, 1982), 28–29.
[5] See James Q. Whitman, "Long Live the Hatred of Roman Law!" *Rechtsgeschichte* 2 (2003): 40–57.

exploitation, founded in mass slavery: With the collapse of the Republic, Friedrich Engels explained, Roman society came to be sharply divided into the two classes of masters and slaves, *domini* and *servi*; and the new form of legal reasoning laid the juridical foundation for centuries of domination through the instrument of law. Nazi ideologues promoted their own version of events. For them, the fall of the Republic signaled the definitive disappearance of the healthy Aryan values of archaic Roman society. The racially pure Aryan Republic was replaced by a cosmopolitan Empire; and that transformation spawned a classical property law that had lost its Aryan character, becoming a vector of social corruption that was destined to spread "semitic" values throughout the law of the West in later centuries.[6]

Those sorts of interpretations have, unsurprisingly, disappeared from the contemporary writings of Roman law scholars. Specialists today typically explain the late republican transformation of Roman property law very differently: as the fruit of an intellectual revolution, which they often credit to the influence of Greek philosophy, or as a response to the growing velocity of commerce. The law, it is said, underwent a process of "juridification," achieving new levels of sophistication in an increasingly sophisticated Roman society.[7] Commercialization in an increasingly wealthy Empire required more supple legal reasoning.[8] The political and social upheavals of the "century of anarchy" play no role in contemporary interpretations. Nor does the literature any longer have much if anything to say on the topic that once focused the attention of scholars and ideologues alike – the triumph of the new terminology of the *dominus*, the "master."

Maybe this is in some ways for the best. Nobody wants to return to the mid twentieth-century Age of Ideologies. But is it fully satisfying? Can we really detach our accounts of the transformation of Roman property law from the political and social history of the fall of the Republic? Is there really nothing of significance to be said about the emergence of the new language of *dominus* and *dominium*?

---

[6] Both discussed below, this chapter.
[7] Luigi Capogrossi Colognesi, *La struttura della proprietà e la formazione dei "iura praediorum" nell'età repubblicana* (Milan, 1969–1976), 1:451–452.
[8] Bruce Frier, *The Rise of the Roman Jurists: Studies in Cicero's Pro Caecina* (Princeton, 1985), 280.

Those are the questions this chapter tackles. The old ideologically driven interpretations were dubious in myriad ways, and I will not defend them in their original form. But it is a mistake to ignore the questions that they posed, even if their answers no longer seem right. The problem of the entry of the *dominus* into the law deserves particularly close attention. There is in fact an important history to be traced about how the "master" assumed his place at the pinnacle of classical Roman property thought. It is not a history that accounts for all the subtleties of classical property law. But it is one that compels us to peer into the cultural gulf that separates ancient property law from modern.

* * *

To understand the interpretations of the transformation of Roman property law that once prevailed among ideologues and interpreters of Roman property law, communist, fascist, and otherwise, we must begin, once again, with the history of the *ager publicus*, the "public land" of Republican Rome. Much of the classic social theorizing of the West concerned the tale of how Rome's originally communal public land eventually fell into the grasping hands of private owners.

The previous chapter introduced the early history of the *ager publicus*. As we saw, early Roman rights in land, like those in most non-Western, nonmodern societies, consisted in "the side-by-side existence of private property and communal property."[9] The private property in question, like that in other societies, was "limited in scope," probably restricted to garden plots.[10] The communal property presumably lay in the *ager publicus*, the "public land," governed by a system of use rights of the kind found in most of the non-Western, nonmodern world.

This archaic property regime did not survive unchanged as Rome underwent its stunning expansion over the latter centuries of the first millennium BCE; but it is a centrally important fact of Roman history that it did not simply disappear either. Even as the emerging Roman state displaced whatever chieftains had allotted rights in the earlier

---

[9] Elinor Ostrom, *Governing the Commons: The Evolution of Institutions for Collective Action* (Cambridge, 1990), 61.

[10] Richard E. Mitchell, "*Ager publicus*: Public Property and Private Wealth during the Roman Republic," in Michael Hudson and Baruch Levine, eds., *Privatization in the Ancient Near East and Classical World* (Cambridge, MA, 1996), 253 [253–291].

The Dominus *Enters the Law* 129

periods, and even as the Italian *ager publicus* grew to spectacular dimensions, the old understanding of the nature of rights in land held on. Indeed, the history of the *ager publicus* in the Middle Republic can be understood as one of an unusually, and possibly uniquely, sophisticated use-rights system, which took complex forms, including, to take one striking example among many, a system for their public auction, with the proceeds going to the state.[11]

In the end, though, the venerable system of use rights in the *ager publicus*, even in its highly sophisticated middle republican instantiations, did not survive the Roman subjection of the Mediterranean world, and especially of the Italian peninsula. As more and more rich Italian land fell under Roman control, the inherited system came under steady pressure, and eventually buckled, as individual Roman families, and in particular the wealthy Roman nobility, succeeded in appropriating permanent private ownership in Rome's conquered territories. By the late second century, large privately held slave plantations, so-called *latifundia*, had emerged in Roman Italy (though it should be emphasized that they were not the only form of holding), the consequence of the appropriation of what had once been public land by Romans of great wealth and power.[12]

This triumph of privatization in the *ager publicus*, and the emergence of great Italian slave plantations, was consummated amid the demise of the Republic,[13] and to later Europeans, for whom the fall of the Roman Republic was perhaps the defining experience of Western history, the two events seemed to have a manifest connection, and to carry a portentous warning for future generations: The fate of Rome's "public land," dismembered and appropriated by wealthy slaveholders, served as an

---

[11] *Ager quaestorius*, discussed in Saskia Roselaar, *Public Land in the Roman Republic: A Social and Economic History of ager publicus in Italy, 396–89 B.C.* (Oxford, 2010), 121–127, esp. 123. See further on the complexities Luigi Capogrossi Colognesi, "*Dominium e possessio* nell'Italia Romana," in Ennio Cortese, ed., *La proprietà e le proprietà* (Milan, 1988), 141–182; and Mario Talamanca, "Considerazioni conclusive," ibid., 183–200. Further general examination in Roselaar, *Public Land*, 86–145.

[12] See above, Chapter 2, for caveats on the use of "plantation."

[13] See Claude Nicolet, "La question agraire," in *Rome et la conquête du monde méditerranéen* (Paris, 1979), 1:117–142; and for the larger historiography, and expressions of skepticism, Roselaar, *Public Land*, 146–149 and *passim*.

object lesson in the precariousness of the common good. It exemplified the danger that unrestricted private property rights posed to liberty.

This belief in the fateful link between the privatization of the *ager publicus* and the death of the Roman Republic was shaped in particular by a key ancient text, the work of the Greek historian Appian, a native of Alexandria who was active as a lawyer in the city of Rome in the mid second century CE. The military victories of the Republican period, Appian explained, perhaps drawing on an earlier account that is now lost,[14] brought a huge influx of slaves who could be put to agricultural labor. The result was the destruction of a healthy Roman tradition of yeoman farmers, and its replacement by a slave order that descended, calamitously, upon Italy:

> The rich ... being emboldened by the lapse of time to believe that they would never be dispossessed, absorbing any adjacent strips and their poor neighbors' allotments, partly by purchase under persuasion and partly by force, came to cultivate vast tracts instead of single estates, using slaves as laborers and herdsmen, lest free laborers should be drawn from agriculture into the army. At the same time the ownership of slaves brought them great gain from the multitude of their progeny, who increased because they were exempt from military service. Thus certain powerful men became extremely rich and the race of slaves multiplied throughout the country, while the Italian people dwindled in numbers and strength, being oppressed by penury, taxes, and military service.[15]

Appian's lament echoed a commonplace view among Roman moralists, expressed most famously in a lapidary phrase of Pliny the Elder: *latifundia perdidere Italiam*, "the great slave plantations destroyed Italy."[16] These jeremiads had a powerful impact on later Western social and political thought. For figures like Thomas More or James Harrington, Appian's bleak description of socio-economic–political transformation offered the

---

[14] Common source for Appian and Plutarch: Roselaar, *Public Land*, 7. For the importance of these passages, and scholarly doubts about their interpretation, see Emilio Gabba, "Sulle strutture agrarie dell'Italia romana fra III e I sec. a.C.," in Emilio Gabba and Marinella Pasquinucci, *Strutture agrarie e allevamento transumante nell'Italia romana (III–I sec. a.C.)* (Pisa, 1979), 17–18.

[15] App. *BC* 1.7, in Brian McGing, ed. and trans., *Appian: Roman History, Vol. I*, Loeb Classical Library 2 (Cambridge, MA, 1912), 17.

[16] Plin. *Nat.* 18.35, in H. Rackham, trans., *Pliny: Natural History*, Loeb Classical Library 330 (Cambridge, MA, 1938), 212. Cf. K. D. White, "Latifundia," *Bulletin of the Institute of Classical Studies* 14 (1967): 62–79.

iconic historical demonstration of the dangers of corruption through excessive wealth, and especially wealth in land, as Alfred Heuss has shown.[17] The fate of the *ager publicus* had a place at the center of Western sociopolitical thinking for generations.

The theory of Karl Marx (who enjoyed reading Appian in Greek in his leisure time) grew out of this tradition too. Marx's interpretations of Roman history must be reconstructed from scattered remarks throughout his voluminous writings, and it is not always easy to be sure precisely what he thought.[18] But as he presented the fall of the Republic in the unfinished final volume of *Das Kapital*, this was an age in which the class structures of exploitation were revolutionized. The patricians who had dominated in the Middle Republic had conducted themselves to at least some degree paternalistically. But those republican patricians now gave way to a new class of ruthless, usurious *nouveaux riches*: "In the place of the old exploiters, whose exploitation was more or less patriarchal ... came a hard, money-hungry upstart [*ein harter, geldsüchtiger, Emporkömmling*]." This late republican, purely profit-driven, ruling class destroyed the values of the older republican order; while agrarian laborers who had once been free peasants were reduced to slavery.[19]

Marx did not directly address the consequences of this new pattern of class exploitation for the conceptual transformation of Roman law, but his comrade Engels did. The rise of the new class order, Engels explained in his *Anti-Dühring*, in a fascinating exercise in legal historical analysis, was directly linked to the new forms of abstract analysis that emerged among the Roman jurists. This happened

---

[17] See Heuss, *Barthold Georg Niebuhrs wissenschaftliche Anfänge* (Göttingen, 1981), 222–233.
[18] For a strong (though in my view strongly overstated) presentation of the case that Roman history, never systematically treated in Marx's writings, did not play a crucial role in his thinking at all, and even that he did not in fact read Appian in the original, see Wilfried Nippel, "Marx and Antiquity," in Danielle Allen, Paul Christesen, and Paul Millet, eds., *How to Do Things with History: New Approaches to Ancient Greece* (Oxford, 2018), 185–208. The fact that there is no sustained analysis of Roman history in Marx's corpus does not imply that his thinking was not shaped by the tradition in which, like everybody else, he was reared.
[19] Marx, *Das Kapital: Kritik der politischen Ökonomie*, Bk. 3, 2nd ed., ed. Friedrich Engels (Hamburg, 1904), 3:133, 134, 136, 138; also in Marx and Engels, *Werke* (Berlin, 1964), 25: 610. Marx's larger analysis, which I do not discuss here, was about the corrosive effects of lending at interest.

because traditional social distinctions were flattened. In the Republic, there had been a variety of social statuses. But "under the Roman Empire, [social distinctions] dissolved, with the exception of that of free and slave." It was the rise of the new form of undifferentiated "free" status that brought with it the rise of absolute private property: "There emerged, at least for the free, the equality of private individuals, on the basis of which Roman law took shape, the most perfect expression of a law based on private property that we know of."[20] With the development of an ancient order that sorted society into the two categories of free and slave, *dominus* and *servus*, the *dominus* class came to live by an ideology of "freedom" and the associated "free" absolute conception of property.

From Marx and Engels onward, the link between the high Roman slave order and the high classical law of private property became a standard Marxist teaching. This is not the place to investigate the full history. I cite, in lieu of many others, one typical author writing in 1904: "The 'classical' system," this Marxist explained, "rested on the slave-system, the exploitation of slaves"; from the "materialist point of view," this was the ancient beginning of a system of exploitation based on the protection of property that carried on through all later centuries of the exploitation of subordinate classes.[21] This was the tradition of analysis that eventually made its way into the interpretation of Orlando Patterson, who explained how the classical "idiom of power" of slavery, with its paradigmatic *dominus*, established the juridical terms for the absolute conception of property of the modern capitalist order.

* * *

The Marxist tradition is by far the best remembered of the older literature. But there were also interpretations in the fascist world, notably in Nazi Germany, and not all of them deserve to be forgotten.[22]

Plenty of what appeared in Germany during the interwar years promoted vile nonsense about race. Nazi ideology, as we saw in the

---

[20] Engels, *Herrn Eugen Dühring's Umwälzung der Wissenschaft*, 3rd ed. (Stuttgart, 1894), 100.
[21] M. Gursky, "Die criminal-soziologische Schule als Kämpferin für die Interessen der herrschenden Klassen," *Die neue Zeit: Wochenschrift der deutschen Sozialdemokratie* 22, no. 2 (1903–1904): 644, 647 [641–648].
[22] For the larger Fascist and Nazi scene, see Thorsten Keiser, *Eigentumsrecht in Nationalsozialismus und Fascismo* (Tübingen, 2005).

previous chapter, held that archaic Rome had been founded by Aryan warriors, whose law rested on "the right of rule over persons free and unfree and large animals";[23] and it was fit to serve as an archaic inspiration for their modern German racial kin. Classical law, by contrast, with its socially corrosive absolute conception of *dominium*, was polluted by racial corruption, the embodiment of a destructive "materialist view of the world"; and Nazi ideologues held that the process of corruption began in earnest with the fall of the Republic. As one lawyer explained in 1931, the assassination of Julius Caesar in 44 BCE marked the turning point. With the death of Caesar came the definitive end of the Republic, and Rome began to succumb to race mixing. The process of degeneration reached its climax in 212 CE, when Roman citizenship was extended to all free persons; and the result was an Empire that became "the cesspool of peoples," in which even "Africans, Arabs and Jews called themselves 'Romans.'" By the time of the final compilation of the Roman texts by Justinian, the "Jewish spirit" had thoroughly infected the law.[24]

That sort of subintellectual rant was common in the age of Nazism. (The same tale was told a year later by Helmut Nicolai, then the leading legal "philosopher" of the Party.)[25] If that were all there were to the German literature of the Nazi era, there would be no point in discussing it at all. But there were also much more thoughtful interpretations. Germany was the home of a magnificent scholarly tradition; and serious scholarship did not come to an abrupt end after 1933. In particular, interpretations of the transformation of Roman property law were offered by two of the greatest legal historians of the twentieth century, Max Kaser and Franz Wieacker, both of whose work deserves close study. Neither spoke of race pollution, as Party ideologues did. Nor did either follow Marx in analyzing the forms of class exploitation. Instead, both made arguments about what Elizabeth

---

[23] Karl Friedrich Thormann, *Der doppelte Ursprung der mancipatio: ein Beitrag zur Erforschung des frühromischen Rechtes unter Mitberücksichtigung des nexum* (Munich, 1943), 64–65.

[24] Albert Halbe, *Eigentum als Verdienst: eine Kampfschrift gegen und für Alle* (Breslau, 1931), 45–46. "Kloake der Völker": The phrase seems to be taken from the German translation of the Baron d'Holbach, *Geschichte der menschlichen Ausartung und Verschlimmerung durch das gesellschaftliche Leben* (Altona, 1796), 2:23.

[25] Helmut Nicolai, *Die rassengesetzliche Rechtslehre: Grundzüge einer nationalsozialistischen Rechtsphilosophie*, 3rd ed. (Munich, 1934), 7–9, first published 1932.

Fox-Genovese and Eugene Genovese famously call "the mind of the master class."[26] For both Kaser and Wieacker, the task was to reconstruct the culture in which wealthy Romans of the Late Republic and Empire came to call themselves *domini*.

Kaser, the greatest of historians of Roman property law, is a man we encountered in the previous chapter. As we saw, in his interpretation of the archaic sources, Kaser took a thoughtful middle position between primitivist and modernist accounts. He steered clear of the primitivist fallacy that the archaic sources were reliable guides to the archaic socio-economic realities. Nevertheless, he did believe that the sources opened windows into the nature of "concept formation" in the early Roman legal mind. As he explained, early Roman law, though the realities could not be recovered, displayed an "undeveloped" pattern of concept formation, which turned on the ownership of *Gesinde und Vieh*, humans and animals.

The same interest in concept formation marked his account of the transformation of the law in the age of the fall of Republic, which he presented in his 1943 classic *Ownership and Possession in Early Roman Law*. This was certainly not a Nazi book, but it was a book of its time. Nazi ideology was soaked in what Fritz Stern called "the politics of cultural despair," which centered on the loss of *Gemeinschaft*, the healthy communal order in which ownership was always understood in terms of its social function.[27] What had collapsed with the fall of the Republic, in the view of Nazi commentators, were the values of a healthy Aryan community, which gave way to a cosmopolitan, anomic, "jew-ified" form of imperial *Gesellschaft*. While Kaser maintained his distance from the Nazi rulers of his young years – in particular, be it stressed, he had nothing to say about Aryans or inferior races – the problem of the demise of traditional *Gemeinschaft*, so central to the anxieties of the time and to Nazi theories of property law, shaped his writings as well.[28]

---

[26] Elizabeth Fox-Genovese and Eugene Genovese, *The Mind of the Master Class* (Cambridge, 2005).

[27] See Stern, *The Politics of Cultural Despair* (Berkeley, 1974), 56n., discussing Lagarde's anticipation of Tönnies' distinction between *Gemeinschaft* and *Gesellschaft*.

[28] Notably in a work of great importance: Kaser, *Römisches Recht als Gemeinschaftsordnung* (Tübingen, 1939). I discuss this text in Whitman, "Long Live the Hatred of Roman Law!" *Rechtsgeschichte* 2 (2003): 40–57.

His interpretation began with the history of Roman procedure. As we have seen, Kaser held that archaic procedures, with their staged battle between two warriors, determined only relative rights: They established only which of the two combatants should prevail, without excluding other possible claimants. What could explain why the Romans of the later Republic left the older, warlike, form of relative rights behind, instead embracing absolute *dominium*? The answer, Kaser argued, was to be sought partly in the growing sophistication of legal argument over possession, which he described with characteristic insight and ingenuity.[29] It was further to be sought in socio-economic change: As Republican Rome grew richer and became integrated into the monetary order of the Hellenistic world, "commercial and industrial acquisition" gained in salience in the lives of wealthy Romans, and the traditional understanding of property gave way to the absolute conception typical of a market order.[30]

But commercialization was clearly not enough by itself to settle the question. Why the term *dominus*? It was here that Kaser turned to "the mind of the [ancient Roman] master class." *Dominus*, he believed, derived from *domare*, "to tame":[31] When Romans of the dying Republic spoke themselves as *domini*, they were embracing the image of "tamers," in the first instance over living creatures, their beasts and slaves, then by extension over their households more broadly. The same language, Kaser observed, entered the Roman understanding of rulership as well: The Romans acquired the habit of calling themselves "masters," "tamers," over all their subjects, both private and imperial.[32]

---

[29] Kaser, *Eigentum und Besitz im älteren römischen Recht* (Weimar, 1943), 277–305.
[30] Ibid., 306.
[31] Kaser relied on the articles "dominus" and "domo" in his source, Alois Walde, *Lateinisches etymologisches Wörterbuch*, 3rd ed., ed. J. B. Hofmann (Heidelberg, 1938), 1:367–368. This was a forced reading of the entries in that text, which at best weakly supports his use of the etymology from *domare*. Most discussions omit *domare* from the etymology; see e.g., Michiel de Vaan, *Etymological Dictionary of Latin and Other Italic Languages* (Leiden and Boston, 2008), s.v. [177], deriving the term simply from *domus*.
[32] Kaser, *Eigentum und Besitz*, 308: "'Dominium' leitet sich von 'dominus' ab, dieses von 'domare.' Darum wird 'dominus' mit Vorliebe von der Herrschaft über Lebewesen, vor allem über Tiere und Sklaven, gebraucht und geht dann auf den gesamten Bereich des Hauses, übertragen auch auf den Staat und sein Oberhaupt, über."

And why did this arresting usage take hold when it did? "It is understandable," Kaser answered, "that precisely in the last two centuries of the Republic, during which social ties began to dissolve in a way that posed the gravest danger to the Roman community [*Gemeinwesen*], the idea of the individual as master [*der Herrengedanke des Einzelnen*] was precipitated in the life of the law."[33] Communal values crumbled, and with them crumbled the older concepts of property as embedded in social relations. Middle republican *Gemeinschaft* gave way to late republican *Gesellschaft*; and Roman owners embraced the imagery of the figure in their society least burdened by concern for others, the absolute master, the tamer, reveling in his rule over his human and animal property.[34]

Kaser's contemporary Wieacker (1908–1994), one of the finest legal minds of the twentieth century, offered his own meditation on the cultural roots of absolute ownership in 1935. Wieacker is the subject of considerable current controversy. After the War, he became a leading figure in the project of creating a post-Nazi legal scholarship, widely admired for his learning, acuity, and *humanitas*. But in the Nazi period during which he made his early career, he advanced rapidly up the academic ranks, coming to count, as Kaius Tuori writes, as one of the "young lions" of legal scholarship under the National Socialist Movement.[35]

This "young lion" made his name as an exceptionally brilliant scholar of property law, with a monograph entitled *The Transformations of the Constitution of Property*, published as a contribution to the leading series of Nazi studies in the law. Carl Schmitt was the general editor of that series, and Wieacker's study deployed the methodology advocated

---

[33] Ibid., 308.
[34] Ibid., 308–309. In his earlier 1938 version of this argument, Kaser contented himself with saying that the dependents of the *paterfamilias* were not being treated as things, but that both powers arose together. Kaser, "Der Inhalt der Patria Potestas," *Zeitschrift der Savigny-Stiftung für Rechtsgeschichte (Romanistische Abteilung)* 53 (1938): 62–87. I read *Eigentum und Besitz* as moving a small step beyond that early argument.
[35] See now Kaius Tuori, *Empire of Law: Nazi Germany, Exile Scholars, and the Battle for the Future of Europe* (Cambridge, 2020), 173–220, tracking Wieacker's movement from "young lion" of the Nazi movement to his postwar role as one of the makers of an idea of Europe founded on the legacy of Roman law, and the strong dissent on the characterization of his young years of Reinhard Zimmermann, "Hero auf dem Felsenturme," *Rechtsgeschichte* 30 (2022): 294–300.

The Dominus Enters the Law

by Schmitt: "concrete" analysis of the law.[36] "Concrete" analysis was intended as an antidote to the legal formalism of the liberal tradition. Where liberal legal thinkers made use of wholly abstract legal reasoning, divorced from the realities of life, "concrete" jurists recognized that no legal rule had any meaning outside the logic of the institutions within which it operated, be those institutions, as Schmitt explained in 1934, the "concrete order of the king or the *Führer*," or the "concrete" institution of the family in the various forms it took in human societies.[37]

Wieacker's youthful study, which swept over the entire history of property law, was, as he later wrote, composed in the midst of the effervescent excitement over the *Rechtserneuerung*, the "refounding of the law," that gripped supporters of regime after 1933; and his discussion of ancient absolute ownership embraced the "concrete" analysis of the day.[38] The law of the Roman owner, the young Wieacker argued, could only be grasped if it was seen in its concrete context; and the context in question encompassed not one institution but two: the household and the state. Roman *domini* did not merely rule in the household, or over their slaves and beasts. They also served as magistrates, engaging in the prestigious business of exercising governmental power in their city as they competed to rise through the *cursus honorum*, the hierarchy of public offices; and their proud psychology of ownership was synonymous with their proud psychology of rulership:

> The relation of masters to their things was the expression of the sense of self [*Selbstgefühl*] of the wealthy Roman nobility. The concrete basis of this lay in a legal community [*Rechtsgemeinschaft*] whose structural principles, alien [to the modern bourgeois conception], were the unconstrained *imperium* of the magistrate on the one hand, and on the other hand *dominium* as the unconstrained power enjoyed by the head of the household.[39]

---

[36] The "great enthusiasm" for "the notion of concrete order" in the period is noted by Tuori, *Empire of Law*, 15.

[37] Schmitt, *Über die drei Arten des rechtswissenschaftlichen Denkens* (Hamburg, 1934), 15, 21; and ibid., 6.

[38] Wieacker's retrospective reflection, "'Wandlungen der Eigentumsverfassung' Revisited," written at the prompting of Paolo Grossi, is reproduced in his *Zivilistische Schriften* (1934–1942), ed. Christian Wollschläger (Frankfurt a.M., 2000), 472–491.

[39] Wieacker, *Wandlungen der Eigentumsverfassung*, Der deutsche Staat der Gegenwart 13, ed. Carl Schmitt (Hamburg, 1935), 17: "Herrschaftlicher Bezug zur Sache war die

This classical Roman understanding of unconstrained power was not to be confused with the liberal conception that took hold with the French Revolution. According to "the ideas of 1789," always a target of Nazi contempt, the institution of absolute private property served a political order dedicated to liberty: By guaranteeing private owners "sole and despotic dominion," the law of liberal societies guaranteed them a form of freedom from the state. But Roman *domini* were not seeking guarantees of freedom from the state. They *were* the state. The Roman conception of absolute ownership was rooted in the *Selbstgefühl*, the haughty sense of self, of the Roman nobility, and that sense of self was shaped by a "concrete" experience of social life in which the high standing of the free man of wealth was on display in all the arenas, public and private, in which he held sway.[40]

* * *

None of these interpretations, whether Marxist or Nazi, whether founded in the history of *latifundia* or in the mind of the Roman master class, feature much or at all in the current literature on Roman law. The challenge of Marxist interpretations continues to engage one leading figure, Aldo Schiavone.[41] But the views of most contemporary scholars are the products of a reaction against all the older approaches, and in particular a reaction against Nazi doctrine.

The history of this reaction dates back to the early 1930s. Its first and most important maker was a man who counted as the preeminent scholar of Roman law in the Germany at the time of the Nazi takeover: Fritz Schulz, incumbent of the chair at the University of Berlin, apex of the German system. Schulz was a man marked out for persecution by the new regime, and for more than one reason. His mother was of Jewish descent, though she converted to Protestantism; and the same was true of his wife, the daughter of an eminent Frankfurt rabbi. Moreover, he had been politically active as an advocate for democracy after 1918. All this resulted in a hail of attacks that began

---

Ausdrucksform des Selbstgefühls der römischen besitzenden Nobilität, das konkret begründet war in einer Rechtsgemeinschaft, deren fremde Strukturprinzipien imperium als Vollrecht des Magistrats und dominium als Vollgewalt des Hausvaters sind." Also available in Wieacker, *Zivilistische Schriften*, 11–122.

[40] See generally Wieacker, *Wandlungen der Eigentumsverfassung*, 12–19.

[41] E.g., Schiavone, *The Invention of Law in the West*, trans. Jeremy Carden and Antony Shugaar (Cambridge, MA, 2012), 362–365.

The Dominus *Enters the Law* 139

in 1933 and ended only with his escape from Germany in 1939. In the face of this assault, Schulz showed himself to be a model of courage, beginning with a famous series of lectures given in Berlin, shortly after Hitler's rise to power in 1933, in which he celebrated what he called the "principles" of Roman law, principles that included "*humanitas, libertas* and *fides* – the epitome," as Wolfgang Ernst observes, "of all the Nazis were about to do away with."[42] Published a year later, Schulz's book, while it refrained from explicitly attacking the Nazis, set the tone for post-Nazi scholarship as it would be practiced throughout the postwar years, becoming, as Ernst writes, "a classic of reasoned veneration of Roman law all over the world."[43]

Nor was it just that Schulz defended liberal and humane values in the face of Nazi dictatorship. His lectures also presented a thesis about the nature of Roman law whose implicit anti-Nazism is emphasized by Renato Sedano Ofri. This was the "isolation" thesis: the argument that "the economic and political circumstances which determined the formation of a given legal rule were ... excluded from juridical consideration."[44] The isolation thesis carried the crucial implication that the law could not be explained reductively as the product of social pressures, political or otherwise – not by Nazi "concrete" thinkers, nor, for that matter, by Marxists.[45] As for the charges laid by both Communists and Fascists against "the Roman concept of property": "they should fall silent once and for all."[46] The Romans never offered

---

[42] Ernst, "Fritz Schulz (1879–1957)," in Jack Beatson and Reinhard Zimmermann, eds., *Jurists Uprooted: German-Speaking Émigré Lawyers in Twentieth-Century Britain* (Oxford, 2004), 123 [105–203].
[43] Ibid., 126.
[44] Sedano Onofri, "Roman Law as Pamphlet: Fritz Schulz and the *Prinzipien des römischen Rechts* between Cesar [sic] and Hitler," História do direito 3 (2022): 21 [3–36].
[45] Schulz, *Prinzipien des römischen Rechts* (Munich, 1934), 13–26. It is important to observe that Schulz's argument was not entirely unrelated to the "concrete" analysis of the day. Indeed, in one crucial passage, Schulz spoke in terms that sound drawn directly from Schmitt: ibid., 104: "Nicht der römische Eigentums*begriff* ist individualistisch gestaltet, sondern die römische Eigentums*rechtsordnung*." For a current statement of Schulz's point, see Éva Jakab, "Property Rights in Ancient Rome," in Paul Erdkamp, Koenraad Verboven, and Arjan Zuiderhoek, eds., *Ownership and Exploitation of Land and Natural Resources in the Roman World* (Oxford, 2015), 107–131.
[46] Schulz, *Prinzipien des römischen Rechts*, 102–103.

any definition of property at all, observed Schulz, any more than they offered definitions of any other legal concept; and in practice real property rights, far from being absolute, were always limited in multiple ways.

Schulz provided what remains the most influential counternarrative to that of the Nazis, but it is important to take note of another as well. This came from the teacher of Wieacker, Fritz Pringsheim. Pringsheim, a Jew, escaped and found a refuge at Oxford, where, in early September of 1942, a few weeks into the Battle of Stalingrad, he delivered a statement of faith in "the unique character of classical Roman law" which has become a classic in the field. Like Schulz, Pringsheim did not deign to mention Nazi doctrine expressly; he simply articulated an alternative. But his alternative was different from Schulz's. Pringsheim did not argue that absolute ownership was in fact not to be found in classical law. Instead, he praised it, in the face of Nazi attacks, as the foremost fruit of high Roman reasoning, the product of a golden classical age in which "jurisprudence attracted the best brains."[47] Before the classical Roman jurists put their minds to the problem, he told his Oxford audience, undoubtedly made up in large part of refugees like himself, no one had grasped what was quite simply the scientific truth at the foundation of property law: the truth that ownership must be absolute, individual, and exclusive.[48]

* * *

The Nazis, let us give eternal thanks, were defeated; and postwar scholars have generally followed on the path laid out by Schulz and Pringsheim, the path of "reasoned veneration," in one way or another presenting classical Roman law as the work of "the best brains" of ancient law, who developed juristic concepts in "isolation," and not susceptible to explanation by reference to the political and social conflicts of the fall of the Republic. The old tradition received its last sustained discussion in 1970, from the Hungarian scholar György

---

[47] By "foremost fruit," I mean the first one that he mentioned in the lecture. For an examination of his larger views on "the superiority of classical Roman law," see Tony Honoré, "Fritz Pringsheim (1882–1967)," in Jack Beatson and Reinhard Zimmermann, eds., *Jurists Uprooted: German-Speaking Émigré Lawyers in Twentieth-Century Britain* (Oxford, 2004), 215–217 [205–232].

[48] Pringsheim, "The Unique Character of Roman Law," *Journal of Roman Studies* 34 (1944): 60–64.

The Dominus *Enters the Law* 141

Diósdi, who did a superb job of combining the older theories with a close reading of the legal sources. It was "the gradual passing of the *ager publicus* into private hands," Diósdi concluded, embracing what had been the view of Marx and so many others, alongside a variety of other developments in an increasingly complex Roman economy, that yielded the new analytic language.[49]

Since Diósdi, though, efforts to situate the transformation of classical law in social and political history, in the way that the older literature did, have almost entirely ended. One important exception is Bruce Frier, the leading American figure in the field. In his 1985 *Rise of the Roman Jurists*, Frier offered an explanation of the transformation of Roman law that was in tune with modern studies in law and society. The Romans of the Late Republic, he argued, faced a rapidly rising flood of litigation, which resulted from the general extension of citizenship throughout Italy in the wake of the Social War of 91–87 BCE. The result was that a new class of wealthy litigants came on the scene, alongside a broader "large and heterogeneous class of the more or less upwardly mobile." The result of this changing social reality was an increase in the sheer volume of business, which encouraged the development of a more abstract and generally applicable law. "A huge surge of commerce ... followed in the wake of Rome's expanding empire; the upper classes of Italy had enjoyed a general rise in their personal wealth, derived from this commerce and from other opportunities imperialism had created."[50] The law was transformed in consequence: In the earlier Republic, reflection on the law had been the province, or perhaps the pastime, of the high patrician nobility, who were expected to protect their clients in disputes. In the Late Republic, by contrast, "there emerged a group of legal professionals, the jurists."[51]

Even Frier's fine interpretation seems to have little resonance in most of the current literature, though. For the most part, the texts you will find on the library shelf point to the influence of Greek

---

[49] György Diósdi, *Ownership in Ancient and Pre-Classical Roman Law* (Budapest, 1970), 136.
[50] Frier, *Rise of the Roman Jurists*, 280. Political instability, too, Frier adds, created an incentive to hive off a "private," rule-bound sphere, untouched by political upheaval. Ibid., 281–282.
[51] Ibid., 272.

philosophy, whose impact on the law is undeniable.[52] In 1946, Schulz highlighted the Greek philosophical practice of making distinctions, *diaireses*, and argued that this was the philosophical source of the Roman juristic practice of making *distinctiones*.[53] Many later writers took up that claim. What happened, specialists argued, is that the Romans, who had formerly managed their law through the rough and ready expedients of men untouched by Greek sophistication, came to recognize "the necessity to make distinctions" that followed from the logic of property itself;[54] ascending to a new plane of juristic comprehension, they grasped the need for "the work of classification that was the task of the jurists."[55] What happened was that Roman law, as Hans Julius Wolff declared in Oklahoma in 1951, began to attain its "elaborate perfection in the hands of skilled specialists."[56] The contemporary scholars who speak in such terms have nothing to say about the entry of the term *dominus* into the legal vocabulary.

* * *

It is impossible not to sympathize with the modern reaction against the old ideologies. Most especially, it is impossible not to sympathize with Schulz and Pringsheim, both voices of sanity in times of horror. It would be absurd to deny the influence of Greek philosophy, or to ignore the commercial pressures toward juridification that are identified by both Kaser and Frier. But it is equally impossible not to worry that something was lost when the old interpretations, from Marx to Wieacker, were discarded. Is there no way to salvage any wisdom from the older scholarship? I want to suggest that there is, and that it is to be found by returning to the abandoned problem of the entry of the *dominus* into the law.

Why, asked Engels, Kaser, and Wieacker, *dominus*? As we hunt for an answer, I think that we must begin by widening the horizons of the discussion beyond the limits of the law itself. The entry of the *dominus*

---

[52] E.g., with extensive citations, Andreas Groten, *Corpus und Universitas. Römisches Körperschafts- und Gesellschaftsrecht: zwischen griechischer Philosophie und römischer Politik* (Tübingen, 2015), 31–34.
[53] Schulz, *The History of Roman Legal Science* (Oxford, 1946), 62–68.
[54] Giovanni Pugliese, "'Res corporales,' 'res incorporales,'" in *Studi in onore di Vincenzo Arangio Ruiz* (Naples, n.d.), 241 [223–260].
[55] Michèle Ducos, "Juristes romains," 121.
[56] Wolff, *Roman Law: An Historical Introduction* (Norman, OK, 1951), 5.

into the law was paralleled by the entry of the same term in other domains as well, both in everyday Latin discourse and in the ideology of imperial rule. All these shifts must be interpreted together; the transformation of the law of ownership must be seen, not in "isolation," but in the context of much more extensive sociocultural change, all involving the same figure of the *dominus*, the "master."

The term *dominus* is derived from an Indo-European root meaning "household" (the Latin *domus*). Some scholars, like Kaser, link it etymologically with *domare*, "to tame."[57] It appeared regularly in later republican authors in the sense of "master" or "lord";[58] and it had a history of use in that sense in earlier periods as well. It was, as all students of Latin know, the commonplace term for "master," with regard to both humans and animals. Alongside its meaning of "master" or "lord," *dominus* carried another intriguing sense, to which I will return: "giver of a feast."[59] Its derivative form *dominium* is given three meanings in the Oxford Latin Dictionary: first "rule"; second "feast or banquet"; and only third "ownership."[60]

The introduction of this word for ruling, feasting, and owning into the language of property law is not entirely easy to date. As early as Plautus, around 200 BCE, *dominus* was used in the sense of "owner."[61] But in the legal sources it is not to be found until much later. The first

---

[57] This is the etymology given in Lewis and Short, s.v. "dominus": "dŏmĭnus ... Sanscr. *damanas*, he who subdues, root dam-; Gr. δαμάω, δάμνημι, v. domo ... one who has subdued or conquered." It is not standard in the literature, which distinguishes between two Indo-European roots, deme-¹, "House, household," and deme-², "To constrain, force especially to break in." Calvert Watkins, *American Heritage Dictionary of Indo-European Roots* (Boston, 1985), 11. See, e.g., Alfred Ernout and Alfred Meillet, *Dictionnaire étymologique de la langue latine* (Paris, 2001), s.v. "dominus" [183]; Michiel de Vaan, *Etymological Dictionary of Latin and Other Italic Languages* (Leiden and Boston, 2008), s.v. "dominus" [177].

[58] Alongside *erus*. For discussion of the two terms, see Luigi Capogrossi Colognesi, *Proprietà e signoria in Roma antica*, 2nd ed. (Rome, 1994), 257–287. As Jhering notes, *erus*, related to the Greek χείρ-, is another term derived from the concept of the seizure by hand. Rudolf von Jhering, *Der Geist des römischen Rechts auf den verschiedenen Stufen seiner Entwicklung*, 5th ed. (Leipzig, 1891), 1:110.

[59] See *Oxford Latin Dictionary* (Oxford, 1982), s.v. "dominus," 2b.

[60] Ibid., s.v. "dominium."

[61] Pl. *Rud.* 956–959, in Wolfgang de Melo, ed. and trans., *Plautus: The Little Carthaginian; Pseudolus; The Rope*, Loeb Classical Library 260 (Cambridge, MA, 2012), 502–503. *Rudens* is a play often treated as a study in the law of property. On these lines in legal context, Luigi Pellecchi, *Per una lettura giuridica della Rudens di Plauto* (Parma, 2012), 42–43. See further now Thomas A. J. McGinn, "The Sea Common to All in Plautus,

possible appearance of the new terminology in a strictly legal context was in the text of a *lex agraria* (a law governing rights in the *ager publicus*) dating to 111 BCE, in the midst of the early crisis of the Republic, of which only bronze fragments survive. There is a lacuna in the text, where a tablet cracked. The resulting gap contained a word, now lost, which the great scholar Theodor Mommsen conjectured must have been a form of *dominus*. If Mommsen was right, this was the first documented occurrence of the term in a property-law context.[62]

The appearance of *dominus* in this late second-century BCE *lex agraria*, if that was indeed the missing word, is uncertain evidence; the next attested use of the term in the law dates nearly a century later.[63] Nevertheless, legal historians accept Mommsen's contention that *dominus* established itself in the law over the course of the late second and first centuries BCE, and it is worth citing a neglected piece of evidence that supports that dating, and that may do something

---

Rudens: Social Norms and Legal Rules," in Ioannis Ziogas and Erica Bexley, eds., *Roman Law and Latin Literature* (London, 2022), 169–188.

[62] Mommsen's conjecture is frequently cited as a securely established instance, e.g., Ernout and Meillet, *Dictionnaire étymologique*, s.v., and e.g., in the current literature, Georgy Kantor, "Property in Land in Roman Provinces," in Kantor, Tom Lambert, and Hannah Skoda, eds., *Legalism: Property and Ownership* (Oxford, 2017), 55–74. The conjecture is accepted by Michael Crawford, *Roman Statutes* (London, 1996), 1:116; Andrew Lintott, *Judicial Reform and Land Reform in the Roman Republic: A New Edition, with Translation and Commentary, of the Laws from Urbino* (Cambridge, 1992), 184 (Lex Agraria 27); Simone Sisani, *L'ager publicus in età graccana* (Rome, 2015), 52; Kirsten Johannsen, "Die lex agraria des Jahres 111 v. Chr.," diss. Munich, 1971, 124. The defective passage reads "COMMVTAV[- - -]MNEIS PRIVATVS ITA VTEI QVOI OPTVMA lege PRIVATVS EST ESTO." Rudorff reconstructed it as "COMMVTAV[it is ager locus o]MNEIS PRIVATVS." A. A. F. Rudorff, "Das Ackergesetz des Spurius Thorius," *Zeitschrift für geschichtliche Rechtswissenschaft* 10 (1839): 157 [1–194]. Mommsen dissented on the grounds that the second syllable of *omnis* must be short, and so proposed "[it is ager locus do]." Mommsen, "Lex agraria," in *Juristische Schriften* (Berlin, 1905), 114 [65–147]. It is worth emphasizing that the *lex agraria* long predates the next attested use of *dominus* in the law. Can we be certain that Mommsen had it right? For a thoughtful discussion of the extent to which this passage in fact expresses an idea of *dominium ex iure quiritium* see Osvaldo Sacchi, *Regime della terra e imposizione fondiaria nell'età dei Gracchi* (Naples, 2006), 346–366.

[63] First appearance in *Digest*: D. 8.3.30. Paul. 4 epit. Alfeni dig.: *quaesitum est, utrum dominium loci ad eum pertineat*. To the extent we understood Alfenus as simply a continuator of the work of Servius Sulpicius Rufus, the usage of the term could be pushed back earlier in the century. But see the doubts expressed by Hans-Jörg Roth, *Alfeni Digesta: eine spätrepublikanische Juristenschrift* (Berlin, 1999), 23–25.

to suggest the context of the new terminology in the social and political conflicts of the time. This is the "Prophecy of Vegoia," an Etruscan text that pronounces an imprecation against those who dare to move sacred boundary stones. This text, which was included in ancient collections of writings by the *gromatici*, the "land-surveyors," describes a supposed archaic prophecy, given by the legendary Etruscan nymph Vegoia:

(Prophecy) of Vegoia, to Arruns Veltymnus: "Know that the sea was separated from the sky. But when Jupiter claimed the land of Aetruria for himself, he established and ordered that the fields be measured and the croplands delimited. Knowing the greed of men and their lust for land, he wanted everything proper concerning boundaries. And at some time, around the end of the eighth saeculum [i.e. in the first century BCE], someone will violate them on account of greed by means of evil trickery and will touch them and move them [...]. But whoever shall have touched and moved them, increasing his own property and diminishing that of another, on account of this crime he will be damned by the gods. If slaves should do it, there will be a change for the worse in status. But if the deed is done with the master's consent, very quickly the master will be uprooted and all of his family will perish. [*Si servi faciant, dominio mutabuntur in deterius. Sed si conscientia dominica fiet, caelerius dominus extirpabitur, gensque eius omnis interiet.*] The ones who move [the boundary stones] will be afflicted by the worst diseases and wounds, and they will feel a weakness in their limbs. Then also the earth will be moved by storms and whirl winds with frequent destruction, crops often will be injured and will be knocked down by rain and hail, they will perish in the summer heat, they will be felled by mildew. There will be much dissension among people. Know that these things will be done when such crimes are committed. Wherefore be not false or double tongued. Keep this teaching in your heart."[64]

Scholars use this wild-eyed source as evidence for Etruscan social and religious history, not for the history of Roman property law.[65]

---

[64] Original and translation in Jean MacIntosh Turfa, *Divining the Etruscan World: The Brontoscopic Calendar and Religious Practice* (Cambridge, 2012), 317. On Vegoia see also Jean-René Jannot, *Religion in Ancient Etruria*, trans. Jane Whitehead (Madison, WI, 2005), 11–13.

[65] Santo Mazzarino argues that the *domini* in question belonged to a peculiarly Etruscan social ordering. Mazzarino, "Sociologia del mondo etrusco e problemi della tarda etruscità," *Historia* 6 (1957): 112–114 [98–122]. I am not equipped to judge this interpretation. The text is commonly thought to have been translated from an Etruscan original. That may be so, but the fact would remain that the translator or author chose *dominus* as his Latin equivalent. For a bathetically less dramatic interpretation, reading the Prophecy as a discussion of plowing accidents, see

Indeed Mommsen condemned the very inclusion of the Prophecy in the same collection with more sober legal texts on land-surveying as the work of a "shameless" late antique compiler.[66] Nevertheless, Nancy Thomson de Grummond argues that it can be "convincingly related" to the fact that "the Etruscans were being overrun by the Romans and a prophecy on boundaries might seem especially pertinent";[67] and other scholars too see the context of the prophecy in early first-century conflicts over land distribution.[68]

If Thomson de Grummond is right, the Prophecy of Vegoia too is an attestation of the term *dominus* in the first century BCE, and one that suggests a context in large-scale conflicts over land, featuring aggressive and self-aggrandizing *domini*, and in the cultic importance of boundary stones as well. (Whether it was a piece of shamelessness to include it in the corpus of the *gromatici* is a question on which I express no view.)

But property law, meanwhile, was not the only realm in which *dominus* came to the fore during the fall of the Republic and rise of the Principate. Over the same period, the same language took hold in other corners of Roman life as well. To begin with, *dominus* established itself in Roman social interactions as a routine form of respectful address. Eleanor Dickey, who has studied this development extensively, recounts the shift, though without reference to the contemporaneous parallels in the law:

> While the word *dominus* (meaning "householder," "owner" or "master") is common from an earlier period, the custom of using *domine* and *domina* as addresses seems to have arisen only in the latter part of the first century B.C. . . . by the middle of the first century A.D. . . . *domine* was such a common form of address that Seneca mentions it as a standard way of greeting people whose names one has forgotten (*Ep.* 3.1) . . .[69]

Louise Adams Holland, "Qui terminus exarasset," *American Journal of Archeology* 31 (1933): 551 [549–553].

[66] Mommsen, "Die Interpolationen des gromatischen Corpus," in *Gesammelte Schriften* (Berlin, 1909) 7:475 [464–482]: "Unverschämtheit."

[67] Thomson de Grummond, "Prophets and Priests," in Thomson de Grummond and Erika Simon, eds., *The Religion of the Etruscans* (Austin, TX, 2006), 31 [27–44].

[68] Alfredo Valvo, *La "Profezia di Vegoia": proprietà fondiaria e aruspicina nel primo secolo a.C.* (Rome, 1988), 103–104.

[69] Eleanor Dickey, "KYPIE, ΔΕΣΠΟΤΑ, DOMINE: Greek Politeness in the Roman Empire," *Journal of Hellenic Studies* 121 (2001): 2 [1–11]. The same term holds on

The Dominus Enters the Law

As a matter of everyday *politesse*, people in this period began to refer to each other as "master." That sort of master/slave language, with its show of ceremonious deference,[70] has appeared in other societies as well: The new *politesse* of the Late Republic and Principate recalls the practice by which medieval Venetians called themselves *schiavo*, "your slave," the term that has since decayed into *ciao*; similarly, *servus*, "your slave," is still used in some German-speaking areas. There is good reason, as Dickey notes, to think that this linguistic shift to a master/slave discourse of *politesse* carried a political charge. Augustus, eager to maintain republican forms, was, Suetonius reports, hostile to the new language of the "master":

> He always abhorred the title of *dominus*, as ill-omened and offensive. And when, in a play, performed at the theatre, at which he was present, these words were introduced, "O just and gracious *dominus*," and the whole company, with joyful acclamations, testified their approbation of them, as applied to him, he instantly put a stop to their indecent flattery, by waving his hand, and frowning sternly, and next day publicly declared his displeasure, in a proclamation. He never afterwards would suffer himself to be addressed in that manner, even by his own children or grandchildren, either in jest or earnest, and forbad them the use of all such complimentary expressions to one another.[71]

The same point was emphasized by Mommsen, in his monumental history of Roman constitutional thinking, *Roman Public Law*: The use of *dominus*, he argued, was in tension with the values of the Republic that Augustus placed at the foundation of his ideology of rule.[72] This demonstrative imperial rejection of the newly fashionable language of deference is the source of the practice of calling the early Empire the

---

vestigially in our own "mister," though we have lost any sense of its original significance.

[70] Cf. Theodor Mommsen, *Römisches Staatsrecht* (Leipzig, 1871–1888), 2.2:737, "als Zeichen zuvorkommender Unterwürfigkeit."

[71] Suet. *Aug.* 53.1, in J. C. Rolfe, trans., *Suetonius: Lives of the Caesars, Vol. I: Julius; Augustus; Tiberius; Gaius Caligula*, Loeb Classical Library 31 (Cambridge, MA, 1914), 230–233.

[72] Tiberius reiterated the refusal to accept address as *dominus*, and the Augustan rule endured throughout the classical period as a matter of court ceremonial, though Caligula and Domitian laid claim to the title *dominus et deus* in the first century. E.g., Andreas Alföldi, "Die Ausgestaltung des monarchischen Zeremoniells," in *Mitteilungen des Deutschen archäologischen Instituts, römische Abteilung* 49 (1934): 45–46 [3–118]. Fuller discussion below, Chapter 8.

"Principate," the monarchy of the *princeps*, the "first citizen," not the *dominus*, while the acceptance of the same term of address for the Emperor leads scholars to call the later Empire the "Dominate," a development to whose significance I will return in Chapter 8.

The political and ideological significance of the term is suggested by another development as well: Over the same period, the same language also rose to prominence in the ideology of imperial rule, which showed a drift of its own toward the master/slave "idiom of power." Kaser noted that the language of the *dominus* entered Roman characterizations of their rule just as it did in their private law; and Roman historians point to the same change. Ari Z. Bryen describes the transition:

While sources from the Republican era betray a tension between various ways of describing the precise status of members of the imperial order – as clients, allies, or slaves – in the Principate the language of slavery is used by Roman writers with far greater ease.[73]

Myles Lavan writes with particular power about the newly emerging ideology of Roman rule in his book *Slaves to Rome*:

The conquest of foreign peoples is often described in terms of breaking animals to harness. The verbs *domare* [to tame], *perdomare* [to tame thoroughly], *subigere* [to force into submission], *frangere* [to break] and *coercere* [to coerce] – all regularly used of taming animals – are widespread in accounts of Roman expansion ... The link is particularly strong in the case of the imagery of the *iugum* [yoke]. The yoke that was forced on the necks of draught animals to attach them to plough or vehicle was a potent symbol of slavery.

"[T]he Roman people," he continues, "is styled the 'conqueror' (*uictor*), 'master' (*dominus*) or 'ruler' (*princeps, imperator* etc.) 'of the peoples' (*gentium*) or 'of all peoples' (*omnium gentium*). These and similar references to the *gentes* represent the empire as a composite of different peoples, united in their subjection to the *populus Romanus*, or *gens Romana*."[74] While the title *dominus* was banned in addressing the Emperor as a matter of domestic rule, the Roman people, in its guise as a community of conquerors, was described as a people of

---

[73] Bryen, "Histories of Violence: Notes from the Roman Empire," in Roderick Campbell, ed., *Violence and Civilization: Studies of Social Violence in History and Prehistory* (Oxford and Oakville, 2014), 137 [125–151].

[74] Myles Lavan, *Slaves to Rome: Paradigms of Empire in Roman Culture* (Cambridge, 2013), 83.

masters, taming and yoking nations just as in the archaic law of *res mancipi* and *occupatio* they tamed and yoked beasts. I will return to this topic in Chapter 5.

The historians who describe these changes in Roman imperial ideology do not note the parallel changes in Roman property law. Indeed, the history of the transformation of Roman property terminology seems to have been almost entirely forgotten among contemporary Roman historians, just as it has been almost entirely forgotten by specialists in Roman law.[75] But their studies suggest that some common shift was at work in the new property law of the *dominus* and changing ideologies of state power during the same transition from republic to monarchy. "Sovereignty and property," Martti Koskenniemi's "yin and yang of power,"[76] entered into some sort of common embrace of the language of *dominus*.

*　*　*

What can account for this shift, which brought the charged hierarchical language of the *dominus* to the juristic analysis of the law, the culture of everyday *politesse*, and the ideology of imperial rule, while banning it from the ceremonial of the Augustan Court? I believe that there is an answer to be found in the work of Roman social historians, especially historians of the family. It is not an answer that neatly bears out the arguments of Marx or Engels, with their focus on the economic structures of exploitation. Instead it is an answer that takes us back to the meditations on the mind of the master class of Kaser and Wieacker; to the "concrete" context of the law of which Wieacker spoke; and to the social sources of Patterson's "idiom of power."

The answer has to do with the transition from one Roman conception of the household, the *familia*, to another, the *domus*. In a well-known 1984 study, Richard Saller showed that *familia* went

---

[75] The literature seems to embody only a fading memory of the debate. See its brief, though thoughtful, mention in Kantor, "Property in Land in Roman Provinces," 56 (discussing Gérard Chouquer, *La terre dans le monde Romain: anthropologie, droit, géographie* (Paris, 2010), 142); and in Ducos, "Les juristes romains," 121, citing (incorrectly) Liv. 45.13.15 as an early instance. While these learned authors flag the importance of the use of *dominium*, none addresses the full amplitude of the older literature.

[76] Koskenniemi, *To the Uttermost Parts of the Earth: Legal Imagination and International Power, 1300–1870* (Cambridge, 2021), 959.

into decline during the transition from the Republic to the Principate, giving way to *domus*. It was Saller's contention that this shift took place because *familia* was associated with the great agnatic lineages that had dominated republican politics, but that lost their political grip in the new regime. The transition to the Principate was also the transition to a newly constituted dominant class of the wealthy, as former outsiders crowded in alongside the old nobility. Like Marx, Saller spoke of an eclipse of an older Republican ruling order:

> Tacitus[] associated *familia* in the sense of lineage mainly with Republican noble families and the imperial house. Such noble families were increasingly rare as the turnover in senatorial families continued at a very rapid pace. Consequently most senators of the empire could not boast a long, illustrious agnatic lineage, nor was there the same need for a great *nomen* [noble family name] since its recognition in the assemblies was no longer of consequence.[77]

Saller did not consider the transformation of Roman property terminology – here again, the rise of the *dominus* in the law seems to have been forgotten by Roman historians – but his argument has a clear bearing on the legal history of this transformative period. Early Roman property law, as we have seen, was thoroughly bound up with the *familia* and its *paterfamilias*. By contrast, the term *dominus* was associated with the term *domus*.[78] A hypothesis suggests itself naturally: The new prominence of the *dominus* in property law, as in other realms of Roman social life, had something to do with the decline of the old noble families that had vested power over the *familia* in the venerable Republican *paterfamilias*, now giving way to a differently composed Roman ruling class that prided itself on its mastery over a differently defined *domus*.

Saller's article has been followed by much subsequent scholarship. Rolf Rilinger offered a stimulating expansion on his interpretation in 1997. The shift from *familia* to *domus*, Rilinger observed, can be documented through archeology; and as Saller suggested, it can be linked to shifts in the practice of power that accompanied the fall of

---

[77] Saller, "'Familia, Domus', and the Roman Conception of the Family," *Phoenix* 38 (1984): 348–349 [336–355].

[78] Cic. *Off.* 1.139: *nec domo dominus, sed domino domus honestanda est*, in Walter Miller, trans., *Cicero: On Duties*, Loeb Classical Library 30 (Cambridge, MA, 1913), 140–141.

the Republic. The *familia* of the Middle Republic was understood primarily to include agnatic kin and slaves, and archeologists have shown that this *familia* was housed in comparatively modest dwellings that presupposed that household structure. The *patresfamiliarum* who ruled over those comparatively modest establishments participated in the practice of Roman power, belonging to the ruling oligarchy of the conquering Republic.

But from the period of the crisis of the Republic onward, this older ruling order lost its direct access to state power. It was during this period of diminishing participation in the state, Rilinger argued, that the *familia* was displaced by the *domus*. The mastery over this *domus* was now understood to imply power over a wider range of persons: It included not merely agnatic kin and slaves, but also cognatic kin (those related through the female line), and also clients and other dependents and supplicants unrelated to the master of the house. The dwelling place of the master of the *domus* now became something more like a quasi-princely court, in which the aristocrats of the late republican and imperial periods, though they no longer enjoyed the political power they had enjoyed in the Middle Republic, ruled over their own substate domains, populated by their own dependents. Correspondingly, the physical form of the *domus* assumed a much grander scale, now designed as a place for aristocrats to hold court. The creation of such palatial houses had not been permitted in the Middle Republic. But by the end of the first century BCE, the period when *dominus* took hold in Roman law and life, they became the new norm.[79]

Rilinger is not alone in focusing on the splendor of imperial *domus*, and their use as theaters for the exercise of power. Andrew Wallace-Hadrill showed in 1989 how this dwelling was the setting for relations between the *dominus* and one important class of dependents in particular, his clients. The *dominus*, "giver of feasts," would periodically feed clients, while the *domus* was designed, architecturally, for the reception of their petitions and pleas for patronage.[80] Kate Cooper offers an especially

---

[79] Rilinger, "*Domus* und *res publica*: die politisch-soziale Bedeutung des aristokratischen 'Hauses' in der späten Römischen Republik," *Historische Zeitschrift: Beihefte* 23 (1997): 73–90.

[80] Wallace-Hadrill, "Patronage in Roman Society," in Wallace-Hadrill, ed., *Patronage in Ancient Society* (London, 1989), 63–87.

powerful account of the culture of this *domus*, focusing on the mentality of the *dominus* who ruled over it:

> The private establishment of a *dominus* involved many elements that were crucial to his ability to attain high standing among his peers, leading in the best of circumstances to public office. Foremost, it was critical to have at his disposal a physical space, the *domus*, appointed in a way that would impress his peers and show himself and his family to advantage. *Domus* referred in Latin both to a physical building and to the cluster of people, paradigmatically but not exclusively kin, who lived there, and ... in an ideal world the *dominus* was possessed of the right sort of dependents, both slaves and children, to go along with the house. Understood as an extension of the *domus* itself were also whatever holdings a man had at his disposal, ideally including rural estates and other money-making enterprises such as brick-works, mines and quarries...[81]

The power of this *dominus* certainly bore a kinship to the power of the republican *paterfamilias*, who also ruled over a "cluster of people," and whose name also incorporated a slave concept, *famulus*. In that sense the *dominus* can be viewed as a sort of juridical evolutionary descendant of the *paterfamilias*. But the *domus*, so much grander than the dwelling places of the older *familia*, was the site of a grander style of the exercise of power. This was the setting in which, as David Hume wrote, "every man of rank was rendered a petty tyrant ... amidst the flattery, submission, and low debasement of his slaves";[82] these were the "posh high-class houses of the Roman aristocracy," which, Max Weber wrote, "consumed slaves in massive quantities."[83] The possession of such a *domus*, Cooper emphasizes, was, moreover, not just a matter of the exercise of "petty tyranny" within the household. It was also essential for the making of a prestigious career as a magistrate, whose attractions were emphasized by Wieacker in 1935:

> The urban house ... was designed to enhance the *auctoritas* of the head of household as he presided over a variety of functions. This meant that

---

[81] Cooper, "Closely Watched Households: Visibility, Exposure and Private Power in the Roman 'Domus,'" *Past & Present* 197 (2007): 5 [3–33]. For a vivid discussion of the *domus* within the larger crowded cityscape of Rome, see Andrew Wallace-Hadrill, "*Domus* and *Insulae* in Rome: Families and Households," in David L. Balch and Carolyn Osiek, eds., *Early Christian Families in Context* (Grand Rapids, 2003), 3–18.

[82] Hume, "Of the Populousness of Ancient Nations," in Hume, *Political Discourses*, 2nd ed. (Edinburgh, 1752), 161–62 [155–262].

[83] Weber, *Wirtschaft und Gesellschaft*, ed. Johannes Winckelmann, 5th ed. (Tübingen, 1985), 798.

possession of the right premises could assist the public man in his rise through the *cursus honorum*. To possess [the accoutrements of the grand *domus*] was a sign not only of the wealth needed to build them, but a self-fulfilling prophecy of the social standing which would make them necessary.[84]

Power public and private, for Cooper as for Wieacker, went hand in hand.

This is literature that cries out for a place in our scholarship on Roman law. The entry of the *dominus* into the law, as in other realms of Roman life, coincided with the displacement of the *familia* by the *domus* identified by Saller, and the emergence of the palatial dwellings so vividly described by Cooper. The image of the *dominus* that Cooper evokes must surely have hovered somewhere in the background imagination when jurists used the term, just as it would have hovered in the background imagination for everybody else.

There is of course no way to reconstruct the mental world of the ancients with any certainty; these are problems that can only be approached essayistically; but both Roman literature and Roman law give us material for reflection. Seneca, in a passage often quoted by historians of Roman slavery, describes a change in mentality that accompanied the change in terminology and household structure. Railing at the behavior of Roman masters, he draws a contrast between the attitudes of a *dominus* and those of a *paterfamilias*:

You are indignant that a slave answered back to you, and a freedman too, and your wife and a client. Then you turn around and complain that the free speech you've destroyed at home has been torn from the commonwealth. Or conversely if a slave you've questioned was silent you call it defiance. Let him speak and be silent – and laugh too! "In the presence of his *dominus*?" you ask. Nay, you should be saying in the presence of a *paterfamilias*. Why shout? Why raise a ruckus? Why go for the whip in the middle of dinner, because slaves are talking, because you don't have in one and the same place a crowd the size of an assembly and silence worthy of a wilderness.[85]

---

[84] Cooper, "Closely Watched Households," 13.

[85] Sen. *Ira* 3.35.1–2: "*Coram domino?*" inquis. *Immo coram patre familiae*, in "On Anger," trans. Robert Kaster, in Kaster and Martha C. Nussbaum, trans., *Seneca: Anger; Mercy; Revenge* (Chicago, 2010), 90 [28–157]. I have altered the translation so that both terms appear in the original. I have also used "Nay you should be saying" in order to give the sense of *immo*, used here in the sense of "nay, I should rather say." Lewis and Short, *Latin Dictionary*, s.v. II.

What Seneca describes, in this contrast between the fulminating *dominus* and what Robert Kaster calls the "normatively benevolent" *paterfamilias*,[86] is not unrelated to Marx's account of the breakdown of a "more or less patriarchal" culture. But most of all it brings to mind the writings of Kaser and Wieacker. The arrogant *dominus* of Seneca is the "tamer" of Kaser, loosed from the social ties of middle republican *Gemeinschaft*. The "concrete" context of domination – so Wieacker might have interpreted Seneca – shifted from *familia* to *domus*, and with it shifted the mentality of Roman household masters.

Alongside Seneca, we can consider another passage contrasting the *dominus* with the *paterfamilias*, this one from the great jurist Ulpian, working at the end of the classical period, some three centuries after *dominus* first intruded into the law. In a fragment dedicated to the definition of the household, Ulpian first provided a careful technical account of *familia*, including the blood relations of parents, children, and grandchildren. He then turned to the imperial society in which he in fact lived, and in which the older *familia* had long since given way to the *domus*. When the law spoke of a *paterfamilias*, did its rules also apply to a *dominus*? "Whoever has rule over the *domus* [*qui in domo dominium habet*]," Ulpian responded, "is called a 'paterfamilias,' and he is correctly called by that name, even if he has no son; for our task is not just to give an account of his person, but also of the law."[87] There were "persons" in Ulpian's Rome who did not fit within the understanding of the world presumed by the ancient law of the Republic. These persons had to be accommodated within a "legal definition," even though that definition, as Saller writes of Ulpian's passage, was one whose language "was essentially archaic."[88] The Ulpian who undertook this labor was not working in isolation from the "economic and political circumstances" of his world. He understood it to be his task to retailor the law, so that it could clothe a powerful figure who had not existed at the time of its origin.

---

[86] Kaster, "On Anger," commenting at 127: "The head of the Roman household was both the formidable *dominus* ('master') ... and the normatively benevolent *paterfamilias*."

[87] D. 50.16.195.2. Ulpianus 46 *ad ed.*: *Pater autem familias appellatur, qui in domo dominium habet, recteque hoc nomine appellatur, quamvis filium non habeat: non enim solam personam eius, sed et ius demonstramus.*

[88] Saller, "Familia, Domus," 338.

The men who "ruled over the *domus*" were men who had outgrown the traditions of the law, and according to Seneca (and Marx) the traditions of the morality, of the Republic. When the jurists spoke of *domini* these are the men of whom they spoke. This does not, let me rush to say, provide an adequate explanation for the transformation of Roman property law, with its spectacular flight into abstract reasoning and the complexities of its doctrine of ownership. The influence of Greek philosophy was palpably at work as well; and so, surely, was the commercialization analyzed by Kaser and Frier. The links between Roman *domini* and Roman property law belong to the history of legal culture, not to the specifics of Roman legal reasoning, and there is no gainsaying the truth that the legal culture of a remote Roman past is difficult to recover.

Nevertheless, the study of legal culture, difficult though it may be, is also a part of the study of legal history. The classical law of *dominium* took shape in a Roman setting under the spell much more broadly of the *dominus*, and we must be attentive to that fact as we try to recapture the jurists' sense of what it meant to be a man "who ruled over a *domus*," free to indulge in "petty tyranny" and free, at least in theory, to disregard "the right of any other individual in the universe." The history of the *dominus* in classical law is the history of an "idiom of power," and one lodged in a culture, so much unlike ours, that placed the figure of the "master" at the center of its imaginative universe.

* * *

There is one more "concrete" institutional context that we must take into consideration if we are to grasp the cultural backdrop to the texts of the law, I think, this time religious. Roman law and Roman religion demand to be studied together, as thoughtful scholars observe,[89] and our understanding of the law also requires an understanding of religious practice.

This is because the *dominus* was also a master in religious matters. His experience was not just the experience of ruling over his *domus* or

---

[89] See for example the essays by leading figures in Clifford Ando and Jörg Rüpke, eds., *Religion and Law in Classical and Christian Rome* (Stuttgart, 2006); Dario Mantovani, *Les juristes écrivains de la Rome antique: les œuvres des juristes comme littérature* (Paris, 2018), 72–76, 133–134. For brief reflections on the challenges presented by the study of law and religion together, see Jörg Rüpke, "Historians of Religion and the Space of Law," in Salvo Randazzo, ed., *Religione e diritto romano* (Rome, n.d. [2014]), 43–49.

climbing the ladder of the *cursus honorum*. It was also the experience of officiating at religious rites, and most especially blood sacrifices.

Collective rites of animal sacrifice lay at the foundation of public religion in the ancient Mediterranean, as elsewhere the ancient world. "Sacrifices, especially blood sacrifices, were in effect at the very heart of religious activity, certainly of any public and official religious activity."[90] Sacrifices were followed by the festive ritual distribution of meat to the community, in a spectacle that dramatized and reinforced the social hierarchy. I quote James Rives:

> The culminating event of the civic religious festivals ... was typically a large-scale public sacrifice followed by a banquet. These festivals were often funded by local benefactors, who also, as the festival's sponsor, officiated at the sacrifice. In so doing, they placed themselves at the center of a dense nexus of religious, cultural, and social associations that were crucial to the self-identity of their communities.[91]

This was a highly prized source of prestige. Local benefactors, as Rives writes,

> were able to display their largesse in a very immediate way: it was their beneficence and wealth, embodied quite literally in the expensive animals that were slaughtered and shared out among the people and their gods, that made the entire festival possible. All the virtues that served to justify and naturalize the power of the elite, their superior piety, benevolence, and patriotism, were thus confirmed through their role as officiants in the ritual of animal sacrifice.[92]

At Rome, there was a ladder of priesthoods that leading citizens aspired to climb just as they aspired to climb the ladder of magistracies; the great man was a man who presided at the public slaughter of ritual victims and the communal feast that followed.[93] Magistracies and priesthoods were indeed closely linked in the

---

[90] Guy Stroumsa, *The End of Sacrifice: Religious Transformations in Late Antiquity*, trans. Susan Emanuel (Chicago, 2009), 57.

[91] Rives, "Between Orthopraxy and Orthodoxy: Constantine and Animal Sacrifice," in G. Bonamente, N. Lenski, and R. Lizzi Testa, eds., *Costantino prima e dopo Costantino/Constantine before and after Constantine* (Bari, 2012), 154 [153–163].

[92] Rives, "Between Orthopraxy and Orthodoxy," 154.

[93] See John Scheid, *An Introduction to Roman Religion*, trans. Janet Lloyd (Edinburgh, 2003), 90–91, for the complexities of the distribution, not made equally or without payment to all.

classifications of the law.⁹⁴ The haughty sense of self of the "wealthy Roman nobility" of which Wieacker wrote was not just the sense of self of the household master and urban magistrate; it was also the sense of self of the operator of blood sacrifices.

This too deserves its place in our account of the "concrete" setting of the classical *dominus*; we must not forget how closely religious identity was bound up with legal identity in the past. And in it, we can perhaps detect, once more, roots in the early human history of hunting that were my subject in Chapters 1 and 2. For it has been argued that classical Greco-Roman religion of blood sacrifice was a realm in which, as Mircea Eliade writes, "warriors, conquerors, and military aristocracies carr[ied] on the symbolism and ideology of the paradigmatic hunter."⁹⁵

Eliade, who died in 1986, is a scholar whose star has darkened in religious studies. He once enjoyed an unchallenged place among the greatest of names in the study of religion. But to contemporary specialists in the field, he represents an outmoded style of grand theory, too much concerned with the general human phenomenon of religion as such, rather than confining himself to the historical particularities in their unconquerable diversity.⁹⁶ Worse yet, he had a history of involvement with fascism in some of its most abhorrent forms.⁹⁷ Nevertheless, his grand theoretical reflections offer too much stimulation for speculation about legal history to be ignored.

Eliade used the phrase "symbolism and ideology of the paradigmatic hunter" because he believed that the practice of blood sacrifice had roots in hunting that were traceable as far back as the Paleolithic. As we saw in Chapter 1, killing animals and distributing their meat in a collective feast has probably gone on since a very early phase in human, and possibly more broadly hominin, history. Classical sacrificial ritual, with its

---

⁹⁴ Cf. D. 1.1.2. Ulpianus 1 *inst.*: *publicum ius in sacris, in sacerdotibus, in magistratibus consistit.*
⁹⁵ Eliade, *A History of Religious Ideas*, trans. Willard Trask (Chicago, 1978), 1:35.
⁹⁶ Vivianne Pirenne-Delforge, *Le polythéisme grec comme objet d'histoire* (Paris, 2018), 15–16; Jonathan Z. Smith, "Morphology and History in Mircea Eliade's 'Patterns in Comparative Religion,'" *History of Religions* 39 (2000): 334 [332–351].
⁹⁷ See now Bruce Lincoln, *Secrets, Lies and Consequences: A Great Scholar's Hidden Past and His Protégé's Unsolved Murder* (Oxford, 2023); Elaine Fisher, "Fascist Scholars, Fascist Scholarship: The Quest for Ur-Fascism and the Study of Religion," in Christian Wedemeyer and Wendy Doniger, eds., *Hermeneutics, Politics, and the History of Religions: The Contested Legacies of Joachim Wach and Mircea Eliade* (Oxford, 2010), 261–283.

associated feasting, was what I called in Chapter 1 a "rite of distribution"; and it bore a resemblance to the practices of what Walter Burkert, the historian of Greek religion, calls *Homo necans*, "man the killer." Religious historians and anthropologists alike perceive the connection: "[T]he principles of sacrifice are prefigured in the hunt."[98]

The implication of the interpretations of Eliade and Burkert is not, of course, that Greco-Roman elites were indistinguishable from Paleolithic hunters. Their point is a subtler one: Greco-Roman religion embodied attitudes and assumptions whose forgotten origins must be tracked back to immensely ancient practices of hunting, killing, and meat sharing. Their point, to quote Daniel Lord Smail, advocate of the study of "deep history," is "that the Paleolithic era, that long stretch of the Stone Age before the turn to agriculture, is part of our history."[99]

And what they say of religion can also be said of law. Roman property law had its own imagery of "warriors, conquerors, and military aristocracies [who] carr[ied] on the symbolism and ideology of the paradigmatic hunter," symbolism most strikingly embodied in the oldest of human lethal weapons, the spear, whose significance for Paleolithic religion is emphasized by Burkert.[100] Religious experience and legal experience can be viewed, in this regard, as of a piece; in both we may see the extraordinary, indeed almost unimaginable, cultural longevity of the hunting orientations that have been the focus of the work of Smail, of evolutionary anthropologists, and that are the focus of Burkert and Eliade as well.

None of this means that the teachings of Roman property law were "religious" in the narrow sense of the term. What it suggests instead is

---

[98] Tim Ingold, "From the Master's Point of View: Hunting Is Sacrifice," *Journal of the Royal Anthropological Institute* 21 (2015): 25 [24–27]. See the extensive discussions in Gerhard J. Baudy, "Hierarchie, oder: die Verteilung des Fleisches," in Burkhard Gladigow and Hans J. Kippenberg, eds., *Neue Ansätze in der Religionswissenschaft* (Munich, 1983), 131–174, and Richard Seaford, *Money and the Early Greek Mind* (Cambridge, 2004), 39–47.

[99] Smail, *On Deep History and the Brain* (Berkeley, 2008), 2. I do not mean to deny the deep-seated differences in the interpretation of religion that divided Eliade and Burkert. See Burton Mack, "Introduction," in Robert G. Hamerton-Kelly, ed., *Violent Origins: Walter Burkert, René Girard and Jonathan Z. Smith on Ritual Killing and Cultural Formation* (Stanford, CA, 1987), 4–5 [1–70].

[100] Burkert, *Homo necans: Interpretationen altgriechischer Opferriten und Mythen*, 2nd ed. (Berlin, 1997), 25–27.

that law and religion shared an idiom of power: Property law teachings were at home in the *domus*; at home in the *cursus honorum*; and at home in a religious culture that centered on the prestigious performance of blood sacrifice by public officiants. To the extent that Eliade and Burkert have it right, their analyses of classical religion add another dimension to our understanding of the culture of classical Roman ownership among wealthy Romans who did indeed think of themselves as "warriors, conquerors, and [members of a] military aristocrac[y]"; just as conversely the law lends weight to their interpretation of classical religion. The law too was in some sense law of *Homo necans*; and to that extent in the law too, despite the immense complexity of Roman economy and society and the great sophistication of the classical jurists, we may be able to make out traces, astoundingly old, of "the lifestyle of Upper Paleolithic hunter-gatherers."[101]

---

[101] Christopher Boehm, *Hierarchy in the Forest* (Cambridge, MA, 1999), 3.

4

Classical Roman Slave Law: The Just Hunt for Human Prey

Classical Antiquity did not have a sacred scripture; but it is often said that Homer came close.[1] "Homer was not a man but a god," students learned to write; philosophers mulled the *Odyssey*; and Alexander the Great took his "carefully guarded, piously regarded *Iliad*," which had been edited for him by Aristotle, and which he reportedly kept under his bedding alongside a dagger, "with him on all his campaigns."[2] So, as we try to understand ancient conceptions of property justice, we can do worse than to begin with the *Iliad*, a poem that revolves around a property dispute.

The property in question is a slave – Briseis, a princess of Lymessus, captured by Achilles when he sacked her city, killing her parents and husband and carrying her off as human war booty. The ensuing action of the epic, like the action of so much of great literature, is a tale of injustice. But the victim of that injustice is not, as modern readers might expect, Briseis, the woman enslaved and raped by her captor.[3] Instead, the victim is the captor, Achilles.

---

[1] H. I. Marrou, *A History of Education in Antiquity*, trans. George Lamb (London, 1956), 224; Félix Buffière, *Les mythes d'Homère et la pensée grecque* (Paris, 1956), 10–13, and 10 n. 3.

[2] Marrou, *History of Education*, 162–163. "Under his bed": Plut. *Alex.* 8.2, in Bernadotte Perrin, trans., *Plutarch: Lives, Volume VII: Demosthenes and Cicero; Alexander and Caesar*, Loeb Classical Library 99 (Cambridge, MA, 1919), 242–243. Cf. also Plut. *Alex.* 26.1, Loeb edition 198–299.

[3] At least presumably raped. That was the ordinary lot of slaves.

Classical Roman Slave Law

The action of the *Iliad* turns on a basic rule in the law of war booty, honored in the western tradition from Antiquity into the nineteenth century. Booty was taken by individual combatants like Achilles. The sack of a city such as Lymessus produced particularly rich hauls of it. According to the standard procedure, observed in the West for thousands of years, the booty carried off by these individual combatants was to be treated as a common pool. Shares in the common pool were then to be distributed, according to the merits of each warrior, by the authority of their chief or captain (or, in the case of the British in eighteenth-century India, by a "prize committee").[4] This was the rule that was violated in the *Iliad*: As the opening book explains, the chief of the Achaeans, Agamemnon, took Briseis, the

---

[4] For this procedure in the Iliad, M. I. Finley, *The World of Odysseus*, new ed. (New York, 2002), 64–65, 73; and for a classic statement of the longer Western tradition with further citations, Hugo Grotius, *De jure praedae commentarius*, ed. Robert Fruin (repr. Clark, N.J., 2003), 139–140 (cap. X); cf., e.g., Plb. 10.16, in W. R. Paton, trans., *Polybius: The Histories, Vol. IV: Books 9–15*, rev. F. W. Walbank and Christian Habicht, Loeb Classical Library 159 (Cambridge, MA, 2011), 156–157. For an example from the palace of Sennacherib at Nineveh, presumably roughly contemporaneous with the form of the *Iliad* as we have it: Frederick Mario Fales, *Guerre et paix en Assyrie: religion et impérialisme* (Paris, 2010), 72, discussing bas-reliefs in which scribes make a tally of the booty, while a commander hands a soldier a share. For a nineteenth-century example, J. N. Creighton, *Narrative of the Siege and Capture of Bhurtpore in the Province of Agra, Upper Hindoostan* (London, 1830), 148–150, complete with details on shares and distribution procedures. "Prize committee": William Dalrymple, *The Anarchy: The East India Company, Corporate Violence, and the Pillage of an Empire* (New York, 2019), 352. On booty in British India more broadly, Rahul Govind, "The King's Plunder, the King's Justice: Sovereignty in British India, 1756–1776," *Studies in History* 33 (2017): 1–36. These procedures seem to be commonplace in human societies; this is a topic that deserves a more searching study. For the sharing of booty in the chilling context of the Polish murderers of Jews during World War II, for example, Andrew Kornbluth, *The August Trials* (Cambridge, MA, 2021), 49. The sharing out of booty was conducted through a rite of distribution, presided over by a chief, much like that of the rite of distribution of the sharing out of meat after the hunt, whose deep human origins were discussed in Chapter 1. For the proposition that meat sharing among hunter-gatherers may be "dependent upon an individual's relative contribution to the kill," see Brian M. Wood and Ian C. Gilby, "From *Pan* to Man the Hunter: Hunting and Meat Sharing by Chimpanzees, Humans, and Our Common Ancestor," in Martin Muller, Richard Wrangham, and David Pilbeam, eds., *Chimpanzees and Human Evolution* (Cambridge, MA, 2017). For a discussion relating Homeric booty distribution to animal sacrifice rites, see Richard Seaford, *Money and the Early Greek Mind* (Cambridge, 2004), 39–47. As Seaford observes of the *Iliad*, "the right to distribute belongs nominally to the people but in fact to the leader." Ibid., 39.

appropriate share of Achilles – Achilles' *geras* or "portion of honor"[5] – for himself. The resulting "rage" of Achilles is the famous subject of the poem.

It is no small challenge for modern readers to enter into the spirit of this Homeric plot. Ancient audiences may have found it possible to empathize with the rage of Achilles. The "right of capture" was a "universally accepted rule" in Greco-Roman Antiquity, and it covered the seizure of the person of the enemy as well as the goods.[6] "Whatever has been captured from the enemy," as the Roman jurist Gaius flatly stated, "is ours by natural reason."[7] But the entitlement to a share of the booty no longer figures in our law of war, and still less in our moral intuitions. A warrior deprived of the slave woman he carried off after slaughtering her family does not make for a sympathetic hero by modern lights.

It is obvious that some sort of imaginative leap is required if we are to grasp the conception of justice in the *Iliad*; and the same is true of ancient Roman property law. The previous two chapters described the grip on Roman law of the principle "whatever has been captured from the enemy is ours." As we saw, property rights were imagined as originating, paradigmatically, in acts like that of Achilles, acts of taking by main force. The terminology and symbolism of early Roman law regularly portrayed owners as warriors and hunters, who had seized goods and creatures with their metaphorical hand; and among the acts of these warriors and hunters, the capture of enemies in war featured especially prominently. The law, as the great legal historian and philosopher Rudolf von Jhering wrote, treated the taking of human booty as its *Hauptfall*, its paradigmatic case exemplifying the claim of right to ownership.[8]

---

[5] Gregory Nagy, *The Best of the Achaeans: Concepts of the Hero in Archaic Greek Poetry*, 2nd ed. (Baltimore, 1999), 132.

[6] Fernand de Visscher, "Droit de capture et *postliminium in pace*," in *Études de droit romain public et privé, 3e. série* (Milan, 1966), 119: "une règle universellement admise par la coutume antique," including "droit de capture sur la personne et le biens de l'ennemi"; cf., e.g., Riccardo Cardilli, "Il problema della libertà naturale in diritto romano," *Derecho animal/Forum of Animal Law Studies* 10, no. 3 (2019): 17 [15–25], and his discussion of the literature at 19 n. 14.

[7] Gai. *Inst.* 2.69: *Ea quoque, quae ex hostibus capiuntur, naturali ratione nostra fiunt.*

[8] Rudolf von Jhering, *Der Geist des römischen Rechts auf den verschiedenen Stufen seiner Entwicklung*, 5th ed. (Leipzig, 1891), 1:110–111, and above, Chapter 2.

Classical Roman Slave Law 163

This chapter centers on the same paradigmatic case of the capture and enslavement of the enemy. But where Chapter 2 focused on the early phases in the development of Roman law, this one puts the focus squarely on the work of the classical jurists of the Empire. Classical Roman law, the magnificent corpus preserved in the *Digest* of Justinian, sophisticated and subtle, was far different in spirit and character from the law found in the archaic sources. Yet for all that, the same paradigm case continued to play much the same leading role. If I may borrow the language of Sigmund Freud, the high classical jurists returned regularly to the primal scene: the scene of the defeated enemy at the feet of the victor. And like other ancient authors from Homer onward, the jurists never expressed doubts about the victor's rights. Quite the contrary: They founded their reasoning on the proposition that the enslavement of defeated enemies was indubitably lawful and just. Indeed, the jurists treated the enslavement of enemies in war as so categorically just that they used it as the basis for analogical reasoning in areas of the law far beyond the limits of the law of slavery as such.

It can be very difficult for us to accept this truth about the ethos of military predation in the classical law – no less difficult than it is for us to enter into the spirit of the *Iliad*. Modern observers commonly suppose that the Romans must have felt *some* need to justify the institution of slavery, by reference to the standards of *some* larger theory of justice or morality beyond the brute fact of victory on the battlefield or booty-taking in the sack of cities. After all, early modern and modern defenders of the institution of slavery always felt such a need. Thinkers such as Grotius and Pufendorf tried to justify enslavement through war on a theory of the morality of consent: Given the choice between death and slavery, they held, the victim had willingly submitted to the latter.[9] Antebellum American ideologues, for their part, invoked, among other justifications,[10] Aristotle's theory of the "natural slave" – the theory that "some people, owing to a deficiency in the reasoning part of their souls,

---

[9] Below, Chapter 9, for some of the complexities of this early modern idea.
[10] S. Sara Monoson, "Recollecting Aristotle: Pro-slavery Thought in Antebellum America and the Argument of *Politics* Book I," in Richard Alston, Edith Hall, and Justine McConnell, eds., *Ancient Slavery and Abolition: From Hobbes to Hollywood* (Oxford, 2011), 247–278. It is also important that it was embraced by the Thomist tradition, beginning with *Summa theologiae* II-II q. 57, a. 3, arg. 2, available at www.corpusthomisticum.org/sth3057.html. See further below, Chapter 8.

could best fulfil their natural potential by serving a master as a slave."[11] The same Aristotelean theory was adopted by the Spanish conquerors of the New World.[12]

Yet neither of these familiar theories is to be found in the classical Roman legal sources. To the classical jurists, triumph in battle or the sack of cities was, in itself, self-evidently sufficient to confer rights to ownership of the vanquished. That does not mean that the jurists recognized no limits on the seizure of human booty. They laid down a crucial stricture, whose importance I will emphasize in this chapter: Capture only justified slavery, they held, if it took place in war. Mere brigands or pirates did not enjoy the legally recognized right to enslave their victims; only warriors could acquire lawful ownership in their prey. But enslavement through capture, as long as it took place in war, deserved unconditional respect from the law.

It is essential that we acknowledge this truth about the classical attitude toward rights in the fruits of victory. It is a truth that matters immensely for the long history of Western slavery. If we do not recognize how untroubled the ancient Romans were by enslavement through war, we will not understand the course of the decline of the legitimacy of slave-taking in the early modern period. For the early modern age of decline, as I will argue in Chapter 9, did not begin in principled abolitionism. It began in the gradual emergence of a sense that enslavement required some justification beyond the mere fact of victory.

To grasp the attitudes of the ancient jurists, with their serene acceptance of enslavement through war, we must overcome two serious misconceptions in the standard literature. The first is that the ancients, like Antebellum slaveholders centuries later, justified slavery through Aristotle's theory of natural inferiority. This claim is often repeated. Even a master historian such as David Brion Davis leads his reader to believe that Aristotle was the accepted ancient authority, and so do other scholars.[13] Yet this is false, and false in ways that are deeply

---

[11] Jeffrey Fynn-Paul, "Empire, Monotheism and Slavery in the Greater Mediterranean Region from Antiquity to the Early Modern Era," *Past and Present* 205 (2009): 14 [3–40].

[12] Below, Chapter 8.

[13] Esp. Davis, *Inhuman Bondage: The Rise of Fall of Slavery in the New World* (Oxford, 2008), 34, though Davis acknowledges that there was some ancient dissent. For another example among many, Fynn-Paul, "Empire, Monotheism and Slavery," 14.

misleading. The introduction of the Aristotelean theory into Roman law was the work, as we shall see in Chapter 9, not of the ancient jurists, but of the early sixteenth-century theologian John Mair. Ancient enslavement was generally understood, not as the lot of the naturally inferior, but as a calamity that could befall persons of all qualities and stations, up to and including princesses. The hunt for human prey could snare anyone. That was the commonplace understanding, and it was the understanding of the classical jurists as well.

The second misconception that we must overcome is equally misleading, and perhaps even more pernicious. This is the notion that the classical jurists, despite the brutality of the society in which they lived, and despite the jubilation in military victory that was so much a part of their culture, were capable of perceiving the timeless verity that the ownership of humans is a radical evil, and were even in some way "pioneers of human rights."[14] Many contemporary specialists in Roman law, eager to proclaim that the sources of modern ideas of justice are to be sought among the skilled specialists of Antiquity, make some version of this claim. Philosophers too, most prominently Martha Nussbaum, offer kindred arguments, maintaining that the roots of human rights thinking lie among the Stoic philosophers who influenced the ancient jurists.[15] At first glance, it may seem that there is solid evidence for such admiring accounts of ancient legal and moral convictions. Most especially, there is a famous line at the opening of the *Digest*: "By natural law," the *Digest* proclaims, stirringly, "all men were born free." This was a phrase with a long echo in later ages. It was repeated by Enlightenment champions of equality such as Rousseau, and it inspired great documents of both the American and French Revolutions. One might easily assume that when the ancient jurists proclaimed that "all men were born free" they were speaking the same moral language that we speak today. And so indeed do scholars say: The Stanford historian of human rights Dan Edelstein, to take a prominent example, declares that this teaching represented "the Romans' own case for abolition."[16]

---

[14] Tony Honoré, *Ulpian: Pioneer of Human Rights* (Oxford, 2002).
[15] E.g., Nussbaum, "Kant and Stoic Cosmopolitanism," *Journal of Political Philosophy* 5 (1997): 1–25.
[16] Edelstein, *On the Spirit of Rights* (Chicago, 2018), 134. Edelstein cites the version of this argument in the *Institutes* of Justinian without an awareness that it repeats

But it is a serious error to ascribe such modern moral meanings to ancient texts. As we shall see in this chapter, freedom meant something quite different in Roman Antiquity. When the ancient jurists spoke of humans as "born free," they were not anticipating Enlightenment ideas. Far from it. They were saying something that will seem, to the modern reader, both bizarre and shocking: They meant that humans were "born free" in the same sense that wild animals are "born free" – that humans were creatures available to be hunted down, at least as long as the hunt was the lawful hunt for human prey that was war. The fact that humans were exposed to the threat of this fate was cause for pity, in the eyes of the Roman jurists, but it was fully consonant with the demands of justice. The history of the juristic concept of "freedom" in Western law does have Roman roots, in a sense; but they are roots in an ancient culture with a thoroughly alien, and to us thoroughly horrifying, normative orientation.

The bulk of the chapter is devoted to recovering these views of the ancient jurists on what the Homeric tradition called "the day of slavery"[17] and the Roman jurists called the "calamity" of reduction to slave status.[18] But the final sections turn to a second question: how the paradigm case of the hunt for human and animal prey was used as a basis for analogical reasoning. As Jhering observed, legal reasoning ordinarily begins from a *Hauptfall*, a principal case upon which it can build analogies. In modern American property law, for example, the ownership of land often serves such a function: In analyzing other forms of property, such as intellectual property, lawyers reason on the basis of the "prototypical example" of "trespass to land."[19] The use of a given "prototypical example" for such analogical purposes is a key measure, perhaps *the* key measure, of its normative centrality: When the teachings of a doctrine are extended analogically, we know that the makers of the legal order in question regard it as offering a secure normative foothold.

classical doctrine. For another example of this commonplace, Richard Schlatter, *Private Property: The History of an Idea* (New Brunswick, N.J., 1951), 26–27.

[17] Hom. *Od.* 17.323, in A. T. Murray, trans., *Homer: Odyssey, Vol. II: Books 13–24*, rev. by George E. Dimock, Loeb Classical Library 105 (Cambridge, MA, 1919), 176–177.

[18] D. 1.5.5.1-2. Marcianus 1 *Inst.*; D. 11.7.36. Pomponius 26 *ad q. muc.*

[19] For the resulting struggles, see Henry Smith, "Intellectual Property as Property: Delineating Entitlements in Information," *Yale Law Journal* 116 (2007): 1745 and *passim* [1742–1822].

The final sections of the chapter show how the jurists used capture through the hunt for prey, animal and human, as a basis for analogical reasoning. These sections begin with the analogical use of *occupatio*: In analyzing the nature of ownership, the jurists turned regularly to the prototypical example of the capture of wild animals, even when discussing problems remote from the hunt. The chapter then turns to the use of the analogy to enslavement in war, focusing on two areas of law: *capitis deminutio*, the law of status changes, and *postliminium*, the law of escape from slavery at the hands of the enemy. These were both domains in which the jurists used the paradigm case of enslavement through war as a model for analyzing legal and social problems that had nothing to do with slavery as such. The practices of hunting down beasts and enslaving enemies seemed to have such normative validity that they suggested themselves as metaphorical models for the analysis of human relations more broadly.

* * *

To enter into the spirit of the conception of justice shared by the *Iliad* and Roman law, we must begin by recognizing that the fate of Princess Briseis was by no means outside the realm of the imaginable in the ancient world. In Greco-Roman Antiquity, it was well understood that high-status persons, even princesses, might find themselves reduced to slavery. It can be difficult for us to appreciate how seriously the ancients took that possibility, especially if we draw our idea of a "slave society" from the one most familiar to modern Americans, the Antebellum South, where the enslavement of white masters was unthinkable. Antebellum slavery was a condition inflicted on a closed caste of persons deemed inherently inferior.

That idea of slavery was not entirely absent in the ancient Mediterranean. Aristotle did indeed propose the theory of natural slavery, and he certainly had followers. But elsewhere in ancient literature, and even in parts of the Aristotelean corpus,[20] slavery was

---

[20] Peter Garnsey, *Ideas of Slavery from Aristotle to Augustine* (Cambridge, 1996), 113–114 and generally 108–127; cf. Myles Lavan, *Slaves to Rome: Paradigms of Empire in Roman Culture* (Cambridge, 2013), 133, for the excessive focus on Aristotle's idea of natural slavery in the literature. See also Aldo Schiavone, *The Invention of Law in the West*, trans. Jeremy Carden and Antony Shugaar (Cambridge, MA, 2012), 454.

treated differently: not as a consequence of natural inferiority, but as the result of misfortune, and especially of the colossal misfortune of defeat in war. That is the idea lying in the background of the tale of Briseis, and it was present throughout the Homeric tradition. "In the *Iliad*, the 'day of slavery' hangs over the women of Troy continually, and in *The Trojan Women* of Euripides and Seneca that day arrives, bringing the pathetic spectacle of noble women facing the prospect of ignominious slavery to the slayers of their husbands and sons."[21]

Ancient literature is packed with ruminations on this "pathetic spectacle" of the mighty in chains. "He who shortly before had shown no pity or consideration for the defeated," Polybius wrote of the Roman general Marcus Atilius Regulus, captured and enslaved by the Carthaginians in 255 BCE, "now had to beg helplessly for his own life."[22] Perhaps the most garish description of such a fall from the height of power involved no less a figure than an emperor, taken captive and cast down into slavery a thousand years after the *Iliad* and described in the Christian author Lactantius' *On the Deaths of Persecutors*. Here is Lactantius cackling over the fate of the pagan Emperor Valerian, captured by the Persians in 260 CE and compelled to serve as a human footstool:

He lost not only that power which he had exercised without moderation, but also the freedom of which he had deprived others; and he wore out the remainder of his days in the vilest condition of slavery: for Shapur, the king of the Persians, who had made him prisoner, whenever he chose to get into his carriage or to mount on horseback, commanded the Roman to bend over and present his back; then, placing his boot on Valerian's shoulders, he said, with a malevolent grin, "This is the truth, not what the Romans write on their wooden tablets or upon their walls."[23]

This scene is certainly a fiction, but that does not make it any less revealing. The calamity suffered by Valerian, and others like him reduced to slavery, was at least as important for the normative

---

[21] William Fitzgerald, *Slavery and the Roman Literary Imagination* (Cambridge, 2000), 90.
[22] Plb. 1.35, in W. R. Paton, trans., *Polybius: The Histories, Vol. I: Books 1–2*, rev. F. W. Walbank and Christian Habicht, Loeb Classical Library 128 (Cambridge, MA, 2010), 106–107.
[23] I have slightly altered the translation in Lactantius, *Of the Manner in Which the Persecutors Died*, ed. David Dalrymple (Edinburgh, 1782), 10.

Classical Roman Slave Law

imagination of ancient slavery as Aristotle's theory of natural inferiority.

Enslavement was not just the lot of "natural slaves." It could also befall the mighty. This was an ancient commonplace, and it had normative implications that fundamentally distinguished ancient attitudes toward slavery from modern ones. In the modern world, we think of slavery as an institution embodying inequality in its foulest form. In Antiquity, by contrast, as in Lactantius' gleeful tale of Valerian, slavery could serve as a great equalizer. In a controversial 1946 book, the American sociologist Frank Tannenbaum argued that Roman slave law was critically different from American slave law because the Romans made manumission relatively easy; as a result, Tannenbaum maintained, the Latin American societies that emerged out of the Roman tradition were less vicious than the society of Jim Crow America. Tannenbaum's thesis may or may not have been correct – many scholars question it[24] – but if he was right, he was only telling half of the story. It is not just that Roman law contemplated relatively easy manumission. It is also that it contemplated relatively easy enslavement.[25]

For "the prospect that anyone at any time might become its victim [i.e. of enslavement]," as Keith Bradley writes, "was far more real than it could ever have been in the slave societies of the New World."[26] Wars produced slaves in reality just as they did in epic poetry: Mass enslavements of the defeated were regular occurrences in the Greco-Roman world.[27] Roman public pageantry paraded the defeated enemy in chains through the streets of the city, kings prominently among them;[28] and the defeated were publicly auctioned.

---

[24] Frank Tannenbaum, *Slave and Citizen: The Negro in the Americas* (New York, 1946). For discussion and doubts, Alejandro de la Fuente and Ariela Gross, "Comparative Studies of Law, Slavery, and Race in the Americas," *Annual Review of Law and Social Science* 6 (2010): 470–472 [469–485].

[25] Wisely observed by Robert Cottrol, *The Long Lingering Shadow: Slavery, Race and the Law in the American Hemisphere* (Athens, GA, 2013), 44.

[26] Bradley, *Apuleius and Antonine Rome: Historical Essays* (Toronto, 2012), 62.

[27] Hans Volkmann, *Die Massenversklavungen der Einwohner eroberter Städte in der hellenistisch-römischen Zeit*, 2nd ed. (Stuttgart, 1990); W. Kendrick Pritchett, *The Greek State at War* (Berkeley, 1974–), 5:170–172, 223–244.

[28] "Kings in chains": Pliny, *Panegyricus* 17.1–3, in Betty Radice, trans., *Pliny the Younger: Letters, Vol. II: Books 8–10; Panegyricus*, Loeb Classical Library 59 (Cambridge, MA, 1969), 362; Richard Brilliant, "'Let the Trumpets Roar!': The

But it must be emphasized that war was not the only danger. There was brigandage as well: Raiders could descend without warning and capture and sell anybody, as a recently discovered letter of St. Augustine, describing his North African region in 428 CE, makes dramatically clear:

> There are so many of those in Africa who are commonly called "slavers" [*mangones*], that they seem to be draining Africa of much of its human population and transferring their "merchandise" to the provinces across the sea. Almost all of these are free persons...
>
> It is said that in a certain small village, in an incursion of this sort, the men were killed and the women and children were carried off to be sold...[29]

Not all eras and regions were as dangerous as this one. Nevertheless, enslavement by bandits or pirates was always an authentic risk in Antiquity; the "hunt for men," as Plato described his ancient Mediterranean world, was a normal part of human affairs, and it was conducted both by armies and by "man-stealers."[30] Travelers by land simply disappeared; being accompanied by bodyguards was no guarantee of safety;[31] even Julius Caesar, to cite the much-repeated ancient example of another mighty figure, was taken captive by pirates.[32]

Alongside war and brigandage, moreover, there were many other roads into slavery as well. Exposed infants, born free, were harvested by slave-traders, raised, and then sold. Straitened circumstances could force free persons to sell themselves, even where the law prohibited them from doing so.[33] Sometimes free children were sold by their

---

Roman Triumph," *Studies in the History of Art* 56, Symposium Papers 34: *The Art of Ancient Spectacle* (1999): 227 [220–229]; Ida Östenberg, *Staging the World: Spoils, Captives and Representations in the Roman Triumphal Procession* (Oxford, 2009), 1–2.

[29] Available at www.classics.upenn.edu/sites/www.classics.upenn.edu/files/Divjak%20Augustine%2010%20Trans.pdf.

[30] Plat. *Soph.* 222c, in Harold North Fowler, trans., *Plato: Theaetetus; Sophist*, Loeb Classical Library 123 (Cambridge, MA, 1921), 284–285.

[31] Brent Shaw, "Bandits in the Roman Empire," *Past & Present*, 105 (1984): 9–10 [3–52]; Werner Riess, *Apuleius und die Räuber: ein Beitrag zur historischen Kriminalitätsforschung* (Stuttgart, 2001), 106–109 with further literature.

[32] Or at least, so the story comes down to us. For its history, and its uses, see Josiah Osgood, "Caesar and the Pirates: or How to Make (and Break) an Ancient Life," *Greece and Rome* 57 (2010): 319–336.

[33] Self-sale was technically permitted in only some ancient legal systems; but in practice it is likely that it went on even where it was prohibited. For a well-known study in

parents. Sometimes parents offered their children as security for their debts. Sometimes, the legal sources reveal, creditors simply seized children in payment even if their parents had not pledged them.[34]

Enslavement was a menace that hovered just over the horizon for free persons, from infancy onward, throughout the ancient world. There was none of the tranquil security of those born white in the American South. "'But I have no master!' you say," writes Seneca in one of his letters, describing the attitude of a callow high-status youth. "You are still young," replies the sage, transmitting the standard ancient wisdom. "Perhaps you *will* have one."[35] Several generations later, the physician Galen, diagnosing the human condition from the more clinical point of view of an ancient medical man, presented life in the same light: For many people, he explained, "harm is inevitable from what they do – this cannot be avoided. Some happen upon such lives through poverty and some through slavery, either coming down to them from their fathers, or by being seized as prisoners through war, or snatched away by bandits."[36]

To be sure, we should be careful not to overstate the frequency of either enslavements or manumissions in reality. It was hardly routine for princesses or emperors to become slaves. Despite the experience of Caesar, the vast majority of high-status persons undoubtedly lived lives safe from the slavers. Conversely, the mass of Roman slaves laboring on plantations had no meaningful hope of obtaining freedom. The risk of enslavement was a bogey of the normative imagination as much as, or more than, it was an aspect of the realities of everyday life – at least

---

Roman law, see Jacques Ramin and Marie-Paul Veyne, "Droit romain et société: les hommes libres qui passent pour esclaves et l'esclavage volontaire," *Historia* 30 (1981): 472–497.

[34] So we can conclude from efforts to forbid these practices. See the discussion of Hans Wieling, "Einleitung," in Wieling, ed., *Corpus der römischen Rechtsquellen zur antiken Sklaverei* (Stuttgart, 1999), 1:16–17.

[35] Sen. *Ep.* 47.12, in Richard M. Gummere, trans., *Seneca: Epistles, Vol. I: Epistles 1–65*, Loeb Classical Library 75 (Cambridge, MA, 1917), 306–309.

[36] Galen, *Hygiene* 2.1, 82K: ἢ αἰχμαλώτοις ληφθεῖσιν ἢ ἁρπαχθεῖσιν, in Ian Johnston, ed. and trans., *Galen: Hygiene, Vol. I: Books 1–4*, Loeb Classical Library 535 (Cambridge, MA, 2018). I have altered Johnston's translation of the final passage, which he renders "by being taken away as prisoners, or being snatched away," in order to bring out more clearly the distinction between the two routes into slavery. For the interpretation of this as "Menschenraub" and the contrast with "Kriegsgefangenschaft," see Heinrich Schlange-Schöningen, *Die römische Gesellschaft bei Galen* (Berlin and New York, 2003), 262.

when it came to the everyday lives of the elite. But the realities are not all that matter. The mere remote risk of enslavement was a ceaseless ancient preoccupation, as was the mere remote prospect of liberation. This was true of ancient literature, religion, and philosophy just as it was true of law; and before turning to the classical Roman law of this vertiginously unstable master/slave hierarchy, it is useful to dwell for a moment on the evidence from these other domains, which helps us get a feel for the ancient moral world in which the jurists operated.

* * *

The imaginative literature, often exploited by historians to reconstruct the cultural context of ancient slavery, makes the best starting point.[37] As the classicist William Fitzgerald writes, the possibility of a sudden enslavement, or a sudden liberation, served as a key plot device for the authors of the Greco-Roman world. Fitzgerald offers a host of examples of literary "crossings of the great divide between slave and free,"[38] and plenty more can be added. Plautus' play *Captivi*, "War Slaves," for example, is a comedy (!) about a man who becomes a slaver in order to seize a high-status victim whom he can trade for his son, who has been enslaved by the enemy. Plautus' play took it for granted that the world was a theater of marauding armies, engaged in a wholly legitimate hunt for human prey. (It includes a joking reference to captured enemies who had recently been marched through Rome in chains.)[39] Many of the examples that scholars find most telling are drawn from ancient novels. In particular, classicists highlight Apuleius' marvelous *Golden Ass*, the tale of the metamorphosis of Lucius, the man transformed into the ass of the title, and subjected to comic/horrific brutality. As Bradley argues in an elegant interpretation, the fate of Lucius serves as "a perfect metaphor for the situation of captive slaves" in an ancient world that took it for granted that slaves were closely comparable to domestic beasts.[40] In romances such as *Daphnis and Chloe* or *Chaereas and*

---

[37] Keith Bradley, "Animalizing the Slave: The Truth of Fiction," *Journal of Roman Studies* 90 (2000): 110–125; Keith Hopkins, "Novel Evidence for Roman Slavery," *Past & Present* 138 (1993): 3–27.

[38] Fitzgerald, *Slavery and the Roman Literary Imagination*, 87.

[39] Matthew Leigh, *Comedy and the Rise of Rome* (Oxford, 2004), 58–96; and K. Wellesley, "The Production Date of Plautus' *Captivi*," *American Journal of Philology* 76 (1955): 298–299 [298–305], on the capture of Boii.

[40] Bradley, "Animalizing the Slave," 110, 114. But contrast Finley, *Ancient Slavery and Modern Ideology*, expanded ed., ed. Brent Shaw (New York, 1998), 167: "Roman

Callirhoe free persons (especially virginal young women like Chloe or Callirhoe) fell, horrifyingly, into the clutches of slavers, only to be happily liberated at the end. The most famous literary crosser of the divide between slave and free received a less sympathetic portrayal. This was of course Trimalchio, the boorish host of the feast in Petronius' *Satyricon*, glorying buffoonishly in his wealth.

Free and slave were, not two closed castes separated by an impassable wall, but two points on a treacherous slope that anybody might clamber up or slip down. Real-life freedmen who had managed the upward climb populated ancient *belles lettres* just as fictional ones did. Some were semilegendary: Both the great king Cyrus of Persia and the great king Servius Tullius of Rome were said to have risen up from slavery.[41] But others were not. One example was Gaius Caecilius Claudius Isidorus, a freedman reported to have acquired such enormous riches that he executed a will "in which he declared that in spite of heavy losses in the civil war he nevertheless left 4116 slaves, 3600 pairs of oxen, 257,000 head of other cattle, and 60 million sesterces in cash."[42] It is worth remarking that the fabulous wealth accumulated by this ex-slave was described in terms of his ownership of humans and animals. Wealthy Romans certainly owned land, as we have seen, and certainly bequeathed it by will; Isidorus could hardly have been a man of great wealth without extensive landholdings. Indeed, the historian P. A. Brunt went to some trouble to calculate exactly how much land he must have owned or at least leased.[43] Nevertheless, the immense wealth of which Isidorus boasted in his will took the form, not of lands, but of tens of thousands of humans and beasts, accumulated by a man who had ascended from bestial slavery himself; we are reminded of other societies in which, as in seventeenth-century Malaya, "the natives reckon[ed] high status and wealth by the quantity of slaves a person owns";[44] or of the European

---

lawyers may have linked slaves and animals in noxal actions and in other property contexts; but no one could for a moment have forgotten that the differences were fundamental."

[41] Fitzgerald, *Slavery and the Roman Literary Imagination*, 94.
[42] Plin. *Nat.* 33.135, in H. Rackham, trans., *Pliny: Natural History, Vol. IX: Books 33–35*, Loeb Classical Library 394 (Cambridge, MA, 1952), 102–103.
[43] Brunt, "Two Great Roman Landowners," *Latomus* 34 (1975): 624–628 [619–635].
[44] Muhammad Ibrahim, *The Ship of Sulaiman*, trans. John O'Kane (London, 1972), 177.

colonizers of Batavia, among whom no one "who wanted to count as somebody could afford to arouse the suspicion that he was skimping on the number of his black slaves."[45] Another much-invoked ancient figure who had made a different kind of passage into wealth was Vedius Pollio, the son of a freedman who made himself notorious for his cruelty to his own slaves, reportedly feeding them to lampreys when they displeased him.[46]

Needless to say, these are not stories that describe the "quotidian reality" of the ancient Mediterranean. They are lurid and thrilling tales of exceptional cases. The point is not that they demonstrate that "crossings of the great divide between slave and free" occurred routinely, but that they belonged to a culture that consumed fabulous tales of the free made slave and the slave made free, and in which the fear of enslavement was omnipresent. Ancient religion had comparable tales. The gods of the eastern Mediterranean sometimes enslaved their devotees, as ancient inscriptions reveal,[47] and so did the God of Abraham. Exodus declared that God had made the Jews His own property, (Exod. 19:5; Deut. 7:6; cf. Eph. 1:14), while granting His people the right to enslave other nations. Abrahamic teachings often described divine slavery as a paradoxical form of liberation: Both Jews and Christians were said to have been enslaved to God as a way of freeing them from enslavement to man.[48] Nevertheless, slavery it was.

Something similar can be said about Greco-Roman philosophers: The proposition that persons might slip from free status into slave provided much of the conceptual timber of their work as well. For

---

[45] Jürgen Osterhammel, *The Transformation of the World*, trans. P. Camiller (Princeton, 2014), 223.

[46] Discussed in Hopkins, "Novel Evidence for Roman Slavery."

[47] W. K. Pleket, "Religious History as the History of Mentality," in H. S. Versnel, ed., *Faith, Hope and Worship: Aspects of Religious Mentality in the Ancient World* (Leiden, 1981), 152–192, esp. 176; Karin Hülsen, "Tempelsklaverei," in "*Kleinasien: ein Beitrag zum Tempeldienst in hellenistischer und römischer Zeit*," diss. Trier, 2007; Felix John, *Der Galaterbrief im Kontext historischer Lebenswelten im antiken Kleinasien* (Göttingen, 2016), 97 on *hierodouloi* as notional slaves. For divine emancipation in Apuleius, Arthur Darby Nock, *Conversion: The Old and the New in Religion from Alexander the Great to Augustine of Hippo* (Oxford, 1933), 140–141. H. S. Versnel, *Inconsistencies in Greek and Roman Religion*, Vol. 1 (Leiden, 1990), 92 sees this pattern gathering strength in the Imperial period, "especially from the second century onwards."

[48] Biblical passages in Francis Lyall, *Slaves, Citizens, Sons: Legal Metaphors in the Epistles* (Grand Rapids, 1984), 27–46.

Plato or the Stoics, as historians of ancient philosophy emphasize, one core ethical question, arguably the core question for the latter, was whether a man might, contemptibly, become a slave to his passions, or he whether he could maintain his status as his own master.[49] More broadly, Hellenistic philosophies of life can be read as philosophies of how to maintain free status in the face of threats of enslavements both metaphorical and real. For the philosophers as for the jurists, the very fabric of society was woven out of relationships of the ownership of some persons by others.

* * *

We cannot comprehend the classical Roman juristic texts unless we read them against this broader ancient cultural background. This is particularly true when it comes to one of the most hotly contested questions in recent Roman law scholarship: whether or not the jurists recognized the radically evil nature of the institution of slavery.

Scholars have struggled mightily with that question over the last few decades. There are specialists in Roman law who insist that the ancient jurists were humane men, devoted to philosophical reflection, troubled by the institution of slavery, and committed to incipient concepts of human rights. Others, by contrast, have responded to such claims dismissively, and sometimes almost angrily: The ancient jurists, they maintain, worked in a world of profound brutality, and they fully accepted slavery, its most brutal institution. They were slave lawyers for slave societies. The only good way to settle the conflict between these warring scholarly camps is to understand the place of the Roman jurists within the normative world of their ancient Mediterranean milieu: They *did* accept the justice of slavery – as long as it resulted, as in the case of Briseis, from capture in war. In other cases, however, they hesitated.

The scholars who believe that the ancient jurists were troubled by slavery, no matter how it arose, certainly have evidence to cite. There is no doubt that the Roman legal texts include some passages that have a humanitarian sound. Most important among these is a line from the jurist Ulpian, a leading figure of the Severan Dynasty (193–235 CE), which ruled Rome during the last decades of the Principate, before the crisis of the mid third century. The Severan age, the last flowering of classical Rome, produced a great deal of philosophizing by leading

[49] Garnsey, *Ideas of Slavery*, 128–152.

jurists, among whom Ulpian stands out. His fragments, which often reflect appealingly humane attitudes, include the ringing declaration that I quoted at the opening of this chapter: "By natural law all men were born free."[50]

That phrase certainly sounds like a grand statement of a belief in universal human dignity, and it has had a long resonance in later Western thought. It reappeared as the powerful opening sentence of Rousseau's *Social Contract* – "man is born free, and everywhere he is in chains" – and made its way from there, in altered form, into the Declaration of the Rights of Man and the Citizen, and eventually into the Universal Declaration of Human Rights in 1948.[51] It hovered in the background of Jefferson's Declaration of Independence as well. All this makes it tempting to trace the history of the idea of "natural" human equality back to the ancient jurists, and most especially to Ulpian.

There are, moreover, other passages in which the jurists held that slavery was contrary to "natural law" or "natural liberty." Classical Roman teachings included the *favor libertatis*, the "presumption in favor of liberty," which in cases of doubt declared persons to be free.[52] There were prohibitions on excessive cruelty toward slaves, especially after the mid second century CE,[53] and there are many fragments of the classical jurists that treat slaves as legal actors with rights and duties fully respected by the law. Among the most notable passages is one in which Ulpian held, in another ringing line, that "with regard to natural law" all men are equal.[54] Not least, as Tannenbaum emphasized in 1946, Roman law contemplated large-scale manumissions.[55]

---

[50] This and related teachings are picked up in *Inst.* 1.2.
[51] Article 1: "All human beings are born free and equal in dignity and rights."
[52] G. Härtel, "Der 'favor libertatis' im Imperium Romanum und sein gesellschaftlicher Zusammenhang nach den Digesten im 2.–3. Jahrhundert u.Z.," *Index* 5 (1974–1975): 282–302.
[53] Detlef Liebs, "Strafrechtlicher Schutz der Sklaven gegen Willkür ihrer Herren," *Tijdschrift voor Rechtsgeschiedenis* 85 (2017): 1–25. For the longer tradition, see also Stefan Knoch, *Sklavenfürsorge im römischen Reich: Formen und Motive* (Hildesheim, 2005), 40–57.
[54] D. 50.17.32. Ulpianus 43 *ad sab.*: *Quod attinet ad ius civile, servi pro nullis habentur: non tamen et iure naturali, quia, quod ad ius naturale attinet, omnes homines aequales sunt.* Cf. *Inst.* 1.2.2., 1.3.2, emphasized by Tony Honoré, "Les droits de l'homme chez Ulpien," in Huguette Jones, ed., *Le monde antique et les droits de l'homme* (Brussels, 1998), 240 [235–244]; and e.g., Ernst Levy, "Natural Law in the Roman Period," in *Natural Law Institute Proceedings* 2 (1949): 58 [43–72].
[55] Tannenbaum, *Slave and Citizen*.

Taken together, these various doctrines, practices, and passages can certainly give the impression of an enlightened, or at least sporadically enlightened, ancient juristic mentality, and leading Roman law scholars have seized on them in order to make the case for the Roman roots of modern human rights thinking. This much-repeated line of interpretation traces the supposedly enlightened teachings of the jurists to Greek philosophical doctrines on "natural law." Historians reconstruct the philosophical history of "natural law" roughly as follows: The later Sophists Thrasymachus and Callicles promulgated a harsh view of "natural law" that enshrined the rights of the strong over the weak, including over slaves.[56] But Plato rejected the teachings of the Sophists, and so did subsequent thinkers. Over the course of subsequent centuries, the sophistic conception of "natural law" as the right of the strong eventually gave way to conceptions founded in much more attractive ideas of human equality. All this culminated in the philosophy of the Greek Stoics, whose ideas acquired highly influential Roman acolytes such as Cicero.[57]

It is this philosophical history that is frequently said to lie in the background of the humane work of the Roman jurists. The Stoics are often credited with having laid the foundations for enlightened philosophies of humanity, by Nussbaum as by many others; and specialists in Roman law have long argued that juristic references to "natural law" or "nature" should be traced to their influence.[58] In 1968, Gerhard Oestreich contended that the sources of the idea of human rights were to be sought among the Stoics.[59] Two decades later, the eminent Oxford jurist Tony Honoré picked up the thread. The Stoics spoke of a "cosmopolis," a universal city including all free men. As the Roman Empire came to encompass that entire Mediterranean world and extended Roman citizenship to all free persons under the

---

[56] Plat. *Gorg.* 483, in W. R. M. Lamb, trans., *Plato: Lysis; Symposium; Gorgias*, Loeb Classical Library 166 (Cambridge, MA, 1925), 382–387.

[57] For a recent account, see Laurens Winkel, "Deux conceptions du droit naturel dans l'antiquité," *Revue historique du droit français et étranger* 93 (2015): 341–350; and for a classic discussion, Felix Flückiger, *Geschichte des Naturrechts* (Zurich, 1954), 1:257–283.

[58] E.g., Guy Haarscher, "Le monde antique et les droits de l'homme," in Jones, ed., *Le monde antique et les droits de l'homme*, 198–199 [197–208].

[59] Oestreich, *Geschichte der Menschenrechte und Grundfreiheiten im Umriß* (Berlin, 1968), 17–18.

Severan Emperor Caracalla in 212 CE, Honoré argues, Ulpian, the "pioneer of human rights," infused the law with Stoic ideals.[60]

Honoré is the most unabashed champion of the idea the ancient Roman jurists "pioneered" human rights. Others are somewhat more restrained, but they too argue that we can trace the roots of modern human rights thinking to the Romans.[61] Roman law, Richard Bauman concedes, was a "patchwork." Nevertheless, he maintains that it reflected, from an early date, the *humanitas*, the "humanity," of the ancient jurists. There were *Human Rights in Ancient Rome*, in the title of his book, and it is right to identify ancient anticipations of the critical tenets of modern human rights thinking.[62] Bauman's approach is echoed elsewhere in the literature.[63] Thus Jacob Giltaij and Kaius Tuori, the scholars who have published the latest word on this question, argue that, while it may be anachronistic to speak of full-blown "human rights" in ancient Rome, it is nevertheless not wrong to see ancient foreshadowings of modern conceptions. The doctrinal history of human rights is a history that begins at Rome, even if it had a long road to walk thereafter.[64]

The most cautious contribution to this line of interpretation comes from one of the finest of historians of property law, Peter Garnsey. The ancient jurists, Garnsey acknowledges, like other ancient authorities, had no inkling of the possibility of abolishing slavery. Nevertheless, they were authentically uneasy about it. Their critiques and doubts were underdeveloped by modern standards, but, read sympathetically, they can be seen to reflect "the moral anxieties and tensions of a slave-owning class engaged in the thoroughgoing and brutal exploitation of their fellow men," and they show that anti-slavery sentiment was not wholly absent from the ancient world.[65] Modern Western ideas of

---

[60] Honoré, *Ulpian*; "Droits de l'homme chez Ulpien."
[61] Jean Gaudemet, "Le monde antique et les droits de l'homme – quelques observations," in Jones, ed., *Le monde antique et les droits de l'homme*, 175–183.
[62] Bauman, *Human Rights in Ancient Rome* (London, 2000).
[63] Jacob Giltaij, "Mensenrechten in het Romeinse Recht?" diss. Rotterdam, 2011; cf. G. Crifò, "Per una prospettiva romanistica die diritti dell'uomo," in Klaus Girardet and Ulrich Nortmann, eds., *Menschenrechte und Europäische Identität: die antiken Grundlagen* (Stuttgart, 2005), 240–269.
[64] Giltaij and Tuori, "Human Rights in Antiquity? Revisiting Anachronism and Roman Law," in Pamela Slotte and Miia Halme-Tuomisaari, eds., *Revisiting the Origins of Human Rights* (Cambridge, 2015), 39–63.
[65] Garnsey, *Ideas of Slavery*, 10.

justice can be traced back, to that extent, thousands of years into the past.

But other scholars reject all such efforts at praising the ancient jurists, no matter how cautiously framed. Unsurprisingly so: Modern classical scholarship has been heavily devoted to documenting the horror of ancient slavery, especially since the publication of M. I. Finley's 1980 *Ancient Slavery and Modern Ideology*, which poured scorn on the work of classicists who minimized that horror in the service of misconceived idealizations of the Greco-Roman heritage.[66] Finley's book was followed by fierce articles from the two leading specialists in Roman slave law, Bradley and Alan Watson.[67] Forty years later, there is no escape from the knowledge that the Roman jurists, however stirring their occasional pronouncements, worked in societies of staggering brutality.

The law may have condemned the cruelty of masters; but we know the truth that these scholars hammer home: Masters continued to be revoltingly cruel.[68] As the scholar of Roman slave law W. W. Buckland once quipped, ancient laws against cruelty to slaves had as much impact as modern laws against cruelty to animals.[69] Nor was the gruesomeness of Roman life restricted to the treatment of slaves: For example, people took pleasure in watching drawn-out executions and inventive forms of death at the Games. In light of the numbing cruelty on daily display at Rome, scholars like Olivia Robinson find it questionable, not to say tasteless, to speak of Roman human rights.[70]

A particularly forceful assault on idealizers of Roman law has come from the Italian scholar Mario Talamanca. It is methodological nonsense, Talamanca argues, to look for ancient anticipations of modern human rights in the relentlessly exploitative society that was Rome.[71] The idea that the jurists were troubled by "moral anxieties

---

[66] Finley, *Ancient Slavery and Modern Ideology*, at e.g., 124–125, 183–185.
[67] Watson, "Roman Slave Law and Romanist Ideology," *Phoenix* 37 (1983): 53–65; Bradley, "The Regular, Daily Traffic in Slaves: Roman History and Contemporary History," *Classical Journal* 87 (1991–1992), 125–138.
[68] Bradley, "Regular, Daily Traffic," 123–129.
[69] Buckland, *A Text-Book of Roman Law*, 2nd ed. (Cambridge, 1950), 64.
[70] Robinson, "Crime and Punishment and Human Rights in Ancient Rome," in Jones, ed., *Le monde antique et les droits de l'homme*, 325–326 [325–334].
[71] Talamanca, "L'antichità e i 'diritti dell'uomo,'" *Atti dei Convegni Lincei* 174 (2001): 41–91.

and tensions" is utterly anachronistic. "The conscience of the Roman jurists, like that of the man in the street, and of the slaves themselves, coexisted tranquilly with the distinction of humans into the free and the slave."[72] Aldo Schiavone speaks in similar terms: When it came to slavery, the Roman mind was "encased in a shell of ethical and cognitive indifference."[73] Bradley puts the point unsparingly: "The reality is that slavery at Rome was an evil, violent and brutalizing institution that the Romans themselves, across a vast interval of time, consciously chose to maintain, for which they themselves were responsible, and whose justification they never seriously questioned."[74]

It is hard indeed to deny the force of such views. The jurists, far from being consistently humane, were capable of displaying a jaw-dropping indifference to the lot of slaves. This is even true of material offered up as evidence for their commitment to human rights: When Honoré argues that Roman law accorded slaves rights, among the examples that he cites is their "natural right" to mutilate themselves, or commit suicide out of desperation![75] And so, we are told, they did: Seneca casually mentions that slaves might throw themselves off a roof in order to be free of a master who relentlessly harangued them, or plunge a shiv into their own gut if they were about to be captured after an attempted escape.[76] Honoré has an explanation for why these nightmare "rights" embodied an ethic of respect for the personhood of the slave: Suicide, he points out, could be the act of an honorable

---

[72] Ibid., 88.
[73] Schiavone, *La storia spezzata: Roma antica e Occidente moderno* (Bari, 1996), 45.
[74] Bradley, "Regular, Daily Traffic," 136.
[75] Honoré, "Droits de l'homme chez Ulpien," 238.
[76] Sen. *Ep.* 4.4: *Alius ante amicae fores laqueo pependit, alius se praecipitavit e tecto, ne dominum stomachantem diutius audiret, alius ne reduceretur e fuga, ferrum adegit in viscera*, in Richard M. Gummere, trans., *Seneca: Epistles, Vol. I: Epistles 1–65*, Loeb Classical Library 75 (Cambridge, MA, 1917), 14–15. It is worth suggesting that it may not be unconnected to the fragment of Ulpian highlighted by Honoré: D. 15.1.9.7. Ulp. 29 *ad ed.*: *Si ipse servus sese vulneraverit, non debet hoc damnum deducere* [i.e. from his *peculium*], *non magis quam si se occiderit vel praecipitaverit: licet enim etiam servis naturaliter in suum corpus saevire*. The phrase *se occiderit vel praecipitaverit* recalls Seneca. Was his epistle a subject of school discussion? A certain casual cruelty is, I suggest, on display in Ulpian's fragment: Masters, as we are told by Gaius, were forbidden to *saevire* to excess. Gai. *Inst.* 1.53. It is difficult not to hear the tones of a brutal lawyer's joke when Ulpian observes that slaves are nevertheless permitted to *saevire* upon themselves. Not, in any case, the voice of a champion of human rights, I think.

person in Antiquity. True enough. Seneca himself committed suicide. But does that really capture a culture that produces such statements? Can anyone seriously maintain that a legal order of such stunning callousness, populated by such wretched human creatures, "pioneered" human rights?

* * *

After decades of debate, Roman law scholarship has thus arrived at an impasse – an impasse of the kind that has become familiar throughout contemporary university classrooms. On the one hand, the ancient Roman jurists, like other heroes of the Western intellectual tradition, sometimes gave wing to soaring sentiments; whatever instinct it is that drives us to seek ancient authority for our modern beliefs seems to lead us straight to the *Corpus iuris civilis*. Yet the same Roman jurists were undeniably involved in what now seems the radical immorality of their societies; and ascribing the origins of human rights to Roman law seems to require an almost superhuman willingness to disregard Roman realities. By the standards of modern human rights law, the case for ancient Rome seems fraught at best.

There is only way out of this impasse: We must judge the Roman jurists by something other than the standards of modern human rights law. The right standards are those of the broader ancient Mediterranean culture whose literature, religion, and philosophy have been the subject of this chapter. The ancient historian Glen Bowersock says that the tales in the Gospels should be read alongside the tales in the ancient novels.[77] The same is true of Roman law, which trafficked in its own tales.[78] The Roman jurists shared the presuppositions of their world. It would be strange if they had not. Lawyers are rarely in the business of questioning the normative foundations of their society. The justice of slavery, in at least some form, was a given. The work of the jurists was only to interpret it, and work out its practical applications.

In approaching that task, they did indeed sometimes display what we would recognize as humane impulses. Garnsey has documented ancient "moral anxieties and tensions" (though in my opinion he may

---

[77] G. W. Bowersock, *Fiction as History: Nero to Julian* (Berkeley, 2018).
[78] Esp. Marie-Thérèse Fögen, *Römische Rechtsgeschichten: über Ursprung und Evolution eines sozialen Systems* (Göttingen, 2002).

ascribe to them too much significance[79]). The jurists believed that slavery was an evil, and it is not wrong to speak of their *humanitas*. But like the philosophers and the novelists, they regarded slavery as an evil that could befall anyone, and that recognition shaped their sense of the demands of justice. Their *humanitas* was not the *humanitas* of a modern human rights lawyer, supposing it to be the task of the law to mount a root and branch assault on a horrifically inegalitarian and brutal institution. It was the more modest *humanitas* of sympathy for the victims – to use a stock Homeric phrase, the jurists "looked on with pity"[80] – and correspondingly their humanitarian commitments were commitments to what Garnsey elegantly calls "slavery eased."[81] It took the form of the belief, not that slavery was incompatible with the "natural" rights of man, but that the law was called upon to intervene, from time to time, to shield some persons from the dreadful calamity of "the day of slavery" – unless they had been enslaved through the one incontestably just act, seizure by the enemy in war. But the justice of enslavement through war was beyond question. Even the jurists' most seemingly enlightened pronouncements on "natural liberty" were premised on the unimpeachable legitimacy of the taking of human prey by the victor.

* * *

The word "calamity" (*calamitas*) is used in the opening pages of the *Digest* of Justinian, which treat the general nature of law. The passage in question is typical of Roman juristic philosophizing, and of Greco-Roman traditions more broadly. When the jurists considered large questions of justice and legal philosophy, it was not the ownership of land that preoccupied them, as it would preoccupy early modern philosophers such as Locke or Rousseau. What preoccupied them was enslavement, just as it was enslavement that preoccupied the epic poets, novelists, and philosophers of the Mediterranean world.

[79] To my mind, Garnsey reads a bit too much into the efforts of the ancients to find a justification for slavery. Property law always seems to require some effort at justification for the ownership of its paradigmatic object. We would be wrong to conclude from contemporary debates over the justification for landownership that moderns are afflicted by deep doubt about the propriety of owning land. The same, I suggest, can be said of ancient justifications for slavery.
[80] See the dissertation of no less a figure than Walter Burkert, "Zum altgriechischen Mitleidsbegriff," diss. Erlangen, 1955, at e.g., 81–134.
[81] Garnsey, *Ideas of Slavery*, 87–106.

In this passage, the compilers of the *Digest* excerpted the *Institutes*, or basic textbook, of Aelius Marcianus, like Ulpian a jurist active during the Severan period. Marcianus addressed a fundamental Roman distinction between two types of law. First, there was the *ius civile*, the personal law of Roman citizens. Alongside it came the *ius gentium*, the "law of all peoples," the body of practices presumptively common to all human polities. Ordinarily, no Roman citizen could be enslaved under the *ius civile*, since free status was a fundamental aspect of citizenship. There was, however, one exception, involving the case where a Roman citizen engaged in fraud, attempting to cheat a buyer by falsely offering himself for sale, in order to appropriate a portion of the price when he was subsequently declared to be a free man. The law punished such acts by enslaving the fraudster.

If enslavement was limited to this one exception under the *ius civile*, however, the same was not true of the *ius gentium*, the "law of all peoples," which fully accepted the legitimacy of enslavement through two routes: either through defeat in war or through birth to a slave mother. Those enslaved through war had no escape, but there was a glimmer of hope for a few of the others:

(1) Slaves are brought under our ownership either by the ius civile or by the ius gentium. This is done by the ius civile where anyone who is over twenty years of age permits himself to be sold for the sake of sharing in his own price. Slaves become our property by the ius gentium when they are either taken from the enemy, or are born of our female slaves. (2) Persons are born free who are born from a free mother, and it is sufficient for her to have been free at the time when her child was born, even though she may have been a slave when she conceived; and, on the other hand, if she was free when she conceived, and was a slave when she brought forth, it has been established that her child is born free, nor does it make any difference whether she conceived in a lawful marriage or through promiscuous intercourse; because the calamity of the mother should not be a visited upon her unborn child.[82]

We are not told what sort of "calamity" might have reduced a woman to slavery during her pregnancy, but that is not what matters. What matters, as Marcianus explained to his students, is

---

[82] D. 1.5.5.1-2. Marcianus 1 *Inst*. Cf. the marvelous D. 40.7.6.1-2. Ulpianus 27 *ad sab*., for an example of such reasoning in cases involving multiple complexities of passages between slavery and freedom. For the "free womb" see also D. 5.4.3. Paulus 17 *ad plaut*.

that the law had the authority, not to question the justice of slavery in general, but to soften the blow of fate in a particular instance not involving war. This was "slavery eased," an expression of the *favor libertatis*, the presumption in favor of liberty, here applied to benefit unborn children.[83] The same presumption was used by the jurists in a variety of other cases. Wills, for example, would be construed in such a way as to favor liberty.[84]

But the one context in which the *favor libertatis* was never applied was in cases of the paradigm cause of enslavement, defeat in war, a disaster that the law could do nothing to remedy. This is true of Marcianus' passage, and it is true elsewhere in the Roman legal corpus as well. While the jurists firmly insisted that slavery could not be legally created through capture by brigands, the "man-stealers" of Plato, they never questioned its creation through capture on the battlefield or the sack of cities.[85] On this point, it is instructive to contrast Marcianus' account of slavery with that of his older contemporary, the physician Galen. For Galen, it was obvious that people fell into slavery in three different ways: "because they are born into it, or because they are captured in war *or snatched away by bandits*."[86] For Marcianus, only the first two of these possibilities counted.

Capture by bandits deserved no legal respect, and in many circumstances the law favored liberty; but enslavement through war could not be second-guessed. Bradley exaggerates a bit when he says that the jurists "never seriously questioned" the justification for slavery. What they never seriously questioned was this *one* justification for slavery.

* * *

[83] For this as an example of *favor libertatis*, see Hans Wieling, ed., *Corpus der römischen Rechtsquellen zur antiken Sklaverei* (Stuttgart, 1999), 1:43. But see W. W. Buckland, *Roman Law of Slavery: The Condition of the Slave in Private Law from Augustus to Justinian* (New York, 1969), 399, suggesting that it is not necessary to appeal to the *favor libertatis* to account for these issues. For Marcianus' treatment see further *D.* 40.11.2.

[84] Härtel, "Favor libertatis"; H. J. Wieling, *Testamentsauslegung im römischen Recht* (Munich, 1972), 115.

[85] *D.* 49.15.19.2. Paulus 16 *ad sab*. *A piratis aut latronibus capti liberi permanent*; *D.* 49.15.24 (Ulpianus 1 *inst*.). Further discussion in Maria Floriana Cursi, *La struttura del "postliminium" nella Repubblica e nel Principato* (Naples, 1996), 136–138. Visscher, "Droit de capture," 119, observes that this is also true of those captured in civil war.

[86] Galen, *Hygiene* 2.1, 82K.

Classical Roman Slave Law

The incontestable legitimacy of enslavement through war was assumed in Marcianus' passage, and the same assumption lay in the background of juristic discussions of "natural law" and "natural liberty." Paradoxical though it may sound, it is even the view that lay in the background of Ulpian's resonant "by natural law all men were born free." Much though that line may sound to modern readers like a sweeping proclamation of natural human liberty and equality, it represented in fact an endorsement of enslavement through war.

To grasp the ancient meaning of Ulpian's apothegm, we must read it in the larger context of Roman juristic argument. The proposition that slavery was "contrary to nature" is found in a number of passages in the *Digest*. Florentinus, probably a generation older than Ulpian and author of a standard textbook, explained that liberty was a "natural faculty," of which "the law of peoples" could deprive persons through slavery. Slavery, Florentinus explained in a famous passage, originated in war. This was revealed by its terminology: Slaves, he observed, were called *servi* or *mancipia*. The first term was used because they were "spared" [*servare*] by the victor in order to be sold, and the second, meaning (as we saw in Chapter 2) "things subject to the hand-gripping power," was used because slaves were persons who had been seized by the victor's triumphant hand:

Liberty is the natural faculty of doing whatever anyone wishes to do unless he is prevented in some way, by force or by law. (1) Slavery is an institution of the ius gentium by means of which anyone may subject one man to the control of another, contrary to nature. (2) Slaves [*servi*] are so called for the reason that military commanders were accustomed to sell their captives, and in this manner to preserve [*servare*] them, instead of putting them to death. (3) They are styled mancipia, because they are taken by the hands of their enemies.[87]

There was a choice to be made, in the account of Florentinus, about whether the captive would be killed or enslaved. But that choice did not belong to the defeated person, as it would for early modern political theorists.[88] There was no morality of consent here. The choice to kill or enslave belonged entirely to the triumphant captor.

---

[87] D. 1.5.4pr.3. Florus 9 *inst.* Cf. Pomponius in D. 50.16.239.1: "*servorum*" *appellatio ex eo fluxit, quod imperatores nostri captivos vendere ac per hoc servare nec occidere solent.*

[88] Below, Chapter 9.

The world of Florentinus, like the world of Plautus' *Captivi*, was a stage on which armies hunted human prey, who were then to be offered for sale. Humans who had not yet been captured enjoyed the "natural faculty" of liberty, but either force or law could put an end to that, subjecting them to the *dominium* of another "against nature." The same idea of "natural" liberty was also referenced by the Severan jurist Claudius Tryphoninus:

D. 12.6.64. Tryphoninus 7 *disp*. Freedom is a part of natural law, and domination has been introduced by the *ius gentium*.

The right of acquisition in war through the *ius gentium* was also regularly remarked, making its way into the basic treatment of the *Corpus iuris civilis*:

Inst. 2.1.17: those things that we seize from the enemy automatically become ours by the *ius gentium*.

The assumption behind all these passages was the same. Humans were "naturally" free; but that "natural" freedom could be terminated if they were defeated and taken captive.

Ulpian's declaration that "all men were born free" belongs to his own statement of this conventional doctrine, so remote from modern human rights thinking. The passage in which Ulpian's line appears was also concerned with the "taking by hand," and it too assumed that the "law of all peoples" conferred legitimacy on enslavement. Like Tannenbaum centuries later, Ulpian emphasized the significance of manumission. Ulpian began, as scholars reconstruct his basic textbook, by distinguishing banditry, in line with the standard view of the jurists, from properly declared war:

[D. 49.15.24] Enemies are those against whom the Roman people have publicly declared war, or who themselves have declared war against the Roman people; others are called robbers, or brigands. Therefore, anyone who is captured by robbers, does not become their slave ... He, however, who has been taken by the enemy, for instance, by the Germans or Parthians, becomes their slave ...[89]

---

[89] *Hostes sunt, quibus bellum publice populus Romanus decrevit vel ipse populo Romano: ceteri latrunculi vel praedones appellantur. Et ideo qui a latronibus captus est, servus latronum non est, nec postliminium illi necessarium est: ab hostibus autem captus, ut puta a Germanis et Parthis, et servus est hostium et postliminio statum*

Not all hope was lost for the enslaved, however. This was partly because they might escape. But it was also because the enslaver might condescend to free them:

[D. 1.1.4 Ulpianus 1 *inst.*] Manumissions are also part of the ius gentium, for manumission is dismissal from the hand [of the master, who was conceived as gripping slaves in his hand], that is to say the bestowal of freedom; for as long as anyone is in servitude he is subject to the hand and to authority, but, once manumitted, he is liberated from that authority. This takes its origin from the ius gentium; since, according to natural law all men were born free, and manumission was not known, as slavery itself was unknown; but after slavery entered [*invasit*] under the ius gentium, the benefit of manumission followed, and while men were designated by one natural name there arose three different kinds under the ius gentium, that is to say freemen, and, in distinction to them, slaves, and as a third class, freedmen, or those who had ceased to be slaves.

Ulpian thus portrayed slavery as the result of a kind of Fall from an original condition of innocence.[90] Universal liberty had once reigned in what later political theorists would call the state of nature, in which humans were born "naturally" free and equal.[91] But subsequently slavery "entered" the primitive natural order under "the law of all peoples," which permitted them to be seized by the hand of the victor. The idea that slavery was the consequence of such an intrusion into the state of nature seems to have been shared by other jurists of the Severan period: For Tryphoninus too, the history of liberty was marked by the moment when slavery was "introduced" into the primitive natural order.

These Severan jurists did not use the phrase "state of nature." Nevertheless, like their early modern successors, they were telling a mythic history that began in a lost age of "natural" innocence, which was terminated by the intrusion of the *ius gentium*, which brought with it enslavement through war; and as we contemplate its

---

pristinum recuperat. For its placement, see Otto Lenel, *Palingenesia iuris civilis* (repr. Frankfurt a.M., 2004), 2: col. 927.

[90] There is of course a danger in using such Christian terminology as "the Fall" to describe ancient juristic teachings, just as there is a danger in using the phrase "state of nature." Nevertheless, this is language that helpfully highlights the historical links among these various Western traditions of reflection on the early history of humanity.

[91] For the observation that this and related passages presupposed a historical development akin to what is found in the literature on the state of nature, see Ugo Nicolini, *La proprietà, il principe e l'espropriazione per pubblica utilità* (Milan, 1940), 10.

mythic character it is helpful, as so often, to turn to a comparison with Roman religion. These are juristic teachings, as Bradley suggestively observes, that shared the vision of human history celebrated in one of the great Roman religious festivals: the Saturnalia, the late December feast of status inversion.[92] The Saturnalia, during which slaves were permitted to dress up in their masters' clothes,[93] and recline alongside them as they dined,[94] told of its own state of nature: The festival celebrated the reign of Saturn, "a time of plenty when there was no distinction between free and slave, which is why during the festival slaves are allowed to act licentiously."[95] Once the festivities were over, however, the slaves were thrust back into subjection, as though the *ius gentium* had once again entered the world. As Bradley's comparison suggests, what Ulpian was offering was what might be called a Saturnalian account of the law of slavery – a tale of a long-ago juristic state of nature, like the lost days of Saturn that flickered briefly back to life during the idle and chilly days of late December.

In any case, an account of the state of nature this was; and in that sense it is entirely correct to see a line of filiation between the thought of Ulpian and the thought of Rousseau and other early modern political thinkers. But it should be obvious that that does not mean that he or other ancient jurists had the same concept of freedom as a Rousseau, and still less that they were "pioneers of human rights" in anything like the modern sense. What these texts reveal, on a sober reading, is, as Schiavone writes, "the inability to transform the ancient theory of natural law into an authentic doctrine of human rights, even in the

---

[92] Keith Bradley, "Roman Slavery and Roman Law," *Historical Reflections* 15 (1988): 479 n. 11 [477–495]; Bradley, "Slavery in the Roman Republic," in John Bodel and Paul Cartledge, eds., *The Cambridge World History of Slavery, Vol. 1: The Ancient Mediterranean World* (Cambridge, 2011), 243 [241–264].

[93] Cassius Dio 60.19.3, in *Roman History*, ed. Earnest Cary (Cambridge, MA, 1924), 7:414.

[94] At least according to Justin. *Epit.* 43.1.3: *Saturnus tantae iustitiae fuisse dicitur, et neque servierit quisquam sub illo neque quicquam privatae rei habuerit ... cuius exemplum memoriam cautum est ut Saturnalibus exaequato ominium iure passum in conviviis servi cum dominis recumbent*.

[95] Macrobius, *Saturnalia* 1.7.26: *Regni eius tempora felicissima feruntur, cum propter rerum copiam tum quod nondum quisquam servitio vel libertate discriminabatur: quae res intellegi potest, quod Saturnalibus tota servis licentia permittitur*, in Robert A. Kaster, trans., Macrobius: Saturnalia, Vol. I: Books 1–2, Loeb Classical Library 510 (Cambridge, MA, 2011), 76.

moment when it seemed closest to being attained."[96] The celebration of human freedom in these passages is a celebration of a freedom as remote, and as definitively terminated, as the mythic past of the reign of Saturn.

To be sure, there is no doubt that the authors of these Severan passages displayed a kind of *humanitas* as they contemplated the tragic history of humanity's Fall, and no doubt that they were cultivated readers of the Stoics. Ulpian in particularly insisted that the law had a humane role to play in responding to the irruption of enslavement into human life. But that role was much like the role imagined by Marcianus in his discussion of the fetus whose mother fell into slavery. The calling of the law was, not to abolish slavery, but to soften it through the *beneficium*, the "good deed," of manumission, accorded in some cases by some masters to some victims. Manumission played something like the part of hope in the myth of Pandora's box (at least, in the modern version of the myth), the wisp of comfort left to a humanity condemned to live with ineradicable evils. Yet those evils really were ineradicable: The Saturnalia always ended, and the jurists never denied that the "law of all peoples" licensed enslavements through war.

And as two leading French scholars, A.-J. Arnaud and Yan Thomas,[97] emphasize, their pronouncements on enslavement through war must be read alongside others that analyze the other form of capture through the "seizure by hand," the hunt for animal prey. The "natural" liberty of humans, in the view of the jurists, was indistinguishable from the "natural" liberty of beasts, which also enjoyed "the faculty of doing whatever [they wished] to do unless [they are] prevented in some way, by force or law." Here again, as Bradley has so compellingly argued, we must understand the ownership of humans alongside the ownership of beasts. Arnaud and Thomas make the point by emphasizing the link between the law of enslavement and the law of *occupatio*, the law of the acquisition of property already discussed in Chapter 2. The account of *occupatio* preserved in the *Digest* makes the connection between

---

[96] Schiavone, *The Invention of Law in the West*, trans. Jeremy Carden and Antony Shugaar (Cambridge, MA, 2012), 457.

[97] Thomas, "L'institution juridique de la nature: remarques sur la casuistique du droit naturel à Rome," in Thomas, *Les opérations du droit*, ed. Marie-Angèle Hermitte and Paolo Napoli (Paris, 2011), 24–40; Arnaud, "Reflexions sur l'occupation du droit romain," *Revue historique du droit* 46 (1968): 183–210.

hunting and enslavement clear. The compilers drew on the mid second-century CE jurist Gaius, writing two generations before the Severans. Like his Severan successors, Gaius began by distinguishing the *ius gentium* from the *ius civile*:

[D. 41.1.1pr.] We obtain the ownership of certain property by the ius gentium, which is everywhere observed among men, according to the dictates of natural reason; and we obtain the ownership of other things by the ius civile, that is to say, by the law of our own community.

But unlike his Severan successors, Gaius did not yet imagine a primitive state of nature in which all men once enjoyed "natural liberty."[98] Instead, according to his mid second-century account, the *ius gentium* already existed from the beginning, having been "born along with the human race itself":

And because the ius gentium is the more ancient, as it was born along with the human race itself [*cum ipso genere humano proditum est*], it is proper that it should be examined first.

And what were the sorts of objects that could be acquired by the "more ancient" *ius gentium*? Gaius' list began with living creatures:

(1) Therefore, all animals which are captured on land, on sea, or in the air, that is to say, wild beasts and birds, as well as fish, become the property of those who take them ... (3) For what does not belong to anyone by natural law becomes the property of the person who first acquires it.

Next, after discussing the law of a wide variety of creatures, from bees to guinea fowl, Gaius turned to war booty, which naturally included slaves:

[D. 41.1.5.7] those things that we seize from the enemy automatically become ours by the *ius gentium* ...

[D. 41.1.7pr.] To such an extent is this true that even men who are free become the slaves of the enemy; but, still, if they escape from the power of the enemy they will recover their pristine liberty.[99]

This was the law of "the mastery of hunters over their game, the mastery of fishers over their catch ... war captives ... and booty" of

---

[98] For the contrast, see Schiavone, *Invention of Law*, 456.
[99] See also the reconstruction in Lenel, *Palingenesia iuris civilis*, 1: cols. 252–253.

which Arnaud speaks.[100] Closely parallel accounts of the relationship between animals and humans featured elsewhere in the ancient fragments as well. Thus the jurists explained that animals too, like human beings, enjoyed "natural liberty" until such time as they were captured.[101] They also found it important to note that animals, like humans, sought to escape.[102]

It is in light of these teachings that we must read our Ulpian. In a famous passage, he defined "natural law" as the law shared by humans and animals:

> D. 1.1.1.3–4: Natural law is that which nature teaches to all animals, for this law is not peculiar to the human race, but affects all creatures which deduce their origin from the sea or the land, and it is also common to birds. From it proceeds the union of male and female which we designate as marriage; hence also arises the procreation of children and the bringing up of the same; for we see that all animals, and even wild beasts, appear to be acquainted with this law. The ius gentium is that used by the human race, and it is easy to understand that it differs from natural law, for the reason that the latter is common to all animals, while the former only concerns men in their relations to one another.

Modern scholars have been understandably fascinated by this biologistic definition of "natural law," and have offered a variety of observations about its ancient sources and its significance for the history of natural law thought. There is certainly no doubt that it is the product of a striking lawyerly mind, and that Ulpian's concerns were not limited to the problem of enslavement. What deserves emphasis, for my purposes here, is that his conception of "natural law" fit comfortably within a tradition that always linked slaves closely with beasts, and treated both not only as creatures that engaged in sexual reproduction, but also as creatures suitable to be hunted down. Ulpian's classification into animals of the land, sea, and air is telling; the same tripartite division appears in the law of *occupatio*, as it does in Genesis, as we saw in Chapter 2. When Ulpian declared that men were originally "born free," he meant that they were born free in the same sense that stags or quail or salmon are

---

[100] Arnaud, "Reflexions sur l'occupation du droit romain," 186.
[101] Gai. *Inst.* 2.67, and D. 41.1.3.2 5pr. Bruce Frier, "Bees and Lawyers," *Classical Journal* 78 (1982–1983): 106 [105–114].
[102] See below, this chapter.

born free. To speak of "natural" liberty was only to say that in the beginning, humans were "natural" beings who, however, after the intrusion of the law of all peoples, were subject to capture and enslavement.

* * *

This is not a teaching that is likely to strike modern readers as enlightened, and it is important to emphasize how different it is both from ancient Stoic doctrines, and from modern human rights thought. The views of these Roman jurists were not, despite the claims of so many scholars, synonymous with Stoic philosophies of human equality. This was by no means "the Romans' own case for abolition," or their blueprint for a cosmopolis dedicated to universal human rights. While it is true that figures like Marcianus and Ulpian accepted, in some sense, the proposition that all humans were naturally equal, it is also true that they endorsed the harsh position that we associate with Thrasymachus and Callicles: They never denied the right of the stronger to enslave the weaker, as long as it was done through war rather than brigandage. By the same token, it is essential to underline the obvious point that none of the juristic ancient passages I have discussed used the terms "nature" or "natural law" or "natural liberty" in the way that figures like Grotius or Pufendorf or Rousseau or Jefferson would use them a millennium and a half later. The point in all of them is not that there are universal human rights, but that humans, who were originally "naturally" free, could, like naturally free wild animals, or for that matter Homeric princesses, be lawfully reduced to the *dominium* of their captors, to be sold on the market, or, as the case may be, to be dragged off to the tent of Achilles and raped.

From the modern point of view, this is appalling. Can we do anything but condemn it as a violation of universal morality? As historians, we are enjoined to cultivate a sympathetic view of alien societies, rather than condemning them outright. In the classic words of Johann Gottfried Herder, we are supposed to engage in *Einfühlung*: We are supposed to "feel our way in" to the values of the foreign culture. But maybe that sort of effort is simply out of place when it comes to fundamental violations of human rights, and in particular when it comes to such "an evil, violent and brutalizing institution" as slavery at Rome.

Nevertheless, let us try. Here we can begin with one great scholar who mounted a defense, of a kind, of Roman slave law: Jhering, the supremely tough-minded legal historian and philosopher who laid the groundwork for the modern study of Roman law, and more broadly for the modern philosophy of law. Writing in 1877, Jhering offered a characteristically unsentimental view of ancient enslavement. It is a basic methodological error, he insisted, to condemn the ancient practice of enslaving defeated enemies as a violation of timeless norms of human rights. On the contrary, seen in proper historical perspective, enslavement represented nothing less than the very *origin* of human rights:

> The victor who spared the life of his vanquished enemy instead of slaughtering him did it because he understood that a living slave is more valuable than a dead enemy. He spared him for the same reason that the proprietor spares his domestic animal ... Recognition of the economic value of human life was the first beginning of humanity in human history. The Romans call a slave "homo" – he is a human being who is nothing more than a human being, a working animal, not a subject of rights ("persona"). The citizen alone is "persona," but "homo" signifies nevertheless the first rise of humanity to human-ness [*Menschlichkeit*].[103]

Jhering's writings never quite lose their capacity to shock; it is easy to see why Nietzsche was one of his readers. There are certainly few more aggressively challenging propositions in the literature of legal history than "recognition of the economic value of the human as a working animal to be enslaved was the first beginning of human rights."

Of course, his thesis is not susceptible of proof one way or another. Who knows whether calling slaves *homo* was really the "first rise of humanity to human-ness"?[104] Nevertheless, Jhering's attitude toward history is instructive. He was right to say that we must shake off

---

[103] I have slightly altered the translation of Isaac Husik, trans., Rudolf Jhering, *Law as a Means to an End* (Union, N.J., 1999), 182–183, by reference to the original, Jhering, *Der Zweck im Recht*, 6th–8th ed. (Leipzig: Breitkopf & Härtel, 1923), 1:188.

[104] The question of how humans become fully human was frequently posed in nineteenth-century Germany, for example by Schiller, *Über die ästhetische Erziehung des Menschen in einer Reihe von Briefen*, ed. Gideon Steinig (Berlin, 2019). For a contemporary of Jhering: Nietzsche, "Vom Nutzen und Nachteil der Historie für das Leben," in *Unzeitgemässe Betrachtungen*, in *Nietzsches Werke: historich-kritische Gesamtausgabe* 3, pt 1 (Berlin, 1972), 249.

modern beliefs about human rights if we are to grapple properly with ancient Roman attitudes, and beyond that the place of slavery in human history. We are the heirs of a complex process of human development, one that has been going on for thousands of years, and one that will continue after we are dead. The concept "humanity" has always been, and will always remain, a moving target. When we insist on viewing ancient slavery by the light of current human rights norms, we only succeed in obscuring it, while sparing ourselves the labor of confronting hard questions about the historical contingency of our own belief systems.

So, following Jhering's lead, let us approach the Roman sources with a dose of historical humility. We revile slavery in the modern world; but we must think through carefully why we revile it; for much of what disturbs us about it makes a shaky basis for evaluating the Romans. We revile slavery, first of all, because it violates the foundational principle that there can be, in the slogan often proclaimed in late eighteenth and nineteenth centuries, "no property in man."[105] The modern conception of property holds, as we saw in Chapter 2, that all objects, entities, and claims can count equally as legal "things" – but with the fundamental, and indefeasible, exception of human beings.

Yet that principle, self-evident as it has come to seem to us since the mid eighteenth century, makes a problematic basis for an attack on Roman slavery. As we saw in the first two chapters, Roman society, like the societies of precolonial Africa, was organized along a "slavery to kinship continuum," in which most persons, including some persons of very high standing, were deemed to be the property of a small stratum of masters.[106] If there is something objectionable in the status of Roman slaves, it cannot be that they suffered some special evil in being human property; that was a widespread juridical condition, and not necessarily a symbolically degrading one.[107]

---

[105] Sean Wilentz, *No Property in Man: Slavery and Anti-slavery at the Nation's Founding* (Cambridge, MA, 2018).

[106] Suzanne Miers and Igor Kopytoff, *Slavery in Africa: Historical and Anthropological Perspectives* (Madison, WI, 1977), 23–24.

[107] These are issues that lie in the background of Orlando Patterson's controversial definition of slavery as constituted by "natal alienation" rather than by the condition of being property.

We revile slavery for a second reason as well: because it exposes its victims to unredressable corporal violence. We think of slaves as persons who are subject to the whip, deprived of all right to defend themselves.[108] Yet here again we must be careful not to bring anachronistic assumptions to the study of the past. The suppression of corporal violence is a very recent development in human history. Many or most Romans, like many or most persons throughout the premodern world, were exposed to beatings, including women, children, and pupils, even ones of the highest social status. To be sure, the worst-off Roman slaves certainly faced forms of brutality that were exponentially more severe. But it is not even the case that all slaves were treated brutally. Some Roman slaves were men of great wealth and power.

Not least, we revile slavery because we live with the shameful memory of the American Antebellum South. Yet Antebellum slavery, as we saw in Chapter 1, operated on the model of what anthropologists call a "closed system": It treated its slaves as a caste of inferiors, permanently excluded from membership in the dominant society. Roman slavery, by contrast, like slavery in precolonial Africa, conformed much more closely to the model of the "open system": Manumission was practiced on a large scale, and properly freed slaves were automatically admitted to Roman citizenship; in that sense, Roman slavery is an example of James L. Watson's "open model."[109] Of course, we must be careful not to view Roman manumission in too starry-eyed a way. The lot of most Roman slaves was hopeless, especially those consigned to labor on the great slave plantations. Nevertheless, Roman slavery did not function purely as an institution of exclusion; on the contrary, it sometimes functioned as an institution of recruitment, bolstering the citizen rolls.

None of that means that it was just fine to be a Roman slave, and the Roman jurists did not think anything of the kind. They regarded enslavement as a profound form of abasement, the definitional

---

[108] See for example the discussion of Pierre Bonnassie, "Survie et extinction du régime esclavagiste dans l'Occident du haut moyen âge (IVe–XIe s.)," Cahiers de civilisation médiévale, 27 (1985): 318 [307–343].

[109] This is the argument of Peter Temin, "The Labor Market of the Early Roman Empire," *Journal of Interdisciplinary History* 34 (2004): 513–538.

deplorable fate.[110] What it does mean is that the condition of the slave was not categorically outside the pale of human rights as they existed in Roman society. Slaves were owned; but so were others. Slaves were beaten; but so were others. The *Odyssey* bewails the "day of slavery" as the moment when a man loses "half his value."[111] Those verses reflect the undoubted fact that the ancients regarded enslavement as a calamity; but is it not striking that the *Odyssey* speaks only of the loss of *half* the value of a man?

There are deep-seated differences between the ancient and modern worlds at work here. Ancient historians are well aware that these differences exist; but they sometimes allow themselves to forget them when it comes time to pass judgment on the morality of Roman slavery. If we bear them in mind, we have a better chance of "feeling our way in" to the values of the Roman jurists.

The teachings of those jurists do indeed look appalling from our point of view, and we are entitled to say so; but they were not entirely devoid of moral content. The ancient jurists were not immune to pity for their fellow humans. But their concerns did not turn on modern values like human dignity. Instead, they turned on the most unconquerable of premodern moral problems, the problem of fate. Fate sometimes visited upon persons the "calamity" of "the day of slavery." That fate was commonly undeserved. If the Romans sacked your city and hauled you off in chains for sale on the slave market, that was ordinarily not the result of any act of your own for which you could be considered at fault. Yet the omnipresence of that harrowing danger, seen in the larger scheme of human affairs, was not a source of unalloyed evil in the world. Enslavement, as we have seen, was a great equalizer; it could strike any person of any station; in that sense, it was akin to the other great equalizers, disease and death, both also undeserved; and like them it had the welcome power to rattle the arrogant. "A man who feels pity for another suffering calamity," so wrote the ex-slave Publilius Syrus, "is reminded of his own precarious lot."[112]

---

[110] See Henrik Mouritsen, *The Freedman in the Roman World* (Cambridge, 2011), 14–15 for discussion and citations.

[111] Hom. *Od.* 17.322–323: ἥμισυ γάρ τ' ἀρετῆς ἀποαίνυται εὐρύοπα Ζεὺς | ἀνέρος, εὖτ' ἄν μιν κατὰ δούλιον ἦμαρ ἕλῃσιν.

[112] *Homo qui in homine calamitoso est misericors meminit sui.* My translation. Text in J. Wight Duff and Arnold M. Duff, eds., *Minor Latin Poets, Vol. I*, Loeb Classical Library 284 (Cambridge, MA, 1982), 46.

Not least, and perhaps most importantly, the jurists resolutely restricted slave-taking to the context of lawful war. That fact is not emphasized by their defenders, but it deserves to be. What may be most remarkable about the classical jurists is their commitment to the proposition that the activities of man as "animal of prey, roving in search of booty and victory" must be conducted with the proper sanction of the Roman state. To us, that breathes barbarism: In our eyes, the fact of state *imprimatur* makes crimes against humanity worse, not better. But we must recognize it for what it was: a form of the rule of law.[113] The most majestic declaration of Ulpian, one might even say, was not "by natural law all men were born free," but "anyone who is captured by robbers does not become their slave."

* * *

Juristic teachings on "natural law" and "the law of all peoples" rested on the idea that enslavement through war was unproblematically just. But the study of the place of war and hunting in Roman law cannot end there. We must also understand how the paradigm case of the hunt served as a basis for analogical reasoning.

The practice of analogical reasoning always offers insight into the normative underpinnings of any sophisticated legal system. As Wael Hallaq, the lucid expositor of classical Islamic Law, writes, "[a]ny system of interpretation ... starts from given or self-evident premises"[114] from which it can generalize; but what count as "given or self-evident" premises noticeably varies from culture to culture. Modern American legal culture, for example, begins from the "given and self-evident premise" that freedom of speech must be safeguarded – and then extends the concept of "speech" to cover a wide, indeed wild, variety of behaviors far removed from the ordinary understanding of the term, from nude dancing to cake baking to gun ownership.[115] The study of the analogical extension of "speech" is a study of how the most basic American values propagate through the medium of the law, taking on the coloration of what legal reason deems "given or self-evident."

---

[113] And one in tune with the *pax romana*. See Philip de Souza, *Piracy in the Graeco-Roman World* (Cambridge, 1999), 195–210.

[114] Hallaq, "Uṣūl al-Fiqh: Beyond Tradition," *Journal of Islamic Studies* 3 (1992): 178 [172–202].

[115] Danny Li, "The First Amendment Weaponized: When Guns Become Public Discourse," *William & Mary Bill of Rights Journal* 30 (2022): 925–961.

What then were the "given or self-evident premises" of classical Roman property law, suitable for the exercise of analogical reasoning? Perhaps unsurprisingly, in light of the cultural orientations described in this chapter and the previous two, the jurists looked, in particular, to the hunt.

The hunt indeed pervades classical reasoning about property. Scholars have often observed that Roman jurists used *occupatio*, the law of "acquiring first possession of wild animals,"[116] as the foundation for analogical reasoning in realms well outside the hunt itself. This shows clearly in the texts of Book 41 of the *Digest*, the principal home of the surviving sources on property law. The account in the *Digest* begins with *occupatio* in its most basic form, the hunting of "all animals which are captured on land, on sea, or in the air, that is to say, wild beasts and birds, as well as fish."[117] The subsequent fragments allow us to follow how the jurists applied the basic model of the capture of animals to a host of other topics.

These included the taking of enemies in war, as we have seen. The *Digest* text, drawn from Gaius, moved, without skipping a beat, from a survey of the capture and ownership of various nonhuman animals to the capture and enslavement of "free men."[118] But the imagery of the hunt extended well beyond that. The jurists took the same tack in analyzing topics such as the birth of offspring to domestic animals. On what basis can the owner of the mother claim ownership of the new creature? The answer was that the newly born calf or sheep was treated as though it were a *res nullius*, a wild thing first sighted and captured at the moment it dropped from its dam.[119] It was as though the owner was a hunter who had spotted and grabbed the newborn when it first came into sight.

The use of the hunting analogy in such a context may not seem wholly odd, since animals are involved. But the analogy was also used in much more unexpected, indeed startling, ways. A famous example is

---

[116] Herbert Hausmaninger and Richard Gamauf, *Casebook on Roman Property Law*, available at https://global.oup.com/us/companion.websites/9780199838677/.

[117] D. 41.1.1.1. Gai. 2 *rer. cott.*

[118] Drawn from Gaius. For the reconstruction of the text, see Lenel, *Palingenesia iuris civilis*, 1: col. 253.

[119] D. 41.1.6. Flor. 6 *inst.*: *Item quae ex animalibus dominio nostro eodem iure subiectis nata sunt.*

specificatio, the problem that arises when a new thing is created through the use of raw materials provided by someone other than its maker.[120] Suppose you cast a statue using my bronze, or make wine from my grapes? To whom does the object so produced belong? This was a question that divided the two great schools of the classical law, the Sabinians and Proculians, as Gaius reports:

D. 41.1.7.7. Gaius, *Common Matters or Golden Things*, Book 2: When someone makes something for himself out of another's materials, Nerva and Proculus [of the Proculian school] are of opinion that the maker owns that thing because what has just been made previously belonged to no one [*antea nullius fuerat*]. Sabinus and Cassius [of the Sabinian school], on the other hand, take the view that natural reason requires that the owner of the materials should be owner of what is made from them, since a thing cannot exist without that of which it is made ...

"The Proculian view in effect," the authors of a leading textbook explain, "treated *specificatio* as a special form of *occupatio*: at the moment of creation the new thing was regarded as a *res nullius*, i.e. owned by no one, and thus open to the first 'occupier' – the creator." It was as though the bronze statue was a creature that suddenly leapt into view when its clay mold was shattered, like a piece of game darting out of the bush, and the sculptor was the first to seize it. This Proculian hunting analogy was not accepted by the rival Sabinian school. As the textbook authors write, the analogy with *occupatio* was "rather strained ...: the created thing can hardly be said to have been a *res nullius* if it was owned as soon as it was created"; and other competing approaches to the problem appeared as well.[121] And it is indeed true that the Proculian analogy to *occupatio* was "strained"; but all analogies strain; that is what makes them analogies rather than identities. The same can be said of the American use of the analogy to land in property law: Like the Roman jurists puzzling over whether a bronze sculpture is *res nullius*, American jurists puzzle over the extent to which intellectual property can be said to be fenced off by "metaphorical boundaries."[122] And like the Roman jurists, the

---

[120] The term itself is postclassical. Anna Plisecka, "*Accessio* and *Specificatio* Reconsidered," *Tijdschrift voor Rechtsgeschiedenis* 74 (2006): 46–47 [45–60].

[121] All from Paul J. Du Plessis, *Borkowski's Textbook on Roman Law*, 6th ed. (Oxford, 2020), 201.

[122] Here quoting from the abstract to Smith, "Intellectual Property as Property."

American ones reach differing conclusions about how far the land metaphor can be extended. All sophisticated legal traditions are riven by debates over the use of basic analogies. What matters for the understanding of legal cultures is that the analogies they debate are not all the same.

It is especially important for my purposes that the Roman jurists resorted to the analogy to *occupatio* in their efforts to conceptualize rights in land. Far from using landownership as the metaphor for understanding other forms of property, as we do, they tackled the problem of land by using the metaphor of the hunt. In part, this involved some odd school problems, of palpably minor economic importance: the accretion of land through the deposit of silt; avulsion resulting from the shift in the course of a stream; and the emergence of an *insula nata*, a new island formed in a sea or river. All of these were treated as cases in which new bits of land had appeared and been seized, like the newborn foal or the newly cast statue.[123] But the most telling material in the *Digest* involves an issue of the greatest economic importance, the acquisition of tracts of land through the taking of possession. As we saw in Chapter 2, the possession of land, most especially in the *ager publicus*, played a part of vast importance in the politics of the Republic. But how was "possession" to be conceptualized? Here again, the classical debates turned on the utility of the analogy of the "possession" of land to the capture of prey in the hunt. This can be seen in texts given at the opening of its treatment of acquisition in the *Digest*. As we saw in Chapter 1, the term *possessio* literally means "sitting" on a parcel of land, and the Severan jurist Paul took that as his starting point. He cited Labeo, a founder of the Proculian school:

D. 41.2.1.pr. Paul, *On the Edict*, Book 54. Possession, as Labeo says, is derived from the term *sedes* [that on which one sits] as it were a kind of putting something in a place, because it is naturally held by him who has it; and this the Greeks designate κατοχήν ["holding"].

But Paul immediately went on to speak, as classical jurists did so often, of the hunt:

D. 41.2.1.1. Nerva, the son, asserts that the ownership of property originated from natural possession, and that the trace of this still remains in the case of

---

[123] D. 41.1.7.1–8. Gai. 2 *rer. cott.*

whatever is taken on the earth, on the sea, and in the air, for it immediately belongs to those who first acquire possession of it. Likewise, spoils taken in war, and an island formed in the sea, gems, precious stones, and pearls found upon the shore, become the property of him who first obtains possession of them.

As Dario Mantovani comments, the possession of land "was seen by Nerva as the form of appropriation typical of a primordial phase of humanity, a trace of which survives in hunting, which ensures ownership of the prey to the person who seizes it by occupation."[124] Land – let me say this once again! – was unquestionably of supreme economic importance, and the law developed many sophisticated doctrines to deal with real estate transactions, as the fragments in the *Digest* unmistakably attest.[125] Nevertheless, when the jurists wrestled with the fundamental of question of how "the external things of the world" can be appropriated, land included, they found it natural to conduct their debates by reference to the analogy promoted by the Nerva and Proculus: the analogy to the primordial human activity of the hunt.

* * *

The same analogical use was made of the special aspect of *occupatio* that has been my subject in this chapter: the case of "men ... who become slaves of the enemy." This is on display in two domains of the classical law: *capitis deminutio*, "loss of head," the law of status changes; and *postliminium*, "return over the threshold," the law of escape from captivity to the enemy. These were two closely related areas of law, both rich in reflection on the fate of those defeated and enslaved in war. Both document the extent to which the jurists treated enslavement through war as a "given and self-evident" starting point for the exercise of juristic reason, to be exploited through analogy and fiction for the legal analysis of human affairs more broadly.

The law of *capitis deminutio*, "loss of head," addressed a problem of basic social importance at Rome. In the complex social hierarchy of Roman society, there were many possibilities of status change. When

---

[124] Mantovani, *Le juriste "historien,"* ch. 3 n. 70, available at https://books.openedition.org/lesbelleslettres/204?lang=en.
[125] For a study of the legal workings, see Dennis Kehoe, *Law and Rural Economy in the Roman Empire* (Ann Arbor, 2007).

subordinate members of a given *familia* entered another *familia*, for example, their legal personality was technically extinguished, as they underwent *emancipatio*, leaving the "hand" of their master. This extinction of their personality was thought of as a form of notional death;[126] and as the jurists explained, it had to be conceptualized as an "imaginary enslavement," entailing what the law called "loss of head":

D. 4.5.3.1. Paulus 11 *ad ed*. When a son or other persons are emancipated, they suffer *capitis deminutio*, since no one can be emancipated without undergoing an imaginary enslavement [*nisi in imaginariam servilem causam deductus*]: But it is different when a slave is manumitted, since a slave head has no rights and therefore cannot be diminished.

Scholars are not sure about the origins of the dramatic metaphor of "head" for describing these "imaginary enslavements." Is it that the family of origin was diminished by one head?[127] In any case, whatever its source, "loss of head" served, in the classical period, as the working paradigm of the jurists for describing all sorts of status changes.

The classical law of *capitis deminutio* had a complexity suitable to the complexity of Roman social relations. Specialists in Roman law have produced a large literature that reconstructs how it worked in practice; this is not the place to review all the details. What matters for my purposes is that, in dealing with their social world, the ancient jurists found it natural to generalize from "imaginary enslavement" as their paradigm case. As we saw in the previous chapter, Roman property terminology and procedures frequently employed the master/slave relationship as a model in conceiving and justifying property rights. "Loss of head" fit snugly within this tradition: It is not that ex-members of the *familia* were in fact enslaved; it is that the paradigm of slavery was so normatively foundational that the law found it right to treat them fictively as though they had been enslaved.

And unsurprisingly, *capitis deminutio* carried close associations with enslavement through war; for as we have seen, it was defeat in war that counted, for the jurists, as the route by which the free became slave. Their primal scene, if I may say it again, was the scene of the

---

[126] Gai. *Inst.* 3.153.
[127] Kaser, *Das römische Privatrecht* (Munich, 1954–1959), 1:235 and 235 n. 9; and generally Kaser, "Zur Geschichte der *Capitis Deminutio*," *IURA* 3 (1952): 48–89.

defeated enemy at the feet of the victor. The link seems to have been a commonplace in ancient Latin: "Those who fall into the power of the enemy," explained the second-century CE grammarian Festus, "are called people who have 'lost head.'"[128] The very word _captivus_, "captive," added Isidore of Seville, in one of his fanciful etymologies, was derived from the fact that anyone taken by the enemy was _capite deminutus_, "shortened by a head."[129] The literary sources made the same connection. Scholars point in particular to the extensive traditions surrounding one iconic war captive, Marcus Atilius Regulus, the general enslaved by the Carthaginians, and invoked by Polybius, as we saw at the beginning of this chapter, as a capital example of how the mighty might fall into slavery: "The calamity of Regulus gives the clearest possible warning that no one should feel too confident of the favors of Fortune, especially in the hour of success."[130] In the Roman literary tradition, Regulus became the exemplar, not only of the blows that fate might visit on the mighty, but also of fortitude in the face of enslavement through war. "[S]ent back to Rome by the Carthaginians ostensibly in order to lead a request for the exchange of prisoners" and having sworn an oath "to return to Carthage should the senate refuse this offer" he heroically urged the Senate "to reject the very proposal he was meant to endorse."[131] Horace painted an affecting scene of the heroic Regulus, on his return to Rome, refusing the kisses of his wife and spurning his children, since "he had lost head";[132] dead to his family, Regulus could no longer accept affection.[133]

The jurists saw the same link between capture by the enemy and "loss of head." They do not seem to have cited the phrase as reflexively

---

[128] Festus, _De significatione verborum_ 70: _Deminutus capite appellatur ... qui in hostium potestatem venit_, in Wallace Lindsay, ed., _Sexti Pompei Festi De verborum significatu quae supersunt_, Teubner (Leipzig, 1913), 61.

[129] Isidore of Seville, _Etymologiarum sive originum libri XX_, ed. Wallace M. Lindsay (Oxford, 1911), 10.54: _Captus captivus dicitur quasi capite deminutus_.

[130] Plb. 1.35, in Evelyn S. Shuckburgh, trans., _Polybius: Histories_ (London and New York, 1889). I have altered the translation to "calamity" from "disaster."

[131] Leigh, _Comedy and the Rise of Rome_, 75.

[132] Hor. _Od._ 3.5.41–44, in Niall Rudd, ed. and trans., _Horace: Odes and Epodes_, Loeb Classical Library 33 (Cambridge, MA, 2004), 160–161.

[133] For other Carthaginian captives as having "lost head" as well: Liv. 22.60.15, in B. O. Foster, trans., _Livy: History of Rome, Vol. V: Books 21–22_, Loeb Classical Library 233 (Cambridge, MA, 1929), 400–401.

as the poets, grammarians, and historians did.[134] Nevertheless, as Boudewijn Sirks argues, when they analyzed the consequences of status changes, they too found it entirely natural to generalize from captivity to the enemy as their paradigm case.[135]

* * *

Capitis deminutio was law of metaphor – metaphors of "head," metaphors of "imaginary enslavements." The law of *postliminium*, "the return over the threshold," the law of captives who returned from slavery at the hands of the enemy,[136] was not law of metaphor to the same degree. *Postliminium* was designed to deal with very real practical problems of war. Nevertheless, it too displayed the pattern of generalizing from the case of enslavement in war to analyze law and society more broadly.

The return of warriors from captivity was a topic of inevitable interest. As Gaius emphasized, implicit in the proposition that persons might be enslaved by the enemy was the possibility that they might subsequently escape, recovering their "pristine liberty."[137] Here again, it is worth signaling the parallel with the law of animals, which also might escape.[138] This possibility meant that a fully worked-out law of enslavement through war also had to include a law of captives and escapees, and the law that the jurists worked out was extensive.

At the core of that law lay a conceptual puzzle. Citizen-warriors taken captive by the enemy were reduced to slavery, as we have seen. Since slavery imported a form of notional death, the rights and duties of those captured were in principle extinguished. Captives, their head lost, had become, like Regulus, corpses in the law. Yet if those captives succeeded in making their way back "across the threshold" of their home, thus reclaiming their "pristine liberty," it seemed that they had, as it were, come back to life. How should these *revenants* from the

---

[134] Luigi Amirante, *Captivitas e postliminium* (Naples, 1950), 24–28; Kaser, "Zur Geschichte der *Capitis Deminutio*," 66.
[135] A. J. B. Sirks, "Noxa caput sequitur," *Tijdschrift voor Rechtsgeschiedenis* 81 (2013): 91 [81–108].
[136] In its earliest form, probably not for captives, but for citizens who had freely left and then returned. Cursi, *La struttura del "postliminium,"* 1–36; Hildegard Kornhardt, "*Postliminium* in Republikanischer Zeit," *Studia et documenta historiae et iuris* 19 (1953): 8, 24–25 [1–37]. The Aelius Gallus quote in Festus refers to *eum, qui liber ... in aliam civitatem abierat.*
[137] D. 41.1.7pr. Gaius 2 *rer. cott.*   [138] D. 9.1.1.10. Ulp. 18 *ad ed.*

juristic grave be treated? The law of *postliminium* responded by declaring the rights and duties of returning captives, within the limits of the possible, as having been merely suspended during the period of their absence/death.

The jurists developed an elaborate set of doctrines on how to treat these warrior rights suspended and then reanimated after a lapse of years: What happened, to take an example that haunted Western law for many centuries,[139] to the marriages of such returning warriors? Were their wives still theirs? What about their children, what about the slaves they had promised to free? It is clear that these doctrines sometimes had practical applications. Warriors did sometimes return, whether because they managed to escape or because they were ransomed.[140] One particularly famous case involved Romans who had been enslaved and sold by Hannibal. Many of these, it was reported, languished in slavery around the Mediterranean. Twelve hundred of them in particular, held as slaves in Greece, were turned over the consul Titus Quinctius Flamininus by their grateful, or intimidated, Greek masters in 194 BCE. These long-suffering warrior-slaves were transported back to Rome, where they were paraded before the Roman public in Flamininus' triumphal procession, decades after their capture, displaying Phrygian caps, the symbol of the newly freed man, on their shaved slave heads, in a joyous inversion of the festive Roman practice of parading the newly defeated and enslaved through the streets.[141]

The law of *postliminium* thus had real cases to resolve; it was a body of practical law for a warring society, even if it was not always easy to make it work.[142] But the practicalities were not all that mattered. Just as the metaphor of "loss of head" was extended to address other legal problems, so too was the metaphor of "return over the threshold." In part, this involved extending *postliminium* to cover the return of property from captivity, as well as the return of warriors. In the

---

[139] Cf., most famously on this timeless problem of premodern life, Natalie Z. Davis, *The Return of Martin Guerre* (Cambridge, MA, 1984).
[140] E.g., Vasile Lica, "'Clades Variana' and 'Postliminium,'" *Historia: Zeitschrift für alte Geschichte* 50 (2001): 496–501.
[141] Plu. *Flam.* 13.5–9, in Bernadotte Perrin, trans., *Plutarch: Lives, Vol. X: Agis and Cleomenes; Tiberius and Gaius Gracchus; Philopoemen and Flamininus*, Loeb Classical Library 102 (Cambridge, MA, 1921), 362–363.
[142] E.g., Lica, "'Clades Variana' and 'Postliminium.'"

earliest texts, the catalogue of property subject to *postliminium* followed the standard archaic model, covering slaves and beasts that could be saddled or yoked, alongside the odd addition of boats: "horses and mules and boats, by the same rationale as slaves."[143] As we saw in the previous chapter, early property catalogues typically omitted land; and that is true of this one as well. But the *postliminium* of property was subsequently extended to cover land. Indeed, as the second-century jurist Pomponius explained, land too could be imagined as suffering the "calamity" of enslavement to the enemy:

D. 11.7.36. Pomponius 26 *ad q. muc.* Where a place is taken by the enemy it ceases to be either religious or sacred, just as freemen pass into slavery. Where, however, such places are freed from this calamity, they are restored to their pristine condition by a kind of *postliminium*, as it were.

The very idea that land might suffer the "calamity" of being "enslaved in war" is testimony to the potent grip of martial metaphor on the Roman legal imagination. Nor did the jurists limit themselves to the case of war, or of sacred property, when applying *postliminium* to land: Marcianus explained that the destruction of a building on the banks of a river restored the land on which the building had been built to its "pristine" status of common property. This was to be understood, he said, "as though under the law of *postliminium*."[144]

Most importantly for the later history of international law, the jurists extended *postliminium* beyond war to cover "the movements of people and property in peacetime." Classical *postliminium* was used to treat not only relations with enemies, but also those with allied and friendly regimes; in this way, it served as normative model for the understanding international relations in the imperial order of the *pax romana* more broadly.[145]

* * *

These various doctrines of "loss of head," of "imaginary enslavement," of taking possession of land as though it were prey taken in the

---

[143] Cursi, *La struttura del "postliminium,"* 251–252.
[144] D. 1.8.6pr. Marcianus 3 *inst.*
[145] Ando, "Aliens, Ambassadors and the Integrity of Empire," *Law and History Review* 26 (2008): 503 [491–519]. Cf. Maxime Lemosse, *Le régime des relations internationales dans le Haut-Empire romain* (Paris, 1967), 9–16; Theodor Mommsen, *Römisches Staatsrecht* (Leipzig, 1871–1888), 3:656 n. 1.

primordial human activity of the hunt, of land restored to its "pristine liberty" "as though under the law of *postliminium*," even though it had suffered the "calamity" of enslavement to the enemy, and so on, clearly belong the law of what is conventionally called a "slave society." The jurists made heavy use of enslavement metaphors because they were accustomed to the institution of slavery and did not imagine its abolition. But it is essential to describe the place of slavery in their normative world carefully. It is not just that they "never seriously questioned" the justification for slavery through war. It is that they treated enslavement through war as their conceptual instrument for explicating the mysteries of society more broadly. Enslavement through war was so much a model that it came naturally to use the metaphor of *postliminium* and its restoration of "pristine liberty" as the basis for the analogical analysis of legal problems far removed from the context of the battlefield, just as it came naturally to speak of status changes as an "imaginary enslavement."

"Concepts, images and actions," to take a phrase from Georges Dumézil, "[were] articulated and, through their connections, form[ed] a kind of net in which, in the law, all the matter of human experience must be caught."[146] The law of these "concepts, images and actions" was certainly law of a slave society in the sense that it treated the ownership of human beings as fundamentally legitimate. But there is more to it than that: It was law of a slave society in the sense that its jurists were drawn to the model of the ownership of human beings as a paradigm of legitimacy, at least as long as it had its source in capture through war. To that extent, the normative reasoning of the "serious poem" that was Roman law, as Giambattista Vico so memorably called it, rested on the "poetic logic" of the hunt for human prey.[147]

---

[146] Dumézil, *L'Héritage indo-européen à Rome* (Paris, 1949), 64–65.
[147] Vico, *La scienza nuova*, ed. Paolo Rossi (Milan, 1958), 507.

5

An Empire of the Chieftainship over People

In his provocatively titled study of Roman imperial ideology, *Slaves to Rome*, Myles Lavan offers a bracing catalogue of the brutal terms and phrases used by the Romans to characterize their rule. I have already quoted him in Chapter 3:

> The conquest of foreign peoples is often described in terms of breaking animals to harness. The verbs *domare* [to tame], *perdomare* [to tame utterly], *subigere* [to subject], *frangere* [to break] and *coercere* [to coerce] – all regularly used of taming animals – are widespread in accounts of Roman expansion ... The link is particularly strong in the case of the imagery of the *iugum* [yoke]. The yoke that was forced on the necks of draught animals to attach them to plough or vehicle was a potent symbol of slavery.[1]

The resemblance between this imperial ideology and the ideology of property law traced in the previous three chapters is unmistakable: We have seen how much the language of Roman ownership turned on what was "seized by hand and subjected to the will" of the owner, in the phrase of Fernand de Visscher, and how deeply associated it was with idiom of taming, capturing, and yoking.[2]

Lavan is not alone in arguing that the "language of slavery" assumed a central place in Roman imperial ideology with the fall of

---

[1] Lavan, *Slaves to Rome: Paradigms of Empire in Roman Culture* (Cambridge, 2013), 83.
[2] Fernand de Visscher, "Mancipium et res mancipi," *Studia et documenta historiae et iuris* 2 (1936): 294 [263–324].

the Republic. Such is the view of Ari Z. Bryen, whom I quote again as well:

While sources from the Republican era betray a tension between various ways of describing the precise status of members of the imperial order – as clients, allies, or slaves – in the Principate the language of slavery is used by Roman writers with far greater ease.[3]

It is also the view of Matthew Roller, who writes that "[t]here are two social relationships in Roman society, those of master to slave and father to child (usually son), that are used pervasively in the Julio-Claudian period as metaphors for the relationship of the emperor to his subjects."[4] In the logic of rulership in the early Principate, Roller argues, the master/slave and father/son relationships constituted the "parent domain," while "my relationship with my ruler" was the "derived domain."[5] There is an imposing body of literature that interprets the spirit of Roman government along such lines. In Lavan's words, the Romans based their conception of rulership on "the paradigmatic power relations of everyday life – notably those of masters and slaves, patrons and clients, and parents and children."[6]

What all these writings suggest is that there were conceptual affinities between Martti Koskeniemmi's "yin and yang of power," sovereignty and property.[7] Those affinities are the subject of this brief chapter. Its aims are modest. Like earlier chapters, this one is an exploration of "social imaginaries,"[8] not of the quotidian workings of Roman rule. I make no effort to reconstruct the realities of government in the vast and long-enduring Roman Empire, a matter of much illuminating work by specialists. I offer no original research. My purpose is only to survey the work of historians whose writings suggest aspects of Roman rule that give it the look of the same sort of

---

[3] Bryen, "Histories of Violence: Notes from the Roman Empire," in Roderick Campbell, ed., *Violence and Civilization: Studies of Social Violence in History and Prehistory* (Oxford and Oakville, 2014), 137 [125–151].
[4] Roller, *Constructing Autocracy: Aristocrats and Emperors in Julio-Claudian Rome* (Princeton, 2001), 213.
[5] Ibid., 218. [6] Lavan, *Slaves to Rome*, 1.
[7] Koskenniemi, *To the Uttermost Parts of the Earth: Legal Imagination and International Power, 1300–1870* (Cambridge, 2021), 959.
[8] Clifford Ando, *Roman Social Imaginaries: Language and Thought in the Context of Empire* (Toronto, 2015).

"chieftainship over people" so clearly present in Roman property law, and that seem to share the master/slave idiom of power discussed in the previous three chapters.

Taking stock of such affinities is, I believe, an essential task in legal history. It is a thought-provoking fact that yin and yang often hang together – that the idiom of power in the understanding of ownership often bears a resemblance to the idiom of power of the nature of rulership. We have seen examples in earlier chapters. The distinction between "chieftainship over people" and "chieftainship over land" laid out in Chapter 1 is as much a distinction in the understanding of rulership as in the understanding of ownership. The term *dominus*, we saw in Chapter 3, became prominent in the ideology of Roman rule in the same period in which it became prominent in the law of ownership. The second Part of this book will offer further examples. In Chapter 8, I will argue that norms of territoriality began to take hold in the legal imagination of both ownership and rulership in Late Antiquity. Charles Maier, as we shall see in Chapter 9, argues that the triumph of the territorial state in the late eighteenth and nineteenth centuries went hand in hand with the triumph of Blackstonian ownership.

None of these examples demonstrates that there is some perfect congruence between the laws of property and sovereignty. Nevertheless, the affinities matter. They matter for our understanding of a premodern world in which we so often encounter the tendency to conceive both property and sovereignty against the background of the social hierarchical order. They matter for our understanding of the modern world as well, in which the idea of the territorial state, as Maier contends, bears a conceptual and historical kinship with ideas of private landownership. Rulers exercise power just as owners do, and time and again we find the two forms of power sharing unspoken assumptions about how the exercise of power works. Histories of property law and the law of the state both must take this into account. As Koskenniemi observes, our field of vision must be wide enough to take in both if we are to take the full measure of the law of either.

At the end of the chapter, I will emphasize that the territorial/ nonterritorial contrast touches on more than just the pattern of rule: It also involves another fundamental issue in the law: whether the law is conceived of as personal or territorial.

An Empire of the Chieftainship over People

* * *

Before describing the classical Roman Empire as a "chieftainship over people," akin to the "chieftainship over people" in Roman property law, it is important to begin with some sensible caveats. Goody's formula cannot be applied without many qualifications. The Roman Empire was spectacularly larger, and far more complex, than any of the precolonial African societies that Jack Goody and other African anthropologists study. The Romans did sometimes describe themselves as ruling over territories, not just over peoples: The Empire encompassed, in a phrase the Romans repeated for centuries, the *orbis terrarum*, the "world of all the lands."[9] Moreover, the Roman "language of power," according to J. S. Richardson, grew steadily more territorial over the course of Roman imperial history: The Roman word *imperium*, which originally described the personal power to command, took on an "increasingly concrete, territorial sense" after the mid first century CE, slowly acquiring something like the territorial sense of "empire" that we give it today.[10] The daily bureaucratic workings of Roman government, documented in papyri and inscriptions, were not the workings of the household rule of a Roman *paterfamilias*. All this counsels against mechanical application of Goody's African anthropology to the case of Rome.

Nevertheless, many historians have argued that the Roman practice of rule in the classical period really did depend on bonds of power over persons, in ways that sharply distinguished the Roman Empire from a modern state, and that lent themselves to the use of concepts taken from the "the paradigmatic power relations of everyday life."

To understand the force of these interpretations, it is important to begin with a rapid review of the basic contrasts between premodern and modern states. The modern state is defined, in the familiar formula of Max Weber, by its capacity to assert the "monopoly of legitimate violence" over a demarcated territory.[11] It follows that the state must

---

[9] Philip Hardie, *Virgil's Aeneid: Cosmos and Imperium* (Oxford, 1986), 378.

[10] Richardson, "*Imperium Romanum*: Empire and the Language of Power," *Journal of Roman Studies* 81 (1991): 1 [1–9]; and the more expansive investigation in his book version, Richardson, *The Language of Empire: Rome and the Idea of Empire from the Third Century* BC *to the Second Century* AD (Cambridge, 2008).

[11] Maier, *Once within Borders: Territories of Power, Wealth and Belonging since 1500* (Cambridge, MA, 2016), e.g., 75–76.

have sharply drawn borders, marking its exclusive zone of control: Modern states, as Maier emphasizes, presuppose the existence of modern maps; in this regard, they resemble modern Blackstonian owners, who locate their holdings on plats and insist on the inviolability of their borders. It further follows that the state must have a substantial administrative capacity: The monopoly of violence of the modern state must be overseen by what Weber called an "administrative staff," a corps of officials capable of exercising coercion throughout its domain; in the absence of such a staff, the state has failed.[12] The modern territorial state must have a third feature as well, though one that is not emphasized by Weber's definition: Its basic conception of law must be territorial and not personal. Individuals who find themselves within the borders of a country, regardless of their community of origin, must be subject to the law promulgated by the law of that country's sovereign.

Weber's "monopoly of violence" formula is sometimes recited as an eternal social scientific verity, true of all states in all times and places; but historians are well aware that it is certainly not. On the contrary, this Weberian form of the territorial state is a late arrival in history, dating only to the later eighteenth century, and perhaps not fully realized, as Maier and Lauren Benton argue, until the second half of the nineteenth.[13] Premodern states looked quite different. As Alain Testart writes, they generally lacked a "territorial base," exercising "primarily power over humans and not over things."[14] Direct territorial control simply exceeded their grasp. "Imperial governments," writes the anthropologist John Gledhill, "always claimed to be masters of all they surveyed." However,

[t]hey lacked the administrative, communicative and military infrastructures to make that claim a reality. "Traditional" states had frontiers rather than borders. The administrative reach of the political centre was relatively low and its control was patchy on the periphery of its domains. The Weberian definition of the state as an institution that possesses a monopoly of the legitimate use of

---

[12] Weber, *Wirtschaft und Gesellschaft*, ed. Johannes Winckelmann, 5th ed. (Tübingen, 1985), 26.
[13] As we shall see in more detail below, it is Maier's argument that the modern state arose simultaneously with the rise of the modern form of fee-simple ownership.
[14] Testart, *Éléments de classification des sociétés* (Paris, 2005), 82.

An Empire of the Chieftainship over People

force within a territorial domain is therefore appropriate only to the modern European state.[15]

It is worth reciting the familiar words of Psalm 2, which sing of this premodern understanding of power. "Ask of me," says the Lord,

> [8] and I will make the nations your inheritance,
> the ends of the earth your possession.
> [9] You will break them with a rod of iron;
> and dash them to pieces like pottery.

Rulership has a territorial ambit of a kind in the Psalm, reaching as far as "the ends of the earth" – in the King James Version "to the uttermost parts"; but at core it means to rule (and break) nations; at core it is Hugo Grotius' "rulership over persons."[16] Even where they did have some territorial base, premodern states did not have the capacity to assert a monopoly of violence of the modern kind.

Nor were they in a position to maintain sharply demarcated borders. Their outer limits, as Gledhill observes, typically consisted in ill-defined frontier zones, kept under quasi-control by forts and patrols: "areas, districts or frontiers, not border lines";[17] the edges of empire were not well-policed customs barriers, but hazardous regions where the power of the central state petered out. "[T]he administrative capabilities of most ancient governments were too limited to extend the rule of law continually and consistently far beyond the city walls into the rural hinterland."[18] Premodern travel, Maier writes, was not the experience of "flashing a passport" while crossing a border separating one securely controlled expanse of sovereign country from another.[19] Instead, the prototypical premodern travel experience was that of joining a caravan or a wagon train. Travelers left the safety of a city or fort, and moved out into lawless and dangerous stretches. Travel was a business of making one's way from one pocket of comparative security to the next.

---

[15] Gledhill, *Power and Its Disguises: Anthropological Perspectives on Politics* (Boulder, 1994), 17.
[16] Grotius, *De jure belli ac pacis*, ed. Jean Barbeyrac (Utrecht, 1773), 1:233–234 (2.3.4.1).
[17] Thongchai Winichakul, *Siam Mapped: A History of the Geo-body of a Nation* (Honolulu, 1994), 74–75.
[18] Arthur M. Eckstein, "Brigands, Emperors, and Anarchy," *International History Review* 22 (2000): 863 [862–879].
[19] Maier, *Once within Borders*, at e.g., 19.

To appreciate the kinship between Roman conceptions of ownership and rulership, we must begin by recognizing that the Roman Empire fit broadly within this pattern of premodern rule. Benjamin Isaac describes the classical Roman conception of empire:

> The Romans conquered peoples, not land. This is clear from the terminology used in numerous sources. Romans talked of the "Imperium Populi Romani," the power of the Roman people, not of the "Imperium Romanum" in any geographical sense. Latin literature invariably speaks of war with a people or its king. The Romans knew client-kings, *not* client-kingdoms.[20]

Roman frontiers were, like frontiers in other premodern states, generally fluid. There were certainly some natural features that marked the limits of the Empire, such as major rivers;[21] but like other premodern empire-builders, the Romans were generally only able to establish frontier zones, imperfectly secured by garrisons. As David Cherry argues, Roman "frontier-zones" were not borders of the modern kind; instead, "the frontiers cannot be shown to have performed any historically recoverable function other than to have accommodated the contact of Roman and indigenous society."[22] The periphery of the Empire was what Richard White, the subtle historian of eighteenth-century North America, famously calls "the middle ground," "the place in between cultures, peoples, and in between empires and the nonstate world of villages."[23] The limits of Roman power in these zones of contact were reflected in the law of *postliminium*, the law of escape from captivity at the hands of the enemy discussed at the close of the previous chapter. As the jurists explained, captives were deemed to have escaped once they came *intra praesidia nostra*, "within our defenses."[24] The word *praesidium* means "fort" or "garrison"; escapees were enjoined, not to cross some fixed border with gates and customs officers, but to get themselves within the cover of Roman troops in a frontier zone.

---

[20] Isaac, *Limits of Empire: The Roman Army in the East*, rev. ed. (Oxford, 2000), 395.
[21] Mark Graham, *News and Frontier Consciousness in the Late Roman Empire* (Ann Arbor, 2006), 57–72.
[22] Cherry, *Frontier and Society in Roman North Africa* (Oxford, 1998), 28.
[23] White, *The Middle Ground: Indians, Empires and Republics in the Great Lakes Region, 1650–1815* (Cambridge, 2010).
[24] D. 49.15.5.1. Pomponius 37 *ad q. muc.* Lewis and Short s.v. "praesidium."

An Empire of the Chieftainship over People 215

Indeed, despite their attachment to the phrase *orbis terrarum*, it is not clear that the Romans thought about their Empire in the sort of territorial terms that are second nature today at all. It has sometimes been argued that Romans had a map that displayed to inhabitants of the imperial city their immense realm;[25] but the current literature raises doubts about whether that was so, and indeed about the extent to which the Romans possessed what scholars call "map consciousness" at all. Historians of mapping distinguish between two ways of viewing the Earth: On the one hand, there is map consciousness, which blocks the planet out, in familiar modern fashion, into bounded territories; on the other hand, there is "itinerary," "hodological," or "linear" consciousness, which provides charts of how to travel from one place to another. (The GPS provides the most familiar modern experience of itinerary consciousness.) The ancient historian Kai Brodersen argues that map consciousness was absent in the classical period:

We simply lack the evidence for 'map consciousness' in the [Greco-Roman] ancient world ... [E]ven the copious ancient writings on strategy and warfare lack all references to maps. There is [however] plenty of evidence ... for the use of 'linear' modes of such perception and presentation of space ...[26]

The same point is made evocatively by the art historian Tonio Hölscher: "Geographical descriptions in antiquity do not present the reader with an overall image of topographical interrelations between different places but follow the routes of traveling, with conquering eyes, through the landscape and along the seaside. Even geographical maps are stamped with this kind of concrete experience, giving precise information on distances of sites along travel routes but totally neglecting the interrelations between the sites of different routes."[27] Such interpretations are not universally accepted;[28] but to the extent

---

[25] See Nicolet, *Space, Geography and Politics in the Early Roman Empire* (Ann Arbor, 1991), 98–111, on the map of Agrippa.
[26] Brodersen, "Mapping (in) the Ancient World," *Journal of Roman Studies* 94 (2004): 185–186 [183–190].
[27] Hölscher, *Visual Power in Ancient Greece and Rome: Between Art and Social Reality* (Berkeley: California, 2018), 4.
[28] For a survey of the literature in a skeptical spirit, P. Arnaud, "Marcus Vipsanius Agrippa and His Geographical Work," in M. R. Cataudella and H.-J. Gehrke, eds., *Brill's Companion to Ancient Geography: The Inhabited World in the Greek and Roman Tradition* (Leiden, 2016), 205–222.

they are correct, the Romans did not experience geopolitical space in the way that now seems natural; they saw the world, as Hölscher says, with different "eyes." Merio Scattola, meanwhile, working carefully through the legal sources, shows that the juristic concept of the boundary in classical Roman law applied only to private holdings. The boundary of the state as such, he argues, was an invention of the early modern period, whose career can only be traced from the late sixteenth century onward.[29]

Not least, the Romans were incapable of asserting anything like a monopoly of violence over the far-flung regions that comprised their Empire. This was not just a matter of the comparative shakiness of the Roman grip at the fringes of the Empire. Something similar was even true of the Mediterranean heartlands. Travelers by sea or land (especially hill country) throughout the Roman world were exposed to ever-present risks of banditry or piracy, which have been memorably reconstructed in the writings of Brent Shaw, and which (as we saw in Chapter 4) threatened to land them in slavery, even if enslavement by bandits was something to which the Roman jurists refused to give the stamp of the law.[30] There is no more dramatically matter-of-fact account of this ancient state of affairs than the one found in Plato's *Sophist*:

THEAETETUS: Is there, then, a hunting of tame creatures?
STRANGER: Yes, if man is a tame animal ...
THEAETETUS: Why, Stranger, I think we are a tame animal, and I agree that there is a hunting of man ...
STRANGER: [P]iracy, man-stealing, tyranny, and the whole art of war [can all be] [defined] collectively as hunting by force.[31]

These were not just realities of the fourth century BCE. Even at the height of the *pax romana*, the Roman Empire was, not a modern state maintaining a full-scale territorial monopoly of violence, but a chain of secure locations scattered across menacing expanses of water and land,

---

[29] Scattola, "Die Grenze der Neuzeit: ihr Begriff in der juristischen und politischen Literatur der Antike und Frühmoderne," in Markus Bauer and Thomas Rahn, eds., *Die Grenze: Begriff und Inszenierung* (Berlin, 1997), 37–69.
[30] Esp. Brent Shaw, "Bandits in the Roman Empire," *Past & Present* 105 (1984): 3–52.
[31] Plat. *Soph.* 222b–c, in Harold North Fowler, trans., *Plato: Theaetetus; Sophist*, Loeb Classical Library 123 (Cambridge, MA, 1921), 284–285.

in which the hunt for the "tame animal," man, was conducted with varying degrees of success in different periods.

But perhaps the single most striking measure of absence of a Roman "monopoly of violence" lies in a famous datum: The Romans lacked the "administrative staff" that Weber deemed indispensable for sovereignty. The staff of the classical Roman Empire was astonishingly small, even by comparison with other premodern empires. Keith Hopkins offers a frequently cited comparison with medieval China: Twelfth-century Sung China, hardly a state juggernaut, "had twenty-five times as many élite administrators at work in the provinces as the Roman government."[32] "The territory of the Roman Empire during the second century A.D.," G. P. Burton calculates, "comprised about 5 million square kilometers." Yet within this vast expanse, "the number of elite officials ... routinely sent to the provinces was about 160."[33] Others give the number as closer to 250, but all the numbers cited are tiny.[34] As this suggests, Roman government was simply not designed for the exercise of direct rule.

To be sure, the Romans had the capacity to apply enormous military force. Indeed, Rome was notorious for her ferocity, especially in sacking cities. The Romans too were known to shatter nations like pottery. There were episodes when they deployed legions in various parts of the Empire, and there were Roman provinces that had standing garrisons, instilling fear in the local population.[35] The threat of possible military intervention always hovered somewhere in the background. Moreover, 160, or 250, while tiny numbers, are not zero. At least a few Roman administrators sat in every part of the Empire, along with their retinues, and local disputants learned that it was worth trying to appeal to those officials for support.[36] Surviving

[32] Hopkins, "Taxes and Trade in the Roman Empire (200 B.C.–A.D. 400)," *Journal of Roman Studies* 70 (1980): 121 [101–125]. Since revised to twenty times in most accounts.
[33] Burton, "Was There a Long Term Trend to Centralisation of Authority in the Roman Empire?" *Revue de philologie* 72 (1998): 7–8 [7–24].
[34] Peter Heather and David Moncur, trans. and ed., *Politics, Empire and Philosophy in the Fourth Century: Select Orations of Themistius* (Liverpool, 2001), 31, seeing a rise to at least three thousand in Late Antiquity.
[35] Vividly described in Ramsay MacMullen, *Soldier and Civilian in the Later Roman Empire* (Cambridge, MA, 1963), 85–89.
[36] E.g., Naphtali Lewis, "Judiciary Routines in Roman Egypt," *Bulletin of the American Society of Papyrologists* 37 (2000): 83–93.

papyri and inscriptions demonstrate that people were eager to claim the rights that Roman government accorded them. Roman governors had extensive, even effectively unbridled, power, and they used it, at times with considerable brutality. The Emperor himself, not wholly unlike itinerant medieval monarchs, would appear from time to time throughout the provinces, accompanied by his court and hearing petitions.[37] William Harris, the hardheaded chronicler of the realities of Roman power, sardonically notes that the imperial government maintained sufficient capacity to assist in the capture of runaway slaves.[38] The power of Rome was certainly never entirely absent.

Nevertheless, it remains the case that Roman administrative personnel were startlingly thin on the ground. As Ramsay MacMullen describes the consequent mystery of Roman imperial government, an "administration of only a few hundred" ruled an empire that may well have been the most geographically vast in the ancient world.[39] How did they do it?

* * *

The answers that Roman historians offer differ in many particulars, but there is a rich vein of scholarship that invites comparison with the property law described in the previous three chapters. The Romans operated, not by direct coercion, but by establishing relationships of personal submission and dependence that bound the lesser rulers of the Empire to them. They exercised, in Testart's phrase, "primarily power over humans."

This involved, in particular, the creation of relations of dependency among urban elites. "The secret of government," write Peter Garnsey and Richard Saller in a 1987 study, "was the system of cities which were self-governing."[40] Direct rule in the Greco-Roman Mediterranean was left in the hands of local urban hierarchies, each master within its own walls, each extracting wealth from its own social inferiors and its own surrounding subject territory. The supremacy of the Romans consisted

---

[37] Fergus Millar, *The Emperor in the Roman World* (Ithaca, N.Y., 1992), 28–40; and for the Emperor's role more broadly, Kaius Tuori, *The Emperor of Law: The Emergence of Roman Imperial Adjudication* (Oxford, 2016).
[38] Harris, *Roman Power: A Thousand Years of Empire* (Cambridge, 2016).
[39] MacMullen, *Corruption and the Decline of Rome* (New Haven, 1988), 121.
[40] Garnsey and Saller, *The Roman Empire: Society, Economy and Culture*, 2nd ed. (Berkeley, 2014), 40.

An Empire of the Chieftainship over People

in ensuring that all these local elites bowed to the ultimate, if distant, authority of Rome. This reading of the nature of Roman rule is what Harris calls "the main consensus doctrine" in his *Roman Power*; and as he emphasizes, it applies not only to the city-state world of the Mediterranean but throughout the Empire. The Romans, Harris notes, were able to attract the loyalty of nonelite populations; but it was their hold on local elites that mattered most:

> Rome succeeded in assimilating and winning over significant portions of the local populations, especially but not only the local elites, in literally every part of the empire. Patronage relationships between emperors and other important figures linked the centre with Italy and the provinces … [O]rdinary people could be consoled by the idea that in the last resort the emperor might respond positively to their appeals over the heads of lesser authorities – and occasionally he did so. But in general local elites cooperated with the central government and its agents. In return they received imperial backing for their own authority as well as marks of distinction.[41]

Such was the "secret of government": The Romans managed to make themselves supreme chiefs over a network of subordinate chiefs, master rulers who could count on the cooperation and submissiveness of lesser rulers. They possessed immense military power, usually massed somewhere offstage, and they stood ready to give "imperial backing" when necessary. But in the ordinary course of affairs, they ruled, in the phrase of Marshall Sahlins, through "the hold on persons."[42]

With that vision of Roman rule in mind, ancient historians focus on the obvious key question: How did Rome "succeed[] in assimilating and winning over" local rulers? What, in the words of J. E. Lendon, were "the practical inducements, whether tangible or psychological, to obedience"?[43] The question can be put in the language of Roman property law: As we have seen, the paradigmatic Roman formula for claiming property rights was "I declare that this man is mine." The imperial rule of the Romans depended on their capacity to make local men *theirs*; and the challenge for Roman historians is to explain how they accomplished that.

---

[41] Harris, *Roman Power*, 154.
[42] Sahlins, *Stone Age Economics*, new ed. (Abingdon and New York, 2017), 84–85.
[43] Lendon, "The Legitimacy of the Roman Emperor," in A. Kolb, ed., *Herrschaftsstrukturen und Herrschaftspraxis* (Berlin, 2006), 53 [53–63].

The interpretations that historians have developed certainly do not fit within the Weberian sociology of the territorial monopolization of violence. Nevertheless, another of Weber's sociological categories does suggest itself: patrimonialism. "Weber," as Julia Adams and Mounira M. Charrad explain,

> developed the concept of patrimonialism, which he often contrasted with rational-legal bureaucracy to explore political systems in which rulers exert power on the basis of family and kinship ties, patron–client relations and chains of personal allegiances, with few formal rules and regulations.[44]

In a Weberian patrimonial order, rulers rule, not through the instrumentality of a bureaucratized "administrative staff" of the modern kind, but through ties of personal dependence and power that bind subordinate power-holders to them. The drift of modern scholarship is precisely to show that the Romans ruled less through direct administration than through "patron–client relations and chains of personal allegiances"; in this respect, as Jonathan Skaff argues, Roman rule was not all that different from rule elsewhere in premodern Eurasia – even in regions Westerners have always imagined as sharply distinct from the "civilized" realm of Rome, such as the east Asian steppe.[45] Rome, for all its hostility toward the steppe, looks, in light of current scholarship, like one among many patrimonial Eurasian premodern polities, founded on the power over persons.[46]

* * *

The task is to explain what sorts of "chains of personal allegiances" the Romans forged, and how those chains succeeded in binding. Here, a distinguished line of scholarship puts the emphasis where Harris does, on "[p]atronage relationships between emperors and other important figures [that] linked the centre with Italy and the provinces through patron–client relations." Of "the paradigmatic power

---

[44] Adams and Charrad, "Introduction," in Adams and Charrad, *Patrimonial Capitalism and Empire* (Bingley, UK, 2015), 1 [1–6].
[45] Skaff, *Sui-Tang China and Its Turko-Mongol Neighbors: Culture, Power and Connections, 580–800* (New York, 2012), 13; cf. David Sneath, *The Headless State* (New York, 2007).
[46] See now the essays in Nicola Di Cosmo and Michael Maas, eds., *Empires and Exchanges in Eurasian Late Antiquity: Rome, China and the Steppe ca. 250–750* (Cambridge, 2018).

An Empire of the Chieftainship over People

relations of everyday life," according to this view, it was the relation between patron and client that provided the principal model for Roman imperial rule.

The dominance of patron–client relations has been one of the master themes of Roman historiography since the 1930s.[47] Roman nobles did favors for their clients; in return the clients formed a network of support. This was not, for the most part, enforced by law, which had comparatively little to say about the mutual obligations of patron and client. Nevertheless, the norms of Roman society imposed an expectation that wealthy Romans would act as generous patrons. Numerous scholars have focused on the centrality of patron–client relations to the organization of Roman society. The Roman *dominus*, historians such as Saller and Andrew Wallace-Hadrill have shown, was not just the master of his own household, but the patron over a crowd of clients; and the Roman *domus* itself was not just the habitation of a *dominus*, master over a slave-to-kin continuum. As we saw in Chapter 3, it was also designed, architecturally, to serve as the stage for patron–client relations. The *dominus* was the "giver of feasts," in particular the giver of feasts at which his clients could hope for at least scraps, and more if they ranked more highly.

It is the same sorts of relationships that are said to have served as the foundation of Roman power on the imperial level in Harris' "main consensus doctrine." Here the most important postwar work was Ernst Badian's 1958 *Foreign Clientelae*, the book, more than any other, that laid out the modern theory of Roman imperial rule through the establishment of "patronage relationships between emperors and other important figures [that] linked the center with Italy and the provinces." Badian's enormously learned study left little

---

[47] The seminal work is Anton von Premerstein, *Vom Wesen und Werden des Prinzipats*, ed. Hans Volkmann (Munich, 1937). This too belonged to the Nazi period, in ways that I leave aside in the text. Premerstein himself was a "highly cultivated, kind and rather soft man," as Karl Christ observes, and no Nazi. Karl Christ, *Römische Geschichte und deutsche Geschichtswissenschaft* (Munich, 1982), 133. Nevertheless, his analysis, which was published posthumously by his hard right-wing student Hans Volkmann, emphasized the oath of loyalty to the leader in ways that, as Volkmann insisted, bore "unmistakable similarities with the present," in which, of course, the Oath to Adolf Hitler featured prominently. Volkmann, "Vorwort," in Premerstein, *Wesen und Werden*, iii. For Volkmann in these years, see the frank discussion of Heinz Bellen, "Hans Volkmann," *Gnomon* 18 (1976): 428 [426–431].

doubt that Roman imperial power during the Republic depended extensively on the establishment of patron–client relations, binding foreign elites to Rome: Powerful Romans did favors for their foreign clients, and expected submission in return. The "pattern" of Roman imperial rule, Badian explained, was taken from the forms of Roman patronal power in domestic life:

> The basis of Roman control was, in an important sense, not political but personal ... The method, ingrained in the Roman character and the oligarchic *Weltanschauung*, had not changed over the centuries. Rome had imposed her pattern on her world, and the latter – especially the tribal societies of the West – easily adapted itself to it.[48]

This Roman pattern, as Badian presented it, was not, importantly, a matter of the exercise of arbitrary personal power wholly alien to the law. It belonged to "the normal working of Roman institutions,"[49] and although it took a variety of forms, it had a rule-governed character that could even influence legal thinking.[50] In subsequent decades, scholars followed Badian's lead, exploring the relatively rule-governed workings of the patron–client relations of the mature Empire.

"It is the web of favors given or owed," as MacMullen writes, summing up the judgment of this line of Roman historiography, "that enables an administration of only a few hundred really to rule an empire."[51] We must be careful not to overstate the explanatory power of such accounts. The Roman Empire lasted for many centuries and covered enormous expanses. There are Roman historians who look past the "main consensus doctrine," reconstructing the operation of Roman power on the ground in ways that have nothing to do with the older analysis of patron–client relations.[52] Nevertheless, among analyses of Roman rule, this is one that has been embraced by some of the most important figures in the field, and it is one that points unmistakably toward the conceptual affinities between yin and yang, Roman rulership and Roman ownership. In MacMullen's description of the "web of favors" we can hear the echo of African anthropology: To quote Antony Hopkins once again, among precolonial chiefs of

---

[48] Badian, *Foreign Clientelae (264–70 B.C.)* (Oxford, 1958), 262.   [49] Ibid., 165.
[50] Ibid., 9–10.   [51] MacMullen, *Corruption and the Decline of Rome*, 121.
[52] Among others, Clifford Ando and Ari Bryen.

An Empire of the Chieftainship over People

Lagos, "[a]llocation of use rights was important as a means of settling followers and of building up a power base of dependents, some free men but most of slave status, by attaching them to the entourage of the chief concerned."[53] The Romans operated on a far grander scale, and they created more complex webs of personal power; but they too, with their "oligarchic *Weltanschauung*," sustained their rule by "building up a power base of dependents," creating entourages throughout the Empire.

Recent literature has pushed the study of this pattern of rule in a direction of particular interest for my theme: Historians now look beyond the mechanics of patrimonial relations to investigate the culture and ideology of Roman rule. Thus Lendon argues that the Romans relied on a highly choreographed logic of personal honor, which he documents beautifully. It is his thesis that we cannot content ourselves with analyzing the workings of "force, authority and patronage"; we must also reckon with "honour and pride, the underpinnings of loyalty."[54] This can be compared with the interpretation of Roman property law offered by Franz Wieacker: As we saw in Chapter 3, Wieacker argued that the "sense of self" of the wealthy Roman nobility rested on their status as both owners and rulers; he too focused on "honour and pride"; and so too do the Roman social historians who try to recapture the culture of the classical *domus*. The same interest in ideology motivates Lavan, Bryen, and Roller, with whom I began. Their writings too rest on the proposition that we must look beyond what Yan Thomas calls the "quotidian reality." As Lavan puts it, the challenge is to understand, not just the socio-economic "structure" of patron–client relations, but the "metaphor": "what matters is how the Romans themselves imagined their social world."[55]

And in this, the place of slavery in Lavan's *Slaves to Rome* bears a resemblance to the place of slavery in Roman property law. As we have seen in the previous chapters, the Roman attachment to images of mastership in property law did not directly reflect the realities of the Roman economy. It is not the case that the Romans really only owned

---

[53] Hopkins, "Property Rights and Empire Building: Britain's Annexation of Lagos, 1861," *Journal of Economic History* 40 (1980): 784 [777–798].
[54] Lendon, *Empire of Honour: The Art of Government in the Roman World* (Oxford, 1997), 13.
[55] Lavan, *Slaves to Rome*, 180.

slaves; it is rather that they took enslavement, alongside the hunting and taming of beasts, as their normative model in "conceiving of and justifying" ownership;[56] it is a matter of "how the Romans imagined their social world." By the same token, the Roman Empire was not really a vast Roman household, with the peoples under its rule really its slaves, broken literally to the Roman harness. The celebration of imperial mastership that Lavan and other scholars describe had to do with the ways in which the Romans conceived of and justified rulership, not with the ways in which they in fact ruled. In both realms, as Lavan contends, the Romans called themselves masters.

The most compelling way to describe this consonance between rulership and ownership is to turn back to Orlando Patterson. The same "idiom of power," founded in the master/slave relationship, that gave meaning to Roman property law is to be found in the way that Romans described their rule. In assessing this kinship between property and sovereignty, *dominium* and *imperium*, it is misleading, I think, to speak, as Roller does, of a "parent domain" and a "derivative domain." It is not that the understanding of rulership derived from the understanding of ownership. What we see in the Roman case, as in the case of the "chieftainship over land" of the later Middle Ages and after, is rather an intimate play of mutual conceptual influence between the two, in a world in which both ownership and rulership rested on the same taken-for-granted normative assumptions. To be an owner, as Wieacker argued, was to be something like a ruler; to be a ruler was to be something like an owner. In both domains, the wealthy Roman was pictured as "the 'conqueror' (*uictor*), 'master' (*dominus*) or 'ruler' (*princeps, imperator* etc.) 'of ... peoples'" – as a figure who, in Kyle Harper's phrase, "participate[d] in the superiority of Roman arms";[57] as a figure who, in the words of Mircea Eliade, belonged to a culture of "warriors, conquerors, and military aristocracies [who] carr[ied] on the symbolism and ideology of the paradigmatic hunter."[58]

* * *

---

[56] Thomas, "Vitae necisque potestas," in Thomas, ed., *Du châtiment dans la cité: supplices corporels et peine de mort* (Rome, 1984): 512 [499–548].
[57] Harper, *Slavery in the Late Roman World*, AD 275–425 (Cambridge, 2011), 34.
[58] Mircea Eliade, *A History of Religious Ideas*, trans. Willard Trask (Chicago, 1978), 1:35.

Let me glance, finally, at a second topic of importance for the proposition that Roman rule was a "chieftainship over peoples," different from what would emerge in later centuries: the personality, rather than territoriality, of Roman law.

Here it is important to clear some methodological underbrush. The distinction between the "personality" and the "territoriality" of law is one of the most basic in legal analysis. There are simpler and subtler ways of stating it. In its simple form, it is a distinction between two sharply different forms of social organization. A society founded wholly on the principle of personality is one in which members of a given community are governed exclusively by the law of that community. A classic example might be a self-governing premodern Jewish community. To the extent that the lives of Jews were to be lived in full disregard of non-Jewish law, the principle of the personality of law would be said to govern. At the limit, the application of this simple principle of personality would imply that those Jews would not even be subject to the criminal law of the country in which they find themselves. A society founded wholly on a simple principle of territoriality, by contrast, is one in which no legal force is accorded to internal communal norms. To stick with the same example, it would be a society whose Jewish inhabitants are entirely subject to territorial law, not only in criminal matters but also, for example, in matters of family law.

When scholars have written about the distinction between "personality" and "territoriality," they have sometimes spoken, in such relatively simple terms, of such sharply contrasting social orders. The idea of a legal order founded purely in the personality of law was especially appealing to scholars of the long Romantic era, from the nineteenth through the early twentieth centuries: To thinkers attached to the idea that the meaning of life had to do with membership in a distinct community, there was a deep attraction to the idea that lives should be ruled, not by the overbearing authority of the territorial state, but by the more richly fulfilling norms of substate human associations.[59] On this assumption, only a society made up entirely

---

[59] For a brilliant and sophisticated statement of this orientation, see classically Eugen Ehrlich, *Grundlegung der Soziologie des Rechts* (Munich and Leipzig, 1913).

of autonomous communal orders would count as one governed by principle of personality.

If we take that Romantic view of the personality of law, the Roman Empire unquestionably does not qualify. It is far from clear that inhabitants of the Empire were governed, or even wished to be governed, exclusively by the law of their community of origin. On the contrary, there is plenty of evidence that they made use of, and submitted to, the law of multiple orders in a world of legal pluralism.[60] This is especially true to the extent that Roman citizenship was widely shared – though scholars disagree about exactly how widely shared it was before 212 CE.[61] There is little sign that the mature Empire was a world in which individual identity was deeply bound up with submission to the law of a single community of origin. In this as in other respects, the Roman Empire resembled other premodern empires, many of which display much the same sort of legal pluralism.

But of course there is no need to think of the principle of personality in such simplistic terms. Inhabitants of the Roman Empire, like those of other premodern empires, may not have felt the necessity to define themselves by membership in a single community; but the law nevertheless treated membership in *some* community, or as the case might be multiple communities, as its organizing principle. Claude Nicolet describes the state of affairs in the Empire in a way intended to capture its complexity, the product of centuries of development. The "fundamental classifications" of Roman law and rule, he writes, were "personal and not territorial";[62] but he adds that those classifications had formed in a city-state context that no longer retained its original significance in the mature Empire. In that sense, the personality of law in the Empire was less a lived reality than an inherited normative assumption – a matter of legal principles, not of social organization

---

[60] Kaius Tuori, "Legal Pluralism and the Roman Empire," in J. W. Cairns and P. du Plessis, eds., *Beyond Dogmatics* (Edinburgh, 2007), 39–52; Clifford Ando, "Legal Pluralism in Practice," in Paul du Plessis, Clifford Ando, and Kaius Tuori, eds., *The Oxford Handbook of Roman Law and Society* (Oxford, 2016), 283–292; and for the broader phenomenon in later periods, Lauren Benton and Richard Ross, eds., *Legal Pluralism in Empires, 1500–1850* (New York, 2015).

[61] Myles Lavan, "The Spread of Roman Citizenship, 14–212 CE: Quantification in the Face of High Uncertainty," *Past & Present* 230 (2016): 3–46.

[62] Nicolet, *Space, Geography and Politics in the Early Roman Empire* (Ann Arbor, 1991), 10.

An Empire of the Chieftainship over People

in the fullest sense. It was the concept of law of an Empire filled with the ghosts of the autonomous *poleis* of the past. As Yan Thomas phrases it, the ultimate point is a negative one: What characterized Roman citizenship law was not a simple form of the personality of law, but "the nonexistence of a territorial principle."[63]

* * *

The (relative) "nonexistence of a territorial principle" has been my topic throughout this chapter, and the previous three. We must be careful not to exaggerate the point. The Romans did describe themselves as ruling the "world of all lands"; it would be no more correct to speak of Roman rulership purely in terms of the "chieftainship over people" than it would be to speak of Roman property law in the same terms; when it comes to property law, the Romans, after all, did own land. Nevertheless, the comparison with Roman property law, as with Goody's precolonial Africa, is inescapable. Regardless of whether the Romans in fact lacked "map consciousness," as Brodersen contends, in practice their rule depended heavily on establishing webs of personal domination. They operated by "building up a power base of dependents." If I may return to a metaphor I offered in Chapter 1, the working map of the law was not just a plat showing fee-simple owners and territorial sovereigns. It was also, and arguably principally, a chart of an Empire-wide multiplicity of dominance hierarchies.

In this, Roman rulership shared its idiom of power with Roman ownership. Before turning, in the next Part of this book, to the problem of how that idiom of power changed, it is worth gesturing one more time in the direction of a great historian of Western normative transformations, Nietzsche. I quote, once again, the notorious passage in the *Genealogy of Morals* in which he described the "blond beast" of Antiquity – the dominant male who behaved as a "magnificent animal of prey, roving in search of booty and victory."[64] Nietzsche's aim was to explain, and deplore, how this ancient predatory morality, which he deemed happy and healthy,

---

[63] "Inexistence d'un 'principe territorial'": Thomas, *"Origine" et "commune patrie": étude de droit public romain (89 av. J.-C.–212 ap. J.-C.)* (Rome, 1996), 181.

[64] Nietzsche, "Zur Genealogie der Moral," in Giorgio Colli and Mazzino Montanari, eds., *Nietzsches Werke: historisch-kritische Ausgabe* (Charlottesville, 1995), 6.2:289.

gave way to the "slave morality" of Christianity. There is certainly no need to endorse Nietzsche's view of either morality or Christianity; but the first Part of this book has indeed traced a normative orientation that imagined, and lionized, the Roman *dominus* as a kind of "animal of prey, roving in search of booty and victory." And the fundamental historical question posed by the *Genealogy of Morals* – the question of how and why that ancient normative attitude perished – is the question to which the next Part turns.

PART II

FROM MASTERS TO LORDS

6

Introduction to Part II: From *Pierson* v. *Post* to *Johnson* v. *M'Intos*h

When beginning American law students open their property casebooks, they encounter two famous cases from the early nineteenth century. Both rely on the ancient Roman law of *occupatio*, the law of how to acquire the ownership of things and creatures that have never been owned before. One of the two cases involves the prime concern of the ancients: acquiring prey in the hunt. The other involves the prime concern of the moderns: acquiring land.

The hunting case, *Pierson* v. *Post*, arose on Long Island in 1805. Its facts are simple, and familiar to every American lawyer: A hunter flushed and chased a fox; while the animal was fleeing, a second hunter swooped in, killed and took it. Called upon to decide the dispute between the two, the Supreme Court of Judicature of New York, after a learned tour through the law of *occupatio*, awarded ownership to the second hunter. As we saw in Chapters 2 and 4, ancient Roman *occupatio* centered on the acquisition of property through the hunt, as well as through war, itself understood as a form of hunting: It was, as A.-J. Arnaud describes it, law of "the mastery of hunters over their game, the mastery of fishers over their catch ... war captives ... and booty,"[1] covering both the taking of animals and the taking of enemies as slaves. The basic rule of this ancient law was that both animals and humans could lose their

---

[1] A.-J. Arnaud, "Reflexions sur l'occupation du droit romain," *Revue historique du droit* 46 (1968): 186 [183–210].

"natural liberty" and be reduced to the *dominium* of their captors once they had been taken by the real or metaphorical hand of the hunter or warrior, which placed them in their captor's *potestas*, his "power."

Pierson v. Post explained why this ancient Roman teaching, whose origins lie in the late Bronze or early Iron Age, and perhaps are to be sought as far back as the Upper Paleolithic, if not even earlier in hominin evolution, made a sound basis for the law of hunting in the Early American Republic. The court used the case of the fox as an occasion for showing off its mastery of the vastness of the Roman legal tradition, stringing together citations from centuries of texts, beginning with the *Institutes* of the sixth-century Emperor Justinian, continuing through the medieval English treatises *Bracton* and *Fleta*, and ending with the seventeenth-century jurist Samuel Pufendorf and his eighteenth-century commentator Jean Barbeyrac. It relied on Pufendorf in particular for its account of the Roman law of "occupancy":

> Puffendorf defines occupancy of beasts *feræ naturæ* [wild by nature] to be the actual corporeal possession of them ... If the first seeing, starting, or pursuing such animals, without having so wounded, circumvented or ensnared the animal, so as to deprive them of their natural liberty, and subject them to the control of their pursuer, should afford the basis of actions against others for intercepting and killing them, it would prove a fertile source of quarrels and litigation.[2]

Pierson v. Post thus held that the ancient Roman doctrine of acquisition through "actual corporeal possession" recommended itself as the basis for a modern property law system – but not for the ancient reason. For the ancient Romans, seizure by the "hand" of the hunter played a key symbolic role in the conceptualization of ownership grounded in the *potestas* of the master, in a legal order rich in hand symbolism. The *Pierson v. Post* court, rewriting ancient law for a modern age, endorsed the Roman rule for a reason more in tune with the practical mentality of Americans: because it served to avert "quarrels and litigation" by laying down a comparatively clear and unambiguous test for awarding title.[3]

---

[2] *Pierson v. Post*, 3 Cai. R. 175 (1805).
[3] As we shall see in Chapter 9, this justification for property rights had a history that traced back to Aristotle, passing by way of Aquinas, the Second Scholastic, and Pufendorf.

As for the early nineteenth-century case involving the acquisition of land: It is the most notorious in the corpus of American decisions on westward expansion. This is *Johnson* v. *M'Intosh*,[4] an 1823 decision in which the Supreme Court, in an opinion by Chief Justice John Marshall, considered the land rights of Native Americans.

Johnson v. *M'Intosh* too based its reasoning on the Roman law of "occupancy," and it too relied on Pufendorf. But the Court, confronting conflicting land claims in Indiana and Southern Illinois, supplemented its Pufendorf with the philosophy of John Locke.[5] As we have seen, the ancient texts on *occupatio* had virtually nothing to say about land; like the *Pierson* v. *Post* court, the *Johnson* v. *M'Intosh* court had to rewrite the ancient law to make it useful in nineteenth-century America. It achieved this purpose by holding that while the Indians had "occupancy" of their lands, "occupancy" as such did not automatically ripen into ownership. "Occupancy" of land became ownership only if the occupiers engaged, in Lockean fashion, in settled agriculture. "As *much Land* as a Man Tills, Plants, Improves, Cultivates," so run Locke's canonical words, "so much is his *Property*."[6] Yet the Indians (so the opinion dubiously asserted) were mere hunters, not agriculturalists. Since they did not till, plant, improve, and cultivate, it followed inexorably that they could not be said to have title to the land they exploited. True title to the lands of America accrued only to their European "discoverers," who could be counted on to put it to productive use.

Two cases from the Early American Republic, reflecting two different stages in the three-thousand-year history of the Roman law of the acquisition of ownership through first possession, fossilized, as it were, in the casebooks. They can be said to illustrate the transition that all of Western property law has undergone over the last two millennia: from an ancient law whose property teachings regularly turned on the hunting of "naturally free" beasts (as well as "naturally free" humans) to a modern law, whose property teachings came to turn on the settlement and tillage of land.

When, and why, did that transition take place?

---

[4] 21 U.S. (8 Wheat.) 543 (1823).   [5] Ibid., at e.g., 569 n. b.
[6] John Locke, *Two Treatises of Government*, ed. Peter Laslett (Cambridge, 1988), 290 (2: §32).

That is the question to which the next three chapters turn. Chapter 7 begins with the most famous explanation for the transformation of Western law on offer. This is the great hypothesis, most closely associated with Karl Marx, that the West, after the fall of the Roman Empire, underwent a socio-economic transition "from slavery to feudalism," from ancient economies founded on the exploitation of slaves to medieval economies founded on the exploitation of serfs tied to the land.

This interpretation of the course of Western history was first proposed in 1822, by Friedrich Carl von Savigny, the most famous Roman lawyer of the nineteenth century. From Savigny it passed to a long roster of leading figures, adopted in some form not only by Marx, but also by Max Weber, Marc Bloch, and many others. But this great hypothesis, once almost universally accepted, is almost universally rejected today. This is primarily because it has been proven false as a matter of economic history. Great advances in our understanding of ancient and medieval economies have been made; Marx, Weber, and Bloch, contemporary historians will say, simply got the economic facts wrong. There never were ancient "slave economies" of the Marxist kind. Nor for that matter were the Middle Ages really "feudal."

But it is the contention of this book that legal history must not be reduced to economic history. Chapter 7 argues that the classic narratives, erroneous though they were, nevertheless point us toward a fundamental truth. The West really has been shaped by a kind of passage from slavery to feudalism. That shift was, however, not one in the economics of the exploitation of labor. It was a shift in basic understandings of the nature of ownership, which took place over many centuries, extending from Late Antiquity into the nineteenth century, when the lawful private ownership of human beings finally disappeared in the West.

Chapters 8 and 9 are studies in critical moments in that long-term shift. Chapter 8 explores developments in Late Antiquity. While the interpretations of Marx and Weber have been generally abandoned, many scholars make a claim that is closely akin: that land and territoriality assumed a new importance in both late antique Roman law and Roman rule. This transition has been linked to one causal factor in particular: the crisis of ancient cities, which suffered as a result of invasions, disease, and climate change. As the chapter aims to show, this urban crisis brought with it departures in the law of both sovereignty and property, yin and yang. New conceptions of property law emerged that reflect a broad pattern of drift away from the cities. New territorial conceptions appeared in the law of rule. But deurbanization, Chapter 8 argues, was not the only force at work: The rise of Christianity played a part as well, contributing to the extinction of a classical culture populated by "warriors, conquerors, and military aristocracies [who] carr[ied] on the symbolism and ideology of the paradigmatic hunter."

But the full realization of the "radical transformation," argues Chapter 9, dates many centuries later. It belongs to the early modern period, beginning in the sixteenth century, but not culminating before the later eighteenth century and after, the age of Blackstone, of *Johnson v. M'Intosh*, of the consolidation of the territorial state, and of the delegitimation of private slavery. Chapter 9 tracks the changes in the law that developed over the early modern centuries, which slowly came to embrace the orientation toward the cultivation of land that we associate with John Locke, and the disappearance of the old law of use rights. The beginnings of the strong orientation toward the cultivation of land, the chapter argues, can be traced back to the Middle Ages; from the early sixteenth century, the shift gathered momentum. The slow decline of the legitimacy of private slavery, for its part, can only be understood against the background of the transformation in the basic understanding of ownership. It must also be viewed against the background of the rise of the territorial state, which contributed in its own way to the ultimate disappearance of the private ownership of human beings.

7

From Slavery to Feudalism: The Great Hypothesis

After two and a half years of terror, "[t]he Soviet political landscape," writes Stephen Kotkin of the year 1938, "resembled a huge forest full of charred stumps":

> Finally, however, with the September–October 1938 rollout of the *Short Course*, the training manual for those who had been chosen to go forward (or just got lucky), the mass terror was, in an important sense, complete.[1]

The *Short Course* (or to give it its full title, *History of the Communist Party of the Soviet Union (Bolsheviks), Short Course*), which was now to be required reading for "the new crop of regional bosses, most of whose predecessors had been put to death,"[2] laid down the orthodox Stalinist line. In particular, it laid down the line on the course of Western socio-economic history. The West, the *Short Course* instructed its students, had undergone a momentous economic revolution after the fall of the Western Roman Empire: from ancient slavery to medieval feudalism. "The basis of the relations of production under the slave system," it explained,

> is that the slave owner owns the means of production; he also owns the worker in production – the slave, whom he can sell, purchase, or kill as though he were an animal ...
>
> The basis of the relations of production under the feudal system is that the feudal lord owns the means of production and does not fully own the worker in

---

[1] Kotkin, *Stalin: Waiting for Hitler, 1929–1941* (New York, 2017), 577.   [2] Ibid., 575.

production – the serf, whom the feudal lord can no longer kill, but whom he can buy and sell ...[3]

Such lessons in Marxist theory were not easy for "the new crop of bosses" to follow: The Politburo was alerted that teachings on "historical and dialectical materialism" could be understood by "[m]any propagandists and district secretaries ... only with the greatest difficulty."[4] Nevertheless, every apparatchik was henceforth obligated to master a view on ancient and medieval socio-economic history. Soviet Communism was to have an ideology informed by the most advanced historical scholarship.

For, murderous and doctrinaire though the Stalinist regime was, the proposition that the course of Western history had been determined by a socio-economic evolution from ancient slavery to medieval feudalism *did* represent the most advanced scholarship of the day, and not only among Marxists. Max Weber offered his own version of the same thesis in 1896. So too, among many others, did the eminent medievalist Marc Bloch, the first installment of whose masterwork, *Feudal Society*, arrived in Paris bookstores in 1939, a few months after Stalin's bosses were handed the *Short Course*. These scholars, and many others whose names are less well remembered, were all believers in the same great hypothesis about the making of the Western world: Where the economies of Greco-Roman Antiquity depended on the exploitation of slaves, the economies of the medieval world underwent a "passage," in the language of the Marxian historian Perry Anderson, to the feudal exploitation of land, ruled by lords and tilled by serfs.[5]

It is obvious that if this hypothesis is correct, it provides a compelling answer to the question posed by this book, and an answer given on the authority of some of the most brilliant minds to have graced our literature: The ancient world had slave-based economies. When these gave way to medieval serf-based economies,

---

[3] Stalin, *History of the Communist Party of the Soviet Union (Bolsheviks)*, in David Brandenberger and Mikhail Zelenov, eds., *Stalin's Master Narrative* (New Haven, 2019), 266–267.
[4] Kotkin, *Stalin*, 576.
[5] Anderson, *Passages from Antiquity to Feudalism* (London, 1974).

the law followed suit, shifting from the ownership of humans to the ownership of land.

But few scholars today believe it is correct. Quite the contrary: The drive of most scholarship over the last half-century, an era of far-reaching revisionism, has been to prove it wrong.

The attacks of the past decades have been relentless. Economic historians today vigorously contest the proposition that the ancient Mediterranean had slave economies of the kind that Marx and Weber supposed. Slaves were certainly in heavy use in classical Greco-Roman Antiquity; but the ancient Mediterranean, particularly under Roman hegemony, boasted a complex and varied economic order that was by no means radically alien to our own.[6] In any case, historians are quick to observe, slavery did not end with the fall of the Western Roman Empire. Classical slaves, as Michael McCormick archly writes, did not "wake up one morning as medieval serfs."[7] The exploitation of slaves persisted, in one form or another, throughout the Middle Ages. The reality is that lawful slavery did not finally disappear from the Western world until the late nineteenth century.

Indeed, contemporary economic historians maintain, slavery did not merely survive into the nineteenth century. It flourished. It is the weight of current opinion that slavery was a highly remunerative economic institution up until the American Civil War, its profitability magnified, not endangered, by transborder capitalism.[8] The high age of the Western slave economy, it might even be suggested, arrived, not during Greco-Roman Antiquity, but around the year 1860. If that is so, what is left of the thesis of the passage from slavery to feudalism after the fall of the Western Roman Empire?

Nor do the critiques end there. The classic literature, Marxist and otherwise, presupposed that medieval societies were "feudal." Yet

---

[6] For a thoughtful statement of the state of play, giving due attention to the social and cultural differences while insisting that "modern theoretical and economic concepts can and should play [a] role," see Paul Erdkamp, Koenraad Verboven, and Arian Zuiderhoek, "Introduction," in Erdkamp, Verboven, and Zuiderhoek, eds., *Capital, Investment and Innovation* (Oxford, 2020), 3 and *passim*.

[7] McCormick, "Slavery from Rome to Medieval Europe and Beyond," in John Bodel and Walter Scheidel, eds., *On Human Bondage: After Slavery and Social Death* (Chichester, 2017), 251 [249–264].

[8] Esp. Seymour Drescher, *Econocide: British Slavery in the Era of Abolition*, 2nd ed. (Chapel Hill, 2003).

contemporary medievalists regard "feudalism" as a highly suspect concept, to be used with caution – a "construct," in the much-cited 1974 words of the sharp-eyed medievalist Elizabeth A. R. Brown, whose "tyranny" has led to misconceived analyses of medieval social and economic history.[9] The system of feudal law, Brown and other critics argue, reached its apogee, not during the Middle Ages, but in the seventeenth century. Indeed, the very idea of "feudalism" as a form of social ordering was not effectively articulated until the eve of the French Revolution. If slavery might be said to have reached its height around 1860, feudalism might, on this interpretation, be said to have reached its height around 1660. As one medievalist mischievously described the state of play in the field a few years ago, "feudalism," after a half-century of such critiques, had become the "F-word," unmentionable at professional gatherings.[10]

The critical onslaught has gone on without respite since the mid 1970s, and it has demolished virtually all support for the old grand narratives of the passage from slavery to feudalism, at least outside the dwindling company of Marxist historians. Understandably so: If slavery did not dominate in the economies and societies of classical Antiquity, and feudalism did not dominate in the economies and societies of the Middle Ages, the doctrine imposed on Stalin's bosses by the *Short Course*, and elaborated in so many other more serious and substantial writings down into the 1970s, seems plainly wrong.

The classic theories have taken such a battering, in fact, that it may seem that there is no longer much point in discussing them at all. Why bother devoting any attention to the supposed passage from slavery to feudalism, when so many careful historians have concluded that it never took place? Yet as this book is dedicated to showing, the West really has undergone a kind of passage, from an ancient law with a persistent imaginative orientation toward the capture and subjugation of humans and other living creatures, and the rule over

---

[9] Brown, "The Tyranny of a Construct: Feudalism and Historians of Medieval Europe," *American Historical Review* 79 (1974): 1063–1088.

[10] Richard Abels, "The Historiography of a Construct: 'Feudalism' and the Medieval Historian," *History Compass* 7, no. 3 (2009): 1022 [1008–1031]. References to literature and thoughtful strictures in Martti Koskenniemi, *To the Uttermost Parts of the Earth: Legal Imagination and International Power, 1300–1870* (Cambridge, 2021), 52–54.

peoples, to a post-ancient law whose "archetypal form of property" is land, and whose states are territorial. Do the classic accounts of Marx, Weber, and Bloch really have nothing to teach us?

They do. In fact, they point us toward fundamentally important truths about Western history. But to see the truth in them, we must understand where they went wrong. The classic theorists were men of profound learning, intimately familiar with the literary and legal traditions of the Western world, and their writings are funds of insight. But they fell prey, all too often, to the same error: They relied too uncritically on the legal sources as evidence for economic history. In the hunt for documentation of socio-economic evolution, figures like Marx, Weber, and Bloch turned to the law – and mistook the imagery and symbolism of the normative texts for evidence of the workings of the economy.

Such indeed has been the burden of many of the most important critiques launched against them: When the classic thinkers theorized about the decline of slavery, Chris Wickham writes, they made the mistake of believing that the legal language in the Code provided a dependable account of the realities;[11] in the words of their greatest modern reader, M. I. Finley, Marx and Weber put too much trust in the "false picture" in the law.[12] Ancient Roman law did locate slavery at the center of its property cosmology; but Rome did not have a Marxian or Weberian "slave economy"; reading the sources as though they supported such a conclusion, as we saw in Part I of this book, is simply a mistake. Critics of Bloch and other medievalists have leveled much the same charge: When scholars like Bloch theorized about medieval "feudalism," Brown and Susan Reynolds complain, they too were taken in by a false picture. They accepted too credulously unreal visions of feudalism manufactured by the authors of the legal treatises of the Middle Ages and especially the early modern period.[13] They allowed themselves to be dazzled by a feudal *fantasia* that was primarily a creation of the lawyers of the seventeenth century.

---

[11] Wickham, *Framing the Early Middle Ages: Europe and the Mediterranean, 400–800* (Oxford, 2007), 523–524, citing and discussing Domenico Vera.

[12] Finley, *Ancient Slavery and Modern Ideology*, expanded ed., ed. Brent Shaw (New York, 1998), 193.

[13] Brown, "Tyranny of a Construct"; Reynolds, *Fiefs and Vassals: The Medieval Evidence Reinterpreted* (Oxford, 1994).

Critiques of this kind have left the grand socio-economic narratives that were once the stuff of most histories of the West in tatters. But, damaging though they are, they do not imply that the classic authors spun their theories out of nothing. The older literature did indeed mistake the "false picture" in the law for the socio-economic reality; Marx, Weber, and their successors were often chasing illusions, both when it came to Antiquity and when it came to the Middle Ages. But false pictures matter; illusions count for something; and as readers of the legal (as well as historical, literary, and philosophical) sources, the classic social theorists produced writings that spoke from the heart of the imaginative orders of the texts they studied. Ancient Rome did not have a slave economy of the kind postulated by Marx or Weber. But Roman law really was suffused with the "symbolism and ideology of the paradigmatic hunter," and marked by the "idiom of power" of the master/slave relationship. "Feudalism" did not abruptly descend upon Europe after the fall of the Western Roman Empire. But the so-called *ius feudale* that ripened slowly in Europe from the High Middle Ages and achieved its mature form in the seventeenth and early eighteenth centuries did put real property at the center of *its* imaginative universe, where it would remain from the time of Blackstone into our own day.

There *is* a kind of grand narrative to be written of a kind of passage from slavery to feudalism in Western law, in short. The classic thinkers were not wrong about that. There is still every reason to read Marx, Weber, and Bloch; and their great authority lends weight to the proposition that I defend in this book: that the property law of the West has undergone a sea change, from a law oriented toward the ownership of humans and other living creatures to a law oriented toward ownership and cultivation of land. That is the transformation of which the classic thinkers caught sight, and it really has taken place. But the right narrative of the passage from slavery to feudalism is not a narrative of socio-economic evolution, as their critics have shown. It is a narrative of transformation in the conceptual order of the law.

* * *

To see both what is mistaken and what is illuminating in the classic theories of Marx, Weber, and their many followers and competitors, it is essential to know their origins. The interpretations of the classic theorists were all formulated in the long wake of the same upheaval, the French Revolution. More particularly, they were all formulated in response to one of the Revolution's most revolutionary measures: the abolition in 1789 of what the revolutionaries decried as *la féodalité*, "feudalism"; and their replacement of that "feudalism" by a resurrected form of the ancient Roman "absolute" conception of ownership. To understand the genesis of the idea of the passage from slavery to feudalism, we must know what the French revolutionaries thought "feudalism" was, why they condemned it as an evil, how they imagined the fall of the Roman Empire, and what version of ancient Roman ownership they proposed to resurrect in its place.

That, in turn, requires us to start long before the Revolution. The revolutionary abolition of "feudalism" grew out of juristic debates about the nature of ownership that began in the High Middle Ages, gathered steam into the early modern period, and fed a conflagration during the summer of 1789, before taking on a new life in the theorizing of Marx, Weber, and their successors.

What then is "feudalism"? The term is sometimes used as a generic descriptor for almost any hierarchically ordered society of the human past or present.[14] But in its original sense, it has to do very specifically with the property law of the Western European Middle Ages. "Feudal" is a word derived from "feod" or "fief," a medieval term for a parcel of real property held by a vassal; and the history of the idea of "feudalism" is bound up with a long record of juristic struggles to meet the challenge of explaining the nature of the fief.

That challenge is, for the modern lawyer, considerable. The fief-form, whose existence can probably be documented in the Latin West from the late ninth century onward,[15] looks, to the modern legal eye, strange and even baffling. As Marx declared, the medieval fief "took land as its basis,"[16] and to that extent it seems to rest on a land-based concept of property just as modern law does. But the fief did not only involve real property rights. It also involved a law of hierarchical

---

[14] For a recent example, Christopher Beckwith, *The Scythian Empire: Central Eurasia and the Birth of the Classical Age* (Princeton, 2023), 17 and often.
[15] Reynolds challenges this in her *Fiefs and Vassals*, though to my mind unconvincingly. I will return to her argument below.
[16] Karl Marx and Friedrich Engels, "Deutsche Ideologie: Manuskripte und Drucke," in *Karl Marx/Friedrich Engels Gesamtausgabe* (Berlin and Boston, 2017), Abt. 1, 5.1:130.

deference governing relations between the vassal and his lord, of a kind completely unknown to modern law. John Hudson, a leading historian of the medieval common law, explains the conceptual contours of the institution. On the one hand, medieval law conferred upon the vassal an enforceable real property claim on the fief, including the right to pass it on to his heirs, subject to certain conditions. But at the same time, it declared the vassal to be the lord's "man," his hierarchical inferior, imposing upon him the obligation to perform ritual ceremonies of "homage and fealty" as well as a variety of services.[17] Lords for their part could function as small-scale rulers, maintaining courts in which they judged disputes among their vassals.[18] Conjoining real property rights and compulsory rituals of status hierarchy, land and lordship, the fief thus looks exceedingly strange from the modern point of view; there is simply nothing like it in our law.

But if we are to make sense of the history of Western property law, we must begin by recognizing that the fief looks much less strange when we view it through the lens of the comparative anthropology of real property. As we learned in Chapter 1, anthropologists have shown that land in nonmodern and non-Western tribal and agricultural societies land has commonly been held in the form of "use rights," allotted by superiors to inferiors in line with the social hierarchical order of the society in question. In such a use rights system, chiefs or other dominant figures grant rights to resources in tracts of land in ways that reflect and reinforce their hierarchical authority, exercising what Marshall Sahlins calls "political control." "Allocation of use rights," as one anthropologist of precolonial Africa describes the pattern, "[is] important as a means of settling followers and of building up a power base of dependents."[19] Such patterns of conditional land tenure, subject to "political control," have been identified throughout the non-Western, nonmodern world. Indeed,

---

[17] Hudson, "Anglo-Norman Land Law and the Origins of Property," in *Law and Government in Medieval England and Normandy: Essays in Honour of Sir James Holt* (Cambridge, 1994), 202–203 [198–222], expressing skepticism about how much practice conformed to the law.

[18] E.g., Karl-Heinz Spieß, "Lehnsgericht," in Adalbert Erler and Ekkehard Kaufmann, *Handwörterbuch zur Deutschen Rechtsgeschichte* (Frankfurt a.M., 1971–), 2: cols. 1714–1717.

[19] Antony Hopkins, "Property Rights and Empire Building: Britain's Annexation of Lagos, 1861," *Journal of Economic History* 40 (1980): 784 [777–798].

the grant of use rights probably represents the most widespread form of real property rights in premodern human history, "shared by many of the hunter-gatherer and agricultural peoples of the world, but radically different from that of [modern] Europeans."[20]

The fief, baffling though it looks to the modern lawyer, fit comfortably within the logic of this commonplace human form of real property rights: The fief too was used "as a means of settling followers and of building up a power base of dependents"; "enfeoffment," as the common law called it, was also a grant of use rights in land by a superior to an inferior. In that sense, fiefs were nothing out of the ordinary in human affairs. Medieval "feudalism" was a variant of the chieftainship over people documented throughout the premodern world. The proposition that rights in land should depend on who is the "man" of whom has been the norm over most of human history.

To say that is not suggest that medieval fiefs were synonymous with the forms of land tenure identified by students of precolonial Africa or colonial New England or anywhere else. The patterns of human rank-ordering are endlessly variable, and European fief-based hierarchies had their own structures, rituals, and dynamics. It is especially important, and perhaps comparatively distinctive, that the vassal held a heritable right to the use of the fief. (As we shall see in a moment, medieval jurists analyzed this feature of the institution by holding that the vassal had the *dominium utile*, the "ownership of the use.") But the basic organizing principle of the institution of the fief was nothing unusual: Rights in much or most real property, in many or most human societies, have been granted out by superiors to inferiors; the use of land in many or most times and places has been conceived "as a function of ... status or position in society."[21]

---

[20] William Cronon, *Changes in the Land: Indians, Colonists and the Ecology of New England* (New York, 1983), 60, 62, 65.

[21] Christian Lund, *Local Politics and the Dynamics of Property in Africa* (Cambridge, 2008), 16. Chris Wickham argues that the "feudal-mode land tenure" that emerged after 800 or so displaced an earlier form that he calls "tribal," in which "a ruler, or local lord, is less the owner of land than the leader of a free people ... who are all tried to him by tight bonds of mutual obligation and loyalty"; the feudal form, by contrast, made "one person ... the owner." Wickham, *Framing*, 304–305; cf., e.g., 339; and for the gift-exchange basis, 538, and for its prevalence in different regions, 540; and

But just how thoroughly feudalized were the Middle Ages? How much of the land of Western Europe was "enfeoffed"? Precisely because "feudal" is the term routinely used by nonspecialists to describe the Middle Ages, it may seem natural to assume that the fief was the exclusive, or at least the dominant, form of real property in medieval societies – that the lands of medieval Western Europe were divided up into a honeycomb of infeudated holdings, in which feudal lords granted lands to their vassals, who in turn subinfeudated the land to their own dependents, creating a vast "pyramid" of land-based hierarchical feudal relations extending from the king down to the mass of the exploited peasantry. So indeed did Stalin assume; so indeed did school textbooks explain to their students in 1974, as Brown complained;[22] so indeed do internet sites still inform those who click on them.[23] So, for that matter, might one conclude from reading property casebooks, or watching TV miniseries, or reading historical novels. But it is essential to underline that this is not so; that is a large part of the reason why contemporary medievalists distance themselves from the "F-word."

There is certainly plenty of good evidence that many lands were held in the form of some kind of fief in various regions of the Latin West in various periods of the Middle Ages, and fascinating work has been done on their operation. There is no doubt that there were feudal hierarchies in many times and places, rituals of homage, and court and local cultures infused with norms that can fittingly be called "feudal."[24] Monarchies in particular were conceptualized in what must be deemed "feudal" terms; there is no way to understand the politics of the Middle Ages without taking seriously the feudal ties that bound kings and popes to their vassals in various times and periods in Western Europe. The "F-word," to that extent, has an undeniable place in the description of medieval societies and the dynamics of medieval power, as most contemporary medievalists would readily acknowledge.[25]

[ ] for the question of whether the transition was the result of growing aristocratic oppression or changing patterns of chieftainly authority, 572.
[22] Brown, "Tyranny of a Construct," 1078.
[23] E.g., https://thehistoryjar.com/tag/feudal-pyramid/.
[24] E.g., Gérard Giordanengo, *Le droit féodal dans les pays de droit écrit: l'exemple de la Provence et du Dauphiné, XIIe–début XIVe siècle* (Rome, 1988).
[25] For some examples of thoughtful use, see Sverre Bagge, Michael H. Gelting, and Thomas Lindkvist, eds., *Feudalism: New Landscapes of Debate* (Turnhout, 2011).

But what is not to be found in the medieval sources is a systematic commitment to the proposition that all of society must be organized, pyramidally, around feudal property relations, or a settled or uniform understanding of the how the law of fiefs was supposed to work. The medieval scene, during the thousand years that we lump together as the "Middle Ages," was much more varied, indeed much more chaotic, than that. Kings may have been conceived as feudal lords in some ways in some periods, but jurists were never willing to agree that they were the superior owners of all land, granting it out on a feudal basis: The orthodox view was that the King possessed, not rights of *dominium*, ownership, but rights of *imperium*, rulership.[26] In any case, disputes over the exact nature of royal rights were legion. Uncertainty reigned on lower levels of society as well: "Fief-holding," as Constance Bouchard writes, "was never tidy, even when most prevalent in the thirteenth century: any modern effort to create lists of what was held from whom or to draw clear boundaries between the areas where one or another lord held dominion will be undercut by the shifting nature of medieval alliances and the prevalence of multiple homage."[27] In any case, careful study shows that lords acted, in practice, in flexible and improvisatory ways; it is a mistake to think in terms of a fixed feudal law.[28] Moreover, alongside fiefs, there were many other kinds of real property, including what medieval law called "allods," lands not held

---

[26] See the learned survey of Ugo Nicolini, *La proprietà: il principe e l'espropriazione per pubblica utilità* (Milan, 1940), 107–126, which traces the practice of ascribing to monarchs universal *imperium* but not universal *dominium*, and esp. 110–111 for the *dissensio* of Bulgarus and Martinus and the "concetto feudale." See also Susan Reynolds, *Before Eminent Domain: Toward a History of Expropriation for the Common Good* (Chapel Hill, 2010), 86–90.

[27] Bouchard, "Three Counties, One Lineage, and Eight Heiresses: Nevers, Auxerre, and Tonnerre, Eleventh to Thirteenth Centuries," *Medieval Prosopography* 31 (2016): 27 [25–46].

[28] See esp. Emily Tabuteau, *Transfers of Property in Eleventh-Century Norman Law* (Chapel Hill, 1988), 228: "[T]he charters give the impression that in legal matters the Normans of the eleventh century were quite flexible. Within the established rules, they could make a wide variety of legal arrangements to meet the needs of particular situations." Tom McSweeney also points me to the discussion of the "malleable and internally contradictory legal culture" of fiefs in Stephen D. White, "The Discourse of Inheritance in Twelfth-Century France: Alternative Models of the Fief in 'Raoul de Cambrai,'" in George Garnett and John Hudson, eds., *Law and Government in Medieval England and Normandy: Essays in Honour of Sir James Holt* (Cambridge, 1994), 177 [173–197].

subject to any feudal obligations. Meanwhile, the real property rights of medieval serfs, the large subject agrarian population, did not take the form of fiefs. While serfs had lords, they did not themselves count as vassals – vassals were juridically free, whereas serfs were not – and the law of serfdom is technically called "manorial" rather than "feudal." In any case, the juridical condition of serfs underwent numerous, and often far-reaching, changes in various periods; there simply was no such thing as "the" medieval serf. Even beyond that, there were many forms of real property rights that were neither "feudal" nor "allodial" nor "manorial" in the immensely variegated agrarian and urban landscapes of medieval Western Europe over its many centuries.[29] Faced with this luxuriant biota of property forms and social practices, "[m]ost students of the Middle Ages," as a leading legal historian writes, if with a bit of exaggeration, "will now agree that the Middle Ages were not feudal."[30]

The belief that the medieval West should be understood as straightforwardly "feudal" is a mistake, critics contend; and it is a mistake that arose for a reason of importance for my tale: It arose because the European authors who created the vision of the feudal Middle Ages put too much faith in what they found in the legal texts. In particular, Brown and Reynolds have influentially argued, they put too much faith in a learned juristic tradition that traces back to the *Libri feudorum*, the "books of fiefs," a text of the High Middle Ages that spawned centuries of theorizing about the nature of "feudal" law and "feudal" society.

The *Libri feudorum* was a slim text, composed in late Milan in the late 1100s, during the twelfth-century Renaissance of learning that transformed the high culture of Western Europe. The twelfth-century Renaissance witnessed many efforts to produce orderly accounts of the law, and the *Libri feudorum* was intended to do that work for the law of fiefs. Compiled around the same time that English lawyers and officials set out to create their own orderly account of the fief-based common law, the *Libri feudorum* opened with a portrayal of a well-articulated

---

[29] Observations and citations in Koskenniemi, *Uttermost Parts*, 66–67.
[30] Dirk Heirbaut, "Feudal Law: the Real *Ius Commune* of Property in Europe, or: Should We Reintroduce *Duplex Dominium*?" *European Review of Private Law* 3 (2003): 306 [301–320].

social hierarchy, in which persons of clearly defined social status granted out fiefs to their equally clearly defined inferiors:

Since we are to treat of fiefs, let us first see who can grant a fief. An archbishop, a bishop, an abbot, an abbess, or other officer of the church, if that person has an ancient customary right, can grant a fief. A march-lord, a count (who is properly called a captain of the king). Others too, who receive fiefs from them (and who are properly called vassals of the king, though today they are given the name captains), can also grant fiefs. But those who receive fiefs from the latter are called minor vassals.[31]

The Milanese jurists thus wove a tapestry of a society organized around a well-understood "feudal" rank order, with lords ecclesiastical and secular, and their subordinate vassals, all disposed in their proper places. There is nothing surprising in the fact that their text takes such a form; lawyers always set out to create orderly frameworks. Among jurists, the orderly account in the *Libri feudorum* initiated a grand tradition of legal analysis, serving as the basis of a growing and elaborate literature of commentary on the lineaments and functioning of the "feudal" legal system that included contributions by many leading medieval figures.[32] The *Libri feudorum* even attached itself to the standard text of the *Corpus iuris civilis*, acquiring the status of foundational law alongside the Roman texts, the indispensable feudal pendant to the classical teachings.

But the tapestry woven by the *Libri feudorum*, and the voluminous subsequent juristic literature that embellished it and commented upon it, Brown and Reynolds argue, was never a faithful representation of the realities. In practice, medieval hierarchical status was often vaguely understood and variably defined, just as rights in land were. If we seek a carefully worked out feudal ranking of society and a law of property

---

[31] *Quia de feudis tractaturi sumus videamus primum, qui feudum dare possunt. Archiepiscopus, episcopus, abbas, abbatissa, praepositus, si antiquitus eorum fuit consuetudo, feudum dare possunt. Marchio, comes, qui proprie regis capitanei dicuntur. Sunt et alii, qui ab ipsis feudum accipiunt, qui proprie regis valvassores dicuntur, sed hodie capitanei appellantur; qui et ipsi feuda dare possunt. Ipsi vero, qui ab eis accipiunt, minores valvassores dicuntur.* Available at https://amesfoundation.law.harvard.edu/digital/CJCiv/LFConsFeud.pdf.

[32] See Kenneth Pennington, "Law, Feudal," in *The Dictionary of the Middle Ages*, Supplement I, ed. William Chester Jordan (New York, 2004), 321–322 [320–323].

rights, tidily ordered and applied, we must wait until the Middle Ages were over.

* * *

In particular, we must wait until the seventeenth century, the true high age of feudal law in the reckoning of Brown and Reynolds. It was in the seventeenth century that the law of social rank was in fact carefully articulated and made the basis of a well-worked-out legal order.

The juristic energies of the seventeenth century were indeed heavily invested in the analysis of feudal law. The complexities of the feudal social hierarchy were the subject of work by great legal minds such as the Frenchman Charles Loyseau and the Englishman John Selden, both leading figures in the early seventeenth century and both rigorous students of what Selden called "titles of honor."[33] As for the feudal land order: The rule that all land must be subject to feudal lordship was another seventeenth-century teaching, promoted by lawyers who included defenders of royal power such as the Scotsman Thomas Craig, a legal propagandist for James I.[34] Most especially it was promoted by the French jurists. French law did eventually proclaim the rule "nulle terre sans seigneur," "every parcel of land must have a lord" – but it did not do so before 1629, when an effort began that continued throughout a progressive seventeenth-century feudalization of France.[35] The feudal pyramid in France was completed, not in the time of St. Louis, but in the time of Louis XIV. Nor was this just a matter of legal theory. Holdings throughout Europe before the French Revolution were routinely governed by feudal law, whose pervasiveness in litigation is now emphasized by historians,[36] and

---

[33] On Selden, see now Ofir Haivry, *John Selden and the Western Political Tradition* (Cambridge, 2017); on Loyseau, Brigitte Basdevant-Gaudemet, *Aux origines de l'état moderne: Charles Loyseau, 1562–1627, théoricien de la puissance publique* (Paris, 1977).

[34] Cited and discussed in Kathleen Davis, *Periodization and Sovereignty: How Ideas of Feudalism and Secularization Govern the Politics of Time* (Philadelphia, 2012), 55.

[35] See Rafe Blaufarb, *The Great Demarcation: The French Revolution and the Invention of Modern Property* (Oxford, 2016), 30–34; and for a sample of controversy, *Traitez de Monsieur Duplessis sur la Coutume de Paris* (Paris, 1699), 167–168, admitting diversity among Coutumes while minimizing it. See also Reynolds, *Before Eminent Domain*, 98, on the history from DuMoulin to Louis XIV.

[36] Yves-Marie Bercé, "Conclusion," in Ghislaine Brunel and Serge Brunei, eds., *Haro sur le seigneur! Les luttes anti-seigneuriales dans l'Europe médiévale et moderne* (Toulouse, 2009), 202–206 [202–209]; Jonathan Dewald and Liana Vardi, "The

whose ins and outs are a topic of basic importance for historians of the events of 1789.[37]

The *ius feudale* was law of seventeenth-century Europe, much more rigorously worked out and extensively applied than it was in the Middle Ages, Brown and Reynolds insist; and it is important to add it was not just law in the European homelands. It was also law that Europeans carried with them in their campaigns of colonialism and conquest. The Europe that began expanding through the rest of the globe in the early modern period was, in many of its basic juristic orientations, a feudal Europe; and early modern European assertions of power overseas were frequently made through the assertion of feudal rights. "Colonialism as Feudalism" is indeed the title of the relevant section of Martti Koskenniemi's *To the Uttermost Parts of the Earth*.[38] The feudal bent was on display in the Iberian conquests, justified by the declaration that the indigenous populations of the New World were the "subjects and vassals" of the Spanish monarchy. It can be seen in the notorious *encomienda* form, a legacy of the feudalized conceptions of the Iberian *Reconquista*, extended into the New World.[39] It can be seen in French expansion into the New World as well, designed to take a "feudal" form in the seventeenth century[40] (and still taking a "feudal" form in French Canada as late as the 1830s, when Tocqueville passed through[41]). It can be seen in the "Bishop of Durham" clauses that governed real property in British North America,[42] and in the Fundamental Constitutions of Carolina in

---

Peasantries of France," in Tom Scott, ed., *Peasantries of Europe from the Fourteenth to the Eighteenth Centuries* (London, 1994), 34–35 [21–47]. I leave the question of the "feudal reaction" aside.

[37] See the survey of Blaufarb, *The Great Demarcation*, 1–8, and David Parker, "Feudalism and Property Rights in the France of Louis XIV," *Past & Present* 179 (2003): 60–96. The same can even be said, as Holly Brewer has recently argued, of seventeenth-century slavery: "[S]lavery was anchored in hierarchical and feudal principles that connected property in land to property in people." Brewer, "Slavery, Sovereignty, and 'Inheritable Blood': Reconsidering John Locke and the Origins of American Slavery," *American Historical Review* 22 (2017): 1043 [1038–1078].

[38] Koskenniemi on "Colonialism as Feudalism": *Uttermost Parts*, 726–736.

[39] Below, Chapter 8.

[40] Koskenniemi, *Uttermost*, 506–517; Dominique Deslandres, "Et loing de France," *Revue d'histoire de l'Amérique française* 64 (2011): 93–117.

[41] Oliver Zunz, *The Man Who Understood Democracy: The Life of Alexis de Tocqueville* (Princeton, 2022), 68.

[42] Koskenniemi on "Colonialism as Feudalism": *Uttermost Parts*, 726–736.

which John Locke had a hand.⁴³ These are all cases in which the feudal law served as a justification, and juridical framework, for colonialism; Europeans of the sixteenth and seventeenth centuries not infrequently understood themselves to be taking feudal possession of the lands of the New World, a matter to which I will return in Chapter 9.

All this points to an unexpected truth, and one that for that very reason must be stated all the more emphatically: Feudalism, much though we are accustomed to thinking of it as a thing of the Middle Ages, was not, in its most rigorously realized form, a phenomenon of the Middle Ages at all. It was a phenomenon of the early modern period. That observation, which sounds so improbable today, was already made in 1887, if only half in jest, by Frederick William Maitland, the pioneer of the history of the medieval common law: "[W]ere an examiner to ask," wrote Maitland, "who introduced the feudal system into England? one very good answer, if properly explained, would be Henry Spelman [author of the 1627 *Archæologus*, which insisted on the 'feudal' character of the common law] ... If my examiner went on with his questions and asked me, when did the feudal system attain its most perfect development? I should answer, about the middle of the last century."⁴⁴ Maitland's jest was echoed in a more serious way by J. G. A. Pocock, in his seminal 1957 study *The Ancient Constitution and the Feudal Law*, which demonstrated how vibrant, and how politically central, feudal law was in sixteenth-century France and especially seventeenth-century England.⁴⁵ Pocock's argument was in turn expanded by Brown in her influential 1974 article, "The Tyranny of a Construct: Feudalism and Historians of Medieval Europe," whose verdict deserves to be quoted in full:

[F]eudalism is, always has been, and always will be, a construct devised in the seventeenth century and then and subsequently used by lawyers, scholars, teachers, and polemicists to refer to phenomena, generally associated more or less closely with the Middle Ages, but always and inevitably phenomena

---

⁴³ Available at https://quod.lib.umich.edu/e/eebo/A48880.0001.001/1:2?rgn=div1; view=fulltext.
⁴⁴ Frederic William Maitland, *The Constitutional History of England*, ed. H. A. L. Fisher (Cambridge, 1908), 14, quoted and discussed in Brown, "Tyranny of a Construct," 1064.
⁴⁵ J. G. A. Pocock, *The Ancient Constitution and the Feudal Law: English Historical Thought in the Seventeenth Century* (Cambridge, 1957).

selected by the person employing the term and reflecting that particular viewer's biases, values, and orientations.[46]

Twenty years later, Brown's attack on the belief in the feudal Middle Ages was elaborated by Reynolds, in her study *Fiefs and Vassals*, now a standard citation. As for the seventeenth-century jurists themselves: They betrayed no awareness that feudalism was supposed to be a purely medieval phenomenon: They "never used the terms 'medieval' or 'Middle Ages,'" as Kathleen Davis pointedly notes, "and would perhaps have found them perplexing ... For them, the ius feudale they studied was customary law of their own time."[47] What Kyle Harper writes of the Black Death can equally be written here: "Plague has an unshakable reputation as a medieval disease, but it was just as much a player in the early modern period. The seventeenth century must be reckoned among the great ages of the plague"[48] – and perhaps as *the* great age of the feudal law.[49]

* * *

Feudalism's "unshakable reputation as a medieval disease" did not in fact establish itself until the mid eighteenth century, in the decades immediately preceding the French Revolution. In trying to account for this eighteenth-century relegation of feudalism to the medieval past, Brown and Reynolds point to Henri de Boulainvilliers, the early eighteenth-century philosopher and defender of the power of the seigneurial nobility, as well as to Montesquieu, both of whom ascribed the rise of feudalism to the Middle Ages, and in particular to the barbarian invasions, as jurists had done since the sixteenth century.[50] But it is important to emphasize that neither man regarded feudalism as the kind of retrograde evil that would be assailed in 1789, the embodiment of the purported ugliness and savagery of the medieval world.

---

[46] Brown, "Tyranny of a Construct," 1086.
[47] Davis, *Periodization and Sovereignty*, 8.
[48] Harper, *Plagues upon the Earth: Disease and the Course of Human History* (Princeton, 2021), 334–335.
[49] This does not, of course, if it needs to be said, imply that feudal law was the only form of law to be found, or that there was an early modern "feudal society" of the Blochian kind.
[50] Brown, "Tyranny of a Construct," 1064–1065; Reyolds, *Fiefs and Vassals*, 7. For summary with citation to further literature, see Blaufarb, *Great Demarcation*, 16–18.

Unambiguously condemnatory views of feudalism as a "medieval disease," fit to be eradicated in a campaign of reform, are very hard to find until we come to a threshold moment in the making of modern social thought, the Scottish Enlightenment.[51] But in the Scottish Enlightenment, as Reynolds observes, we find them.[52] Here the key figure, as far as I can determine, was Henry Home, Lord Kames, the brilliant Scottish jurist now best remembered as one of the makers of the four-stage theory of human history, which presented humanity as progressing from hunting to pastoralism to agriculture to commerce.[53] Kames mounted a seminal attack on the feudal law in 1745, and in a noteworthy historical context: He was writing in the wake of the Jacobite Rebellion, an uprising aimed at the restoration of the Stuart monarchy that was violently suppressed by the English. The conflict surrounding the Jacobite Rebellion was, in important ways, conflict over the feudal system in Scotland: After suppressing the rebellion, the English took the step of abolishing the jurisdictions of the Highland Lairds, a measure intended to put an end to the Scottish problem once and for all.[54] The statute in question, the Heritable Jurisdictions Act, stimulated much debate; its working assumption was that there was something deeply dangerous about feudal lordly power. The Scotsman Kames, writing in the immediate aftermath of the uprising, penned an essay blaming the English themselves, and in particular William the Conqueror, for the introduction of the feudal law into the British Isles in the Middle Ages. Seventeenth-century commentators had often accused the Normans of imposing the "feudal yoke" on England, and Kames now made this the basis of an enlightened denunciation of feudalism more broadly – "a Constitution," as he put it, "contrary to all the Principles which govern Mankind."[55]

---

[51] For an interesting possible early example from Lyons, see Noel Chomel, *Supplement au Dictionnaire œconomique* (Commercy, 1741), 233–234. Blaufarb cites, quite appropriately, Voltaire's *Commentaire sur l'esprit des loix*. *Great Demarcation*, 38. This was, however, a significantly later text.
[52] Reynolds, *Fiefs and Vassals*, 7, pointing to Adam Smith.
[53] See the discussion in Andreas Rahmatian, *Lord Kames: Political and Social Theorist* (Edinburgh, 2015), 142–150.
[54] Heritable Jurisdictions (Scotland) Act 1746 c. 43 (Regnal. 20 Geo 2).
[55] Kames, *Essays upon Several Subjects Concerning British Antiquities ... composed anno 1745*, 2nd ed. (London, 1749), 1 [1–25]. Cf. Rahmatian, *Lord Kames*, 261, and frequently on the feudal law. On the "Norman Yoke" see for a classic discussion

Thereafter, the idea gained strength among Kames and the Scottish Enlightenment thinkers who followed him that the feudal system belonged to an ugly "medieval" past that must be superseded, in the modern world, by the sort of commercial order increasingly defended by Scottish thinkers such as Adam Smith. Readers of *The Wealth of Nations* may recall Smith's association of the feudal law with "rapine and violence."[56] But the figure who was probably most influential in the later eighteenth century is one less well remembered today: This was William Robertson, author of the 1769 *History of Charles V*, in which he castigated the feudal laws as a legacy of the "barbarous" and "destructive" work of the Germanic invaders who ravaged ancient Rome.[57] Robertson's view of the "medieval disease," as we shall see shortly, would prevail in the age of the French Revolution as well; in time, it would make its way into the theorizing of Marx and others.

* * *

Before passing to post-mid-eighteenth-century denunciations of "violent" and "barbarous" "medieval" feudalism, though, it is necessary to return to the High Middle Ages, working through some of the details of medieval juristic thought on the nature of fiefs.

The doctrines that the learned lawyers of the Middle Ages crafted, from the twelfth century onward, addressed a crucial puzzle in the analysis of feudal real property rights. Fiefs could not be said to be "owned" in the ancient Roman sense: Since both lord and vassal had some sort of claim, neither could be designated "the" owner. In the centuries-old phrase used in the English common law, medieval fiefs were not owned, but instead "held of" a lord; that is why common law real property rights came to be called "tenures," from the French *tenir* or Latin *tenere*, "to hold."[58] In order to analyze the complex of shared rights in such "holdings," the English lawyers of the Middle Ages

---

Christopher Hill, "The Norman Yoke," in *Puritanism and Revolution* (New York, 1964), 50–123.

[56] Smith, *An Inquiry into the Nature and Causes of the Wealth of Nations*, ed. Edwin Cannan (New York, 1994), 413.

[57] Robertson, *History of the Reign of the Emperor Charles V, with a View of the Progress of Society in Europe, from the Subversion of the Roman Empire to the Beginning of the Sixteenth Century* (London, 1840), 1:11–16.

[58] Medieval European law had a special technical vocabulary for describing the rights of vassals to "hold" their fiefs: French and English lawyers said that the vassal enjoyed "seisin." German lawyers used an equivalent German term, "Gewere."

developed the doctrine of "estates in land," which over time attained baroque levels of complexity: Various persons, including not only lord and vassal but also others, in particular members of future generations, were said by common lawyers to hold "estates" in the parcel in question, existing in different time frames, and subject to complex rules and conditions.[59]

The jurists of the Continent faced the same analytic problem; and for them, the difficulties were especially challenging, since they had to find some means of interpreting fiefs in Roman legal terms. As we saw in Chapter 3, classical Roman law featured its notoriously "absolute" conception of property, which presupposed the unlimited control of the *dominus*, the "master," over all his possessions, inanimate, animal, and human. This was imagined, in its most dramatic form, as the power to destroy: The ancient Roman owner/master enjoyed, in principle if not in practice, the right of *usus* and *abusus*, the power to dispose of and destroy his inanimate things at will; and in a parallel way he enjoyed, in principle if not in practice, the *vitae necisque potestas*, the power of life and death; he could "kill" his things just as he could kill his people. We also saw that this "absolute" conception of the powers of the *dominus*, while it was pervasively present in the ancient Roman texts, did not correspond to Roman social realities; it belonged to the "myths" of classical Roman property law, not the working rules of Roman daily life; it was, in the phrase of Yan Thomas, "not a quotidian reality, but a pure concept."[60]

When the learned study of classical Roman law revived in the universities of the Continent from the early twelfth century onwards, jurists rediscovered the "pure concept" of ownership in the ancient Roman texts upon which they commented and taught. Yet they had to recognize that that concept, despite the fact that it could claim the towering authority of Rome, could not possibly be used to analyze fiefs, since neither lord nor vassal enjoyed the exclusive powers of an ancient *dominus*. The problem was especially difficult to avoid because the text of the *Libri feudorum* was appended to the *Corpus iuris civilis*. Since Roman law and feudal law were both found in the same

---

[59] E.g., Jesse Dukeminier, James Krier, Gregory Alexander, Michael Schill, and Lior Strahilevitz, *Property*, 10th ed. (New York, 2022), 269–272.

[60] Thomas, "Vitae necisque potestas," in Thomas, ed., *Du châtiment dans la cité: supplices corporels et peine de mort* (Rome, 1984): 512 [499–548].

authoritative set of texts, it was imperative, according to the standards of medieval learning, to resolve the contradictions between them. Faced with this challenge, Continental jurists contorted the ancient law into a new shape, creating one of the most famous of medieval property law doctrines: *duplex dominium* or *dominium divisum*, "twofold" or "split" ownership. Under this teaching, which probably took its mature form as jurists worked through the *Libri feudorum*,[61] the problem was solved by holding that lord and vassal were each a sort of *dominus*, but of two distinct kinds. The vassal, the jurists held, had been granted the *dominium utile*, the "ownership of the use" of the fief; but his lord had retained the *dominium directum*, the "direct" ownership.

These medieval doctrines on the two-headed fief, the single parcel of land with two masters, one the hierarchical superior and the other his inferior, his "man," remained at the center of Western property law for centuries. Indeed, the feudal conception of split property, whether in its common law or civil law variant, has set the terms for the law of property in both of the great modern Western legal traditions down to the present. On the common law side, it is a familiar fact that property law has never wholly cut ties with the "feudal" past, even in the twenty-first century; the common law is still governed by what Bernard Rudden calls "the feudal calculus," and students must still master the doctrine of estates. The casebooks they are assigned retain the focus on land that has always been the stuff of feudal law – though of course they have let the old law of hierarchical rank-ordering, no longer intelligible to us, drop.[62]

The modern civil law of property, by sharp contrast, has taken the opposite path, defining itself self-consciously and aggressively against the feudal tenures of the past, and in particular against the doctrine of

---

[61] See, with discussion of the larger literature, Robert Feenstra, "Les origines du *dominium utile* chez les glossateurs," in Feenstra, *Fata iuris romani: études d'histoire du droit* (Leiden, 1974), 234–239. A fuller account of this teaching than I will give it here would investigate the use of the same distinctions in the debates over *dominium* and *usus* surrounding the Franciscans. For a learned discussion see Annabel Brett, *Liberty, Right and Nature* (Cambridge, 1997), 49–87. Somewhat reluctantly, I have decided to omit discussion of this centrally important debate, in the interests of keeping this book within manageable limits.

[62] Rudden, "Things as Things and Things as Wealth," *Oxford Journal of Legal Studies* 14 (1994): 81–97.

split ownership; and it is in the civil law tradition of anti-feudalism, and the determination to restore Roman absolute ownership to its rightful place, that the immediate origins of the property law of the French Revolution, and of the classic theories of the passage from slavery to feudalism, are to be sought.

Here, once again, it is developments in France that matter most. The French jurists of the sixteenth century took a lively interest in the study of both feudal and manorial rights, producing treatises and historical essays, as well as new commentaries on the venerable *Libri feudorum*, which continued to be appended to the humanist edition of the *Corpus iuris civilis*.[63] These sixteenth-century texts inspired an outpouring of systematic theory on "feudal law" in the seventeenth century, as Pocock, Brown, and Reynolds recount. The high medieval doctrine of *duplex dominium* was still the law of those texts; no one was prepared to discard the centuries-old law that governed the real property of France, as of Europe more broadly. Questioning the validity of *duplex dominium* would, after all, have thrown every title on the Continent into doubt, plunging Europe into what could only be called a revolution.

But that does not mean that seventeenth-century jurists were entirely comfortable with the doctrine. The beneficiaries of much humanist scholarship on Roman law, they could not avoid knowledge of the irksome fact that the medieval teaching was not in fact a doctrine to be found in the classical texts. François Hotman, the influential humanist jurist who produced some of the most important Protestant political writing of the sixteenth century, flatly stated the classical truth: "*dominium* is the right and power to use or destroy anything whatsoever in accordance with what is permitted by Roman law."[64] This truth seemed manifest to any careful Renaissance reader of the Roman texts. As another humanist, Hermann Vultejus, put it,

---

[63] Denys Godefroy, ed., *Corpus iuris civilis a Dio. Gothofredo recognitum* ([Geneva], 1614), 2:551–603.
[64] Hotman, *Novus commentarius de verbis iuris* (Basil, 1563), 117: "dominium est ius ac potestas, re quapiam tum utendi, tum abutendi, quatenus iure civili permittitur." Cf. Robert Feenstra, "Historische aspecten van de private eigendom als rechtsinstituut," *Rechtsgelehrd Magazin Themis* 1976, 249–254. On Hotman see also Pocock, *Ancient Constitution*, 15–16, 27–28.

the jurists of the Middle Ages had polluted the pure classical law with "excremental incrustations" that had to be scraped away.[65]

None of this was lost on the working jurists of the seventeenth and eighteenth centuries, learned men who were perfectly well aware that the property order of their times could not be squared with the classical Roman tradition. As one French writer acknowledged in 1657, the "most common opinion" was that the doctrine of split property, though its legitimacy in practice was beyond question, represented bad classical law. Nevertheless, neither he nor any other writer suggested taking the radical step of overthrowing the land law of France.[66]

The same was true of the leading legal theorists of the age, all of whom were both good humanists and sensible lawyers. Hugo Grotius is, as always, a key example. The great Dutch jurist responded to the advances in humanist scholarship by abandoning the old language of *dominium directum* and *dominium utile*. But it would be difficult to point to passages in his work that questioned the existing land relations of his time, and he developed flexible doctrines of property law that could accommodate them.[67] His follower Samuel Pufendorf is another leading case, and a particularly interesting one. Pufendorf offered a ringing statement of the classical conception. But he did so in a revealing context. It was in the course of his defense of the proposition that defeated enemies in war could be enslaved that Pufendorf described "property" as a right that knew no limits:

[T]he Property I claim over a Thing, implies a Right of using, spoiling, and consuming it, to procure my Advantage, or to satisfy my Pleasure; so that what way soever I dispose of it, to say it was my own, shall be a sufficient Excuse.[68]

Pufendorf felt the need to proclaim this classical rule in order to prove that the victor possessed the right to kill the man he vanquished,

---

[65] Vultejus, *In Institutiones juris civilis commentarius*, new ed. (Marburg, 1630), 153: "ex fecibus posteriorum seculorum."

[66] Claude Henrys, *Oeuvres*, 6th ed. (Paris, 1772), 653, describing "la plus commune opinion."

[67] There is much to Grotius on property that I do not discuss here. For a survey, see Bart Wauters, "Property," in Randall Lesaffer and Janne Nijman, eds., *The Cambridge Companion to Hugo Grotius* (Cambridge, 2021), 492–512.

[68] Pufendorf, *Of the Law of Nature and Nations*, trans. anon. (Oxford, 1703), Bk. 6, ch. 3, paragraph 7, p. 125.

which established the basis for the continuing legitimacy of enslavement through war. Yet in his treatment of the land law of his own time, he did not see fit to take the radical step of questioning the feudal order.[69] Neither did Jean Domat, the great Jansenist jurist and friend of Blaise Pascal, who offered a classicizing definition of ownership while insisting that it could not capture the complexities of ownership in the living world.[70] The same remained true of William Blackstone, whose 1766 treatment of property theory has puzzled his commentators. Like his learned early modern predecessors, Blackstone opened his discussion of property with a definition that trumpeted the Roman classical conception, now framed by him as "sole and despotic dominion." In his detailed treatment of the workings of property rights, however, he, like everybody else, aired no doubts about the validity of the feudal realities on the English ground.[71]

Nevertheless, eighteenth-century discomfort with the medieval distortion of pure classic Roman law was palpable. Among jurists, the most influential doubts were expressed by the Robert Joseph Pothier, still well remembered among European lawyers for his reflections on the un-Roman character of the clumsy doctrine of *duplex dominium*.[72] Among social reformers, the most important figures, at least in France, were the physiocrats, eager to reorder French land relations in order to permit improvement. They too flirted with classical revivalism: In order to engage in unencumbered improvement, owners must be accorded exclusive rights of the classical Roman kind.[73] In the latter part of the century, these eighteenth-century mutterings about the correct classical analysis of ownership coincided with the assaults on "the feudal system" of Enlightenment authors such as Robertson; and by the 1770s, it was common wisdom among educated persons that *dominium directum* was a postclassical term, a travesty of the classical law employed to characterize the

---

[69] E.g., Samuel Pufendorf, *De jure naturae et gentium libri octo* ([Amsterdam], 1672) 4.4.2, p. 454, continuing to make use of *dominium directum* and *dominium utile*.
[70] Domat, *Les loix civiles dans leur ordre naturel*, 2nd ed. (Paris, 1695), 1:67–68.
[71] David Schorr, "How Blackstone Became a Blackstonian," *Theoretical Inquiries in Law* 10 (2009): 103–126; Carol Rose, "Canons of Property Talk, or Blackstone's Anxiety," *Yale Law Journal* 108 (1998): 601–632.
[72] E.g., Vincenzo Mannino, *Questioni di diritto* (Milan, 2007), 454.
[73] Arnaud, *Les origines doctrinales du Code civil français* (Paris, 1969), 174–177; Blaufarb, *Great Demarcation*, 40–46.

lordship seized violently by the barbarian invaders after the fall of the Western Roman Empire – a product, as Voltaire said shortly before his death in 1778, of "feudal anarchy."[74] As the *Grand vocabulaire françois*, a 1773 conspectus of the knowledge of the Enlightenment marketed to the cultivated general public, explained to its readers, "the conquerors," having displaced the Roman property order, "made themselves lords over both the persons and the goods of the vanquished," and with them arrived the barbarism of *duplex dominium*.[75]

This late eighteenth-century contempt for medieval doctrine, and belief that the *ius feudale* was a legacy of violence of the barbarian conquerors, set the legal stage for the property law of the French revolutionaries, who embarked on the thoroughgoing program of classical revivalism before which earlier jurists had quailed. Among the Revolution's earliest and most radical measures was a decree abolishing "feudalism" (*la féodalité*), voted by an exhilarated National Assembly after a feverish all-night session on August 4, 1789. The word "feudalism" was a new coinage, and there was by no means clarity on what it meant;[76] but the abolitionist program that followed focused strongly on property law; and what it demanded was a revival of the pure classical Roman conception of *dominium*.

This revolutionary neoclassicism came to fruition fifteen years later, in the Civil Code promulgated by Napoleon in 1804, the founding text of the modern civil law tradition, and an enactment dedicated to insuring, in the words of the French lawyer Marcel Planiol, that "every trace of the feudal hierarchy of persons and land" should disappear.[77] Precisely because "feudal hierarchy" was associated with the practice of tolerating plural "owners," the law of the Civil

---

[74] Voltaire, *Commentaire sur l'esprit des lois de Montesquieu* (Paris, 1819), 46 (originally 1778).

[75] *Grand vocabulaire françois* (Paris, 1773), 26:170, col. 2, s.v. "Seigneurie." The author is speaking of the Franks, and echoing the analysis of public and private *seigneurie* of Loyseau. On this, see Blaufarb, *Great Demarcation*, 23–28. For the context and the publisher, the encyclopedia publicist Charles-Joseph Pancoucke, www.cairn.info/revue-ela-2011-3-page-325.htm.

[76] See James Q. Whitman, "The Seigneurs Descend to the Rank of Creditors: The Abolition of Respect, 1790," *Yale Journal of Law and Humanities* 6 (1994): 249–283.

[77] Planiol, quoted in James Gordley, "Myths of the French Civil Code," *American Journal of Comparative Law* 42 (1994): 492 [459–505].

Code enshrined its own version of the classical "absolute" conception: It insisted that there must be only one owner, with the unhampered classical Roman right of *usus* and *abusus*, the right to use and destroy his inanimate possessions – though not of course the *vitae necisque potestas*; the owners of the Civil Code could destroy their lifeless objects at will, just as they could exploit their lands without regard for the interests or use rights of any others; but unlike their Roman predecessors they could no longer claim the authority to put their dependents to death.

The Revolution thus conjured the ancient Roman *dominus* back from the tomb. In practice, as scholars often observe, this revolutionary resurrection of "pure," absolute ownership, like the ancient Roman commitment to absolute ownership on which it was based, has turned out to have more to do with ideology than with legal reality. The civil law finds plenty of ways of tolerating plural interests in practice,[78] and plenty of ways of limiting owners' right to use and destroy; absolute ownership is, as the great comparative lawyer James Gordley writes, in truth one of the "myths of the French Civil Code."[79] But as Gordley also observes, it is a myth, like so many we have examined, of foundational importance: The civil law of property is unintelligible unless we know its ideological origins in the overthrow of the law of fiefs on the night of August 4, 1789, and the determination to bring back the classical Roman form of ownership, conceived of as the untrammeled power of *usus* and *abusus*, the power to use, abuse, and destroy.

* * *

This centuries-long history of debate and conflict over the law of ownership, culminating in the resurrection of the Roman *dominus* in the French Civil Code of 1804, is the soil out of which the leading theories of the passage "from slavery to feudalism" grew. Those theories, from Marx to Weber and beyond, all formed in the shadow of the abolition of 1789, and they were all designed to speak to the great historical question effectively posed by that abolition.

---

[78] This was true from the very beginning. See Jean-Étienne-Marie Portalis, *Discours préliminaire du premier project de Code civil* (1801), 55, available at https://mafr.fr/IMG/pdf/discours_1er_code_civil.pdf.
[79] Gordley, "Myths of the French Civil Code," 492.

That question seemed, to anybody familiar with the law, a crucial one in the making of the Western world: How, to put it in humanist terms, had the darkness of the feudal form of split ownership descended upon medieval Europe after the fall of Rome? How had Europeans lost their knowledge of what Fritz Pringsheim called, in 1942, "the precision of the classical conception"?[80] The answer that the revolutionaries themselves presupposed, embracing a vision of European history that went back to Robertson, was that feudalism had been imposed by the "violence, rapine and disorder" of the invading barbarians who destroyed the Empire, bringing with them a Dark Ages for law. The genius of the classical theorists of the passage from slavery to feudalism lay in their efforts to give subtler answers, founded in more searching accounts of ancient and medieval socio-economic history.

The leading nineteenth- and early twentieth-century efforts to explain how the feudal darkness had descended upon the West fell broadly into two chronological schools of thought. Marx and Weber remained faithful to the humanist chronology of Western history that prevailed among the revolutionaries, dating the origins of feudalism to the decline and fall of the Western Roman Empire. As Rome tottered and finally collapsed, both men believed, though for different reasons, ancient slavery became nonviable, and in the latter centuries of the Empire incipient forms of serfdom appeared, in which agrarian laborers were tied to the soil. Over time, this matured into the full-scale land-based feudalism of the Middle Ages.

The second school of thought, which commanded the allegiance of most professional medievalists, shifted the focus to a later period: to what Bloch called "the first feudal age," beginning in the late ninth century and continuing into the twelfth. Believers in this medievalist chronology generally pointed to the collapse of the Carolingian Empire, a half-millennium after the fall of the Roman West. For them, the tale was one of the emergence of a class of armed warlords, which they typically linked to the breakdown of Carolingian authority under the pressure of Viking, Avar, and Magyar depredations. The decisive decline of Carolingian authority by the 880s or so led to the

---

[80] Pringsheim, "The Unique Character of Classical Roman Law," *Journal of Roman Studies* 34 (1944): 62 [60–64].

takeover of power by local strongmen; and it was this appropriation of state functions by private lords that explained the appearance of the feudal form of real property tenures: *Duplex dominium* took hold when a new class of lords, the emerging feudal *domini* of the Middle Ages, seized what had once been the power of the Carolingian rulers, granting out parcels of land to their armed followers.

This chapter is not the place to explore all of these theories, whose complexities have been the subject of two centuries of searching scholarship among both medievalists and ancient historians. My sole purpose is to understand how the idea of the passage from slavery to feudalism emerged out of the reforms of the French Revolution; and to that end, I will focus only a few leading accounts – that of Friedrich Carl von Savigny; those of Marx and Weber; and those of Bloch and the oft-cited Jean-Louis Ganshof.

* * *

I begin with Savigny.

Today, the idea that the decline and fall of the Western Roman Empire triggered a passage from slavery to feudalism is most closely associated with Marx – so much so that it is almost taken for granted that it is a Marxist teaching.[81] But it was first aired when Marx was no more than a toddler, and by a man whose ideas he despised: Savigny, the most celebrated Roman lawyer of the nineteenth century; and to grasp the genesis of the theories of both Marx and Weber, and their roots in reflection on the long history of Roman law, it is with Savigny that we must begin.

Friedrich Carl von Savigny (1779–1861) was an iconic figure in his time, deemed the greatest jurist of the age on both sides of the Atlantic. A figure of considerable charisma, he belonged, as a young man, to a community of dashing Romantics: His wife was Kunigunde Brentano, sister both of the poet Clemens Brentano and of the multifaceted artist Bettina von Arnim, herself a friend of Goethe, Beethoven, Schleiermacher, and a long list of other artistic and cultural eminences. The young Savigny burst onto the German scene in 1803, with a study on the Roman law of possession. A lawyer among

---

[81] Adriaan Verhulst and Monique Bourin, "Europe carolingienne et Europe méridionale: le point de vue d'Adriaan Verhulst," *Médiévales* 21 (1991): 55–61.

poets, painters, musicians, and philosophers in the Germany of *Dichter und Denker*, writers and thinkers, Savigny is mostly remembered today for his career in later life, when he became an archconservative who put his talents in the service of the reactionary Prussian monarchy in the 1840s. He is further remembered as a founding figure of the Historical School of Jurisprudence, which united learned investigation of the history of Roman law with analyses of its application to contemporary problems, and as a vocal opponent of codification in the age of Romantic idealization of the *Volksgeist*, the "spirit of the people."[82]

He deserves to be remembered for another reason as well: as the pioneer of the social scientific study of the passage from slavery to feudalism. In an immensely influential 1822 lecture, he was the first to focus attention on a historical development that has stood at the center of scholarly debate ever since: the appearance, in the latter centuries of the Roman Empire, of a new class of agricultural laborers who were bound to the soil.[83]

These mysterious late antique laborers, who went by the name *coloni*, began cropping up in the Roman legal sources of the fourth century CE, after the crisis of the third century that marked the end of the classical period. Called *adscripticii* in late Latin officialese, "persons listed on the rolls," they were attached to a parcel of land for what scholars now believe to be tax reasons.[84] Attached to the land as they were, these late antique agrarian workers bore an intriguing resemblance to medieval serfs; and that made their presence in the

---

[82] For an overview with references to further literature, Gerhard Kleinheyer and Jan Schröder, eds., *Deutsche und Europäische Juristen aus neun Jahrhunderten*, 6th ed. (Tübingen, 2017), 380–388.

[83] Savigny, "Über den römischen Colonat," in *Vermischte Schriften* (repr. Aalen, 1981), 2:1–53. Savigny did not cite, and I assume did not know, the treatment of Joachim Potgieser, *De conditione et statu servorum apud Germanos* (Cologne, 1707). His main secondary source was Davide Winspeare, *Storia degli abusi feudali* (Naples, 1811).

[84] For current efforts to explicate the mysteries of the late antique colonate, see Boudewijn Sirks, "The Colonate in the Later Roman Empire," *Tijdschrift voor Rechtsgeschiedenis* 90 (2022): 125–147; Sirks, "The Colonate in Justinian's Reign," *Journal of Roman Studies* 98 (2008): 120–143; Cam Grey, "Contextualizing *Colonatus*: The *Origo* of the Late Roman Empire," *Journal of Roman Studies* 97 (2007): 155–175; Sirks, "Reconsidering the Roman Colonate," *Zeitschrift der Savigny-Stiftung für Rechtsgeschichte (Romanistische Abteilung)* 110 (1993): 331–369.

waning centuries of the Empire a topic of intense interest in the German-speaking world, where the problem of the origins of serfdom carried a heavy political charge.

When Savigny delivered his lecture in 1822, the "feudalism" whose abolition was voted by the French in August of 1789 was by no means dead east of the Rhine. The bulk of the German countryside was still dominated by lords, claiming seigneurial rights that they traced back for centuries. This was so despite the fact that the French revolutionary armies had brought a measure of change to the parts of Germany where they had imposed the Civil Code. Notwithstanding more than a decade of French occupation and indirect control, agrarian dependency was still widely entrenched; in that sense, the Revolution had visibly failed in most of the German-speaking lands. The power of German seigneurs over peasants would ebb only slowly, after the Revolutions of 1830 and 1848; indeed, beyond the Elbe, where Junkers dominated, it would not be fully broken until the twentieth century. The question of the origins and nature of agrarian feudalism was correspondingly high on the nineteenth-century political agenda, and it would command the attention, and shape the thought and careers, of German revolutionaries, reformers, and social thinkers, Marx and Weber prominently among them, for generations. Agrarian feudalism was not just a subject for historians; it was a live issue in German politics down into the 1930s.[85]

Savigny's seminal 1822 lecture on the emergence of late antique *coloni* laid down many of the basic guidelines for the succeeding generations of debate, and launched the study of ancient and medieval history on a wholly new trajectory. Unlike his predecessors among the Roman lawyers of the early modern period and the French Revolution, Savigny did not confine himself to the juristic business of parsing the doctrinal distinction between the ancient "absolute" and the medieval "split" forms of ownership, or with deploring the medieval garbling of the clarity and purity of the ancient doctrines. Instead, he devoted himself to a new kind of socio-economic history, setting out to nail down a precise historical record of how, when, and

---

[85] James Q. Whitman, *The Legacy of Roman Law in the German Romantic Era: Historical Vision and Legal Change* (Princeton, 1990), 151–199.

why the classical Roman order had given way to the barbarized medieval one.

To that end, he began with a basic definitional task: establishing a careful legal distinction between two kinds of agrarian laborers, slaves and serfs. That distinction, so obviously fundamental to any analysis of the transition from slavery to feudalism, is frustratingly elusive.[86] There have been many oppressed persons in the course of agrarian history who might plausibly be deemed either "slaves" or "serfs." *Servus*, the very Latin word for "slave" most commonly used both during and after Antiquity,[87] eventually came to mean "serf" in European usage. The distinction between the two forms of oppression remains difficult for scholars to specify today; and it was certainly obscure in the law before 1822. Indeed, Grotius and Pufendorf, the greatest of early modern authorities, saw no difficulty in extending the term *servus* to cover all workers, as we shall see in Chapter 9.[88]

Nor was it just a matter of technical legal terminology. In politics too, "slavery" was a term of opprobrium tossed around with promiscuous zest at the end of the eighteenth and beginning of the nineteenth centuries. "Slaves," in the rhetoric of the era of the Atlantic revolutions, could include those who tilled the soil – those "luckless peasants born the slaves of the great," as one French lover of liberty bewailed their lot in 1791.[89] The American revolutionaries, led by merchants and plantation owners – those "drivers of Negroes," in the familiar mocking phrase of Samuel Johnson, from whom "we hear the loudest yelps for liberty"[90] – even protested, without evident irony, that they themselves were facing "enslavement" at the hands of King George III. German idealist philosophers could be accused of their own peculiar sin of conceptual mushiness: They liked to speak in grandiose generalities of the history of Freedom and Unfreedom, especially under the influence of Hegel, one of Savigny's Berlin colleagues, and a man for whom he had hearty contempt.[91] Hegel's

---

[86] And it still gives scholars fits. See M. I. Bush, ed., *Serfdom and Slavery: Studies in Legal Bondage* (New York, 1996).

[87] Alongside, to take terms discussed earlier, *famulus* and *mancipium*.

[88] Below, Chapter 9. [89] J. J. Regnault, *Siècle de Louis Seize* (Bar-le-Duc, 1791), 121.

[90] Samuel Johnson, *Political Writings*, ed. Donald J. Greene, The Yale Edition of the Works of Samuel Johnson (New Haven, 1957-), 14:454.

[91] Though he did not attack him by name in his scholarship. See Christoph Kletzer, "Custom and Positivity: An Examination of the Philosophical Ground of the

famous 1807 dialectic of "Herr und Knecht," "master and servant," in particular, was hopelessly foggy about whether its "servant" was a slave or a serf or some other phenomenological genre of subordinate.[92]

Savigny, the exacting professor of Roman law, insisted on a higher standard of rigor. "In the most diverse periods and among the most diverse peoples," he began his lecture by observing, in a phrase that would resound through the writings of his nineteenth-century successors, "the cultivation of the soil has given rise to peculiar class relations [*eigenthümliche Standesverhältnisse*]."[93] The later Roman Empire was an example of how such soil-based "peculiar class relations" could emerge. In high classical Antiquity, the workers at the bottom of the social scale had been slaves, and the law of slavery had formed a corresponding focus of the classical Roman law of labor. The new *coloni* who came to the fore in the late Roman age of imperial decline were different. In many ways, careful examination of the legal sources revealed, their lot had improved over that of their enslaved predecessors: Among other things, they had more secure property rights, and unlike slaves they could form legally recognized families.[94] Nevertheless, they were still subject persons: Although formally free, in the sense that they were not the property of another, they were nonetheless treated by the law as mere human appurtenances to a parcel of real property.

Late Antiquity was thus the scene of a metamorphosis in the "class relations" governing agrarian labor, documentable by careful study of the classical and late antique legal sources: As classical Roman civilization crumbled, slavery began giving way to serfdom. This transformation, Savigny argued, could not be explained in the way that Robertson or Smith had tried to explain it. The emergence of the colonate was not simply the result of barbarian rapine and violence.

Hegel-Savigny Controversy," in Amanda Perreau Saussine and James Bernard Murphy, eds., *The Nature of Customary Law: Legal, Historical and Philosophical Perspectives* (Cambridge, 2007), 126–127 [125–148].

[92] Henning Ottmann, "Herr und Knecht bei Hegel: Bemerkungen zu einer mißverstandenen Dialektik," *Zeitschrift für philosophische Forschung* 35 (1981): 365–384. Savigny's distaste for Hegel was reciprocated. See Schiavone, *The Invention of Law in the West*, trans. Jeremy Carden and Antony Shugaar (Cambridge, MA, 2012), 108–110.

[93] Savigny, "Über den römischen Colonat," 2.   [94] Ibid., 12, 28–29, and *passim*.

On the contrary – and here was the historiographical coup of Savigny's lecture – the legal sources revealed that the transformation had already been underway before the invaders arrived. Late antique *coloni* had long existed "alongside the class of slaves, which they gradually limited and eventually replaced."[95] The invasions certainly mattered, in Savigny's telling; but their consequence was to accelerate an internal metamorphosis that Roman society was already undergoing. The invaders had this impact because they brought their own form of serfdom with them. The "peculiar class relations" of soil-bound subordination [*Hörigkeit*], Savigny explained, were found among the Germanic barbarians as well as among the later Romans, and "[a]fter the conquest of the Western Empire by Germanic peoples, the two institutions came into unmediated contact. An amalgamation [*Vermischung*] of the two was unavoidable. This hastened the final decline of ancient slavery, the way for which had already been paved by the introduction of *coloni*."[96]

The medieval agrarian property order was thus the offspring of an "amalgamation" between the warlike invaders from the northern forests and Rome in her later period of decline. This was a very different account from the one given by Robertson; but its implication was still the one drawn by the French revolutionaries: Only a revival of Roman law in its pure high classical absolute form could bring justice to Germany, still suffering under the barbarization of rural property relations that took place with the miscegenation between violent Germanic invaders and a languishing postclassical Rome a millennium and a half earlier.

* * *

It is easy to forget how much impact a scholarly lecture on Roman law could have in the nineteenth century, when Roman history haunted the self-understanding of political actors; but Roman law had no less significance in German political and intellectual life than it did in France. "The controversy ignited by Savigny," so Weber described

---

[95] Ibid.
[96] Ibid., 53: "Nach der Eroberung des westlichen Reichs durch die deutschen Völker kamen beide Institute in unmittelbare Berührung, und eine Vermischung derselben war unvermeidlich. Dadurch aber wurde der gänzliche Untergang der alten Sklaverey beschleunigt, welcher schon durch die Einführung des Colonats vorbereitet worden war."

the impact of this lecture in 1891, "has never since been put to rest";[97] and the same would remain true for decades thereafter. Savigny's analysis of the rise of the late antique colonate stimulated more than a century of German, and more broadly European, controversy over whether the decay and final fall of the Western Roman Empire had resulted in a mutation of the property-law foundations of exploitation, causing a formative transition from classical slavery, and classical absolute ownership, to medieval serfdom and feudal property law – a transition that had already begun with the slow disintegration of the socio-economic order in the later centuries of the Empire itself, before the barbarians descended.

Marx and Weber were the "axial figures" in the German strain of this debate, though they were not the only ones.[98] Both were men whose social and economic thought developed to a notable extent in response to "the controversy ignited by Savigny." Marx, who attended Savigny's Berlin courses as a law student in the 1830s, dismissed the Historical School of Jurisprudence just as derisively as he did virtually all the intellectual movements of his time, and he was certainly no fan of Savigny's politics. Nevertheless, the truth is that he wrote, in some sense, as Savigny's disciple throughout his career. Indeed, it could be said that Savigny's analysis of the emergence of the ancient colonate was the original locus out of which Marx built his historical thinking. He fully embraced the idea that history was a record of metamorphoses in the legal form of unfreedom, as one species of "peculiar class relations" gave way to the next. He also seized enthusiastically on a critical implication of Savigny's analysis (though one that Savigny himself would have abjured): that classical Roman absolute ownership was first and foremost the ownership of slaves. Not least, he followed Savigny in the hunt for clues in the legal sources that seemed to offer the most revealing documentation of socio-economic change.

Of course Marx, a man of colossal intellectual ambition, expanded the tale to cover all of human history; and where Savigny restricted

---

[97] Weber, *Die römische Agrargeschichte in ihrer Bedeutung für das Staats- und Privatrecht* (Stuttgart, 1891), 3.

[98] "Axial": Kyle Harper, *Slavery in the Late Roman World*, AD 275–425 (Cambridge, 2011), 6–7, though speaking only of Weber. For a survey of nineteenth-century theories, see Adolph Wagner, *Lehr- und Handbuch der politischen Ökonomie*, 2nd ed. (Leipzig, 1894), 1:69–70.

himself to an examination of the law, Marx painted from a much more varied palette of economic and social theory. Still, his fundamental idea remained substantially the one first expounded in Savigny's famous 1822 lecture on the transformation of Roman law, and he never abandoned Savigny's belief in the pivotal importance of the sociolegal transformation of Late Antiquity, the putative period of decline that brought with it the incipient passage from the stage of slavery to the stage of serfdom, to be fully consummated under the pressure of the barbarian invasions.

Marx never published a systematic statement of his theoretical views, but scholars glean them from his scattered published and unpublished writings.[99] Beginning with the unpublished material from the 1840s later assembled into the text known as "The German Ideology,"[100] Marx pursued his lifelong commitment to explaining the full sweep of history. At the origins of human society, he argued, following the ancient tradition described in Chapter 1, there was primitive communism – a social order in which there was no ownership at all, and therefore no form of unfreedom. The stage of primitive communism was followed by the rise of ancient slave economies, for which Marx's capital examples were Athens and Rome. Again faithful to ancient tradition, he focused on the fall of the Roman Republic and the rise of mass plantation slavery. As we saw in Chapter 2, ancient authors such as Appian lamented the triumph of slave plantations in the formerly common lands of the Roman *ager publicus*: "Certain powerful men became extremely rich and the race of slaves multiplied throughout the country, while the Italian people dwindled in numbers and strength, being oppressed by penury, taxes, and military service."[101] Marx followed those accounts in his explanation of the rise of the late republican and imperial economy, in which, he wrote, injecting the language of economic analysis into the study of ancient history, the ownership of slaves became "the basis of

---

[99] See the discussion above, Chapter 3.
[100] For the problems in treating this text, traditionally credited to Marx and Engels but assembled long after the deaths of the authors, see Sarah Johnson, "Farewell to the German Ideology," *Journal of the History of Ideas* 83 (2022): 143–170, discussing the edition in Karl Marx and Friedrich Engels, "Deutsche Ideologie: Manuskripte und Drucke," in *Karl Marx/Friedrich Engels Gesamtausgabe* (Berlin and Boston, 2017), Abt. 1, 5.1.
[101] App. *BC* 1.7.

From Slavery to Feudalism 271

all production."[102] This was accompanied by a transformation of the Roman ruling class: The old order had been dominated by the patricians of the Middle Republic, who lived according to traditional Roman norms. The new one was dominated by a "money-hungry" wealthy class, dedicated to the extraction of profit, in a Rome whose erstwhile simplicity of manners has vanished amidst the riches of rule. Slave-based economics and a market-oriented commodity-lust took hold together in the age of the corrupted and collapsing Republic.[103]

The ancient slave "basis of all production" did not, however, survive the decline and fall of the Western Empire. In explaining the transformations that attended the collapse of classical civilization, Marx, like Savigny, continued to ascribe a critical role to the barbarian invasions. Indeed, he laid somewhat greater weight on the invasions than Savigny had. Marx's emphasis on the consequences of the invasions reflected developments in nineteenth-century German legal thought, which underwent rapid change after the early 1820s. In the years after Savigny's lecture, conflict broke out between two Romantic-era schools: the "Romanists" and the "Germanists." The Romanists followed Savigny's lead in embracing the law of the ancients, suitably reframed as law for a modern world. The Germanist school developed a competing nationalistic theory, in which they drew an ever-sharpening contrast between Roman legal principles (which they deplored) and the "Germanic" ones supposedly deducible from medieval legal texts.[104] By the time that Marx

---

[102] Marx and Engels, "Deutsche Ideologie," *Karl Marx/Friedrich Engels Gesamtausgabe*, Abt. 1, 5.1:106–107: "In Italien ... war durch die Konzentration des Grundeigentums ... und Verwandlung desselben in Viehweiden ... die freie Bevölkerung fast verschwunden, die Sklaven selbst starben immer wieder aus und mußten stets durch neue ersetzt werden. Die Sklaverei blieb die Basis der gesamten Produktion..."

[103] Marx, *Das Kapital: Kritik der politischen Ökonomie*, Bk. 3, 2nd ed., ed. Friedrich Engels (Hamburg, 1904), 3:136. For a helpful concise account from an early twentieth-century anti-Marxist, see Emil Hammacher, *Das philosophisch-ökonomische System des Marxismus* (Leipzig, 1909), 603. I am offering an admittedly speculative reading of Marx here, in suggesting that his conception of the commodity orientation drew in some measure on the traditional view of the breakdown of Roman republican frugality.

[104] See generally Gerhard Dilcher, "Römisches Recht oder Deutsches Recht?" in Dilcher, *Die Germanisten und die historische Rechtsschule: bürgerliche Wissenschaft zwischen Romantik, Realismus und Rationalisierung* (Frankfurt, 2017), 143–157.

embarked on his career, the contrast between the "principles" of Roman law and the "principles" of "Germanic" law counted as cutting-edge legal scholarship, and that scholarship informed his account, which now made feudalism out to be a more essentially "Germanic" institution than it was for Savigny.

When the Germanic peoples descended on Rome, Marx argued in his *Grundrisse* of 1857–1859, they brought with them the institution of serfdom. "The Germanic barbarians, who lived in isolation on the land and for whom agriculture with serfs [*Leibeigenen*] was the traditional production, could impose these conditions on the Roman provinces all the more easily as the concentration of landed property which had taken place there had already entirely overthrown the earlier agricultural relations."[105] Internal Roman developments certainly still counted in Marx's analysis. Rome, he believed, had fatally weakened herself through dependence on slave plantations, and so was vulnerable to the invaders from the north. Nevertheless, the invasions now played the critical role in the transformation of the law into a more "Germanic" form. As the Germans descended, carrying with them their practices of serfdom, there followed a transformation in the patterns of economic exploitation: German war-bands converted themselves into feudal nobilities, whose power depended on "feudal property" with its accompanying "power over serfs."[106]

---

[105] Karl Marx, "Ökonomische Manuskripte 1857/58," *Marx/Friedrich Engels Gesamtausgabe* (Berlin and Boston, 1981), Abt. 2.1.1: 34.

[106] Karl Marx and Friedrich Engels, "Deutsche Ideologie: Manuskripte und Drucke," in *Karl Marx/Friedrich Engels Gesamtausgabe* (Berlin and Boston, 2017), Abt.1 5.1: 130–133: "Wenn das Altertum von der Stadt und ihrem kleinen Gebiet ausging, so ging das Mittelalter vom Lande aus ... Die letzten Jahrhunderte des verfallenden römischen Reichs und die Eroberung durch die Barbaren selbst zerstörten eine Masse von Produktivkräften; der Ackerbau war gesunken, die Industrie aus Mangel an Absatz verfallen, der Handel eingeschlafen oder gewaltsam unterbrochen, die ländliche und städtische Bevölkerung hatte abgenommen. Diese vorgefundenen Verhältnisse und die dadurch bedingte Weise der Organisation der Eroberung entwickelten unter dem Einflusse der germanischen Heerverfassung das feudale Eigentum. Es beruht, wie das Stamm- und Gemeindeeigentum, wieder auf einem Gemeinwesen, dem aber nicht wie dem antiken die Sklaven, sondern die leibeignen kleinen Bauern als unmittelbar produzierende Klasse gegenüberstehen. Zugleich mit der vollständigen Ausbildung des Feudalismus tritt noch der Gegensatz gegen die Städte hinzu. Die hierarchische Gliederung des Grundbesitzes und die damit

From Slavery to Feudalism

The transition from a slave-based, classical-Roman-law-governed Antiquity to a land-based, Germanic-law-governed Middle Ages was eventually followed, in the vision of Marx, by a second transformation. This came in 1789, with the final abolition, after a millennium of feudal property law, of the "Germanic" institution of the fief. When the Revolution proclaimed its revival of the absolute Roman concept of property, it did so in furtherance of the interests of the bourgeoisie: The romanized conception of the revolutionaries, no longer founded on the ownership of slaves, but now entirely on the ownership of commodities, laid the property law foundation for capitalist exploitation.[107]

Marx's narrative of the transitions from the "peculiar class relations" of slavery to those of feudalism and then bourgeois capitalism, this grand rereading of a juristic debate over the nature of ownership that began in late twelfth-century Milan before passing to sixteenth- and seventeenth-century jurists, Enlightenment reformers, French Revolutionaries, and nineteenth-century German legal historians, served as the outline for all later Marxist historical theorizing down to Stalin and beyond. But Marx left the labor of creating a systematic economic history of the shifting "bases of production" to his disciples from Engels onwards, who developed the familiar theory of the successive stages of the modes of the ownership of the means of production that would be recited in the *Short Course* in 1938.

* * *

Weber, writing several decades later, was, like Marx, trained as a student of Roman law; like Marx, he devoted much of his early intellectual energy to "the controversy ignited by Savigny," as well as to the nature of Roman landholding and the problems of agrarian exploitation in nineteenth-century Germany; and he too dated the origins of feudalism to the decline and fall of the Western Empire. But his analytic approach diverged significantly. For both Savigny and Marx the late antique collapse of classical civilization was the consequence, in at least some measure, of the barbarian invasions. It

---

zusammenhängenden bewaffneten Gefolgschaften gaben dem Adel die Macht über die Leibeigenen."

[107] Above, Chapter 3.

followed, for Marx in particular, that Europe had been born out of the collision between the Latin and Germanic "peoples," as nineteenth-century historians often put it,[108] which meant that the writing of medieval history required disentangling the threads of its Roman and Germanic heritages. In line with those beliefs, Marx treated the study of "feudalism" largely as the study of its legal historical genetics, as it were: He set out to identify the indigenous "Germanic" legal practices that were the seeds of feudalism, carried into the lands of Rome by the barbarian invaders "for whom agriculture with serfs was the traditional production."[109]

Weber, by contrast, let the barbarian invasions drop from his account, abandoning the legal historical genetics of Marx. Like other late nineteenth-century scholars, especially in France,[110] Weber believed that feudalism had to be understood through the study of its historical "sociology," not its supposed "Germanic" roots. Accordingly, he now sought the causes of the transition from slavery to serfdom wholly in internal Roman socio-economic developments, decisively abandoning the focus on the barbarian invasions that dated back to Robertson and beyond him to the jurists of the Renaissance.

To that end, he focused on warfare, so pervasively present in the Greco-Roman legal and literary texts. Classical Rome, Weber argued, was, like other ancient Mediterranean societies, ruled by a predatory warring aristocracy, which prospered by exploiting the labor of enslaved enemies. "In Antiquity, war is always also a hunt for slaves."[111] It was this "hunt for slaves" that lay at the foundation of the classical socio-economic order.

This was a proposition that Weber fleshed out, beginning in the early 1900s, in one of his most important social historical constructs, the "consumer city hypothesis," over which it is important to linger for a moment. The consumer city hypothesis was a product of the

---

[108] E.g., Leopold von Ranke, *Geschichte der romanischen und germanischen Völker von 1494 bis 1535* (Leipzig and Berlin, 1824).

[109] For critique: Francesco Calasso, "Diritto volgare, diritti romanzi, diritto comune," in *Introduzione al diritto comune* (Milan, 1951), 207–232.

[110] In particular in the work of two great figures whom I do not have space to discuss, Jacques Flach and Numa Denis Fustel de Coulanges, both of whom rejected the study of Germanic and Roman legal sources in favor of sociology.

[111] Weber, "Die sozialen Gründe des Untergangs der antike Kultur," in *Gesammelte Aufsätze zur Sozial- und Wirtschaftsgeschichte* (Tübingen, 1924), 293 [289–311].

From Slavery to Feudalism

primitivist approach to economic history, already described in Chapter 2. As we saw, primitivist economic history started from a denial that ancient economies were market economies of the modern kind, populated by market-oriented actors of the modern sort. Instead, primitivists reached various versions of the same conclusion, namely that the ancient Greco-Roman world had "*oikos*-economies," centered on the semi-autarkic household and associated with the "master's right of the slaveholder."[112]

The consumer city hypothesis extended the primitivist analysis to the explanation of the nature of ancient urbanism. First presented by Karl Bücher in 1903, the hypothesis held that, where modern market-oriented cities are centers of industrial production and finance, ancient cities were centers of military predation. Ancient elites were not industrialists or bankers, but warriors, dedicated to booty-taking, and their cities were "citadels," in which *Gewaltherren*, "rulers by violence," collected and distributed the take from their campaigns. It followed that ancient cities, instead of serving as production centers of deal-making and trade, functioned as consumption centers – fortified camps for warriors feasting on the profits of war. Rome and Athens in particular, Bücher wrote, lived by their *Herrscherberufe*, their predatory "vocation to rule."[113]

In his own history of the West, Weber followed Bücher's lead, though his ideal type of the consumer city rang some significant changes on Bücher's original. Weber put a heavier accent on slaving as the basis of ancient economies, rather than on other forms of booty. He also shifted the emphasis somewhat toward ideology: Rather than speaking of the actual practice of war, he spoke of a more diffuse ethos of predation. Weber's consumer city was not necessarily the fortified citadel of an elite that was itself actively engaged in campaigning. Instead, it was the home of a leisured nobility that fed on the fruits of conquest as well as on other forms of wealth-extraction, living off the fat of a subject countryside as well

---

[112] Bücher, *Die Entstehung der Volkswirtschaft* (Tübingen, 1893), 23, 27–28.

[113] Bücher, *Die Entstehung der Volkswirtschaft: Vorträge und Versuche* (Tübingen, 1910), 368; cf. Bücher, *Beiträge zur Wirtschaftsgeschichte* (Tübingen, 1922), 38. The consumer city theory is discussed at length in M. I. Finley, "The Ancient City: From Fustel de Coulanges to Max Weber and Beyond," *Comparative Studies in Society and History* 19 (1977), 315–317 [305–327].

off the labor of enslaved enemies.[114] In that sense, Weber departed from narrowly socio-economic and military history, putting the focus on the broader history of elite values and culture; and in the next chapter, I will suggest that his consumer city hypothesis is best reread as an argument about the cultural history of the law, rather than about economics.

Nevertheless, the economics of the "hunt for slaves" remained at the center of Weber's interpretation; and it was from that starting point that he built his explanation of the passage from slavery to feudalism. Since classical civilization relied on slaving to satisfy its labor needs, it could flourish only so long as it could continue to engage in the successful hunt for human prey. Yet slaving on a large scale eventually became impossible; and the downfall of classical civilization inevitably followed. Kyle Harper summarizes the argument that Weber published in 1896, in a work that did much to make his name as a preeminent German scholar. Weber put particular weight on a point emphasized by Savigny in 1822: the fact that the legal sources showed that late antique *coloni*, unlike slaves, could form legally recognized families:

[T]he rise of the Roman empire created a system of slave labor which was a direct outgrowth of imperial conquest. Even the control of slave labor was a continuation of war, organized on plantations that were run as army barracks, with celibate male slaves chained together. The end of conquest, then, was nothing less than "the turning point" of ancient civilization. The end of military expansion catalyzed a process in which the slave supply withered, and consequently the price of labor rose. In turn, the slave system began to mutate internally, as slave-owners allowed slaves to form families, and slaves dissolved into the undifferentiated mass of rural dependents. These changes, in step with

---

[114] This Weberian consumer city was, it must be emphasized, a Weberian ideal type: Weber never argued that all ancient cities were "consumer cities" in every respect; it was rather that they approximated more closely the type of the "consumer city" than later cities did. In particular, he drew a contrast with the "producer city" that dominated in the Middle Ages, a center of production, often ruled by guilds. See generally Finley, "The Ancient City," 305–327; Paul P. M. Erdkamp, "Beyond the Limits of the 'Consumer City': A Model of the Urban and Rural Economy in the Roman World," *Historia: Zeitschrift für alte Geschichte* 50 (2001): 333 [332–356]; Andrew Wallace-Hadrill, "Back to M. I. Finley's Ancient City: Town and Country, Landowners and the Rest at Pompeii," *Journal of Roman Archaeology* 32 (2019): 718–723.

From Slavery to Feudalism

the development of the colonate, led to the gradual emergence of medieval serfdom.[115]

The late antique Roman countryside no longer featured barracks housing an exclusively male slave population, consisting in defeated enemies toiling under the whips of overseers. Instead, there were cottages housing proto-serf families; the "mutation" in the "peculiar class relations" of Late Antiquity was one that transformed a system that exploited the enslaved enemies of the classical Empire, who had been treated, as it were, as gelded plantation beasts, to be worked to death and then replaced by new enslaved victims, into a system that exploited sexually active serfs, who reproduced for the benefit of their lords. The passage from slavery to feudalism was thus a passage to a new mode of replenishing the labor supply: from capturing workers to breeding them – from the hunting of wild workers, if you will, to the husbandry of domesticated ones.

The shift to an incipiently feudal form of land-based exploitation, founded on the natural increase of the subordinate population rather than on slaving wars, followed naturally. Laborers had to be able to feed themselves and their offspring, which meant that they had to have some claim on the fruits of their allotment of soil. The form of agrarian lordship that thus emerged was still effectively found, Weber hinted broadly, among the East Prussian Junkers of the late nineteenth century.[116]

* * *

Marx and Weber both sought the origins of feudalism where Savigny had sought them, in the decline and fall of the Western Empire. Most medievalists looked later: to the period from the late ninth to the early thirteenth century – the "first feudal age," in the chronology of Bloch, when ancient slavery, though already in decline in Late Antiquity, in fact definitively "came to an end."[117]

---

[115] Harper, *Slavery in the Late Roman World*, 6.
[116] Weber, "Agrarverhältnisse im Altertum," in *Gesammelte Aufsätze zur Sozial- und Wirtschaftsgeschichte* (Tübingen, 1924), 278 [1–288].
[117] Bloch, "Comment et pourquoi finit l'esclavage antique," *Annales: économies, sociétés, civilisations* 2 (1947): 32 [30–44]: "dès le ix siècle." Bloch's famous article is sometimes cited, somewhat mysteriously to me, as though it identified Late Antiquity as the critical moment of transition. While it is true that Bloch weighed late antique developments, the ultimate argument of his article puts the center of gravity in the later period.

This is an interpretation received its canonical statement from Ganshof, in his 1944 book *What Is Feudalism?* Published in the midst of chaos of the last months of World War II, *What Is Feudalism?* offered a concise account of feudalism as a product of the post-Carolingian chaos a thousand years earlier. "Feudalism," in Ganshof's much-cited definition, took hold when local strongmen seized control as central authority collapsed, offering protection to followers. As such, it comprised

> a body of institutions creating and regulating the obligations of obedience and service – mainly military service – on the part of a free man (the vassal) towards another free man (the lord), and the obligations of protection and maintenance on the part of the lord with regard to his vassal. The obligation of maintenance had usually as one of its effects the grant by the lord to his vassal of a unit of real property known as a fief.[118]

The feudal institutions that took hold in this region certainly had Carolingian antecedents, since Carolingian rulers had given their agents temporary grants of real property holdings. But the fully formed feudal system was different, since fiefs had become heritable, a development that could be dated to the last decades of the failing Empire in the late ninth century.[119] Because he regarded feudalism as a form of military order, Ganshof had little to say about serfs. His account was focused on the men in arms, not on the cultivators of the soil.

Bloch too located the heartland of what he called "the first feudal age" in the Loire–Rhine region in the wake of Carolingian collapse. But he belonged to the high French intellectual tradition, exemplified by the sociology and anthropology of Émile Durkheim and Marcel Mauss, that was committed to explaining what Mauss called "total" facts, lodged in social systems.[120] In line with that tradition, Bloch refused to restrict his account to the military relation of lord and vassal, writing instead of a total social order that he called "feudal society"; and he set out to produce an account that restored the place of economics in the history of feudalism, and in particular the economics of real property.

---

[118] Ganshof, *Feudalism*, trans. Philip Grierson, 3rd ed. (New York, 1961), xvi.
[119] The source commonly cited is the Capitulary of Quierzy, 877.
[120] Mauss, *Essai sur le don: forme et raison de l'échange dans les sociétés archaiques* (Paris, n.d.), 234.

From Slavery to Feudalism

What lay in the background of the rise of "feudal society," according to Bloch, was not just the fragmentation of central government authority, but also the disappearance of a cash economy, which gave rise to a form of social system based, not on salary, but on the "service tenement" in real property. It was this that explained the turn toward a law "that took land as its basic point of departure": The triumph of feudalism was the consequence of a post-Carolingian liquidity crisis. In-kind, land-based compensation governed life on the manor as much as it governed military relations; feudalism was not just a matter of the law of fiefs, but a general organizing principle of society. By including manorial relations, Bloch was able to reintroduce peasant servitude, the dominant concern of the Marxist tradition, into his account of feudalism. "Feudal society" comprised, in Bloch's own famous definition:

A subject peasantry; widespread use of the service tenement (i.e. the fief) instead of a salary which was out of the question; the supremacy of a class of specialized warriors; ties of obedience and protection which bind man to man, and within the warrior class, assume the distinctive form called vassalage; fragmentation of authority – leading inevitably to disorder and, in the midst of all this, the survival of forms of association, family and State, of which the latter, during the second feudal age, was to acquire renewed strength.[121]

In Bloch's "second feudal age," dating after 1100 or so, state authority reemerged. So too did a cash economy, which led to the gradual transformation of feudalism into a system of financial exploitation of a subject peasantry, generally called "seigneurialism" or sometimes "bastard feudalism." Lords continued to engage in such financial exploitation for centuries thereafter; this was the form of "feudalism" whose abolition was finally decreed in the French Revolution.

* * *

Many of these accounts of the origins and nature of "feudalism" continue to be repeated by nonspecialists, prominent among them American law professors, who most commonly cite either Ganshof or Bloch.[122] But professional ancient historians and medievalists alike

---

[121] Bloch, *Feudal Society*, trans. L. Manyon (Chicago, 1974), 446.
[122] E.g. (meaning no disrespect!), Alfred C. Yen, "Western Frontiers or Feudal Society? Metaphors and Perceptions of Cyberspace," *Berkeley Technology Law Journal* 17 (2002): 1232–1234 [1207–1263].

now distance themselves from all these arguments, whether in the versions of Marx, Weber, Ganshof, or Bloch. The interpretations in the older literature have certainly not been disavowed wholesale. Marxist history is still written. Scholars have not lost all interest in the project of dating the transition from slavery to serfdom.[123] Nevertheless, the old standard interpretation of Western socio-economic history as the chronicle of a passage from slavery to feudalism, after a half-century of critical bombardment, has been left more or less a derelict on the academic waters.

The economic histories of Marx and Weber have proven to be especially fat targets. The most telling objections to their work have to do with their accounts of the economies of the classical world, which have aged badly. This is largely because new sorts of evidence have come to the fore since they wrote. Nineteenth-century studies of Roman history were overwhelmingly based on legal and literary sources.[124] Both Marx and Weber, despite their immense originality and sophistication, and despite their determination to develop more socio-economically informed theories and to use the widest range of evidence, received a nineteenth-century neo-humanist education in the Greek and Latin classics as schoolboys, and in Roman law as university students; both took their inspiration from Savigny; and in the end, their interpretations bore the impress of the same sorts of sources that Westerners had relied upon from the twelfth century onward, such as Appian, Aristotle, and of course the riches of the *Corpus iuris civilis*.

Since the nineteenth century, however, historians have come to exploit a much wider range of evidence, particularly through archeology and papyrology, two fields that have made stunning progress. We now understand that slaves were a smaller proportion of the labor force than nineteenth-century Europeans believed, and that those slaves were not primarily acquired through war in the mature Empire, despite the occasional large-scale victory that flooded the slave markets. In any case, the old confidence that we can reconstruct the economic significance of Roman slavery has evaporated; as John Bodel writes, given the fragility of the evidence,

---

[123] Jean-Pierre Poly and Éric Bournazel, *La mutation féodale, X^e–XIIe siècle* (Paris, 2004).
[124] Along with numismatics and other "antiquarian" evidence, including of course inscriptions. The use of these forms of evidence extends back to the Bollandists of the seventeenth century.

"we must approach the question as primarily a cultural rather than an economic issue."[125] Meanwhile, historians, applying the techniques developed in economics departments, have come to see the economy of the Roman Empire was vigorous and varied, attaining levels of commercial development that would not be matched until the end of the Middle Ages.[126] Archeologists, for their part, have chiseled away at the foundations of the consumer city hypothesis of Bücher and Weber, identifying many productive, and even arguably quasi-industrial, urban workshops.[127] These are advances that have made the interpretations of Marx and Weber seem musty and quaint.

Our understanding of the latter centuries of the Empire has changed as well: Historians no longer speak of late antique "decline" in the humanistic way that Savigny, Marx, and Weber did – though there is some controversy on that point, as we shall see in the next chapter. What we now call "Late Antiquity" is typically studied, not as a period when civilization crumbled, but as a culturally and often economically vigorous time, displaying many continuities with the classical period.[128] To be sure, the latter centuries of the Roman Empire are still regarded as different from what came before, and scholars have not uniformly dropped the idea that there was a transformation of property law underway, and perhaps even scattered signs of what might be called transitions from slavery to serfdom.[129] But the

---

[125] Bodel, "Slave Labour and Roman Society," in Bodel and Paul Cartledge, eds., *The Cambridge World History of Slavery, Vol. 1: The Ancient Mediterranean World* (Cambridge, 2011), 314 [311–336]; similarly Keith Bradley, "Slavery in the Roman Republic," ibid., 245 [241–264]: "[T]he proportion of slaves in the overall Roman population during the conquest remains indeterminate. What continue to be important therefore are institutional indicators of the predominance of slavery in Roman culture."

[126] See Paul Erdkamp, Koenraad Verboven, and Arian Zuiderhoek, eds., *Capital, Investment and Innovation in the Roman World* (Oxford, 2020), and more broadly the publications in the series Oxford Studies in the Roman Economy.

[127] See Wallace-Hadrill, "Back to M. I. Finley's Ancient City," 723.

[128] Though with debate between "catastrophist" and "continuist" schools. See Bryan Ward-Perkins, "Continuists, Catastrophists and the Towns of Post-Roman Northern Italy," *Papers of the British School at Rome* 65 (1997): 157–176.

[129] Chris Wickham, "Marx, Sherlock Holmes, and Late Roman Commerce," *Journal of Roman Studies* 78 (1988): 183–193, reviewing A. Giardina, *Società romana e impero tardoantico III: Le merci; gli insediamenti*; Wickham, "The Other Transition: From the Ancient World to Feudalism," *Past & Present* 103 (1984): 3–36; and Wickham, *Framing*, 259–260.

unavoidable reality is that slavery did not vanish. On the contrary, it remained an economically important institution in Late Antiquity,[130] and persisted in the early Middle Ages, arguably playing a critical economic role in the Carolingian period,[131] and long after.

Nor do scholars think of the barbarian invasions in the way they once did. There is no doubt that the establishment of barbarian kingdoms brought profound changes to what had been the Western Empire; but there can hardly be anyone who takes seriously the belief of Savigny and Marx that when the barbarians arrived they brought with them serfdom. Indeed, scholars no longer believe that there were clearly ethnically defined "Germanic" nations that carried a common "Germanic" customary law with them into a collapsing Empire at all.[132] While the laws of the early medieval kingdoms include some forms of use rights that might suggest an orientation toward some inchoate kind of feudal land tenure,[133] they also unmistakably include slavery. Indeed, it has been argued that slaves were treated even more brutally in the barbarian kingdoms than they had been in classical Rome.[134]

As for believers in medieval feudalism: They have been the targets of Brown, Reynolds, and others. We have already seen the tenor of these attacks: The classic interpretations anachronistically projected concepts of feudalism from the early modern period onto the past. Brown, a great connoisseur of the complexities of medieval societies, mocks believers in Bloch's "feudal society"; while Reynolds is particularly fierce in attacking interpretations of Bloch's "first feudal age."

Reynolds mounts a critique too important not to summarize, since it speaks directly to my theme: the problem of the interpretation of the

---

[130] Harper, *Slavery in the Late Roman World*.
[131] Michael McCormick, *Origins of the European Economy: Communications and Commerce* A.D. 300–900 (Cambridge, 2002).
[132] See Patrick Geary, *The Myth of Nations: The Medieval Origins of Europe* (Princeton, 2001). Noel Lenski, in new work, challenges this orthodoxy.
[133] For a remarkably confident linkage of feudalism to Germanic *Gewere*, see Hilton Root, *Network Origins of the Global Economy: East vs. West in a Complex Systems Perspective* (Cambridge, 2020), 124 (with Cameron Harwick).
[134] Bonnassie, "Survie et extinction," 317–320; Hermann Nehlsen, *Sklavenrecht zwischen Antike und Mittelalter: **germanisches und römisches Recht in den germanischen** Rechtsaufzeichnungen* (Göttingen, 1972).

legal sources. Legal records of the ninth through eleventh centuries, she observes, included a variety of terms, many of them in Latin, many of them ambiguous, by no means all of them forms of either "fief" or "vassal." Their ambiguities were assumed away by scholars who, under the hypnotic spell of the tradition that traces back the *Libri feudorum*, simply took it for granted that "feudalism" was what explained them. Indeed, in her most recent work, Reynolds has challenged the belief that medieval real property rights consisted in "tenures" whose form of "ownership" was different from the modern form at all.[135]

Reynolds goes much further than most medievalists would go (and too far for me[136]); but her critique is only one in what has become a large literature of skepticism about what the medieval legal sources can tell us about the supposed workings of "feudalism." Contemporary medievalists, even ones who do not follow Reynolds in her attacks on the very existence of fiefs, have largely lost the old faith in the sources as reliable evidence for socio-economic history. To be sure, most medievalists would acknowledge that there were numerous social practices that can properly be called "feudal." For the most part, though, medievalists have become sharply conscious that anyone who speaks of "fiefs," "vassals," or any other aspect of medieval "feudalism" is treading on philological thin ice.

The fundamental problem is the one flagged by Reynolds, as well as by another highly influential scholar, Dominique Barthélemy:[137] All interpretations, whether written in the spirit of Marx or Bloch, inevitably depend on deciphering ambiguous terms in the surviving documentation from the early and central Middle Ages; but we lack evidence from the early and central Middle Ages for how to decipher them.[138] The most important of these philological problems, for my

---

[135] Reynolds, *Fiefs and Vassals*; and Reynolds, "Tenure and Property in Medieval England," *Historical Research* 88 (2015): 563–576.

[136] The burden of Reynolds' argument in "Tenure and Property," I take it, is that in the absence of any clear statement on the nature of ownership in the sources, there is no reason to assume that medieval conceptions were different from our own. But as I have argued throughout, there is indeed a reason: Use rights represent the most common form of land rights, and they may therefore rightly be assumed to explain the sources.

[137] Barthélemy, *La mutation féodale, a-t-elle eu lieu?* (Paris, 1997).

[138] For the common law, see John Hudson, "Imposing Feudalism on Anglo-Saxon England: Norman and Angevin Presentation of Pre-conquest Lordship and Landholding," in S. Bagge, M. H. Gelting, and T. Lindkvist, eds., *Feudalism: New Landscapes of Debate* (Turnhout, 2011), 115–134.

purposes, infects the semantic history of a term that is at the top of the list for any study of the supposed socio-economic passage from slavery to serfdom, *servus*. *Servus*, used throughout the centuries, unambiguously meant "slave" in classical Antiquity; by some point, it had come to mean "serf," the form in which it still exists in modern languages. But when? And how clearly? Ambiguities in the meaning of *servus* already abound in the sources from Late Antiquity. The *Code of Justinian*, for example, declares that both *coloni* and *servi* are *in domini potestate*,[139] "in the power of the *dominus*." The terms *dominus* and *potestas* were already more than half a millennium old at the time, as we saw in earlier chapters; what did they mean as a matter of sixth-century realities? The answer is not obvious to us, and it was not even obvious in Late Antiquity. Justinian did his autocratic best to settle the question, but his answers are puzzling.[140] Savigny may have thought he could specify a precise distinction between serfs and slaves on the basis of the legal texts, but the ancients found it a struggle, and so do contemporary specialists. As a leading student of the period, Domenico Vera, colorfully complains, trying to get at the social and economic realities of late antique agrarian relations "starting from the Codes," as Savigny did, "is like crushing water in a mortar."[141]

Nor does the task grow easier when we arrive in the early Middle Ages: As Alice Rio argues, the early medieval meaning of *servus* is elusive, since actors used their inherited Roman terminology in wholly opportunistic ways.[142] They no more had a definitive understanding of the difference between slaves and serfs than their late antique predecessors did. The same remained true for hundreds of years thereafter. Ruth Mazo Karras describes the challenge in interpreting the term in thirteenth-century northern France:

> It is pointless to ask when the term *servus* changes in meaning, for the medieval people who used it would not have seen its various meanings as mutually exclusive ... Beaumanoir's thirteenth-century Coutumes de Beauvaisis speak of *sers* as one class of people, although "this manner of people are not all of one condition, but there are several conditions of servitude."[143]

---

[139] C. 11.52.1.   [140] Generally Sirks, "The Colonate in Justinian's Reign."
[141] Quoted in Wickham, *Framing*, 524.
[142] McCormick, *Origins of the European Economy*, 734–735.
[143] Karras, *Slavery and Society in Medieval Scandinavia* (Philadelphia, 1988), 8.

Specialists in other regions make parallel observations.[144] A semantic shift in the meaning of *servus* may eventually have taken hold in the later Middle Ages. Charles Verlinden argued in 1943 that it was complete in thirteenth-century Italy.[145] But there are reasons to doubt that he resolved the question. As late as the seventeenth century, Grotius and Pufendorf were using *servus* to cover workers of all sorts.[146] The unsettling truth is that a sharp and carefully specified distinction between slaves and serfs was not really clearly drawn until Friedrich Carl von Savigny tried to do so in the year 1822. At least as matter of semantic history, it was in his Berlin lecture hall, more than a thousand years after the fall of the Western Roman Empire, that the passage from slavery to feudalism finally took place.

* * *

Into these troubled waters of interpretation, I venture to cast two more stones of doubt. The first involves the very idea that we can assign any date at all to the transition "from slavery to serfdom"; and the second involves the genesis of the classic theories.

To begin with the first: The classic thinkers were determined to identify the momentous era in historical time when slaves underwent the "mutation" that transformed them into serfs – the era when exploitation through the ownership of human beings, under the pressure of socio-economic change, gave way to exploitation through the ownership of land. This was the project embarked upon by Marx, Weber, and Bloch alike. Yet there is good reason to deny that there ever was any such single transformative era. The truth is that there have been numerous passages from some form of slavery to some form of serfdom, occurring in numerous periods. Some of them date to Late Antiquity, and some date to Bloch's first feudal age. Some, as French critics of Bloch argue, date to the late tenth century and after.[147] Thoughtful medievalists today can all see

---

[144] Robert Boutruche, *Seigneurie et féodalité* (Paris, 1959) 1:126–135 and 371; Poly and Bournazel, *La mutation féodale*, 195–198, esp. 196; and Michel Parisse, "Histoire et sémantique: de *servus* à *homo*," in Paul Freedman and Monique Bourin, eds., *Forms of Servitude in Northern and Central Europe* (Turnhout, 2005), 19–56.

[145] Verlinden, "L'origine de *sclavus* = esclave," *Bulletin Du Cange* 17 (1943): 97–128, and the discussion in Stephen Epstein, *Speaking of Slavery: Color, Ethnicity and Human Bondage in Italy* (Ithaca, N.Y., 2001), 18–20.

[146] Below, Chapter 9.   [147] Poly and Bournazel, *La mutation féodale*.

the unavoidable truth: There was never any single medieval moment of mutation.

But we cannot restrict ourselves to the Middle Ages. We can identify such passages from slavery to serfdom at later points in history as well. Consider the Iberian conquest of the New World: Initial efforts to enslave indigenous populations gave way to practices that effectively tied the subject population in various places to the soil, a point to which I will return in Chapter 9. The same scene was replayed in later history as well – for example, in the history of Haiti, after its Revolution. There too, slavery gave way to a kind of serfdom, as former slaves were bound to labor on sugar plantations.[148] Not least, it was replayed in the history of the nineteenth-century United States: The abolition of slavery in the American South did not end labor oppression. It gave way to sharecropping and numerous other practices that permitted forms of effective enserfment.[149]

As these examples suggest, the passage from slavery to serfdom has certainly taken place; but there was never any single socio-economic mutation that can be dated to some single moment in historical time. The passage from slavery to serfdom (and sometimes back again) is a reiterated process – one is tempted to say, an endlessly reiterated process – found in orders based on agrarian exploitation, throughout human history. It is a fact; but it is a fact about general agrarian sociology, not about some particular age of change in Western socio-economic history, whether ancient or medieval. The oscillation between oppression through the ownership of humans and oppression through the ownership of land is a historical perennial, which ended (if it has ended) only in the latter part of the nineteenth century.

The second stone of doubt that I would like to cast follows from the intellectual history recounted in this chapter. The classic socio-economic theories of the origins and nature of feudalism were all framed, in one way or another, as responses to the reforms of the French Revolution; and their makers all worked in some way from

---

[148] On the *fermage* system, see Philippe Girard, *Haiti: The Tumultuous History – from Pearl of the Caribbean to Broken Nation* (New York, 2010), 66.

[149] For basic materials, see Bridget Carr, Anne Milgram, Kathleen Kim, and Stephen Warnath, *Human Trafficking Law and Policy* (Durham, N.C., 2014), 21–41.

the assumption, inherited from critics of *duplex dominium* from the Renaissance onward, that feudal land tenure was a historically aberrational form of real property rights, whose displacement of the pure and correct classical Roman absolute concept required explanation. It is such an explanation that their theories were designed to supply.

It was the hunt for such an explanation that led Marx to seek the "Germanic" origins of serfdom, imposed on a decaying Rome in the course of the barbarian invasions. It was the same hunt that led Weber to emphasize the need of late antique lords to control a class of agrarian laborers capable of reproducing and feeding themselves; that led Bloch to suggest that both feudal and manorial tenures should be understood as a response to the demands of a cash-poor economy; and that led scholars such as Ganshof to link the rise of feudalism to the collapse of Carolingian authority, as warlords arrogated the powers of the disintegrating Carolingian state to themselves and distributed fiefs to their vassals.

All these men were scholars of daunting learning, and there is always much to be learned from their various writings. Nevertheless, lying behind their post-1789 efforts to understand feudal land tenure, and to explain how it could have arisen, was a dubious supposition: the supposition that we should be puzzled by the phenomenon of real property rights that are a function of the hierarchical relationship between superiors over inferiors. Yet seen in large historical and anthropological perspective, there is simply nothing anomalous about feudal land tenure. *Many or most real property rights, in many or most human societies*, to say it again, *have been granted out by superiors to inferiors*. The hierarchically based distribution of land rights is not a medieval aberration, but the historically normal form in human societies. It is the "absolute" conception of ownership found in the classical Roman legal sources and revived in the French Civil Code, not the medieval conception of land tenure "held subject to superior right," that is historically exceptional, and that must be explained.

* * *

Yet for all that, we should not conclude that there is no point in reading the classic literature, or even no point in studying the process of the passage from slavery to feudalism. The lessons of the large body of critical literature that has grown up since Brown mounted her seminal attack on the "tyranny of a construct" in 1974 must be stated carefully. Medievalists sometimes declare that the "F-word" has no place in serious discussions of medieval history; but that is not in fact what the revisionist literature demonstrates. What the revisionist literature demonstrates is, not that there was no feudalism in the Middle Ages – in plenty of respects, there was – but that the history of feudalism *did not end* with the Middle Ages. On the contrary, feudalism continued to play a potent part in Western history, into the seventeenth century, which marks its acme, and on into the French Revolution and its aftermath. What that inescapably implies is that the proper study of "feudalism" is not a study of medieval socio-economic realities. It is a study in a powerful and enduring ideational formation in the law, a juristic "construct" that provided a framework for political and social thought for more than a thousand years, and that continued to offer itself as an alternative to slavery deep into the modern centuries.

The proper study of "feudalism," to put it differently, is a study in what the historian Fernand Braudel called the *longue durée* in the culture of the law. Braudel's famous scheme for thinking about historical time will be familiar to most of my readers. It distinguishes among three different chronological levels or "durations" that can structure our writing of history: events, conjunctures, and the *longue durée*. Events are of brief duration, constituting the "glittering surface" of history, as Braudel famously put it; and *l'histoire événementielle*, the history of events, the main topic of traditional political history, is ill-equipped to grapple with the deeper forces at work in the making of human societies.[150] Conjunctures and the *longue durée* both call for the investigation of deeper currents. "Conjuncture" is a term that Braudel borrowed from economic history. It refers to medium-term trends and developments such as cyclic price fluctuations, which occur over decades.[151] As for Braudel's *longue durée*: As its name suggests, it takes place over longer, indeed vast, periods, which cover the multi-century or multi-millennium history of matters such as trade routes.

---

[150] Braudel, "Histoire et sciences sociales: la longue durée," *Annales: économies, sociétés, civilisations* 13 (1958): 738 [725–753].
[151] Ibid., 727.

From Slavery to Feudalism

When Marx, Weber, Bloch, and so many others set out to explain the transition from slavery and serfdom, what they were hunting for were Braudelian conjunctures: They took it to be their task to identify processes of socio-economic structural change that worked themselves out, if not over decades, at most over a few centuries. By contrast, the next two chapters will explore a *longue durée* of cultural change in the law. Braudel believed that the "immense domain of culture" is peculiarly a realm of the *longue durée*; it is of the essence of culture, he argued, that it changes with glacial slowness, as tales and *topoi* are repeated and varied over generations. Such was the case, he thought, in particular, of the European high classical tradition: The example that he gave was the history of Latin literary culture as recounted in Ernst Robert Curtius' classic 1948 study *European Literature and the Latin Middle Ages*.[152] European literary culture, in Curtius' portrayal, was the home of centuries of oceanically slow change, of variation and meditation on passages and images from ancient authors and artists such as Ovid, Virgil, and Praxiteles, a classicizing culture that did not enter upon its era of decisive decline until the mid eighteenth century.[153]

The next two chapters offer a legal history that bears a resemblance to Curtius' literary history, the history of a high cultural system whose origins lie in classical Antiquity, and whose great vehicle was the Roman legal tradition. This tradition did experience significant change in Late Antiquity, just as Marx and Weber argued. As we shall see in the next chapter, many scholars have pointed to a partial decay in the classical understanding of property law, and a shift toward land and territoriality in both ownership and rulership in Late Antiquity. But that change did not take place for the reasons Marx and Weber supposed, and it did not amount to a complete transformation. Like the tales and *topoi* of literature, the tales and *topoi* of the law maintained their grip on the legal imagination for more than a thousand years. For the full-scale reordering of the law, we must look to developments in "the immense domain of [legal] culture" that gathered momentum in the early modern controversies that have

---

[152] Ibid., 732, citing E. R. Curtius, *Europäische Literatur und lateinisches Mittelalter* (Bern, 1948).
[153] Curtius, *Europäische Literatur*, 397–398.

been the subject of this chapter, and reached their culmination from the mid eighteenth century onward, the same period to which Curtius dated the decisive decline of the classical literary tradition. The full realization of the passage from slavery to feudalism, and more broadly from a law centered on the ownership of living creatures to a law centered on the ownership of land, dated to the early modern centuries, and in the end to the lifetimes of Marx and Weber themselves. And as I will suggest in the closing chapter, the resulting transformation helped foster the single most important development in the modern law of human rights: the end of lawful slavery.

8

From Masters to Lords in Late Antiquity

The beginnings of what we now call "Late Antiquity" are customarily said to lie in the reign of the Emperor Diocletian, who seized power in 284, after the chaotic and crisis-ridden middle decades of the third century CE, and succeeded in establishing a stable and lasting regime for the first time in two generations.[1] The centuries that followed are no longer described in the way that Karl Marx and Max Weber once did, as an age of the crisis of an ancient slave economy. Classical slaves, in Michael McCormick's epigrammatic summation of the post-Marxist wisdom of modern scholarship, did not "wake up one morning as medieval serfs."[2]

But if few scholars still think of Late Antiquity as a period when an ancient slave economy collapsed, giving way to serfdom, many make an intriguingly similar argument: that both owners and rulers came to exercise new sorts of what Chris Wickham calls "land-based" power.

---

[1] For the conventional focus, Jill Harries, *Imperial Rome, AD 204–363: The New Empire* (Edinburgh, 2012), 5. Debate over the crisis of the third century: J. H. W. G. Liebeschuetz, "Late Antiquity and the Concept of Decline," *Nottingham Medieval Studies* 45 (2001): 1–11; and for a skeptical discussion, Christian Witschel, *Krise–Rezession–Stagnation? Der Westen des römischen reiches im 3. Jahrhundert* (Frankfurt a.M., 1999), 7–11 and *passim*. See further Olivier Hekster, *Rome and Its Empire, AD 193–284* (Edinburgh, 2015).

[2] McCormick, "Slavery from Rome to Medieval Europe and Beyond," in John Bodel and Walter Scheidel, eds., *On Human Bondage: After Slavery and Social Death* (Chichester, 2017), 251 [249–264], and generally Kyle Harper, *Slavery in the Late Roman World, AD 275–425* (Cambridge, 2011).

Wickham, a giant of Marxist historiography, argues that late antique elites were drawn out of declining cities and into the countryside, where they began to orient themselves more toward the exploitation of their rural landholdings, becoming something more like medieval lords.[3] Peter Sarris, similarly, speaks of the "retreat" of Roman owners "from *civitas* to *villa*."[4] As Marx himself put it in his early unpublished writings, "where Antiquity took the city and its small subject territory as its basis, the Middle Ages took land as its basis."[5] A related interpretation was mounted more than fifty years ago by the masterful Italian legal historian Paolo Grossi: After the end of the classical period, Grossi argued, the "juridical experience" of property law began a slow shift toward a new, more rural, orientation.[6]

Historians of Roman imperial rule write of similar developments, identifying a newly territorial drive. Claudia Rapp and H. A. Drake speak of a "great shift in political thought," which spurred a conceptual transition "from *polis* to *imperium*."[7] An older form of city-based rule entered an age of decline, on their interpretation, and the Empire came to be conceived in more territorial terms. Mark Graham argues that "a change occurred in the Roman way of thinking about territory ... Specifically from the third century onward, the Romans [began] to think of their holdings in terms of bounded territories and not just divisions between peoples."[8] We shall see in this chapter that newly territorial conceptions entered the law of rulership as well.

---

[3] Wickham, *Framing the Early Middle Ages: Europe and the Mediterranean, 400–800* (Oxford, 2005), 595, 602. For "land-based," ibid., 58–62. Wickham uses the term to analyze state power, but I hope he would not regard it as an abuse to extend it to the "private" power of lords as well.

[4] Sarris, "The Origins of the Manorial Economy: New Insights from Late Antiquity," *English Historical Review* 119 (2004): 311 [297–311].

[5] Marx and Engels, "Deutsche Ideologie: Manuskripte und Drucke," in *Karl Marx/Friedrich Engels Gesamtausgabe* (Berlin and Boston, 2017), 5.1:130: "Wenn das Altertum von der Stadt und ihrem kleinen Gebiet ausging, so ging das Mittelalter vom Lande aus."

[6] Grossi, *Le situazioni reali nell'esperienza giuridica medievale* (Padua, 1968).

[7] Rapp and Drake, "Polis–Imperium–Oikoumenē: A World Reconfigured," in Rapp and Drake, eds., *The City in the Classical and Post-Classical World: Changing Contexts of Power and Identity* (Cambridge, 2014), 6 [1–13].

[8] Graham, *News and Frontier Consciousness in the Late Roman Empire* (Ann Arbor, 2006), 45.

None of this literature bears out the claims of the classic social thinkers about the supposed economic passage from slavery to feudalism, but all of it speaks of change; and what it suggests is that the search for the beginnings of a land-based orientation in the conception of ownership, and of a territorial orientation in the conception of rulership, both so familiar in modern law, ought properly to start where Marx and Weber started, in Late Antiquity.

This chapter sets out on that search. Late Antiquity was certainly not the scene of some wholesale transformation. Classical law survived, just as classical slavery did. But there were many less dramatic changes – what I will call "departures." New doctrines appeared alongside classical law; and they were new doctrines that would prove to be of great importance in later Western legal history. The law, as Grossi argued, became somewhat less law of the city and somewhat more law of the country. The Empire, as I will try to show, was reconceived on the model of classical property law, taking on the look of a private landholding, while the emperor himself was redescribed, like classical owners, as a *dominus*. A major restatement of the foundations of the law of property appeared during the reign of Diocletian, in the form of a fragment known as *ex hoc iure*, which would serve as the basis for the analysis of both territorial rulership and land-based ownership for centuries. None of this transformed the law utterly, but all of it paved the way for later developments.

In trying to account for these departures, I will start where so many scholars start: with the decline of classical cities. In Chapter 3, I drew on the work of the great legal historian Franz Wieacker, who located the "concrete" context of classical property law in a culture of urban elites, masters over their households and ambitious for advancement in urban magistracies. That culture, I will argue in this chapter, faltered. Classical elites were gradually drawn out of the cities, into the countryside and perhaps also into high imperial office, while urban magistracies lost their attraction. The tale of late antique change in the law, on this reading, was not one of a crisis of a classical slave economy. It is the tale of a crisis of Aristotle's *zōon politikon*, the human animal that had lived in, and ruled from, classical cities.

This crisis of the *zōon politikon* is, however, only a part of the story. In the latter part of the chapter, I will turn to a second factor: the triumph of Christianity. This too has been the subject of much discussion among scholars aiming to understand the newly territorial orientation of imperial rule: The Empire, they argue, came to be conceived as a single vast Christian realm. To their work, I will add two arguments. The first has to do with change in the foundations of elite status. The classical dominus was a figure, as I argued in Chapter 3, whose social prestige was bound up, in part, with the performance of ritual sacrifices. The triumph of Christianity, with its suppression of classical sacrificial practices, brought on the decline of that classical religious culture. At the close of the chapter, I will propose another, admittedly highly speculative, interpretation of the link between law and religion, drawing on the work of Mircea Eliade: Christianity arguably displaced an ancient hunting orientation, bringing with it a new agricultural orientation also to be found in the law.

* * *

The decline of the classical urban order is certainly the obvious factor to consider if we are hunting for interpretations of late antique property law that sound in cultural change, rather than in some economic mutation in the practices of labor exploitation. Cities, as historians often remark, played a supremely important cultural role in the Greco-Roman societies of the classical period.[9] Wickham sums up the centrality of the urban orientation in the Principate of the first, second, and early third centuries CE, the high age of the classical Principate:

The whole of the world of culture was bound up in city-ness, *civilitas* in Latin, from which come our words "civilized" and "civilization," and which precisely implied city-dwelling to the Romans. The empire was in one sense a union of all its cities (some thousand in number) each of which had its own city council (*curia* in Latin, *boulē* in Greek) that was traditionally autonomous...[10]

Nor was the *polis* orientation just a matter of city autonomy. The classical Empire itself was sometimes described as a vast conceptual extension of the city of Rome, the "common town" or "common

---

[9] E.g., Susan E. Alcock, *Graecia Capta: The Landscapes of Roman Greece* (Cambridge, 1993), 130.
[10] Wickham, *The Inheritance of Rome: Illuminating the Dark Ages, 400–1000* (New York, 2010), 24.

patria"¹¹ – "the city," in the words of a famed second-century oration by Aelius Aristides, "that is become the whole world."¹²

To be sure, the cultural primacy of the urban orientation in this "city that is become the whole world" must be described carefully. There is no doubt that classical economies were agrarian; and no doubt that country life featured prominently in classical literature. City-based elites owned, exploited, and prided themselves on country estates, and poets waxed poetic about shepherds. What historians accordingly argue is, not that the countryside did not matter economically or culturally in the classical Empire, but that participation in high elite culture depended on the possession of what Wickham calls an "urban base." The countryside villas of the wealthy Roman city elite, each lording it over his portion of the Italian countryside, may have been savored by their owners; but rustics, persons living entirely in the country with no city presence, were regarded with withering contempt. Urban culture, as Ramsay MacMullen vividly writes, defined itself by the contrast between "the fitting, the graceful, the citified" and the uncouthness, regarded as nearly subhuman, of the "clumsy, ill-shorn peasants" who constituted the vast majority of the population of the Roman world."¹³

It is a commonplace that classical Roman law had its home within this "city that is become the world." This is particularly so because the law turned on the figure of the Roman citizen. The Roman texts speak of various kinds of "law"; but Roman law in its narrow sense was the *ius civile*, the law of the citizens, the *cives*, of the city of Rome. It is one of the key facts of Roman history that the Romans, over the course of their creation of "the city that is become the world," extended this law of privilege and triumph beyond the original community of free Romans themselves. In the Early and Middle Republic, Rome developed a distinctive program of granting (or imposing) full or partial citizenship on outsiders. By the first century BCE, all the free

---

[11] Cic. *Leg.* 2.5, in Clinton W. Keyes, trans., *Cicero: On the Republic; On the Laws*, Loeb Classical Library 213 (Cambridge, MA, 1928), 374–375.

[12] For the Roman Oration on the proposition that Rome should "administer the *oikoumenê* as if it were a single polis," see Daniel Richter, "Cosmopolitanism," in Richter and William A. Johnson, eds., *Oxford Handbook to the Second Sophistic* (Oxford, 2017), 91–93 [81–98].

[13] MacMullen, *Roman Social Relations, 50 B.C. to A.D. 284* (New Haven, 1974), 30.

inhabitants of Italy had become Roman citizens. Further extensions continued throughout the Empire;[14] high status often involved the acquisition of a measure of Roman legal identity. In 212 CE, the broad extension of citizenship culminated in the *Constitutio Antoniniana*, which made all free persons of the Empire Roman citizens. Of course, the connection to Rome as a physical city was tenuous for most of these citizens of the mature Empire. The link was a notional one; the law was law of the idea of Rome, not of the reality.

This law of privileged participation in the notional city had one feature that deserves emphasis: by contrast with most of the modern law of citizenship, its working conception of citizenship was not territorial. Modern lawyers distinguish two varieties of birth-right citizenship: citizenship by virtue of the *ius soli*, the "right of soil," acquired through birth in a particular territory; and citizenship by virtue of the *ius sanguinis*, the "right of blood," by birth to citizens. As early as the fourth century BCE, it is perhaps possible that the descent-based conception of citizenship may have been flagging in the Greek world,[15] but scholars emphasize that it was not replaced by a territorial conception in the classical Empire: The "fundamental classifications," in the judgment of Claude Nicolet, remained "personal and not territorial,"[16] enduringly modeled as they were on the forms of an older, descent-based, city-state world. The *polis* still hovered, spectrally, behind the classical Empire. Yan Thomas, similarly, speaks of "the nonexistence of a territorial principle" in classical law.[17]

Classical Roman law was thus city law in the simple sense that it was the law of *cives*, the juridically free ruling class of a notional Empire-wide city. But it is important to think of it as city law in

---

[14] These grants were made in particular to whole communities; but the Romans also had various practices that resulted in the conferral of citizenship to individuals.
[15] Cf. Isoc. 4.50: "The name 'Hellenes' is given rather to those who share our *paideia* than to those who share a common blood." Not too much weight should be put on this passage. George Norlin, trans., *Isocrates: To Demonicus; To Nicocles; Nicocles or the Cyprians; Panegyricus; To Philip; Archidamus*, Loeb Classical Library 209 (Cambridge, MA, 1928), 148–149.
[16] Nicolet, *Space, Geography and Politics in the Early Roman Empire* (Ann Arbor, 1991), 10.
[17] "Inexistence d'un 'principe territorial'": Thomas, *"Origine" et "commune patrie": étude de droit public romain (89 av. J.-C.–212 ap. J.-C.)* (Rome, 1996), 181.

a larger cultural sense as well. Here I would like to turn back to the work of two figures discussed in earlier chapters, Max Weber and Wieacker. As we have seen, both were scholars who laid great weight on the culture of urban privilege and rule in the classical Empire. In the case of Weber, this was expressed in the consumer city hypothesis that he shared with Karl Bücher; in the case of Wieacker, it was expressed in his analysis of the "concrete" context of classical ownership.

Bücher and Weber, as we saw, argued that ancient cities were not commercial or industrial centers of the modern type; instead, they were the "citadels" of ancient warrior elites dedicated to seizing booty, exploiting the labor of enslaved enemies, and extracting wealth from the subject countryside – the walled resorts of *Gewaltherren*, rulers by violence, as Bücher put it, "preying on the world outside the city walls," but always returning to their strongholds.[18] Weber offered his own, subtler version, putting the accent more on the mentality of ancient elites rather on than their active practice of warmaking. But both Bücher and Weber described a warrior culture: Their *zōon politikon* was a more emphatically predatory figure than the *zōon politikon* of Aristotle.

Economic historians and archeologists today generally (though not universally) reject the consumer city hypothesis, and I will not try to defend it in its original form. This is one of the topics on which Weber was probably simply wrong on the economics. But it is a theme of this book that while Weber may have been mistaken as an economic historian, he was a brilliant reader of the legal sources that inspired so much of his work; and his consumer city hypothesis deserves to be reread, and defended, as an account of the imaginative order that underlay classical property law.

The predatory "rulers by violence" of the Athens and Rome of Bücher and Weber may or may not have existed in socio-economic reality; but they are the *domini* of the classical legal texts described by Kaser in his interpretation of Roman property law, when he said that the Romans had a taste for calling themselves "masters," ruling both in their households and in the Empire at large. They are the predatory elite whose "idiom of power," in the judgment of

---

[18] Above, Chapter 7.

Patterson, was the idiom of the master/slave relationship; and the same predatory elite who liked to speak of their imperial rule as the rule of masters who had enslaved the peoples of the world. For that matter, they are the embodiments of MacMullen's "fitting ... graceful [and] citified" rulers, contemptuous of its subordinate rural population.

They are also the *domini* of Wieacker, who, as we saw, identified the city as the locus of the "concrete basis" of classical *dominium* in 1935. Wieacker's Roman property law was law bound up with the psychology of men who ruled, not merely as *domini* in the household, but also as urban magistrates. It is important to emphasize how little his interpretation, for its own part, had to do with economic analysis. Wieacker's focus was on the social-psychological context of the experience of rule, not on narrowly economic interests. It is further important to note that his interpretation bore on the "concrete basis" of elite life outside the confines of the city of Rome itself. The experience of urban rulership was not reserved to wealthy Romans. As Wickham emphasizes, membership in the *curia* or *boulē* was important for the sense of self of the wealthy elite throughout the urban Mediterranean "system of cities which were self-governing."

* * *

The arrogant and extractive classical urban culture described by Weber, Wieacker, Kaser, and MacMullen, suffused with Badian's "oligarchical *Weltanschauung*," belonged to an "urban culture" that "lost momentum nearly everywhere,"[19] in Wickham's judgment, after the crisis of the third century; and with the loss of momentum came change in the law, though certainly not any radical transformation.

"Loss of momentum" is a judiciously chosen phrase. Cities certainly did not vanish or lose their significance as a legal matter. In the East in particular they seem to have held up well until the seventh century.[20] Nevertheless, the dimming of the old urban order is much remarked. In a process often reiterated in the history of the premodern world, the

---

[19] Wickham, *Framing*, 687.
[20] Mark Humphries, *Cities and the Meanings of Late Antiquity* (Leiden, 2019), 32–33, 45.

later Empire experienced a measure of deurbanization.²¹ Premodern cities were frequently abandoned, or semi-abandoned, under the pressure of war, disease, or climate change; this was part of the systole and diastole of ancient civilizations, and it took place in the late antique Mediterranean as well. Invasions, the focus of Marx, certainly played a role: "[I]ncreased political insecurity in the face of barbarian invasions from the third century onwards," Mark Humphries writes, resulted in the "construction of new urban fortifications, many of them encompassing urban centers that often were much reduced in area by comparison with the early Roman empire."²² But current scholarship emphasizes that plagues figured well, as did the end of the "Roman Climate Optimum," which had produced favorable circumstances for centuries.²³

Historians disagree, sometimes almost bitterly, about how to characterize the consequent changes in Roman society. Gian Pietro Brogiolo and Bryan Ward-Perkins are defenders, along with the eminent ancient historian Wolf Liebeschuetz,²⁴ of a highly controversial term, "decline," to portray the fate of classical cities:

Towns were so central to Roman styles and structures of life and culture that they were particularly hard hit ... From the perspective of any research into urbanism that starts with the Roman period, it is very difficult to view developments in the sixth and seventh centuries, except for the late-antique christianization of the city, as part of some neutral (or even positive) "transformation." The changes that occurred in urban life generally look more like the dissolution of a sophisticated and impressive experiment in how to order society – an experiment developed by the Greeks and Romans and centered on the Mediterranean.²⁵

---

²¹ E.g., Mario Liverani, *The Ancient Near East: History, Society and Economy*, trans. Soraia Tabatabai (Abingdon, 1988), 185–186, 469–470; Michael R. Smith, "Mesoamerican State Formation in the Postclassic Period," in Benjamin Kedar and Merry Wiesner-Hanks, eds., *Cambridge World History, Vol. 5: Expanding Webs of Exchange and Conflict, 500 CE–1500 CE* (Cambridge, 2015), 610–637.
²² Humphries, *Cities and the Meanings of Late Antiquity*, 31–32.
²³ Kyle Harper, *The Fate of Rome: Climate, Disease and the End of an Empire* (Princeton, 2017).
²⁴ Liebeschuetz, *The Decline and Fall of the Roman City* (Oxford, 2001); particularly aggressively in Liebeschuetz, "Late Antiquity and the Concept of Decline," *Nottingham Medieval Studies* 45 (2001): 7 [1–11].
²⁵ Brogiolo and Ward-Perkins, "Introduction," in *The Idea and Ideal of the Town between Late Antiquity and the Early Middle Ages* (Leiden, 1999), xv–xvi [xii–xvi].

Other scholars bristle at the use of "decline,"[26] and at phrases like "sophisticated and impressive experiment"; most students of ancient history today are committed to the proposition that Late Antiquity had its own intrinsic value, and they are sometimes (though not always) sensitive to the darker side of classical urban domination. I take no sides in this debate. What matters for my purposes is that the city culture of the classical period faded in importance after the third century – on that point there is little quarrel[27] – and that its (at least relative) decline arguably operated to undermine the power, and the culture, of the classical urban elite described by Weber and Wieacker.

This is especially so because Late Antiquity was marked by a development much discussed among contemporary specialists: the tendency of elites to drift away from the cities and more into the countryside. The "urban base" that Wickham deems so central became less important. This late antique drift was, it must be emphasized, a drift only toward a *more* ruralized system. "[T]he Roman ideal of the city as *the* paramount center and social, political and cultural life was in practice eroded," as Brogiolo and Ward-Perkins put it.[28] Wickham describes this erosion as a decay of classical assumptions about the proper seat of elite power. The cities did not vanish. But elites became increasingly comfortable with the possibility of having either an "urban or [a] rural base."[29] It became acceptable to live primarily as a countryside lord in a way that had not been the case before.

Wickham offers an engrossing interpretation of the causes, course, and consequences of the gravitational pull into the countryside. The shift was partly the consequence of the new governmental practices:

The traditional autonomy [of the cites] had meant in the early empire that being a city councilor (*curialis* in Latin, bouleutēs in Greek) was the height of local ambition. This was less so by the fourth century, however ...[30]

---

[26] Humphries, *Cities and the Meanings of Late Antiquity*, 16, 87.
[27] Though see, e.g., Anthony Kaldellis, *The New Roman Empire: A History of Byzantium* (Oxford, 2023), 229.
[28] Brogiolo and Ward-Perkins, "Introduction," xiv.   [29] Wickham, *Framing*, 595, 602.
[30] Wickham, *Inheritance of Rome*, 23–24.

As A. H. M. Jones, the pioneer of the modern study of the later Roman Empire, emphasized more than a half century ago, in the classical period, leading citizens had gloried in their membership in the ruling *curia* or *boulē* of their city. Whether at Rome or elsewhere, service in the city hierarchy was a coveted mark of distinction. By contrast, in Late Antiquity we find signs of elite efforts to escape curial membership.[31] The proposition that this was the result of anything properly called "the decline and fall of the Roman city" has been contested: Anthony Kaldellis interprets these changes as an aspect of the displacement of power from *polis* to *imperium*. What happened was not that Romans fled to the countryside, but that they were drawn to the greater opportunities for status and power in the newly assertive late antique Roman imperial state.[32] Kaldellis' argument is powerful, but it is not inconsistent with Wickham's; both could easily be true; and Wickham is concerned with a wider range of phenomena taking place over a much longer stretch of time. In any case, on either argument, urban office came to matter less, and the contrast with the classical Empire is clear: Persons of wealth and power who flee civic office are no longer the persons of wealth and power whose sense of self constituted the concrete basis of the classical property law of Wieacker, and whose ambitions to climb the *cursus honorum* depended on the possession of the classical *domus* described by Kate Cooper.[33]

The economic calculus was changing as well, Wickham argues. Classical elites had been drawn to living in cities, not only for reasons of prestige, but also because classical Roman civilization was "tax-based" rather than "land-based." Taxes were a preeminent source of wealth and power in classical Antiquity, and cities were centers of tax collection. As the urban framework of the Western Empire failed, however, the tax regime failed as well, in different ways and degrees in different regions in different periods; and elites, now typically comparatively poor by comparison with their classical predecessors, gradually shifted to direct exploitation of the countryside, transforming themselves, over the course of several centuries, into

---

[31] Jones, *The Later Roman Empire, 284–602* (repr. Baltimore, 1986), 1:753–757. Studies of this phenomenon now push its history further back before Jones' later Roman Empire. See Harries, *Imperial Rome*, 13–15.
[32] Kaldellis, *The New Roman Empire*, 229.   [33] Above, Chapter 3.

what would eventually become feudal lords. A related argument is made by Peter Sarris:

> The demise of the Roman state as a tax-raising structure, combined with the widespread decline of urbanism ... would have ... severely curtail[ed] the incentives for great landowners to engage in commodified production. The consequent retreat of landowners in much of the west from *civitas* to *villa* meant that a form of estate structure that had arisen in the context of the highly urbanized, highly monetized, and highly commercialized world of the fourth century came to take on an increasingly autarkic aspect. In the medieval phrase, a lord would be expected "to live off his own."[34]

This is an interpretation of considerable power, which permits Wickham and Sarris to salvage some of the classic Marxist chronology. If there was no decisive shift from slave labor to serf labor in Late Antiquity, we can nevertheless point to important changes. But they undertake this salvage operation in a way that departs tellingly from the presuppositions of Marx: They turn their attention away from the exclusive focus on the structures of labor coercion, to consider changes in the incentives and behavior of the men who did the coercing. In effect, they ask us to shift our gaze from the exploited to the exploiters.[35] In effect, they invite us to ask, not how slaves became serfs, but how masters became lords.

And they are able to cite some archeological evidence that seems to chart the change they describe. There were notable alterations in the face of the countryside in the late antique and early medieval rural West. As Sarris writes, the classical Roman countryside featured the villa, a well-appointed country house owned by members of the urban elite and dominating its surrounding agricultural holdings. Archeologists have been able to document how the villa, this key institutional expression of domination of the countryside by the city, was transformed. Over the course of the early Middle Ages, which were marked in most regions by declining elite wealth, the ancient villa tended to become something new: the medieval village. The classical country house was (probably) broken up into separate dwellings, as it

---

[34] Sarris, "Origins of the Manorial Economy," 311.
[35] Cf. also, in a much less sophisticatedly argued account, Ellen Meiksinis Wood, *From Citizens to Lords: A Social History of Western Political Thought from Antiquity to the Late Middle Ages* (London, 2011).

also (perhaps) came to accommodate a church;[36] the villa was, as it were, swallowed up by the countryside it had once ruled.

Parallel developments touched the Church, as scholars have shown. In classical Antiquity, the center of gravity of Christianity lay, unsurprisingly, in the cities.[37] That pattern seems to have held in the early centuries of Late Antiquity. "Throughout the 4th and first half of the 5th c.," the archeologists Kim Bowes and Adam Gutteridge note, "the Church remained largely an urban phenomenon in the West."[38] Moreover, the "values and attitudes" of the Church also seem to have fit within the broader "intellectual culture" of "city-ness"; the most famous literary expression of the theology of the idea of the city is of course St. Augustine's *City of God* – even though Augustine himself was a figure notable for his burgeoning interest in reaching out to country folk.[39] Some of the same reflexive contempt for rustics that characterized the urban elites of the classical period probably lies, revealingly, behind the bit of Christian jargon that derided unbelievers as "pagans," meaning literally "country-dwellers" or "worshipers of countryside gods." "The educated pagans," in the invective of Christians, "become the rustici, untaught and inarticulate."[40]

But, like other ancient institutions, the Church was pulled more into the countryside over the course of Late Antiquity and the early Middle Ages. "[B]y the later 5th and particularly the 6th c., ecclesiastical organization of the countryside began to gain momentum: it was around this time that the first documentation for nascent parish systems appears in N Italy, central and S Gaul, and, slightly later, in Hispania, alongside the first significant numbers of rural churches."[41] During the same period, Christianizing changes were underway in the

[36] See Kim Bowes, "'... Nec sedere in villam': Villa-Churches, Rural Piety and the Priscillianist Controversy," in Thomas S. Burns and John W. Eadie, eds., *Urban Centers and Rural Contexts in Late Antiquity* (East Lansing, MI, 2001), 323–378.
[37] Wayne Meeks, *The First Urban Christians: The Social World of the Apostle Paul* (New Haven, 2003).
[38] Bowes and Gutteridge, "Rethinking the Later Roman Landscape," *Journal of Roman Archaeology* 18 (2005): 412 [405–414].
[39] See Jack Tannous, *The Making of the Medieval Middle East: Religion, Society and the Simple Believers* (Princeton, 2018), 18.
[40] E. G. Clark, "Pastoral Care: Town and Country in Late Antique Preaching," in Burns and Eadie, eds., *Urban Centers and Rural Contexts*, 277 [265–284].
[41] Bowes and Gutteridge, "Rethinking the Later Roman Landscape," 412.

cities themselves. Hendrik Dey traces an evolution by which classicizing cities in what is now Southern France and Spain, which had had "regular street grids, porticoes, forums, baths, atrium houses, basilicas, temples, senate houses ... theaters, arenas and circuses,"[42] were converted into stages for Christian ceremonies, organized around churches and processions; there were parallel developments, he observes, in cities like Constantinople. There are many similar studies of various regions in the formerly Roman world, where "from the fourth century onward," cities came to boast "a cathedral and other churches replacing the temples."[43] Cities certainly did not vanish on the argument of any of these scholars; but their "meanings," in the words of Humphries' thoughtful review of the literature, changed.[44]

* * *

How might this much-chronicled drift into the countryside, elite migration to villas, and change in the "meanings" of classical cities, have mattered for the law? There is a famous hypothesis about the decay of classical property law in Late Antiquity, proposed by the legal historian Ernst Levy in 1951. Levy believed that he could demonstrate that classical Roman property law was progressively forgotten in late antique and early medieval Italy. It is often said that the greatest achievement of classical Roman property law was the development of the distinction between ownership and possession.[45] Levy argued that that key distinction now became blurred: The "vulgar" law of these centuries began to use "possession" for what would once have been carefully specified as *dominium*.[46] If Levy is right, the sources show an unmistakable weakening of the classical property law tradition, now being progressively forgotten.

For purposes of this chapter, though, I would like to focus, in the spirit of Wickham and other historians, not so much on doctrinal history as on broader questions in the changing cultural background

---

[42] Dey, *The Afterlife of the Roman City: Architecture and Ceremony in Late Antiquity and the Early Middle Ages* (Cambridge, 2015), 3.
[43] Wickham, *Inheritance of Rome*, 24.
[44] Humphries, *Cities and the Meanings of Late Antiquity*.
[45] For a classic statement, see Fritz Pringsheim, "The Unique Character of Classical Roman Law," *Journal of Roman Studies* 34 (1944): 62 [60–64].
[46] Ernst Levy, *West Roman Vulgar Law: The Law of Property* (Philadelphia, 1951). Levy's analysis is challenged in Sarah Vandendriessche, *Possessio und Dominium im postklassischen römischen Recht* (Hamburg, 2006).

to the law. Here we can draw on the work of some exceptionally fine legal scholars, among them Grossi, Caroline Humfress, Nicolet, and Thomas, all of whom point to revealing change.

To be sure, we must not exaggerate the extent of the change that took place. If urban life began to yield to ruralization, if the wealthy started to flee the cities and civic magistracies, if the Empire became in important respects more territorial, it is still not the case that the "territorial principle" that Thomas deemed "nonexistent" in the classical period now became the sole basis of the law. To my knowledge, no scholar would make such an assertion. Instead, scholars identify subtler alterations in late antique law that suggest that the classical *polis* orientation waned without fully disappearing. Just as classical slavery survived, classical law survived; but it came to share the stage with alternative conceptions, partly territorial in nature.

Thus it has long been argued that Roman law, after the general extension of citizenship to free persons in 212 CE, progressively sustained influence from *Volksrecht*, "folk law," the indigenous law of local populations in the eastern Mediterranean.[47] Local practices such as eastern Mediterranean bride-price, absent from the classical *ius civile*, began to work their way into the law as jurists found ways to accommodate them.[48] *Volksrecht* is not the law of a modern type of territorial sovereign; but it is not the personal law of a classical *polis* citizen body either.

More broadly, it has long been argued that custom began to establish itself as a source of law alongside the classical *ius civile*. The classical Roman jurists spoke of certain "customs," and in certain cases accorded those customs a certain legal standing; but as Humfress explains, "whilst early Imperial jurists used numerous arguments from custom in order to develop the Roman *ius civile*, they were not, it seems, especially concerned with elaborating the idea of a 'customary law' as a source of legal obligation in and of itself."[49] That began to

---

[47] Mario Amelotti, "Reichsrecht, Volksrecht, Provinzialrecht," *Studia et documenta historiae et iuris* 65 (1995): 211–215.

[48] Ludwig Mitteis, *Reichsrecht und Volksrecht in den östlichen Provinzen des römischen Kaiserreichs* (Leipzig, 1891), 256–312, on the *donatio propter nuptias*.

[49] Humfress, "Law and Custom under Rome," in Alice Rio, ed., *Law, Custom, and Justice in Late Antiquity and the Early Middle Ages* (London, 2012), 25 [23–46]; cf.

change. Custom became, to a new degree, an acknowledged source of law in Late Antiquity, and the pattern survived in Western law in the Middle Ages:[50] It is widely agreed that the learned systems of the Middle Ages treated "customary law" as a primary source in a way that classical Antiquity never did;[51] this counts as one of the crucial developments in the transition from classical to medieval law.

The budding emergence of custom as a source of law does not mean that the classical understanding of the *ius civile* completely disappeared in Late Antiquity. There were, after all, still cities, and Roman citizenship had been extended to all free persons. What scholars instead argue is that the classical idea of citizenship lost some of its monopoly on juristic thinking; just as it became possible for elites to take up a primary rural residence, it became possible to understand membership in the political community outside the confines of the historic *polis* framework. "Moving from the principate to the dominate," as Humfress summarizes the change, "we seem to [see] a shift from a legal world of 'citizens' to one of 'citizens and subjects.'"[52]

* * *

Some especially sensitive and interesting work on the changes of this age of transition "from *polis* to *imperium*" has been done by Grossi, the great Italian legal historian and later justice of the Italian Constitutional Court, who published a 1968 study, now rarely read outside Italy, of what he called the changing "juridical experience" of property in the West.[53] Grossi's book tackles the same contrast between ancient and medieval property law that captured the attention of Marx, Weber, Marc Bloch, and other analysts of the

---

classically A. A. Schiller, "Custom in Classical Roman Law," *Virginia Law Review* 24 (1938): 281, 270–271 [268–282].
[50] Humfress, "Law and Custom," 35–36, with appropriate caution.
[51] Franck Roumy, "Lex consuetudinaria, jus consuetudinarium: recherche sur la naissance du concept de droit coutumier aux XIe et XIIe siècles," *Revue historique du droit français et étranger* 79 (2001): 257–291. See now the innovative discussion of Ada Kuskowski, *Vernacular Law-Writing and the Reinvention of Customary Law in Medieval France* (Cambridge, 2022).
[52] Caroline Humfress, "Laws' Empire: Roman Universalism and Legal Practice," in Rapp and Drake, eds., *The City in the Classical and Post-Classical World*, 99 [81–108].
[53] Grossi, *Le situazioni reali*.

purported passage from slavery to feudalism examined in the previous chapter. But as the phrase "juridical experience" suggests, he frames his interpretation, not as a study of economic change, but as a study of change in the mentality of ownership. Ancient Roman *dominium*, Grossi argues, following in the interpretive tradition of Kaser, was defined by the personal power of the *paterfamilias*, whose control over persons was conceptually "extended to the world of things."[54] But by the early Middle Ages, the "juridical experience" of owning property began to assume a new shape, coming to center on land: To be a medieval property holder was no longer to exercise sole rule over dependent persons. Instead, it was to enjoy rule over realty, a change that Grossi tries to trace through careful reading of the sources from the peninsula of Italy.[55] From that early medieval starting point, land increasingly came to dominate the culture of ownership, Grossi argues, in a process he follows into the High Middle Ages, when juristic concepts like *duplex dominium* revolved unmistakably around land.

Grossi offers a particularly striking argument tying this conceptual change to the late antique shift toward a law based on custom. Custom, he argues, is inherently linked with land: It is always understood as "the custom of a region, the custom of a place, the custom of a land, the custom of a farm."[56] So it was that where classical ownership turned on the individualistic will of the master, the privileged citizen of a *polis* conscious of his uncabined power, early medieval ownership, increasingly centered in the countryside, came to turn on the collective customary law associated with a particular locale. The passage to a "juridical experience" centered on land was thus one of the consequences of the ruralization of late Antique and early medieval life; the law became law of farms.

This is a memorable thesis, and there is certainly an intuitive appeal to the proposition that custom is somehow linked to territorial place. That said, it is not clear how many scholars would be prepared to embrace Grossi's claims without reservation. It is not obvious that custom is necessarily understood as "custom of a place"; it could, after all, also be "custom of a people"; *Volksrecht* is arguably exactly that. Moreover, the ultimate test of his thesis depends on the interpretation of late antique and early medieval sources whose

[54] Ibid., 19, 23. [55] Ibid., 68. [56] Ibid., 68.

terminology, as we saw in the last chapter, is nearly unconquerably opaque.

Still, Grossi is an uncommonly cultivated reader of the sources, and his interpretation accords well with other accounts of the diminishing (but not completely vanishing) cultural centrality of the classical city and its citizen culture. Even if we cannot be sure that the emergence of custom as a source of law necessarily implied a strong orientation toward land, we can recognize that it brought with it the "partial erosion" of a concept of law rooted in the classical *ius civile*, with its understanding of law as a body of citizen privileges and its associated culture of ownership. In all these changes in the law we can see signs of the same "dissolution of a sophisticated and impressive experiment in how to order society" so much mourned by Brogiolo and Ward-Perkins, and so much bound up with the cultural and political supremacy of the privileged urban *domini* of the classical Empire.

And in all these ways, we catch glimpses of the transition from masters to lords so elegantly analyzed by Wickham. The arguments of Wickham and Grossi are particularly well paired. Let me emphasize again, if emphasis is still needed, that no such analysis of the culture of Roman property law could be fully adequate to understanding the "quotidian reality." In practice, the law operated in many contexts, many of them urban or commercial, many of them involving actors who could not be said to belong to the wealthy elite, many of them unquestionably relevant to the economics of labor coercion. Togas were still worn, even as trousers appeared.[57] People were still conscious of themselves as living in Rome. But where Wieacker-style "concrete" analysis has special value is in laying the groundwork for the study of the impact on the law of the decay, or at least partial decay, of the culture of the classical city, which arguably carried with it the decay, or at least partial decay, of the culture of the classical *dominus*, in an age of an incipient shift from masters to lords.

* * *

Let me turn now to rulership. Here, the reign of Diocletian deserves particular attention: It witnessed the appearance of ideas and doctrines that would shape centuries of later land-oriented legal thought.

---

[57] Documented most dramatically by the 397 ban within the city of Rome in the *Theodosian Code*, CTh. 14.10.3.

It is important to set the scene by returning to the interpretations of classical Roman rule discussed in Chapter 5. As we saw, historians of Roman government in the classical Empire commonly describe a system of collaborative oligarchical exercise of power. In an Empire woefully short of administrative personnel on the ground, the practicalities of rule were mostly left to local elites, bound primarily by patronage relations to the center, and given a relatively free hand in ruling and exploiting their localities. "Rome," as William Harris summarizes "the main consensus doctrine," "succeeded in assimilating and winning over significant portions of the local populations, especially but not only the local elites, in literally every part of the empire. Patronage relationships between emperors and other important figures linked the centre with Italy and the provinces."[58] The ties that bound the oligarchs of Rome to the urban oligarchies of the Empire were particularly important, in the view of Richard Saller and Peter Garnsey: "The secret of government was the system of cities which were self-governing."[59] These are not the only analyses of classical Roman rule on offer. Roman historians also explore the day-to-day workings of power, and the presence and pressures of imperial government. Nevertheless, as we saw in Chapter 5, many Roman historians have argued that what Ernst Badian called the "oligarchical *Weltanschauung*" did indeed bind the greater rulers of Rome to the lesser rulers of the Empire.

This order too, based on the web of relations between Roman and local oligarchies, experienced a "partial erosion": the new Empire of Diocletian assumed a newly quasi-territorial form, which has been the subject of much study by historians. This begins with a major administrative innovation: the establishment in Diocletian's reign of the "Tetrarchy," the "Rule of Four," under which two senior co-Emperors and two junior colleagues took command of an Empire now divided into four realms.[60] This territorialization of the Empire

---

[58] William Harris, *Roman Power: A Thousand Years of Empire* (Cambridge, 2016), 154.
[59] Garnsey and Saller, *The Roman Empire: Society, Economy and Culture*, 2nd ed. (Berkeley, 2014), 40.
[60] There is much controversy over the question of how the Tetrarchy (the term is a modern coinage) formed, and exactly how the role of Diocletian should be understood. For a rapid survey, see Frank Kolb, "La Tetrarchia: struttura, fondamento e ideologia del potere imperial," in Werner Eck and Salvatore Puliatti, eds.,

may not have been wholly unprecedented. J. S. Richardson, as we have seen, argues that the Roman "language of power" had already become increasingly territorial over the course of the history of the classical Empire. Nevertheless, within the conceptual order of the law, the Tetrarchy represented a very large departure from classical patterns – and a shocking one, in the view of one of our key witnesses for the period, the Christian theologian whose full name was probably Lucius Caecilius Firmianus Lactantius.[61] Lactantius denounced the Tetrarchy as a vandalization of the classical order. The Emperor's act of "dividing the world into four parts (*in quatuor partes orbe diviso*)," so he inveighed, did nothing less than "subvert the whole world."[62]

The Tetrarchy did not survive for long after Diocletian's reign, since its four corulers inevitably warred against each other for sole control; but the territorializing drive did. This brought with it, in particular, the division of older provinces into smaller administrative units, to be governed by new imperial officers, whose ranks increased exponentially.[63] As we saw in Chapter 5, the classical Empire was characterized by an extraordinary paucity of its governmental personnel. "[A]n administration of only a few hundred," as Ramsay MacMullen writes, "rule[d] an empire."[64] By contrast, "[b]etween c. 250 and 400 AD, the number of attractive jobs in the imperial bureaucracy increased from about two hundred and fifty overall to at least three thousand per generation in each half of the

---

Diocleziano: la frontiera giuridica dell'impero (Pavia, 2018), 5–7 [3–43]. For the invention of the term and the vicissitudes of interpretation, see Hartmut Leppin, "Zur Geschichte der Erforschung der Tetrarchie," in Dietrich Boschung and Werner Eck, eds., *Die Tetrarchie: ein neues Regierungssystem und seine mediale Präsentation* (Wiesbaden, 2006), 13–30. For a skeptical discussion of the use of the term, see Bill Leadbetter, *Galerius and the Will of Diocletian* (New York, 2009), 1–5.

[61] For the name, Anthony P. Coleman, *Lactantius and the Doctrine of Providence* (Piscataway, N.J., 2017), 9. On Lactantius more broadly, emphasizing his classicizing tendency, Elizabeth DePalma Digeser, *The Making of a Christian Empire: Lactantius and Rome* (Ithaca, N.Y., 2000).

[62] Lactantius, *De mortibus persecutorum*, ed. and trans. J. L. Creed (Oxford, 1984), 10 (7.2), quoted and discussed in Harries, *Imperial Rome*, 50–51, whose translation I have slightly altered; and further 51–52 on the haphazardness of the changes in question over the expanse of the Empire. See also her discussion at 139–140.

[63] For a detailed review, see Werner Eck, "Die Neuorganisation der Provinzen und Italiens unter Diokletian," in Eck and Puliatti, eds., *Diocleziano*, 133–149 [111–151].

[64] MacMullen, *Corruption and the Decline of Rome* (New Haven, 1988), 121.

Empire, a twenty-fold increase."[65] Lactantius denounced the new swarm of new administrators too, as part of a program to "terrorise the Empire":[66]

And to fill everywhere with terror, the provinces too were cut up into fragments, many governors and even more bureaucratic burdens were loaded onto individual regions, even cities, and in addition many finance officers (*rationales*) and masters [of the imperial estates?] and deputies (*vicarii*) of the prefects.[67]

Even cities. As Wickham writes, the new realities of Late Antiquity were such that cities, once centers of power with a largely free hand, "[were now] finding that more decisions were taken over their heads."[68]

These shifts, whether or not we view them with Lactantius' horror, add up to a watershed in the history of Roman rule. They represent something of a watershed in legal history as well. Diocletian's "division of the world into four parts," so scandalous in the eyes of Lactantius, was the first of many territorial divisions in later centuries, notable among them one to which I will turn in the next chapter: Pope Alexander VI's division of the New World between the Spanish and Portuguese in 1493, an act that he undertook as the "vicar," deputy, of Christ, territorial king of the globe.[69] As for the late antique butchering of the Empire into fragments: That included the creation of the dioceses still with us in the Catholic Church. We shall see more examples of the long resonance of the shifts of the reigns of Diocletian and his successors as we go along.

How should we interpret the appearance of this new conceptualization of imperial power? As a matter of political history, the answer may seem straightforward: Old practices of collaborative oligarchical rule suffered, and power was displaced toward the imperial center. But new forms of the exercise of power are not invented out of nothing. They require legal

---

[65] Peter Heather and David Moncur, *Politics, Philosophy and Empire in the Fourth Century: Select Orations of Themistius* (Liverpool, 2001), 31.
[66] Harries, *Imperial Rome*, 50.   [67] Lactantius, *De mortibus persecutorum*, 12 (7.4).
[68] Wickham, *Inheritance of Rome*, 23–24.
[69] I do not mean to suggest that Diocletian directly inspired "Inter caetera," but merely to highlight the historic importance of the break in practice of his reign. That said, the term "vicar" for the popes, first used by Pope Gelasius I in the late fifth century, may have had a model in late antique governmental practices. I am grateful to Conrad Leyser for confirming in a personal communication that this might be the case.

justifications and conceptual models; and I think we should recognize that the late antique practice of government had a model: the model of classical property law. The innovations of Diocletian were not just events in the history of Roman Empire. They were events in the history of Martti Koskenniemi's yin and yang, sovereignty and property: The new Empire came to be described in terms that classical jurists had previously used to describe private landholding, while the emperor himself came to be imagined as something more like a classical owner.

This begins with boundaries – with the emerging Roman tendency "to think of [imperial] holdings in terms of bounded territories and not just divisions between peoples."[70] The law of the classical period had much to say about boundaries, which were marked, as we have seen, by sacred boundary stones, the recipients of annual sacrifices. But the classical jurists did not devote themselves to "public" law in the way that modern lawyers do,[71] and their primary concern was with the doings of private citizens. As Merio Scattola observes, the boundaries of the classical jurists were boundaries of private holdings, not of governmental territories.[72] While there were classical "territories" of rule in a sense, Scattola argues, they established only the limits of the application of magistratial or religious authority.[73] In effect, they created zones of the control over persons, not zones of territorial rule.

That understanding altered from the mid third century onward: The Empire, as Graham argues, came to have juridical boundaries too, displaying what he calls an altered "late Roman cosmology of space and frontiers."[74] The shift is interestingly attested in the early fifth-century appearance of a new species of administrative literature: "late imperial

---

[70] Graham, *News and Frontier Consciousness*, 45.
[71] For a general account of what they did consider, see Boudewijn Sirks, "Public Law," in David Johnston, ed., *The Cambridge Companion to Roman Law* (Cambridge, 2015), 332–352.
[72] Scattola, "Die Grenze der Neuzeit: ihr Begriff in der juristischen und politischen Literatur der Antike und Frühmoderne," in Markus Bauer and Thomas Rahn, eds., *Die Grenze: Begriff und Inszenierung* (Berlin, 1997), 41 and *passim* [37–69]. See further the discussion in Alan Watson, *The Law of Property in the Later Roman Republic* (Oxford, 1968), 110–124. There were of course also boundary stones marking the limits of state power, going back centuries before the Romans. The point is only one about what was considered an appropriate subject for juristic analysis.
[73] Scattola, "Die Grenze der Neuzeit," 38.
[74] Graham, *News and Frontier Consciousness*, 46. Richardson and others date the change to a significantly earlier period.

booklets" carrying the noteworthy titles "The Division of the Lands of the World" and "The Measurement of the Provinces."[75] These are brief texts, upon which too much weight should not be laid; but they make for revealing reading against the background of classical law. Division had been practiced for centuries: Classical Roman law included *iudicia divisoria*, actions for "dividing up" property. But those classical actions applied strictly to private matters – dividing up inheritances or common holdings.[76] Dividing up "the lands of the world" was new. (As we shall see shortly, some historians argue that the rise of such boundary-thinking was accompanied by a dramatic conceptual shift: the emergence of a "map consciousness" that had not previously existed.)[77]

What can be said of boundaries can also be said of measurement. The classical period boasted a body of literature by authors known as the *agrimensores*, the "land measurers." But classical land measurement was the measurement of private holdings, not of provinces.[78] It is worth quoting once again the first-century BCE Prophecy of Vegoia, discussed in Chapter 3, which gives an aromatic whiff of classical attitudes. Here speaks the nymph Vegoia:

Know that the sea was separated from the sky. But when Jupiter claimed the land of Aetruria for himself, he established and ordered that the fields be measured and the croplands delimited. Knowing the greed of men and their lust for land, he wanted everything proper concerning boundaries.[79]

The classical gods may have divided the sea from the sky and claimed lands like Etruria for themselves. But in the world of

---

[75] "Late imperial booklets": P. Arnaud, "Marcus Vipsanius Agrippa and His Geographical Work," in M. R. Cataudella and H.-J. Gehrke, eds., *Brill's Companion to Ancient Geography: The Inhabited World in the Greek and Roman Tradition* (Leiden, 2016), 208 [205–222], and the texts in Alexander Riese, *Geographi Latini minores* (Heilbronn, 1878), 9–20.
[76] E.g., Heinrich Honsell, Theo Mayer-Maly, and Walter Selb, *Römisches Recht*, 4th ed. (Berlin, 1987), 256–257.
[77] Below, this chapter.
[78] Along with other surveying tasks. See Jan Burin, "Surveyors," *Brill's New Pauly*, available at https://referenceworks.brillonline.com/search?s.f.s2_parent=s.f.book.brill-s-new-pauly&search-go=&s.q=surveyors. Texts in Carolus Thulin, ed., *Corpus agrimensorum Romanorum*, Vol. 1 fasc. 1, *Opuscula agrimensorum veterum*, Teubner (Leipzig, 1913).
[79] Jean MacIntosh Turfa, *Divining the Etruscan World: The Brontoscopic Calendar and Religious Practice* (Cambridge, 2012), 317.

mortals, it was the holdings of private owners, not rulers, that were the subjects of division and measurement.

To be sure, we should not read too much into these late antique departures. It would be a mistake to conclude that the emergence of large-scale "division," "measurement," and directly administered "fragments," perhaps bringing with it "map consciousness," converted the Empire into a full-scale territorial state; the transformation was not so far-reaching. As Scattola and many other scholars argue, the emergence of fully realized territorial states is a phenomenon of the late eighteenth century and after, a view that the next chapter will endorse. Nevertheless, change there was; and it was change that matters for our legal histories. The new Empire of Diocletian and his successors was not becoming a modern Weberian territorial state. But in the eyes of the law, it was becoming something more akin to a classical private landholding.

* * *

The figure of the Emperor, meanwhile, was changing as well, and in ways that suggest the same pattern.

Change in the figure of the emperor has been one of the main themes in studies of Late Antiquity, and one of the most hotly controverted. This involves one development in particular: the ruler's adoption of the form of address *dominus*. As we saw in Chapter 3, *dominus*, "master," established itself in classical Roman property law in the first century BCE, during the same period in which it established itself in Roman *politesse* and the rhetoric of imperial rule. The term was, however, banned from the imperial court at Rome, being condemned as unacceptably un-Republican by Augustus; *dominus* was a title assumed by classical aristocrats, not monarchs. The ban held in the courts of later classical emperors over the next three centuries, despite efforts by Caligula and Domitian to defy the Augustan norm.[80] But in the early third century, at the tail end of the classical period, the Emperor Septimius Severus once again laid claim to the title, and over the subsequent century his successors began to do so as well.[81]

---

[80] With the exceptions of Caligula and Domitian. For a classic account, Andreas Alföldi, "Die Ausgestaltung des monarchischen Zeremoniells," in *Mitteilungen des Deutschen archäologischen Instituts, römische Abteilung* 49 (1934): 45–46 [3–118].

[81] Harries, *Imperial Rome*, 83–84.

The collapse of Augustan practice was complete in the later Empire: *Dominus* became the obligatory form of imperial address from Diocletian onward. Justinian in particular declared himself to be *dominus mundi*, "master/owner of the world," in a phrase that carried much significance for the development of legal thinking on monarchical power in later centuries.[82]

These are developments that have loomed large in the thinking of Roman historians, who have come to call the later Empire, when the Emperor became a *dominus*, the "Dominate," said to have displaced the classical "Principate," in which the Emperor was deemed merely *princeps*, "first citizen." This is a reading of Roman history promoted by late nineteenth-century German historians,[83] the most important of whom was the greatest scholarly name of the age, Theodor Mommsen (1817–1903), the preeminent Roman historian of Europe (and the winner of the second Nobel Prize in Literature, in an age when scholarship was regarded with more awe than it is today). In his *Roman Public Law*, a massive effort to explain Roman history through the reconstruction of its supposed constitutional development, Mommsen argued that the triumph of *dominus* in court ceremonial was the defining marker of late antique constitutional change. The classical Empire, in Mommsen's account, had been organized around the preservation of republican forms, among which Augustus' refusal to accept address as *dominus* played a crucial symbolic role. The institutionalization of that form of address by Diocletian decisively put paid to the republican tradition, and the result was "an even greater break" in Roman history than the transition three centuries earlier from the Republic to the Augustan Principate.[84] This introduction of unrepublican, indeed antirepublican, symbolism into the language

---

[82] See James Muldoon, *Empire and Order: The Concept of Empire, 800–1800* (New York, 1999), 87–100 and often. Ari Bryen observes to me that Antoninus Pius had already referred to himself as κοσμοῦ κύριος in the context of law of the sea. D. 14.2.9.

[83] See Christian Gizewski, "Dominatus," in *Brill's New Pauly*, available at https://referenceworks.brillonline.com/entries/der-neue-pauly/dominat-e322320#.
Alongside Mommsen should be mentioned Otto Seeck. See Stefan Lorenz, "Otto Seeck und die Spätantike," *Historia: Zeitschrift für alte Geschichte* 55 (2006): 234 [228–243].

[84] This is the characterization of Alexander Demandt, *Geschichte der Spätantike* (Munich, 1989), 252. Cf. Jochen Bleicken, *Prinzipat und Dominat: Gedanken zur Periodisierung der römischen Kaiserzeit* (Wiesbaden, 1978).

of Diocletian's court, Mommsen emphasized, was accompanied by the introduction of forms of court ceremonial utterly alien to Augustus' practice. As a number of late antique authors reported, the later Empire adopted such ostentatious practices as dressing the Emperor in silk robes adorned with gold and precious stones.[85] This was widely described as an "orientalization" of the Roman court, amid borrowings from Persian practice, and its result, in Mommsen's judgment, was to convert the imperial court, which had once been a theater of classical Greco-Roman values, into an "Asiatic sultanate."[86]

Specialists today are more than a little uncomfortable with this story. To the modern eye, the Mommsenian approach looks too legalistic, too neat, and too much a product of the worldview of nineteenth-century liberalism, always eager to define itself against "despotism," and especially, since the classical Greeks, against "Asiatic" Persian despotism.[87] Moreover, scholars are sharply aware that the term *dominus* had been used before Diocletian; aware as well that emperors had long claimed some kind of divine status;[88] and conscious of the unavoidable fact that the republican forms of the Principate were a façade, not a working body of constitutional rules. The radical break between Principate and "Dominate" that structured Mommsen's Roman constitutional history, though it is still used, is used with many caveats.

And there is certainly no doubt that Mommsen's scheme was too tidy, and that he was too sanguine about the prospect that nineteenth-century liberal historians could reconstruct the history of human liberty since the Greeks. Still, he was a very great scholar, whose intuitions should not be casually disregarded. The symbolism of legal language carries real power; so too does ceremonial, both private and public; and the triumph of *dominus* in the imperial court, though its value for the periodization of Roman history, and its supposedly "orientalized" character, may be questioned, deserves a place in our

---

[85] Demandt, *Spätantike*, 53.
[86] Ibid., 66; and his further defense of the concept of the "orientialization" at 273–274.
[87] Ibid., 588, on Mommsen's liberal presuppositions driving this interpretation. For the self-definition of Greek and subsequent Western tradition against Persia, see James Q. Whitman, "The World-Historical Significance of European Legal History: An Interim Report," in Heikki Pihlajamäki, Markus D. Dubber, and Mark Godfrey, eds., *The Oxford Handbook of European Legal History* (Oxford, 2018), 6–7.
[88] E.g., Harries, *Imperial Rome*, 83–84.

From Masters to Lords in Late Antiquity 317

legal histories. Like the rise of "division" and "measurement," it is a signal that concepts that had been used to describe classical owners were infiltrating the postclassical understanding of rule. What had once been the terminology of private despotic dominion, banished from court ceremonial with few exceptions until the third century, did indeed now become the language of public despotic dominion. This too set the stage for later developments: Medieval emperors would defend their claims to power on the ground that they too were *domini*;[89] as we shall see in the next chapter, the question of whether monarchs possessed the power of *dominium* was crucial in the development of medieval and early modern legal thinking.

* * *

The reign of the Emperor/*dominus* Diocletian, finally, witnessed something of an opening act in the religious history of Late Antiquity, and one that further bears on the question of the interrelated fates of ownership and rulership in the new order: In 303, Diocletian unleashed the last of the major persecutions of Christians; and as Lactantius reports, that Persecution began in a way of high interest for the history of property law: The Emperor chose to initiate it on the Terminalia, the feast of boundary stones:

A suitable and auspicious day was sought for carrying the business out, and the festival of the *Terminal* ... was chosen, so that a *terminus*, so to speak, would be imposed on this religion.[90]

The Terminalia, as we have seen, was an ancient festival in which neighbors joined to crown their boundary stones with garlands and offer them grain, honeycombs, and wine, while sacrificing a lamb or suckling pig upon which to dine together. These *termini*, bearing a *numen*, a godhead, which had been erected in ditches into which sacrificial blood had been spilled, stood alongside innumerable other monuments indicating divine ownership of various parcels of land. All these stone markers, dotting the lands of the Empire, served as reminders that mortals and immortals were coproprietors of the Earth. "A stroll in the countryside," as Béatrice Caseau writes, would

---

[89] Muldoon, *Empire and Order*.
[90] Lactantius, *De mortibus persecutorum*, 19–20 (12.1). I have slightly altered the translation of Creed.

"reveal an intense sacralization of space," in which "fields were limited by consecrated 'boundary markers.'"[91] As I argued in Chapter 2, this sacralization of the landscape is telling evidence of the fact that the ancient experience of landownership was not like ours.

Why did Diocletian open his Great Persecution on the Terminalia, the festival of consecrated boundary stones? Lactantius declared, presumably rhetorically, that the date was chosen to place a symbolic *terminus* on Christianity. That idea was picked up by Edward Gibbon in his *Decline and Fall of the Roman Empire*, and it has been repeated by subsequent scholarship.[92] Perhaps it is correct. Perhaps the date was chosen because the Terminalia was a moment when private persons throughout the Empire offered sacrifices. When better to insist on the inviolability of traditional religion? Perhaps, for that matter, the choice of the Terminalia had no significance at all. But I think that a bit of further speculation is called for. This is because the choice of the Terminalia is not the only piece of evidence of a Diocletianic concern with boundaries and boundary stones.

The same period in which the Persecution was proclaimed also saw a historic change in the juristic analysis of the primeval state of nature. As we saw in Chapter 3, when the jurists of the classical period spoke of the state of nature (though without using the phrase), they spoke of slavery: They described a primordial time when humans, like other animals, enjoyed "natural liberty." This state of "natural liberty," was, however, terminated by the intrusion of the *ius gentium*, which introduced servitude into the state of nature, as the Severan jurist Ulpian explained. This was a legal teaching, as Keith Bradley remarks, that shared a mystic vision of human history with a great religious festival: the Saturnalia, the December carnival of role reversals, which celebrated a time of primordial natural liberty, the age of Saturn, now vanished.[93]

---

[91] Caseau, "Sacred Landscapes," in G. W. Bowersock, Peter Brown, and Oleg Grabar, eds., *Interpreting Late Antiquity: Essays on the Postclassical World* (Cambridge, MA, 2001), 24 [21–59].

[92] Gibbon, *History of the Decline and Fall of the Roman Empire* (New York, 1893), 2:223; and e.g., Paul Allard, *La Persécution de Dioclétien* (Paris, 1900), 1:156, and J. H. W. G. Liebeschuetz, *Continuity and Change in Roman Religion* (Oxford, 1979), 247.

[93] Above, Chapter 4.

Ulpian's Saturnalian tale of the death of the state of nature contrasts strikingly with a new tale, offered by a leading jurist in Diocletian's court, Aurelius Hermogenianus. Hermogenianus was a high official, the compiler of a major collection of imperial pronouncements that projected the new style of power.[94] Like the classical jurists, this mandarin of the new regime was also an author of learned writings on the law, fragments of which eventually found their way into the *Digest* of Justinian. One of them is of special historical significance. Probably at the beginning of the fourth century, Hermogenianus composed a new statement of the primeval development of the law. Unlike his predecessor Ulpian three quarters of a century earlier, he did not write of the extinction of "natural liberty" and the introduction of slavery. Instead, he wrote of the rise of monarchy and land boundaries, along with commerce:

D. 1.1.5 (Hermogenianus 1 *juris epit.*): By the ius gentium [*ex hoc iure*] wars were introduced; peoples were distinguished; kingdoms founded; domains of ownership distinguished [*dominia distincta*]; boundary stones placed in fields [*agris termini positi*[95]], buildings set in place, trade, buying and selling, letting and hiring, and obligations instituted ...[96]

Scholars treat this fragment, cited as *ex hoc iure*, as little more than a bland restatement of learning of the classical period. As Peter Haggenmacher presents it, for example, *ex hoc iure* was merely a shorthand summary of the "undoubtedly more searching" work of Ulpian, which must have appeared in writings that have now been lost.[97]

---

[94] E.g., Simon Corcoran, *The Empire of the Tetrarchs* (Oxford, 1996), 25–42.
[95] This is generally translated as "establishing boundaries" or some similar phrase, but I suggest that it is important to bear in mind its literal sense. For *termini positi*, cf. D. 47.22.2: *Divus Hadrianus in haec verba rescripsit: Quin pessimum factum sit eorum, qui terminos finium causa positos propulerunt, dubitari non potest.*
[96] Otto Lenel, *Palingenesia iuris civilis* (repr. Frankfurt a.M., 2004), 1: col. 265, dating the fragment probably to the early fourth century.
[97] Haggenmacher, *Grotius et la doctrine de la guerre juste* (Paris, 1983), 316: "Les compilateurs de Justinien semble l'avoir intercalé en cet endroit en manière de résumé, afin d'abréger la discussions sans doute plus fouillée d'Ulpien." The assimilation of Hermogenianus to the earlier tradition was already made by Savigny, *System des heutigen Römischen Rechts* (Berlin, 1840), 1:415, and seems to have held on in the literature despite the revolution in our understanding of Late Antiquity. As far as I can see, there is no basis for this speculation about lost writings of Ulpian. Merio Scattola also minimizes the extent to which *ex hoc iure* represents a departure, observing that it did not yet introduce the idea of public, as opposed to private, boundaries, which

Ex hoc iure, on this interpretation, would be an example of what David Johnston calls "epiclassical law," late antique law whose differences from the earlier juristic tradition were slight – a mere derivative bit of late antique regurgitation of classical Ulpianic learning.[98]

Yet as Annabel Brett observes, this is a strange reading of the fragment. *Ex hoc iure* clearly seems to represent a view of the law different from that of Ulpian.[99] She is right: It offers something quite new. Hermogenianus' late antique tale of the rise of kingdoms, distinct domains of ownership, and boundaries marked by *termini* was, to be sure, in a certain sense not unprecedented. It had classical *literary* antecedents. Virgil, as we have seen, spoke of the beginnings of human society as a time when "no tillers subjugated the land: even to mark possession of the plain or apportion it by boundaries was sacrilege..." and classical authors such as Seneca and Tibullus recycled the same fable (as would Rousseau and Marx, centuries later).[100] In that sense, we can describe *ex hoc iure* as the product of an infiltration of classical literary *topoi* into the law.

But within the law it represented yet another departure, and a large one, at the threshold of Late Antiquity. And as we try to make sense of that departure, I think we must bear in mind its late antique context. Hermogenianus' reference to the "founding of kingdoms" was composed against the backdrop of the Emperor's division of the Empire into four realms, and his carving of its territories into

---

would only emerge in the early modern period. Scattola, "Die Grenze der Neuzeit," 41 and *passim*. This is both persuasive and important, but it risks understating the novelty of Hermogenianus' passage in other respects, and its context in the law of the Dominate. For a larger study of the man, see Serena Connolly, *Lives behind the Laws: The World of the Codex Hermogenianus* (Bloomington and Indianapolis, 2010).

[98] Johnston, "Epiclassical Law," in Alan Bowman, Averil Cameron, and Peter Garnsey, eds., *Cambridge Ancient History* 12, 2nd ed. (Cambridge, 2008), 200–211. Cf. Dario Mantovani, *Les juristes écrivains de la Rome antique: les œuvres des juristes comme littérature* (Paris, 2018), 41.

[99] If cautiously. Brett, *Changes of State: Nature and the Limits of the City in Early Modern Natural Law* (Princeton, 2011), 75–76.

[100] Verg. G. 1.121–129, in H. Rushton Fairclough, trans., *Virgil: Eclogues; Georgics; Aeneid: Books 1–6*, rev. G. P. Goold, Loeb Classical Library 63 (Cambridge, MA, 1916), 106–107; cf. Sen. Oct. 398–406, in John G. Fitch, ed. and trans., *Seneca: Tragedies, Volume II: Oedipus; Agamemnon; Thyestes; Hercules on Oeta; Octavia*, Loeb Classical Library 78 (Cambridge, MA, 2004), 548–551; Tib. 1.3.43–44, in F. W. Cornish, J.P. Postgate, and J. W. Mackail, trans., *Catullus; Tibullus; Pervigilium Veneris*, rev. G. P. Goold, Loeb Classical Library 6 (Cambridge, MA, 1913), 206–207.

fragments. The erection of *termini* in his tale of the *ius gentium* recalls the same Emperor's initiation of the Great Persecution on the day of the Terminalia. There is no way of establishing these connections with any certainty; but these are pieces of evidence that demand to be considered side by side. What they suggest, if only tantalizingly, is some sort of concern with a somehow charged question of boundaries and boundary stones, laden with some sort of social and religious significance, in the court of the Emperor, alongside some sense that the erection of private *termini* had a conceptual link to the founding of kingdoms. What Hermogenianus was offering was, if you will, a Terminalian tale of the death of the state of nature, fit for the days of Diocletian, to be contrasted with the Saturnalian tale of Ulpian.

In any case, whatever its precise context in the reign of Diocletian, *ex hoc iure* had a long future before it. Like the Emperor's "division of the world into four parts," it set the stage for centuries of later land-oriented law. "[A] very large and fruitful fragment," as Koskenniemi describes it, it "would come in handy to explain the legal status of a number of institutions that could be met more or less everywhere in the world known to the medieval jurists."[101] In particular, those medieval jurists relied upon *ex hoc iure* in their treatment of the doctrine of *duplex dominium*, the division of feudal property into *dominium directum* and *dominium utile* whose importance was discussed in Chapter 7.[102] Medieval theologians, for their part, would conduct their debates over the nature of *dominium* with regular reference to *ex hoc iure*'s account of the division of the earth into *dominia distincta*, "distinct domains of ownership."[103] Nor was

---

[101] Koskenniemi, *To the Uttermost Parts of the Earth: Legal Imagination and International Power, 1300–1870* (Cambridge, 2021), 75. For medieval citations, Ugo Nicolini, *La proprietà: il principe e l'espropriazione per pubblica utilità* (Milan, 1940), 23–24. The medieval use was filtered through Isidore, *Etym.* 5.6: *Ius gentium est sedium occupatio, aedificatio, munitio, bella, captivitates, servitutes, postliminia, foedera pacis, indutiae, legatorum non violandorum religio, conubia inter alienigenas prohibita. Et inde ius gentium, quia eo iure omnes fere gentes utuntur*, in Wallace M. Lindsay, ed., *Isidore of Seville: Etymologiarum sive originum libri XX* (Oxford, 1911), 183.

[102] E.g., Baldus degli Ubaldi, *In primam Digesti Veteris partem commentaria* (Venice, 1599), 1:111r *ad* 31. For other examples, see Ugo Nicolini, *La proprietà*, 28.

[103] For a discussion focusing on the great Franciscan controversies, with citations to larger literature, Jonathan Robinson, *William of Ockham's Early Theory of Property* (Leiden and Boston, 2013), 122–174.

the significance of *ex hoc iure* merely medieval. The next chapter, drawing on the scholarship of Brett, will trace its impact on the thought of Vitoria, Grotius, Pufendorf, Locke, and others. It is on the road laid by *ex hoc iure* that we can follow most clearly the movement from the law of Late Antiquity into the Middle Ages and on into the early modern period, when the echoes of Hermogenianus' Terminalian tale would sound in Rousseau's own tale of the end of the state of innocence: "The first person who, having enclosed a plot of land, took it into his head to say this is mine and found people simple enough to believe him was the true founder of civil society."[104]

* * *

The literature I have surveyed so far puts the focus on the relative decline of classical urban culture, and the consequent emergence, at least tentatively, of a more territorial understanding, both in Roman property orientations and in Roman rule. But students of the "great shift" also point to another factor in the history of religion: the rise of Christianity.

Christianity came, of course, to dominate in the societies of the Roman world over the generations after Constantine declared its formal toleration in the early fourth century, perhaps in part under the guidance of Lactantius, who had joined his court.[105] How, if at all, would that have mattered for the changing orientation of the law of ownership? There is an old idea, promoted by the nineteenth-century French abolitionist Henri Wallon (and long before him by Jean Bodin), that it was the triumph of the new religion that doomed classical slavery.[106] If that thesis were correct, there might be a comparatively straightforward story to tell about the impact of Christianity: Christianity was inherently abolitionist, and consequently slavery began an inexorable decline with the Christianization of the Roman world.

But scholars have long since rejected Wallon's thesis. While it is true that some ancient Church teachings discouraged holding Christians in

---

[104] Jean-Jacques Rousseau, *Discourse of the Origin of Inequality*, trans. Donald Cress (Indianapolis, 1992), 44.
[105] See DePalma Digeser, *Making of a Christian Empire*, 133–134.
[106] Wallon, *Histoire de l'esclavage dans l'antiquité* (Paris, 1867), e.g., at 3:365–368; on Bodin, see, e.g., Henry Heller, "Bodin on Slavery and Primitive Accumulation," *Sixteenth Century Journal* 25 (1994): 55 [53–65].

slavery; and while it is true that ancient Christianity celebrated ceremonies of manumission; and while, in later centuries, there were important medieval bans on selling Christians to pagans,[107] or taking Christians as slaves;[108] it is impossible to mount a convincing argument that the ancient Church was categorically opposed to the institution. Historians cite much evidence to the contrary. This includes, to take one example distressing to modern ears, Pope Gregory the Great's instructions to one of his priests to purchase some English slave boys. Gregory's letter betrays none of the modern revulsion at the traffic in humans.[109] Most generally, there is simply no doubt that the institution of slavery survived the triumph of Christianity handily. Christianity did have a major impact on the abolitionism of the eighteenth and nineteenth centuries; but that, of course, was more than a thousand years later. Christianity played a crucial role, but it did so only over an enormously *longue durée* that stretched into the nineteenth century.

But that does not mean that the rise of Christianity in Antiquity had no significance at all. Contemporary scholars are quite sure that it did; but they take a tack different from the one taken by Wallon. Instead of arguing that Christianity caused the institution of ancient slavery to decline precipitously, scholars today point to a different development: what Rapp and Drake call the "great shift in political thought" that brought with it a new orientation toward land and territoriality. Christianity, on this account, participated in, and amplified the impact of, the decay of classical urban culture and the movement into the countryside that this chapter has been discussing.

The argument of Rapp and Drake draws on the work of legal historians of late antique citizenship, but reframes it in light of religious change. The late antique shift from "*polis* to *imperium*" was a shift from the Empire imagined as a notional city, to an Empire imagined as a territory subject to the rule of one Emperor, the great

---

[107] McCormick, *Origins of the European Economy*, 748.
[108] Usefully surveyed in Luis Rivera-Pagán, "Freedom and Servitude: Indigenous Slavery and the Spanish Conquest of the Caribbean," in J. Sued-Badillo, ed., *General History of the Caribbean* (New York, 2003), 316–362.
[109] Gregory, epistle to the priest Candidus, in Arthur West Haddan and William Stubbs, eds., *Councils and Ecclesiastical Documents Relating to Great Britain and Ireland* (Oxford, 1871), 3:5.

territorial *dominus* described above, and it was Christian in tenor. What marked the new understanding was the belief that the Emperor ruled over one realm just as heaven and earth were ruled by one God. "In religious terms," as Arnaldo Momigliano writes, "one can easily see that Christianity was bound to insist on the parallelism between the unity of the Empire and the unity of the Christian Church."[110]

This shift to a monotheistic, and therefore territorial/imperial conception, in the view of Rapp and Drake, "reconfigured" political membership, displacing the older form of citizenship: "[M]embership in a world state, an *oikoumenē*, replaced the *polis* as the conceptual framework in which the ancient Mediterranean peoples thought about their relationship to each other."[111] Where persons had understood themselves to be privileged rights-holders in a city-state community, they now came to understand themselves to be Christian inhabitants of a godly state that encompassed the lands of the entire world, conceived as a vast territory with Jerusalem at its center.[112]

To make their case, Rapp and Drake draw on a range of scholarship. The conceptual apparatus of citizenship, Susanna Elm shows, was repurposed in ways such that Christendom, rather than the *polis*, became the realm of the citizen.[113] At the same time, in a development of particular interest for historians of property law, Late Antiquity may have seen the emergence of a new style of Christian "map consciousness." As we saw in Chapter 5, scholars such as Kai Brodersen deny that the classical Empire possessed "map consciousness." "Geographical descriptions in antiquity," Tonio Hölscher argues, "do not present the reader with an overall image of topographical interrelations between different places but follow the routes of traveling, with conquering eyes."[114] The Romans of the classical period, as Emily Albu summarizes this view, "do not seem to have used maps to plot their travels through the world. Instead, they

---

[110] Momigliano, "The Disadvantages of Monotheism for a Universal State," in *Ottavo contributo alla storia degli studi classici e del mondo antico* (Rome, 1987), 314 [313–328].
[111] Rapp and Drake, "Polis–Imperium–Oikoumenē," 2.   [112] Id., 6
[113] Elm, "Church–Festival–Temple: Reimagining Civic Topography in Late Antiquity," in Rapp and Drake, eds., *The City in the Classical and Post-Classical World*, 167–183.
[114] Hölscher, *Visual Power in Ancient Greece and Rome: Between Art and Social Reality* (Berkeley, 2018), 4.

thought in terms of itineraries that led them along their vast route network."[115] They charted paths from city to city, not yet imagining their Empire as territorial entity.

But it is Albu's contention that that changed in Christian Late Antiquity: "Under the powerful influence of the new religion, the Roman itinerary mind, with its linear thought, yields to a different kind of spatial thinking, a Christian mapping mentality on a scale encompassing the known inhabited world (the *oikoumenē*)."[116] "By emphasizing territories rather than cities," as Rapp and Drake put it, following Albu's work, "Christians in late antiquity achieved a 'conceptual leap' that, once imperial authority waned in the West, opened the way for Christian maps to serve 'as signifiers of dominion over the earth.'"[117]

All fascinating. Rapp, Drake, and Albu do not cite Marx when they postulate this "conceptual leap" to "territories rather than cities" and "dominion over the earth"; but their argument might be read as a gloss on his dictum that "where Antiquity took the city and its small subject territory as its basis, the Middle Ages took the land as its basis." Rapp and Drake's argument might be read as a gloss on Grossi as well. Customary law may or may not necessarily be understood as embodying "the custom of a region, the custom of a place, the custom of a land, the custom of a farm."[118] But the emergence of custom as a source of law accompanied the cultural decline of the classical *polis*; and that decline opened the way for a different Christian mode of imagining the planet.

* * *

To these interpretations of the impact of Christianity, I would like to add two more, both, to be sure, speculative. The first has to do with the decline in the culture and standing of classical elites described throughout this chapter. The second has to do with the Christian assault on ritual sacrifice.

In Chapter 3, I proposed that the "concrete" context of the classical law of the *dominus*, to use Wieacker's language, should be sought in

---

[115] Albu, "The Battle of the Maps in the Christian Empire," in Rapp and Drake, eds., *The City in the Classical and Post-Classical World*, 203 [202–216].
[116] Ibid.   [117] Rapp and Drake, "Polis–Imperium–Oikoumenē," 10.
[118] Grossi, *Le situazioni reali*, 68.

the classical *domus*, whose displacement of the older *familia* has been the subject of much investigation by social historians of the Roman family. One of those historians, Kate Cooper, argues that Late Antiquity worked yet another change. Cooper emphasizes the challenges that the new religion posed to the power of the classical *dominus*. The classical *domus*, she writes, was "a central arena for the social, economic, and even political negotiations in which its members participated." But the triumph of Christianity implied deep change in the "vision" underlying the exercise of power: The *paterfamilias* "essentially ceded to the Christian bishop his role as arbiter in matters of piety and justice,"[119] while subordinate members of the household could claim a new kind of independence and authority upon conversion.[120] On this account, what mattered about Christianity for the history of property law is that it endangered the classical culture of domination at its household foundations.

This is a powerful argument indeed; and alongside it I think we might consider another aspect of late antique change, already foreshadowed in Chapter 3: Christianity also endangered the ritual role of the *dominus*. The classical household master presided over ritual sacrifices, both in the home and in the city; in Chapter 3 I argued that this religious function played an important part in what Wieacker called the wealthy Roman nobility's "sense of self": "Sacrifices, especially blood sacrifices," as Guy Stroumsa writes, "were in effect at the very heart of religious activity, certainly of any public and official religious activity";[121] and the performance of blood sacrifices was emblematic of the sociocultural supremacy of a man of high standing. By officiating at major sacrifices, members of local elites "placed themselves at the center of a dense nexus of religious, cultural, and social associations that were crucial to the self-identity of their communities."[122] It was not just that the man of power

---

[119] Cooper, *The Fall of the Roman Household* (Cambridge, 2007), 97, ix.
[120] Cooper, "Relationships, Resistance, and Religious Change in the Early Christian Household," in John Doran, Charlotte Methuen, and Alexandra Walsham, eds., *Religion and the Household* (Woodbridge, Suffolk, 2014), 5–22.
[121] Stroumsa, *The End of Sacrifice: Religious Transformations in Late Antiquity*, trans. Susan Emanuel (Chicago, 2009), 57.
[122] James Rives, "Between Orthopraxy and Orthodoxy: Constantine and Animal Sacrifice," in G. Bonamente, N. Lenski, and R. Lizzi Testa, eds., *Costantino prima e dopo Costantino/Constantine before and after Constantine* (Bari, 2012), 154 [153–163].

ruled as master over his *domus* and magistrate in his city. It was also he, if he rose high enough in the ritual hierarchy, who had the high privilege of killing the victim and distributing its meat, decked out before the community as *Homo necans*.

And of course opposition to blood sacrifice was one of the defining features of the new religion. Persecutions of Christians were mounted on the basis of their refusal to participate in sacrifices – including those of the Terminalia – and the triumph of the new religion led to "the end of sacrifice," in the title of Stroumsa's lectures on the topic, with the destruction, largely complete by the early fifth century, of classical ritual practice. The older culture did not come to a swift end everywhere.[123] But the end did come; and as we weigh the impact of Christianity, I suggest that we might consider the blow it landed on the ritual role of Wieacker's wealthy Roman nobility. The magnificence of the classical *dominus* was on display in the performance of blood sacrifice as in other realms; and the assault on blood sacrifice, accompanied by the establishment of a new priesthood that displaced the old religious ruling order, did something to cut the heart out of the classical culture of ownership.

If that is the right way, or one of the right ways, to view the impact of the new religion, it brings to mind one of the most unsavory hypotheses about the significance of Christianity. This is Nietzsche's claim that the new religion embodied a "slave morality," founded in an *Umwertung aller Werte*, an inversion of all the values of the classical ruling orders.[124] There are plenty of reasons to reject Nietzsche's proposition that Christianity was the expression of a "slave morality," just as there are plenty of reasons to resist so many of his ideas. But it is true that the triumph of the new religion was a triumph over the ritual primacy of a classical elite that had indeed, in some sense, "rove[d]," in the imagination of the law, "in search of booty and victory."[125]

* * *

---

[123] E.g., Garth Fowden, *Empire to Commonwealth: Consequences of Monotheism in Late Antiquity* (Princeton, 1994), 48.

[124] E.g., Nietzsche, "Der Antichrist," §5, in Giorgio Colli and Mazzino Montanari, eds., *Nietzsches Werke: historisch-kritische Ausgabe* (Charlottesville, 1995), 6.3:171.

[125] Nietzsche, "Zur Genealogie der Moral," in Colli and Mazzino Montanari, eds., *Nietzsches Werke*, 6.2:289.

There is one last way of thinking about the impact of Christianity as well. This takes us back the work of Mircea Eliade, and into the realm of large-scale, indeed dizzying, speculation about the history of law and religion both.

In his unfinished magnum opus, *The History of Religious Ideas*, Eliade proposes a grand history of religious change that extends back to the Paleolithic. In the ancient world, he argues, there were two contrasting forms of ritual: On the one hand, there were sacrificial rites, which had roots in hunting practices reaching back thousands of years; on the other hand, there were rites with roots in the agricultural revolution, also of course reaching back thousands of years. Sacrificial ritual, with its slaughter of animals and distribution of meat, emerged out of the activities of Walter Burkert's Paleolithic *Homo necans*, and it reflected the fact that the religion of paleolithic hunters turned on the deaths of their animal prey. Ritual sacrifice of those animals was understood to be necessary to propitiate the gods; and as Burkert and René Girard argue, it was further necessary in order to channel the aggressive instincts of hunters who might otherwise turn their weapons on each other.[126]

But agriculture yielded, according to Eliade, a different form of religious practice: Rituals oriented toward agriculture were centered on land, and revolved around "birth, death and rebirth,"[127] the life cycle of the cultivated crop, which seemed to die in the winter only to be reborn in the spring. "[T]he 'mystery' of vegetation" lay at its religious core, as Eliade argues, echoing the interpretations commonly offered by late nineteenth- and early twentieth-century scholars:[128]

It is a mystery that demands the "death" of the seed in order to insure it a new birth, a birth all the more marvelous because accompanied by an astonishing multiplication. The assimilation of human existence to vegetable life finds expression in images and metaphors drawn from the drama of vegetation

---

[126] See esp. the presentation of their ideas in Robert G. Hamerton-Kelly, ed., *Violent Origins: Walter Burkert, René Girard and Jonathan Z. Smith on Ritual Killing and Cultural Formation* (Stanford, 1987).

[127] Eliade, *A History of Religious Ideas*, trans. Willard Trask (Chicago, 1978), 1:41.

[128] Classically Wilhelm Mannhardt, *Wald- und Feldkulte*, 2 vols. (Berlin, 1875–1877); James George Frazer, *The Golden Bough: A Study in Magic and Religion* (New York, 1941).

(life is like the flower of the field, etc.) ... The agrarian cultures develop what may be called a *cosmic religion*, since religious activity is concentrated around the central mystery: *the periodic renewal of the world.*[129]

Where hunting religion ritualized death, agrarian religion ritualized death succeeded, endlessly, by rebirth. Eliade sees archaic agrarian forms reappearing in Christianity among others, the religion of the death and rebirth of Jesus, rich in agricultural symbolism.[130]

Eliade's approach does not enjoy much support among contemporary specialists in religious studies, who doubt that his generalizations can capture the complexity of lived religion, or indeed that comparative religious history in the grand style, sweeping over long centuries, is a proper subject for careful scholars at all.[131] His work is certainly subject to challenge and emendation. His understanding of the nature of agricultural ritual is not the only possible one. Fertility cults no longer play the role in the thinking of scholars that they once did.[132] In any case, social scientists now

---

[129] Eliade, *History of Religious Ideas*, 1:41.
[130] Ibid., e.g., at 2:367–368. For the hunting/agriculture contrast, see further Mircea Eliade, *The Sacred and the Profane: The Nature of Religion*, trans. Willard R. Trask (New York, 1959), 17 and often on hunting.
[131] E.g., Jonathan Z. Smith, "Morphology and History in Mircea Eliade's 'Patterns in Comparative Religion,'" *History of Religions* 39 (2000): 334 [332–351].
[132] For the departure from the older emphasis on fertility cults in the intellectual history of earlier ideas, Ronald Hutton, "The Neolithic Great Goddess: A Study in Modern Tradition," *Antiquity* 71 (1997): 91–99; Lynn Meskell, "Goddesses, Gimbutas and New Age Archaeology," *Antiquity* 69 (1995): 74–86. Some of the most interesting work suggests that early agricultural religion functioned as a means of mobilizing agrarian labor, since "domestication of animals and plants fosters increasingly routinized forms of collaborative labour" that required religious rituals that fostered sustained collective solidarity. Quentin D. Atkinson and Harvey Whitehouse, "The Cultural Morphospace of Ritual Form: Examining Modes of Religiosity Cross-culturally," *Evolution and Human Behavior* 12 (2011): 59 [50–62]. For another approach, see Jacques Cauvin, *The Birth of the Gods and the Origins of Agriculture*, trans. Trevor Watkins (Cambridge, 2000). The current literature emphasizes the prevalence of Neolithic symbolism featuring "wild and dangerous animals" even in the midst of the slow shift toward agriculture, with "agricultural symbolism" not coming to the fore for thousands of years. Ian Hodder and Lynn Meskell, "A 'Curious and Sometimes a Trifle Macabre Artistry,'" *Current Anthropology* 52 (2011): 235–263; Hodder, "The Lady and the Seed," in Mehmet Özdogan, Harald Hauptmann, and Nezih Basgelen, *From Village to Cities* (Istanbul, 2003), 133 [129–137]. See further William Johnsen, "Mimetic Theory, the Wall Paintings, and the Domestication, De-domestication, and Sacrifice of Cattle at Çatalhöyük," in Ian Hodder, ed., *Violence and the Sacred in*

recognize that hunter-gatherers often engage in some kind of agriculture; there is no perfectly neat distinction between the two patterns of subsistence.[133] Specialists have, moreover, grown more wary of the idea of an agricultural "revolution" than scholars of Eliade's time were. The development of plant (and animal) domestication, we now know, transpired incrementally, over thousands of years during the Holocene.[134] As Ian Hodder jocularly puts it, it is better to speak of the agricultural "gradual process" than an agricultural revolution.[135]

But whatever its failings, Eliade's account of general religious history lends itself provocatively to comparison with the history of law – too provocatively to be ignored. Eliade sees the decline of a form of religion founded in blood sacrifice, with roots in the mentality of the hunt, giving way, after many thousands of years, to a form of religion with roots in agriculture. The law too witnessed, after many thousands of years, the decline of the ideology of "the paradigmatic hunter," as the center of gravity of the ancient world was displaced into the agrarian countryside. In both domains, we seem to see the consequences of a large-scale imaginative shift from hunting to agriculture – a shift, to borrow the language of Ian Morris' evolutionist history of "human values," from foragers (i.e. hunter-gatherers) to farmers.[136]

Offering such an interpretation means asking scholars to accept a proposition that is difficult to digest. It means asking them to believe that the cultural impact of the invention of agriculture only made itself fully felt over a process of change that lasted on the order of ten thousand years, not entering its decisive phase of the displacement of the hunting orientation until Late Antiquity. It means, that is, speaking of a *longue durée* of almost unimaginable *longueur* –

---

  the Ancient Near East (Cambridge, 2019), 153–164, and more generally the other contributions to the same volume.
[133] E.g., Hodder, "The Lady and the Seed," 132.
[134] L isa Maher, Tobias Richter, and Jay T. Stock, "The Pre-Natufian Epipaleolithic: Long-Term Behavioral Trends in the Levant," *Evolutionary Anthropology* 21 (2012): 69–81; Melinda Zeder, "Religion and the Revolution: The Legacy of Jacques Cauvin," *Paléorient* 37 (2011): 39–60.
[135] Hodder, "The Lady and the Seed," 132.
[136] Ian Morris, *Foragers, Farmers and Fossil Fuels: How Human Values Evolve* (Princeton, 2015).

difficult indeed to accept, I know, even if both law and religion have histories that must be measured in millennia.

* * *

But then, none of the interpretations that I have discussed is easily proven. The developments surveyed in this chapter certainly suggest, in the phrase of a famous account of a very different period of cultural upheaval, "great psychological changes."[137] Stroumsa, in his lectures on "the end of sacrifice," speaks of "a profound psychological transformation,"[138] just as Rapp and Drake speak of "a great shift in political thought." But it is in the nature of things that "profound psychological transformations" and "great shifts in political thought" taking place over vast regions and long centuries in remote Antiquity are next to impossible to document securely.

Nevertheless, taken together, the work of scholars does testify to a transition, though no more than an incipient one, from an older property law orientation, whose "concrete basis" lay in the urban culture of an exploitative elite, to a more territorial or "ruralized" one, broadly in line with Marx's observation that property relations moved out of the city and into the countryside, if not for the reasons Marx himself gave.[139]

But what the various accounts I have surveyed in this chapter reflect is not a transition in the economics of labor exploitation from slavery to serfdom, but a gathering transformation in the culture of the law, whose sources can be linked to a crisis in the culture of a classical urban elite, the transformation of practices of rule in the Dominate, and the rise of a new religion. This is not inconsistent with the proposition that there was socio-economic change. On the contrary, it accords well with

---

[137] Paul Hazard, *La crise de la conscience européenne (1680–1715)* (Paris, 1942), chapter 1: "les grands changements psychologiques."
[138] Stroumsa, *End of Sacrifice*, 8.
[139] Perhaps other evidence could be cited as well. One late text deserves mention because of its importance in the medieval literature. This is Isidore, *Etym*. 5.2: *Fas lex divina est; ius lex humana. Transire per agrum alienum fas est, ius non est*, in Wallace M. Lindsay, ed., *Isidore of Seville: Etymologiarum sive originum libri XX* (Oxford, 1911), 183. This reappeared in Gratian, *Decr*. 1, and stimulated the fascinating commentary of Johannes Teutonicus: *Fas est: idest aequum est ... item iure divino licitum est comedere uvas in agro alterius sed non exportare; contenere spicas et comedere licitum est, sed non mittere falcem ... non est ius, idest ius non dat civilem actionem. Ubi enim aliquid michi prodest et tibi non nocet aequum est ut michi non prohibeas, licet ius ibi deficiat.*

Wickham's account of the shift from a "tax-based" to a "land-based" order; and perhaps the case could be made for other socio-economic theories as well.

But none of these interpretations presupposes an ancient slave economy, or a medieval feudal one. These are not accounts of the transformation of economically conditioned patterns in the exploitation of labor. They are accounts of the early stages in the rise of a different sort of elite, from classical urban masters to a new kind of lord, and of a new cultural orientation, in which the power of ownership, like the power of rulership, was coming to be imagined as power over land.

9

From the Law of Owning Humans to the Law of Owning Land: The Early Modern Culmination

By 1787, James Madison was arguing that it would be "wrong to admit in the Constitution the idea that there could be property in men." This was a matter of plain legal logic, as his biographer Michael Signer explains his views: Humans, Madison observed, "were not like merchandize, consumed &c."[1] William Blackstone, the greatest of legal authorities in the common law world, had expressed his own opposition to slavery two decades earlier: "It is repugnant to reason, and the principles of natural law, that [slavery] should subsist anywhere."[2] A decade before that, in 1752, David Hume was condemning slavery as "disgusting" and "barbarous."[3]

These have all become conventional, indeed self-evident, views today, even if it took a distressingly long time for them to take hold in Madison's United States. Slavery, we can all now clearly see, is repugnant, disgusting, and barbarous. It is obvious that people cannot be owned in the way that inanimate objects or nonhuman animals can be owned; it is obvious that humans cannot be bought and sold like "merchandize, consumed &c." It is repellant that anyone

---

[1] Madison, "Power of Congress to Prohibit the Slave Trade" ([25 August] 1787), discussed in Signer, *Becoming Madison: The Extraordinary Origins of the Least Likely Founding Father* (New York, 2015), 205. Available at https://founders.archives.gov/documents/Madison/01-10-02-0106.

[2] Blackstone, *Commentaries on the Laws of England, Book I: Of the Rights of Persons*, ed. David Lemmings (Oxford, 2016), 272.

[3] Hume, "Of the Populousness of Ancient Nations," in *Political Discourses*, 2nd ed. (Edinburgh, 1752), 161–162 [155–262].

should suggest otherwise. A moral and conceptual Enlightenment has dawned that separates us from our ancestors.

But that dawn came late. What is obvious to us now was not obvious before the time of Hume. Ancient Roman slave law, as Aldo Schiavone writes, was "encased in a shell of ethical and cognitive indifference."[4] The Romans did not perceive the treatment of humans as things as any sort of contradiction in terms; most especially, as we saw in Chapter 4, they were wholly untroubled by slave-taking through war. As for early modern Westerners before the age of Hume: Even extraordinarily thoughtful ones such as Hugo Grotius and John Locke did not see any logical impossibility in the enslavement of human beings.

Our perception of ownership, and its permissible objects, has undergone, as A.-J. Arnaud puts it in the phrase I have often quoted, "a radical transformation that operated on the foundation and form of our conception of property"; we simply see the morality of ownership differently from the way in which our ancestors saw it. But the consummation of that "radical transformation" cannot be dated before the latter decades of the eighteenth century. How did this upheaval in our perception of "the external things of the world" unfold? This chapter gives an answer that extends over three early modern centuries, running from the Iberian incursions into the New World, and continuing up until the late eighteenth century.

Over this long period, Schiavone's "shell of ethical and cognitive indifference" cracked. But it cracked slowly. Western legal and political thinkers were the children of the ancient legal and religious sources, and those sources did nothing to encourage the understanding, so self-evident to us today, that there could be "no property in men." Classical Roman law left no doubt about the legitimacy of enslavement through war. The Old Testament, for its part, spoke in passage after passage of the ownership of "many slaves and servants and flocks" (Gen. 26:14) and the like. These were inescapable references in a Western world that was self-consciously both Roman and Christian, and until the mid eighteenth century, virtually no thinker, no matter how brilliant, was able to see past them completely. The tale of the decline of the inherited view of

---

[4] Schiavone, *La storia spezzata: Roma antica e Occidente moderno* (Bari, 1996), 45.

slavery is, for that reason, not a simple tale of how moral and conceptual Enlightenment dawned. It is a tale of how legal and religious scholars picked their way through the thickets of the ancient legal and scriptural sources. And as I will argue in this chapter, it is a tale marked by irony. For the decline of the ancient law of slavery did not begin with principled objections to the ownership of human beings as such. It began as early modern legal and religious scholars sought *justifications* for slavery not to be found in the ancient legal sources. It began as Western thinkers abandoned the classical teaching that enslavement through war was self-evidently just, and embraced instead two new justificatory theories: the doctrine of natural slavery and the doctrine of the consent of the defeated enemy to accept enslavement rather than death.

That is one part of the story this closing chapter tells. The second involves the other side of Arnaud's "radical transformation," the growing dominance of an orientation toward land and territoriality. In part, this involves the legal doctrine that was Arnaud's subject, *occupatio*. As we saw in Chapters 2 and 4, classical *occupatio* was law centered on the hunt for living prey. Over the course of the early modern period, it assumed its familiar modern form, as law oriented toward the acquisition of land. This transformation in *occupatio*, from the "occupation" of prey to the occupation of real estate and regions, will feature prominently in this chapter; but it is only one aspect of a larger early modern legal history of the ascendancy of a land orientation. The feudal tradition played a major part as well. In Chapter 5, we saw that the feudal law, which put the control of land squarely at the center of its analysis of rights, reached its acme of authority in the early modern period. The feudal tradition too offered an alternative to slavery, and the history of transformation of early modern law is partly the history of the success of that alternative: There was a kind of imaginative passage from slavery to feudalism, whose beginnings can already be detected in the Iberian New World conquests. A third crucial development marked these centuries too: From the sixteenth century onward, free-soil teachings established themselves. The free-soil tradition, which reached its culmination in the American Civil War, offered a land-based alternative to slavery just as feudalism did.

These developments propelled property law toward its modern focus on the ownership of land: They converged in the making of a law in which "in the modern West we tend to assume that land is the archetypal form of property."[5] They were paralleled by change in the understanding of the state. By the late eighteenth century, states, like Blackstonian private owners, were coming to embrace an unambiguously territorial orientation. Yin and yang, as we have seen so often in this book, shifted in tandem. At the close of the chapter, I will argue that the rise of these territorial states contributed in its own way to the most important development of all: the final disappearance of the legitimacy of the ownership of human beings.

* * *

It is appropriate to begin this many-sided tale of early modern transformation in 1512, with one of the most studied, and most deplored, events of early modern legal history: the Junta of Burgos, called by King Ferdinand II of Castile to debate the novel legal problems posed by the discovery and exploitation of the New World.

The decision to call the Junta was triggered by a Christian denunciation of the brutal treatment of the indigenous peoples in the Caribbean, given in a Christmas sermon in 1511 at Santo Domingo, amidst the human misery on the island of Hispaniola, by the Dominican Antonio de Montesinos. Montesinos, speaking in the ramshackle church building that had been erected on the conquered island, thundered at the assembled Spaniards that they were on the road to damnation – *"Are these people not humans? Do they not have a soul, and reason?"* – after which, facing ferocious anger, he returned to Castile to consult with the royal court.[6]

The deliberations that followed at Burgos aimed to bring settled juristic order to the *Asuntos de Indias*, the matter of the Indies. Various questions were debated, but one stands out: whether the "Indians" of the New World could be enslaved. This was a problem that had only been tentatively resolved, at best, over the twenty years since the

---

[5] Georgy Kantor, Tom Lambert, and Hannah Skoda, "Introduction," in Kantor, Lambert, and Skoda, eds., *Legalism: Property and Ownership* (Oxford, 2017), 10 [1–27].

[6] For a vivid and up-to-date account, see Christiane Birr, "*Dominium* in the Indies: Juan López de Palacios Rubios' *Libellus de insulis oceanis quas vulgus indias appelat* (1512–1516)," *Rechtsgeschichte* 26 (2018): 264–283.

From Owning Humans to Owning Land

landfall in 1492. Columbus and some of his men had conceived the project of extracting profit from their discoveries by selling Taino on European markets, and in 1495 they shipped five hundred of them to Iberia with that in mind. But in 1500, after a few years of stumbling uncertainty, Queen Isabella put a stop to this venture, intervening to restore the freedom of any captives shipped to the Old World for sale: These were, she declared, not human merchandise available for the taking, but her own vassals, and they were to be sent home.[7] On Hispaniola itself, meanwhile, the governor Nicolas de Ovando regularized the *encomienda*, a feudalized form of lordship that had been used in the *Reconquista* of Iberia, as the proper institution for the conversion, control, and exploitation of the indigenous population in 1502.[8] This institution turned indigenous peoples over to the exploitative care of *encomenderos*, who were granted a quasi-fiefdom in a particular holding.[9] In 1503, Isabella ratified its use for the indigenous populations.[10]

There were thus two approaches on offer for dealing with the conquered population of Hispaniola in 1512: on the one hand, enslavement, on the other the "semi-feudal" grant of *encomiendas*, with its roots in medieval practice.[11] Neither had been the subject of careful legal or theological analysis. Both had essentially emerged as *ad*

---

[7] Anthony Pagden, *The Fall of Natural Man: The American Indian and the Origins of Comparative Ethnology* (Cambridge, 1982), 33–34.

[8] For the "neo-feudal" character of the *encomienda* in debates surrounding the conquista, Juan Pérez de Tudela y Bueso, "Ideas juridicas y realizaciones politicas en la historia indiana," in *Annuario de la Asociación "Francisco de Vitoria"* 13 (1960–1961): 164 [137–171]. It was certainly not fully feudal, in the sense that the *encomienda* was not heritable. See Margarita Herrera Ortiz, "La encomienda indiana y sus repercussiones," in *Derechos contemporáneos de los pueblos indios: justicia y derechos étnicos en México* (Mexico City, 1992), 133 [131–142]. See further Lesley Byrd Simpson, *The Encomienda in New Spain* (Berkley, 1982). For the reconquista roots, Lauren Benton, *Law in Colonial Cultures: Legal Regimes in World History* (Cambridge, 2004), 51; and for the roots in medieval feudal grants, Robert S. Chamberlain, *Castilian Backgrounds of the Repartimiento-Encomienda* (Washington, D.C., 1939).

[9] José Maria Ots y Capdequi, *España in America: el régimen de tierras en la época colonial* (Mexico City, 1959), 83–96.

[10] E.g., Aldo Andrea Cassi, *Ius commune tra Vecchio e Nuovo Mondo: mari, terre, oro nel diritto della Conquista* (Milan, 2004), 175–176.

[11] "Semi-feudal": Woodrow Borah, *Justice by Insurance: The General Indian Court of Colonial Mexico and the Legal Aides of the Half-Real* (Berkeley, 1983), 19.

hoc responses to new (though by no means wholly unprecedented[12]) questions, and the problem of enslavement remained open enough that it was subject to serious discussion at Burgos.

That ensuing debate was marked, infamously, by the presence of one great classical authority: Aristotle on natural slavery. Aristotle's ugly theory had recently been promoted by the learned and clever Paris theologian John Mair.[13] It would lend itself to centuries of Western racism; it featured prominently in the discussions of 1512; and its sheer monstrousness has made it the natural focus of most of the scholarship on Burgos.

And it is of course entirely understandable that scholars should focus on the theory of natural slavery at Burgos: Its use in the deliberations place the Junta at the headwaters of centuries of the horrors of modern enslavement, and beyond that modern racism. Nevertheless, we must not neglect the fact that it was not the only legal theory available. The analysis of the conquered Caribbean peoples as natural slaves had to compete with the feudalized characterization of them as "vassals," and their semi-feudal subjection to *encomenderos* as well; and if we are to take proper stock of the significance of Burgos for Western legal history, we must remember that it was the feudalizing analyses that ultimately won the day.

We have no detailed record of the deliberations, but we do have a report given some decades later by Bartolomé de las Casas, and knowledge of the views of two of the participants. One, a pitiless gentleman named Gregorio, took the hard line that the Indians could be enslaved because they were pagans: Since they were "idolators," "Your Majesty may justly punish them with the penalty of slavery."

---

[12] For the background in expansion to the Canaries and Africa, see José Luis Egío García and Christiane Birr, "Before Vitoria: Expansion into Heathen, Empty, or Disputed Lands in Late-Mediaeval Salamanca Writings and Early 16th-Century Juridical Treatises," in Jörg Tellkamp, ed., *A Companion to Early Modern Spanish Imperial Political and Social Thought* (Leiden, 2020), 53–77.

[13] For Mair, see below. See Bartolomé de las Casas, *Historia de las Indias* (Madrid, 1875), 3:392. See the account in Matías de Paz, *Acerca del dominio sobre los indios (Libellus circa dominium super indos)*, ed. and trans. Paulino Castañeda, José Carlos Martín de la Hoz, and Eduardo Fernández (Salamanca, 2017). On Mair, David Lantigua, *Infidels and Empires in a New World Order* (Cambridge, 2020), 78–81.

The second defended a view that was at least somewhat milder: Following Isabella's 1500 assertion of royal rights, Bernardo de Mesa, while he too accepted the Aristotelean doctrine of natural slavery, nevertheless insisted that the Indians were "vassals of Your Majesty, and not slaves."[14] After several sessions, the Junta produced the Laws of Burgos, regulating the status of the subject peoples. Those Laws ratified the free condition of the Amerindians, as Isabella had done. At the same time, however, they left in place the *encomienda*.

The judgment at Burgos was then distilled into one of the most notorious, and riveting, documents in the history of Western expansion. This was the *Requerimiento*, the "Requirement," probably drafted by an elderly canon lawyer who served as a royal councilor, Juan López de Palacios Rubios. The *Requerimiento* was the declaration to be read out, in Castilian or Latin, to the peoples of the New World, in order to put their subjection on a proper legal footing. God, it proclaimed, had entrusted the rulership over the world to St. Peter. In turn, Pope Alexander VI, St. Peter's successor and the vicar of Christ, had determined in 1493 that the New World should be divided between the Spanish and Portuguese monarchies, granting "the islands of the ocean sea" to the former. In consequence, the local inhabitants were now legally "subjects and vassals" of the rulers of Castile.

As "vassals," they were not slaves. To be a vassal of the monarch was to enjoy a form of protected status within the feudal order, as Queen Isabella had made clear in 1500. But that did not mean that the possibility of enslavement was off the table. The status of "vassals," the herald was to announce to indigenous peoples, would be theirs only so long as they chose to obey:

[I]f you do not [submit], and maliciously make delay in it, I certify to you that, with the help of God, we shall powerfully enter into your country, and shall make war against you in all ways and manners that we can, and shall subject

---

[14] Las Casas, *Historia de las Indias*, 3:392. Mesa is occasionally presented as having promoted the theory of natural slavery, Mariano Delgado, "Die Indios als Sklaven von Natur? Aristoteles-Rezeption in der Amerika-Kontroverse im Schatten der spanischen Expansion," in Günter Frank and Andreas Speer, eds., *Der Aristotelismus in frühen Neuzeit: Kontinuität oder Wiederaneignung?* (Wiesbaden, 2007), 359-360 [353-382], but we must be careful to see the full picture: Las Casas' text clearly describes him as defending the status of vassals.

you to the yoke and obedience of the Church and of their Highnesses; we shall take you and your wives and your children, and shall make slaves of them, and as such shall sell and dispose of them as their Highnesses may command; and we shall take away your goods, and shall do you all the mischief and damage that we can, as to vassals who do not obey, and refuse to receive their lord, and resist and contradict him.[15]

So runs one of landmark documents, jaw-dropping in its arrogance, redolent of tragedy, in the history of the West.

These are not events that anybody would cite as belonging to the history of abolitionism. There is not the slightest sign in the *Requerimiento*, or the Junta, or any of the other pronouncements of the time, of any commitment to the enlightened proposition that there can be "no property in man"; the "repugnance" of Blackstone and the "disgust" at the "unbounded dominion" of the ownership of human beings that would be voiced by Hume a quarter millennium later are nowhere to be heard. The illogic of the proposition that humans could be "merchandize, consumed &c." was not apparent to any of the participants. Isabella may have insisted that her "vassals" were not subject to private enslavement. But the throne would continue to decree that "cannibals" and those captured in a just war could be reduced to slavery. The *Requerimiento* may have offered the conquered the status of vassals. But it did so against the background threat of merciless enslavement. Even if the Junta determined that the inhabitants of the Antilles were vassals, no one seems to have thought that that status was inconsistent with the proposition they were also "natural slaves," much though the *Requerimiento* may have graciously accorded them the opportunity to avoid enslavement by submitting.[16] The decimation of the indigenous populations went on unabated; the reading of the *Requerimiento* showed itself to be the tragico-farcical prelude to horrifying depredations; and, not least, the Junta was eventually followed by the massive importation of African captives that scars the moral history of the West.

For all those reasons, Burgos represents the beginning of the horrific history of early modern slavery, not the end. Yet if the Junta of Burgos

---

[15] Translation available at https://nationalhumanitiescenter.org/pds/amerbegin/contact/text7/requirement.pdf.
[16] Pagden, *Fall of Natural Man*, 48.

and the *Requerimiento* are not documents in the rise of enlightened abolitionism, they *are*, paradoxically, documents in the history of the decline of slavery in the Western world. *These are my vassals*, declared Isabella, *not your slaves. Be vassals*, commanded the *Requerimiento*, *or be slaves*. Conquered persons in classical Antiquity faced the prospect of enslavement, plain and simple; no one offered them the option of entering into a juridical status called "vassal" instead. Something different was at work in the early sixteenth century: The *encomenderos* may have brutalized the wretches in the territories granted to them in ways that left them no better off than slaves; but as a technical legal matter, the grant of the *encomienda* was the grant of a territory. The *Requerimiento*, monstrous though it was, offers a glimpse of a shift in the legal imagination, if not in the cruel realities of life on the ground: a passage from slavery to feudalism, at the dawn of the early modern era, presented as an ugly choice to an uncomprehending population under the heel of conquest.[17]

The promises made in the *Requerimiento* were utterly hollow; but Karl Marx was right to say that the passage from slavery to serfdom bespeaks a conceptual reordering of the terms of oppression. The change was no more than incipient in 1512, but the glint of change was visible, if only faintly. For all its arrogance, for all the tragedy that followed, for all the brutality of the *encomenderos*, the *Requerimiento* was a way station in Arnaud's "radical transformation," the transformation from a legal imagination whose understanding of power was founded in the ownership of humans and other living creatures, to a legal imagination whose understanding of power was founded in rights in, and lordship over, land.

* * *

The subsequent three centuries of legal and theological debate allow us to trace the progress of that imaginative transformation.

After the Junta, the King commissioned two treatises, one by the aged canon lawyer Palacios Rubios, and one by the theologian Matías de Paz. Both texts make it clear how difficult it was, at the beginning of the sixteenth century, to work out a land-based, feudalized, conception

---

[17] A full account would of course continue with the New Laws of 1542. I have resisted the temptation to dive more deeply into the question, which would burst the bounds of this book.

of power, despite the long history of the analysis of feudal law running back to the High Middle Ages, and despite the technically feudal tenor of the *Requerimiento*.

I will turn to Paz later in the chapter. For now, I begin with the treatise of López de Palacios Rubios. Palacios Rubios, the presumed draftsman of the infamous *Requerimiento*, was long denounced as "one of the villains in the drama of the Americas' conquest"; and given the horror of that document it is easy to see why. Nevertheless, recent scholarship portrays him in a more sympathetic light.[18] Born in 1440 in the village of Palacios Rubios from which he took his name, he made his way as a young man to the University of Salamanca, the leading Iberian institution of higher learning. He rose to a professorship at Salamanca, and remained there for many decades, acquiring the nickname "El Doctor" for his mastery of canon law. The learned monograph on "the islands of the ocean sea" that the elderly *Doctor* composed, by order of the King, was never printed in his own lifetime, but it circulated widely in manuscript. A partial copy made by Las Casas was rediscovered in the nineteenth century and recently given its first scholarly edition.[19]

Current scholarship emphasizes that Palacios Rubios, no monster, defended some comparatively humane views; and he cannot be described as an advocate of ruthless depredation.[20] Nevertheless, the analysis that his labors yielded showed how elusive, at the beginning of the sixteenth century, were legal arguments that could support the orientation of the *Requerimiento*. The burden of that baleful document was to declare the Amerindians "vassals" of the monarch, and to ratify the use of the semi-feudal *encomienda* as the proper means of controlling them. Yet for the most part, Palacios Rubios only found ways to talk about slavery. This is partly because he, like others of the day, endorsed the Aristotelean theory of natural slavery, if with slight reservations.[21] But his approach to the problem of slavery

---

[18] Birr, "*Dominium* in the Indies," 264; Lorenzo Milazzo, *La Conquista attraverso il diritto: contributi sul discorso ispano-americano* (Milan, 2014), 16–18, and the elegant discussion of Pagden, *Fall of Natural Man*, 50–56.

[19] Juan López de Palacios Rubios, *De las islas del mar océano (Libellus de insulis oceanis)*, eds. Paulino Castañeda Delgado, José Carlos Martín de la Hoz, and Eduardo Fernández (Pamplona, 2013).

[20] Lantigua, *Infidels and Empires*, 62–64.   [21] Pagden, *Fall of Natural Man*, 51–52.

was not just a matter of his use of Aristotle. Other sources mattered to this learned man too. In his legal analysis, he embraced the classical analysis of *occupatio*, with its focus on the capture of slaves and beasts. Not least, as a matter of the will of God, he cited scriptural authority that took the same approach.

This begins with his treatment of the law of *occupatio*, which betrays his debt to Mair, the advocate of the theory of natural slavery. A Scottish theologian of great energy and ingenuity teaching in early sixteenth-century Paris, Mair was the target of much humanist abuse, as a supposed embodiment of benighted Parisian scholasticism, still plunged in medieval darkness. He even earned the supreme honor of being lampooned by Rabelais. Nevertheless, as current scholarship argues, he very much belonged to his humanist age, devoting himself to an unsuccessful effort to master Greek; and his exploitation of Aristotle can appropriately be called a feat of humanism.[22] What Mair engineered was a momentous fusion of ancient law and ancient philosophy: He combined the classical Roman law of *occupatio* with Aristotle's theory of natural slavery. "The first to occupy them [*primus eos occupans* – i.e. the peoples of the Antilles]," he explained in Paris teachings first published in 1510, "justly rules them, for there are clearly slaves by nature ... for as Aristotle says, some are manifestly by nature slaves and some free."[23] This Aristoteleanization of the law was, it must be emphasized, something that the Roman jurists themselves had never attempted. As we saw in Chapter 3, there is no sign of the Aristotelean theory of natural slavery in the ancient juristic texts; for the Romans, enslavement was a fate that could befall anyone, not the lot of natural slaves. Mair's theory was a creative reinterpretation, a bravura display of humanist villainy.

Presumably following his lead, Palacios Rubios too embraced the theory of natural slavery, and like Mair he founded his argument on the Roman law of *occupatio*. To that end, he, like Mair, offered an

---

[22] See James K. Farge, "John Mair: An Historical Introduction," in John Slotemaker and Jeffrey Witt, eds., *A Companion to the Theology of John Mair* (Leiden, 2015), 13–22, and more broadly the other contributions to the same volume.

[23] *Joannes Major in Secundum sententiarum* (n.p., n.d.), *Distinctio* 40, q.3 (Google Books edition, p. 205). There may of course have been anticipations of this analysis of which I am not aware. In any case, the significance of Mair is emphasized by current scholarship.

analysis of *occupatio* that focused almost entirely on the capture of humans and beasts, rather than on the acquisition of land. In so doing, it is important to recognize, he deviated noticeably from medieval tradition.[24] Like Mair, Palacios Rubios belonged to an era of humanist reinterpretation.

To see why, we must bear in mind the fact that the Roman juristic sources offered their early sixteenth-century reader more than one possibility. The texts in the *Digest* of Justinian, as we saw in Chapters 4 and 8, included two different ways of understanding the foundations of ownership. Classical jurists such as Ulpian treated *occupatio* as law of the hunting of humans and animals alike. This was in tune with Ulpian's account of the primeval history of the law, in which humans were originally born free but became subject to enslavement. Late Antiquity, however, saw an important departure, as Aurelius Hermogenianus, a high official of the Emperor Diocletian in the early fourth century, composed the fragment known as *ex hoc iure*. *Ex hoc iure*, produced in the midst of Diocletian's territorializing reforms, focused, not on slavery, but on boundary stones and kingdoms:

> By the ius gentium (*ex hoc iure*) wars were introduced; peoples were distinguished; kingdoms founded; domains of ownership distinguished; boundary stones placed in fields ...[25]

This "large and fruitful" late antique fragment, as Martti Koskeniemmi calls it, with its focus on the ownership of land rather than of living creatures, served as the foundation for medieval analyses of both feudal land relations and monarchy in subsequent centuries,[26] and Palacios Rubios too could presumably have built his analysis upon it, developing a wholly feudal approach to the New World. This would have comported both with the use of the *encomienda*, and with the

---

[24] This is not to deny the medieval roots of the *Requerimiento*. See most recently Yanay Israeli, "The *Requerimiento* in the Old World: Making Demands and Keeping Records in the Legal Culture of Late Medieval Castile," *Law and History Review* 40 (2022): 37–62. For a discussion of other accounts of the medieval roots, Lauren Benton, *They Called It Peace: Worlds of Imperial Violence* (Princeton, 2024), introduction to part I.

[25] D. 1.1.5 Hermogenianus. 1 *juris epit.*, and for the placement Otto Lenel, *Palingenesia iuris civilis* (repr. Frankfurt a.M., 2004), 1: col. 265.

[26] Notably, from a great master, Baldus degli Ubaldi, *In primam Digesti Veteris partem commentaria* (Venice, 1599), 1:10v–11r, developing the doctrine with regard to both private holdings and monarchies.

treatment of Taino as royal vassals. He did not.[27] Turning his back on three centuries of medieval learning on the use of *ex hoc iure* for the analysis of feudal law, he cited the fragment for its account of the introduction of war, which, he argued, justified enslavement.[28]

Slavery thus deeply penetrated his interpretation of the Roman legal texts. But *el Doctor* did not concern himself exclusively with Roman law. He was a canonist, and alongside the Roman legal authorities, he also consulted scripture. Here again, though, the dominion over living creatures played the principal part. The question that Palacios Rubios faced was a familiar one in Iberia, after centuries of war against the Muslims of the peninsula, and decades of overseas expansion by Iberian monarchies. The standard view was that war on infidels was justified for the purpose of spreading the faith. Those were the terms on which the Papacy sanctioned Portuguese expansion, for example,[29] and the same was true of treatments of expansion within Iberia. To take one example, the Italian jurist Oldradus de Ponte declared that war against the Saracens was just – but only because the word of Christ must go "to the ends of the earth." Oldradus cited Psalm 8:

All are subject to Christ, sheep and cattle and beasts of the field, as Psalm 8 tells us ... By "sheep" we understand Christians, of whom the Savior says he is the pastor, and a good shepherd ... But by "beasts of the field" we understand Saracens, who, like beasts lacking reason, abandon the true God and worship idols.[30]

The implication was that lands could be taken, up to "the ends of the earth," but not for the purpose of acquiring land as such. The purpose was to diffuse the faith among peoples, not least among bestial infidels.

---

[27] For the use he did make of it, in connection with Genesis 13, see below.
[28] Palacios Rubios, *De las islas del mar océano*, 98. For a similar focus on war in *ex hoc iure* from a great humanist, see the discussion of Andreas Alciati in Susan Longfield Karr, *Jus Gentium in Humanist Jurisprudence: On Justice and Right* (Leiden and Boston, 2022), 275–276.
[29] E.g., Bull "Dudum cum" of 1436, Bull "Inter caetera" of 1456. The texts of both are conveniently reproduced in Pius Onyemechi Adiele, *The Popes, the Catholic Church, and the Transatlantic Enslavement of Black Africans, 1418–1839* (Hildesheim, 2017), 499, 511.
[30] Oldradus de Ponte, "Consilium LXXII," in Norman Zacour, *Jews and Saracens in the Consilia of Oldradus de Ponte* (Toronto, 1990), 81. Discussed in James Muldoon, "Papal Responsibility for the Infidel: Another Look at Alexander VI's 'Inter caetera,'" *Catholic Historical Review* 64 (1978): 173–174 [168–184].

Palacios Rubios continued to work within this established tradition of theorizing Reconquest and Conquest, putting the focus on the mission of the Church. He began his scriptural analysis by placing the discovery of the New World in the context of sacred history. In the immediate aftermath of the Fall, he explained, God had exercised personal rule over the world. It was only after the flood that human dominion appeared. This had a critical implication for the analysis of the situation on Hispaniola: The appropriate scriptural text for analyzing the parameters of human ownership must be the postdiluvian grant of rights by God to Noah, and Palacios Rubios cited it as such: "Then God blessed Noah and his sons, saying to them, 'Be fruitful and increase in number and fill the earth. The fear and dread of you will fall on all the beasts of the earth, and on all the birds in the sky, on every creature that moves along the ground, and on all the fish in the sea; they are given into your hands" (Gen. 9:1–2).[31] This could possibly be stretched to apply to the taking of land in the Indies. "Filling the earth" formed part of God's directive, and to that extent the passage suited itself to the conquests in the Caribbean. Nevertheless, the burden of God's grant to Noah was clearly on the dominion over living creatures; and that is how Palacios Rubios treated it, directing his reader to St. Augustine's discussion of this command to humankind to "be masters of the beasts."[32]

The rule over living creatures was thus the firm basis of his scriptural analysis, just as it was of his Roman law. Nevertheless, Palacios Rubios did identify one scriptural passage that spoke of the division of land. This was the story of Abram and Lot, who, according to Genesis 13, divided up pasturelands *ut ne litigarent*, as the Vulgate put it, "in order that they should not dispute." Genesis 13 had been highlighted a few years earlier by the Tübingen theologian Konrad Summenhart, another man with a considerable influence on Iberian thinking;[33] and as we shall see, in the generations after Palacios Rubios it would become the

---

[31] Palacios Rubios, *De las islas del mar océano*, 98, on the role of Noah, following Konrad Summenhart, *Tractatus de contractis licitis atque illicitis* (Venice, 1580), 36 (Trac.I, q.10).

[32] Palacios Rubios, *De las islas del mar océano*, 96, citing Augustine, *De Genesi contra Manichaeos* 20, in Corpus Scriptorum Ecclesiasticorum Latinorum 91, ed. Dorothea Weber (Vienna, 1998), 98–99.

[33] Summenhart, *Tractatus de contractis licitis*, 39 (Trac.I, q.12). On Summenhart's treatment of this question, see Jussi Varkemaa, *Conrad Summenhart's Theory of Individual Rights* (Leiden and Boston, 2011), 190–197.

critical proof text in the making of early modern property law oriented toward land. The history of the rise of the land orientation in early modern law is, indeed, in many ways the history of the interpretation of the tale told in Genesis 13.

This fertile biblical passage began by describing the wealth of Abram and Lot, in the familiar scriptural way, as consisting primarily in beasts:

> ² Now Abram was very rich in livestock, in silver, and in gold. ...
>
> ⁵ Now Lot, who went with Abram, also had flocks and herds and tents.

It was their great wealth in "livestock" and "flocks and herds" that compelled them to divide the land:

> ⁶ and the land could not support both of them living together because their possessions were so great that they could not live together.
>
> ⁷ Thus strife [*rixa*, "brawling," in the Latin of the Vulgate] arose between the herders of Abram's livestock and the herders of Lot's livestock ...
>
> ⁸ Then Abram said to Lot, "Let there be no strife between you and me and between your herders and my herders, for we are kindred.
>
> ⁹ Is not the whole land before you? Separate yourself from me. If you take the left hand, then I will go to the right, or if you take the right hand, then I will go to the left."

The resulting division was a fateful one:

> ¹² Abram settled in the land of Canaan, while Lot settled among the cities of the plain and moved his tent as far as Sodom.

Here was a passage, the first in the Genesis narrative, that clearly spoke of some sort of division of land – and one that resulted, fatefully, in Lot's settlement by Sodom and Abram's in the hills of Canaan. Palacios Rubios noted that the tale of Abram and Lot could be read alongside *ex hoc iure*, and used to provide a justification for private property: Genesis 13 sanctioned the division of lands, he argued, following a suggestion in Summenhart, "because things held in common are naturally neglected."³⁴ This was the first of many early

---

³⁴ Palacios Rubios, *De las islas del mar océano*, 98, 124. Cf. Summenhart, *Tractatus de contractis licitis atque illicitis*, 31 (Tract. 1, q. 9): *quod communitatis est, negligitur*. Summenhart elsewhere mentioned that private property was expedient because otherwise lands would remain *inculte*. This was, however, only one of four justifications he ultimately offered. As Varkemaa translates it, "First the earth would have remained uncultivated and become a desert. Second, the path would be open to fraud

modern Iberian efforts to defend private property in land on this biblical basis, and it hinted at the familiar modern justification for the ownership of land as giving incentives to improve. Nevertheless, Palacios Rubios did not make all that much of it. Genesis 13 came long after the original grant of property rights to Man by God; and he discussed it essentially only in passing. The accent, in his reading of scripture as in his reading of Roman law, was on slavery and the mastery over beasts.

Why did dominion over land not figure more prominently in *el Doctor*'s effort to give technical legal substance to the commands of the Junta? Why did he cite so much authority justifying enslavement? Why did he not simply rely on the familiar text of *ex hoc iure* as he explicated the feudal law of the *Requerimiento*, as medieval jurists would presumably have done before him? Why did not he not simply embrace "Colonialism as Feudalism"?[35]

One possible answer, of course, is that he was entirely under the spell of John Mair, and so a participant in a dawning European culture of racism. But his analysis was by no means limited to the theory of natural slavery, and there is also another possibility: He was a prisoner of his scriptural sources. Confronted by the novel challenges of governing "the ends of the earth," Palacios Rubios felt constrained to seek wisdom from God; and almost all of the texts from Genesis, as we saw in Chapter 2, omitted land from their recitations of the nature of ownership, which was repeatedly described as consisting in "sheep and cattle... and slaves male and female" and the like. Any attentive reader of Genesis would naturally be led to the conclusion that dominion was properly dominion over living creatures, both human and animal. This seemed indeed clear from the very first creation of humanity: "God said, 'Let us make mankind in our image, in our likeness, so that they may rule over the fish in the sea and the birds in the sky, over the livestock and all the wild animals, and over all the creatures that move

---

and malice. Third, the good [people] would always have less and the bad more. Fourth, there would never be peace among mankind." Varkemaa, *Summenhart*, 192. The first and fourth are the ones upon which Vitoria would seize. This teaching was foreshadowed in William of Ockham. See Richard Scholz, ed., *Wilhelm von Ockham und sein Breviloquium* (repr. Stuttgart, 1952), 127 (Bk. 3, chapter 7): *a pluribus communia minus diliguntur* ("what is communally owned, is neglected").

[35] Martti Koskenniemi, *To the Uttermost Parts of the Earth: Legal Imagination and International Power, 1300–1870* (Cambridge, 2021), 726–736.

along the ground'" (Gen. 1:26). Only with chapter 13, very late in the Genesis narrative, did the division of land come into the picture. It was no easy task to build a land-oriented property law out of such biblical timber.

* * *

There were thus two considerable obstacles to the development of a law oriented toward the rule over land rather than the rule over living creatures, one philosophical and one scriptural. The philosophical obstacle lay in the Aristotelean theory of natural slavery, which counted, with the work of John Mair, as cutting-edge humanist science. The scriptural obstacle lay in the texts of Genesis, which introduced the division of land into their account of history only in chapter 13. Both obstacles were overcome in the following decade, by one of the great figures in the Western legal tradition, Francisco de Vitoria, the luminescent Thomist mind best remembered today for his *Relectio de Indis* of 1539, which vigorously defended the humanity of the conquered peoples of the New World and denied that they could be enslaved. Vitoria showed the path to a different reading of Aristotle, based on something other than the theory of natural slavery; and he succeeded in making the tale of Abram and Lot the most important source of biblical authority for property law. In so doing he paved the way to a law that would focus squarely on the ownership of land, rather than on the ownership of humans, in subsequent generations. As we shall see, he paved the way for the political theory of John Locke as well.

Vitoria made his arguments in lectures that he gave on St. Thomas Aquinas' *Summa theologiae* at Salamanca in the 1520s, which were never published in his lifetime but which were clearly known to the scholars of Salamanca and elsewhere. He was, of course, a Thomist; St. Thomas was, of course, an Aristotelean; and to understand both the complexity and the ingenuity of his argument, we must first acquaint ourselves with certain theories of Aristotle and Aquinas.

I begin with Aristotle. The texts of Aristotle offer, it goes without saying, more than just the theory of natural slavery. In Book 2 of the *Politics*, Aristotle mounted, in particular, a defense of the institution of the private ownership of land – one that is little remembered among property theorists today, but that served as the chief justification for private property in land for more than a millennium, down into the mid nineteenth century.

This once-dominant Aristotelean defense of landownership took a very different form from the justifications offered in classrooms and law reviews today. Modern theorists, as we saw in Chapter 1, generally justify private property in land (and other resource-rich territories) as a response to the threat of the tragedy of the commons. "Farmlands, pastures, hunting or fishing territories," according to modern theory, must be exclusively owned, because in the absence of exclusive rights to territories, their resources will be exploited by competing users to the point of exhaustion. Aristotle had an entirely different problem in mind. His defense of private property in land had nothing to do with the dangers of resource exhaustion in the absence of exclusive ownership. Instead, it was his argument that individual ownership was necessary in order to preserve resource-*sharing* in societies prone to interpersonal conflict.

The analysis of the *Politics* started from the un-Blackstonian proposition that the use of the fruits of the land must be shared in common: It was essential that all members of the community be able to draw on the resources of the territories claimed by the community as a whole. But the imperative of common use could not be met through what might seem the most natural approach (and the one favored by Plato), communism. To show why this was so, Aristotle began by describing three forms of the organization of land and resource rights, all involving some variety of communism:

Should the farms be separate property but the farm-produce be brought into the common stock for consumption (as is the practice with some non-Greek peoples); or on the contrary should the land be common and farmed in common, but the produce be divided for private use (and this form of communism also is said to prevail among some of the barbarians); or should both farms and produce be common property?

If there was to be communism, should it be communism of resources, communism of land, or both? The question did not present itself, Aristotle continued, in a system that could rely on the labor of slaves or helots: "[I]f the tillers of the soil be of a different class there might be another and easier system." In a society in which slaves were burdened with all the work, the class of free persons could share harmoniously together, living off the sweat of coerced labor. But in the absence of large-scale agrarian slavery, it was necessary to come up with some solution that would preserve the common interest in resources even though the work had to be done by free individuals themselves.

Yet no such solution could depend on the communal ownership of land. For where there was common ownership among free persons, there was a grave risk that social life could take an ugly turn:

If the citizens do the work for themselves, the regulations for the common ownership of property would give more causes for grumbling and resentment [δυσκολία]; for if both in the enjoyment of the produce and in the work of production they prove not equal but unequal, complaints are bound to arise between those who enjoy or take much but work little and those who take less but work more. And in general to live together and share all our human affairs is difficult, and especially to share such things as these ...

Traveling companions, for example, Aristotle pointed out, often squabbled; and what was true of travelers was true of all communal settings. The only possible safeguard lay in the private ownership of land:

Community of property therefore involves these and other similar difficulties; and the present system [i.e. of private ownership of land], if further improved by good morals and by the regulation of correct legislation, would be greatly superior. For it will possess the merit of both systems, by which I mean the advantage of property being common and the advantage of its being private. For property ought to be common in a sense but private speaking absolutely. For the superintendence of properties being divided among the owners will not cause these mutual complaints, and each will busy himself with his own;[36] while on the other hand virtue will be exercised to make "friends' goods common goods," as the proverb goes, for the purpose of use.[37]

Private property in land was indispensable to forestall the δυσκολία, the "grumbling and resentment," that would otherwise disrupt communal solidarity in societies that did not have the luxury of

---

[36] Arist. *Pol.* 1263a, in H. Rackham, trans., *Aristotle: Politics*, Loeb Classical Library 264 (Cambridge, MA, 1932), 84–87. The Loeb translation has "and will improve the more because each will apply himself to it as to private business of his own." I have altered this rendering, which risks implying a culture of improvement that did not clearly take hold until later centuries.

[37] *Pol.* 1262b–1263, trans. Rackham, 81–87.

saddling slaves with all the work. But if Aristotle saw private property as necessary for the avoidance of conflict in a society that did not enjoy the blessings of mass agrarian slavery, he also saw it as worrisome, since it threatened to endanger the imperative of common use. One possible response was legislation – a possibility upon which Grotius and Blackstone would later expand: As we shall see, this is the Aristotelean source for a critical modern doctrine for preserving the common interest in resources, eminent domain. But Aristotle's principal solution was that the human impulse to share, at least among friends, would guarantee that the undoubted necessity of common use would be met even in a private property regime.

Private property in land was necessary because it permitted communities to avoid δυσκολία – what the *Pierson* v. *Post* court, in 1805, would call "quarrels and litigation"[38] – even as the norms of friendship guaranteed that the imperative of sharing resources would be met. As its appearance in *Pierson* v. *Post* suggests, this Aristotelean argument remained at the heart of property thought for more than two thousand years. But the theory underwent a significant change in the hands of Aristotle's successors. For Aristotle, the imperative of the sharing of resources was to be met through the norms of friendship, a favorite topic of his. Christian commentators, from Aquinas to Vitoria and beyond, by contrast, put their faith in the command of God to exercise charity. And from Grotius onward, the answer was sought in a new doctrine: eminent domain.

* * *

Christian theory was theory of sin. It held that private property was a depraved institution, which only appeared after humankind's Fall from the state of innocence. This was a teaching that drew on the broader Greco-Roman tradition of belief in "primitive communism," described in Chapter 1. Primitive communism, as we saw, was something of an article of faith in Greco-Roman Antiquity, among pagans and Christians alike. A particularly influential statement came from Cicero, who declared that land was "by nature common property," and only artificially appropriated and distributed. "There

---

[38] *Pierson* v. *Post*, 3 Cai. R. 175 (1805).

is," Cicero insisted, "no such thing as private ownership established by nature."[39]

This was the tradition that the Latin Christian tradition integrated into the sacred history of the Fall, ascribing the golden age of primitive communism to the state of innocence in the Garden of Eden. Peter Garnsey describes how St. Ambrose Christianized the teachings of Cicero in the fourth century. "Ambrose," he writes, brought "the Fall into play." God created a world full of things that were all too liable to inspire, in fallen men, sinful thoughts of avarice:

And God said: "Let the waters bring forth creeping things that have life, and birds that fly above the earth in the firmament of heaven" ... Alas, even before the arrival of man, there had appeared worldly allurements, the source of our extravagant living. Pleasures came first, man afterwards. Man's temptations were in place before man made his appearance ... However Nature was not at fault: it furnished nourishment for man but did not lay down that he should be vicious.

"Nature," railed Ambrose at his listeners, anticipating Marx on commodity-lust, "provided things for you to share, not to claim as your own."[40] Yet "vicious" humans continued to desire and acquire, destining themselves to damnation.

The Fall of Man was a fall from virtuous communism, which only Christ could repair. Garnsey makes a particular point of arguing for the Aristotelean sources of the Christian communism proclaimed in Acts 4:32–34: "All the believers were one in heart and mind. No one claimed that any of their possessions was their own, but they shared everything they had ... there were no needy persons among them. For from time to time those who owned land or houses sold them and brought money from the sales." This Christian ideal of communism, Garnsey argues, was "a theme taken over from the classical philosophical tradition":

We think of Plato, *Republic*; of Aristotle on friendship in the *Nichomachean Ethics*, citing what he calls "the common tags," "friends are of one soul," and "friends have goods in common"; and also of Cicero *On Duties*.[41]

---

[39] Cic. *Off.* 1.21, in Walter Miller, trans., *Cicero: On Duties*, Loeb Classical Library 30 (Cambridge, MA, 1913), 22–23.

[40] Garnsey, *Thinking about Property: From Antiquity to the Age of Revolution* (Cambridge, 2007), 61. For the fuller treatment, Ambrose, *Expositio de Psalmo CXVIII*, Corpus Scriptorum Ecclesiasticorum Latinorum 62 (Vienna, 1913), 163–164.

[41] Garnsey, *Thinking about Property*, 61.

Garnsey is, as always, a most welcome guide. We can indeed trace a line of influence from Aristotelean friendship to Christian communism, and from there to Christian charity. But it deserves emphasis that the conversion of Aristotelean friendship into Christian charity had far-reaching implications.

Those implications can be seen in the work of Aristotle's greatest Christian expositor, Thomas Aquinas. In considering the question of private property, Aquinas relied, as so often, on "the philosopher"; but following his practice he Christianized him, and in two ways. First, as Garnsey suggests, Aquinas altered the analysis of the imperative of sharing: The key question became, not what friends were naturally inclined to share among themselves, but what charity required all owners to share with all "needy persons." Second, Aquinas historicized the problem, integrating it, as Ambrose had done, into sacred history. For Aristotle, the question had been the synchronic one of how private property orders function in a community that cannot offload the labor onto slaves; for Aquinas, the question became the diachronic one of how the private property order arose in the first place.

His principal attack on the problem appears in the first Part of his *Summa theologiae*, dating to sometime after 1265. Aquinas, like the ancient Church Fathers, now treated private property as a consequence of the Fall. There had been no private property in Eden; only after the expulsion from Paradise had ownership entered the world.[42] But he was no longer content simply to treat private property as Ambrose had done, as the fruit of the sin of avarice. Instead, wielding the analytic tools he had acquired from Aristotle, Aquinas set out to explain the precise social mechanism that had given rise to private ownership. The δυσκολία, the "grumbling and resentment," of the *Politics* now became *discordia*, "strife."[43] This was a somewhat more ominous word that, as we shall see, might easily cover violence. It is a term that must be seen against the background of what Heiko Oberman describes as the

---

[42] Ibid., 93–94.
[43] I am not certain of the source of Aquinas' use of this term. William of Morbeke, Aristotle's thirteenth-century translator, used *difficultates* and *accusationes*. Aristotle, *Politica*, trans. Morbeke (Cologne, March 8, 1492), ad loc. (Google incunabulum, p. 45). Similarly in the text of *Aristoteles Latinus*, ed. Petrus Michaud-Quantin (Bruges and Paris, 1961), by an uncertain translator, 30.

"particularly intensive" "longing for peace" among medieval theologians; for peace went by the name, not just of *pax*, but of *concordia*.[44] It was the threat of its opposite, *discordia*, Aquinas held, that had required the "division of possessions" after the Fall:

> In our present [fallen] state a division of possessions is necessary on account of the multiplicity of owners (*domini*), inasmuch as community of possession is a source of *discordia*, as the Philosopher says (Politic. ii, 5). In the state of innocence, however, the will of men would have been so ordered that without any danger of *discordia* they would have used in common, according to each one's need, those things of which they were owners – a state of things to be observed even now among many good men.[45]

The division of possessions, an institution of human, not divine or natural, law, was indispensable for averting *discordia* in a world of sin. That said, this *divisio* did not, of course, eliminate the obligation of charity to others, commanded in Acts and so many other Christian texts. As Aquinas put it, anticipating a famous line from Locke to which we will return: "whatever some people have in superabundance is owed by natural law to the sustenance of the poor" (II-II q. 66, a. 7).

* * *

With this, Aquinas established the basic terms for early modern land-focused property thought as it emerged in the neo-Thomist tradition of the Second Scholastic of sixteenth-century Iberia, whose most brilliant and innovative early figure was Vitoria.

Let us see, then, what Vitoria made of Aristotle and Aquinas in the lectures he held at Salamanca in the fourth decade of Iberian presence "at the ends of the earth." The Christian tradition had always held that the "state of innocence" had been a state of primitive communism, which had only given way to private property after the Fall. Aquinas

---

[44] Oberman, *Dawn of the Reformation: Essays in Late Medieval and Early Reformation Thought* (Edinburgh, 1986), 30.

[45] *Summa theologiae* I-I q. 68: in statu isto, multiplicatis dominis, necesse est fieri divisionem possessionum, quia communitas possessionis est occasio discordiae, ut philosophus dicit in II Politic. Sed in statu innocentiae fuissent voluntates hominum sic ordinatae, quod absque omni periculo discordiae communiter usi fuissent, secundum quod unicuique eorum competeret, rebus quae eorum dominio subdebantur, cum hoc etiam modo apud multos bonos viros observetur. This critically important passage appears in Aquinas' discussion of generation (whence multiplicatis dominis). Available at www.corpusthomisticum.org/sth1090.html.

had given Aristotelean analytic substance to the tale of the rise of private property *after* the Fall, explaining that it was necessary in order to avert *discordia*. Vitoria now took St. Thomas' approach a bold step further: He set out to explain, not just the sociolegal dynamics of the rise of private property after the Fall, but the sociolegal dynamics of the state of innocence itself. His analysis, which pried open, as it were, the black box of innocence, carried implications, not only for property law, but also for political theory as it would develop down into the writings of Locke.

Vitoria framed his problem in the conceptual terms of what I have been calling "the chieftainship over people." As we have seen throughout earlier chapters, most human property orders have assumed what Marshall Sahlins calls "political control": Rights in land are distributed by the authority of a chief. Vitoria began by assuming the necessity of just such a system. In the beginning, he observed, echoing Ulpian, "all men were equal by natural law." This primitive state of equality had an important consequence: It made private property impossible. This is a statement sure to baffle modern readers. Why should equality be incompatible with private property? Surely, we would say, the opposite is the case. The answer is that ownership, for Vitoria, remained dependent, in the first instance, on political control. Private property required a division of goods, as Aquinas had explained. Yet there could not be any division of goods in the state of innocence, since such a division could only be ordered by a chief: "there was no chief (*princeps*) by natural law: therefore nobody could order the necessary division."[46]

---

[46] Vitoria, *Comentarios a la Secunda secundae de Santo Tomaso*, ed. Vicente Beltran de Heredia (Salamanca, 1934), 3:77 (=commentary on q.62, Art.1, n.21). Vitoria was drawing, once again, on Summenhart, *Tractatus de contractis licitis atque illicitis*, 39 (Tract. I, Quaestio 12). The deeper history extends to William of Ockham, whose account focused on the moment in which God granted humans the *potestas rectores eligendi iurisdictionem habentes*. See Richard Scholz, *Wilhelm von Ockham als Politischer Denker und sein "Breviloquium de Principatu tyrannico"* (Stuttgart, 1952), 128, and generally the *Breviloquium*, Bk. III, chapters 7–11, at 125–132. Ockham, sticking close to the scriptural sources, did not, however, speak of the ownership of land as such. For a useful general account of his theory, see Jürgen Miethke, *Ockhams Weg zur Sozialphilosophie* (Berlin, 1969), 467–477. Here again it is with some reluctance that I leave aside the fuller history of Franciscan controversies in order to keep this book within reasonable limits. For further discussion of this theory in Vitoria, see Annabel Brett, *Liberty, Right and Nature* (Cambridge, 1997), 131.

There was no prince in Paradise, and therefore no private property. How then had division eventually come to pass? Vitoria's answer lay in original sin: After the Fall, Adam became the chief. "After leaving Paradise, since he was a *paterfamilias*, he could make the division of possessions with the consent of his sons (*ex consensu filiorum*), and he divided them as seemed to him appropriate at that time."[47] The Fall produced, for the first time, *patria potestas*, and with it a system of hierarchical authority without which private property rights could not exist. Stepping through the gates of Paradise, Adam emerged into the age of sin with the power to divide: just as Diocletian would divide "the whole world into four parts" after him; just as Pope Alexander VI, acting as chief of all the globe in his role as the vicar of Christ, would divide the New World between the Spanish and the Portuguese in 1493.[48]

Yet even Adam had acted "with the consent of his sons"; he was, as it were, a constitutional chieftain. Moreover, the operation of chieftainship after the Fall had many mansions. It was also possible for humans to choose, by common consent, a chief who could undertake the necessary division. What is more, and most importantly in Vitoria's analysis, there was a third route to division, which did not require the action of a chief at all. This came through division by mere consent, undertaken, in the spirit of Aristotle and Aquinas, in order to prevent discord.

It was here that Vitoria shifted the emphasis within Genesis squarely to the tale of Abram and Lot in Genesis 13. As we saw, Abram and Lot, disturbed by the "brawling" between their herdsmen, divided up pasturelands "in order that they should not dispute." This was a biblical text that suited itself admirably to the Aristotelean/Thomist approach founded in the threat of *discordia*: The tale was of nothing other than *discordia* and division. That said, it is important to emphasize the contrast between this Old Testament text and the theory of Aristotle: Aristotle believed that private property was necessary in order to permit humans to live together. The implication

---

[47] Vitoria, *Comentarios*, 3:78. He drew here on Summenhart's arguments, which can be found in *Tractatus de contractis licitis atque illicitis*, 31–40 (Tract. 1, qq. 1–9).

[48] The connection was clear enough to François I, who offered the famous sour commentary "Je voudrais bien voir la clause du testament d'Adam qui m'exclut du partage du monde."

of the division between Abram and Lot, by contrast, was that humans must live apart. *Discordia*, unlike δυσκολία, was too powerful a solvent to permit communal coexistence.

In any case, Genesis 13 was a precedent that permitted private ownership of a momentous kind. For the implication of the doings of Abram and Lot was that division was possible *even in a society with no supreme political authority*, through the operation of mere consent.[49] Vitoria was careful to note the limitations of his scriptural proof text. It was true that Abram and Lot had succeeded in a peaceable division of lands; but dealings between them were easy, since they were only two, and "brothers" to boot.[50] Was such a procedure possible when humans numbered in the thousands? Yes, held Vitoria, in a move with powerful implications, since the larger number could impose its will on the smaller.[51] Finally, and crucially, a system of tacit consent to division could occur through *occupatio*. But it is essential to emphasize how this tacit division took place in Vitoria's account. The acquisition of land through *occupatio* was achieved, not merely through presence on the land, but through tillage: The division developed as some men began to "cultivate certain lands" and others began to cultivate others.[52] It was the investment of agricultural labor that justified ownership.

With this vision of the emergence of private property after the Fall, we arrive at a crucial moment in the early modern history of the law of *occupatio*, and more broadly in the history of property law. Land now occupied the foreground. For Palacios Rubios a decade and a half earlier, *occupatio* had been principally what it was for the classical jurists, for the compilers of Genesis, and for John Mair: a law of the dominion over living creatures – a law, in St. Augustine's terms, of "masters over beasts." Vitoria's *occupatio* was becoming what it

---

[49] This followed a suggestion made by Summenhart, though without delving as deeply into the text: Genesis 13 demonstrated that lands could be divided merely "through the common consent of men." Summenhart, *Tractatus de contractis licitis atque illicitis*, 39 (Trac.I, q.12).
[50] Actually uncle and nephew. For discussion of the theological background, see Dan Rickett, *Separating Abram and Lot: The Narrative Role and Early Reception of Genesis 13* (Leiden, 2020), 158–182.
[51] Vitoria, *Comentarios*, n. 22, at 3:78–79.
[52] Ibid., n. 23, at 3:79. This was a substantial expansion of the brief mention of this issue by Summenhart at *Tractatus de contractis licitis atque illicitis*, 31 (Tract.I, q.9).

would be thereafter, for Grotius, for Locke, for Kant, and for modern property law: a law primarily of the settlement of land. Equally importantly, it was becoming what it would be within the Lockean tradition down to the Supreme Court's decision in *Johnson v. M'Intosh*: the law of acquisition through tillage. And the law of acquisition through tillage was law of ownership with politically radical implications: It could exist independently of any system of organized political power with the authority to divide.

Still, Vitoria's commitment to the land orientation went only just so far. He was, as Annabel Brett emphasizes, by no means a Blackstonian. His *Relectio de Indis*, the great text that acknowledged the property rights of the indigenous populations of the New World, also denied them the Blackstonian right to exclude: Vitoria insisted on the right of "travel" (*peregrinari*); the lands could not be closed to the Iberian arrivals, who retained the right to engage in missionizing, and also the right to seek out "unoccupied" resources, precious metals among them.[53] Borders remained porous for Vitoria; rights were rights in resources, which ripened only upon *occupatio*. That implied that resources that had not yet been subjected to "actual corporeal possession" by the inhabitants of the New World could not be denied to their colonizers. As Lauren Benton and Benjamin Straumann remark, mineral resources were to be treated as though they were the wild animal prey of classical Roman property law.[54] Tragedy, as we all know, followed for the indigenous populations.

How troubled Vitoria was by that tragedy is hard to say. Certainly there is no doubt that the law of *occupatio*, in his hands, proved to be less than a law of justice. In any case, his capacious analysis laid out the basic set of arguments that would reappear in later early modern authors, in Iberia and elsewhere. Brett has given us a superb study of those arguments. As she shows, Vitoria's successors came to insist on the power of the holder of *dominium* to exclude, distancing themselves from Vitoria's right to travel. In that sense, they began to push the understanding of territoriality in a more Blackstonian direction. But

---

[53] Annabel Brett, *Changes of State: Nature and the Limits of the City in Early Modern Natural Law* (Princeton, 2011), 14, taking some issue with Antony Anghie, *Imperialism, Sovereignty and the Making of International Law* (Cambridge, 2005).

[54] Benton and Straumann, "Acquiring Empire by Law: From Roman Doctrine to Early Modern European Practice," *Law and History Review* 28 (2010): 22 [1–36].

the change, as Brett demonstrates, was by no means without limits: Vitoria's successors, both in Iberia and elsewhere, continued to insist that the power to exclude was tempered by the Christian obligation of charity, which dictated some measure of the sharing of the use of resources. In particular, it required a kind of law of free movement for the beggars who were populating the roads and countryside of early modern Europe.[55]

An especially important statement came from Vitoria's younger Salamanca colleague, and another great figure in the making of modern property law, Domingo de Soto. In his writings of the 1550s, de Soto, a cleric of sufficient stature to be the confessor of Emperor Charles V, began by echoing Aristotle and Vitoria on the division of the soil: Division was necessary in order that fallen men might live in peace. But he now put the accent on another consideration: Private property, he argued, echoing Summenhart, was necessary *ut agri colentur*, "*in order that* the fields should be cultivated."[56] With this, we see what may be the first really forceful statement of a doctrine that would continue powerfully into the late eighteenth century, and from there into present-day property theory: Private property in land was indispensable, not only in order to keep the peace in face of the threat of *discordia*, but in order to guarantee that fields were put to productive use.[57]

In that sense, de Soto was pioneering the modern conception of ownership, and he was doing so in another sense as well, as Brett emphasizes: In de Soto's view, unlike Vitoria's, the division of land into *dominia* conferred the right to exclude.[58] Borders, in principle, could be closed. Yet for all that, it is essential to emphasize the limits of de Soto's claims: Only use rights, he continued to hold, had existed under the natural law that reigned before the Fall: "by natural law [as in the state of innocence] that which previously belonged to no one

---

[55] Brett, *Changes of State*, 15–19 and often.
[56] De Soto, *De iustitia et iure* (Lyons, 1569), 42 (1.5.4): "[I]f man, a fallen creature, lives in a state of communism, he will not diligently cultivate fields, nor will he live in peace."
[57] This was, to be sure, once again an expansion of the argument of Summenhart. See above, n. 34. For the older proposition in John of Paris that "industry" justified property rights, see Janet Coleman, "*Dominium* in Thirteenth- and Fourteenth-Century Political Thought and Its Seventeenth-Century Heirs: John of Paris and Locke," *Political Studies* 33 (1985): 73–100.
[58] Brett, *Changes of State*, 24–25.

becomes the possession of the first possessor, but not with regard to the rights of ownership (*dominium*). The first possessor acquires only the right of first use. By natural law, all things are held in common."[59] This primordial imperative of common use had never entirely vanished. Even after the Fall, the right to exclude was always accompanied by the duty to give succor to beggars, the "travelers" of metropolitan Europe.[60] For de Soto, as for Aquinas and Vitoria, the natural law of use rights was transmuted into a moral imperative of charity.

* * *

The subsequent juristic literature developed many elegant arguments, generally amid citations of Hermogenianus' late antique *ex hoc iure* and Genesis 13, always endorsing the power to exclude while acknowledging the demands of charity and especially the claims of beggars.[61] I leave the details of those arguments, which are presented with crisp and admirable learning by Brett, aside, to focus on the contributions of Hugo Grotius, which pushed property law dramatically toward its familiar modern Blackstonian form.

As Stephen Buckle has observed, Grotius, the genius already celebrated for his learning when he was a child, held, like his predecessors running back to Aquinas and Vitoria, that property originally consisted in use rights, with an obligation to share; but his argument took him well beyond that starting point.[62] Now drawing on historical and ethnographic argument, in the style of brilliant late sixteenth-century predecessors such as Michel de Montaigne and Jean Bodin, he brought the discussion of the origins of private property a large step further out of the domain of sacred history.

To be sure, Grotius still depended on scriptural authority. In particular, he was guided, as was his predecessor Vitoria, by the tale of the strife between the herders of Abram and Lot.[63] But he now

---

[59] De Soto, *Relectio de dominio*, 142, my translation.
[60] Brett, *Changes of State*, 27, in de Soto's view of the right to beg. See also Maureen Flynn, *Sacred Charity: Confraternities and Social Welfare in Spain, 1400–1700* (Ithaca, N.Y., 1989), 96.
[61] E.g., Brett, *Changes of State*, 34, on Luís de Molina; 201–202 on Molina and Alberico Gentili.
[62] Stephen Buckle, *Natural Law and the Theory of Property: Grotius to Hume* (Oxford, 2002), 11.
[63] Ibid., 39–40, also pointing to the Tower of Babel.

treated this scriptural exemplum in a new way, as evidence for the early course of human social evolution. The brawling between the people of Abram and the people of Lot was brawling between pastoralists, not agriculturalists; and Grotius concluded that after the Flood there was private property in *pecora*, domesticated beasts, but not yet in land.[64] This was of course a belief that seemed well supported by the remains of archaic Roman law. With time, however, Grotius explained, in line with the Genesis narrative, beasts became more numerous, and it became necessary to divide land among families, as Abram and Lot had done.[65]

Following Vitoria, Grotius believed that this process of division need not necessarily have been ordered by a chief. It could have taken place tacitly, through *occupatio* alone: "This happened not by a mere act of will, for one could not know what things another wished to have, in order to abstain from them – and besides several might desire the same thing – but rather by a kind of agreement, either by division, or tacitly, as by *occupatio*."[66] Again like Vitoria, Grotius now interpreted the law of *occupatio*, in the first instance, as law of land. His full account of the law of *occupatio* thus began with the possession of "places as yet not cultivated" before turning only in the second place to the beasts, fish, and birds that were the objects of ancient *occupatio*.[67] Here we see Arnaud's "radical transformation" working its spell on the mind of the great seventeenth-century jurist.

And what about the obligation of charity? For Grotius as for the Thomists, there remained no doubt about the "duty to share with those in need."[68] But Grotius placed this duty on a new basis, pioneering a doctrine with a great future before it, eminent domain.[69] In the original state of nature, he explained, reciting the standard view, there had only been a right of use, which meant that those in need could always supply themselves. But the rise of private property changed that primitive state of affairs: Owners now held the

---

[64] Grotius, *De jure belli ac pacis*, ed. Jean Barbeyrac (Utrecht, 1773), 1:209–210 (2.2.3–4).
[65] Ibid. [66] Ibid., 1:210 (2.2.5). [67] Ibid., 1:213 (2.2.4): *loca multa inculta adhuc*.
[68] Steven Forde, "The Charitable John Locke," *Review of Politics* 71 (2009): 439 [428–458].
[69] For Grotius' originality, Susan Reynolds, *Before Eminent Domain: Toward a History of Expropriation for the Common Good* (Chapel Hill, 2010), 92–96.

fundamental power to exclude. To be sure, not all persons chose to exercise this fundamental power. Communism did sometimes exist in human societies. Exclusionary ownership was not present among the ancient Scythians, who still lived in wholly primitive circumstances, and the same was true of the natives of the New World.[70] Most importantly, the power to exclude had been renounced by the Essenes and primitive Christians of Acts.

But the Scythians and New World Indians were what Europeans of Grotius' age regarded as savages; and the Essenes and primitive Christians were people, Grotius wrote, capable of *eximia caritas*, "superlative charity."[71] This was more than could be expected of most persons. How then was the duty to share to be met? The answer, Grotius held, drawing on a medieval tradition that was reconstructed with great learning by Ugo Nicolini in 1940,[72] was that the king retained the right to make of use of property in cases of extreme necessity. Medieval jurists had broadly agreed that the king was not the "owner" of the lands of Christendom. His power, they generally argued, was the power of rule, *imperium*, not of the power of ownership, *dominium*. Grotius, by contrast, now held that his powers did indeed give the king a certain form of circumscribed *dominium*, a "royal property right for the common good": "[W]ith regard to the things of private persons, the *dominium* of the king is superior, as to the common good (*ad bonum commune*), to the rights of private owners." This was the *facultas eminens*, or *supereminens dominium*, the "eminent power" or "supereminent ownership," and through its exercise the common right of use survived the rise of private property rights.[73] This represented, wrote Grotius, "a kind of benign reception of primitive rights" in the law of regal power.[74]

[70] Grotius, *De jure belli ac pacis*, ed. Barbeyrac, 1:206–208 (2.2.1).
[71] Ibid., 1:206 (2.2.1).
[72] Nicolini, *La proprietà: il principe e l'espropriazione per pubblica utilità* (Milan, 1940), 126–127, and generally the valuable discussion at 126–134.
[73] Vitoria, as Feenstra points out, had already used the phrase *dominium eminens*, but without evident influence on Grotius. Robert Feenstra, "Der Eigentumsbegriff bei Hugo Grotius im Licht einiger mittelalterlicher und spätscholastischer Quellen," in Okko Behrends, Malte Dießelhorst, Hermann Lange, Detlef Liebs, Joseph Georg Wolf, and Christian Wollschläger, eds., *Festschrift für Franz Wieacker zum 70. Geburtstag* (Göttingen, 1978), 219 [209–234].
[74] Grotius, *De jure belli ac pacis*, ed. Barbeyrac, 1:215 (2.2.6.4): *cum benigna quadam receptione primitivi iuris*. Feenstra expresses some reservations about Nicolini's

The state was the "benign receptacle" of the primordial common right of the use that had existed before the Fall. Here was Grotius' answer to the problem first bruited by Aristotle in the *Politics*. Aristotle had tried to solve the problem by looking to norms of friendship, necessary to resolve the conflicts of a society unable to depend on slave labor and prone to squabbling. The Thomist theological tradition had looked instead to the Christian duty of charity. Grotius now located the solution in the state, through the exercise of eminent domain, which was to allow, in the words of the U.S. Constitution, "private property [to] be taken for public use."

With Grotius' invention of eminent domain, we reach another critical moment in the development of what would become Blackstonian exclusive ownership. And it is essential to see that this doctrine did smooth the way for Blackstone. In effect, Grotius detached the duty to share from the rights of ownership. In pre-Grotian thought, private owners had the obligation, as a matter of conscience, to share; and as Christians they risked their salvation if they failed to do so. Grotius eliminated this source of moral anxiety. His private owners were no longer weighed down by the burdensome obligation to give charity as a condition of their enjoyment of property rights.[75] They could devote themselves to their own interests, while leaving concern for the common good to the operation of the state, the benign receptacle of the duty of charity. The creation of the doctrine of eminent domain cleared the moral theological terrain for Blackstonian ownership. The point deserves some emphasis, since we tend today to think of the doctrine of eminent domain as in deep tension with Blackstonian ownership. The historical truth is different: The invention of eminent domain made the triumph of Blackstonian ownership possible.

The Grotian proposition that the state, through its exercise of eminent domain, "ownership for the public good," was the proper

---

reading of this passage as bearing entirely on the question of eminent domain, and observes that Grotius' views involved subtleties that I do not discuss here. Feenstra, "Histoire du droit savant, expropriation et *dominium eminens* chez Grotius," in *L'expropriation*, Recueils de la Société Jean Bodin 67 (Brussels, 1999), 133–153.

[75] This does not mean, let me emphasize, that Grotius thought there was no duty of charity. It means only that the duty of charity was not a condition of the enjoyment of property rights.

home of charity established itself as standard thereafter in the literature. Pufendorf, whose analysis was to inspire both Locke and Hume, summed up the advances in property thinking since the sixteenth century. Lands had to be divided into mine and thine. This was for the reason given since Aquinas, and attested by Genesis 13: Without the division of lands, there would be strife and war.[76] The individual *occupatio* of land was valid only if the land in question was cultivated; tillage was the determinant of ownership.[77] No chief was necessary. As for the broader interests of humanity in the use of the land: They should be safeguarded through eminent domain.[78] Authorities of the later seventeenth and early eighteenth century agreed.[79] So too, eventually, did Blackstone, to whose treatment of eminent domain I will turn shortly.

First, though, it is necessary to pause over another figure of the greatest importance: John Locke. In some ways, Locke was the very embodiment of the developments I have been describing, the arch-example of the shift from norms of social dominance to norms of territoriality. His theory, after all, was pitched as a refutation of the *Patriarcha* of Robert Filmer; and the *Patriarcha* was nothing other than a theory founded in the classical conception of ownership, and the primary norm of social dominance: Adam, as Filmer argued, had "by right of fatherhood, royal authority over [his] children," and that right, "as large and as ample as the absolutest dominion of any monarch," served as the foundation of the rights of patriarchal kings.[80] Filmer's theory can usefully be read against the background of early modern property thought. He was seizing on a possibility implicit in the theology of Vitoria: Adam had emerged after the Fall with *patria potestas*, and *patria potestas*, the juristic expression of the chieftainship over people, remained the foundation of law and government thereafter.

---

[76] Samuel Pufendorf, *De jure naturae et gentium libri octo* (Amsterdam, 1672), 4.4.6, 4.4.14 (pp. 460–462, 476–477).
[77] Ibid., 4.4.6 (pp. 460–462).
[78] On both Pufendorf and Bynkershoek, and their somewhat more restrictive view of the doctrine than Grotius', see Reynolds, *Before Eminent Domain*, 97.
[79] Reynolds, *Before Eminent Domain*, 97–98.
[80] Filmer, *Patriarcha and Other Writings*, ed. Robert Sommerville (Cambridge, 1990), 6–7.

Locke's assault on Filmer can be understood, for its part, as a campaign to substitute a conception of property rights founded in the cultivation of land for a conception of property rights founded in *patria potestas*. He too was reasoning against the background of early modern property thought. Rights for him were rights that began in the division of land; and that division of land, as Vitoria had explained, did not require a chief at all, since it could be achieved through the tacit process of *occupatio* justified through tillage. Within the conceptual structure of Vitorian thought, *occupatio* through tillage was, indeed, the only possible alternative to political control. Locke's focus on land can thus be viewed as a statement, not only about the acquisition of property as such, but also about political theory. "As *much Land* as a Man Tills, Plants, Improves, Cultivates ... so much is his *Property*" was a recapitulation of a doctrine first enunciated by Vitoria more than a century and a half earlier; and in the thought of Vitoria, and after him Grotius, the "tacit" taking of land through tillage effectively eliminated any need for absolute monarchical authority.

Locke's attitude toward the problem of charity and use rights also continued the older tradition. Locke had an enduring fidelity to the belief in the imperative of sharing resources. This is a fact that deserves to be emphasized, since he is still sometimes decried as a representative of what C. B. MacPherson calls "possessive individualism."[81] As James Tully argues, Locke, like all his early modern predecessors, always understood property to be limited by a primordial obligation to share use. The original right of property given to Adam was "a right of use only, not of use, abuse and alienation."[82] This provided the moral theological context for the famous passage in the *Two Treatises* in which Locke declared that there must always be "still enough, and as good left" for the use of others.[83]

In both his focus on the tillage of land and his commitment to a concept of property limited to what "a Man ... can use the Product of," Locke was putting a gloss on what had become the standard view

---

[81] MacPherson, *The Political Theory of Possessive Individualism: Hobbes to Locke* (Oxford, 1962).
[82] Tully, *A Discourse on Property: John Locke and His Adversaries* (Cambridge, 1980), 61. Contrasted with Pufendorf, 72.
[83] John Locke, *Two Treatises of Government*, ed. Peter Laslett (Cambridge, 1988), 291 (2: §33).

over the previous two centuries. There is a straight road from Vitoria to the *Second Treatise*, passing via Grotius and Pufendorf. Yet if Locke was only one in a long line of early modern property theorists, he was a strangely reticent philosophical contributor to the tradition. He noticeably failed to rise to the challenge that had engaged his predecessors. Unlike all his philosophical forerunners, from Aristotle to Aquinas to Grotius to Pufendorf, he left the nature of the duty to share, and the mechanism for its management, unspecified. There was no theory of friendship, no theory of charity, no theory of the royal power to safeguard the common good through eminent domain. The vague moralizing of his text has puzzled his readers ever since.[84]

* * *

Perhaps Locke's philosophical silence reflected an unspoken discomfort with the very idea of the obligation of charity. In any case, a duty founded on no explicit legal theory is a duty fated to go unenforced. To that extent, at least, we might view Locke as a representative of possessive individualism. Blackstone, by contrast, did offer a legal theory for the exercise of eminent domain, but he now endorsed the requirement of just compensation;[85] and that made the doctrine a noticeably more restricted one than it had been in the hands of his predecessors. The spirit of possessive individualism moves far more visibly through the pages of the *Commentaries on the Laws of England* than through those of the *Second Treatise*.

Blackstone's *facultas eminens*, now located in the legislature rather than in the King, had withered dramatically since Grotius. He began with a scornful dismissal of "the general good of the whole community," of a kind that would have puzzled, and even shocked, his predecessors:

So great ... is the regard of the law for private property, that it will not authorize the least violation of it; no, not even for the general good of the whole community. If a new road, for instance, were to be made through the grounds of a private person, it might perhaps be extensively beneficial to the public; but

---

[84] On this, I share the sense of dissatisfaction in Reynolds, *Before Eminent Domain*, 100–101.
[85] The sources of this in French thought are discussed in Arthur Lenhoff, "The Development of the Concept of Eminent Domain," *Columbia Law Review* 42 (1942): 601–603 [596–638].

the law permits no man, or set of men, to do this without consent of the owner of
the land. In vain may it be urged, that the good of the individual ought to yield to
that of the community . . .

The moral imperative of charity that had motivated Thomist theory
was now banished from the law:

. . . for it would be dangerous to allow any private man, or even any public
tribunal, to be the judge of this common good, and to decide whether it be
expedient or no. Besides, the public good is in nothing more essentially interested, than in the protection of every individual's private rights, as modelled by
the municipal law. In this, and similar cases the legislature alone, can, and
indeed frequently does, interpose, and compel the individual to acquiesce.

The state had the Grotian power to intervene; but only in a way
subject to the norms of the market:

But how does it interpose and compel? Not by absolutely stripping the subject
of his property in an arbitrary manner; but by giving him a full indemnification
and equivalent for the injury thereby sustained. The public is now considered
as an individual, treating with an individual for an exchange. All that the
legislature does is to oblige the owner to alienate his possessions for
a reasonable price; and even this is an exertion of power, which the legislature
indulges with caution, and which nothing but the legislature can perform.[86]

There may be no passage that more perfectly captures the spirit of
Blackstonian ownership than this one laying out its limits, and in a way
profoundly at odds with the great tradition extending back to Aristotle.

Blackstone was only one representative of a far broader tendency in
late eighteenth-century thought. We have already seen how the
conception of absolute ownership achieved a crucial modern triumph
in the French Civil Code of 1804, which discarded the old regime of use
in favor of a new regime of use and abuse, founded on the classical
Roman law of *dominium*.[87] Many other texts could be cited; the
transformation in the understanding of ownership lies at the heart of
Karl Polanyi's larger *Great Transformation* that accompanied the rise
of modern market society.[88] I do not want to load this chapter down
with too many examples, but it is worth highlighting one of special

---

[86] Blackstone, *Commentaries on the Laws of England, Book I: Of the Rights of Persons*,
ed. David Lemmings (Oxford, 2016), 1:94.
[87] Above, Chapter 5.   [88] Polanyi, *The Great Transformation* (New York, 1944).

interest. This is Kant's 1797 defense of private property, which offered a curiously scholastic argument for exclusive rights in land.

Kant on property, we might say, put the final philosophical nail in the coffin of the use rights tradition. The venerable understanding of rights in land, as we have seen, presupposed that they were rights in resources, not rights to land as such. Kant unconditionally dismissed that understanding. The soil, he explained, was the "substance," whereas the resources on the soil were the "inherence." This logically entailed that *only* the owner could make use of them. *Occupatio*, argued Kant, now fully inhabiting the "radical transformation," must by its nature be *occupatio*, in the first instance, of the soil:

The First Acquisition of a Thing can only be that of the Soil
By the Soil is understood all habitable Land. In relation to everything that is moveable upon it, it is to be regarded as a substance, and the mode of the existence of the Moveables is viewed as an Inherence in it. And just as, in the theoretical acceptation, Accidents cannot exist apart from their Substances, so, in the practical relation, Moveables upon the Soil cannot be regarded as belonging to any one unless he is supposed to have been previously in juridical possession of the Soil so that it is thus considered to be his.

If the law were to yield to the use rights of nonowners, the very concept of private property would become meaningless. Yet private property was necessary for the realization of human freedom:

For, let it be supposed that the Soil belongs to no one. Then I would be entitled to remove every moveable thing found upon it from its place, even to total loss of it, in order to occupy that place, without infringing thereby on the freedom of any other; there being, by the hypothesis, no possessor of it at all. But everything that can be destroyed, such as a Tree, a House, and such like – as regards its matter at least – is moveable; and if we call a thing which cannot be moved without destruction of its form an immoveable, the Mine and Thine in it is not understood as applying to its substance, but to that which is adherent to it, and which does not essentially constitute the thing itself.[89]

Rights in land were rights in resources; but it was a matter of the plain logic of substance and inherence that those resources could only accrue to a private owner, who would otherwise not count as an "owner," participating in the full freedom of Kantian man, at all.

* * *

---

[89] Kant, *The Philosophy of Law*, trans. W. Hastie (Edinburgh, 1887), 87.

The early modern triumph of a law oriented toward the "occupation" of land, from Vitoria through Grotius to Blackstone and Kant, is one part of the story of the progress of Arnaud's "radical transformation." The second has to do with the slow disappearance of the classical Roman law of slavery, the cracking of the shell of indifference.

That disappearance really was slow. In this respect, the authority of ancient cultural traditions held remarkably firm until the latter decades of the eighteenth century. This is particularly true of Roman teachings on the lawfulness of the enslavement of defeated enemies. We have already seen this among the jurists of the Junta of Burgos. Whatever doubts about slavery the participants in the Junta may have entertained, they, and the Spanish Monarchy, did not question the proposition that defeated enemies could be enslaved, at least as long as the war fought against them was just.[90]

The same remained true for a century and a half thereafter. Even the most adventurous thinkers, such as Grotius, did not reject the ancient teaching that war captives could be enslaved. It was true of others as well, with the great and honorable exception of Bodin.[91] It was true of François Connan, writing in late sixteenth-century France.[92] It was true of Hobbes, who, following the classical jurists, held that humans could be reduced to servitude by force just as animals could be.[93] It was true of Pufendorf, who, as we saw in Chapter 5, promoted a strong version of the Roman absolute conception of ownership in order to justify it. (Pufendorf also made a point of noting that slavery through capture in war was accepted by the Turks just as it was accepted by the Europeans.[94]) It was also true of Locke, whose distaste for slavery, recently highlighted by Holly Brewer, did not prevent him from accepting the logic that war permitted enslavement.[95] He was no

---

[90] For the Thomist tradition, see Frederick H. Russell, *The Just War in the Middle Ages* (Cambridge, 1975), 279–280.

[91] Jean Bodin, *Les six livres de la République* (Paris, 1986), 1:85 (Bk. 1, chapter 5).

[92] Brett, *Changes of State*, 100.   [93] Ibid., 111.

[94] Pufendorf, *De jure naturae et gentium libri octo*, 841–843 (6.3:5–6), and 841 for the citation to Augerius Gislenius Busbequius, *Epistola quatuor* (Hanover, 1605), 120 on the Turks.

[95] Locke, *Two Treatises*, 284 (2: §22), offering an argument that shifts the focus to the consent of the victim: "[H]aving by his fault forfeited his own life by some act that deserves death, he to whom he has forfeited it may, when he has him in his power, delay to take it, and make use of him to his own service; and he does him no injury by it. For, whenever he finds the hardship of his slavery outweigh the value of his life, it is

more able than any other author of his time to manage a full escape from the classical tradition.

To say that the ancient teaching of the legitimacy of enslavement through war survived is not, however, to say that the law remained static. It certainly did not. Classical Roman doctrine was in fact undermined in a critically important way in the early modern tradition. Even if we cannot find abolitionism in many texts before the latter half of the eighteenth century, we can see the law of slavery begin to form fissures.

This is because early modern authors felt the need for a more searching justification for enslavement through war than the ancients had to offer. For the classical jurists, the legitimacy of enslavement through war required no justification beyond the fact of war itself: As we saw in Chapter 4, they regarded the rights of conquest as self-evident. Human booty, like all other forms of booty, accrued to the victor by simple virtue of the law of victory. There was certainly a choice to be made about whether defeated persons would be killed or enslaved, in the eyes of the classical jurists. But that choice belonged, not to the defeated persons themselves, but to their triumphant captors:

D. 1.5.4.2. Slaves (*servi*) are so called for the reason that military commanders were accustomed to sell their captives, and in this manner to preserve (*servare*) them, instead of putting them to death.

If it was profitable for the captor to sell his victim, the victim would be sold rather than killed. The very word *servus*, slave, signified "one who was spared." The jurists of the early modern tradition, still beholden to the authority of the ancient texts, took the same primal scene of the defeated warrior at the feet of the victor as their starting

in his power, by resisting the will of his master, to draw on himself the death he desires." Holly Brewer, "Slavery, Sovereignty, and 'Inheritable Blood': Reconsidering John Locke and the Origins of American Slavery," *American Historical Review* 122 (2017): 1038–1078, minimizes the significance of Locke's acceptance of this doctrine in light of the larger opposition to slavery that she ascribes to him. I read it differently: as evidence of the undoubted acceptance of enslavement through war even in the eyes of an author made deeply uncomfortable with it. Locke's theory in effect held that those who had willingly committed crimes, in war as in other domains, had exposed themselves to the danger of enslavement. This was, we might say, a theory of second-order consent, consent to the *risk* of enslavement. In any case, Locke put the accent throughout on the free will of the victim in a way alien to the ancient understanding.

point. But they engineered a great reversal: They now assigned the choice of death or slavery to the victim.

This tendency is one that we can already detect in the notorious *Requerimiento*. Enslavement, under the *Requerimiento*, was analyzed, not as a self-understood consequence of defeat, but as the result of a free choice by persons who refused to submit. "[I]f you do not [submit] ... we shall ... take you and your wives and your children, and shall make slaves of them." Slavery was, in that sense, the product of consent. *You may **choose** to be vassals, or you may **choose** to be slaves.*

The same focus on consent also marked the analysis of a second man asked by the King to compose a monograph after the Junta, the theologian Matías de Paz. Paz is a memorable figure.[96] A *converso*, a Jew converted to Catholicism, he belonged to a feared and persecuted community in Spain. Despite that, he managed to rise high in the Dominican Order and the King's counsels. Like other Dominicans such as Montesinos and Las Casas, Paz was a champion of the cause of the conquered peoples on Hispaniola, the island whose very capital, Santo Domingo, had been named for the founder of his order. His discussion set out some of the leading themes of the literature, which would reappear in the more famous work of Las Casas, beginning with the insistence that the Indians had rights to property that had to be respected. As for their potential enslavement: Paz's argument took a striking, and even moving, form, coming as it did from a *converso*. Conversion, he held, should protect them. No person's juridical condition should be worsened after accepting Christ. It followed that the embrace of Christianity by the Indians saved them from the threat of slavery: "those who willingly convert to faith in Christ" could not be done the injury of enslavement.[97] In this too we see norms of consent offered as a justification for the institution. *You may **choose** Christ, or you may **choose** slavery.*

The pattern of argument grounded in norms of consent continued to develop over later generations. Grotius is, as so often, the seminal figure. He effectively subjected enslavement to the norms of contract

---

[96] See esp. José Luis Egío García, "Matías de Paz and the Introduction of Thomism in the *Asuntos de Indias*: A Conceptual Revolution," *Rechtsgeschichte* 26 (2018): 236, 237 [236–262].

[97] Paz, *Acerca del dominio sobre los indios*, ed. Castañeda et al., 141.

law. Grotius did not deny the classical teaching that those captured in war could be enslaved against their will. Nevertheless, he strongly intimated that consent was the most proper route into slavery.[98] Indeed, as Johan Olsthoorn and Laurens van Apeldoorn show, Grotius' analysis extended into a far-reaching reconceptualization of the juridical roots of enslavement.[99]

Grotius began from the proposition, founded in a Christian rereading of Roman law, that persons could not sell themselves as though they were things. The ultimate rights in human beings lay with God; consequently a person could not sell himself as though he were a *res*. How then was slavery possible? The answer, he held, was that slavery was not an *in rem* right, but an *in personam* right: It was a perpetual right, not to the body of the enslaved person, but to the enslaved person's services. Persons could surrender the perpetual right to their labor, without surrendering themselves as though they were mere inanimate things. Slavery, in that sense, was perfectly compatible with the special ontological status of human beings, and with the supreme norm of consent.

This analysis had a significant consequence. It allowed Grotius, and indeed obliged him, to subsume slavery under the larger rubric of labor relations. All workers granted rights in their services, not just slaves. What made slaves *slaves*? The distinguishing feature of slavery was that slaves were what Grotius called "perfect" *servi*, since their labor belonged entirely and perpetually to their master. Other laborers were "imperfect" *servi*. Every slave was a kind of "perfect" worker; conversely, every worker was a partial slave.[100] This did not solve all the difficulties, since it provided no obvious answer to the heritability of slave status, a topic on which Grotius had to seek other arguments.[101] But it did permit a measure of contractualization of

---

[98] Grotius, *De jure belli ac pacis*, ed. Barbeyrac, 1:842: non soli qui se dedunt aut servitutem promittunt per servos habentur; sed omnes omnino bello solenni publico capti (3.7.2): "Not only those who surrender or agree to servitude are held to be slaves; but all those taken captive in a lawful war." My italics. Grotius' preference to turn to norms of consent shows in this formulation and elsewhere in his discussion.
[99] Olsthoorn and Van Apeldoorn, "'This Man Is My Property': Slavery and Political Absolutism in Locke and the Classical Social Contract Tradition," *European Journal of Political Theory* 21 (2022): 253–275.
[100] I follow in these paragraphs the account ibid.
[101] Grotius, *De jure belli ac pacis*, ed. Barbeyrac, 1:666–663 (2.21.14).

the analysis of slavery. Grotius' analysis was adopted by Pufendorf, who elaborated at length on the distinction between "perfect" *servi* and other laborers.[102] This analysis continued to reign in the eighteenth century. One result was that the term *servus* acquired early modern clouds of ambiguity that would not be dispelled until Friedrich Carl von Savigny distinguished slaves from serfs in 1822.

There is a paradox in the rise of these consent norms that deserves every emphasis. The breakdown in the inherited understanding of the legitimacy of slavery did not begin in a campaign for wholesale abolition. It began with early modern efforts to justify slavery on the basis of some theory not to be found in the classical Roman texts. In that sense, consent theories went hand in hand with the theories of natural slavery, radically different though the two may seem. Both responded to the same felt need: the need for arguments that could justify the institution of slavery for reasons that went beyond the mere fact of victory. Both betrayed the same early modern discontent with the classical rule: "Whatever has been captured from the enemy is ours by natural reason."[103]

* * *

Servi, in the Grotian analysis, were now not things, but workers; the law of slavery was effectively a branch of contract law rather than property law, and it was founded in norms of consent. This shift should be viewed alongside another change, which brought the law of land, once again, to the fore. Over the course of the same early modern period, the free-soil doctrines that would eventually determine the law of Antebellum America took hold as well.

The rise of free soil counts as perhaps the most dramatic example of the "radical transformation that operated at the foundation and form of the conception of property": It was the great theoretical vehicle by which subjugation of workers ceased to belong to the rule over humans and came to belong to the rule over lands. Free-soil doctrines have been extensively studied by historians of slavery, most especially by Seymour Drescher in his absorbing magnum opus *Abolition*; I will not go into the full details here.[104] The law of free soil probably dates

---

[102] On this pattern of analyses, see generally Maria Luisa Pesante, *Come servi: figure del lavoro salariato dal diritto naturale all' economia politica* (Milan, 2013).
[103] Gai. Inst. 2.69.
[104] Drescher, *Abolition: A History of Slavery and Anti-Slavery* (Cambridge, 2009) at, e.g., 245.

back to the thirteenth century, when it is documented in Toulouse (and also, I note, in Bologna and other Italian cities).[105] This medieval free-soil doctrine may have been in some degree an expression of the principle, intermittently honored, that goes by the modern name *Stadtluft macht frei*, that taking breaths of city air conferred free status on unfree persons. In that sense, free soil began within the feudal tradition.[106]

The question of how these medieval traditions made their way into early modern law is the subject of some perplexities, which I will not describe.[107] In any case, by the later sixteenth century free-soil doctrines were well entrenched in France, promoted notably by Bodin. They established themselves in the Netherlands as well, and in England they reappeared in Somerset's Case, the 1772 decision that opened the way for British abolitionism. As the opinion declared, British "air" was "too pure for slaves to breathe in it."[108] Free-soil doctrines then served as the foundation for sectional coexistence in the United States until *Dred Scott* v. *Sandford*.

As Drescher has powerfully argued, the history of the spread of free soil can be told as the history of the decline of slavery itself: Abolition was a process by which the denial that slavery was possible on the free soil of Europe was slowly extended to the non-European world as well; the history of the decline of slavery is the history of globalization of a doctrine of free soil. By the same token, living on the peculiarly free soil of Europe provided the context for early abolitionist thinking.

---

[105] See the account of the *Liber Paradisus* of Bologna in Paolo de Stefani, "The *Liber Paradisus*: A Vision of Good Governance," in Markku Suksi, Kalliope Agapios-Josephides, Jean-Paul Lehners, and Manfred Nowak, eds., *First Fundamental Rights Documents in Europe* (Cambridge, Antwerp, and Portland, OR, 2015), 49–51 [39–55]. The context, as de Stefani presents it, lay in social conflict and Christian theology, not in any version of *Stadtluft macht frei*.

[106] The phrase is a nineteenth-century coinage. For discussion and literature, see Dieter Werkmüller, "Luft macht eigen – Luft macht frei," in Adalbert Erler and Ekkehard Kaufmann, *Handwörterbuch zur deutschen Rechtsgeschichte* (Frankfurt a. M.: Erich Schmidt, 1971–), 3: cols. 92–98. For a survey of abolitions in thirteenth-century Italian cities, see Antonio Pertile, *Storia de diritto italiano*, 2nd ed. (Turin, 1894), 3:87–8.

[107] On this, I have benefited from personal communications from E. A. R. Brown and Daniel Lord Smail, kindly shared with me by Sara McDougall.

[108] *Somerset* v. *Stewart*, 98 ER 499 (1772). See the discussion in Daniel Hulsebosch, "Somerset's Case at the Bar: Securing the 'Pure Air' of English Jurisdiction within the British Empire," *Texas Wesleyan Law Review* 13 (2006–2007): 699–710.

Bodin is an important example: It was as a theorist of free soil in France that he proposed his critique of the institution of slavery.[109] The same can be said of David Hume's eloquent essay "Of the Populousness of Ancient Nations" of 1752, which I have quoted before. By that mid eighteenth-century date, Hume found it natural to contrast the law of the ancients and the law of the moderns – and to do so expressly as a man living in the free lands of Europe:

> The chief difference between the domestic œconomy of the ancients and that of the moderns consists in the practice of slavery, which prevailed among the former, and which has been abolished for some centuries throughout the greater part of Europe.

Hume made a point of emphasizing that the morally corrupting effects of mastership still persisted in the New World. New World slavery was an atavistic survival on soils not yet free: "The remains which are found of domestic slavery, in the American colonies, and among some European nations, would never surely create a desire of rendering it more universal."[110] By the end of the century, and especially in the middle decades of the next, his view would become commonplace among thoughtful Westerners.

* * *

The triumph of free soil too can be understood as a manifestation of Arnaud's "radical transformation that operated at the foundation and form of our conception of property"; and the same can be said of a last development, much studied by recent historians, among whom Benton and Maier stand out: the early modern consolidation of the territorial conception of the state.

As we saw in the previous chapters, the idea of territorial rule was certainly not unknown in earlier periods. A kind of quasi-territorial rule emerged in the late antique Roman Empire, beginning with the establishment of the Tetrarchy in the reign of Diocletian; as Chapter 8 argued, the Empire came to be imagined as something more like a private landholding. Nevertheless, it is widely accepted that sovereignty in the West was not reconceptualized in wholly territorial

---

[109] Bodin, *Six livres de la République*, 1:85 (Bk. 1, chapter 5).
[110] Hume, "Of the Populousness of Ancient Nations," in *Political Discourses*, 2nd ed. (Edinburgh, 1752), 161–162 [155–262].

terms before the later eighteenth century, the period in which all the developments described in this chapter reached their culmination.

I have often quoted Grotius' 1625 statement: "Rulership [*imperium*] can take two possible subject matters. The primary subject matter is rulership over persons … as for example over a horde of men, women and children seeking a new place to settle. The secondary subject matter is rulership over a place, which is called 'territory.'"[111] Edward Keene regards this as an account of the nature of sovereignty in Grotius' own time: Grotius, he argues, thought of "rulership over persons" as the primary form in the seventeenth century.[112] It is not clear to me that Keene is right: It is possible that the passage should be read as an account of a historical movement from the primary to the secondary form.[113] The drive toward a land-oriented law in Grotius' highly original work is unmistakable.

But whatever we make of this statement from Grotius, the relative absence of territorial thinking among his early modern successors is manifest, and it has been widely remarked. Hobbes' Leviathan, as Brett observes in comments on the famous frontispiece of his book, was composed of myriad persons; "[t]he silence about territory," in the chapters of the book itself, "is almost total."[114] Among early modern political theorists more broadly, she adds, there was "very little interest either in the concept of territory, or in place more generally."[115] Benton, the leading legal historian of European overseas expansion, warns, similarly, against "project[ing] backward in time the post-nineteenth-century idea that territoriality was not just one element of sovereignty but its defining element":

Although control of territory formed an important part of early modern constructions of sovereignty, European powers often asserted and defended imperial dominion on the basis of strategic, symbolic, and limited claims while recognizing the incomplete and tentative nature of more expansive spheres of influence. Some legal practices, including rituals defining subjecthood and acts controlling criminality had only an indirect relation to dominion of territory.

---

[111] Grotius, *De jure belli ac pacis*, ed. Barbeyrac, 1:233–234 (2.3.4.1).
[112] Edward Keene, *Beyond the Anarchical Society: Grotius, Colonialism and Order in World Politics* (Cambridge, 2002), 56–57.
[113] Such at least is the conclusion suggested, I think, by the phrase *interdum sufficit*, which suggests Grotius' concern that the rulership over people might not suffice.
[114] Brett, *Changes of State*, 170, 212.   [115] Ibid., 170.

Even over the "long nineteenth century," she continues, territoriality established itself only unevenly.[116] Maier too sees "modern territoriality" taking full form only in the eighteenth century and after, though with roots that extend back to Bodin in the sixteenth.[117] Roughly the same chronology was proposed almost fifty years ago by Dietmar Willoweit, who concluded that the principle of supreme territorial power displaced the multiple rulerships of the early modern world only in the second half of the eighteenth century.[118]

These scholars lay out a case of fundamental importance, not only for the history of the state, but also for legal history more broadly. The unambiguously territorial state is hard indeed to find before the late eighteenth century – much more so, as Benton rightly complains, than most modern lawyers are prepared to recognize. There is one example that deserves particular emphasis. This is the Peace of Westphalia of 1648, which put an end to the Thirty Years' War. Westphalia is notoriously misinterpreted by international lawyers, who routinely claim that it laid the foundations for a law of sovereign nation-states of the modern form. As specialists point out again and again, to little apparent avail, it did nothing of the kind.[119] As we saw in Chapter 7, the seventeenth century counts as the high age of feudal law, and that was so of the conception of the state as an international actor. The subjects of the Peace were not modern nation-states at all, but monarchs and other feudal potentates. The organizing principle of Westphalia was dynastic, and it presupposed throughout the more or less feudal norms of dynastic rule over subjects that were the unchallenged law of the seventeenth century. Grotius' "rulership over persons" remained the primary form; the Westphalian state of legend is

---

[116] Lauren Benton, *A Search for Sovereignty: Law and Geography in European Empires, 1400–1900* (Cambridge, 2010), 3–4.

[117] Charles Maier, *Once within Borders: Territories of Power, Wealth and Belonging since 1500* (Cambridge, MA, 2016).

[118] Willoweit, *Rechtsgrundlagen der Territorialgewalt: Landesobrigkeit, Herrschaftsrechte und Territorium in Rechtswissenschaft der Neuzeit* (Cologne and Vienna, 1975), 348–349.

[119] See Karl-Heinz Ziegler, "Die Bedeutung des Westfälischen Friedens für das europäische Völkerrecht," in *Fata iuris gentium: kleine Schriften zur Geschichte des europäischen Völkerrechts* (Baden-Baden, 2008), 312–314; Heinhard Steiger, "Rechtliche Strukturen der europäischen Stattsordnung 1648–1792," *Zeitschrift für ausländisches öffentliches Recht und Völkerrecht* 59 (1999): 609–645.

a product of the late eighteenth and nineteenth centuries, projected anachronistically back on the past.

As all these studies suggest, the later eighteenth and nineteenth centuries were the decisive age of territorialization in the conception of the state. To say it again, this was not wholly without precedent. As far back as the third century CE, "Romans [began] to think of their holdings in terms of bounded territories and not just divisions between peoples";[120] and as I argued in Chapter 8, private-law norms of the *dominium* of land crept into the understanding of late antique rulership. The passage from the "rulership over persons" to the "rulership over a place," like the passage from slavery to serfdom, cannot be neatly confined to some single conjunctural moment of change, whether in the late eighteenth century or otherwise. There was an ongoing, and at times turbulent, oscillation between Grotius' primary and secondary forms in Western law over a very *longue durée*. Nevertheless, the conclusions drawn by the current literature, when it comes to the early modern period, are compelling: The territorial state, as we are familiar with it today, did not unambiguously become the "primary" form before the end of the eighteenth century at the earliest.

* * *

Maier makes a particularly stimulating argument that this transformation in the understanding of rulership went hand in hand with a transformation in the understanding of ownership. In Chapter 7, we saw that the analysis of ownership underwent far-reaching change in the latter decades of the eighteenth century. The feudal conception of split ownership, with its *dominium utile* and *dominium directum*, continued to govern Continental European real property relations up until the French Revolution. Early modern jurists were not so bold, or so foolhardy, as to jettison the *ius feudale*. Nevertheless, there was considerable pressure for change. As a doctrinal matter, jurists from the sixteenth century onward recognized, and deplored, the absence of the classical Roman absolute conception, with its insistence that there must be only one owner, possessing the unbounded power of *usus* and *abusus*. In the eighteenth century, agrarian reformers, among them notably English

---

[120] Mark Graham, *News and Frontier Consciousness in the Late Roman Empire* (Ann Arbor, 2006), 45.

enclosers and French physiocrats, preached their own version of the same doctrine, arguing for the extinction of use rights in the name of improvement.[121]

It is Maier's claim, in his *Once within Borders*, that the same drive toward "improvement" through exclusive ownership was also at work in the late eighteenth-century transformation of the state. The new states, like the new Blackstonian owners, were dedicated to the unencumbered exploitation of the resources of their land:

> [Modern territoriality] came to involve systematic exploitation of economic resources in the eighteenth, and it triumphed as the principle for organizing collective life (at least among Europeans and their American offshoots) in the second half of the nineteenth century and the first two thirds of the twentieth. The changes that took place from the Renaissance onward augmented its persuasive hold on the imagination of state and rulers by adding new economic and technological possibilities for the political organization of global space. They also helped render alternatives unviable.[122]

As owners became unchecked and exclusive exploiters of their lands, states became unchecked and exclusive exploiters of their territories; in both domains, territoriality took "persuasive hold on the imagination." To put it in Weberian terms, the emergence of the territorial state came to involve not just the monopolization of violence, but also a monopolization of resource extraction.

The logic of Maier's important argument, linking ownership and rulership, must be stated carefully. One might read him to say that there was a causal arrow running from state monopolization of resources to the household monopolization of resources: As rulers insisted on their exclusive extractive control over their territories, owners learned to do the same, imagining themselves as small-scale monarchs. The ultimate motor of legal change, on this theory, should be sought in the history of the state.[123] An argument of just that form has been made by one of the great scholars of the history of political thought, Richard Tuck. In his *Rights of War and Peace*, Tuck contends that the legal analysis of the rights of individuals among the leading

---

[121] Above, Chapter 5.   [122] Maier, *Once within Borders*, 12.
[123] As Matthew Roller would put it, the law of the rulership was the "parent domain," while the law of ownership was the "derived domain." Roller, *Constructing Autocracy: Aristocrats and Emperors in Julio-Claudian Rome* (Princeton, 2001), 213.

early modern jurists drew on "the real and imaginatively vivid example" of states as they operated in international relations.[124] The makers of contracts were conceptualized by reference to the makers of treaties. One might possibly claim that the owners of land modeled their conduct on the same "real and imaginatively vivid example."

As I understand it, Maier does not make that kind of causal argument, however, and, appealing though it may seem, I do not think it would be the right kind of argument to make. It is not the case that the transformation in property law was driven by the transformation in the state. There are too many other sources for the emergence of Blackstonian ownership of land for that to be so. The right interpretation sounds in a less causal vein: It is that the territorial understanding of sovereignty and Blackstonian ownership emerged in parallel. Something shifted contemporaneously, tectonically, in the understanding of both yin and yang, just as had happened before.

* * *

Nevertheless, the rise of Maier's territorial state may have played a causal role in Arnaud's radical transformation in a different way: It may have been instrumental in the decline of lawful private slavery. With some careful thought, we can recognize the role of the rise of the new state in the modern history of slavery, in a pattern already on display at Burgos: Servitude did not in fact vanish; but it did become a monopoly of the newly triumphant territorial state.

To see why, we must begin by giving a careful legal historical definition to the decline of slavery – a more careful one than it always receives in the literature. It is commonly asserted that the nineteenth century witnessed the abolition of "slavery [and] involuntary servitude," in the words of the Thirteenth Amendment to the U.S. Constitution. But that is not quite correct. What the nineteenth century witnessed was the abolition of the *private* ownership of slaves and the *private* imposition of involuntary servitude – what Hume carefully specified as "domestic" slavery. Involuntary servitude to the state did not disappear at all. Quite the contrary: It grew in scale as private enslavement declined.

---

[124] Tuck, *Rights of War and Peace: Political Thought and the International Order from Grotius to Kant* (Oxford, 2001), 8.

There are two principal examples: penal servitude and mass conscription. To begin with the first: It is a fact of fundamental importance that the expansion of free soil never brought with it the abolition of forms of penal servitude. This was true of galley slavery and comparable forms in Continental Europe. It was also true of the Anglophone abolitionist tradition that took wing with Somerset's Case in 1772. The report of the case did indeed declare that the island's "air" was "too pure for slaves to breathe in it." But in the same paragraph, it included a telling exception: "Slavery imposed for the performance of public works for civil crimes, is much more defensible, and rests on quite different foundations."[125] *Public* slavery remained perfectly acceptable. Only private owners were forbidden the ownership of humans. The endorsement of effective slavery when "imposed ... for crimes" survived in England thereafter, notably in the Penal Servitude Acts of the mid nineteenth century.[126]

It survived in the United States as well. The Northwest Ordinance, promulgated in 1787 under the Articles of Confederation, declared the territories that were its subject to be free soil. But it also carefully specified that public slavery remained acceptable: "There shall be neither slavery nor involuntary servitude in the said territory, *otherwise than in punishment of crimes whereof the party shall have been duly convicted.*"[127] That language made its way, lightly edited, into the Thirteenth Amendment to the United States Constitution: "Neither slavery nor involuntary servitude, *except as a punishment for crime whereof the party shall have been duly convicted*, shall exist within the United States, or any place subject to their jurisdiction."[128] This remains the law of the United States down to this day: Convicted persons still have the effective status of slaves of the state, and the state still claims the authority, in some circumstances, to take their lives. To be sure, their status is not heritable; in that sense they are certainly not

---

[125] Both Hargrave, in *Somerset v. Stewart*, 500.

[126] James Q. Whitman, *Harsh Justice: Criminal Punishment and the Widening Divide between America and Europe* (New York, 2003), 176–178.

[127] Northwest Ordinance, Art. 6., emphasis added. Available at www.archives.gov/milestone-documents/northwest-ordinance. For discussion of its use in the formulation of the Thirteenth Amendment, see Jack M. Balkin and Sanford Levinson, "The Dangerous Thirteenth Amendment," *Columbia Law Review* 112 (2012): 1477–1479 [1459–1500].

[128] U.S. Const., Amend. XIII, emphasis added.

slaves. Moreover, the Continental tradition, as I have shown elsewhere, resolutely rejects slave status for convicts.[129] Nevertheless, in the common law world the trend embodied in the Thirteenth Amendment, and the law that preceded it from Somerset's Case on, is clear.

A similar tale can be told about mass conscription, a form of involuntary state servitude that, like conviction for a crime, also extends to the authority to take the very life of the subject person. Universal conscription too emerged contemporaneously with the decline of private servitude. Linda Colley has written about the rise of mass conscription from the late eighteenth century onward, arguing that it played a crucial role in the emergence of constitutionalism. Her thesis is that constitutions justified conscription through norms of a kind of consent, and the case she makes is powerful.[130] Nevertheless, we must not lose sight of the reality that conscription is a form of involuntary subjection. It must be seen, not only against the background of constitutionalism, but also against the background of slave law.

Indeed, in episode after historical episode we see the abolition of private slavery shadowed by the rise of that state conscription that is Colley's subject. This was true of the French Revolution, which abolished both feudalism and slavery while introducing the *levée en masse*.[131] It was true of the American Civil War, which brought with it both the end of private slavery *and* the first introduction of mass conscription, despite the protests of some white American draftees that they were being subjected to unconstitutional involuntary servitude.[132] Other nineteenth-century examples can be given as well, prominent among them Imperial Russia, the scene of what Elise Kimerling Wirtschafter calls the transition "from serf to Russian soldier."[133] What happened in such cases, over the course of the long nineteenth century, was not that involuntary servitude ended. What

---

[129] Whitman, *Harsh Justice*, 97–150.
[130] Colley, *The Gun, the Ship and the Pen: Warfare, Constitutions and the Making of the Modern World* (Princeton, 2021).
[131] See the comparative reflections of David A. Bell, "When the Levée Breaks," *World Affairs* 170 (2008): 59–68.
[132] *Kneedler v. Lane*, 45 Pa. 238 (1863).
[133] Wirtschafter, *From Serf to Russian Soldier* (Princeton, 1990).

happened was the state assumed the sole authority to commandeer the resources of coerced human labor, definitively displacing the slavemasters of the past.

These are facts of legal history that must not be read out of our histories of slavery: It is literally false to say that "slavery and involuntary servitude" were eliminated from the law by the end of the nineteenth century. What was banished from the law was private slavery and involuntary servitude; involuntary servitude to the state experienced significant growth.[134] In that sense, the decline of slavery took the form that we can already glimpse in 1512: *These are my vassals*, declared the territorial states of the nineteenth and twentieth centuries, *not your slaves*.

---

[134] The juristic background to this development can be traced back through the same early modern authors whose work features in Maier's account. Bodin viewed the state as a competitor with private slaveowners for the use of compelled labor. See the discussion in Malick Ghachem, *The Old Regime and the Haitian Revolution* (Cambridge, 2012), 50–52. Charles Loyseau, the great theorist of seventeenth-century feudalism, devoted considerable attention to the distinctions between private and public lordship. Loyseau, *Traité des seigneuries* (Chateaudun, 1610), 6–7; Brigitte Basdevant-Gaudemet, *Aux origines de l'état moderne: Charles Loyseau, 1562–1627, théoricien de la puissance publique* (Paris, 1977), 119–123; Rafe Blaufarb, *The Great Demarcation: The French Revolution and the Invention of Modern Property* (Oxford, 2016), 23–28.

Conclusion: From Man the Killer to Man the Tiller

The ancient historian M. I. Finley once organized a forum to discuss "Roman investment in property." Finley believed that studies of the ancient economy should put the focus on ancient elite mentalities, and his symposium was designed to test the proposition that ancient and modern mentalities differed: The question he put to the participants was "just what the notion of 'investment' meant in Roman society." "[N]o presuppositions about maximization of income and the like," he added, "were implicit in the choice of the word."[1]

The classicist Elizabeth Rawson, biographer of Cicero and connoisseur of late republican social history, responded with an essay that focused on attitudes toward land. Her essay contrasted two different cultures of wealth: on the one hand, that of Rome in the time of Cicero; on the other hand, that of England in the time of Jane Austen. Land certainly mattered financially to the nobles of Ciceronian Rome, she wrote: "The Roman upper class [was] not only deeply concerned with real property, its main form of investment, but indeed feverishly engaged in property deals."[2] Cicero himself, as she well knew, spoke evocatively of his own "fatherland" of Arpinum.[3] Nevertheless, the very fact that wealthy Romans made deals so

---

[1] Finley, "Introduction," in Finley, ed., *Studies in Roman Property* (Cambridge, 1976), 1 [1–6].

[2] Rawson, "The Ciceronian Aristocracy and Its Properties," in Finley, ed., *Studies in Roman Property*, 86 [85–102].

[3] Rawson, *Cicero: A Portrait* (London, 1975), 1–2.

feverishly suggested that they did not experience the kind of attachment to their landed estates that the upper class portrayed in Austen's novels did. The relation of Romans to their land, in her judgment, was "much less emotional."[4] In "late eighteenth- or nineteenth-century England," wrote Rawson, whose own ancestors included a Yorkshire family whose lineage could be traced back centuries, "it was ... distasteful and inglorious to sell one's country estate."[5] The English had come to invest land with an emotional significance that it lacked among the more coldly calculating nobles of late republican Rome.

Rawson did not mention William Blackstone in her account of how land stirred English emotions; but his classic description of how the right of property "engages the affections" comes immediately to mind. Blackstone began, in his famous passage, by observing that there was "no foundation in nature or in natural law" for the right of property; in this he was echoing David Hume, who had argued thirty-five years earlier that ownership has no "natural" form.[6] This absence of any natural basis for property, Blackstone continued, was a disturbing truth – too disturbing for owners to admit to themselves. Here is his near-novelistic account of the institution of property in later eighteenth-century England. It does not suffer from comparison with the best of Austen:

There is nothing which so generally strikes the imagination, and engages the affections of mankind, as the right of property ... And yet there are very few, that will give themselves the trouble to consider the original and foundation of this right. Pleased as we are with the possession, we seem afraid to look back to the means by which it was acquired ... We think it enough that our title is derived by the grant of the former proprietor, by descent from our ancestors, or by the last will and testament of the dying owner; not caring to reflect that (accurately and strictly speaking) there is no foundation in nature or in natural law, why a set of words upon parchment should convey the dominion of land; why the son should have a right to exclude his fellow creatures from a determinate spot of ground, because his father had done so before him; or why the occupier of a particular field or of a jewel, when lying on his death-bed

---

[4] Rawson, "Ciceronian Aristocracy," 89.   [5] Ibid., 87.
[6] Hume, "A Treatise of Human Nature," ed. David Fate Norton and Mary J. Norton (Oxford, 2000), 315.

and no longer able to maintain possession, should be entitled to tell the rest of the world which of them should enjoy it after him.[7]

This is a scene, with its dying owner, to be savored, not just for its hardheaded dismissal of the idea that there is some natural foundation for ownership, not just for its clinical dissection of English property psychology, but also for its emotional atmospherics. The owner lying on his deathbed was a figure to stir the feelings of all consumers of the poetry and sentimentalist painting of the later eighteenth century: "A death-bed's a detector of the heart," wrote the poet Thomas Young in his "Night-Thoughts."[8]

John Locke did not have the literary gifts of an Austen or a Blackstone or a Young. But eighty years earlier his thoughts too ran to deathbeds, and he too spoke of "desire." "The first and strongest desire God planted in Men," he wrote in his stolid prose,

and wrought into the very Principles of their Nature [is] Self-preservation ... But next to this God planted in Men a strong desire also of propagating their Kind, and continuing themselves in their Posterity, and this gives Children a Title, to share in the Property of their Parents, and a Right to Inherit their Possessions.[9]

And by "Possessions" he had in mind, of course, "a Parcel of Land."[10]

Rawson believed that the "affections" and "strong desires" of such Englishmen were different from those of late republican Romans. Her "wealthy Romans," we might say – I do not know whether she would have agreed – were at home in Max Weber's consumer city, the citadel of a predatory elite. Their "bases," in Chris Wickham's terms, were urban, and their view of their agrarian holdings was, as Weber's hypothesis argues, fundamentally extractive. As rulers, they "conquered peoples, not land";[11] as both rulers and owners, they

---

[7] Blackstone, *Commentaries on the Laws of England, Book II: Of the Rights of Things*, ed. Simon Stern (Oxford, 2016), 1.
[8] Young, *Night-Thoughts* (1742–1745), 2:641. For the owner on his deathbed in Austen, *Sense and Sensibility*, chapter 1.
[9] John Locke, *Two Treatises of Government*, ed. Peter Laslett (Cambridge, 1988), 206–207 (1: §88).
[10] Locke, *Two Treatises*, 291 (2: §33).
[11] Benjamin Isaac, *Limits of Empire: The Roman Army in the East*, rev. ed. (Oxford, 2000), 395.

called themselves "masters"; and in both their religious and their legal imagination they played the part of "warriors, conquerors, and military aristocracies [who] carr[ied] on the symbolism and ideology of the paradigmatic hunter."[12] Their claims of ownership, in the midst of their sophisticated and economically complex society, were often symbolized by the spear; and their paradigmatic assertion of ownership was *I declare that this man is mine*.

As for their status in the social order of their society: They did not boast of the ownership of a family estate held for generations. When they "showed themselves in public," they conspicuously expended wealth so that "a great crowd of slaves would walk in front of them (*anteambulones*), another would follow them (*pedisequi*); the *nomenclator* would give them the names of those they encountered who wished to be greeted"; and in their "posh high-class houses they consumed slaves in massive quantities."[13]

* * *

Rawson, I have tried to show in this book, was right: Cultural attitudes toward ownership have undergone a transformation in the West, from an ancient Roman world whose legal imagination presupposed the values described by Weber – the values of a predatory urban elite whose conception of power, and social status, rested on the "control over people" – to a modern legal imagination populated by the owners and rulers of land. Our property law is a palimpsest. As we read it today, it speaks a language of landownership. But it is written on parchment on which an earlier law, though scraped away, is still discernible. That earlier law is the law of hunters of slaves and beasts.

None of this is in any simple way a matter of the economic realities. It is a matter of the "symbolism and ideology" of the law; it is a matter of Orlando Patterson's "idioms of power." It is a matter of Finley's elite mentalities, and of all the power that elite mentalities have to shape societies. The Roman economy did not really depend on the hunt for human prey in wars of enslavement, as Weber erroneously concluded. Nor was it based on the slave mode of production. The

---

[12] Mircea Eliade, *A History of Religious Ideas*, trans. Willard Trask (Chicago, 1978), 1:35.
[13] Karl Bücher, *Die Entstehung der Volkswirtschaft* (Tübingen, 1893), 27; Max Weber, *Wirtschaft und Gesellschaft*, ed. Johannes Winckelmann, 5th ed. (Tübingen, 1985), 798.

Roman upper class was indeed "feverishly engaged" in real estate deals. The significance of the symbolism and ideology of the law does not lie in what it tells us about the day-to-day workings of the economy. It lies in the ways in which the human institution of ownership has been conceived and justified.

The ways in which ancient Roman ownership was conceived and justified did indeed differ from those of the law of the age of Blackstone and Austen, and of our own. They can only be fully understood if we avail ourselves of the tools of anthropology. Like innumerable other nonmodern traditions, Roman law displayed a strong orientation toward Jack Goody's "chieftainship over people," both in its vocabulary of ownership and in its vocabulary of rulership. The hunt and war, the characteristic activities of the all-male bands of traditional societies, as Weber remarked,[14] played a foundational imaginative role as modes of the acquisition of property. There is no more dramatic example than the classical law of *occupatio*, which concerned itself with problems in the capture of prey that anthropologists trace back at least to the Upper Paleolithic. Such teachings, with their profound roots in human history, continued to provide the paradigm for thinking about numerous aspects of property law into the high age of the classical Empire: Even when they spoke of the acquisition of land, the classical jurists were drawn to the analogy of the hunt. In their law of slavery, they never questioned the legitimacy of taking human booty in war. Quite the contrary: They used the model of the capture and enslavement of enemies as the conceptual frame for analyzing some of their most basic social relations. In their ideology of rule, the Romans spoke of enslaving the peoples of their world.

This Roman law must also be seen in its broader Roman cultural context. Its imagery echoed the imagery of Roman art, visual and verbal, that celebrated hunters and warriors. The law bore an especially revealing kinship with classical Greco-Roman religion. Classical ritual practice was, in the phrase of Walter Burkert, religion infused with the values of *Homo necans*, "man the killer," the spear-wielder. Burkert coined that phrase because he, like many anthropologists and religious historians, believed that classical sacrificial practice was religion of killing whose origins can be

---

[14] Weber, *Wirtschaft und Gesellschaft*, 154.

tracked back to the hunter-gatherers of the Paleolithic. "[T]he principles of sacrifice," as anthropologist Tim Ingold writes, "are prefigured in the hunt."[15] The comparison with the law imposes itself. The "paradigmatic hunter," *Homo necans*, moved through the forests of the legal imagination just as he did through those of religious practice.

In all these respects, the Roman property imagination had what historian Daniel Lord Smail calls a "deep history," extending back to "the Paleolithic era, that long stretch of the Stone Age before the turn to agriculture."[16] This may seem a difficult proposition to accept; but the law of the Romans was not so different from ours. Our property law too is shaped by memories, centuries old, of feudalism. The workings of property law in the West have always turned on some remote past.

The transformation that marks later legal history can only be grasped if we are willing to take a view that extends over yet further millennia – a view of what Fernand Braudel called the *longue durée*, extending into the nineteenth century. Taking *longue durée* views never comes easily to specialists, nervous as they are when venturing outside their zones of expertise. But there *has* been *longue durée* change, and if we have the courage to step back and consider it, there is no mistaking what we see: We see, as A.-J. Arnaud writes in the phrase I have so often quoted, "a radical transformation that operated on the foundation and form of our conception of property."

The beginnings of that transformation, I have argued, can plausibly be detected in Late Antiquity. They can be linked with late antique deurbanization, which was accompanied by a territorialization of imperial rule and the relative decline of urban oligarchies, as elites drifted into the countryside, becoming something more like lords. They can also be linked with the triumph of Christianity, which, among its many consequences, led to the suppression of the classical practice of blood sacrifice in which classical elites played a preeminent role. None of these developments led to an utter collapse of the classical legal order; but taken together they tended to undermine the

---

[15] Ingold, "From the Master's Point of View: Hunting Is Sacrifice," *Journal of the Royal Anthropological Institute* 21 (2015): 24–27.
[16] Smail, *On Deep History and the Brain* (Berkeley, 2008), 2.

culture of the classical *dominus*, while fostering a tentative turn toward territoriality and "land-based" conceptions of power.

The shift continued through the slow – immensely slow – decline of a conception of ownership infused with the values of the capture and mastery over humans and beasts, giving way over many centuries to a conception of ownership embodied in John Locke's paradigmatic cultivator of land. Medieval property law experienced an unmistakable, if incomplete, shift toward a land orientation. That shift continued into the seventeenth and early eighteenth centuries, the high age of European feudal law. It made itself felt in the thinking of early modern theorists from Vitoria to Grotius to Locke. It further made itself felt in the rise of doctrines of free soil. The same shift was at work in the understanding of rulership. From the late eighteenth century onward, the conception of the state became fully territorial, decisively leaving behind a premodern order in which states exercised "primarily power over humans."[17] The same period, from the late eighteenth century onward, witnessed the greatest of events in modern legal history, the end of lawful private slavery.

This centuries-long transformation is by no means easy to explain. It can fairly be called astonishing. But it has the look of a transition paralleled by a transformation in Western religion. Christianity can be viewed as a religion that displaced older hunting values, substituting an orientation founded, as Mircea Eliade argued, in the values of agriculture. The law too experienced a shift from law whose values were values of the hunt to a law whose values were the values of the cultivation of the soil. We might speak of it as a shift from a law of *Homo necans*, "man the killer," to a law of *Homo arans*, "man the tiller."

* * *

But in any case, it is not a shift that can be understood if we think only in terms of the "maximization of income and the like." We must also make sense of Rawson's emotions, of Blackstone's affections, of Locke's strong desires. Those emotions, affections, and desires must figure in our interpretation of property law because the human grasp of "the external things of the world" can indeed never be fully described through the psychology of wealth maximization. Finley was right to question whether "investment" carries the same sense in every human

[17] Alain Testart, *Éléments de classification des sociétés* (Paris, 2005), 82.

society. What William Ewald calls the "framework of cognition" of human animals is shaped by a more complex set of impulses.

Those impulses have certainly always included the pursuit of wealth, and economic theory is always necessary for the analysis of property law. To the extent that Finley thought otherwise, his arguments have been wisely abandoned by economic historians. But the impulses underlying the human institution of ownership have always also included orientations toward status and power that are not reducible to wealth maximization. What Aquinas called the "voluptuous life," the life of "affluence in the external things of the world" has always consisted, not only in "riches," but also in "honors."[18] The human orientations toward these two voluptuous pleasures, riches and honors, can, I have argued, often be better described using the language of animal ethology than using the language of economics. We can discern vestiges – *vestigia*, "footprints" in Latin – of animal behavior in the history of Western property law. They are the footprints of human animals whose cognitive grasp of the "external things of the world" must be interpreted in light of two basic patterns in animal ethology, social dominance and territoriality.

It goes without saying that there is something disquieting in speaking of humans in this way, as dominant or territorial animals, rather than as the rational market actors of economic theory or the thoughtful moral agents of Kantian philosophy. *Vestigia terrent*, as the Roman poet Horace wrote in a famous line: "the footprints are frightening." To speak of humans as animals is, one worries, to abandon the hope of creating a just and peaceful society. It is to raise the specter of evolutionism, feared and condemned by contemporary humanist scholars. It is to stir up ugly memories of the rants of the Nazis, that terrifying sect of Darwinians.

But we can contemplate the *longue durée* developments that have so clearly shaped human history without surrendering to crude Darwinianism, Nazi or otherwise. We can generalize about human societies without forgetting that they are extraordinarily complex and varied. We can study the ethological roots of property law without asserting that human property orders mechanically obey

---

[18] Thomas Aquinas, *Summa theologiae* I-II q. 69, a. 3, obj. 5: *Consistit enim voluptuosa vita in duobus. Primo quidem, in affluentia exteriorum bonorum, sive sint divitias, sive sit honores*, available at www.corpusthomisticum.org/sth2055.html.

some fixed set of rules determined by species nature. We can recognize, not least, that human animals are entirely capable of acting with grace and decency. "No man is so savage that he cannot be tamed," opined Horace in the same famous poem, in a startling burst of optimism for a man living in first-century BCE Rome.[19] We can hope that he was right.

* * *

There is truth in what Patterson said when he described the Roman law of the *dominus* as bound up with a master/slave idiom of power. There is truth in Weber's portrayal of the predatory *domini* of classical Antiquity, ruling and raiding from their consumer cities. There is truth in Franz Wieacker's 1935 analysis of the "concrete" basis of Roman *dominium*, which turned on the psychology of power of Roman rulers whose perception of "the external things of the world" was tailored to fit their haughty sense of self.

These are not truths that we will grasp if we imagine that the Romans (or anybody else) thought only in terms of "the maximization of income and the like." We must reckon with a much wider range of human motivations and beliefs.

This is so even when it comes to a subject as deeply colored by wealth maximization, and as seemingly the proper province of economists, as the law of property. Thorstein Veblen, the theorist of conspicuous consumption, laid the charge against economics in 1909. Economists, he wrote, assume "a few large and simple pieces of institutional furniture." These "cultural elements ... so tacitly postulated as immutable precedents to economic life are ownership and free contract"; and they are "for the purposes of the theory, conceived to be given a priori in unmitigated force. They are part of the nature of things; so that there is no need of accounting for them or inquiring into them, as to how they have come to be such as they are, or how and why they have changed and are changing, or what effect all this may have on the relations of men who live by or under this cultural situation."[20]

---

[19] Hor. *Ep.* 1.1.39: *nemo adeo ferus est ut non mitescere possit*, in H. Rushton Fairclough, trans., *Horace: Satires, Epistles and Ars Poetica*, Loeb Classical Library 194 (Cambridge, MA, 1929), 255.

[20] Veblen, "The Limitations of Marginal Utility," *Journal of Political Economy* 17 (1909): 624 [620–636].

And yet they change and are changing.

The most important lesson to be drawn from this history of change in the "cultural element" that is ownership is, I think, the lesson taught by the most momentous development in the making of modern law, the end of lawful private enslavement. The drive of modern scholarship is to credit that upheaval in our perception of justice to the conscious efforts of Enlightenment reformers and of Christian abolitionists. And there can be no doubt about their moral courage, or about the impact of their campaigns. But the disappearance of lawful slavery was not just the consequence of conscious campaigns for reform. It was the consequence of a slow, and essentially unconscious, transformation in the legal imagination.

The great abolitionists were convinced that we can be the masters of our own world: that we can look upon evil, denounce it, and end it. But the truth of legal history is that we are not wholly masters of our world. We are not even wholly masters of our conscious thought. We are the subjects of processes of cultural change that extend over thousands of years, and that possess a power to shape human relations that ultimately dwarfs the power of our ambitions for moral reform.

Bibliography

Classical texts are cited according to the standard abbreviations used in the Perseus Digital Library, www.perseus.tufts.edu/hopper/, in which they are easily available. I have generally made use of Loeb translations, though I have altered them where necessary, as indicated in the footnotes. Where I have consulted other editions, they are cited in the footnotes.

Abels, Richard. "The Historiography of a Construct: 'Feudalism' and the Medieval Historian," *History Compass* 7, no. 3 (2009): 1008–1031.
Acheson, James. "Private Land and Common Oceans: Analysis of the Development of Property Regimes," *Current Anthropology* 56 (2015): 28–55.
Acheson, James M. and Roy J. Gardner. "Strategies, Conflict, and the Emergence of Territoriality: The Case of the Maine Lobster Industry," *American Anthropologist* 106 (2004): 296–307.
Adams, Julia and Mounira M. Charrad. "Introduction," in *Adams and Charrad, Patrimonial Capitalism and Empire*. Bingley, UK: Emerald, 2015, 1–6.
Adams Holland, Louise. "Qui terminus exarasset," *American Journal of Archeology* 31 (1933): 549–553.
Adiele, Pius Onyemechi. *The Popes, the Catholic Church, and the Transatlantic Enslavement of Black Africans, 1418–1839*. Hildesheim: Olms, 2017.
Albu, Emily. "The Battle of the Maps in the Christian Empire," in Claudia Rapp and H. A. Drake, eds., *The City in the Classical and Post-Classical World: Changing Contexts of Power and Identity*. Cambridge: Cambridge University Press, 2014, 202–216.
Alcock, Susan E. *Graecia Capta: The Landscapes of Roman Greece*. Cambridge: Cambridge University Press, 1993.

Alföldi, Andreas. "Die Ausgestaltung des monarchischen Zeremoniells," in *Mitteilungen des Deutschen archäologischen Instituts, römische Abteilung* 49 (1934): 3–118.
Allard, Paul. *La Persécution de Dioclétien.* Paris: Lecoffre, 1900.
Ambrosino, Rodolfo. "Le applicazioni innovative della 'mancipatio,'" in *Studi in memoria di Emilio Albertario.* Milan: Giuffrè, 1953, 2, 575–617.
Amelotti, Mario. "Reichsrecht, Volksrecht, Provinzialrecht," *Studia et documenta historiae et iuris* 65 (1995): 211–215.
Amirante, Luigi. *Captivitas e postliminium.* Naples: Jovene, 1950.
Anderson, Perry. *Passages from Antiquity to Feudalism.* London: NLB, 1974.
Ando, Clifford. "Aliens, Ambassadors and the Integrity of Empire," *Law and History Review* 26 (2008): 491–519.
Ando, Clifford. "Legal Pluralism in Practice," in Paul du Plessis, Clifford Ando, and Kaius Tuori, eds., *The Oxford Handbook of Roman Law and Society.* Oxford: Oxford University Press, 2016, 283–292.
Ando, Clifford. *Roman Social Imaginaries: Language and Thought in the Context of Empire.* Toronto: University of Toronto Press, 2015.
Ando, Clifford and Jörg Rüpke, eds., *Religion and Law in Classical and Christian Rome.* Stuttgart: Steiner, 2006.
Anghie, Antony. *Imperialism, Sovereignty and the Making of International Law.* Cambridge: Cambridge University Press, 2005.
Anon. [Une Société de Gens de Lettres]. *Grand vocabulaire françois.* Paris: De Thou, 1773.
Ardrey, Robert. *The Territorial Imperative: A Personal Enquiry into the Animal Origins of Property and Nations.* New York: Atheneum, 1966.
Arnaud, André-Jean. *Les origines doctrinales du Code civil français.* Paris: LGDJ, 1969.
Arnaud, André-Jean. "Réflexions sur l'occupation du droit romain," *Revue historique du droit* 46 (1968): 183–210.
Arnaud, P. "Marcus Vipsanius Agrippa and His Geographical Work," in M. R. Cataudella and H.-J. Gehrke, eds., *Brill's Companion to Ancient Geography: The Inhabited World in the Greek and Roman Tradition.* Leiden: Brill, 2016, 205–222.
Arnold, Jeanne E. "The Archaeology of Complex Hunter-Gatherers," *Journal of Archaeological Method and Theory* 3 (1996): 77–126.
Atkinson, Quentin D. and Harvey Whitehouse. "The Cultural Morphospace of Ritual Form: Examining Modes of Religiosity Cross-culturally." *Evolution and Human Behavior* 12 (2011): 50–62.
Augustine, Saint. *De Civitate Dei, Libri I-X*, Corpus Christianorum, series Latina 47. Turnhout: Brepols, 1955.
Badian, Ernst. *Foreign Clientelae (264–70 B.C.).* Oxford: Oxford University Press, 1958.
Bagge, Sverre, Michael H. Gelting, and Thomas Lindkvist, eds. *Feudalism: New Landscapes of Debate.* Turnhout: Brepols, 2011.

Bailey, Robert. *The Behavioral Ecology of Efe Pygmy Men in the Ituri Forest, Zaire*, Anthropological Papers, Museum of Anthropology, University of Michigan 86. Minneapolis: University of Michigan Press, 1991.
Baldus degli Ubaldi. *In primam Digesti Veteris partem commentaria*. Venice: n.p. 1599.
Balkin, Jack M. and Sanford Levinson. "The Dangerous Thirteenth Amendment," *Columbia Law Review* 112 (2012): 1459–1500.
Banner, Stuart. *How the Indians Lost Their Land: Law and Power on the Frontier*. Cambridge, MA: Harvard University Press, 2009.
Banner, Stuart. "Two Properties, One Land: Law and Space in Nineteenth-Century New Zealand," *Law and Social Inquiry* 24 (1999): 807–852.
Barros, Benjamin. "Home as a Legal Concept." *Santa Clara Law Review* 46 (2006): 255–306.
Barthélemy, Dominique. *La mutation féodale, a-t-elle eu lieu?* Paris: Fayard, 1997.
Basdevant-Gaudemet, Brigitte. *Aux origines de l'état moderne: Charles Loyseau, 1562–1627, théoricien de la puissance publique*. Paris: Economica, 1977.
Baudy, Gerhard J. "Hierarchie, oder: die Verteilung des Fleisches," in Burkhard Gladigow and Hans J. Kippenberg, eds., *Neue Ansätze in der Religionswissenschaft*. Munich: Kösel, 1983, 131–174.
Bauman, Richard. *Human Rights in Ancient Rome*. London: Routledge, 2000.
Beckwith, Christopher. *The Scythian Empire: Central Eurasia and the Birth of the Classical Age*. Princeton: Princeton University Press, 2023.
Behrends, Okko. "Bodenhoheit und privates Bodeneigentum im Grenzwesen Roms," in Behrends and Luigi Capogrossi Colognesi, eds., *Die römische Feldmesserkunst*. Göttingen: Vandenhoek & Ruprecht, 1992, 192–284.
Bell, David A. "When the Levée Breaks," *World Affairs* 170 (2008): 59–68.
Bell, Sinclair and Paul du Plessis, eds. *Roman Law before the Twelve Tables: An Interdisciplinary Approach*. Edinburgh: Edinburgh University Press, 2020.
Bellen, Heinz. "Hans Volkmann," *Gnomon* 18 (1976): 426–431.
Benton, Lauren. *Law in Colonial Cultures: Legal Regimes in World History, 1400–1900*. Cambridge: Cambridge University Press, 2002.
Benton, Lauren. *A Search for Sovereignty: Law and Geography in European Empires, 1400–1900*. Cambridge: Cambridge University Press, 2010.
Benton, Lauren. *They Called It Peace: Worlds of Imperial Violence*. Princeton: Princeton University Press, 2024.
Benton, Lauren and Richard Ross, eds. *Legal Pluralism in Empires, 1500–1850*. New York: New York University Press, 2015.
Benton, Lauren and Benjamin Straumann. "Acquiring Empire by Law: From Roman Doctrine to Early Modern European Practice," *Law and History Review* 28 (2010): 1–36.

Bercé, Yves-Marie. "Conclusion," in Ghislaine Brunel and Serge Brunei, eds., *Haro sur le seigneur! Les luttes anti-seigneuriales dans l'Europe médiévale et moderne.* Toulouse: Presses universitaires du Mirail, 2009, 202–209.

Berdan, Frances. *The Aztecs of Central Mexico: An Imperial Society.* New York: Holt, Rinehart and Winston, 1982.

Birks, Peter. "The Roman Law Concept of Dominium and the Idea of Absolute Ownership," *Acta juridica* (1985): 1–37.

Birr, Christiane. "*Dominium* in the Indies: Juan López de Palacios Rubios' *Libellus de insulis oceanis quas vulgus indias appelat* (1512–1516)." *Rechtsgeschichte* 26 (2018): 264–283.

Blackstone, William. *Commentaries on the Laws of England, Book I: Of the Rights of Persons*, ed. David Lemmings. Oxford: Oxford University Press, 2016.

Blackstone, William. *Commentaries on the Laws of England, Book II: Of the Rights of Things*, ed. Simon Stern. Oxford: Oxford University Press, 2016.

Blaufarb, Rafe. *The Great Demarcation: The French Revolution and the Invention of Modern Property.* Oxford: Oxford University Press, 2016.

Bleicken, Jochen. *Prinzipat und Dominat: Gedanken zur Periodisierung der römischen Kaiserzeit.* Wiesbaden: Steiner, 1978.

Bloch, Marc. "Comment et pourquoi finit l'esclavage antique," *Annales: économies, sociétés, civilisations* 2 (1947): 30–44.

Bloch, Marc. *Feudal Society*, trans. L. Manyon. Chicago: University of Chicago Press, 1974.

Bodel, John. "Slave Labour and Roman Society," in John Bodel and Paul Cartledge, eds., *The Cambridge World History of Slavery, Vol. 1: The Ancient Mediterranean World.* Cambridge: Cambridge University Press, 2011), 311–336.

Bodin, Jean. *Les six livres de la République.* Paris: Fayard, 1986.

Boehm, Christopher. *Hierarchy in the Forest.* Cambridge, MA: Harvard University Press, 1999.

Bonfante, Pietro. *Corso di diritto romano.* Rome: Sampaolesi, 1926.

Bonfante, Pietro. *Storia del diritto romano.* Milan: Giuffrè, 1958.

Bonnassie, Pierre. "Survie et extinction du régime esclavagiste dans l'Occident du haut moyen âge (IVe–XIe s.)," *Cahiers de civilisation médiévale* 28 (1985): 307–343.

Borah, Woodrow. *Justice by Insurance: The General Indian Court of Colonial Mexico and the Legal Aides of the Half-Real.* Berkeley: California, 1983.

Borges, Jorge Luis. "The Analytic Language of John Wilkins," in Borges, *Other Inquisitions, 1937–1952*, trans. Ruth L. C. Simmons. New York: Simon and Schuster, 1968.

Botteri, Paula. "La définition de l'*ager occupatorius*," *Cahiers du Centre Gustave Glotz* 3 (1992): 45–55.

Bouchard, Constance. "Three Counties, One Lineage, and Eight Heiresses: Nevers, Auxerre, and Tonnerre, Eleventh to Thirteenth Centuries," *Medieval Prosopography* 31 (2016): 25–46.
Boutruche, Robert. *Seigneurie et féodalité*. Paris: Fernand Aubier–Éditions Montaigne, 1959.
Bowersock, G. W. *Fiction as History: Nero to Julian*. Berkeley: University of California Press, 2018.
Bowes, Kim. "'... Nec sedere in villam': Villa-Churches, Rural Piety and the Priscillianist Controversy," in *Urban Centers and Rural Contexts in Late Antiquity*. East Lansing: Michigan State University Press, 2001, 323–378.
Bowes, Kim and Adam Gutteridge. "Rethinking the Later Roman Landscape," *Journal of Roman Archaeology* 18 (2005): 405–414.
Bradley, Keith. "Animalizing the Slave: The Truth of Fiction," *Journal of Roman Studies* 90 (2000): 110–125.
Bradley, Keith. *Apuleius and Antonine Rome: Historical Essays*. Toronto: University of Toronto Press, 2012.
Bradley, Keith. "The Regular, Daily Traffic in Slaves: Roman History and Contemporary History," *Classical Journal* 87 (1991–1992): 125–138.
Bradley, Keith. "Roman Slavery and Roman Law," *Historical Reflections* 15 (1988): 477–495.
Bradley, Keith. "Slavery in the Roman Republic," in John Bodel and Paul Cartledge, eds., *The Cambridge World History of Slavery, Vol. 1: The Ancient Mediterranean World*. Cambridge: Cambridge University Press, 2011, 241–264.
Brandenberger, David and Mikhail Zelenov, eds. *Stalin's Master Narrative*. New Haven: Yale University Press, 2019.
Braudel, Fernand. "Histoire et sciences sociales: la longue durée," *Annales: économies, sociétés, civilisations* 13 (1958): 725–753.
Bretone, Mario. "Sesto Elio et le Dodici Tavole," *Labeo* 41 (1995): 66–82.
Brett, Annabel. *Changes of State: Nature and the Limits of the City in Early Modern Natural Law*. Princeton: Princeton University Press, 2011.
Brett, Annabel. *Liberty, Right and Nature*. Cambridge: Cambridge University Press, 1997.
Brewer, Holly. "Slavery, Sovereignty, and 'Inheritable Blood': Reconsidering John Locke and the Origins of American Slavery," *American Historical Review* 122 (2017): 1038–1078.
Brilliant, Richard. "'Let the Trumpets Roar!' The Roman Triumph," *Studies in the History of Art* 56, Symposium Papers 34: *The Art of Ancient Spectacle* (1999): 220–229.
Brodersen, Kai. "Mapping (in) the Ancient World," *Journal of Roman Studies* 94 (2004): 183–190.
Brogiolo, Gian Pietro and Bryan Ward-Perkins, eds. *The Idea and Ideal of the Town between Late Antiquity and the Early Middle Ages*. Leiden: Brill, 1999.

Brown, Elizabeth A. R. "The Tyranny of a Construct: Feudalism and Historians of Medieval Europe," *American Historical Review* 79 (1974): 1063–1088.

Brown, Jerram. "The Evolution of Diversity in Avian Territorial Systems," *Wilson Bulletin* 76, no. 2 (1964): 160–169.

Brunt, P. A. "Two Great Roman Landowners," *Latomus* 34 (1975): 619–635.

Bryen, Ari Z. "Histories of Violence: Notes from the Roman Empire," in Roderick Campbell, ed., *Violence and Civilization: Studies of Social Violence in History and Prehistory*. Oxford and Oakville: Oxbow, 2014, 125–151.

Bücher, Karl. *Beiträge zur Wirtschaftsgeschichte*. Tübingen: Laupp, 1922.

Bücher, Karl. *Die Entstehung der Volkswirtschaft*. Tübingen: Laupp, 1893.

Bücher, Karl. *Die Entstehung der Volkswirtschaft: Vorträge und Versuche*. Tübingen: Laupp, 1910.

Buckland, W. W. *Roman Law of Slavery: The Condition of the Slave in Private Law from Augustus to Justinian*. New York: AMS, 1969.

Buckland, W. W. *A Text-Book of Roman Law*, 2nd ed. Cambridge: Cambridge University Press, 1950.

Buckland W. W. and Arnold D. McNair. *Roman Law and Common Law*. Cambridge: Cambridge University Press, 2008.

Buckle, Stephen. *Natural Law and the Theory of Property: Grotius to Hume*. Oxford: Clarendon, 2002.

Buffière, Félix. *Les mythes d'Homère et la pensée grecque*. Paris: Belles Lettres, 1956.

Burkert, Walter. *The Creation of the Sacred: Tracks of Biology in Early Religions*. Cambridge, MA: Harvard University Press, 1988.

Burkert, Walter. *Homo necans: Interpretationen altgriechischer Opferriten und Mythen*, 2nd ed. Berlin: De Gruyter, 1997.

Burkert, Walter. "Zum altgriechischen Mitleidsbegriff," diss. Erlangen, 1955.

Burton, G. P. "Was There a Long Term Trend to Centralisation of Authority in the Roman Empire?" *Revue de philologie* 72 (1998): 7–24.

Busbequius, Augerius Gislenius. *Epistola quatuor*. Hanover: Typis Wechelianis, 1605.

Bush, M. I., ed. *Serfdom and Slavery: Studies in Legal Bondage*. New York: Longman, 1996.

Bynkershoek, Cornelis van. *Opuscula*. Leiden: Luchtmans, 1752.

Calasso, Francesco. "Diritto volgare, diritti romanzi, diritto comune," in *Introduzione al diritto commune*, Milan: Giuffrè, 1951, 207–232.

Capogrossi Colognesi, Luigi. "Alcuni problem di storia romana arcaica: *ager publicus*, *gentes* e *clienti*," *Bolletino dell'Istituto di diritto romano* 12 (1980): 29–65.

Capogrossi Colognesi, Luigi. "*Dominium* e *possessio* nell'Italia Romana," in Ennio Cortese, ed., *La proprietà e le proprietà*. Milan: Giuffrè, 1988, 141–182.

Capogrossi Colognesi, Luigi. "Ownership and Power in Roman Law," trans. Thomas Roberts, in Paul J. DuPlessis, Clifford Ando, and Kaius Tuori, eds., *Oxford Handbook of Roman Law and Society*. Oxford: Oxford University Press, 2016, 524–536.

Capogrossi Colognesi, Luigi. *Proprietà e signoria in Roma antica*, 2nd ed. Rome: La Sapienza, 1994.

Capogrossi Colognesi, Luigi. "Le regime de la terre à l'époque républicaine," in *Terre et paysans dépendants dans les sociétés antiques* (Paris: Éditions du CNRS, 1979), 313–388.

Capogrossi Colognesi, Luigi. *La struttura della proprietà e la formazione dei "iura praediorum" nell'età repubblicana*. Milan: Giuffrè, 1969–1976.

Cardilli, Riccardo. "Il problema della libertà naturale in diritto romano," *Derecho animal/Forum of Animal Law Studies* 10, no. 3 (2019): 15–25.

Carr, Bridget, Anne Milgram, Kathleen Kim, and Stephen Warnath. *Human Trafficking Law and Policy*. Durham: Carolina Academic, 2014.

Caseau, Béatrice. "Sacred Landscapes," in G. W. Bowersock, Peter Brown, and Oleg Grabar, eds., *Interpreting Late Antiquity: Essays on the Postclassical World*. Cambridge, MA: Harvard University Press, 2001, 21–59.

Cashdan, Elizabeth. "Territoriality among Human Foragers: Ecological Models and an Application to Four Bushman Groups," *Current Anthropology* 24 (1983): 47–66.

Cashdan, Elizabeth. "Territoriality," in David Levinson and Melvin Ember, eds., *Encyclopedia of Cultural Anthropology* (1996) 4:1301–1305.

Cassi, Aldo Andrea. *Ius commune tra Vecchio e Nuovo Mondo: mari, terre, oro nel diritto della Conquista*. Milan: Giuffrè, 2004.

Cauvin, Jacques, *The Birth of the Gods and the Origins of Agriculture*, trans. Trevor Watkins. Cambridge: Cambridge University Press, 2000.

Chabot-Hanowell, Benjamin and Eric Alden Smith. "Territorial and Non-territorial Routes to Power: Reconciling Evolutionary Ecological, Social Agency, and Historicist Approaches," in James Osborne and N. Parker Van Valkenburgh, eds., *Territoriality in Archaeology*. Washington, D.C.: Archaeological Papers of the American Anthropological Association, 2015, 72–86.

Chamberlain, Robert S. *Castilian Backgrounds of the Repartimiento-Encomienda*. Washington, D.C.: Carnegie Institute, 1939.

Chanock, Martin. *Law, Custom and Social Order: The Colonial Experience in Malawi and Zambia*. Portsmouth, N.H.: Heinemann, 1998.

Chapais, Bernard. "Competence and the Evolutionary Origins of Status and Power," *Human Nature* 26 (2015): 161–183.

Chapoutot, Johann. "The Denaturalization of Nordic Law: Germanic Law and the Reception of Roman Law," in Kaius Tuori and Heta Björklund, eds., *Roman Law and the Idea of Europe*. London: Bloomsbury, 2019, 113–126.

Cherry, David. *Frontier and Society in Roman North Africa*. Oxford: Oxford University Press, 1998.

Chomel, Noel. *Supplement au Dictionnaire œconomique*. Commercy: Thomas, 1741.
Chouquer, Gérard. *La terre dans le monde romain: anthropologie, droit, géographie*. Paris: Errance, 2010.
Christ, Karl. *Römische Geschichte und deutsche Geschichtswissenschaft*. Munich: Beck, 1982.
Clark, E. G. "Pastoral Care: Town and Country in Late Antique Preaching," in Thomas S. Burns and John W. Eadie, eds., *Urban Centers and Rural Contexts in Late Antiquity*. East Lansing: Michigan State University Press, 265–284.
Coleman, Anthony P. *Lactantius and the Doctrine of Providence*. Piscataway, N.J.: Gorgias, 2017.
Coleman, Janet. "*Dominium* in Thirteenth- and Fourteenth-Century Political Thought and Its Seventeenth-Century Heirs: John of Paris and Locke," *Political Studies* 33 (1985): 73–100.
Colley, Linda. *The Gun, the Ship and the Pen: Warfare, Constitutions and the Making of the Modern World*. Princeton: Princeton University Press, 2021.
Connolly, Serena. *Lives behind the Laws: The World of the Codex Hermogenianus*. Bloomington and Indianapolis: Indiana University Press, 2010.
Cooper, Kate. "Closely Watched Households: Visibility, Exposure and Private Power in the Roman 'Domus.'" *Past & Present* 197 (2007): 3–33.
Cooper, Kate. *The Fall of the Roman Household*. Cambridge: Cambridge University Press, 2007.
Cooper, Kate. "Relationships, Resistance, and Religious Change in the Early Christian Household," in John Doran, Charlotte Methuen, and Alexandra Walsham, eds., *Religion and the Household*. Woodbridge, Suffolk: Boydell Press, 2014, 5–22.
Corbin, Arthur L. "Legal Analysis and Terminology," *Yale Law Journal* 29 (1919): 163–173.
Corcoran, Simon. *The Empire of the Tetrarchs*. Oxford: Oxford University Press, 1996.
Corni, Gustavo and Horst Gies, eds. *Blut und Boden: Rassenideologie und Agrarpolitik im Staat Hitlers*. Idstein: Schulz-Kirchner, 1994.
Cottrol, Robert. *The Long Lingering Shadow: Slavery, Race and the Law in the American Hemisphere*. Athens: University of Georgia Press, 2013.
Cover, Robert. "Nomos and Narrative," *Harvard Law Review* 97 (1982): 4–68.
Crawford, Michael. "'*Pecunia*' in the Twelve Tables," in Martin Price, Andrew Burnett, and Roger Bland, eds., *Essays in Honour of Robert Carson and Kenneth Jenkins*. London: Spink, 1993, 135–138.
Crawford, Michael. *Roman Statutes*. London: Institute of Classical Studies, 1996.

Creighton, J. N. *Narrative of the Siege and Capture of Bhurtpore in the Province of Agra, Upper Hindoostan*. London: n.p., 1830.
Crifò, G. "Per una prospettiva romanistica die diritti dell'uomo," in Klaus Girardet and Ulrich Nortmann, eds., *Menschenrechte und europäische Identität: die antiken Grundlagen*. Stuttgart: Steiner, 2005, 240–269.
Cronon, William. *Changes in the Land: Indians, Colonists and the Ecology of New England*. New York: Hill and Wang, 1983.
Cursi, Maria Floriana. *La struttura del "postliminium" nelle Repubblica e nel Principato*. Naples: Jovene, 1996.
Curtius, Ernst Robert. *Europäische Literatur und lateinisches Mittelalter*. Bern: Francke, 1948.
Dalrymple, William. *The Anarchy: The East India Company, Corporate Violence, and the Pillage of an Empire*. New York: Bloomsbury, 2019.
Davis, David Brion. *Inhuman Bondage: The Rise of Fall of Slavery in the New World*. Oxford: Oxford University Press, 2008.
Davis, Kathleen. *Periodization and Sovereignty: How Ideas of Feudalism and Secularization Govern the Politics of Time*. Philadelphia: University of Pennsylvania Press, 2012.
Davis, Natalie Z. *The Return of Martin Guerre*. Cambridge, MA: Harvard University Press, 1984.
de la Fuente, Alejandro and Ariela Gross. "Comparative Studies of Law, Slavery, and Race in the Americas," *Annual Review of Law and Social Science* 6 (2010): 469–485.
de las Casas, Bartolomé. *Historia de las Indias*. Madrid: Ginesta, 1875.
de Soto, Domingo. *De iustitia et iure*. Lyons: Jacob, 1569.
de Soto, Domingo. *Relecciones y opusculos*, ed. Jaime Brufau Prats. Salamanca: San Esteban, 1995.
de Souza, Philip. *Piracy in the Graeco-Roman World*. Cambridge: Cambridge University Press, 1999.
de Stefani, Paolo. "The *Liber Paradisus*: A Vision of Good Governance," in Markku Suksi, Kalliope Agapios-Josephides, Jean-Paul Lehners, and Manfred Nowak, eds., *First Fundamental Rights Documents in Europe*. Cambridge, Antwerp, and Portland, OR: Intersentia, 2015, 39–55.
de Zulueta, Francis, ed. and trans. *The Institutes of Gaius*. Oxford: Clarendon, 1946.
Delgado, Mariano. "Die Indios als Sklaven von Natur? Aristoteles-Rezeption in der Amerika-Kontroverse im Schatten der spanischen Expansion," in Günter Frank and Andreas Speer, eds., *Der Aristotelismus in frühen Neuzeit: Kontinuität oder Wiederaneignung?* Wiesbaden: Harassowitz, 2007, 353–382.
Demandt, Alexander. *Geschichte der Spätantike*. Munich: Beck, 1989.
Demsetz, Harold. "Toward a Theory of Property Rights," *American Economic Review* 57 (1967): 347–359.

DePalma Digeser, Elizabeth. *The Making of a Christian Empire: Lactantius and Rome*. Ithaca, N.Y.: Cornell University Press, 2000.

Deslandres, Dominique. "Et loing de France," *Revue d'histoire de l'Amérique française* 64 (2011): 93–117.

Dewald, Jonathan and Liana Vardi. "The Peasantries of France," in Tom Scott, ed., *Peasantries of Europe from the Fourteenth to the Eighteenth Centuries*. London: Longman, 1994, 21–47.

Dey, Hendrik. *The Afterlife of the Roman City: Architecture and Ceremony in Late Antiquity and the Early Middle Ages*. Cambridge: Cambridge University Press, 2015.

Di Cosmo, Nicola and Michael Maas, eds. *Empires and Exchanges in Eurasian Late Antiquity: Rome, China and the Steppe ca. 250–750*. Cambridge: Cambridge University Press, 2018.

Dickey, Eleanor. "ΚΥΡΙΕ, ΔΕΣΠΟΤΑ, DOMINE: Greek Politeness in the Roman Empire," *Journal of Hellenic Studies* 121 (2001): 1–11.

Dilcher, Gerhard. "Römisches Recht oder Deutsches Recht?" in Dilcher, *Die Germanisten und die historische Rechtsschule: bürgerliche Wissenschaft zwischen Romantik, Realismus und Rationalisierung*. Frankfurt: Klostermann, 2017, 143–157.

Diósdi, György. "Familia pecuniaque," *Acta antiqua Academiae scientarum hungaricae* 12 (1964): 87–105.

Diósdi, György. *Ownership in Ancient and Pre-Classical Roman Law*. Budapest: Akadémiai Kiadó, 1970.

Domar, Evsey. "The Causes of Slavery or Serfdom: A Hypothesis." *Journal of Economic History* 30 (1970): 18–32.

Domat, Jean. *Les loix civiles dans leur ordre naturel*, 2nd ed. Paris: Coignard, 1695.

Dowling, J. H. "Individual Ownership and the Sharing of Game in Hunting Societies," *American Anthropologist* 70 (1968): 502–507.

Drescher, Seymour. *Abolition: A History of Slavery and Anti-Slavery*. Cambridge: Cambridge University Press, 2009.

Drescher, Seymour. *Econocide: British Slavery in the Era of Abolition*, 2nd ed. Chapel Hill: University of North Carolina Press, 2003.

Drews, Carlos. "The Concept and Definition of Dominance in Animal Behaviour," *Behaviour* 125 (1993): 283–313.

du Plessis, Paul and Andrew Borkowski. *Borkowski's Textbook on Roman Law*, 5th ed. Oxford: Oxford University Press, 2015.

Ducos, Michèle. "Les juristes romains et le domaine agraire," in Ella Hermon, ed., *La question agraire à Rome: droit romain et société*. Como: New Press, 1999, 121–129.

Dukeminier, Jesse, James Krier, Gregory Alexander, Michael Schill, and Lior Strahilevitz. *Property*, 10th ed. New York: Aspen, 2022

Dulckeit, Gerhard. "Zur Lehre vom Rechtsgeschäft im klassischen Römischen Recht," in *Festschrift Fritz Schulz*. Weimar: Böhlau, 1951, 1:148–190.

Dumézil, Georges. *L'héritage indo-européen à Rome*. Paris: Gallimard, 1949.
Duplessis. *Traitez de Monsieur Duplessis sur la Coutume de Paris*. Paris: Gosselin, 1699.
Dyson-Hudson, Rada and Eric Alden Smith. "Human Territoriality: An Ecological Reassessment," *American Anthropologist* 80 (1978): 21–41.
Eck, Werner. "Die Neuorganisation der Provinzen und Italiens unter Diokletian," in Eck and Salvatore Puliatti, eds., *Diocleziano: la frontiera giuridica dell'impero*. Pavia: Pavia University Press, 2018, 111–151.
Eck, Werner, Antonio Cabbalos, and Fernando Fernández. *Das senatus consultum de Cn. Pisone patre*. Munich: Beck, 1996.
Eckstein, Arthur M. "Brigands, Emperors, and Anarchy," *International History Review* 22 (2000): 862–879.
Edelstein, Dan. *On the Spirit of Rights*. Chicago: University of Chicago Press, 2018.
Egío García, José Luis. "Matías de Paz and the Introduction of Thomism in the *Asuntos de Indias*: A Conceptual Revolution," *Rechtsgeschichte* 26 (2018): 236–262.
Egío García, José Luis and Christiane Birr. "Before Vitoria: Expansion into Heathen, Empty, or Disputed Lands in Late-Mediaeval Salamanca Writings and Early 16th-Century Juridical Treatises," in Jörg Tellkamp, ed., *A Companion to Early Modern Spanish Imperial Political and Social Thought*. Leiden: Brill, 2020, 53–77.
Ehrlich, Eugen. *Grundlegung der Soziologie des Rechts*. Munich and Leipzig: Duncker & Humblot, 1913.
Eliade, Mircea. *A History of Religious Ideas*, trans. Willard Trask. Chicago: University of Chicago Press, 1978.
Eliade, Mircea. *The Sacred and the Profane: The Nature of Religion*, trans. Willard R. Trask. New York: Harcourt, Brace, 1959.
Ellickson, Robert. "Property in Land," *Yale Law Journal* 102 (1993): 1315–1400.
Elm, Susanna. "Church–Festival–Temple: Reimagining Civic Topography in Late Antiquity," in Claudia Rapp and H. A. Drake, eds., *The City in the Classical and Post-Classical World: Changing Contexts of Power and Identity*. Cambridge: Cambridge University Press, 2014, 167–183.
Engbring-Romang, Udo. *Karl Rodbertus (1805–1875)*. Pfaffenweiller: Centaurus, 1990.
Engels, Friedrich. *Der Ursprung der Familie, des Privateigenthums, und des Staats*. Hottingen-Zürich: Schweizerische Volksbuchhandlung, 1884.
Engels, Friedrich. *Herrn Eugen Dühring's Umwälzung der Wissenschaft*, 3rd ed. Stuttgart: Dietz, 1894.
Engels, Friedrich. "Vorwort," in Karl Marx, *Das Kapital, Band II: Das Circulationsprocess des Kapitals*. Hamburg: Meissner, 1885, iii–xxiii.
Engerman, Stanley. "Some Considerations Relating to Property Rights in Man," *Journal of Economic History* 33 (1973): 43–65.

Epstein, Stephen. *Speaking of Slavery: Color, Ethnicity and Human Bondage in Italy.* Ithaca, N.Y.: Cornell University Press, 2001.

Erdkamp, Paul. "Beyond the Limits of the 'Consumer City': A Model of the Urban and Rural Economy in the Roman World," *Historia: Zeitschrift für Alte Geschichte* 50 (2001): 332–356.

Erdkamp, Paul, Koenraad Verboven, and Arian Zuiderhoek. "Introduction," in Erdkamp, Verboven, and Zuiderhoek, eds., *Capital, Investment and Innovation in the Roman World.* Oxford: Oxford University Press, 2020.

Ernout, Alfred and Alfred Meillet. *Dictionnaire étymologique de la langue latine.* Paris: Klincksieck, 2001.

Ernst, Wolfgang. "Fritz Schulz (1879–1957)," in Jack Beatson and Reinhard Zimmermann, eds., *Jurists Uprooted: German-Speaking Émigré Lawyers in Twentieth-Century Britain.* Oxford: Oxford University Press, 2004, 105–203.

Ewald, William. "Comparative Jurisprudence (I): What Was It Like to Try a Rat?" *University of Pennsylvania Law Review* 143 (1995): 1889–2149.

Fales, Frederick Mario. *Guerre et paix en Assyrie: réligion et impérialisme.* Paris: École pratique des hautes études, 2010.

Farge, James K. "John Mair: An Historical Introduction," in John Slotemaker and Jeffrey Witt, eds., *A Companion to the Theology of John Mair.* Leiden: Brill, 2015, 13–22.

Fedele, Dante. *The Medieval Foundations of International law: Baldus de Ubaldis (1327–1400).* Leiden: Brill, 2021.

Feenstra, Robert. "Les origines du dominium utile chez les glossateurs," in Feenstra, *Fata iuris romani: études d'histoire du droit.* Leiden: Leiden University Press, 1974, 234–239.

Feenstra, Robert. "Der Eigentumsbegriff bei Hugo Grotius im Licht einiger mittelalterlicher und spätscholastischer Quellen," in Okko Behrends, Malte Dießelhorst, Hermann Lange, Detlef Liebs, Joseph Georg Wolf, and Christian Wollschläger, eds., *Festschrift für Franz Wieacker zum 70. Geburtstag.* Göttingen: Vandenhoeck & Ruprecht, 1978, 209–234.

Feenstra, Robert. "Histoire du droit savant, expropriation et *dominium eminens* chez Grotius," in L'expropriation, Recueils de la Société Jean Bodin 67. Brussels: De Boeck Université, 1999, 133–153.

Feenstra, Robert. "Historische aspecten van de private eigendom als rechtsinstituut," *Rechtsgelehrd Magazin Themis* (1976): 249–54.

Feuvrier-Prévotat, Claire. "Le concept de la *familia pecuniaque* dans la loi des XII Tables," in Ella Hermon, ed., *La question agraire à Rome: droit romain et société.* Como: New Press, 1979, 59–79.

Filmer, Robert. *Patriarcha and Other Writings,* ed. Robert Sommerville. Cambridge: Cambridge University Press, 1990.

Finley, M. I. "The Ancient City: From Fustel de Coulanges to Max Weber and Beyond," *Comparative Studies in Society and History* 19 (1977), 305–327.

Finley, M. I. *The Ancient Economy*, ed. Walter Scheidel and Sitta von Reden. New York: Routledge, 2002.
Finley, M. I. *Ancient Slavery and Modern Ideology*, expanded ed., ed. Brent Shaw. New York: Wiener, 1998.
Finley, M. I., ed. *Studies in Roman Property*. Cambridge: Cambridge University Press, 1976.
Finley, M. I. *The World of Odysseus*, new ed. New York: NYRB, 2002.
Fisher, Elaine. "Fascist Scholars, Fascist Scholarship: The Quest for Ur-Fascism and the Study of Religion," in Christian Wedemeyer and Wendy Doniger, eds., *Hermeneutics, Politics, and the History of Religions: The Contested Legacies of Joachim Wach and Mircea Eliade*. Oxford: Oxford University Press, 2010, 261–283.
Fitzgerald, William. *Slavery and the Roman Literary Imagination*. Cambridge: Cambridge University Press, 2000.
Fitzmaurice, Andrew. *Sovereignty, Property and Empire*. Cambridge: Cambridge University Press, 2014.
Flannery, Kent and Joyce Marcus. *The Creation of Inequality: How Our Prehistoric Ancestors Set the Stage for Monarchy, Slavery and Empire*. Cambridge, MA: Harvard University Press, 2012.
Flückiger, Felix. *Geschichte des Naturrechts*. Zurich: Evangelischer Verlag, 1954.
Flynn, Maureen. *Sacred Charity: Confraternities and Social Welfare in Spain, 1400–1700*. Ithaca, N.Y.: Cornell Universtiy Press, 1989.
Fögen, Marie-Therèse. *Römische Rechtsgeschichten: über Ursprung und Evolution eines sozialen Systems*. Göttingen: Vandenhoeck & Ruprecht, 2002.
Forde, Steven. "The Charitable John Locke," *Review of Politics* 71 (2009): 428–458.
Fowden, Garth. *Empire to Commonwealth: Consequences of Monotheism in Late Antiquity*. Princeton: Princeton University Press, 1994.
Fox-Genovese, Elizabeth and Eugene Genovese, *The Mind of the Master Class*. Cambridge: Cambridge University Press, 2005.
Franciosi, Gennaro. "Gentiles familiam habento," in Franciosi, ed., *Ricerche sulla organizzazione gentilizia romana*. Naples: Jovene, 1995, 5–49.
Franciosi, Gennaro. *Studi sulle servitù prediali*. Naples: Jovene, 1967.
Frazer, James George. *The Golden Bough: A Study in Magic and Religion*. New York: MacMillan, 1941.
Fried, Morton. *The Evolution of Political Society: An Essay in Political Anthropology*. New York: McGraw-Hill, 1967.
Frier, Bruce. "Bees and Lawyers," *Classical Journal* 78 (1982–1983): 105–114.
Frier, Bruce. *The Rise of the Roman Jurists: Studies in Cicero's Pro Caecina*. Princeton: Princeton University Press, 1985.

Frier, Bruce and Thomas McGinn. *A Casebook on Roman Family Law*. Oxford: Oxford University Press, 2004.

Fynn-Paul, Jeffrey. "Empire, Monotheism and Slavery in the Greater Mediterranean Region from Antiquity to the Early Modern Era," *Past & Present* 205 (2009): 3–40.

Gabba, Emilio and Marinella Pasquinucci. *Strutture agrarie e allevamento transumante nell'Italia romana (III–I sec. a.C.)*. Pisa: Giardini, 1979.

Gallo, Filippo. "Osservazioni sulla signoria del 'paterfamilias,'" in *Studi in onore di Pietro de Francisci*. Milan: Giuffrè, 1956, 2:195–236.

Ganshof, Jean-Louis. *Feudalism*, trans. Philip Grierson, 3rd ed. New York: Harper, 1961.

Garnsey, Peter. *Ideas of Slavery from Aristotle to Augustine*. Cambridge: Cambridge University Press, 1996.

Garnsey, Peter. *Thinking about Property: From Antiquity to the Age of Revolution*. Cambridge: Cambridge University Press, 2007.

Garnsey, Peter and Richard Saller, *The Roman Empire: Society, Economy and Culture*, 2nd ed. Berkeley: California, 2014.

Gaudemet, Jean. "Le monde antique et les droits de l'homme – quelques observations," in Huguette Jones, ed., Le monde antique et les droits de l'homme. Brussels: Centre de droit comparé et d'histoire du droit, 1998, 175–183.

Geary, Patrick. *The Myth of Nations: The Medieval Origins of Europe*. Princeton: Princeton University Press, 2001.

Gehl, Walther. *Geschichte: 6. Klasse. Oberschulen/Gymnasien und Oberschulen in Aufbauform*. Bresau: Hirt, 1940.

Ghachem, Malick. *The Old Regime and the Haitian Revolution*. Cambridge: Cambridge University Press, 2012.

Gibbon, Edward. *History of the Decline and Fall of the Roman Empire*. New York: Harper, 1893.

Giglio, Francesco. "The Concept of Ownership in Roman Law," *Zeitschrift der Savigny Stiftung für Rechtsgeschichte (Romanistische Abteilung)* 135 (2018): 76–107.

Girard, Philippe. *Haiti: The Tumultuous History – from Pearl of the Caribbean to Broken Nation*. New York: Palgrave Macmillan, 2010.

Giltaij, Jacob. "Mensenrechten in het Romeinse Recht?" diss. Rotterdam, 2011.

Giltaij, Jacob and Kaius Tuori. "Human Rights in Antiquity? Revisiting Anachronism and Roman Law," in Pamela Slotte and Miia Halme-Tuomisaari, eds., *Revisiting the Origins of Human Rights*. Cambridge: Cambridge University Press, 2015, 39–63.

Gintis, Herbert. "The Evolution of Private Property," *Journal of Economic Behavior and Organization* 64 (2006): 1–16.

Giordanengo, Gérard. *Le droit féodal dans les pays de droit écrit: l'exemple de la Provence et du Dauphiné, XIIe–début XIVe siècle*. Rome: École française de Rome, 1988.

Girard, Paul Frédéric. *Manuel élémentaire du droit romain*, 3rd ed. Paris: Rousseau, 1901.
Gledhill, John. *Power and Its Disguises: Anthropological Perspectives on Politics*. Boulder: Westview, 1994.
Godefroy, Denys, ed. *Corpus iuris civilis a Dio. Gothofredo recognitum*. [Geneva]: Stoer, 1614.
Godelier, Maurice. "Territory and Property in Primitive Society," in Cranach, M. von, K. Foppa, W. Lepenies, and D. Ploog, eds., *Human Ethology: Claims and Limits of a New Discipline*. Cambridge: Cambridge University Press, 1979, 133–155.
Goody, Jack. *Technology, Tradition and the State in Africa*. Oxford: Oxford University Press, 1971.
Gordley, James. "Myths of the French Civil Code," *American Journal of Comparative Law* 42 (1994): 459–505.
Govind, Rahul. "The King's Plunder, the King's Justice: Sovereignty in British India, 1756–1776," *Studies in History* 33 (2017): 1–36.
Graham, Mark. *News and Frontier Consciousness in the Late Roman Empire*. Ann Arbor: University of Michigan Press, 2006.
Greer, Allan. *Property and Dispossession: Natives, Empires and Land in Early Modern North America*. Cambridge: Cambridge University Press, 2018.
Grey, Cam. "Contextualizing *Colonatus*: The *Origo* of the Late Roman Empire," *Journal of Roman Studies* 97 (2007) 155–175.
Grimm, Jakob. *Von der Poesie im Recht*. Darmstadt: Gentner, 1957.
Grossi, Paolo. *Le situazioni reali nell'esperienza giuridica medievale*. Padova: CEDAM, 1968.
Groten, Andreas. *Corpus und Universitas. Römisches Körperschafts- und Gesellschaftsrecht: zwischen griechischer Philosophie und römischer Politik*. Tübingen: Mohr Siebeck, 2015.
Grotius, Hugo. *De jure belli ac pacis*, ed. Jean Barbeyrac. Utrecht: Schoonhoven, 1773.
Grotius, Hugo. *De jure praedae commentarius*, ed. Robert Fruin. repr. Clark, N.J.: Lawbook Exchange, 2003.
Guerreau, Alain. *Le féodalisme: un horizon théorique*. Paris: Sycomore, 1980.
Gursky, M. "Die criminal-soziologische Schule als Kämpferin für die Interessen der herrschenden Klassen," *Die neue Zeit: Wochenschrift der Deutschen Sozialdemokratie* 22, no. 2 (1903–1904): 641–648.
Haarscher, Guy. "Le monde antique et les droits de l'homme," in Huguette Jones, ed., *Le monde antique et les droits de l'homme*. Brussels: Centre de droit comparé et d'histoire du droit, 1998, 197–208.
Haggenmacher, Peter. *Grotius et la doctrine de la guerre juste*. Paris: PUF, 1983.
Haivry, Ofir. *John Selden and the Western Political Tradition*. Cambridge: Cambridge University Press, 2017.

Halbe, Albert. *Eigentum als Verdienst: eine Kampfschrift gegen und für Alle*. Breslau: Trewendt und Granier, 1931.
Hallaq, Wael. "Uṣūl al-Fiqh: Beyond Tradition," *Journal of Islamic Studies* 3 (1992): 172–202.
Hämäläinen, Pekka. *The Comanche Empire*. New Haven: Yale University Press, 2009.
Hamerton-Kelly, Robert G., ed. *Violent Origins: Walter Burkert, René Girard and Jonathan Z. Smith on Ritual Killing and Cultural Formation*. Stanford: Stanford University Press, 1987.
Hammacher, Emil. *Das philosophisch-ökonomische System des Marxismus*. Leipzig: Duncker & Humblot, 1909.
Hardie, Philip. *Virgil's Aeneid: Cosmos and Imperium*. Oxford: Clarendon, 1986.
Hardin, Garrett. "The Tragedy of the Commons," *Science* (N.S.) 162 (1968): 1243–1248.
Harper, Kyle. *The Fate of Rome: Climate, Disease and the End of an Empire*. Princeton: Princeton University Press, 2017.
Harper, Kyle. *Plagues upon the Earth: Disease and the Course of Human History*. Princeton: Princeton University Press, 2021.
Harper, Kyle. *Slavery in the Late Roman World, AD 275–425*. Cambridge: Cambridge University Press, 2011.
Harries, Jill. *Imperial Rome, AD 204–363: The New Empire*. Edinburgh: Edniburgh University Press, 2012.
Harries, Jill. "Lawyers and Citizens from Republic to Empire: Gaius on the Twelve Tables and Antonine Rome," in Claudia Rapp and H. A. Drake, eds., *The City in the Classical and Post-Classical World: Changing Contexts of Power and Identity*. Cambridge: Cambridge University Press, 2014, 62–80.
Harris, William. *Roman Power: A Thousand Years of Empire*. Cambridge: Cambridge University Press, 2016.
Härtel, G. "Der 'favor libertatis' im Imperium Romanum und sein gesellschaftlicher Zusammenhang nach den Digesten im 2.–3. Jahrhundert u.Z.," *Index* 5 (1974–1975): 282–302.
Haushofer, Heinz. *Ideengeschichte der Agrarwirtschaft und Agrarpolitik*. Munich, Bonn, and Vienna: Bayerischer Landwirtschaftsverlag, 1958.
Hausmaninger, Herbert and Richard Gamauf, *Casebook on Roman Property Law*, available at https://global.oup.com/us/companion.websites/9780199 838677.
Hazard, Paul. *La crise de la conscience européenne (1680–1715)*. Paris: Fayard, n.d.
Heather, Peter and David Moncur, trans. and ed. *Politics, Empire and Philosophy in the Fourth Century: Select Orations of Themistius*. Liverpool: Liverpool University Press, 2001.
Hedemann, Justus Wilhelm. *Die Fortschritte des Zivilrechts im XIX. Jahrhundert*. 3 vols. Berlin: Haymann, 1910–1935.

Heirbaut, Dirk. "Feudal Law: The Real *Ius Commune* of Property in Europe, or: Should We Reintroduce *Duplex Dominium?*" *European Review of Private Law* 3 (2003): 301–320.

Hekster, Olivier. *Rome and Its Empire, AD 193–284*. Edinburgh: Edinburgh University Press, 2015.

Heller, Henry. "Bodin on Slavery and Primitive Accumulation," *Sixteenth Century Journal* 25 (1994): 53–65.

Heller, Michael and James Salzman. *Mine! How the Hidden Rules of Ownership Control Our Lives*. New York: Doubleday, 2021.

Henrys, Claude. *Oeuvres*, 6th ed. Paris: Libraires associés, 1772.

Hermon, Ella. "Approches historiographiques," in Hermon, ed., *La question agraire à Rome: droit romain et société*. Como: New Press, 1979, 19–29.

Herrera Ortiz, Margarita. "La encomienda indiana y sus repercussiones," in *Derechos contemporáneos de los pueblos indios: justicia y derechos étnicos en México*. Mexico City: Universidad Nacional Autónoma, 1992, 131–142.

Heuss, Alfred. *Barthold Georg Niebuhrs wissenschaftliche Anfänge*. Göttingen: Vandenhoeck & Ruprecht, 1981.

Hill, Christopher. "The Norman Yoke," in *Puritanism and Revolution*. New York: Schocken, 1964, 50–123.

Hodder, Ian. "The Lady and the Seed," in Mehmet Özdogan, Harald Hauptmann, and Nezih Basgelen, eds., *From Village to Cities*. Istanbul: Arkeoloji ve Sanat Yayınlar, 2003, 129–137.

Hodder, Ian and Lynn Meskell. "A 'Curious and Sometimes a Trifle Macabre Artistry,'" *Current Anthropology* 52 (2011): 235–263.

Hoebel, E. Adamson. "Fundamental Legal Concepts as Applied in the Study of Primitive Law," *Yale Law Journal* 51 (1942): 951–966.

Hoebel, E. Adamson. *The Law of Primitive Man: A Study in Comparative Legal Dynamics*. Cambridge, MA: Harvard University Press, 1967 (orig. 1954).

Holbach, Paul Henri Thiry, *Geschichte der menschlichen Ausartung und Verschlimmerung durch das gesellschaftliche Leben*, trans. C. L. Paaltzow, 2 vols. Altona: Verlagsgesellschaft, 1795–1796.

Hölscher, Tonio. *Visual Power in Ancient Greece and Rome: Between Art and Social Reality*. Berkeley: California, 2018.

Honoré, Tony. "Fritz Pringsheim (1882–1967)," in Jack Beatson and Reinhard Zimmermann, eds., *Jurists Uprooted: German-Speaking Émigré Lawyers in Twentieth-Century Britain*. Oxford: Oxford University Press, 2004, 205–232.

Honoré, Tony. "Les droits de l'homme chez Ulpien," in Huguette Jones, ed., *Le monde antique et les droits de l'homme*. Brussels: Centre de droit comparé et d'histoire du droit, 1998, 235–244.

Honoré, Tony. *Ulpian: Pioneer of Human Rights*. Oxford: Oxford University Press, 2002.

Honsell, Heinrich, Theo Mayer-Maly, and Walter Selb. *Römisches Recht*, 4th ed. Berlin: Springer, 1987.
Hopkins, Antony. "Property Rights and Empire Building: Britain's Annexation of Lagos, 1861," *Journal of Economic History* 40 (1980): 777–798.
Hopkins, Keith. *Conquerors and Slaves*. Cambridge: Cambridge University Press, 1978.
Hopkins, Keith. "Novel Evidence for Roman Slavery," *Past & Present* 138 (1993): 3–27.
Hopkins, Keith. *Sociological Studies in Roman History*, ed. Christopher Kelly. Cambridge: Cambridge University Press, 2018.
Hopkins, Keith. "Taxes and Trade in the Roman Empire (200 B.C.–A.D. 400)," *Journal of Roman Studies* 70 (1980): 101–125.
Hotman, François. *Novus commentarius de verbis iuris*. Basil: Nicolaus, 1563.
Howley, Joseph. "Why Read the Jurists? Aulus Gellius on Reading across Disciplines," in Paul J. Du Plessis, ed., *New Frontiers: Law and Society in the Roman World*. Edinburgh: Edinburgh University Press, 2013, 9–30.
Hudson, John. "Anglo-Norman Land Law and the Origins of Property," in *Law and Government in Medieval England and Normandy: Essays in Honour of Sir James Holt*. Cambridge: Cambridge University Press, 1994, 198–222.
Hudson, John. "Imposing Feudalism on Anglo-Saxon England: Norman and Angevin Presentation of Pre-conquest Lordship and Landholding," in S. Bagge, M. H. Gelting, and T. Lindkvist, eds., *Feudalism: New Landscapes of Debate*. Turnhout, Belgium: Brepols, 2011, 115–134.
Hülsen, Karin. "'Tempelsklaverei' in Kleinasien: ein Beitrag zum Tempeldienst in hellenistischer und römischer Zeit," diss. Trier, 2007.
Hulsebosch, Daniel. "Somerset's Case at the Bar: Securing the 'Pure Air' of English Jurisdiction within the British Empire," *Texas Wesleyan Law Review* 13 (2006–2007): 699–710.
Hume, David. "Of the Populousness of Ancient Nations," in Hume, *Political Discourses*, 2nd ed. Edinburgh: Fleming, 1752, 155–262.
Hume, David. *A Treatise of Human Nature*, ed. David Fate Norton and Mary J. Norton. Oxford: Oxford University Press, 2000.
Humfress, Caroline. "Law and Custom under Rome," in Alice Rio, ed., *Law, Custom, and Justice in Late Antiquity and the Early Middle Ages*. London: King's College, 2012, 23–46.
Humfress, Caroline. "Laws' Empire: Roman Universalism and Legal Practice," in Claudia Rapp and H. A. Drake, eds., *The City in the Classical and Post-Classical World: Changing Contexts of Power and Identity*. Cambridge: Cambridge University Press, 2014, 81–108.
Humphries, Mark. *Cities and the Meanings of Late Antiquity*. Leiden: Brill, 2019.

Hutchinson, Sharon. "The Cattle of Money and the Cattle of Girls among the Nuer, 1930–83," *American Ethnologist* 19 (1992): 294–316.
Hutton, Ronald. "The Neolithic Great Goddess: A Study in Modern Tradition," *Antiquity* 71 (1997): 91–99.
Ibrahim, Muhammad. *The Ship of Sulaiman*, trans. John O'Kane. London: Routledge, 1972.
Ingold, Tim. *The Appropriation of Nature: Essays on Human Ecology and Social Relations*. Iowa City: University of Iowa Press, 1987.
Ingold, Tim. "From the Master's Point of View: Hunting Is Sacrifice," *Journal of the Royal Anthropological Institute* 21 (2015): 24–27.
Isaac, Benjamin. *Limits of Empire: The Roman Army in the East*, rev. ed. Oxford: Oxford University Press, 2000.
Israeli, Yanay. "The *Requerimiento* in the Old World: Making Demands and Keeping Records in the Legal Culture of Late Medieval Castile," *Law and History Review* 40 (2022): 37–62.
Jakab, Éva. "Property Rights in Ancient Rome," in Paul Erdkamp, Koenraad Verboven, and Arjan Zuiderhoek, eds., *Ownership and Exploitation of Land and Natural Resources in the Roman World*. Oxford: Oxford University Press, 2015, 107–131.
Jannot, Jean-René. *Religion in Ancient Etruria*, trans. Jane Whitehead. Madison: University of Wisconsin Press, 2005.
Jefferson, Thomas. *Notes on the State of Virginia*. Baltimore: Pechin, 1800.
Jhering, Rudolf von. *Der Geist des römischen Rechts auf den verschiedenen Stufen seiner Entwicklung*, 5th ed. Leipzig: Breitkopf und Härtel, 1891.
Jhering, Rudolf von. *Der Zweck im Recht*, 6th–8th ed. Leipzig: Breitkopf & Härtel, 1923.
Jhering, Rudolf von. *Law as a Means to an End*, trans. Isaac Husik. Union, N.J.: The Lawbook Exchange, 1999.
Johannsen, Kirsten. "Die lex agraria des Jahres 111 v. Chr.," diss. Munich, 1971.
John, Felix. *Der Galaterbrief im Kontext historischer Lebenswelten im antiken Kleinasien*. Göttingen: Vandenhoeck & Ruprecht, 2016.
Johnsen, William. "Mimetic Theory, the Wall Paintings, and the Domestication, De-domestication, and Sacrifice of Cattle at Çatalhöyük," in Ian Hodder, ed., *Violence and the Sacred in the Ancient Near East*. Cambridge: Cambridge University Press, 2019, 153–164.
Johnson, Samuel. *Political Writings*, ed. Donald J. Greene, The Yale Edition of the Works of Samuel Johnson. New Haven: Yale University Press, 1957.
Johnson, Sarah. "Farewell to the *German Ideology*," *Journal of the History of Ideas* 83 (2022): 143–170.
Johnston, David. "Epiclassical Law," in Alan Bowman, Averil Cameron, and Peter Garnsey, eds., *Cambridge Ancient History* 12, 2nd ed. Cambridge: Cambridge University Press, 2008, 200–211.

Jones, A. H. M. *The Later Roman Empire, 284-602*. repr. Baltimore: Johns Hopkins, 1986.
Kaldellis, Anthony. *The New Roman Empire: A History of Byzantium*. Oxford: Oxford University Press, 2023.
Kamath, Ambika and Ashton Wesner. "Animal Territoriality, Property and Access: A Collaborative Exchange between Animal Behaviour and the Socials Sciences," *Animal Behaviour* 164 (2020): 233–239.
Kames, Henry Home, Lord. *Essays upon Several Subjects Concerning British Antiquities ... composed anno 1745*, 2nd ed. London: Cooper, 1749.
Kant, Immanuel. *Philosophy of Law*, trans. W. Hastie. Edinburgh: Clark, 1887.
Kantor, Georgy. "Property in Land in Roman Provinces," in Georgy Kantor, Tom Lambert, and Hannah Skoda, eds., *Legalism: Property and Ownership*. Oxford: Oxford University Press, 2017, 55–74.
Kantor, Georgy, Tom Lambert, and Hannah Skoda, eds., *Legalism: Property and Ownership*. Oxford: Oxford University Press, 2017.
Karr, Susan Longfield. *Jus Gentium in Humanist Jurisprudence: On Justice and Right*. Leiden and Boston: Brill, 2022.
Kaster, Robert, trans. "On Anger," in Kaster and Martha C. Nussbaum, trans., *Seneca: Anger, Mercy, Revenge*. Chicago: University of Chicago Press, 2010), 28–157.
Karras, Ruth. *Slavery and Society in Medieval Scandinavia*. Philadelphia: University of Pennsylvania Press, 1988.
Kaser, Max. *Das römische Privatrecht*. Munich: Beck, 1954–1959.
Kaser, Max. "Der Inhalt der Patria Potestas," *Zeitschrift der Savigny-Stiftung für Rechtsgeschichte (Romanistische Abteilung)* 53 (1938): 62–87.
Kaser, Max. *Eigentum und Besitz im älteren römischen Recht*. Weimar: Böhlau, 1943.
Kaser, Max. *Römisches Recht als Gemeinschaftsordnung*. Tübingen: Mohr, 1939.
Kaser, Max. "Über 'relatives Eigentum' im altrömischen Recht," *Zeitschrift der Savigny Stiftung für Rechtsgeschichte (Romanistische Abteilung)* 102 (1985): 1–39.
Kaser, Max. "Zur Geschichte der *Capitis Deminutio*," *IURA* 3 (1952): 48–89.
Kaufmann, John H. "On the Definitions and Functions of Dominance and Territoriality," *Biological Review* 58 (1983): 1–20.
Keene, Edward. *Beyond the Anarchical Society: Grotius, Colonialism and Order in World Politics*. Cambridge: Cambridge University Press, 2002.
Kehoe, Dennis. *Law and Rural Economy in the Roman Empire*. Ann Arbor: Michigan University Press, 2007.
Keiser, Thorsten. *Eigentumsrecht in Nationalsozialismus und Fascismo*. Tübingen: Mohr Siebeck, 2005.
Kelley, Donald R. "Gaius Noster: Substructures of Western Social Thought," *American Historical Review* 84 (1979): 619–648.

Kishigami, Nobuhiro. "A New Typology of Food-Sharing Practices among Hunter-Gatherers, with a Special Focus on Inuit Examples," *Journal of Anthropological Research* 60 (2004): 341–358.

Kleinheyer, Gerhard and Jan Schröder, eds. *Deutsche und europäische Juristen aus Neun Jahrhunderten*, 6th ed. Tübingen: Mohr Siebeck, 2017.

Kletzer, Christoph. "Custom and Positivity: An Examination of the Philosophical Ground of the Hegel–Savigny Controversy," in Amanda Perreau Saussine and James Bernard Murphy, eds., *The Nature of Customary Law: Legal, Historical and Philosophical Perspectives*. Cambridge: Cambridge University Press, 2007, 125–148.

Knoch, Stefan. *Sklavenfürsorge im römischen Reich: Formen und Motive*. Hildesheim: Olms, 2005.

Kolb, Frank. "La Tetrarchia: struttura, fondamento e ideologia del potere imperial," in Werner Eck and Salvatore Puliatti, eds., *Diocleziano: la frontiera giuridica dell'impero*. Pavia: Pavia University Press, 2018, 3–43.

Kornbluth, Andrew. *The August Trials*. Cambridge, MA: Harvard University Press, 2021.

Kornhardt, Hildegard. "*Postliminium* in republikanischer Zeit," *Studia et documenta historiae et iuris* 19 (1953): 1–37.

Koskenniemi, Martti. *To the Uttermost Parts of the Earth: Legal Imagination and International Power, 1300–1870*. Cambridge: Cambridge University Press, 2021.

Kotkin, Stephen. *Stalin: Waiting for Hitler, 1929–1941*. New York: Penguin, 2017.

Kratochwil, Friedrich. "Of Systems, Boundaries, and Territoriality: An Inquiry into the Formation of the State System," *World Politics* 39 (1986): 27–52.

Kuskowski, Ada. *Vernacular Law-Writing and the Reinvention of Customary Law in Medieval France*. Cambridge: Cambridge University Press, 2022.

Lagerlöf, Nils-Petter. "Slavery and Other Property Rights," *Review of Economic Studies* 76 (2009): 319–342.

Lantigua, David. *Infidels and Empires in a New World Order*. Cambridge: Cambridge University Press, 2020.

Lavan, Myles. *Slaves to Rome: Paradigms of Empire in Roman Culture*. Cambridge: Cambridge University Press, 2013.

Lavan, Myles. "The Spread of Roman Citizenship, 14–212 CE: Quantification in the Face of High Uncertainty," *Past & Present* 230 (2016): 3–46.

Leacock, Eleanor B. "The Montagnais 'Hunting Territory' and the Fur Trade," *American Anthropologist* 56, no. 5, pt. 2, memoir no. 78 (October 1954).

Leadbetter, Bill. *Galerius and the Will of Diocletian*. New York: Routledge, 2009.

Lee, Richard B. and Irven DeVore, eds. *Man the Hunter*. Chicago: Aldine, 1968.

Lee, Richard B. and Irven DeVore. "Problems in the Study of Hunters and Gatherers," in Lee and DeVore, eds., *Man the Hunter*. Chicago: Aldine, 1968, 3–12.

Leigh, Matthew. *Comedy and the Rise of Rome.* Oxford: Oxford University Press, 2004.
Lemosse, Maxime. *Le régime des relations internationales dans le Haut-Empire romain.* Paris: Sirey, 1967.
Lendon, J. E. *Empire of Honour: The Art of Government in the Roman World.* Oxford: Oxford University Press, 1997.
Lendon, J. E. "The Legitimacy of the Roman Emperor," in A. Kolb, ed., *Herrschaftsstrukturen und Herrschaftspraxis.* Berlin: Akademie, 2006, 53–63.
Lenel, Otto. *Palingenesia iuris civilis.* repr. Frankfurt a.M.: Vico, 2004.
Lenhoff, Arthur. "The Development of the Concept of Eminent Domain," *Columbia Law Review* 42 (1942): 596–638.
Leppin, Hartmut. "Zur Geschichte der Erforschung der Tetrarchie," in Dietrich Boschung and Werner Eck, eds., *Die Tetrarchie: ein neues Regierungssystem und seine mediale Präsentation.* Wiesbaden: Reichert, 2006, 13–30.
Leroi-Gourhan, André. *Le geste et la parole: technique et langage.* Paris: Albin Michel, 1964.
Levy, Ernst. "Natural Law in the Roman Period," *Natural Law Institute Proceedings* 2 (1949): 43–72.
Levy, Ernst. *West Roman Vulgar Law: The Law of Property.* Philadelphia: American Philosophical Society, 1951.
Lewis, Naphtali. "Judiciary Routines in Roman Egypt," *Bulletin of the American Society of Papyrologists* 37 (2000): 83–93.
Leyhausen, Paul. "Dominance and Territoriality as Complemented in Mammalian Social Structure," in A. H. Esser, ed., *Behavior and Environment: The Use of Space by Animals and Men.* New York: Plenum, 1971, 22–33.
Li, Danny. "The First Amendment Weaponized: When Guns Become Public Discourse," *William & Mary Bill of Rights Journal* 30 (2022): 925–961.
Lica, Vasile. "'Clades Variana' and 'Postliminium,'" *Historia: Zeitschrift für alte Geschichte* 50 (2001): 496–501.
Liebeschuetz, J. H. W. G. *Continuity and Change in Roman Religion.* Oxford: Oxford University Press, 1979.
Liebeschuetz, J. H. W. G. *The Decline and Fall of the Roman City.* Oxford: Oxford University Press, 2001.
Liebeschuetz, J. H. W. G. "Late Antiquity and the Concept of Decline," *Nottingham Medieval Studies* 45 (2001): 1–11.
Liebs, Detlef. "Strafrechtlicher Schutz der Sklaven gegen Willkür ihrer Herren," *Tijdschrift voor Rechtsgeschiedenis* 85 (2017): 1–25.
Liebs, Detlef. "Wenn Fachliteratur Gesetz wird," *Zeitschrift der Savigny-Stiftung für Rechtsgeschichte (Romanistische Abteilung)* 135 (2018): 395–473.

Lincoln, Bruce. *Secrets, Lies and Consequences: A Great Scholar's Hidden Past and His Protégé's Unsolved Murder.* Oxford: Oxford University Press, 2023.

Linklater, Wayne L. "Territorial Tuatara? – A Hypothesis Still to Be Tested," *New Zealand Journal of Ecology* 35 (2011): 308–311.

Linnekin, Jocelyn. "The Hui Lands of Keanae: Hawaiian Land Tenure and the Great Mahele," *Journal of the Polynesian Society* 92 (1983): 169–188.

Lintott, Andrew. *Judicial Reform and Land Reform in the Roman Republic: A New Edition, with Translation and Commentary, of the Laws from Urbino.* Cambridge: Cambridge University Press, 1992.

Liverani, Mario. *The Ancient Near East: History, Society and Economy,* trans. Soraia Tabatabai. Abingdon: Routledge, 1988.

Locke, John. *Two Treatises of Government,* ed. Peter Laslett. Cambridge: Cambridge University Press, 1988.

Lorenz, Stefan. "Otto Seeck und die Spätantike," *Historia: Zeitschrift für alte Geschichte* 55 (2006): 228–243.

Lovejoy, Arthur. "The Communism of St. Ambrose," *Journal of the History of Ideas* 3 (1942): 458–468.

Loyseau, Charles. *Traité des seigneuries.* Chateaudun: L'Angelier, 1610.

Lund, Christian. *Local Politics and the Dynamics of Property in Africa.* Cambridge: Cambridge University Press, 2008.

Lyall, Francis. *Slaves, Citizens, Sons: Legal Metaphors in the Epistles.* Grand Rapids: Academie, 1984.

Mack, Burton. "Introduction," in Robert G. Hamerton-Kelly, ed., *Violent Origins: Walter Burkert, René Girard and Jonathan Z. Smith on Ritual Killing and Cultural Formation.* Stanford: Stanford University Press, 1987, 1–70.

MacMullen, Ramsay. *Corruption and the Decline of Rome.* New Haven: Yale University Press, 1988.

MacMullen, Ramsay. *Roman Social Relations, 50 B.C. to A.D. 284.* New Haven: Yale University Press, 1974.

MacMullen, Ramsay. *Soldier and Civilian in the Later Roman Empire.* Cambridge, MA: Harvard University Press, 1963.

MacPherson, C. B. *The Political Theory of Possessive Individualism: Hobbes to Locke.* Oxford: Clarendon, 1962.

Maher, Christine R. and Dale F. Lott. "Definitions of Territoriality Used in the Study of Variation in Vertebrate Spacing Systems," *Animal Behaviour* 6 (1995): 1581–1597.

Maher, Lisa, Tobias Richter, and Jay T. Stock. "The Pre-Natufian Epipaleolithic: Long-Term Behavioral Trends in the Levant," *Evolutionary Anthropology* 21 (2012): 69–81.

Maier, Charles. *Once within Borders: Territories of Power, Wealth and Belonging since 1500.* Cambridge, MA: Harvard University Press, 2016.

Maine, Henry. *Ancient Law: Its Connection with the Early History of Society and Its Relation to Modern Ideas*, 10th ed. London: Murray, 1908.
Maitland, Frederic William. *The Constitutional History of England*, ed. H. A. L. Fisher. Cambridge: Cambridge University Press, 1908.
Malinowski, Bronisław. *Crime and Custom in Savage Society*. London: Harcourt, Brace, 1926.
Mannhardt, Wilhelm. *Wald- und Feldkulte*. Berlin: Gebrüder Borntraeger, 1875–1877.
Mannino, Vincenzo. *Questioni di diritto*. Milan: Giuffrè, 2007.
Mantovani, Dario. *Les juristes écrivains de la Rome antique: les œuvres des juristes comme littérature*. Paris: Docet Omnia, 2018.
Mantovani. *Le juriste "Historien,"* available at https://books.openedition.org/lesbelleslettres/204?lang=en.
Marquardt, Joachim. *Privatleben der Römer*. Leipzig: Hirzel, 1879.
Marrou, Henri-Irénée. *A History of Education in Antiquity*, trans. George Lamb. London: Sheed and Ward 1956.
Marshall, Bridget. "Romanticism, Gothic and the Law," in Kieran Dolin, ed., *Law and Literature*. Cambridge: Cambridge University Press, 2018, 142–156.
Marx, Karl. *Das Kapital: Kritik der politischen Ökonomie*, Bk. 3, 2nd ed., ed. Friedrich Engels. Hamburg: Meissner, 1904; also in Karl Marx and Friedrich Engels, *Werke*. Berlin: Dietz, 1964.
Marx, Karl. *The Ethnological Notebooks of Karl Marx (Studies of Morgan, Phear, Maine, Lubbock)*, transcribed and ed. with an introduction by Lawrence Krader. Assen: Van Gorcum, 1974.
Marx, Karl and Friedrich Engels. "Deutsche Ideologie: Manuskripte und Drucke," in *Karl Marx/Friedrich Engels Gesamtausgabe*. Berlin and Boston: De Gruyter, 2017, Abt. 1, 5.1.
Massen, Jörg, Lisette van den Berg, Berry Spruit, and Elizabeth Sterk. "Generous Leaders and Selfish Underdogs: Prosociality in Despotic Macaques," *PLoS One* 5 (2010): e9734.
Mastrocinque, Attilio. "Propriété foncière archaïque et modèles d'interprétation modernes," in Ella Hermon, ed. *La question agraire à Rome: droit romain et société*. Como: New Press, 1979, 101–109.
Mauss, Marcel. *Essai sur le don: forme et raison de l'échange dans les sociétés archaiques*. Paris: PUF, n.d.
Mazzarino, Santo. "Sociologia del mondo etrusco e problemi della tarda etruscita." *Historia* 6 (1957): 98–122.
McCormick, Michael. *Origins of the European Economy: Communications and Commerce A.D. 300–900*. Cambridge: Cambridge University Press, 2002.
McCormick, Michael. "Slavery from Rome to Medieval Europe and Beyond," in John Bodel and Walter Scheidel, eds., *On Human Bondage: After Slavery and Social Death*. Chichester: John Wiley and Sons, 2017, 249–264.

McGinn, Thomas A. J. "The Sea Common to All in Plautus, *Rudens*: Social Norms and Legal Rules," in Ioannis Ziogas and Erica Bexley, eds., *Roman Law and Latin Literature*. London: Bloomsbury, 2022, 169–188.

Meeks, Wayne. *The First Urban Christians: The Social World of the Apostle Paul*. New Haven: Yale University Press, 2003.

Meissel, Franz-Stefan. "Deutsche Rechtsgeschichte im nationalsozialistischen Staat," in Ulrike Davy, Helmut Fuchs, Herbert Hofmeister, Judith Marte, and Ilse Reiter, eds., *Nationalsozialismus und Recht*. Vienna: Orac, 1990, 412–426.

Merrill, Thomas. "The Property Strategy," *University of Pennsylvania Law Review* 160 (2012): 2061–2095.

Meskell, Lynn. "Goddesses, Gimbutas and New Age Archaeology," *Antiquity* 69 (1995): 74–86.

Meuli, Karl. "Griechische Opferbräuche," in *Gesammelte Schriften*, ed. Thomas Gelzer. Basel: Schwabe, 1975, 2:907–1021.

Miers, Suzanne and Igor Kopytoff. *Slavery in Africa: Historical and Anthropological Perspectives*. Madison: University of Wisconsin Press, 1977.

Miethke, Jürgen. *Ockhams Weg zur Sozialphilosophie*. Berlin: De Gruyter, 1969.

Milazzo, Lorenzo. *La Conquista attraverso il diritto: contributi sul discorso ispano-americano*. Milan: Mimesis, 2014.

Millar, Fergus. *The Emperor in the Roman World*. Ithaca, N.Y.: Cornell University Press, 1992.

Miller, Joseph C. "Breaking the Historiographical Chains: Martin Klein and Slavery," *Canadian Journal of African Studies/Revue canadienne des études africaines* 34 (2000): 512–531.

Mitchell, Richard E. "*Ager publicus*: Public Property and Private Wealth during the Roman Republic," in Michael Hudson and Baruch Levine, eds., *Privatization in the Ancient Near East and Classical World*. Cambridge, MA: Peabody Museum, 1996, 253–291.

Mitteis, Ludwig. *Reichsrecht und Volksrecht in den östlichen Provinzen des römischen Kaiserreichs*. Leipzig: Teubner, 1891.

Mitteis, Ludwig. *Römisches Privatrecht bis auf die Zeit Diokletians*. Leipzig: Duncker & Humblot, 1908.

Miziur-Moździoch, Maja. "How a Sheep Turned into a Giraffe: The Case of Deuteronomy 14:5," *Vetus Testamentum* 70 (2020): 753–758.

Momigliano, Arnaldo. "The Disadvantages of Monotheism for a Universal State," in *Ottavo contributo alla storia degli studi classici e del mondo antico*. Rome: Edizioni di Storia e Letteratura, 1987, 313–328.

Momigliano, Arnaldo. "New Paths of Classicism in the Nineteenth Century," in Momigliano, *Studies on Modern Scholarship*, eds. G. W. Bowersock and T. J. Cornell. Berkeley: California, 1994, 223–285.

Momigliano, Arnaldo. "The Origins of Rome," in A. E. Astin, F. W. Walbank, M. W. Frederiksen, and R. M. Ogilvie, eds., *Cambridge Ancient History* 7.2 (Cambridge: Cambridge University Press, 1989), 52–112.

Mommsen, Theodor. *Gesammelte Schriften*. Berlin: Weidmann, 1909.
Mommsen, Theodor. *Juristische Schriften*. Berlin: Weidmann, 1905–1907.
Mommsen, Theodor. *Römisches Staatsrecht*. Leipzig: Hirzel, 1871–1888.
Monier, Raymond. "Du *mancipium* au *dominium*: essai sur l'apparition et le développement de la notion de propriété en droit romain," in "Cours de droit," unpublished manuscript, 1947.
Monier, Raymond. "La date d'apparition du 'dominium,'" in *Studi in onore di Siro Solazzi*. Naples: Jovene, 1948, 357–374.
Monoson, S. Sara. "Recollecting Aristotle: Pro-Slavery Thought in Antebellum America and the Argument of Politics Book I," in Richard Alston, Edith Hall, and Justine McConnell, eds., *Ancient Slavery and Abolition: From Hobbes to Hollywood*. Oxford: Oxford University Press, 2011, 247–278.
Morgan, Lewis Henry. *Ancient Society, or Researches in the Lines of Human Progress from Savagery, through Barbarism to Civilization*. New York: Henry Holt, 1877.
Morley, Neville. "Slavery under the Principate," in John Bodel and Paul Cartledge, eds., *The Cambridge World History of Slavery, Vol. 1: The Ancient Mediterranean World*. Cambridge: Cambridge University Press, 2011, 265–286.
Morris, Ian. *Foragers, Farmers and Fossil Fuels: How Human Values Evolve*. Princeton: Princeton University Press, 2015.
Mouritsen, Henrik. *The Freedman in the Roman World*. Cambridge: Cambridge University Press, 2011.
Muldoon, James. *Empire and Order: The Concept of Empire, 800–1800*. New York: St. Martin's, 1999.
Muldoon, James. "Papal Responsibility for the Infidel: Another Look at Alexander VI's 'Inter caetera,'" *Catholic Historical Review* 64 (1978): 168–184.
Nagy, Gregory. *The Best of the Achaeans: Concepts of the Hero in Archaic Greek Poetry*, 2nd ed. Baltimore: Johns Hopkins, 1999.
Nehlsen, Hermann. *Sklavenrecht zwischen Antike und Mittelalter: germanisches und römisches Recht in den germanischen Rechtsaufzeichnungen*. Göttingen: Musterschmidt, 1972.
Nicholas, Barry. *An Introduction to Roman Law*, rev. and ed. Ernest Metzger. Oxford: Oxford University Press, 2008.
Nicolai, Helmut. *Die Rassengesetzliche Rechtslehre: Grundzüge einer nationalsozialistischen Rechtsphilosophie*, 3rd ed. Munich: Eher, 1934.
Nicolet, Claude. *Rome et la conquête du monde méditerranéen*. Paris: PUF, 1979.
Nicolet, Claude. *Space, Geography and Politics in the Early Roman Empire*. Ann Arbor: University of Michigan Press, 1991.
Nicolini, Ugo. *La proprietà: il principe e l'espropriazione per pubblica utilità*. Milan: Giuffrè, 1940.
Niebuhr, Barthold Georg. *Römische Geschichte, neue Ausgabe*. Berlin: Calvary, 1873.

Nietzsche, Friedrich. *Werke: historisch-kritische Ausgabe*, ed. Giorgio Colli and Mazzino Montanari. Charlottesville: Intelex, 1995.
Nippel, Wilfried. "Marx and Antiquity," in Danielle Allen, Paul Christesen, and Paul Millet, eds., *How to Do Things with History: New Approaches to Ancient Greece*. Oxford: Oxford University Press, 2018, 185–208.
Nock, Arthur Darby. *Conversion: The Old and the New in Religion from Alexander the Great to Augustine of Hippo*. Oxford: Oxford University Press, 1933.
Nussbaum, Martha. "Kant and Stoic Cosmopolitanism," *Journal of Political Philosophy* 5 (1997): 1–25.
Oberman, Heiko. *Dawn of the Reformation: Essays in Late Medieval and Early Reformation Thought*. Edinburgh: Clark, 1986.
Oestreich, Gerhard. *Geschichte der Menschenrechte und Grundfreiheiten im Umriß*. Berlin: Duncker & Humblot, 1968.
Olson, Mancur. *The Logic of Collective Action*. Cambridge, MA: Harvard University Press, 1965.
Olsthoorn, Johan and Laurens van Apeldoorn. "'This Man Is My Property': Slavery and Political Absolutism in Locke and the Classical Social Contract Tradition," *European Journal of Political Theory* 21 (2022): 253–275.
Osgood, Josiah. "Caesar and the Pirates: or How to Make (and Break) an Ancient Life," *Greece and Rome* 57 (2010): 319–336.
Östenberg, Ida. *Staging the World: Spoils, Captives and Representations in the Roman Triumphal Procession*. Oxford: Oxford University Press, 2009.
Osterhammel, Jürgen. *The Transformation of the World*, trans. P. Camiller. Princeton: Princeton University Press, 2014.
Ostrom, Elinor. *Governing the Commons: The Evolution of Institutions for Collective Action*. Cambridge: Cambridge University Press, 1990.
Ots y Capdequi, José Maria. *España in America: el régimen de tierras en la época colonial*. Mexico City: Fondo de Cultura Económica, 1959.
Ottmann, Henning. "Herr und Knecht bei Hegel: Bemerkungen zu einer mißverstandenen Dialektik," *Zeitschrift für philosophische Forschung* 35 (1981): 365–384.
Pagden, Anthony. *The Fall of Natural Man: The American Indian and the Origins of Comparative Ethnology*. Cambridge: Cambridge University Press, 1982.
Palacios Rubios, Juan López de. *De las islas del mar océano (Libellus de insulis oceanis)*, eds. Paulino Castañeda Delgado, José Carlos Martín de la Hoz, and Eduardo Fernández. Pamplona: EUNSA, 2013.
Parker, David. "Feudalism and Property Rights in the France of Louis XIV," *Past & Present* 179 (2003): 60–96.
Parisse, Michel. "Histoire et sémantique: de *servus* à *homo*," in Paul Freedman and Monique Bourin, eds., *Forms of Servitude in Northern and Central Europe*. Turnhout: Brepols, 2005, 19–56.
Patterson, Orlando. *Slavery and Social Death*. Cambridge, MA: Harvard University Press, 1982.

Paz, Matias de. *Acerca del dominio sobre los indios (Libellus circa dominium super indos)*, ed. and trans. Paulino Castañeda Delgado, José Carlos Martín de la Hoz, and Eduardo Fernández. Salamanca: San Esteban, 2017.

Peabody, Sue. *There Are No Slaves in France: The Political Culture of Race and Slavery in the Ancien Régime*. Oxford: Oxford University Press, 1996.

Peabody, Sue and Keila Grinberg, eds. *Free Soil in the Atlantic World*. New York: Routledge, 2015.

Pellecchi, Luigi. *Per una lettura giuridica della Rudens di Plauto*. Parma: Casanova, 2012.

Pennington, Kenneth. "Law, Feudal," in *The Dictionary of the Middle Ages*, Supplement I, ed. William Chester Jordan. New York: Scribner, 2004, 320–323.

Pérez de Tudela y Bueso, Juan. "Ideas juridicas y realizaciones politicas en la historia indiana," in *Annuario de la Asociación "Francisco de Vitoria"* 13 (1960–1961): 137–171.

Pertile, Antonio. *Storia de diritto italiano*, 2nd ed. Turin: Unione Tipografico Editrice, 1894.

Pesante, Maria Luisa. *Come servi: figure del lavoro salariato dal diritto naturale all' economia politica*. Milan: FrancoAngeli, 2013.

Peterson, Nicolas. "Demand Sharing: Reciprocity and the Pressure for Generosity among Foragers," *American Anthropologist* 95 (1993): 860–874.

Piccaluga, Giulia. *Terminus: i segni di confine nella religione romana*. Rome: Edizioni dell'Ateneo, 1974.

Pierson, Christopher. *Just Property: A History in the Latin West*. Oxford: Oxford University Press, 2013.

Pirenne-Delforge, Vivianne. *Le polythéisme grec comme objet d'histoire*. Paris: Collège de France, 2018.

Pistor, Katharina. *The Code of Capital*. Princeton: Princeton University Press, 2019.

Pleket, W. K. "Religious History as the History of Mentality," in H. S. Versnel, ed., *Faith, Hope and Worship: Aspects of Religious Mentality in the Ancient World*. Leiden: Brill, 1981, 152–192.

Plisecka, Anna. "*Accessio* and *Specificatio* Reconsidered," *Tijdschrift voor Rechtsgeschiedenis* 74 (2006): 45–60.

Pocock, J. G. A. *The Ancient Constitution and the Feudal Law: English Historical Thought in the Seventeenth Century*. Cambridge: Cambridge University Press, 1957.

Polanyi, Karl. *The Great Transformation*. New York: Farrar and Rinehart, 1944.

Poly, Jean-Pierre and Éric Bournazel. *La mutation féodale, X^e–XIIe siècle*. Paris: PUF, 2004.

Portalis, Jean-Étienne-Marie. *Discours préliminaire du premier project de Code civil*, 1801, available at https://mafr.fr/IMG/pdf/discours_1er_code_civil.pdf.

Pospisil, Leopold. *Anthropology of Law: A Comparative Theory*. New York: Harper and Row, 1971.
Pothos, Emmanuel, Andy J. Wills, John Paul Minda, and J. David Smith. "Prototype Models of Categorization: Basic Formulation, Predictions, and Limitations," in Emmanuel Pothos and Andy J. Wills, eds., *Formal Approaches in Categorization*. Cambridge: Cambridge University Press, 2011, 40–64.
Potgieser, Joachim. *De conditione et statu servorum apud Germanos*. Cologne: Promper, 1707.
Premerstein, Anton von. *Vom Wesen und Werden des Prinzipats*, ed. Hans Volkmann. Munich: Beck, 1937.
Pringsheim, Fritz. "The Unique Character of Roman Law," *Journal of Roman Studies* 34 (1944): 60–64.
Pritchett, W. Kendrick. *The Greek State at War*. Berkeley: California, 1974.
Pufendorf, Samuel. *De jure naturae et gentium libri octo*. [Amsterdam]: Junghans, 1672.
Pufendorf, Samuel. *Of the Law of Nature and Nations*, trans. anon. Oxford: Lichfield, 1703.
Pugliese, Giovanni. "'Res corporales,' 'res incorporales,'" in *Studi in onore di Vincenzo Arangio Ruiz*. Naples: Jovene, n.d., 223–260.
Radin, Margaret Jane. "Property and Personhood," *Stanford Law Review* 34 (1982): 957–1015.
Rahmatian, Andreas. *Lord Kames: Political and Social Theorist*. Edinburgh: Edinburgh University Press, 2015.
Ramin, Jacques and Marie-Paul Veyne. "Droit romain et société: les hommes libres qui passent pour esclaves et l'esclavage volontaire," *Historia* 30 (1981): 472–497.
Ranke, Leopold von. *Geschichte der romanischen und germanischen Völker von 1494 bis 1535*. Leipzig and Berlin: Reimer, 1824.
Rapp, Claudia and H. A. Drake, eds. *The City in the Classical and Post-Classical World: Changing Contexts of Power and Identity*. Cambridge: Cambridge University Press, 2014.
Rapp, Claudia and H. A. Drake. "Polis–Imperium–Oikoumenē: A World Reconfigured," in Claudia Rapp and H. A. Drake, eds., *The City in the Classical and Post-Classical World: Changing Contexts of Power and Identity*. Cambridge: Cambridge University Press, 2014, 1–13.
Rathbone, D. W. "The Control and Exploitation of *ager publicus* in Italy under the Roman Republic," in J.-J. Aubert, ed., *Tâches publiques et entreprises privées dans le monde romain*. Neuchâtel: Droz, 2003, 135–178.
Rawson, Elizabeth. *Cicero: A Portrait*. London: Allen Lane, 1975.
Rawson, Elizabeth. "The Ciceronian Aristocracy and Its Properties," in M. I. Finley, ed., *Studies in Roman Property*. Cambridge: Cambridge University Press, 1976, 85–102.

Reden, Sitta von. *Money in Classical Antiquity*. Cambridge: Cambridge University Press, 2010.
Regnault, J. J. *Le siècle de Louis Seize*. Bar-le-Duc: Moucheron et Duval, 1791.
Reynolds, Susan. *Before Eminent Domain: Toward a History of Expropriation for the Common Good*. Chapel Hill: University of North Carolina Press, 2010.
Reynolds, Susan. *Fiefs and Vassals: The Medieval Evidence Reinterpreted*. Oxford: Oxford University Press, 1994.
Reynolds, Susan. "Tenure and Property in Medieval England," *Historical Research* 88 (2015): 563–576.
Richardson, J. S. "*Imperium Romanum*: Empire and the Language of Power," *Journal of Roman Studies* 81 (1991): 1–9.
Richardson, J. S. *The Language of Empire: Rome and the Idea of Empire from the Third Century BC to the Second Century AD*. Cambridge: Cambridge University Press, 2008.
Richter, Daniel. "Cosmopolitanism," in Richter and William A. Johnson, eds., *Oxford Handbook to the Second Sophistic*. Oxford: Oxford University Press, 2017, 81–98.
Rickett, Dan. *Separating Abram and Lot: The Narrative Role and Early Reception of Genesis 13*. Leiden: Brill, 2020.
Riese, Alexander. *Geographi Latini minores*. Heilbronn: Henninger, 1878.
Riess, Werner. *Apuleius und die Räuber: ein Beitrag zur historischen Kriminalitätsforschung*. Stuttgart: Steiner, 2001.
Rilinger, Ralf. "*Domus* und *res publica*: die politisch-soziale Bedeutung des aristokratischen 'Hauses' in der späten römischen Republik," *Historische Zeitschrift: Beihefte* 23 (1997): 73–90.
Rivera-Pagán, Luis. "Freedom and Servitude: Indigenous Slavery and the Spanish Conquest of the Caribbean," in J. Sued-Badillo, ed., *General History of the Caribbean*. New York: Palgrave Macmillan, 2003, 316–362.
Rives, James. "Between Orthopraxy and Orthodoxy: Constantine and Animal Sacrifice," in G. Bonamente, N. Lenski, and R. Lizzi Testa, eds., *Costantino prima e dopo Costantino/Constantine before and after Constantine*. Bari: Edipuglia, 2012, 153–163.
Robertson, William. *History of the Reign of the Emperor Charles V, with a View of the Progress of Society in Europe, from the Subversion of the Roman Empire to the Beginning of the Sixteenth Century*. London: Cadell, 1840.
Robinson, Jonathan. *William of Ockham's Early Theory of Property*. Leiden and Boston: Brill, 2013.
Robinson, Olivia. "Crime and Punishment and Human Rights in Ancient Rome," in Huguette Jones, ed., *Le monde antique et les droits de l'homme*. Brussels: Centre de droit comparé et d'histoire du droit, 1998, 325–334.
Rodbertus, Johann Karl. "Zur Geschichte der römischen Tributsteuern," *Jahrbücher für Nationalökonomie und Statistik* 4 (1865): 341–427.

Roller, Matthew. *Constructing Autocracy: Aristocrats and Emperors in Julio-Claudian Rome*. Princeton: Princeton University Press, 2001.
Root, Hilton. *Network Origins of the Global Economy: East vs. West in a Complex Systems Perspective*. Cambridge: Cambridge University Press, 2020.
Rose, Carol. "Canons of Property Talk, or Blackstone's Anxiety," *Yale Law Journal* 108 (1998): 601–632.
Rose, Carol. "The Comedy of the Commons: Custom, Commerce, and Inherently Public Property," *University of Chicago Law Review* 53 (1986): 711–781.
Rose, Carol. *Property and Persuasion: Essays on the History, Theory and Rhetoric of Ownership*. New York: Routledge, 1994.
Roselaar, Saskia. *Public Land in the Roman Republic: A Social and Economic History of ager publicus in Italy, 396–89 B.C.* Oxford: Oxford University Press, 2010.
Roth, Hans-Jörg. *Alfeni Digesta: eine Spätrepublikanische Juristenschrift*. Berlin: Duncker & Humblot, 1999.
Roumy, Franck. "Lex consuetudinaria, jus consuetudinarium: recherche sur la naissance du concept de droit coutumier aux XIe et XIIe siècles," *Revue historique du droit français et étranger* 79 (2001): 257–291.
Rousseau, Jean-Jacques. *Discourse of the Origin of Inequality*, trans. Donald Cress. Indianapolis: Hackett, 1992.
Rudden, Bernard. "Things as Things and Things as Wealth," *Oxford Journal of Legal Studies* 14 (1994): 81–97.
Rudorff, A. A. F. "Das Ackergesetz des Spurius Thorius," *Zeitschrift für geschichtliche Rechtswissenschaft* 10 (1839): 1–194.
Rückert, Joachim, Michael Stolleis, and Dieter Simon, eds. *Rechtsgeschichte im Nationalsozialismus: Beiträge zur Geschichte einer Disziplin*. Tübingen: Mohr Siebeck, 1989.
Rüpke, Jörg. "Historians of Religion and the Space of Law," in Salvo Randazzo, ed., *Religione e diritto romano*. Rome: Libellula, n.d. [2014], 43–49.
Russell, Frederick H. *The Just War in the Middle Ages*. Cambridge: Cambridge University Press, 1975.
Sacchi, Osvaldo. *Regime della terra e imposizione fondiaria nell'età dei Gracchi*. Naples: Jovene, 2006.
Sahlins, Marshall. *The New Science of the Enchanted Universe*. Princeton: Princeton University Press, 2023.
Sahlins, Marshall. *Stone Age Economics*, new ed. New York: Routledge, 2017.
Said, Edward. *Culture and Imperialism*. New York: Knopf, 1993.
Saller, Richard. "'Familia, Domus,' and the Roman Conception of the Family," *Phoenix* 38 (1984): 336–355.
Sarris, Peter. "The Origins of the Manorial Economy: New Insights from Late Antiquity," *English Historical Review* 119 (2004): 297–311.
Savigny, Friedrich Karl. *System des heutigen Römischen Rechts*. Berlin: Veit, 1840.

Savigny, Friedrich Karl. *Vermischte Schriften.* repr. Aalen: Scientia, 1981.
Scanlan, Padraic X. *Slave Empire: How Slavery Built Modern Britain.* London: Robinson, 2020.
Scattola, Merio. "Die Grenze der Neuzeit: ihr Begriff in der juristischen und politischen Literatur der Antike und Frühmoderne," in Markus Bauer and Thomas Rahn, eds., *Die Grenze: Begriff und Inszenierung.* Berlin: Akademie, 1997, 37–69.
Scheel, H. von. "Die wirtschaftlichen Grundbegriffe im Corpus Iuris Civilis," *Jahrbücher für Nationalökonomie und Statistik* 6 (1866): 325–344.
Scheid, John. *An Introduction to Roman Religion,* trans. Janet Lloyd. Edinburgh: University of Edinburgh Press, 2003.
Schiavone, Aldo. *The Invention of Law in the West,* trans. Jeremy Carden and Antony Shugaar. Cambridge, MA: Harvard University Press, 2012.
Schiavone, Aldo. *La storia spezzata: Roma antica e Occidente moderno.* Bari: Laterza, 1996.
Schiller, Arthur A. "Custom in Classical Roman Law," *Virginia Law Review* 24 (1938): 268–282.
Schiller, Friedrich. *Über die ästhetische Erziehung des Menschen in einer Reihe von Briefen,* ed. Gideon Steinig. Berlin: De Gruyter, 2019.
Schlange-Schöningen, Heinrich. *Die römische Gesellschaft bei Galen.* Berlin and New York: De Gruyter, 2003.
Schlatter, Richard. *Private Property: The History of an Idea.* New Brunswick, N.J.: Rutgers University Press, 1951.
Schmitt, Carl. *Über die drei Arten des rechtswissenschaftlichen Denkens.* Hamburg: Hanseatische Verlagsanstalt, 1934.
Schmitt, Carl. *The Nomos of the Earth in the International Law of the Jus Publicum Europaeum,* trans. G. L. Ulmen. Candor, N.Y.: Telos, 2003.
Schmitthenner, Walter. "Über eine Formveränderung der Monarchie seit Alex. d. Gr.," *Saeculum* 19 (1968): 32–46.
Scholz, Richard. *Wilhelm von Ockham als politischer Denker und sein "Breviloquium de Principatu tyrannico."* Stuttgart: Hiersemann, 1952.
Schorr, David. "How Blackstone Became a Blackstonian," *Theoretical Inquiries in Law* 10 (2009): 103–126.
Schulz, Fritz. *The History of Roman Legal Science.* Oxford: Oxford University Press, 1946.
Schulz, Fritz. *Prinzipien des römischen Rechts.* Munich: Duncker & Humblot, 1934.
Seaford, Richard. *Money and the Early Greek Mind.* Cambridge: Cambridge University Press, 2004.
Sedano Onofri, Renato. "Roman Law as Pamphlet: Fritz Schulz and the *Prinzipien des römischen Rechts* between Cesar [sic] and Hitler," *História do direito* 3 (2022): 3–36.
Seidl, Ursula. *Die babylonischen Kudurru-Reliefs: Symbole mesopotamischer Gottheiten.* Göttingen: Vandenhoeck & Ruprecht, 1989.

Selden, John. *Mare Clausum, seu de Dominio Maris.* Leiden: Maire, 1636.
Service, Elman. *Primitive Social Organization: An Evolutionary Perspective,* 2nd ed. New York: Random House, 1971.
Shaik, Carel P. van and Judith Burkart. "Mind the Gap: Cooperative Breeding and the Evolution of Our Unique Features," in Peter M. Kappeler and Joan B. Silk, eds., *Mind the Gap: Tracing the Origins of Human Universals.* Berlin: Springer, 2009, 477–496.
Sharfstein, Daniel. "Atrocity, Entitlement and Personhood in Property," *Virginia Law Review* 98 (2012): 635–690.
Shaw, Brent. "Bandits in the Roman Empire," *Past & Present* 105 (1984): 3–52.
Shaw, Brent. "Raising and Killing Children: Two Roman Myths," *Mnemosyne* Ser. 4, 54 (2001): 31–77.
Shryock, Andrew and Daniel Smail. *Deep History: The Architecture of Past and Present.* Berkeley: California, 2011.
Signer, Michael. *Becoming Madison: The Extraordinary Origins of the Least Likely Founding Father.* New York: Public Affairs, 2015.
Simpson, Lesley Byrd. *The Encomienda in New Spain.* Berkley: California, 1982.
Sirks, Boudewijn. "The Colonate in Justinian's Reign," *Journal of Roman Studies* 98 (2008): 120–143.
Sirks, Boudewijn. "The Colonate in the Later Roman Empire," *Tijdschrift voor Rechtsgeschiedenis* 90 (2022): 125–147.
Sirks, Boudewijn. "Noxa caput sequitur," *Tijdschrift voor Rechtsgeschiedenis* 81 (2013): 81–108.
Sirks, Boudewijn. "Public Law," in David Johnston, ed., *The Cambridge Companion to Roman Law.* Cambridge: Cambridge University Press, 2015, 332–352.
Sirks, Boudewijn. "Reconsidering the Roman Colonate," *Zeitschrift der Savigny-Stiftung für Rechtsgeschichte (Romanistische Abteilung)* 110 (1993): 331–369.
Sisani, Simone. *L'ager publicus in età graccana.* Rome: Quasar, 2015.
Skaff, Jonathan. *Sui-Tang China and Its Turko-Mongol Neighbors: Culture, Power and Connections, 580–800.* New York: Oxford University Press, 2012.
Smail, Daniel. *On Deep History and the Brain.* Berkeley: California, 2008.
Smith, Adam. *An Inquiry into the Nature and Causes of the Wealth of Nations,* ed. Edwin Cannan. New York: Bantam, 1994.
Smith, Christopher. "Becoming Political: Middle Republican Quandaries," in Seth Bernard, Lisa Maria Mignone, and Dan-el Padilla Peralta, eds., *Making the Middle Republic: New Approaches to Rome and Italy, c. 400–200 BCE.* Cambridge: Cambridge University Press, 2023, 253–269.
Smith, Henry. "Exclusion and Property Rules in the Law of Nuisance," *Virginia Law Review* 90 (2004): 965–1049.

Smith, Henry. "Exclusion versus Governance: Two Strategies for Delineating Property Rights," *Journal of Legal Studies* 31 (2002): S453–S487.
Smith, Henry. "Intellectual Property as Property: Delineating Entitlements in Information," *Yale Law Journal* 116 (2007): 1742–1822.
Smith, Jonathan Z. "The Bare Facts of Ritual," *History of Religions* 20 (1980): 112–127.
Smith, Jonathan Z. "Morphology and History in Mircea Eliade's 'Patterns in Comparative Religion,'" *History of Religions* 39 (2000): 332–351.
Smith, Michael R. "Mesoamerican State Formation in the Postclassic Period," in Benjamin Kedar and Merry Wiesner-Hanks, eds., *Cambridge World History, Vol. 5: Expanding Webs of Exchange and Conflict, 500 CE–1500 CE*. Cambridge: Cambridge University Press, 2015) 610–637.
Sneath, David. *The Headless State*. New York: Columbia University Press, 2007.
Spieß, Karl-Heinz. "Lehnsgericht," in Adalbert Erler and Ekkehard Kaufmann, *Handwörterbuch zur deutschen Rechtsgschichte*. Frankfurt a.M.: Erich Schmidt, 1971–, 2: cols. 1714–1717.
Steiger, Heinhard. "Rechtliche Strukturen der europäischen Sttatsordnung 1648–1792," *Zeitschrift für ausländisches öffentliches Recht und Völkerrecht* 59 (1999): 609–645.
Steinmetzer, Franz X. *Die babylonischen Kudurru als Urkundenform*. Paderborn: Schöningh, 1922.
Stern, Fritz. *The Politics of Cultural Despair*. Berkeley: University of California Press, 1974.
Stern, Stephanie. "Residential Protectionism and the Legal Mythology of Home," *Michigan Law Review* 107 (2009): 1093–1144.
Stroumsa, Guy. *The End of Sacrifice: Religious Transformations in Late Antiquity*, trans. Susan Emanuel. Chicago: University of Chicago Press, 2009.
Summenhart, Konrad. *Tractatus de contractis licitis atque illicitis*, Venice: Ziletto, 1580.
Sweet, James H. "Defying Social Death: The Multiple Configurations of African Slave Family in the Atlantic World," *William and Mary Quarterly* 70 (April 2013): 251–272.
Syme, Ronald. *The Roman Revolution*. Oxford: Oxford University Press, 1939.
Tabuteau, Emily. *Transfers of Property in Eleventh-Century Norman Law*. Chapel Hill: University of North Carolina Press, 1988.
Talamanca, Mario. "Considerazioni conclusive," in Ennio Cortese, ed., *La proprietà e le proprietà*. Milan: Giuffrè, 1988, 183–200.
Talamanca, Mario. "L'antichità e i 'diritti dell'uomo,'" *Atti dei Convegni Lincei* 174 (2001): 41–91.
Tannenbaum, Frank. *Slave and Citizen: The Negro in the Americas*. New York: Vintage, 1946.

Tannous, Jack. *The Making of the Medieval Middle East: Religion, Society and the Simple Believers.* Princeton: Princeton University Press, 2018.
Temin, Peter. "The Labor Market of the Early Roman Empire," *Journal of Interdisciplinary History* 34 (2004): 513–538.
Testart, Alain. *Éléments de classification des sociétés.* Paris: Éditions Errance, 2005.
Testart, Alain. "Game Sharing Systems and Kinship Systems among Hunter-Gatherers," *Man* (N.S.) 22 (1987): 287–304.
Testart, Alain. "The Significance of Food Storage among Hunter-Gatherers: Residence Patterns, Population Densities, and Social Inequalities," *Current Anthropology* 23 (1982): 523–537.
Thapar, Romila. *From Lineage to State.* Oxford: Oxford University Press, 1984.
Thomas, Yan. *Les opérations du droit*, ed. Marie-Angèle Hermitte and Paolo Napoli. Paris: Seuil/Gallimard, 2011.
Thomas, Yan. *"Origine" et "commune patrie": étude de droit public romain (89 av. J.-C.–212 ap. J.-C.).* Rome: École française de Rome, 1996.
Thomas, Yan. "*Res*, chose et patrimoine (note sur le rapport sujet–objet en droit romain)," *Archives de philosophie du droit* 25 (1980): 413–426.
Thomas, Yan. "Vitae necisque potestas," in Thomas, ed., *Du châtiment dans la cité: supplices corporels et peine de mort.* Rome: École française de Rome, 1984, 499–548.
Thomson de Grummond, Nancy. "Prophets and Priests," in de Grummond and Erika Simon, eds., *The Religion of the Etruscans.* Austin: University of Texas Press, 2006, 27–44.
Thormann, Karl Friedrich. *Der doppelte Ursprung der mancipatio: ein Beitrag zur Erforschung des frühromischen Rechtes unter Mitberücksichtigung des nexum.* Munich: Beck, 1943.
Thornton, John. *Africa and Africans in the Making of the Atlantic World, 1400–1680.* Cambridge: Cambridge University Press, 1992.
Tuck, Richard. *Rights of War and Peace: Political Thought and the International Order from Grotius to Kant.* Oxford: Oxford University Press, 2001.
Tully, James. *A Discourse on Property: John Locke and His Adversaries.* Cambridge: Cambridge University Press, 1980.
Tuori, Kaius. *The Emperor of Law: The Emergence of Roman Imperial Adjudication.* Oxford: Oxford University Press, 2016.
Tuori, Kaius. *Empire of Law: Nazi Germany, Exile Scholars and the Battle for the Future of Europe.* Cambridge: Cambridge University Press, 2020.
Tuori, Kaius. "Legal Pluralism and the Roman Empire," in J. W. Cairns and P. du Plessis, eds., *Beyond Dogmatics.* Edinburgh: Edinburgh University Press, 2007, 39–52.
Turfa, Jean MacIntosh. *Divining the Etruscan World: The Brontoscopic Calendar and Religious Practice.* Cambridge: Cambridge University Press, 2012.

Vaan, Michiel de. *Etymological Dictionary of Latin and Other Italic Languages*. Leiden: Brill, 2008.

Valeri, Valerio. "Wild Victims: Hunting as Sacrifice and Sacrifice as Hunting in Huaulu," *History of Religions* 34 (1994): 101–131.

Valvo, Alfredo. *La "Profezia di Vegoia": proprietà fondiaria e aruspicina nel primo secolo a.C.* Rome: Istituto italiano per la storia antica, 1988.

Vandendriessche, Sarah. *Possessio und Dominium im postklassischen römischen Recht*. Hamburg: Dr. Kovac, 2006.

Varkemaa, Jussi. *Conrad Summenhart's Theory of Individual Rights*. Leiden and Boston: Brill, 2011.

Veblen, Thorstein. "The Limitations of Marginal Utility," *Journal of Political Economy* 17 (1909): 620–636.

Veblen, Thorstein. *The Theory of the Leisure Class: An Economic Study of Institutions*. New York: MacMillan, 1902.

Verene, Donald Phillip. *Vico's New Science: A Philosophical Commentary*. Ithaca, N.Y.: Cornell University Press, 2016.

Verene, Donald Phillip. *Vico's Science of Imagination*. Ithaca, N.Y.: Cornell University Press, 1981.

Verhulst, Adriaan and Monique Bourin. "Europe carolingienne et Europe méridionale: le point de vue d'Adriaan Verhulst," *Médiévales* 21 (1991): 55–61.

Verlinden, Charles. "L'origine de *sclavus* = esclave," *Bulletin Du Cange* 17 (1943): 97–128.

Versnel, H. S. *Inconsistencies in Greek and Roman Religion, Vol. 1*. Leiden: Brill, 1990.

Vico, Giambattista. *La scienza nuova*, ed. Paolo Rossi. Milan: Rizzoli, 1958.

Vitoria, Francisco de. *Comentarios a la Secunda secundae de Santo Tomaso*, ed. Vicente Beltran de Heredia. Salamanca: Biblioteca de Teólogos Españoles, 1932–.

Visscher, Fernand de. *Études de droit romain public et privé, 3e série*. Milan: Giuffrè, 1966.

Visscher, Fernand de. "Mancipium et res mancipi," *Studia et documenta historiae et iuris* 2 (1936): 263–324.

Volkmann, Hans. *Die Massenversklavungen der Einwohner eroberter Städte in der hellenistisch-römischen Zeit*, 2nd ed. Stuttgart: Steiner, 1990.

Voltaire [François-Marie Arouet]. *Commentaire sur l'esprit des lois de Montesquieu*. Paris: Delaunay, 1819.

Vultejus, Hermann. *In Institutiones juris civilis commentarius*, new ed. Marburg: Egenolph, 1630.

Wagner, Adolph. *Lehr- und Handbuch der politischen Ökonomie*, 2nd ed. Leipzig: Winter, 1894.

Walde, Alois. *Lateinisches etymologisches Wörterbuch*, 3rd ed., ed. J. B. Hofmann. Heidelberg: Winter, 1938.

Wallace-Hadrill, Andrew. "Back to M. I. Finley's Ancient City: Town and Country, Landowners and the Rest at Pompeii," *Journal of Roman Archaeology* 32 (2019): 718–723.
Wallace-Hadrill, Andrew. "*Domus* and *Insulae* in Rome: Families and Households," in David L. Balch and Carolyn Osiek, eds., *Early Christian Families in Context*. Grand Rapids: Eerdmans, 2003, 3–18.
Wallace-Hadrill, Andrew. "Patronage in Roman Society," in Wallace-Hadrill, ed., *Patronage in Ancient Society*. London: Routledge, 1989, 63–87.
Wallon, Henri. *Histoire de l'esclavage dans l'antiquité*. Paris: Imprimerie Royale, 1867.
Ward-Perkins, Bryan. "Continuists, Catastrophists and the Towns of Post-Roman Northern Italy," *Papers of the British School at Rome* 65 (1997): 157–176.
Washburn, Sherwood and Chet Lancaster. "The Evolution of Hunting," in Richard B. Lee and Irven Devore, eds., *Man the Hunter*. Chicago: Aldine, 1968, 293–303.
Watkins, Calvert. *American Heritage Dictionary of Indo-European Roots*. Boston: Houghton Mifflin, 1985.
Watkins, Thomas H. "Coloniae and *ius italicum* in the Early Empire," *Classical Journal* 78 (1983): 319–326.
Watkins, Thomas H. "Roman Citizen Colonies and Italic Right," in C. Deroux, ed., *Studies in Latin Literature and Roman History, I*. Brussels: Collections Latomus, 1979: 59–99.
Watson, Alan. *The Law of Property in the Later Roman Republic*. Oxford: Clarendon, 1968.
Watson, Alan. "Roman Slave Law and Romanist Ideology," *Phoenix* 37 (1983): 53–65.
Watson, Alan. *Rome of the XII Tables: Persons and Property*. Princeton: Princeton University Press, 1975.
Watson, James L. "Slavery as an Institution, Open and Closed Systems," in Watson, ed., *Asian and African Systems of Slavery*. Berkeley: California, 1980, 1–15.
Wauters, Bart. "Property," in Randall Lesaffer and Janne Nijman, eds., *The Cambridge Companion to Hugo Grotius*. Cambridge: Cambridge University Press, 2021, 492–512.
Weber, Max. *Die römische Agrargeschichte in ihrer Bedeutung für das Staats- und Privatrecht*. Stuttgart: Enke, 1891.
Weber, Max. "Die sozialen Gründe des Untergangs der antike Kultur," in Weber, *Gesammelte Aufsätze zur Sozial- und Wirtschaftsgeschichte*, Tübingen: Mohr, 1924, 289–311.
Weber, Max. *Gesammelte Aufsätze zur Sozial- und Wirtschaftsgeschichte*. Tübingen: Mohr, 1924.
Weber, Max. *Wirtschaft und Gesellschaft*, ed. Johannes Winckelmann, 5th ed. Tübingen: Mohr, 1985.

Wellesley, K. "The Production Date of Plautus' *Captivi*," *American Journal of Philology* 76 (1955): 298–305.
Werkmüller, Dieter. "Luft macht eigen – Luft macht frei," in Adalbert Erler and Ekkehard Kaufmann, eds., *Handwörterbuch zur deutschen Rechtsgschichte*. Frankfurt a.M.: Erich Schmidt, 1971–, 3: cols. 92–98.
White, K. D. "Latifundia," *Bulletin of the Institute of Classical Studies* 14 (1967): 62–79.
White, Richard. *The Middle Ground: Indians, Empires and Republics in the Great Lakes Region, 1650–1815*. Cambridge: Cambridge University Press, 2010.
White, Stephen D. "The Discourse of Inheritance in Twelfth-Century France: Alternative Models of the Fief in 'Raoul de Cambrai,'" in George Garnett and John Hudson, eds., *Law and Government in Medieval England and Normandy: Essays in Honour of Sir James Holt*. Cambridge: Cambridge University Press, 1994, 173–197.
Whitman, James Q. "Aux origines du 'monopole de la violence,'" in C. Colliot-Thélène and J.-F. Kervégan, eds., *De la société à la sociologie*. Lyons: ENS Éditions, 2002.
Whitman, James Q. *Harsh Justice: Criminal Punishment and the Widening Divide between America and Europe*. New York: Oxford University Press, 2003.
Whitman, James Q. *The Legacy of Roman Law in the German Romantic Era: Historical Vision and Legal Change*. Princeton: Princeton University Press, 1990.
Whitman, James Q. "Long Live the Hatred of Roman Law!" *Rechtsgeschichte* 2 (2003): 40–57.
Whitman, James Q. "The Seigneurs Descend to the Rank of Creditors: The Abolition of Respect, 1790," *Yale Journal of Law and Humanities* 6 (1994): 249–283.
Whitman, James Q. "The Two Western Cultures of Privacy: Dignity versus Liberty," *Yale Law Journal* 113 (2004): 1151–1221.
Whitman, James Q. *The Verdict of Battle: The Law of Victory and the Making of Modern War*. Cambridge, MA: Harvard University Press, 2012.
Whitman, James Q. "The World-Historical Significance of European Legal History: An Interim Report," in Heikki Pihlajamäki, Markus D. Dubber, and Mark Godfrey, eds., *The Oxford Handbook of European Legal History*. Oxford: Oxford University Press, 2018.
Wickham, Chris. *Framing the Early Middle Ages: Europe and the Mediterranean, 400–800*. Oxford: Oxford University Press, 2007.
Wickham, Chris. *The Inheritance of Rome: Illuminating the Dark Ages, 400–1000*. New York: Penguin, 2010.
Wickham, Chris. "Marx, Sherlock Holmes, and Late Roman Commerce," *Journal of Roman Studies* 78 (1988): 183–193.

Wickham, Chris. "The Other Transition: From the Ancient World to Feudalism," *Past & Present* 103 (1984): 3–36.
Wieacker, Franz. *Wandlungen der Eigentumsverfassung*, Der deutsche Staat der Gegenwart 13, ed. Carl Schmitt. Hamburg: Hanseatische Verlagsanstalt, 1935.
Wieacker, Franz. *Zivilistische Schriften (1934–1942)*, ed. Christian Wollschläger. Frankfurt a.M.: Klostermann, 2000.
Wieling, Hans, ed. *Corpus der römischen Rechtsquellen zur antiken Sklaverei*. Stuttgart: Steiner, 1999.
Wieling, H. J. *Testamentsauslegung im römischen Recht*. Munich: Beck, 1972.
Wilentz, Sean. *No Property in Man: Slavery and Anti-slavery at the Nation's Founding*. Cambridge, MA: Harvard University Press, 2018.
Williams, Eric. *Capitalism and Slavery*. Chapel Hill: University of North Carolina Press, 1944.
Willoweit, Dietmar. *Rechtsgrundlagen der Territorialgewalt: Landesobrigkeit, Herrschaftsrechte und Territorium in Rechtswissenschaft der Neuzeit*. Cologne and Vienna: Böhlau, 1975.
Winichakul, Thongchai. *Siam Mapped: A History of the Geo-body of a Nation*. Honolulu: University of Hawaii Press, 1994.
Winkel, Laurens. "Deux conceptions du droit naturel dans l'antiquité," *Revue historique du droit français et étranger* 93 (2015): 341–350.
Winspeare, Davide. *Storia degli abusi feudali*. Naples: Erani, 1811.
Wirtschafter, Elise Kimerling. *From Serf to Russian Soldier*. Princeton: Princeton University Press, 1990.
Witschel, Christian. *Krise–Rezession–Stagnation? Der Westen des römischen Reiches im 3. Jahrhundert*. Frankfurt a.M.: Marthe Klauss, 1999.
Wolff, Hans Julius. *Roman Law: An Historical Introduction*. Norman: University of Oklahoma, 1951.
Wood, Brian M. and Ian C. Gilby. "From *Pan* to Man the Hunter: Hunting and Meat Sharing by Chimpanzees, Humans, and Our Common Ancestor," in Martin Muller, Richard Wrangham, and David Pilbeam, eds., *Chimpanzees and Human Evolution*. Cambridge, MA: Harvard University Press, 2017, 339–382.
Wood, Ellen Meiksinis. *From Citizens to Lords: A Social History of Western Political Thought from Antiquity to the Late Middle Ages*. London: Verso, 2011.
Wrangham, Richard. "The Evolution of Coalitionary Killing," *American Journal of Physical Anthropology* 110 (1999): 1–30.
Wrangham, Richard. *The Goodness Paradox: The Strange Relationship between Virtue and Violence in Human Evolution*. New York: Vintage, 2019.
Yen, Alfred C. "Western Frontiers or Feudal Society? Metaphors and Perceptions of Cyberspace," *Berkeley Technology Law Journal* 17 (2002): 1207–1263.

Zacour, Norman. *Jews and Saracens in the Consilia of Oldradus de Ponte*. Toronto: Pontifical Institute, 1990.
Zartaloudis, Thanos. *The Birth of Nomos*. Edinburgh: Edinburgh University Press, 2018.
Zeder, Melinda. "Religion and the Revolution: The Legacy of Jacques Cauvin," *Paléorient* 37 (2011): 39–60.
Ziegler, Karl-Heinz. *Fata iuris gentium: kleine Schriften zur Geschichte des europäischen Völkerrechts*. Baden-Baden: Nomos, 2008.
Ziegler, Karl-Heinz. "Grenze," in *Reallexikon für Antike und Christentum*. Stuttgart: Hiersemann, 1950–2022, 12: cols. 1095–1107.
Zimmermann, Reinhard. "Hero auf dem Felsenturme," *Rechtsgeschichte* 30 (2022): 294–300.
Zunz, Oliver. *The Man Who Understood Democracy: The Life of Alexis de Tocqueville*. Princeton: Princeton University Press, 2022.
Zyl, D. H. van. *History and Principles of Roman Private Law*. Durban: Butterworths, 1983.

Index

Africa, precolonial
   slavery in, 59–61
Ager publicus, 83, 88–90, 128–131, 141, 200
   as governed by use rights, 89–90
Agriculture
   religion of, 328–330
Alexander VI, Pope, 311, 339, 357
Althusser, Louis, 18
Ambrose, Saint, 353
Animal sacrifice, 91, 390
   classical priesthoods of, 155–157
   decline in Late Antiquity, 326–327
   related to hunt, 53, 158
Appian of Alexandria, 130, 270
Apuleius, 172
Aquinas, Saint Thomas, 354–355, 392
Ardrey, Robert, 9
Aristotle, 293, 297
   on natural slavery, 163–164, 338, 342
   on private ownership of land, 349–352
   on war as hunting, 14
Arnaud, André-Jean, 19, 122, 189, 341, 390
Augustine, Saint, 27, 170
Austen, Jane, 12, 386

Badian, Ernst, 222
Benton, Lauren, 377
Blackstone, William, 1, 78, 259, 333, 386–387
   on eminent domain, 367–368
   on slavery, 11
Blackstonian ownership, 380
   and eminent domain, 364
Bloch, Marc, 234, 237, 278–279
Blood sacrifice. *See* Animal sacrifice
Blut und Boden, 5, 39
Bodin, Jean, 322, 370, 375–376
Borders
   of private holdings, 163–164, 312
   of states, 213, 312–313
Boundary stones, 44, 312
   in Roman religion, 91
Braudel, Fernand, 288, 390
Brett, Annabel, 320, 359, 377
Brown, Elizabeth A. R., 239, 240, 247, 251–252, 288
Bücher, Karl, 72, 99, 275, 297
Burkert, Walter, 50, 53, 158, 328, 389

Capitis deminutio, 201–204
Capogrossi Colognesi, Luigi, 87
Castle doctrine, 3, 12
Chieftainship over people, 6, 21, 59, 80, 210, 356, 389
Christianity
   and decline of slavery, 25, 322–323
   and idea of territorial *oikoumenē* in Late Antiquity, 325
   teachings on primitive communism, 42
Church
   drift into countryside from Late Antiquity, 303–304

435

Cicero, Marcus Tullius, 42, 93, 121
Cities
  cultural and administrative centrality in classical Antiquity, 294–295
  decline of attraction of council in Late Antiquity, 300–301
  loss of momentum in Late Antiquity, 298–302
Coloni, 264–265, 267
Common law
  feudal character, 256
Conscription, 384
Consumer city hypothesis, 274–276, 297–298, 387
Cooper, Kate, 151, 326
Cursus honorum, 137, 152–153, 301
Curtius, Ernst Robert, 289
Customary law, 305–306, 307–308

Diocletian, 291, 357
  Persecution of, 317–318
  reign of, 309–322
Discordia
  contrasted with δυσκολία, 354–355, 358
  in thought of Aquinas, 354–355
Domar, Evsey, 71
Domat, Jean, 259
Dominance. *See* Social dominance
Dominium
  as term for property, 20, 21–22, 126, 137
  range of meanings in Latin, 143
Dominium directum. See Split ownership
Dominium utile. See Split ownership
Dominus
  as deferential form of address, 148
  as form of address for Emperor, 314–317
  as term for owner, 20
  challenge to household dominance in Late Antiquity, 326
  classical figure revived in French Revolution, 260–261
  contrasted with *paterfamilias*, 153–154
  etymology of, 143
  in Roman ownership ideology, 20–21
  in Roman rulership ideology, 148–149
  medieval usage, 21–22
  range of usage in Late Republic and Early Prinicipate, 149

Dred Scott v. *Sandford*, 375
Dumézil, Georges, 207
Duplex dominium. See Split ownership

δυσκολία, 352
Economic history, primitivist school of, 98–99
Eliade, Mircea, 15, 158, 224, 328–330, 391
  on agricultural religion, 329
Eminent domain, 352
  as doctrinal precondition for Blackstonian ownership, 364
  in thought of Grotius, 362–364
Encomienda, 337–338
Engels, Friedrich, 18, 97, 127, 132
Enslavement
  as threat to high-status persons, 167–169
  founded in natural inferiority of victim, 163–164
  justified by consent of the victim in early modern period, 371–374
  justified by consent of victim, 163
  of exposed infants, 170
  of peoples of New World, 337
  through capture by brigands, 170, 216
  through seizure by creditors, 171
  through war in early modern period, 370–371
Ewald, William, 17, 392
Ex hoc iure, 319–321, 344, 347
Exemplar theory, cognitive psychology, 8

Familia, 95
  gives way to *domus* in Late Republic and Principate, 149–153
  primitivist interpretations of Roman term, 96–101
Feasting, 52, 143, 158, 221
Feudalism, 242–244
  abolition of in French Revolution, 242, 260–261
  as basis for colonialism and imperialism, 250–251
  as long-enduring ideational formation in the law, 288
  as phenomenon of seventeenth century, 249–252
  conceptual uncertainty in Middle Ages, 245–247
  whether it existed in Middle Ages, 239

Index 437

Fief, 242–244, 254–256
  as form of use rights, 244
  Reynolds on, 283
Finley, M. I., 15, 16, 79, 179, 240, 385, 388
Free soil, 23–25, 374–376
French Revolution, 239, 242
  Marx on, 273
Frier, Bruce, 141

Gaius, 108, 116, 190–191
  on capture of slaves as exemplary form of acquisition, 115
Galen, 171, 184
Ganshof, François-Louis, 278
Garnsey, Peter, 178, 181–182, 218, 309, 353–354
Genesis 13, 346–348, 357–358
  as interpreted by Grotius, 361–362
Gibbon, Edward, 108, 318
Giraffe meat
  whether kosher, 120
Girard, René, 328
Goody, Jack, 6, 13, 59, 71, 211
Grossi, Paolo, 292, 306–308, 325
Grotius, Hugo, 13, 163, 213, 258, 361–364, 372–374, 377

Hand, symbolism of, 107, 185–187, 232
Hegel, Georg Wilhelm Friedrich, 267
Herder, Johann Gottfried, 192
Hermogenianus, 319
Hobbes, Thomas, 370, 377
Horace, 203, 393
Hotman, François, 257
Humans, ownership of, 7
  extends beyond slavery, 73, 194
  in precolonial Africa, 6
  in Roman law, 5, 11
Hume, David, 17, 152, 333, 376, 386
  on lack of natural basis for property, 8, 104
Hunt
  used as basis for analogical reasoning, 167, 198–204

Isabella I, Queen of Castile, 337

Jefferson, Thomas, 17, 176
Jhering, Rudolf von, 112, 162, 193
  on capture of slaves as exemplary form acquisition, 115

on relative rights in early Roman law, 112
Johnson v. *M'Intosh*, 233, 359
Junta of Burgos, 336–341
Jurists, Roman
  as pioneers of human rights, 165
  controversy over attitudes toward slavery, 175–181

Kames, Henry Home, Lord, 253
Kant, Immanuel, 369
Karras, Ruth Mazo, 284
Kaser, Max, 77, 79, 102–105, 307
  on relative rights, 114
  on rise of *dominus*, 134–136
Kopytoff, Igor, 60–61, 75
Koskenniemi, Martti, 13, 149, 209, 312, 321
  on legal imagination, 17

Lactantius, 168, 310, 318
Land
  acquired as war booty, 92
  used as basis for analogical reasoning, 166
Land, ownership of
  as "archetypal form," 37
  in Germany, 4
  in Rome, 16
  in the United States, 2–3
  justified through tillage, 358
  theological justification through Genesis 13, 346–348
Land, rights in
  as rights in resources, 48
  as use rights, 41, 54–57
  fief as form of use rights, 244
  in nonmodern, non-Western societies, 57–59
  use rights as commonplace form in human societies, 287
  use rights as solution to tragedy of commons, 67
las Casas, Bartolomé de, 338, 342
Late Antiquity
  whether age of decline, 300
Latifundia, 83, 129
Lavan, Myles, 15, 208
Legal imagination, 17
  contrasted with economic analysis, 10
Legis actio sacramento in rem, 108–111

Levy, Ernst, 304
Libri Feudorum, 247–248, 257
Living creatures
  as exemplary objects of acquisition, 123
Locke, John, 18, 92, 365–367, 387
Longue durée, 288
Loyseau, Charles, 249

Madison, James, 333
Maier, Charles, 378, 379–380
Maine, Henry, 43, 82, 97
Mair, John, 338, 343
Maitland, Frederick William, 251
Malinowski, Bronislaw, 54
Manus, power of gripping hand, 106–111
Mapping, 212, 313
  map consciousness *versus* itinerary consciousness, 215–216, 324–325
Marx, Karl, 10, 16, 97, 126, 131, 234, 292, 325, 331
  ancient economic history outdated, 280–281
  on fall of Roman Republic, 270–271
Miers, Suzanne, 60–61, 75
Momigliano, Arnaldo, 102, 324
Mommsen, Theodor, 315–316
  on first appearance of *dominus* in law, 144
Monopoly of violence, 211–213
Morgan, Lewis Henry, 43

Natural slavery. *See* Aristotle
Nazi era, legal history during, 99–101, 113
Nazism
  property ideology of, 127, 132–133
Niebuhr, Bartold Georg, 117
Nietzsche, Friedrich, 15, 82, 227, 327
Nomos, 38, 39, 52

Occupatio, 198, 231–233, 343–345, 359
  as acquisition of land, 19
  as acquisition of living creatures, 19–20
  as interpreted by Grotius, 362
  in Roman law, 123
Old Testament
  catalogues of property in, 103–104, 345–346
Ostrom, Elinor, 66, 88
Ovando, Nicolas de, 337

Ownership
  absolute conception of, roots in Roman law, 77
  and right to use violence, 13
  Blackstonian, 48
  conceptual affinities with rulership, 13, 74, 209–210, 222, 309–322
  of prey, 50–52, 124

Palacios Rubios, Juan López de, 339, 342–349
Passage from slavery to feudalism, 234, 237
  in early Iberian conquest of New World, 341
  Marc Bloch on, 278–279
  Marx on, 269–273
  Savigny on, 268
  Weber on, 273–277
Passage from slavery to serfdom, 27. *See also* Passage from slavery to feudalism
  contrasted with passage from masters to lords, 302
  repeated occurrence in agrarian history, 264–268
Paterfamilias
  contrasted with *dominus*, 153–154
  supposed right of life and death, 15, 16, 76
Patrimonialism, 220
Patron–client relations, 221
Patterson, Orlando, 5, 18, 77, 126, 132, 224, 388
Paz, Matías de, 341, 372
Pecunia, 95, 96, 98, 101
Penal servitude, 382–383
Personality of law
  contrasted with territoriality of law, 23, 227
Physiocrats, 259
Pierson v. Post, 232, 352
Plato, 14, 216
Plautus, 143, 172
Pocock, J. G. A., 251
Polanyi, Karl, 368
Postliminium, 204–206, 214
Pothier, Robert Joseph, 259
Primitive communism, 41–43, 320, 353
  in thought of Grotius, 363
  Marx on, 270

Index

supposedly present in archaic Roman law, 86–87
Pringsheim, Fritz von, 140, 262
Property
  abstract conception of, roots in Roman law, 126
  as consisting in incommensurable categories, 94–95
  abstract conception of, 94
Prototype theory, cognitive psychology, 8
Pufendorf, Samuel, 78, 163, 258, 365

Rawson, Elizabeth, 385–386
Requerimiento, 339–340, 342, 372
Res mancipi and *nec mancipi*, 95, 120
Reynolds, Susan, 240, 247, 252, 283
Rio, Alice, 284
Robertson, William, 254, 262, 267
Rodbertus, Johann Karl, 98
Roman law
  as law of Roman citizens, 295–296
  mastership as idiom of power, 15
  orientation toward ownership of living creatures, 14–15
Romanists vs. Germanists in German legal thought, 271
Rose, Carol, 2, 76
Rousseau, Jean-Jacques, 41, 176, 322
Rulership
  conceptual affinities with ownership, 13, 74, 209–210, 222, 309–322, 380
  over people vs. over territory, 13, 22–23, 213, 377–378

Sahlins, Marshall, 7, 55, 219, 356
Saller, Richard, 150, 218, 309
Saturnalia, 188, 318
Savigny, Friedrich Carl von, 234, 263–268, 285, 374
  influence on Marx, 269
Schiavone, Aldo, 188, 334
Schmitt, Carl, 37, 61, 136–137
Schulz, Fritz, 138–140
Scottish Enlightenment, 253–254
Selden, John, 249
Seneca, Lucius Annaeus, 153–154, 171, 180

Serfs
  distinguished from slaves, 266
Servus, 266
  ambiguities in meaning of, 285
  in work of Grotius and Pufendorf, 372–374
Slave
  as exemplary form of property, 110
Slave economy
  in nineteenth century, 238
  whether it existed in classical Antiquity, 238
Slavery
  as form of prestige display, 72–73
  in Roman rulership ideology, 148–149
  justified by victory, 164
  open model vs. closed model, 60, 195
Slaves
  close association with beasts, 14
  distinguished from serfs, 266
Smail, Daniel Lord
  on deep history, 26
Smith, Adam, 9, 27, 254, 267
  on decline of slavery, 25
Social dominance, 62–65
Somerset's Case, 375
Soto, Domingo de, 360–361
Specificatio, 199
Split ownership, 256, 307, 321
  dominium utile as use right, 256
Stalin, Joseph, 236–237
State of nature
  ancient juristic idea of, 188
Stoics, 165, 177–178, 192
Summenhart, Konrad, 346–348

Tannenbaum, Frank, 169, 176
Terminalia, 91, 317–318
Termini. See Boundary stones
Territoriality of law
  relative absence in classical Antiquity, 296
Territorial state, 22–23
  role in decline of slavery, 381–384
Territoriality, 40–41, 44–47
  defendability hypothesis, 47
Territoriality of law
  contrasted with personality of law, 225–227

Tetrarchy, 309
Thomas, Yan, 123, 189, 223, 227
Tragedy of the commons, 65–69, 350
Tuck, Richard, 381

Ulpian, 154, 175, 186–187, 191–192, 344, 356
Use rights. *See* Land, rights in

Veblen, Thorstein, 73, 393
Vegoia, Prophecy of, 146, 313
Vico, Giambattista, 76, 82, 97, 207
Violence
  lawful use of in the past, 63, 195
Visscher, Fernand de, 118, 208
Vitae necisque potestas. See Paterfamilias
Vitoria, Francisco de, 349
  on ownership, 355–360
Volksrecht, 305
Voltaire, 260
Vultejus, Hermann, 258

War
  as form of hunting, 14, 274
War booty, 15, 92, 160–162, 190
  land as, 92
  rules for distribution, 160–162
Weber, Max, 10, 16, 72, 98, 123, 211, 220, 234, 237, 269, 297–298, 387
  ancient economic history outdated, 280–281
  on war as hunt for slaves, 14, 274
Westphalia, Peace of, 378–379
Wickham, Chris, 292, 294, 298, 302, 311, 332
Wieacker, Franz, 134, 136–138, 223, 224, 293, 298
  on classical Roman ownership mentality, 138
Willoweit, Dietmar, 378
Wolff, Hans Julius, 84

Studies in Legal History
(Continued from page ii)

Edgardo Pérez Morales, *Unraveling Abolition: Legal Culture and Slave Emancipation in Colombia*

Lyndsay Campbell, *Truth and Privilege: Libel Law in Massachusetts and Nova Scotia, 1820–1840*

Sara M. Butler, *Pain, Penance, and Protest: Peine Forte et Dure in Medieval England*

Michael Lobban, *Imperial Incarceration: Detention without Trial in the Making of British Colonial Africa*

Stefan Jurasinski and Lisi Oliver, *The Laws of Alfred: The Domboc and the Making of Anglo-Saxon Law*

Sascha Auerbach, *Armed with Sword and Scales: Law, Culture, and Local Courtrooms in London, 1860–1913*

Alejandro de La Fuente and Ariela J. Gross, *Becoming Free, Becoming Black: Race, Freedom, and the Law in Cuba, Virginia, and Louisiana*

Elizabeth Papp Kamali, *Felony and the Guilty Mind in Medieval England*

Jessica K. Lowe, *Murder in the Shenandoah: Making Law Sovereign in Revolutionary Virginia*

Michael A. Schoeppner, *Moral Contagion: Black Atlantic Sailors, Citizenship, and Diplomacy in Antebellum America*

Sam Erman, *Almost Citizens: Puerto Rico, the U.S. Constitution, and Empire*

Martha S. Jones, *Birthright Citizens: A History of Race and Rights in Antebellum America*

Julia Moses, *The First Modern Risk: Workplace Accidents and the Origins of European Social States*

Cynthia Nicoletti, *Secession on Trial: The Treason Prosecution of Jefferson Davis*

Edward James Kolla, *Sovereignty, International Law, and the French Revolution*

Assaf Likhovski, *Tax Law and Social Norms in Mandatory Palestine and Israel*

Robert W. Gordon, *Taming the Past: Essays on Law and History and History in Law*

Paul Garfinkel, *Criminal Law in Liberal and Fascist Italy*

Michelle A. McKinley, *Fractional Freedoms: Slavery, Intimacy, and Legal Mobilization in Colonial Lima, 1600–1700*

Karen M. Tani, *States of Dependency: Welfare, Rights, and American Governance, 1935–1972*
Stefan Jurasinski, *The Old English Penitentials and Anglo-Saxon Law*
Felice Batlan, *Women and Justice for the Poor: A History of Legal Aid, 1863–1945*
Sophia Z. Lee, *The Workplace Constitution from the New Deal to the New Right*
Mitra Sharafi, *Law and Identity in Colonial South Asia: Parsi Legal Culture, 1772–1947*
Michael A. Livingston, *The Fascists and the Jews of Italy: Mussolini's Race Laws, 1938–1943*

For EU product safety concerns, contact us at Calle de José Abascal, 56–1°, 28003 Madrid, Spain or eugpsr@cambridge.org.

www.ingramcontent.com/pod-product-compliance
Lightning Source LLC
LaVergne TN
LVHW041206250326
834689LV00002BA/32